Sex Differences in Labor Markets

Sex differences abound in labor markets. In the United States three differences in particular have attracted the most attention: the earnings gap, occupational segregation, and the greater responsibility of women for child care and housework, and consequential lower participation in the labor market.

This volume brings together David Neumark's work of the past fifteen years: in it he tries to understand and analyze the relative importance of family economic decision-making and sex discrimination in generating sex differences in labor markets. Neumark's research covers three main levels of inquiry. The first studies nondiscriminatory sources of sex differences in labor markets; the second grapples with the problem of sex discrimination; while the third evaluates policies to combat and reduce sex differences in labor markets.

David Neumark is one of the most important labor economists working today. He has produced a body of work that deserves to be read as a whole. With this volume, Neumark will leave readers from economics, sociology, and gender studies backgrounds with some incredibly important lessons as well as adding fuel to future research.

David Neumark is Senior Research Fellow in Economics at the Public Policy Institute of California, a Professor of Economics at Michigan State University, and a Research Associate at the National Bureau of Economic Research, USA.

Routledge Research in Gender and Society

Sex Differences in Labor Markets

David Neumark

Routledge
Taylor & Francis Group

LONDON AND NEW YORK

First published 2004
by Routledge
2 Park Square, Milton Park, Abingdon, Oxfordshire OX14 4RN

Simultaneously published in the USA and Canada
by Routledge
711 Third Avenue, New York, NY 10017

Routledge is an imprint of the Taylor & Francis Group, an informa business

First issued in paperback 2012

© 2004 David Neumark editorial matter and
selection; individual chapters, the authors

Typeset in Times New Roman by
Newgen Imaging Systems (P) Ltd, Chennai, India

British Library Cataloguing in Publication Data
A catalogue record for this book is available from the British Library

Library of Congress Cataloging in Publication Data
A catalog record for this book has been requested

ISBN13: 978-0-415-70013-9 hardback
ISBN13: 978-0-415-65168-4 paperback

To DE

Contents

Illustrations

Figures

Tables

Acknowledgments

As the contents of this volume illustrate, my research on sex differences and sex discrimination in labor markets has been a collaborative effort with many outstanding researchers to whom I am indebted. My co-authors run the full gamut of relationships that a researcher forms and benefits from in the course of his career. My co-authors include fellow students from graduate school (Sanders Korenman and McKinley Blackburn), a student (Michele McLennan), colleagues at the two universities where I have been employed (Andrew Postlewaite and Harry Holzer), a professor from graduate school (David Bloom), and others (Kenneth Troske and Kim Bayard). I am especially grateful to Judith Hellerstein, with whom I have had a remarkably productive collaboration over the years that will continue into the future. Our "match" was arranged by our late mentor and friend Zvi Griliches, who recognized our common interest in working on these questions and our willingness to develop new data sources to do so. His presence and guidance are sorely missed, but I have to believe that Zvi would have been satisfied with the results.

The views and conclusions expressed in this volume are mine and those of my co-authors. They do not reflect the views or conclusions of the Public Policy Institute of California. I am grateful to Robert Langham for encouraging me to undertake this project, and to Vincent Antony, Terry Clague, and Aaron Sparrow for their help with the manuscript and other details.

The author and publishers wish to thank the following organizations for permission to reprint previously published material:

Journal of Human Resources (University of Wisconsin Press, USA) for permission to reprint articles used in Chapters 1, 2, 3, 6, 7 and 11; *Journal of Population Economics* (Springer-Verlag, Germany) for permission to reprint the article used in Chapter 4; *Journal of Public Economics* (Elsevier, the Netherlands) for permission to reprint the article used in Chapter 5; *Quarterly Journal of Economics* (MIT Press, USA) for permission to reprint the article used in Chapter 8; *Journal of Labor Economics* (University of Chicago Press, USA) for permission to reprint articles used in Chapters 9, 12 and 13; *Industrial Relations* (Blackwell, UK) for permission to reprint the article used in Chapter 10; and *Industrial and Labor*

Relations Review (Cornell University, USA) for permission to reprint the article used in Chapter 14.

Finally, my greatest thanks go to my wife Donna who, since early in graduate school, has unfailingly supported me through the hard work, long hours, and too-frequent uprooting of our family that have accompanied my research career.

Sex differences in labor
markets—introduction

Introduction

Sex differences in labor markets are pervasive. In the United States three differences, in particular, have attracted the most attention from economists: the earnings gap between women and men; occupational segregation of women and men; and the greater responsibility of women for child care and housework, or "home production," and concomitant lower participation in market work.

Although these sex differences in earnings, occupations, and work in the United States have decreased over the past few decades, sharp differences persist. The earnings of women relative to men hovered in the 60 percent range from the 1970s through the 1980s, but then climbed to around 75 percent in the 1990s.[1] Women made up 83 percent of workers in administrative support and clerical occupations in 1972, and the number fell only trivially to 82 percent by 1995, although in other occupations—such as executive, administrative, and managerial jobs–women's representation increased substantially. The greatest convergence between women and men has occurred in labor force participation; in 1960, women's participation rate was 34 percent compared to 86 percent for men, whereas the comparable numbers for 1995 were 59 and 75 percent. Furthermore, the increased participation of women was by far the strongest among married women with small children, a group with low participation initially. Yet despite this increased participation—and this may help to explain the slower progress with respect to wages and occupational segregation—women, on average, devote far more time than men to housework. Although the available data are not as recent, figures for 1978 indicate that women spent 27 hours per week at housework vs. 6.1 hours for men; in 1988, the comparable figures were 21 hours for women and 7 hours for men.

Labor economists have devoted immense effort to research on sex differences in labor markets. Broadly speaking, this research covers three areas of inquiry. The first attempts to understand the sources of sex differences in labor markets without resorting to explanations based on labor market discrimination. The dominant focus in this research is on how family economic decision making regarding the allocation of time and human capital investment may generate the observed differences between women and men in wages, occupations, participation, and nonmarket work.[2] The second principal area of inquiry in research on sex differences in labor markets grapples with the problem of discrimination. This research originally focused on how the overall wage or earnings gap could be "parsed" into a component due to discrimination and a component due to productivity differences.[3] But in response to concerns about the validity of measuring discrimination from these wage gap decompositions, research on discrimination has moved well beyond this method, to more convincing tests. Finally, the third main area of inquiry evaluates policies to combat discrimination or more generally to reduce sex differences in labor markets. These policies include requirements of equal pay for the same work, equal opportunity in employment, Affirmative Action, and comparable worth.[4]

My own studies of sex differences and sex discrimination in labor markets span all of these areas of inquiry. The purpose of this chapter is to explain how the various studies fit together and to synthesize their findings. The emphasis is on my own work rather than a review of the literature *per se*, although much contact is made with the existing literature and the individual studies provide more extensive literature reviews. Research is a cumulative process, and for me, like many researchers, often picks up where a previous study left off—developing new or better data, improving on the empirical analysis, incorporating new theoretical insights, or simply turning to a new question that helps to flesh out a research agenda. That is certainly the case with my studies of sex differences and sex discrimination in labor markets. My hope is that by tying these studies together, I can strengthen the contribution of the collective body of work and identify or clarify some of the most important avenues for future research.

Some background on discrimination

There are many models of discrimination in labor markets, but none approaches the significance of the models developed by Becker in *The Economics of Discrimination* (Becker, 1971), in particular his model of employer discrimination. Although this chapter is not the appropriate venue for a review of theoretical models of discrimination, a brief discussion of Becker's employer discrimination model is extremely helpful in framing the discussion that follows, as this model is either implicitly or explicitly at the heart of much of the empirical literature on sex discrimination.

Consider a wage-taking firm with a production function Y that uses two inputs: the labor of men, M, and the labor of women, F. Employers have a distaste for hiring female workers and do not maximize profits but rather maximize utility defined as

$$U(\pi, M, F) = P \cdot Y(M, F) - w_M M - w_F F - d \cdot (F/M), \tag{1}$$

where d is the discrimination coefficient capturing this distaste, P is output price, π is profits, and w_M and w_F are the market wages of men and women, respectively. Short-run utility maximization then implies

$$\text{MRP}_F - d/M = w_F,   \text{MRP}_M + d \cdot (F/M^2) = w_M. \tag{2}$$

The marginal revenue product of male labor is set below its input price, because male labor increases the employer's utility, whereas the marginal revenue product of female labor is discounted by the non-pecuniary cost of discrimination to the employer and hence is above the input price of female labor. The discrimination coefficient d will lead the firm in the short run to hire fewer women and more men than profit maximization would dictate.[5] In other words, Becker models discrimination as a price differential needed to induce employers to hire women, which in turn leads to wage and employment differences between women and men that would not exist absent the discrimination.

After developing this static framework, Becker goes on to describe the critical implication that, under some conditions, market forces will cause discrimination to disappear in the long run. If product markets are perfectly competitive, and there are sufficient potential employers with nondiscriminatory tastes, then discrimination will disappear over time through competition in product markets. If product markets are not perfectly competitive but some entry is possible, then discrimination will be competed away if there are nondecreasing returns to scale and at least one potential employer has nondiscriminatory tastes. In the case of total barriers to entry in product markets, even with decreasing returns to scale, if businesses are transferable and there is a potential nondiscriminating employer, discrimination may disappear through competition in the market for firms. Finally, Becker notes that if employers' tastes are nepotistic rather than discriminatory, then discrimination will not be eliminated by competition in the market for firms, although product market competition may still suffice (1971, p. 44).

Numerous researchers have used Becker's arguments about market forces and discrimination to dismiss or at least seriously downplay the possibility that part of the wage gap between women and men reflects discrimination. For example, Fuchs (1988) writes, "[I]f women were as valuable as men to employers, the firms that persist in hiring men should be driven out of business by their competitors who hire women" (p. 54) Similarly, O'Neill (1994) asserts that in a situation where men are paid more because of discrimination, "The expansion of nondiscriminating firms would increase the demand for women . . . and eventually bid up their wages, a process that would narrow and potentially eliminate a discriminatory wage gap" (p. 13). However, this perspective glosses over the important qualifications Becker raised concerning barriers to entry, transferability of assets, and discriminatory vs. nepotistic tastes. Thus, Becker's argument that discrimination should be competed away is best viewed as a hypothesis to be tested, not as a theoretical result. One of the studies discussed below looks at evidence on this hypothesis; but the important point at this juncture is that whether or not discrimination helps to explain sex differences in labor markets should remain an empirical question, and not one prejudged based on the argument that discrimination cannot persist in competitive markets.

At the same time, the Becker model challenges those who would downplay discrimination to explain the observed sex differences in labor markets. Insights from the economics of the family have played a critical role in attempting to construct a nondiscriminatory explanation of these differences.

Family economics and sex differences in labor markets

Although noneconomists frequently view discrimination-based explanations of sex differences in labor markets as compelling, economists have entertained alternative explanations more seriously. Their greater skepticism on this point, I believe, derives from Becker's seminal work on the economics of discrimination. Becker's original work focused on wage differences, but it has led economists to question discriminatory explanations of other sex differences in labor markets as well. Many theoretical approaches have been considered to attempt to explain how sex differences in labor markets can arise in the absence of discrimination. None, however, has been more central than that based on the family as the unit of economic decision making.

One key assumption underlies the explanation of sex differences in labor markets based on the economics of the family: that women are more committed than men to childrearing and are therefore more likely to interrupt their careers for childrearing. In some sense, this a priori assumption is intellectually unsatisfying because it uses an assumed sex difference to explain another sex difference. Reference is typically made to given biological differences, such as women caring more than men about their children (Fuchs, 1988, ch. 4). Economists, however, have typically tried to avoid explanations of observed behavior based on differences in tastes.[6] Becker (1981) offers the more interesting conjecture that women have a comparative advantage in home production because of complementarity between childbearing and childrearing as "a mother can more readily feed and watch her older children while she produces additional children than while she engages in most other activities" (p. 22). Finally, Becker also allows for the possibility that discrimination is itself the source of comparative advantage for men in the labor market, which, even if slight, could generate large differences in behavior owing to specialization (1985, p. S41). In this case, though, the economics of the family does not offer a fundamentally "different" hypothesis, but simply explores further implications of discrimination.

Whatever the basis for this assumption, a host of theoretical predictions can be derived from the notion of weaker labor market commitment among women. First, efficient allocation by households will lead to specialization. In particular, women (especially married women) will devote less effort per unit of time allocated to the labor market, generating lower wages for women even if we condition on the usual control variables (Becker, 1985). Second, Becker (1981) shows that there is likely to be specialization in human capital investment, with men more likely to develop human capital that is rewarded in the labor market. Third, the expectation and realization of career interruptions—in particular for childbirth and childrearing— will affect the pattern of human capital investment among women. Among other things, career interruptions make it less likely that standard predictions regarding the implications of human capital for wage growth (Mincer, 1974) will hold for women. This, in turn, implies that comparisons of the shapes of women's and men's earnings functions as tests for differential treatment by employers can be misleading (Mincer and Polachek, 1974).

The standard economic theory of consumption and labor supply applied to the family has also been used to explain changes in married women's labor force participation over time. Even if women specialize in home production, their behavior over time will respond to exogenous changes in the factors affecting the allocation of time to the home and the market. Mincer (1962) explored how women's labor force participation would be expected to respond to changes in market wages and the productivity of time spent in the home as well as to the substitutability of market-bought goods and services for home production. Subsequently, numerous researchers have concluded that these factors can account for some but not all of the increase in married women's participation in the labor force in the latter part of the twentieth century (e.g. Smith and Ward, 1985).

Each of my chapters summarized in this section relates to some aspect of the economics of the family and its implications for sex differences in labor markets. The first set of chapters addresses elements of the specialization hypothesis, exploring the consequences of marriage and childbearing for women's and men's wages.

In "Does Marriage Really Make Men More Productive?" (Chapter 1), we explore whether the standard 10–15 percent wage premium earned by married men can be explained as resulting from a productivity difference that most likely reflects greater labor market specialization among married men compared to non-married men. There are two principal alternative hypotheses. The first is that the higher wage earned by married men does not reflect a causal effect of marriage at all, but instead reflects a selection process whereby higher-wage men are those who tend to become married, presumably because of their greater desirability in the marriage market. The second, which is causal, is that employers for one reason or another discriminate in favor of married men, perhaps out of concern that married men have families to support.

Two types of evidence are presented. The first uses data from a company personnel file. The evidence indicates that married men earn more because they get promoted into higher-paying positions at a faster rate, but that these promotion rates are attributable to higher performance ratings. Although ruling out explanations based on discrimination is difficult (as discussed in more detail later in this chapter), this evidence is more consistent with a productivity-enhancing effect of marriage than with discrimination. The second type of evidence comes from longitudinal data. This evidence shows that men who marry experience a rise in earnings, which is inconsistent with the selection argument. Together, the combined evidence suggests that married men earn higher wages because in a very general sense their productivity increases with marriage. There is additional, indirect evidence that the increased earnings of married men stem specifically from specialization in human capital investment; in particular, we find that the higher earnings of married men emerge because once married their wages grow faster, as would be predicted by increased human capital investment.

In "Marriage, Motherhood, and Wages" (Chapter 2) and "Sources of Bias in Women's Wage Equations" (Chapter 3), the analysis turns from men to women. The stylized fact that can be regarded as consistent with specialization among women is that their wages are negatively associated with children, and especially young children. Standard empirical results suggest that at least part (and sometimes a major share) of the wage penalty associated with childbearing is the result of reduced time in the labor market; that is, controlling for experience and tenure in wage equations reduces the child penalty substantially. These apparent direct effects of children on labor supply are consistent with some forms of specialization, but not with the direct negative effects of children on wages predicted by Becker's (1985) model of the allocation of effort. In these chapters, we use refined statistical techniques (panel data, instrumental variables, and sample-selection-correction estimators) to probe more fully the relationships between children and wages.

The combined evidence lends credence to the view that, even if we consider labor supply differentials associated with children, women with children earn lower wages.[7] In particular, because direct negative effects of children on wages in turn lead to lower labor supply, simply controlling for experience and tenure leads to overly strong estimates of the effects of low experience and tenure on wages, and hence overly weak estimates of the effects of children on wages. Thus, these findings lead to the conclusion that continued labor force attachment of women with children would be unlikely to fully offset the negative effects of children on women's wages—a conclusion that is consistent with lower alloca-tion of effort to the labor market among women with children, as in Becker's model.

The more complex questions of the effects of women's career interruptions on women's human capital accumulation and wages are taken up in "Fertility Timing, Wages, and Human Capital" (Chapter 4). The starting point for this chapter is the fact that women who have their first child relatively late in life earn higher wages than other women. This stylized fact is consistent with what we might expect from interactions between the timing of career interruptions and human capital investment, if young women who plan to begin childbearing later have human capital investment paths that are more similar to men's. In this chapter, we develop the theory underlying this conjecture more completely. In particu-lar, we derive the conditions under which women anticipating a later first birth will indeed engage in more human capital investment early in their career; we also suggest that these conditions are likely to hold. Finally, we present empirical evidence consistent with this prediction, as numerous proxies for human cap-ital investment are higher for later childbearers and explain a sizable portion of the higher wages earned by late childbearers, even when we try to account for numerous differences (including family background) between early and late childbearers.

Together, the four chapters just described lend empirical support to the hypoth-esized roles for specialization and human capital investment in explaining sex differences in wages. However, this research only helps to establish that specializa-tion and human capital investment play *some* role in generating these differences. It does not rule out an important and perhaps even a primary role for discrim-ination, the analysis of which is the central concern of many of the chapters discussed later.

The final chapter in this section on the economics of the family is concerned not so much with sex differences *per se*, but with advancing our understanding of changes in the labor force participation of married women. Of course, insofar as women's and men's participation have converged, this question bears in a fundamental way on sex differences in labor markets, as many of these differences—as suggested by the theoretical and empirical chapters discussed above—may hinge on the greater likelihood that husbands rather than wives will be primarily committed to the labor market.

Although the Mincer (1962) model of labor force participation has successfully accounted for much of the increase in married women's labor force participation, most research finds that the entire increase cannot be accounted for by the factors that the neoclassical model identifies as important. Consequently, in "Relative Income Concerns and the Rise in Married Women's Employment" (Chapter 5), we consider whether interactions among women's labor force participation decisions could account for the faster than expected rise in the overall participation rate. The specific mechanism we study is a concern over relative income; that is, when incomes of other families go up as wives enter the labor market, a woman may be more likely to enter the labor market herself to preserve the relative ranking of her family's income.[8] A theoretical model is developed to show that this type of concern over relative income can lead to increases in married women's entry into the labor market beyond what would be generated solely from the individualistic neoclassical model.

To assess the evidence on whether relative income concerns drive married women's labor force participation, we look at women and their sisters-in-law. Sisters-in-law are of interest because they provide a likely comparison family, yet are less likely to share unobservables with the reference women in the study. Consistent with the existence of relative income concerns—which, as noted, could help explain the rapid rise in married women's labor force participation—women are more likely to work when their sisters-in-law work. In an alternative test, we find that women are more likely to work when their sister's husband earns more than their own husband, again consistent with relative income concerns.

Theoretical and empirical research on the economics of the family has been fruitfully extended to consider numerous questions related to sex differences in labor markets and women's labor market behavior more generally. This research agenda is unlikely to have run its course, however, as continuing changes in sex roles and family structures—perhaps most interestingly the emergence of a sizable number of families in which women are the primary breadwinner (e.g. Winkler, 1998), and increasing numbers of families with gay and lesbian parents—open up new avenues for research (e.g. Kurdek, 1993). Nonetheless, although the economics of the family points to possible nondiscriminatory explanations of sex differences in labor markets, neither it nor the long-run implications of Becker's model of employer discrimination rule out discriminatory explanations of these differences. Thus, direct attempts to assess the role of discrimination remain critical.

Testing for discrimination

The most-studied question in research on sex discrimination is whether the wage gap between women and men reflects discrimination, and more specifically, what share of the gap is attributable to discrimination. By far the predominant workhorse in empirical studies of discrimination is the "residual wage" approach developed by Blinder (1973) and Oaxaca (1973). Because this approach serves as background for much of the ensuing discussion, I describe it in some detail.

The simplest residual wage approach is to estimate a wage equation of the form

$$\ln(w) = X\gamma + F\beta + \varepsilon, \tag{3}$$

where X is a vector of control variables, presumed to capture individual differences in productivity, and F is a dummy variable equal to 1 for women. β then captures the residual or unexplained wage gap, which is interpreted as reflecting discrimination. The implication of the specification in equation (3) is that the wage differential between women and men is restricted to be constant (in percentage terms) for all values of the X's. However, this restriction may fail to capture, for example, variation in the wage gap with the level of education or experience. Thus, the Oaxaca–Blinder procedure is to estimate two wage regressions

$$\ln(w_F) = X\beta_F + \varepsilon_F, \tag{4}$$

and

$$\ln(w_M) = X\beta_M + \varepsilon_M, \tag{5}$$

where X includes the unit vector, and hence the intercept can differ by sex.

In this case, the sex wage differential varies depending on where it is evaluated, and the residual part of the wage differential now includes not just the difference between the intercepts, but also the difference between the coefficients on X. Because regression lines go through the means, if b_j, $j = F, M$ are the vectors of estimates of β_F and β_M, and μ_j, $j = F, M$ denote the means of X for women and men, then the difference between the average log wages of men and women can be written in one of two ways:

$$\mu_M b_M - \mu_F b_F = \mu_M(b_M - b_F) + (\mu_M - \mu_F)b_F, \tag{6}$$

or

$$\mu_M b_M - \mu_F b_F = \mu_F(b_M - b_F) + (\mu_M - \mu_F)b_M. \tag{7}$$

Intuitively, what is the difference between these alternative decompositions? The last term in each equation captures the difference in wages that would remain even if the wage regressions were the same for men and women (i.e. $b_F = b_M$), because there would still be differences in characteristics between men and women that might lead to a wage differential. But estimating the contribution of the differences in characteristics requires an assumption about what the wage structure would be in the absence of discrimination. The first decomposition assumes that the wage structure in the absence of discrimination would be β_F, whereas the second assumes it would be β_M. The first term in each equation then measures the share of the wage gap attributable to differences in coefficients, which in this approach is interpreted as the discriminatory component of the wage gap. These differences in coefficients must be evaluated at a vector of means, μ_M or μ_F, dictated by the choice of the wage structure used in evaluating the differences in characteristics, as shown in equations (6) and (7).

The residual wage approach is subject to numerous criticisms, each of which is, in one way or another, a starting point for each of the chapters discussed in this section. The first criticism is that the Oaxaca–Blinder approach to estimating wage discrimination leads to ambiguous empirical answers because of an inherent arbitrariness in choosing the "base" with which to compare the present wage structure. To see this, as I show in "Employers' Discriminatory Behavior and the Estimation of Wage Discrimination" (Chapter 6), a more general wage gap decomposition is

$$\mu_M b_M - \mu_F b_F = [\mu_M(b_M - b) - \mu_F(b_F - b)] + (\mu_M - \mu_F)b, \qquad (8)$$

where b is the "no discrimination" wage structure. If $b = b_F$ then the first decomposition results, while the second results if $b = b_M$ (see also Cotton, 1988). I show that each of these two cases can be rationalized in terms of Becker's model of employer discrimination: the first when employers are nepotistic toward men; and the second when they discriminate against women. More importantly, though, there are alternative equally or more plausible assumptions regarding employers' discriminatory tastes that lead to different decompositions (i.e. different "no discrimination" wage structures), and hence to different empirical answers to the question of what share of the wage gap is due to discrimination. The point is not that there is a "better" decomposition than those proposed by Oaxaca and Blinder, but rather that without some assumption—untested and likely arbitrary—regarding the form of discriminatory tastes and the implied wage structure in the absence of discrimination, these decompositions cannot be interpreted as measuring discrimination, even ignoring the additional problems discussed here.[9]

A second criticism of the residual wage approach is that some of the differences in productivity-related variables—for example, lower experience and shorter tenure of women—are themselves a reflection of responses to discrimination. According to this "feedback hypothesis," the residual wage approach will generally underestimate the contribution of discrimination to the wage gap; specifically, it will fail to account for the role of discrimination in generating some of the observed differences between women and men and instead regard the portion of the wage gap associated with these differences as nondiscriminatory.

In "Sex Discrimination and Women's Labor Market Outcomes" (Chapter 7), we try to examine whether there is evidence consistent with these feedback effects. Ideally, we would have some objective measure of whether a woman experiences discrimination and data that allow us to measure whether she responds to this discrimination in ways suggested by the feedback hypothesis. Using differences in outcomes (such as lower wages) as proxies for discrimination is problematic; in this case, we would effectively be reversing a wage regression, using a measure of some productivity-related characteristics that might be influenced by discrimination (such as tenure) as the dependent variable and the wage as the independent variable. Although this may be the underlying relationship we have in mind, we would then face two simultaneous equations—in this case in wages and tenure. Unraveling the causality is problematic, because it is difficult to come up with instrumental variables (IVs) that affect wages but not labor market attachment, or vice versa.[10]

Instead, we use self-reports of discrimination as our exogenous measure of discrimination. We examine the effect of experiencing discrimination (as reported by respondents) on a wide variety of outcomes that are often suggested as sources of lower wages for women, including experience, tenure (or turnover), marriage, childbearing, etc. Using reported discrimination avoids the simultaneity problem discussed earlier. But self-reports are potentially problematic because there may be heterogeneity in the propensity to report discrimination that may be correlated with the dependent variables; for example, if women who are more committed to the labor force are more likely to report discrimination, there would be a bias against finding evidence of feedback effects. To mitigate this problem, we control for a fixed propensity to report discrimination by focusing on a subsample of women who initially report no discrimination, and identify the effects of discrimination from those who subsequently switch to reporting discrimination.

Using this strategy, we find some evidence consistent with the feedback hypothesis. In particular, women who switch to reporting discrimination are more likely to separate from their employer and to subsequently marry and have children. Not all of the evidence points in this direction, however, and even the evidence that does fails to provide a clear estimate of how much standard wage decompositions understate wage discrimination. Nonetheless, this research does suggest that some of the observable differences between women and men that are used to explain the sex wage gap may instead result from discriminatory forces that help generate sex differences in productivity-related characteristics.

The third key criticism of the residual wage approach to studying discrimination is that one can always posit some unobservable that differs on average between women and men and therefore could help explain the residual wage gap.[11] One response to this problem inherent to the residual wage approach has been audit studies, which are based on comparisons of outcomes for matched job applicants of different races or sexes. In a sense, audit studies can be viewed as an alternative approach to the problem of missing data on productivity. Residual wage discrimination studies attempt to solve this missing data problem by means of regression analysis; in the case of sex discrimination, these studies start with women and men whose productivity may differ on average and try to introduce an extensive set of control variables that, while not measuring productivity directly, may serve as adequate proxies for productivity. Because residual wage discrimination studies use data drawn from a population of individuals in which real differences between groups may exist, the need to adjust via regression is unavoidable. The audit study approach, in contrast, creates an artificial pool of labor market participants among whom there are no average differences by sex. This is a potentially powerful strategy because simple comparisons of means—with no need for regression adjustments that may at any rate be inadequate—can yield decisive evidence regarding discrimination.

Most audit studies of labor market discrimination have focused on minority hiring (e.g. Turner *et al.*, 1991). But in "Sex Discrimination in Restaurant Hiring: An Audit Study" (Chapter 8) I use this tool to study sex discrimination. In particular, the chapter focuses on discrimination in the restaurant industry, exploring whether the underrepresentation of women in very high-price restaurants—where incomes of waitstaff are highest—is attributable to discrimination. Using male and female testers in sixty-five audits of restaurants in Philadelphia, a strong pattern of discrimination occurred, with men receiving job offers in 48 percent of the audits in high-price restaurants compared to 9 percent for women, a difference that was statistically significant. Women fared somewhat worse in medium-price restaurants but better in low-price restaurants. Although limited to a particular industry in one geographical area, this study provides rather compelling evidence of discrimination. But the price of a very clean experiment is often less generalizability.[12]

Aside from the typically limited scope of audit studies, they suffer from two other potentially important inherent limitations. First, audit studies by their nature are restricted to an examination of the initial interview and hiring process and are therefore useful only in assessing discrimination in interviewing and hiring for jobs that do not require reference checks, resume validation, personal recommendations, and so on. Second, as has been noted by Heckman (1998), even if audit studies detect some discrimination, this result does not imply that the marginal employer discriminates, and it is the marginal employer that, at least in Becker's model of discrimination, determines wages. Thus, the detection of unequal treatment in audit studies does not necessarily imply a discriminatory wage gap.[13]

Audit studies respond to the absence of actual productivity measures in the residual wage approach by constructing artificial samples in which there are no productivity differences between women and men. In contrast, in "Wages, Productivity, and Worker Characteristics: Evidence from Plant-Level Production Functions and Wage Equations" (Chapter 9), we develop an alternative approach using a matched employer–employee data set. This data set permits the measurement of the demographic characteristics of establishments' workforces as well as the estimation of production functions and can therefore be used to infer productivity differentials between workers in different groups. Comparisons of these productivity differentials with wage differentials then provide a test for wage discrimination.

To motivate the approach to testing for wage discrimination using matched employer–employee data, consider a simple model illustrating the relationship between wages and productivity under perfect competition. Assume that plants produce output Y with a technology that utilizes female labor L_F and male labor L_M, which are assumed to be perfectly substitutable. The production function of each plant is

$$Y = F(L_M + \phi L_F), \tag{9}$$

where ϕ is the marginal productivity of female labor relative to male labor.[14] These plants are assumed to operate in perfectly competitive spot labor markets, and labor supply is assumed to be completely inelastic. The price of the output Y is normalized to equal 1. Wages of female workers and male workers are w_F and w_M, respectively, with the relative wage rate λ defined as w_F/w_M. The proportional mix of the two types of labor in each plant will be determined by the relationship between ϕ and λ. If $\phi = \lambda$, then under profit maximization or cost minimization plants will be indifferent to the proportional mix of the two types of labor in the plant. If there is a wedge between the relative marginal product and the relative wage so that $\phi \neq \lambda$, then profit-maximizing or cost-minimizing plants will be at a corner solution, hiring either only male workers (if $\phi < \lambda$) or only female workers (if $\phi > \lambda$). The only equilibrium in this model, therefore, is when wages adjust so that $\phi = \lambda$, and plants are indifferent between the two types of labor.

Evidence that $\phi \neq \lambda$ is inconsistent with the assumption that we are observing profit-maximizing or cost-minimizing plants in a competitive spot labor market. Most importantly, Becker's model of employer discrimination predicts that $\phi > \lambda$ (see equation (2)), so that a natural alternative interpretation of such evidence is that there is discrimination against women.[15]

This approach can be implemented using matched data on employers and employees, when the resulting matched data set provides information on demographic characteristics of the employer's workforce, labor costs, and the output and input measures needed to estimate standard production functions. The matched employer–employee data set that we used for this purpose is the Worker Establishment Characteristics Database (WECD). The WECD, constructed at the US Census Bureau, links information for a subset of individuals responding to the long form of the 1990 Decennial Census of Population to information about their employers in the 1989 Longitudinal Research Database (LRD), with matches based on the physical location and detailed industry of the worker's reported place of work and similar information on establishments. The LRD is restricted to manufacturing plants. This matching procedure yields data on 3,102 manufacturing plants and 129,606 workers in those plants. The matched data are used to estimate variants of the plant-level production function simultaneously with plant-level wage equations to obtain estimates of parameters corresponding to ϕ and λ.

The results regarding wage discrimination against women are quite strong. The baseline estimate of ϕ, the relative productivity of women, is 0.84, which is significantly less than one. But the baseline estimate of λ is 0.55, significantly less than 1 and, more important, much less than the estimate of ϕ, indicating that women are underpaid relative to their productivity. The p-value for the test of equality of these two parameters is effectively zero, indicating that the null hypothesis of no discrimination is rejected in favor of the hypothesis of wage discrimination against women. Across alternative specifications, the estimate of λ is robust. The estimate of ϕ varies somewhat more, between a range of about 0.71 to 1.01, but the test of the null of no discrimination is rejected in nearly all cases, in favor of the hypothesis that $\phi > \lambda$. The estimates imply that US women working in manufacturing may be less productive than men, but the pay gap is considerably larger than the productivity gap. That outcome, of course, is predicted by Becker's model of employer discrimination against women.

This section has discussed four different approaches to assessing the role of discrimination against women in generating sex differences in labor markets. Each addresses potential flaws with the preceding approach or approaches. What is striking, however, is that all the methods provide evidence consistent with a significant role for discrimination in explaining sex differences in wages. I therefore regard the case for the existence of discrimination as quite strong.

One can construct counter-arguments to each specific type of evidence. Indeed, one characterization of the progression of research on sex differences in labor markets is the initial presentation of evidence from a test for discrimination, followed by criticism of that method of testing for discrimination, leading to the development of improved methods, in turn followed by more refined criticisms and more decisive tests.[16] When these newer tests also provide evidence of discrimination, the objections to evidence of discrimination are eroded, but perhaps never eliminated, as critics of the evidence adopt more refined and—depending on one's perspective—more tortured alternative explanations. In my view, however, it seems more compelling to accept a relatively simple explanation of most of the evidence, older and newer: that it is generated by labor market discrimination.[17]

Testing models of discrimination

Even if one accepts that there is compelling evidence of labor market discrimination against women, critical questions remain. One important question concerns the nature of discrimination. Better understanding of the underlying discriminatory behavior can help in constructing and interpreting tests of discrimination, and can help address policy issues regarding how government might respond to discrimination. A second important question, taken up in the next section, concerns the effectiveness of the policies that have been chosen to combat discrimination.

To this point, the model of discrimination that has received the most attention is Becker's model of employer discrimination. An alternative to the taste discrimination model is statistical discrimination. In early models of statistical discrimination, wage differences between the sexes (or races) emerge because the reliability of information about different groups varies. If, for example, the information about women available to those making hiring decisions is less reliable than the information about men, then among those with above-average qualifications women are paid less than comparable men, and among those with below-average qualifications women are paid more than comparable men. In the simplest models, average pay equals average productivity, so there is no "group discrimination." However, Lundberg and Startz (1983) point out that the less reliable information for women implies lower returns on their investments in human capital, which could lead women to underinvest in their skills. Group discrimination would then result, because "groups with equal average initial endowments of productive ability do not receive equal average compensation in equilibrium" (Lundberg and Startz, 1983, p. 342).

The distinction between taste discrimination and statistical discrimination has implications for both policy and empirical tests for discrimination. If taste discrimination accounts for the unexplained lower wages of women, then policies targeting discriminatory behavior directly may be the most appropriate response. But if statistical discrimination is important, then policies that reduce informational imperfections can also play a role; indeed, as discussed here, one role of Affirmative Action may be to encourage improved information (Holzer and Neumark, 2000b). At the same time, Lundberg and Startz also show that equal pay laws may increase efficiency in their statistical discrimination setting, because a policy that forbids unequal wage schedules for women and men shifts some investment to women, for whom marginal costs are lower.

The implications of the alternative models for tests for discrimination were elucidated by Foster and Rosenzweig (1993). They use data sets for developing countries in which the same workers are sometimes paid time rates, and sometimes paid piece rates, for doing the same kind of work. It would seem that these data present a simple test for taste discrimination. In particular, we could use piece-rate work as a productivity measure and estimate a regression of time rates on piece rates and a dummy variable for women to see whether women are paid less conditional on their productivity. In fact, though, if there is imperfect information in labor markets, in which case statistical discrimination is a possibility, this test for taste discrimination fails. To see this, let w denote the time-rate wage, define F as a dummy variable for females, and let μ denote actual productivity measured by piece-rate earnings.

It seems natural to estimate the regression

$$w = F\beta + \mu\gamma + \varepsilon, \tag{10}$$

and interpret a negative estimate of β as reflecting employer taste discrimination. However, if there is imperfect information, we expect employers to set wages based on expected productivity μ^*, which is unobserved. If, as is typical in statistical discrimination models, we assume that

$$\mu = \mu^* + \nu, \tag{11}$$

where ν is orthogonal to μ^*, then the estimate of γ in equation (10) is biased downward. If women are in fact less productive than men, the estimate of β will be overly negative, providing spurious evidence that taste discrimination leads to underpayment of women. Finally, because Foster and Rosenzweig do not have a measure of expected productivity, they propose an instrumental variables estimate that gives an unbiased estimate of β, which, in their data, provides much weaker evidence of taste discrimination.

In "Wage Differentials by Race and Sex: The Roles of Taste Discrimination and Labor Market Information" (Chapter 10), I carry out related analyses of statistical discrimination, using a data set for the United States. This data set contains data on starting wages w_s, current wages w, and employers' current performance ratings of employees P, which I take as a measure of productivity. These data refer to the last worker hired. It is a relatively straightforward matter to use these data in the Foster–Rosenzweig framework. In these data, however, women and men have very similar average performance ratings, so that statistical discrimination cannot explain a wage gap for women conditional on P.

However, these data also permit an assessment of whether information problems are more severe for female workers, which, as explained earlier, could help to explain women's lower wages in richer models of statistical discrimination. The question of differential information can be addressed by estimating the regression

$$w_s = \alpha P + \epsilon \tag{12}$$

for women and men separately, obtaining both OLS and instrumental variables estimates (using as instruments variables such as training requirements that affect P, but do not affect wages conditional on P). Denoting true productivity as P^*, the reliability of information on new workers can be estimated as the ratio of the OLS estimate of $\alpha(a_{\text{OLS}})$ to the instrumental variable estimate (a_{IV}), since

$$\text{plim}(a_{\text{OLS}}/a_{\text{IV}}) = \text{Var}(P^*)/\text{Var}(P). \tag{13}$$

To this point I have suggested that if the estimate of α changes upon instrumenting, it is because I am using actual rather than expected productivity. Another alternative is that there is no information problem—so that expected and actual productivity are the same—but there is simply measurement error in what the econometrician observes. In this case, instrumental variables could also cause the estimate of α to change. Before drawing conclusions about the evidence being consistent with statistical discrimination (when the estimate of α becomes larger after instrumenting), it would be useful to try to rule out this alternative hypothesis. I do this by comparing results for workers with and without a probationary period. The underlying assumption is that for workers with a probationary period, employers have more difficulty assessing productivity at the outset, so that information is worse. Thus, if the problem is truly one of information, rather than pure measurement error, we would expect to find the ratio $a_{\text{OLS}}/a_{\text{IV}}$ higher for nonprobationary workers; that is, instrumenting has a bigger effect on the estimate for probationary workers.

The evidence from this analysis ultimately does suggest that employers have worse information about women than about men, and that the problem is one of statistical discrimination and not just measurement error. This suggests that policies intended to target the wage gap need to consider the possible role of statistical discrimination, and also that—at least in other data sets—evidence consistent with employer taste discrimination based on use of an individual productivity measure could be problematic.

In "Market Forces and Sex Discrimination" (Chapter 11), we take a more general look at the empirical evidence for Becker's employer discrimination model. We focus in particular on the role of market competition in eliminating discrimination, both statically and dynamically. This question also informs policy, as direct government action to reduce discrimination is less important if market competition can accomplish the same goal. In the Becker model, if competition undermines discrimination, there are two implications. First, there is a static implication that discrimination is likely to exist only where there is product market power, and that, conversely, product market competition hinders discrimination. Second, there is a dynamic implication that when firms with product market power can "afford" to discriminate in the short run, market forces eliminate the discrimination over the long run. However, as noted earlier, competition has these implications only if particular conditions hold, and therefore these implications should be tested.

Using the matched data described earlier, we begin with a simple test for sex discrimination. If there is no discrimination against women, there should be no cross-sectional relationship between profitability and the sex composition of the workforce. Any sex difference in wages must reflect only observed or unobserved productivity differentials between women and men, and firms or plants that employ more women should earn no higher profits. Evidence that plants or firms that employ relatively more women earn higher profits, in contrast, would be consistent with sex discrimination. This test, not surprisingly, parallels the production function-based test described in the previous section. Then, moving on to the implications of the Becker model for the role of market forces, we first test whether—as the Becker model predicts—there is a positive short-run relationship between profitability and the sex composition of the workforce only among plants with product market power, because only among such plants are there positive economic profits that may be exploited to indulge the discriminatory tastes of some employers. Finally, we use longitudinal data on the plants in our data set to test the dynamic implication of Becker's model, asking whether nondiscriminatory plants—those which, according to the cross-sectional evidence, employ more women and earn higher profits—grow faster or are less likely to undergo a change of ownership compared with discriminatory plants.

With regard to the test for discrimination, we find that irrespective of variations in the sample, variable construction, and the use of plants or firms, the proportion female in the workforce is positively and significantly related to profitability. Next, we find that the positive relationship between employment of women and profitability holds for plants with considerable product market power, whereas for plants with little market power the relationship is nonexistent or at least weaker. This positive relationship between the proportion of female employees and profitability among plants with high output share is consistent with the static implication of Becker's model. In plants that operate in a competitive output market, there is no performance advantage to hiring women; because discriminatory employers are unable to indulge their tastes for discrimination, wages in this sector are quickly bid to equality with marginal products. But in (typically larger) plants where there is market power and where plants can discriminate if they wish, at least in the short run, those that do not discriminate and hire more women—who cost less—achieve better performance.

Finally, we look at evidence regarding the dynamic implication of the Becker model for the plants with relatively high output share (located in the top quartile of the distribution of this market power measure), for which there is evidence of discrimination from the static analysis. For these plants, we estimate regressions for growth of both employment and shipments and probits for ownership change as functions of, among other things, the proportion female in a plant's workforce—which should be inversely related to the degree of discrimination exercised by the employer. We find no evidence that sex discrimination in wages is reduced or eliminated by market forces that cause nondiscriminatory plants to expand relative to discriminatory plants. We do find that higher relative employment of women in the base year has a negative relationship with the probability of changing ownership between 1990 and 1995, consistent with plants employing fewer women being more likely to change ownership, as predicted by Becker's model. However, the relationship is not statistically significant. Overall, then, these results provide little evidence that market forces act over time to erode the sex discrimination reflected in the cross-sectional relationship between profitability and the proportion female for plants with product market power. On the basis of this evidence, there is no empirical case for concluding that product market competition alone will suffice to eliminate wage discrimination.

The literature testing alternative models of discrimination has scarcely begun to develop. In my view, however, this is one of the most promising and most important avenues for research on sex differences and sex discrimination in labor markets. Because the competitive implications of the Becker employer discrimination model provide in some sense the theoretical foundation for nondiscriminatory explanations of sex differences in labor markets, evidence on the validity of this model is critical. Such evidence would be even more valuable if it spoke to the validity of other models, in particular those with different implications regarding the persistence of discrimination (e.g. Black, 1995). Furthermore, as elucidated at greater length in the next section, if we accept that sex differences reflect discrimination, then policy choices in response to sex differences in labor markets need to be conditioned on better understanding of the discriminatory behavior that generates these differences.

Evaluating policy responses to sex differences and sex discrimination

There are three basic tools in the arsenal of public policies to combat discrimination against women (and minorities) in the United States. The Equal Pay Act of 1963 addressed pay discrimination within jobs, requiring employers to pay equal wages for substantially equal work, while noting some exceptions. Hiring discrimination and more general labor market discrimination is addressed by Equal Employment

Opportunity (EEO) legislation and Affirmative Action. EEO legislation began with Title VII of the Civil Rights Act of 1964, which made it illegal to discriminate in hiring, discharge, compensation, etc., on the basis of race, color, religion, sex, or national origin, and evolved further with the Equal Employment Opportunity Act (EEOA) of 1972. The groundwork for Affirmative Action was put in place not via legislation, but through a set of presidential Executive Orders governing employers contracting with the federal government.[18] Finally, a fourth policy that has taken hold in other industrialized countries and occasionally at the local or state level in the United States is comparable worth, which tries to equalize pay not simply across similar jobs, but across dissimilar but "equally valuable" jobs within firms or establishments, based on efforts to value the jobs independently of the wages they pay. There seems virtually no likelihood, however, that comparable worth will become more widespread in the United States.

In "New Evidence on Sex Segregation and Sex Differences in Wages from Matched Employer–Employee Data" (Chapter 12), we explore evidence on the nature of the sex wage gap to address the question of which policies are most useful in closing this gap. In particular, we extend the methods we have developed to match employer and employee data using Census data sources to create a broad and nationally representative data set with which to estimate the contributions of sex segregation by industry, occupation, and occupation-establishment cell (job cell), and the contribution of within-job-cell wage differences to the sex wage gap.

This decomposition of the wage gap can be used to guide policy. In particular, if within the narrowly defined occupations that we study the jobs performed by women and men require substantially equal skill, effort, responsibility, and working conditions, yet wages differ by sex, then enforcement of the Equal Pay Act still has a fundamental role to play in closing the wage gap between women and men. In contrast, if segregation along various dimensions accounts for most of the sex wage gap, then policies along the lines of comparable worth, equal opportunities in employment and promotion, and Affirmative Action would be central to any further closing of this gap, and stronger equal pay provisions would not be effective.

Our findings indicate that a sizable fraction of the overall sex gap in wages is accounted for by the segregation of women into lower-paying occupations, industries, establishments, and occupations within establishments. For example, using the most-detailed occupational classification, 4 percent of the gap is attributable to occupational segregation, 11 percent to industry segregation, 18 percent to establishment segregation, and 24 percent to segregation across occupations within establishments. However, a substantial part of the sex wage gap remains attributable to the individual's sex—in this example, 40 percent, with other estimates ranging up to around 50 percent. These latter estimates suggest that equal pay laws and enforcement still likely have a critical role to play in reducing discrimination that lowers the relative pay of women.

Of course, this evidence does not in any way negate the potentially important role of policies to combat discrimination in hiring, promotion, and other dimensions of employment. The final two chapters discussed in this introductory chapter evaluate the effectiveness of Affirmative Action.

Although one can distinguish EEO and Affirmative Action as separate policies, the distinction is not so sharp (Holzer and Neumark, 2000a). Even in the text of EEO law, EEO and Affirmative Action are intertwined. In particular, whereas Title VII of the Civil Rights Act of 1964, which established EEO as law, is mainly focused on the prohibition of discrimination in employment, the act also allows the courts, when finding that an employer is engaging in an unlawful employment practice, to "order such Affirmative Action as may be appropriate, which may include reinstatement or hiring of employees...."[19]

The difference is muddied further in practice because many employment discrimination cases concern hiring and are based on evidence of "disparate impact," according to which underrepresentation of women or minorities—relative to some suitably defined pool of job candidates—is sufficiently large to support an inference of discrimination. Much of the argument in such cases concerns the definition of the appropriate candidate pool. But regardless of how this issue is settled, employers concerned with a possible disparate impact discrimination claim would rationally seek to ensure that women and minorities are adequately represented among their hires. Indeed, EEOC guidelines for defining disparate impact essentially establish a system of numerical yardsticks, embodied in the "80 percent" or "four-fifths" rule, which states that "A selection rate for any race, sex, or ethnic group which is less than four-fifths... of the rate for the group with the highest rate will generally be regarded by the Federal enforcement agencies as evidence of adverse impact...."[20] As a consequence, when analyzing Affirmative Action in the labor market, it is more constructive not to limit attention solely to the effects associated with contractor status, but to focus more generally on policies or actions that induce increased hiring or promotion of women (or minorities).

A central issue in the debate over Affirmative Action is whether it leads to favorable treatment of unqualified women (or minorities) at the expense of more-qualified white males. Such outcomes might be objectionable on grounds of either efficiency or fairness. In "Are Affirmative Action Hires Less Qualified? Evidence from Employer–Employee Data on New Hires" (Chapter 13), we look at measures of individual employees' credentials or performance to see whether or not Affirmative Action generates gaps in performance between white male and other hires. We compare a variety of measures of employee credentials and performance, with the former including educational attainment (absolute levels and relative to job requirements), and the latter including wage or promotion outcomes as well as a subjective supervisor's performance measure. In particular, we evaluate whether or not observed gaps in credentials and performance between white males and females or minorities are larger among establishments that practice Affirmative Action in hiring than among those that do not; the relative comparison across the two types of establishments is critical because there may be population differences between white males and females or minorities.

The results indicate virtually no evidence of weaker credentials or performance among females in the Affirmative Action sector, relative to those of males within the same racial groups. But looking at minority females relative to white males (as well as minority males relative to white males), we find quite clear evidence of weaker educational credentials among minorities. However, we find relatively little evidence of weaker performance.

Our results generate the following puzzle: how could it be that Affirmative Action results in minority female (and male) hires with weaker credentials but not weaker performance, if educational credentials generally are meaningful predictors of performance? In "What Does Affirmative Action Do?" (Chapter 14), we consider the various mechanisms by which firms engaging in Affirmative Action might offset the expected productivity shortfalls among some workers hired from "protected groups." We find, among other things, that firms engaging in Affirmative Action: (1) recruit more extensively; (2) screen more intensively, and pay less attention to characteristics such as welfare recipiency or limited work experience that usually stigmatize candidates; (3) provide more training after hiring; and (4) evaluate worker performance more carefully. Thus, under Affirmative Action firms tend to cast a wider net with regard to job applicants, gather more information that might help uncover candidates whose productivity is not fully predicted by their educational or other credentials, and then invest more heavily in the productivity of those whom they have hired.

Overall, the evidence implies that Affirmative Action need not just "lower the bar" on expected performance of employees hired, and generally does not appear to do so, especially with respect to white women. Rather, a more benign view of Affirmative Action emerges, in which traditional means of recruitment and hiring are challenged, opening up the process to demographic groups less favored by these traditional means. This view does not mean that Affirmative Action never has perverse effects of causing outright favoritism toward women (or minorities)— reverse discrimination that may be no more defensible than the discrimination that Affirmative Action is intended to counter. But this critique of Affirmative Action is not supported by the data, suggesting that, if anything, it pertains to isolated cases rather than the operation of Affirmative Action in general. Of course, one might argue that a system in which women or minorities occasionally get the nod because of their sex or skin color, while not perfect, mirrors opposite cases in which white males are favored. Less polemically, while neither type of scenario can be justified, it is inappropriate to criticize Affirmative Action on the basis of isolated incidents of the former type without balancing them off against occurrences of the latter type.[21]

I have no doubt that attempts to understand and assess the operation of Affirmative Action will be a primary concern of researchers focusing on labor market discrimination. However, the findings regarding within-job sex wage gaps should serve as a reminder that strengthening equal pay laws—which are far less controversial than Affirmative Action—continues to have a very important and likely underappreciated role in reducing sex differences in labor markets. It should be recognized, though, that laws requiring higher pay for women that operate in isolation from laws promoting equal opportunity in employment may effectively act as a tax on female labor. Thus, a stronger focus on equal pay enforcement should not necessarily be viewed as a substitute for or come at the expense of equal opportunity enforcement.

Conclusions

Together with the many, many fine researchers who study sex differences and sex discrimination in labor markets, we have made tremendous progress in constructing economic explanations of different sex roles in labor markets and in evaluating these explanations. We have also taken strides toward a better understanding of the difficulties involved in trying to establish evidence of discrimination and in overcoming some of these difficulties. Finally, we have assembled an array of evidence on the effects of government policies to combat sex discrimination in labor markets and on the contributions and effectiveness of alternative policies.

Despite this progress, there is still a lack of consensus regarding the source of sex differences in labor markets, and perhaps even more so regarding government policies to reduce these differences. I would argue that the research emanating from the economics of the family generated some very clever and compelling explanations for sex differences in labor markets, in particular differences in wages and occupational choice. Although there is some evidence consistent with these explanations, this evidence does not rule out an important role for discrimination in generating sex differences in labor markets.

I also believe that the lack of consensus regarding the existence of discrimination is partly inertial. By this, I mean that the many empirical studies of discrimination using the wage regression approach, which documented a large wage gap between women and men and often attributed a sizable proportion of this gap to discrimination, are not viewed as very compelling. At the same time, the newer literature carrying out more convincing tests of discrimination—and, in my view, establishing rather compelling evidence of discrimination—is less well known. It is also possible, however, that this newer research is by its nature less likely to shift economists' priors about sex differences writ large because it sometimes focuses on very specific labor markets (such as the markets for concert musicians, or waiters and waitresses).

Finally, policy responses remain contentious not only because of disputes over whether they are appropriate in principle (i.e. whether there is discrimination), but also because the cure is sometimes viewed as worse than the disease. As an example, I would conjecture that among labor economists who are quite convinced women suffer from wage discrimination, many would nonetheless not endorse comparable worth. And the conflict over Affirmative Action at the time of writing shows signs only of sharpening.

I hope, of course, that my research has helped to answer some questions regarding sex differences in labor markets, sex discrimination, and policy responses.

But just as my own research is cumulative, so is the much wider body of research of which mine is only a part. Much of our knowledge on this topic remains to be discovered by future researchers, and I will be delighted if my past research helps to spark some of those discoveries.

Acknowledgments

I am grateful to Peter Richardson and Kenneth Troske for comments on this chapter.

Notes

1 These figures and those directly following are taken from Blau *et al.* (1998), who also indicate that similar trends to those described here occurred in other economically advanced countries. There are numerous outstanding reviews of empirical evidence on the evolution of sex differences in labor markets in the United States. See also Goldin (1990); O'Neill (1985); and Smith and Ward (1985).

2 The classic work on this topic, which spawned innumerable studies, is Schultz (1974).

3 See Oaxaca (1973) and Blinder (1973).

4 For an accessible—but skeptical—discussion of these policies, see Fuchs (1988).

5 This formulation comes from Arrow (1973). In Becker's original model d simply multiplies F in the employer's utility function, in which case variation in d across employers generates an equilibrium with complete sex segregation across all employers except those whose value of d equals the market wage differential between women and men. The utility function based on the relative number of female workers generates an equilibrium with less complete segregation, more consistent with observed employment patterns.

6 For a strong statement of this view, see Stigler and Becker (1977). They argue that "no significant behavior has been illuminated by assumptions of differences in tastes. Instead, they . . . have been a convenient crutch to lean on when the analysis has bogged down" (p. 89).

7 The analysis in Chapter 3 indicates that this conclusion is stronger for white than for black women.

8 Other sources of such interactions are also plausible. For example, the utility of leisure may decrease as one's friends enter the labor market, increasing the relative value of market work.

9 Oaxaca and Ransom (1994) provide an integrated discussion of alternative decompositions, and offer some arguments for which should be preferred.

  Another important criticism not pursued in the chapters discussed in this section, but covered implicitly in the previous section, is that coefficient estimates may differ for reasons unrelated to discrimination. As an example, Mincer and Polachek (1974) criticized early wage residual estimates using potential experience as a control variable because, given the more extensive labor market interruptions of women, potential experience overstates the actual experience—and hence human capital—of women relative to men, and hence the coefficient on potential experience should be lower for women. The residual wage gap approach, however, incorrectly attributes this difference to discrimination.

10 But see Gronau (1988) for such an attempt. Blau and Ferber (1991) also report estimates of a two-equation system using data from a survey of business students. The regression most relevant to the feedback hypothesis has the number of years women plan to work

full time as its dependent variable, with expected salary growth over twenty years plus other control variables on the right-hand side. The feedback hypothesis predicts that projected lower wage growth would lead to fewer planned years of work, insofar as the lower projected wage growth is in part due to discrimination. Because Blau and Ferber's survey asks about salary growth assuming *continuous* work, it does not suffer from endogenous determination with the expected participation variable. Yet they do not recognize this, and report only IV estimates. They also attempt to test the human capital model using their equation with expected salary growth as a dependent variable and planned work on the right-hand side. But again, because the salary growth expectation conditions on continuous work, there is no reason to expect to find the positive relationship predicted by the human capital model.

11 This criticism is perhaps best illustrated by Becker's (1985) effort allocation model.

12 As another example illustrating this point, Goldin and Rouse (2000) study discrimination against female musicians in orchestras, using an experimental design that is very much in the spirit of an audit study.

13 On the other hand, Black (1995) shows that in a search model, discriminatory tastes on the part of some employers can result in a wage gap, even when the discriminatory employers do not hire any minorities and are therefore not the marginal employers.

14 In the empirical work, we account for other inputs and other characteristics of workers and use a translog production function.

15 Some other interpretations—generally based on unmeasured variables correlated with the sex composition of plants' workforces—are considered in the chapter and rejected.

16 See Holzer and Neumark (2000a) for more elaboration on this argument.

17 I am struck by the parallels between this characterization of the debate over labor market discrimination and the debate over the efficient markets hypothesis—with the null hypothesis of efficient markets replacing the null of competition precluding or eliminating discrimination. See Shleifer (2000) for an outstanding discussion of the efficient markets debate.

18 See Holzer and Neumark (2000a) for a more complete discussion of Affirmative Action.

19 This occurred, for example, in *Firefighters Local Union No. 1784* v. *Stotts*.

20 See *Code of Federal Regulations*, Title 28, Volume 2, Section 50.14 (2001).

21 This has some parallels to discussions of inferring discrimination in audit studies. Heckman and Siegelman (1993) point out discrimination should be inferred not every time a white gets a job offer and a minority does not, but instead from "asymmetric treatment"—that is, more audits where the white gets a job offer and a minority does not, than audits in which the opposite outcome occurs. In contrast to audit studies, though, in the case of Affirmative Action there is the added possibility that the worker ultimately hired was less qualified.

References

Arrow, Kenneth J. 1973. "The Theory of Discrimination." In *Discrimination in Labor Markets*, eds Orley Ashenfelter and Albert Rees, pp. 3–33. Princeton, NJ: Princeton University Press.

Bayard, Kimberly, Judith Hellerstein, David Neumark, and Kenneth Troske. "New Evidence on Sex Segregation and Sex Differences in Wages from Matched Employer–Employee Data." Forthcoming in *Journal of Labor Economics*.

Becker, Gary S. 1971. *The Economics of Discrimination*, 2nd edn. Chicago, IL: The University of Chicago Press.

Becker, Gary S. 1981. *A Treatise on the Family*. Cambridge, MA: Harvard University Press.
——. 1985. "Human Capital, Effort, and the Sexual Division of Labor." *Journal of Labor Economics* 3(1, part 2): S33–58.
Black, Dan A. 1995. "Discrimination in an Equilibrium Search Model." *Journal of Labor Economics* 13(2): 309–34.
Blackburn, McKinley L., David E. Bloom, and David Neumark. 1993. "Fertility Timing, Wages, and Human Capital." *Journal of Population Economics* 6(1): 1–30.
Blau, Francine D. 1998. "Trends in the Well-Being of American Women, 1970–1995." *Journal of Economic Literature* 36(1): 112–65.
——. and Marianne A. Ferber. 1991. "Career Plans and Expectations of Young Men and Women." *Journal of Human Resources* 26(4): 581–607.
——, Marianne A. Ferber, and Anne E. Winkler. 1998. *The Economics of Men, Women, and Work*, 3rd edn. Upper Saddle River, NJ: Prentice-Hall, Inc.
Blinder, Alan S. 1973. "Wage Discrimination: Reduced Form and Structural Estimates." *Journal of Human Resources* 8(4): 436–55.
Cotton, Jeremiah. 1988. "On the Decomposition of Wage Differentials." *Review of Economics and Statistics* 70(2): 236–43.
Foster, Andrew D. and Mark R. Rosenzweig. 1993. "Information, Learning, and Wage Rates in Low-Income Rural Areas." *Journal of Human Resources* 28(4): 759–90.
Fuchs, Victor R. 1988. *Women's Quest for Economic Equality*. Cambridge, MA: Harvard University Press.
Goldin, Claudia. 1990. *Understanding the Gender Gap: An Economic History of American Women*. New York, NY: Oxford University Press.
—— and Cecilia Rouse. 2000. "Orchestrating Impartiality: The Impact of 'Blind' Auditions on Female Musicians." *American Economic Review* 90(4): 715–41.
Gronau, Reuben. 1988. "Sex-related Wage Differentials and Women's Interrupted Labor Careers—the Chicken or the Egg." *Journal of Labor Economics* 6(3): 277–301.
Heckman, James J. 1998. "Detecting Discrimination." *Journal of Economic Perspectives* 12(2): 101–16.
——. and Peter Siegelman. 1993. "The Urban Institute Audit Studies: Their Methods and Findings." In *Clear and Convincing Evidence: Measurement of Discrimination in America*, eds Michael Fix and Raymond J. Struyk, pp. 187–258. Washington, DC: The Urban Institute.
Hellerstein, Judith K. and David Neumark. "Using Matched Employer—Employee Data to Study Labor Market Discrimination." In *Handbook on the Economics of Discrimination*, ed. William Rodgers. Aldershot, UK: Edgar Elgar, forthcoming.
Hellerstein, Judith K., David Neumark, and Kenneth Troske. 1999. "Wages, Productivity, and Worker Characteristics: Evidence from Plant-Level Production Functions and Wage Equations." *Journal of Labor Economics* 17(3): 409–46.
——. 2002. "Market Forces and Sex Discrimination." *Journal of Human Resources* 37(2): 353–80.
Holzer, Harry and David Neumark. 1999. "Are Affirmative Action Hires Less Qualified? Evidence From Employer—Employee Data on New Hires." *Journal of Labor Economics* 17(4, Part 2): 534–69.
——. 2000a. "Assessing Affirmative Action." *Journal of Economic Literature* 38: 483–568.
——. 2000b. "What Does Affirmative Action Do?" *Industrial and Labor Relations Review* 53(2): 240–71.

——. "EEO Law and Affirmative Action." In *Handbook on the Economics of Discrimination*, ed. William Rodgers. UK: Edgar Elgar, forthcoming.

Korenman, Sanders and David Neumark. 1991. "Does Marriage Really Make Men More Productive?" *Journal of Human Resources* 26(2): 282–307.

——. 1992. "Marriage, Motherhood, and Wages." *Journal of Human Resources* 27(2): 233–55.

Kurdek, Lawrence A. 1993. "The Allocation of Household Labor in Gay, Lesbian, and Heterosexual Married Couples." *Journal of Social Issues* 49(3): 127–39.

Lundberg, Shelly J. and Richard Startz. 1983. "Private Discrimination and Social Intervention in Competitive Labor Markets." *American Economic Review* 73(3): 340–7.

Mincer, Jacob. 1962. "Labor Force Participation of Married Women: A Study of Labor Supply." In *Aspects of Labor Economics*, ed. H. Gregg Lewis, pp. 63–97. Princeton, NJ: Princeton University Press.

——. 1974. *Schooling, Experience, and Earnings*. New York, NY: National Bureau of Economic Research.

Mincer, Jacob and Solomon Polachek. 1974. "Family Investments in Human Capital: Earnings of Women." In *Economics of the Family*, ed. T.W. Schultz, pp. 397–429. Chicago, IL: The University of Chicago Press.

Neumark, David. 1988. "Employers' Discriminatory Behavior and the Estimation of Wage Discrimination." *Journal of Human Resources* 23(3): 279–95.

——. 1996. "Sex Discrimination in Hiring in the Restaurant Industry: An Audit Study." *Quarterly Journal of Economics* 106(3): 915–42.

——. 1999. "Labor Market Information and Wage Differentials by Race and Sex." *Industrial Relations* 38(3): 414–45.

Neumark, David and Sanders Korenman. 1994. "Sources of Bias in Women's Wage Equations: Results from Sibling Data." *Journal of Human Resources* 29(2): 379–405.

Neumark, David and Michele McLennan. 1995. "Sex Discrimination and Women's Labor Market Outcomes." *Journal of Human Resources* 30(4): 713–40.

Neumark, David and Andrew Postlewaite. 1998. "Relative Income Concerns and the Rise in Married Women's Employment." *Journal of Public Economics* 70(1): 157–83.

Oaxaca, Ronald L. 1973. "Male–Female Differentials in Urban Labor Markets." *International Economic Review* 14(3): 693–709.

Oaxaca, Ronald L. and Michael R. Ransom. 1994. "On Discrimination and the Decomposition of Wage Differentials." *Journal of Econometrics* 61(1): 5–21.

O'Neill, June. 1985. "The Trend in the Male–Female Wage Gap in the United States." *Journal of Labor Economics* 3(1, Part 2): S91–116.

O'Neill, June Ellenoff. 1994. "Discrimination and Income Differences." In *Race and Gender in the American Economy*, ed. Susan F. Feiner, pp. 13–7. Englewood Cliffs, NJ: Prentice Hall.

Schultz, Theodore W., ed. 1974. *Economics of the Family: Marriage, Children, and Human Capital*. Chicago, IL: The University of Chicago Press.

Shleifer, Andrei. 2000. *Inefficient Markets*. Oxford, UK: Oxford University Press.

Smith, James P. and Michael P. Ward. 1985. "Time-Series Growth in the Female Labor Force." *Journal of Labor Economics* 3(1, Part 2): S59–90.

Stigler, George J. and Gary S. Becker. 1977. "De Gustibus Non Est Disputandum." *American Economic Review* 67(2): 76–90.

Turner, Margery Austin, Michael Fix, and Raymond J. Struyk. 1991. "Opportunities Denied, Opportunities Diminished: Racial Discrimination in Hiring." Urban Institute Report 91–9. Washington, DC, The Urban Institute.

Winkler, Anne E. 1998. "Earnings of Husbands and Wives in Dual-Earner Families." *Monthly Labor Review* April: 42–8.

Part I

Family economics and sex differences in labor markets

1 Does marriage really make men more productive?

(with Sanders Korenman)

Introduction

Labor economists have long noted that married men earn substantially more per hour worked than men who are not currently married. These cross-sectional wage differentials persist when controls are introduced for education, race, region, age, or work experience, and even occupation and industry. Typically, differentials are in the 10–40 percent range—roughly as large as race, firm-size, and union wage differentials, as well as differentials across industries, all of which have been extensively studied. The marriage premium is of particular interest for estimating gender-based discrimination in labor markets, as the male marital pay premium accounts for about one-third of estimated gender-based wage discrimination in the United States (e.g. Neumark, 1988).[1] More generally, efforts to explain the marriage wage premium can contribute to achieving a better understanding of the determination of individual wages. Marital status differentials in labor market outcomes may also be of increasing interest in light of trends toward delaying (and perhaps foregoing) entry into first marriage, increased divorce rates, and sharply higher labor force participation rates among married women (especially those with young children). If marital status pay differentials reflect productivity differences, then changes in the marital status composition of the labor force potentially can affect the productivity of the labor force.

While there is widespread agreement that cross-sectional marriage differentials for men are sizable, there is much less agreement about their source. In fact, in a recent review of gender wage differentials, Goldin (1990, p. 102) concluded that "...the role of marriage in enhancing the earnings of male workers is still only dimly understood." One major hypothesis is that earnings differentials result from productivity differentials: that is, marriage *per se* makes workers more productive (Greenhalgh, 1980; Becker, 1981, 1985; Kenny, 1983). Another hypothesis attributes these differentials to employer favoritism (Hill, 1979; Bartlett and Callahan, 1984), and a third to selection into marriage on the basis of wages or personal characteristics that are valued in labor markets (Keeley, 1977; Becker, 1981; Nakosteen and Zimmer, 1987).[2]

This chapter presents new descriptive evidence that permits appraisal and refinement of hypotheses regarding the source of marriage pay premiums for white males.[3] The evidence is drawn from two sources: the National Longitudinal Survey of Young Men (NLSYM), and the company personnel file of a single large US manufacturing firm. The longitudinal data are used to examine how wages of individuals change as they change marital statuses, and to examine how wages change for individuals with each additional year spent in a particular marital state. The company personnel data allow us to examine marital status differences within a fairly homogeneous set of occupations (managers and professionals) and environments (i.e. within a single firm), thereby controlling implicitly for important characteristics of workers and jobs that can potentially vary across persons of different marital statuses. These data also include information unavailable from more standard labor market data sources, such as an employee's position (or job grade) in the company, and the performance rating he is given by his supervisor.

In the following section we review the existing empirical literature on male marriage pay differentials. The next two sections describe the NLS data and present the estimation procedures and results. The penultimate section describes the company personnel data and presents empirical findings. A discussion and concluding remarks follow in the final section.

Empirical studies of the marriage wage differential

That married men earn more than otherwise comparable single men is among the most robust findings from human capital wage equations. A comprehensive review of the multitude of studies that have estimated cross-sectional wage equations with marital status controls would, therefore, be a monumental task, and is beyond the scope of this chapter.[4] To cite an example, Schoeni (1990) documents that male marital pay differentials are large and statistically significant in each of the twelve industrialized countries that he studies. This section presents a brief and selective review of cross-sectional studies of the marriage wage premium, and a more detailed review of research that explicitly addresses hypotheses regarding the sources of these premiums.

First-generation studies (cross-sectional wage studies)

Hill (1979), using data from the 1976 Panel Study of Income Dynamics, finds that married men have higher wages than widowed, divorced, or separated men who, in turn, have higher mean wages than never-married men. Her regression analyses include very detailed controls for human capital, work history, health status, occupation, industry, and number of children. In (log) hourly wage regressions for white men, the estimated coefficient of the dummy variable for currently married men is 0.29 with a standard error of 0.04, while it is 0.27 with a standard error of 0.06 for those who are widowed, divorced, or separated.

Greenhalgh (1980) analyzes cross-sections of British workers for the years 1971 and 1975 and finds similar (though somewhat smaller) marital premiums. She attributes the "unexplained" portion of the differentials between married and single men to family role specialization. However, the unexplained portion could also result from other causes such as selection into marriage or employer favoritism.

Bartlett and Callahan (1984) study a sample of men aged 55–64 in 1977, drawn from the National Longitudinal Survey of Older Men, and find that married men earn 20–32 percent more than otherwise comparable unmarried men. Continuously married men, and men who married between 1966 and 1977, had faster wage growth between 1976 and 1977 than other men in the sample. A limitation of this sample of older men is that the effect of first marriages on earnings cannot be estimated; only four men in the sample changed from single to married status in the period covered.

Using wage surveys of three English establishments, Siebert and Sloane (1981) find unadjusted wage differentials favoring married men that range from 15 to 50 percent. Wage equations estimated separately for each of the three establishments (including controls for experience, company tenure, and education) yield differentials of 11, 12, and 27 percent, with corresponding t-statistics of 1.3, 2.0, and 3.9.

Second-generation studies

Two studies use techniques that go beyond the (essentially) cross-sectional analyses reviewed in the previous section, and therefore warrant a more detailed review.

Kenny (1983) uses retrospective data for men aged 30–40 in 1969 to compare mean monthly growth rates of earnings in married as compared to not-married months. He regresses the difference between the rate of growth of a man's wages in his married and not-married months, on age growth, and on the rate of growth of the general level of manufacturing wages, in the same months. The positive (and significant) *intercepts* are interpreted as indicating that wage growth is higher in the married months as compared to the not-married months. Adding controls for race, education, age at marriage, verbal ability, and wife's education makes the intercept negative and statistically insignificant. Kenny concludes that higher wage growth rates in the married months indicate that "a very large fraction of the wage differential between married males and never-married males appears to be attributable to the additional investment in human capital that occurs during marriage" (p. 229). Although faster wage growth is consistent with the hypothesis that greater investment in human capital takes place after marriage, Kenny presents no direct evidence on human capital investment. For example, Kenny does not estimate a marriage effect *net* of measured human capital (e.g. experience and tenure), so it is impossible to determine how much of the marital pay differential is attributable to greater accumulation of human capital. Finally, his findings are also consistent with relatively higher "returns" to—rather than greater investment in—human capital in married months that could result from factors such as favoritism, or from changes associated with marriage in tastes, prices, or effort levels.

Nakosteen and Zimmer (1987) correctly point out that "A possibility exists that marital status is determined stochastically by a process whose random unobservable component is correlated with unobservables in the wage/earnings function. In such a case conventional least squares estimates of the wage function, in particular the marital status coefficient and its standard error, are biased and inconsistent" (p. 249). To account for this problem, Nakosteen and Zimmer specify and estimate two-stage models in which endogeneity between marital status and earnings is allowed. The model that receives the most attention in the paper consists of an annual earnings equation for both married and unmarried men, containing a dummy variable for marital status, and a reduced form probit equation for marital status.[5]

Turning to their results, Ordinary Least Squares (OLS) estimation of the (log) annual earnings equation yields a coefficient on the marital status dummy variable of 0.370, with a standard error of 0.186. In the estimates that allow for endogeneity of the form described earlier, the marital status coefficient rises slightly to 0.410, while its standard error balloons to 0.695. Furthermore, the estimated coefficient of the selectivity variable is insignificantly different from zero, negative, and imprecisely estimated. (The point estimate is −0.190, with a standard error of 4.75.) The authors conclude, despite the large effect of marital status on earnings implied by their point estimates, that "the significant effect of married status disappears when the model is estimated free of selectivity bias, while the remaining coefficients continue to be largely unaffected. Thus, despite the apparent lack of significance of the selectivity term itself, these estimates indicate that marital status per se . . . fails to significantly shift the earnings profile" (p. 262).

This conclusion seems unjustified. The only real change in going from the single equation model to the model with endogeneity is a large increase in the standard error of the marital status coefficient. This seems an insufficient reason to discard the point estimate of the effect of marital status, which is, after all, a consistent estimate. In addition, their results indicate that the statistical experiment may be flawed.[6]

In summary, studies generally find substantial and statistically significant marriage wage premiums for males. The authors differ most widely in the interpretation of their empirical findings. The review suggests to us that, despite the contributions that these studies have made to a better understanding of marital pay differentials, continued research is needed to evaluate and refine hypotheses that are consistent with marital pay differentials. The remainder of the chapter is devoted to this task.

NLS data and summary statistics

The NLSYM followed men aged 14 to 24 in 1966 for fifteen years. Data from 1976, 1978, and 1980 are used to obtain repeated observations on individuals,[7]

Table 1.1 Summary statistics for white young men classified by marital status in 1976

Characteristics in 1976	Marital status in 1976		
	Married spouse present	Divorced or separated	Never married
Hourly wage ($)	6.57	6.90	5.56
	(0.08)	(0.40)	(0.17)
Schooling completed (years)	13.6	13.6	14.7
	(0.1)	(0.3)	(0.1)
Actual work experience (years)	6.6	6.2	4.2
	(0.2)	(0.6)	(0.3)
Age (years)	28.8	30.0	27.1
	(0.1)	(0.4)	(0.2)
Lives in South (%)	30.7	25.3	32.3
Lives in urban area (SMSA) (%)	70.6	84.8	79.9
Is covered by collective bargaining (%)	33.8	40.5	23.2
Has non-spouse dependent(s) (%)	77.6	51.9	3.7
Usual hours worked per week	43.7	43.6	41.5
	(0.2)	(1.1)	(0.6)
Weeks worked per year	50.7	48.8	49.5
	(0.2)	(1.0)	(0.6)
Years married	7.7	5.0	NA
	(0.1)	(0.4)	
Years divorced or separated	0.2	3.4	NA
	(0.0)	(0.3)	
Marital status in 1978, 1980 (%)			
Married, spouse present 1978	94.6	35.4	21.1
Married, spouse present 1980	92.0	53.2	29.1
Divorced or separated 1978	5.4	64.6	0.5
Divorced or separated 1980	7.9	46.6	2.1
Sample size	960	79	189

Source: National Longitudinal Survey, Young Men's Cohort.

which are required for estimation of the fixed-effects models presented later. We use the later years to capture the post-schooling labor market experience of a large portion of the sample. (The youngest men were 24 years old in 1976.) The sample is restricted to white men who completed schooling by 1976, and for whom all needed variables are available for the three years.[8] Attrition between 1966 and 1980 reduced the original sample of 5,225 men to 3,438. Data requirements further reduced the sample to 1,541; of these 1,228 are white.[9]

Sample statistics appear in Table 1.1. The first row of the table presents mean hourly wages in dollars according to marital status (the dependent variable in the regressions that follow is the natural logarithm of the hourly wage). Wages are available as hourly wages for hourly workers, and are constructed from weekly or annual earnings divided by the appropriate hours measure for those who report weekly or annual earnings. Never-married men appear to have much lower wages than men in the two other marital status groups (married, spouse present; and divorced or separated).

The figures in Table 1.1 also indicate that non-wage characteristics differ according to a man's marital status. For example, single men in the sample are younger and have completed more years of schooling, whereas married men have accumulated more work experience.[10] On average, married men worked about two hours more per week and one week more per year than never married men in the sample. The sample captures a fair number of marital status changes. Nearly one-third of the men who were single in 1976 had married by 1980 (29.1 percent plus 2.1 percent, using figures for 1980 marital status from the third column), over one-half of the men who were divorced or separated in 1976 were "remarried" by 1980, and at least 8 percent of married men had separated from their wives by 1980.

The figures in Table 1.1 also serve as a reminder that divorced and separated men have spent a substantial number of years married.[11]

NLS empirical findings

Methods

A leading explanation of marriage wage differentials is the selection hypothesis, which suggests that omitted, unmeasured characteristics that lead to higher wages are also positively correlated with marriage. For expository purposes, define the "true" model as

$$\ln(W_{it}) = \alpha \cdot X_{it} + \gamma \cdot MST_{it} + A_i + \epsilon_{it}, \tag{1}$$

where W_{it} is the wage of individual i in year t, A_i is an unobserved characteristic of individual i, which is assumed to be time-invariant (for illustrative purposes only one marital status variable (MST), and one other observable characteristic (X), are shown).[12] The selection of men with wage-enhancing attributes into marriage suggests that $\text{Corr}(MST_{it}, A_i) > 0$. In this case $\hat{\gamma}$, estimated by least squares from a model in which A_i is part of the error structure, is an upwardly biased estimate of γ. A standard solution to this problem (e.g. Freeman, 1984; Nakamura and Nakamura, 1985) is "within" or fixed-effects estimation of the model:

$$\ln(W_{it}) - \ln(W_{i\cdot}) = \alpha \cdot (X_{it} - X_{i\cdot}) + \gamma \cdot (MST_{it} - MST_{i\cdot}) + v_{it}, \tag{2}$$

where, for any variable Z, $Z_{i\cdot}$ denotes the mean of Z for individual i across the years t of the survey.[13]

Although estimation of this model removes individual fixed-effects, the possibility remains of serially correlated errors for an individual. Estimation of fixed-effects models in the presence of serially correlated disturbances is not trivial. Since in most panel data sets the number of periods is small, a consistent estimate of the residual covariance matrix is unavailable. We therefore use a consistent GLS estimator proposed by Keifer (1980) that yields consistent estimates of coefficients and their standard errors. This estimator assumes an error structure where residuals are uncorrelated across individuals, but correlated across time for each individual. More specifically, stacking the data so that observations for each individual are grouped together, the covariance matrix of the residuals is $(I_N \otimes \Sigma_T)$, where N is the number of individuals, T is the number of periods, I_N is the $N \times N$ identity matrix, Σ_T is a symmetric, positive semi-definite $T \times T$ matrix, and $\otimes$ is the Kronecker product operator. Forming the "within" differences as in equation (2) makes Σ_T a singular matrix, so that the GLS estimator requires a generalized inverse. Keifer shows that such an estimator can be obtained by forming the within differences, dropping data for one year,[14] and computing the GLS estimates, using the covariance matrix $(I_N \otimes \Sigma_{T-1})$.

Empirical findings

Estimation of the potentially misspecified (pooled) cross-sectional wage equation (1) (with A_i "omitted") confirms the presence of marriage premiums in the data. The first column of Table 1.2 presents these cross-sectional estimates, which closely resemble estimates from earlier studies. Married white men with spouse present earn about 11 percent more per hour than never-married men, controlling for survey year, labor market experience and its square, completed schooling (five dummy variables), union (covered) status, year of birth (ten dummy variables), South and urban residence, the presence of non-spouse dependents, and single-digit occupation and industry (nineteen dummy variables). Divorced or separated men earn about 9 percent more than never-married men.[15] Coefficients of these two marital status dummy variables are statistically significant at conventional levels.

Regressions (not reported) that also included years of service on the current job, and hours and weeks worked, yielded nearly identical results. Moreover (also not shown), dropping the control for non-spouse dependents raises the married coefficient somewhat, but leaves the divorced coefficient unchanged; and dropping the occupation and industry controls has no noticeable effect on the marital status coefficients. This latter finding provides partial evidence against the hypothesis that marital status simply reflects unmeasured worker or job characteristics, since the occupation and industry dummy variables should control for average differences in these characteristics across (broad) occupations and industries.

Column (1′) of Table 1.2 presents coefficients from longitudinal (fixed-effects) estimation of equation (2). Men who marry experience about an 8 percent wage increase, while those who divorce experience roughly a 2 percent decrease (e.g. 0.04 minus 0.06). Clearly the longitudinal estimates (and the implied t-statistics) of the effects of marriage are much smaller than the cross-sectional estimates. The much lower estimates of the marriage premium found in the longitudinal analysis are consistent with the hypothesis that a good portion (roughly one-half) of the cross-sectional marriage premium is associated with fixed (econometrically) unobservable characteristics of individuals that are positively correlated with both marriage and wages. The differences between the cross-sectional and longitudinal marriage premiums, however, could also result from an important misspecification

Table 1.2 Estimates of marriage premiums from NLS wage regressions, white males, 1976, 1978, 1980. Dependent variable equals Ln(hourly wage) or change in Ln(hourly wage). GLS coefficients (standard errors in parentheses)

	Dummy variable specifications		Years married specifications	
	Cross-sectional[a] (1)	Longitudinal[b] (1′)	Cross-sectional[a] (2)	Longitudinal[b] (2′)
Married, spouse	0.11	0.06	0.04	0.03
present	(0.02)	(0.03)	(0.03)	(0.03)
Divorced or	0.09	0.04	0.05	0.04
separated[c]	(0.03)	(0.04)	(0.03)	(0.04)
Years married,			0.023	0.022
spouse present			(0.006)	(0.009)
Years married,			−0.085	−0.096
squared/100			(0.028)	(0.034)
Years divorced or			−0.011	−0.025
separated			(0.006)	(0.011)
Has non-spouse	0.04	0.02	0.02	0.00
dependents	(0.02)	(0.02)	(0.02)	(0.02)
Degrees of freedom	3,639	2,427	3,636	2,424

Notes

a Also included in the cross-sectional regressions are actual experience and its square, South, urban, union (covered), schooling (5), year (3), year of birth (10), and single-digit occupation (8) and industry (11) dummy variables.

b Except for schooling and cohort dummy variables, the longitudinal regressions include the controls listed above, entered as deviations from their mean values from 1976, 1978, and 1980. Because the sample is restricted to those who have completed school, schooling variables do not deviate from their mean values and are excluded. Birth year is also constant over time.

c The category divorced or separated includes a few men who are widowed or married, spouse absent.

of the earnings equation that could contaminate the statistical experiment. In particular, it is possible that the attenuation of the marriage premium results from a time-dependent effect of marriage on wages (as suggested by Kenny, 1983). In contrast to the benefits of starting a unionized job, for example, which should accrue to a member quickly, there is no reason to believe that the labor market returns to marriage are reaped upon utterance of the words "I do." This consideration suggests that the diminution of the marriage premium in longitudinal estimation may be due to a shorter duration of marriage for those who marry between 1976 and 1980 than for those who are observed married at a given time. In our sample, a person who married between 1976 and 1978 accumulated about one and one-half years of marriage, on average, while those who were married in 1978, for example, had been married for an average of about twelve years. Therefore, a longitudinal marriage wage differential of 6 percent is consistent with a 4 percent yearly wage growth premium (in the early years of marriage) accruing to married, as compared to never-married men.

Columns (2) and (2′) of Table 1.2 report coefficients from cross-sectional and longitudinal regressions where marriage premiums are allowed to vary by marital duration.[16] The most striking result is that there is no longer a sizable or significant *intercept* shift associated with any particular marital status. Rather, the effect of marriage appears gradually, increasing wages (cross-sectionally) 2.3 percent per year married in the early years of marriage, and roughly 1–2 percent per year at the mean of years married.[17,18] The wage premium earned by divorced or separated men compared to never-married men appears to be explained by the advantages gained from time spent married; there is a negative and significant cross-sectional effect on wages of years divorced or separated. The fixed-effects results also reveal a significant negative association between years divorced and wages of 2.5 percent per year (compared to continuously never-married men).

Calculations of marital premiums for persons who change marital states lend additional support for the idea that the reduction of the marital status premium from 0.11 in column (1), to 0.06 in column (1′) is due to a misspecification of the wage equation. As noted, a man who married between 1976 and 1978 accumulated 1.5 years of marriage, on average. Using this figure in conjunction with the coefficients presented in column (2) yields a marriage premium for these newlyweds of 0.07, and the coefficients reported in column (2′) imply a premium of 0.06,[19] very similar to the fixed-effects coefficient reported in column (1′). Columns (2) and (2′), however, suggest that the marriage premium continues to grow with each year married, indicating that the 0.06 percent figure understates the marriage wage differential. This point is brought out more fully by Table 1.3.

In Table 1.3, we use the cross-sectional and longitudinal coefficient estimates from Table 1.2, columns (2) and (2′), to summarize the marriage wage premium in two ways: first, as the sum of the coefficient on the dummy variable plus the years effect (evaluated at the unconditional sample means for the appropriate group); and second, as this figure, plus the coefficient on the dependents dummy. The

Table 1.3 Summary of cross-sectional and longitudinal estimates of marital pay premiums at mean years married, NLS young men, whites, 1976, 1978, 1980. Estimated wage premiums (percent)[a]

	Married vs. single			Married with non-spouse dependents vs. single with no non-spouse dependents		
	Cross-section	Longitudinal	Ratio	Cross-section	Longitudinal	Ratio
Years married specification[b] Table 1.2, column (2) vs. (2′)	16.6	14.8	0.92	18.1	15.2	0.84
Dummy variable specification Table 1.2, column (1) vs. (1′)	10.6	6.1	0.58	14.8	8.2	0.55

Notes

a Estimates of wage premiums are calculated using coefficient estimates from Table 1.2. For regression details, see footnotes to Table 1.2.

b Estimates are evaluated at the unconditional sample mean of "Years Married" for the appropriate group.

latter calculation compares a married man with non-spouse dependents to a single man with no dependents. (For comparison, corresponding figures from the dummy variable specifications in columns (1) and (1′) of Table 1.2 are reproduced in the second panel of Table 1.3.) Table 1.3 indicates that the longitudinal estimates are much closer to the cross-sectional estimates for the "years married" specification than for the dummy variable specification. Evaluated at the sample mean years of marriage, the longitudinal estimate of the marriage premium is between 80 and 90 percent as large as the cross-sectional estimate.

To summarize findings from the NLS data, there appears to be a significant increase in wages associated with marriage for white males, even correcting for selectivity into marriage based on fixed unobservables; over 80 percent of the estimated impact of marriage on earnings survives the fixed-effects estimation. Moreover, large marriage premiums persist even after adding controls to wage equations that should capture differences across marital statuses in labor supply or in investment in human capital (e.g. occupation, industry, hours and weeks worked, and tenure on the current job).

Although the fixed-effects estimates suggest that the selectivity hypothesis alone does not account for a major share of the marriage premium, at least not in the simple "fixed unobservables" form of the hypothesis, it is possible that a more complex selection process underlies the marriage premium. For example, selection into marriage on the basis of unmeasured potential wage growth could account for the remaining marriage premiums. The possibility also exists that causation could run from wages to marital status. If the marriage premium resulted from selection of men with high wage *levels* into marriage, then we would not expect to have found that marriage wage premiums result from wages rising with years married. On the other hand, if the marriage wage growth premiums were due to selection of men with high wage *growth rates* into marriage, then unmarried men with relatively high wage growth in a period should be more likely to marry thereafter. Korenman (1988, chapter III) found no evidence of such an effect in these data; controlling for other observable characteristics, unmarried men in this sample who had high wage growth between 1975 and 1976 were (insignificantly) *less* likely than other men to marry between 1976 and 1980.

In the remainder of the chapter we present analyses of data drawn from a company personnel file in order to illuminate further the marriage differential in general, and the "years married" effect in particular.

Company personnel data and empirical findings

Data

This section briefly describes data from the personnel file of a large US manufacturing firm described in detail in Medoff and Abraham (1981). The data are for white male managers and professionals working within a single firm for the year 1976. Sample statistics are reported in Appendix Table 1.A2. Because the data pertain to a fairly homogeneous set of occupations (managers and professionals) and work environments (a single firm), they allow us to control implicitly for important characteristics of workers and jobs that potentially vary across persons of different marital status. Most of the variables are self-explanatory as they are common in labor market data sets.

The data are unique in that they obtain supervisor performance ratings that provide an additional measure of worker productivity, aside from a worker's wage. The performance of each manager or professional employee is rated each year by his immediate supervisor.[20] Supervisors are instructed to rate employees on "current performance and contributions based on requirements of his present assignment" (Medoff and Abraham, 1981, p. 189). Ratings are to reflect performance relative to the "standards" of the job, and relative to "others performing similar work at similar levels," but are not to reflect "[c]areer potential and promotability" (Medoff and Abraham, 1981, p. 189). On a six-point scale, six is the highest performance rating. Each employee is also ranked relative to other workers in comparable jobs, by several different supervisors, all of whom are familiar with his work. In order to ensure the consistency of performance ratings by immediate supervisors with these "consensus rankings," both are reviewed by managers at the next higher level of the corporation.

Another somewhat nonstandard variable contained in the data is the employee's job grade. According to a company salary manual, a job's grade reflects its relative value to the company, and "positions of similar value are placed in the same classification level" (Medoff and Abraham, 1981, p. 191). (In practice, job grade dummy variables alone account for roughly 85 percent of the variation across workers in the log of annual salaries in this company.)

Given these definitions of performance ratings and job grades, Medoff and Abraham are "comfortable assuming that, within a given grade level, those with high performance ratings or high rankings were more productive than those with low performance ratings or rankings" (Medoff and Abraham, 1981, p. 191).

Estimation and empirical findings

Table 1.4 presents estimates from earnings equations in 1976, using the natural log of annual salary as the dependent variable. The second column shows sizable and significant annual earnings differentials of about 12 percent favoring both married and divorced men, controlling for pre-company experience and its square, company service and its square, and dummy variables for region and education. Because performance ratings are valid only for workers doing comparable jobs (i.e. controlling for job grade), performance ratings can be meaningfully related to worker productivity only if job grade dummies are added to the wage regressions. Adding job grade dummy variables alone (column (3)) diminishes the marriage premium substantially; although the coefficients remain statistically different from zero, they imply that married men earn only about 2.5 percent more per year than otherwise comparable single men working in similar jobs.[21] Thus, most of the return to marriage, whatever its source. takes the form of location of married

Table 1.4 Estimated coefficients from cross-sectional earnings regressions. Company personnel data, white male managers and professionals.[a,b] Dependent variable is Ln (annual salary as of December 1976)

	OLS coefficients (SEs)			
	(1)	*(2)*	*(3)*	*(4)*
Married	0.226	0.119	0.025	0.019
	(0.014)	(0.012)	(0.004)	(0.004)
Divorced	0.182	0.115	0.022	0.022
	(0.027)	(0.021)	(0.008)	(0.007)
Widowed	0.224	0.069	0.020	0.013
	(0.042)	(0.034)	(0.013)	(0.012)
Other included variables:				
Pre-company experience and its square, company service and its square	No	Yes	Yes	Yes
Region (3) and education (4) dummies				
Grade dummies (11)	No	No	Yes	Yes
Performance rating dummies (5)	No	No	No	Yes
R^2	0.03	0.38	0.91	0.93

Notes
a The sample size is 8,235. The reference category is "Single."
b Means of variables used in the regressions appear in Table 1.A2.

workers in higher paying job grades within the company, rather than higher pay for a given performance level within a job grade.[22]

The preceding results imply that we should direct our attention to the association between marriage and job grades—and not to the effects of marriage on wages within job grades. Why are single men relatively concentrated in the lower grades? On the one hand, marital status could determine the grades into which workers are hired or promoted, or whether they experience job separations. On the other hand, the concentration of married workers in higher grades may be coincidental, simply reflecting a company lifecourse whereby young workers are hired into lower grades, progress through the corporate hierarchy based on a combination of tenure and performance, and tend to get married along the way. If this last scenario is correct, then there should be no discernible marriage pattern of hiring, promotion, pay, or performance once controls are introduced for other worker characteristics and company tenure.

To explore the first possibility, we examine a sample of "recent hires" (workers with two or fewer years of company service). There is at most a slight marriage pattern to hiring; over 90 percent of recent hires are found in four job grades (two through five); single workers comprise 32 percent of the recent hires in grade two, and 29 percent of recent hires in each of grades three through five. Further, estimates of earnings equations for this sample, presented in Table 1.5, confirm that hiring practices are not responsible for the marriage premiums. In particular, there is no significant wage differential favoring married "recent hires," controlling for

Table 1.5 Estimated coefficients from cross-sectional earnings regressions. Company personnel data, white male managers and professionals, recent hires.[a,b,c] Dependent variable is Ln (annual salary as of December 1976)

| | OLS coefficients (SEs) | | | |
	(1)	(2)	(3)	(4)
Married	0.030	−0.004	0.002	0.000
	(0.015)	(0.013)	(0.010)	(0.010)
Other included variables:				
Pre-company experience and its square, company service and its square	No	Yes	Yes	Yes
Region (3) and education (3) dummies				
Grade dummies (3)	No	No	Yes	Yes
Performance rating dummies (4)	No	No	No	Yes
R^2	0.01	0.40	0.63	0.64

Notes

a The sample size is 280. The reference category is "Single."

b "Recent Hires" are people with two or fewer years of company service.

c The smaller number of grades here than in Table 1.4 reflects the concentration of "Recent Hires" in the lower grades. Only one recent hire received the lowest performance rating, hence he and the category were dropped from the sample.

the worker characteristics listed above, whether or not grade dummy variables or performance ratings are included in the regressions.[23]

Turning to the possibility of different chances of promotion into higher grades, or job separation, on the basis of marital status, we estimate multinomial logit models of the probability of promotion and job separation of recent hires between year-end 1976 and year-end 1977, including controls for characteristics of workers as of 1976. Results are summarized in Table 1.6. In the first panel, where performance ratings variables are excluded from the analysis, marriage is associated with a substantially higher probability of promotion, and a slightly lower probability of separation from the company, controlling for pre-company experience and its square, company service, and dummy variables for education, region, and job grade. Although neither coefficient is statistically significant (the asymptotic *t*-statistic for the promotion–marriage coefficient is about 1.5, and for the job separation–marriage coefficient, about 0.6), the implied partial derivative of the probability of promotion with respect to marriage is sizable; controlling for the above characteristics, the probability of promotion for a married man is 10.5 percentage points higher than for a single man (column (2)). Compared to the sample mean probability of promotion, married men are about 34 percent more likely to be promoted (41.2 versus 30.7), all else (except rated performance) held constant.[24]

Coefficients from analyses that include performance dummy variables are reported in the second panel. Strikingly, the marriage promotion premium virtually disappears when performance ratings are added; the separation premium also grows somewhat (in absolute value). As these figures suggest, and as multinomial logit analyses of performance ratings confirm (Panel 3), married workers are more likely to win high performance ratings, and higher performance ratings are positively related to the probability of promotion.[25]

The third panel of Table 1.6 summarizes results from these performance rating logits (the top two and bottom two performance rating categories are combined). The figures indicate that marriage increases by almost 50 percent the probability that a recent hire will receive one of the top two performance ratings (compared to the median rating category), controlling for education, job grade, Southern location, company service, and pre-company experience.

In short, married men are substantially more likely than their single counterparts to receive high performance ratings; high performance ratings, in turn, appear

Table 1.6 Estimated coefficients from multinomial logit models of promotion and job separation, and models of rated performance, recent hires. Company personnel data, white male managers and professionals, 1976 (standard errors in parentheses)[a]

	Married coefficient (SE)	*Partial with respect to marriage (percent)*	*Percent change in probability (at sample mean)*
1 Without performance controls[b,c]			
Job separation	−0.223	−2.8	−16.9
	(0.378)		
Promotion	0.499	10.5	34.3
	(0.332)		
2 With performance controls			
Job separation	−0.318	−4.1	−24.7
	(0.339)		
Promotion	0.052	1.0	3.4
	(0.368)		
3 Performance rating[d]			
Low	−0.636	−13.2	−43.0
	(0.358)		
High	0.791	19.3	46.2
	(0.355)		

Notes

a "Recent Hires" have two or fewer years of company service. The sample size is 280. The partial derivatives are evaluated at sample means.

b Other variables included in the promotion and separation equations are: pre-company experience and its square, company service, and dummy variables for education (3), region (3), job grade (3), and a constant. Performance controls are four rating dummy variables.

c In the sample, 16.4 percent of recent hires had job separations, and 30.7 percent were promoted. The reference category is "retained without promotion."

d Other variables included in the performance equations are: pre-company experience and its square, company service, dummy variables for education (3), South, job grade (3), and a constant. In the sample, 30.7 percent were rated "Low" and 41.9 percent were rated "High," that is, below or above the median (reference) category.

to increase promotion probabilities so that married men are also more likely to be promoted. The large and statistically significant marital pay premiums for managerial and professional workers within a single firm suggest that marriage wage differentials do not compensate married men for working under adverse conditions. While it is possible that these managers and professionals need to be compensated for undertaking the greater responsibility that accompanies promotion, it seems plausible that promotions to higher paying positions are used to reward workers who are perceived to be performing well.

These results also provide evidence that is consistent with the NLS data, which indicate that a steeper wage profile, rather than an intercept shift, best describes marriage wage premiums. The evidence presented therefore calls for future research to focus on job assignment or promotion, in additon to wages, in exploring marriage pay differentials. Because these findings are based on analysis of the company personnel file of a single firm, caution should be exercised in drawing more general conclusions from these data until additional firm-level analyses are conducted.

Conclusions

In this chapter we have attempted to bring new evidence to bear on the male marital pay premium. We have five principal findings to report.

First, hourly wage premiums paid to married men are large and persist even when detailed human capital controls (such as actual labor market experience) are included in wage equations.

Second, marriage premiums seem to arise slowly, resulting more from faster wage growth for married men as compared to never-married men, than from an intercept shift associated with any particular marital status. This finding suggests that an appropriate specification allows for a relationship between marriage and wages that varies according to the number of years a man is married.

Third, taking as our "true" model a specification that incorporates a "years married" effect, comparisons of cross-sectional and fixed-effects estimates indicate that selection on the basis of fixed unobservable characteristics accounts for less than 20 percent of the observed wage premium.

Fourth, data drawn from a company personnel file indicate that the marriage wage premiums persist even within a single firm, for a relatively homogeneous group of occupations (managers and professionals). The marriage premium appears to be due to the location of married workers in higher paying job grades within the company, rather than to married workers receiving higher pay than single workers within the same job grades.

Finally, married workers in this company receive higher performance ratings from their supervisors. These higher performance ratings increase their promotion chances, allowing them to enter the higher paying job grades. When we controlled for supervisor performance ratings, however, the marriage promotion premium disappeared.

Although these findings do not represent a tightly constructed test of a theory of marital pay differentials, they do lend greater support to some hypotheses than to others. In particular, selection of men into marriage on the basis of wages, wage growth, or other wage-enhancing characteristics receives little support as an explanation of the observed marital pay premiums. Wages rise after marriage, fixed-effects estimates of marriage premiums in properly specified wage equations are nearly as large as their cross-sectional counterparts, and in the sample and period we studied, unmarried men's wage growth appears unrelated to the probability that they marry.

While it may be fair to interpret our findings as providing support for the hypothesis that marriage enhances men's labor market productivity, a definitive judgment requires more direct evidence about the processes or causal mechanisms linking marriage to men's productivity.

Appendix

Table 1.A1 Sample statistics by years married, ever married men, 1976. Means (standard errors of means in parentheses)

Characteristics in 1976	Two or fewer	Two to five	Five to ten	Ten or more
Hourly wage	5.51	6.02	6.77	7.22
	(0.36)	(0.13)	(0.13)	(0.17)
Schooling completed	13.9	14.1	13.8	12.7
(years)	(0.3)	(0.1)	(0.1)	(0.1)
Actual work experience	3.9	4.4	6.3	10.3
(years)	(0.5)	(0.2)	(0.2)	(0.3)
Age (years)	26.9	26.5	28.7	32.1
	(0.3)	(0.1)	(0.1)	(0.1)
Percentage who				
Live in South	27.1	25.0	33.6	31.5
Live in urban areas (SMSAs)	83.1	74.7	69.1	70.1
Are covered by collective				
bargaining	47.5	29.8	35.3	34.6
Have non-spouse dependents	35.6	47.6	86.6	98.4
Hours worked per week	42.5	42.8	44.4	43.8
	(1.1)	(0.4)	(0.4)	(0.4)
Weeks worked per year	49.2	50.0	50.8	51.0
	(1.3)	(0.4)	(0.3)	(0.3)
Married, spouse present (%)	64.4	93.2	92.4	98.0
Divorced or separated (%)	35.6	6.8	7.6	2.0
Years married spouse present	1.1	3.7	7.7	13.0
	(0.1)	(0.1)	(0.1)	(0.1)
Years divorced or separated	1.8	0.4	0.4	0.2
	(0.4)	(0.1)	(0.1)	(0.1)
Sample size	59	292	434	254

Table 1.A2 Means for white male managers and professionals, company personnel data, 1976 (standard deviations in parentheses)

	All	Single	Married	Divorced	Widowed
Number	8,235	337	7,730	126	42
Salary in 1976 ($)	26,629	21,384	26,873	25,594	26,936
	(7,183)	(5,731)	(7,159)	(6,347)	(8,119)
Ln(annual salary)	10.15	9.94	10.17	10.12	10.16
	(0.25)	(0.24)	(0.25)	(0.23)	(0.27)
Less than high school diploma	0.02	0.01	0.02	0.01	0.10
High school diploma	0.34	0.09	0.35	0.36	0.43
College	0.45	0.52	0.44	0.42	0.38
MA	0.15	0.29	0.14	0.18	0.10
PhD	0.04	0.09	0.04	0.03	0.00
Years of pre-company experience	5.2	2.9	5.3	4.9	5.9
	(5.3)	(3.0)	(5.4)	(4.9)	(5.9)
Years of company service	19.5	8.5	19.9	16.4	31.1
	(11.3)	(10.4)	(11.0)	(10.9)	(8.2)
Northeast	0.14	0.14	0.14	0.06	0.29
South	0.75	0.71	0.75	0.81	0.67
Midwest	0.02	0.03	0.02	0.02	0.00
West	0.09	0.13	0.09	0.10	0.05
Job grade distribution					
Bottom quartile	11.5	17.2	11.3	11.9	19.1
Second quartile	51.5	65.9	50.8	55.5	47.7
Third quartile	30.2	14.9	31.0	26.9	23.8
Top quartile	6.8	2.0	6.9	5.6	9.6
Performance ratings					
Low (1–3)	40.1	38.0	40.2	39.7	52.4
High (4–6)	59.9	62.0	59.8	60.3	47.6

Acknowledgment

The authors are grateful to James Medoff for making available an extract from the company personnel file.

Notes

1 The standard technique for estimating wage discrimination (Blinder, 1973; Oaxaca, 1973) decomposes a wage differential between two groups into a part due to differences in average characteristics, and a part due to different coefficients in separate wage regressions. The part resulting from differences in coefficients is commonly interpreted as discriminatory. Marital status coefficients for men are large and positive, while those for women are typically close to zero.

2 Our review of published research in this area indicates that these categories, broadly defined, cover the majority of hypotheses that have been advanced to date. Additional hypotheses exist, however, that do not fall into one or more of these three

categories. Reed and Harford (1988) have suggested that the marriage premium may be a "compensating differential" needed to bribe married men to work under adverse conditions.

3 Korenman and Neumark (1990, 1988) explore the relationships between marriage and pay for women and minority men, respectively.

4 For partial summaries see Nakosteen and Zimmer (1987), Kenny (1983), and Bartlett and Callahan (1984).

5 This is the "treatment effects" model of Barnow *et al.* (1980). The procedure used to obtain consistent estimates of the wage equation parameters is (i) to estimate the probit; (ii) to construct from this probit a "marriage selectivity" variable related to the probability of being married; and (iii) to include this variable on the right-hand side of the wage equation, and to estimate this equation by least squares (correcting the standard errors of the coefficient estimates).

6 A potentially important problem is that the selectivity term is itself correlated with marital status, by construction. This source of collinearity may lie behind the large increase in the standard error of the marital status coefficient, as well as the imprecision with which the coefficient of the selectivity term is estimated. Suggestive of other problems are: very large returns to experience (25 percent per year), negative returns to schooling, and the use of annual earnings with a sample of 16–24 year olds, many of whom may not have completed their schooling.

7 Surveys were not conducted in 1977 and 1979.

8 Griliches (1976, 1978) discusses problems in using these data for younger men. While our choice of 1976–80 permits us to study post-schooling labor market behavior, it entails some reduction in the sample size and the number of marital status changers.

9 As mentioned in the introduction, Korenman and Neumark (1988) report results for blacks. We limit the present analysis to white men because the company personnel data set analyzed below contains no information on blacks. Separate analysis by race also seems advisable given evidence that patterns of family formation and marriage differ greatly between black and white Americans (Evans, 1986; Bennett *et al.*, 1989).

10 "Actual Experience" measures post-schooling work experience, in years or fractions of years, based on weeks worked. This measure includes work experience of those who were enrolled in school part-time, but who did not report school as their primary activity. It was constructed using retrospective job history questions, and where these were incomplete, contemporaneous survey questions, whenever possible.

11 Construction of the "years married" and "years divorced or separated" variables entailed a combination of contemporaneous and retrospective questions. For men who married for the first time prior to the first survey year, retrospective questions on the number and durations of marriages, divorces, and separations allowed construction of marital histories covering up to two marriages prior to 1966. Fewer than 20 percent had been married at least once by the 1966 survey.

12 In the empirical analysis, the model will be expanded to include many "human capital" variables, as well controls for different marital states, and in some specifications, for the number of years spent in each marital state.

13 We often refer to the results from such models as longitudinal estimates.

14 We drop data for 1976, although the results do not depend on the year chosen.

15 The category divorced or separated includes a few men who are widowed or "married, spouse absent."

16 Corresponding sample statistics by years married are presented in Table 1.A1 in the Appendix.

17 The quadratic functional form for years married was adopted after examining specifications with single-year dummy variables for each year of marriage.

18 In regressions that included both the total duration in each marital state and the duration in the current marital state, duration in current state did not enter significantly.

19 Using the coefficients reported in column (2′), the relevant calculation is

$$0.06 = 0.03 + (1.5) \cdot (0.022) + (1.5)^2 \cdot (-0.096)/100.$$

20 This section summarizes, in part, section I of Medoff and Abraham (1981).

21 These regressions were also run separately for the twelve individual job grades. The coefficient on the married dummy variable changed somewhat from grade to grade, but was generally about the same size as the coefficient for the overall sample, controlling for job grade. There was no striking correlation between job grade and the size of the marriage premium.

22 That single workers are disproportionately represented in lower job grades is apparent from the job grade distribution reported in Table 1.A2.

23 The sample was restricted to four grades that contain over 92 percent of the company's "recent hires," as well as to men who were married or single (eliminating two divorced men), and who received better than the lowest performance rating (eliminating one employee).

24 This finding is consistent with Goldin's (1990, p. 102) evidence from the Depression era suggesting that employers promoted married office workers more frequently.

25 In particular, the promotion logits indicate large and statistically significant relationships between the probability of promotion and the four included performance rating dummy variables (2, 3, 4, and 6, there are no "1s" in the sample, 5 is the reference category). The derivatives of the probability of promotion with respect to these four dummy variables are: $-21.4, -45.0, -16.5$, and 16.7; the ratios of the coefficients to standard errors (corresponding to the coefficients used to calculate the derivatives) are: $-1.5, -4.4, -2.1$, and 1.7, respectively.

References

Barnow, Burt, Glen Cain, and Arthur Goldberger. 1980. "Issues in the Analysis of Selectivity Bias." In *Evaluation Studies Review Annual*, Vol. 5, ed. Ernst Stromsdorfer and George Farkas, pp. 43–59. Beverly Hills: Sage Publications.

Bartlett, Robin and Charles Callahan. 1984. "Wage Determination and Marital Status: Another Look." *Industrial Relations* 23(1): 90–6.

Becker, Gary. 1981. *A Treatise on the Family*. Cambridge: Harvard University Press.

——. 1985. "Human Capital, Effort, and the Sexual Division of Labor." *Journal of Labor Economics* 3(1, Part 2): S33–58.

Bennett, Neil, David Bloom, and Patricia Craig. 1989. "The Divergence of Black and White Marriage Patterns." *American Journal of Sociology* 95(3): 692–722.

Blinder, Alan. 1973. "Wage Discrimination: Reduced Form and Structural Estimates." *Journal of Human Resources* 8(4): 436–55.

Evans, M. D. R. 1986. "American Fertility Patterns: White-Nonwhite Comparisons." *Population and Development Review* 12(2): 267–93.

Freeman, Richard. 1984. "Longitudinal Analyses of the Effects of Trade Unions." *Journal of Labor Economics* 2(1): 1–26.

Goldin, Claudia. 1990. *Understanding the Gender Gap*. New York: Oxford University Press.

Greenhalgh, Christine. 1980. "Male-Female Wage Differentials in Great Britain: Is Marriage an Equal Opportunity?" *Economic Journal* 90(360): 751–75.

Griliches, Zvi. 1976. "Wages of Very Young Men." *Journal of Political Economy* 84(2): S69–85.

——. 1978. "Earnings of Very Young Men." In *Income Distribution and Inequality*, ed. Zvi Griliches *et al.* Frankfurt: Campus Verlag.

Heckman, James. 1978. "Dummy Endogenous Variables in Simultaneous Equations Systems." *Econometrica* 46(4): 932–59.

Hill, Martha. 1979. "The Wage Effects of Marital Status and Children." *Journal of Human Resources* 14(4): 579–94.

Keeley, Michael. 1977. "The Economics of Family Formation." *Economic Inquiry* 15(2): 238–50.

Keifer, Nicholas. 1980. "Estimation of Fixed Effect Models for Time Series of Cross-Sections with Arbitrary Intertemporal Covariance." *Journal of Econometrics* 14(2): 195–202.

Kenny, Lawrence. 1983. "The Accumulation of Human Capital During Marriage by Males." *Economic Inquiry* 21(2): 223–31.

Korenman, Sanders. 1988. "Empirical Explorations in the Economics of the Family." PhD Dissertation, Department of Economics, Harvard University.

Korenman, Sanders, and David Neumark. 1988. "Does Marriage Really Make Men More Productive?" Finance and Economics Discussion Paper No. 29, Federal Reserve Board, May.

——. 1990. "Marriage, Motherhood, and Wages." NBER Working Paper No. 3473, October.

Medoff, James and Katharine Abraham. 1981. "Are Those Paid More Really More Productive? The Case of Experience." *Journal of Human Resources* 14(2): 186–216.

Nakamura, Alice and Masao Nakamura. 1985. "Dynamic Models of the Labor Force Behavior of Married Women Which Can Be Estimated Using Limited Amounts of Past Information." *Journal of Econometrics* 27(3): 273–98.

Nakosteen, Robert and Michael Zimmer. 1987. "Marital Status and Earnings of Young Men." *Journal of Human Resources* 22(2): 248–68.

Neumark, David. 1988. "Employers' Discriminatory Tastes and the Estimation of Wage Discrimination." *Journal of Human Resources* 23(3): 279–95.

Oaxaca, Ronald. 1973. "Male–Female Wage Differentials in Urban Labor Markets." *International Economic Review* 14(3): 693–709.

Reed, W. Robert and Kathleen Harford. 1988. "The Marriage Premium and Compensating Wage Differentials." Texas A&M Department of Economics Working Paper, #88–14.

Schoeni, Robert. 1990. "The Earnings Effects of Marital Status: An International Comparison." Paper presented at the Annual Meetings of the Population Association of America, Toronto, May.

Siebert, W. S. and Sloane, P. J. 1981. "The Measurement of Sex and Marital Status Discrimination at the Workplace." *Economica* 48(190): 125–41.

2 Marriage, motherhood, and wages

(with Sanders Korenman)

Introduction

Cross-sectional studies find little association between a woman's marital status and her wage rate, but often a negative relationship between children and wages. The negative relationship between children and wages is reduced and sometimes eliminated by inclusion in wage equations of detailed controls for "labor force attachment" such as experience and tenure.

There are, however, a number of reasons to be cautious in drawing causal inferences from these cross-sectional relationships. First, labor market experience and tenure may be endogenous if labor supply is responsive to wages. Because the estimated effect of children on wages is sensitive to the inclusion of controls for experience and tenure, it is important to explore whether experience and tenure are in fact exogenous variables in wage equations. Second, economic theories of fertility and marriage (e.g. Butz and Ward, 1979; Easterlin, 1980; Becker, 1981) suggest that marital status and number of children may also be endogenous with respect to wages. Third, estimated wage effects of marriage or children may be biased by unmeasured heterogeneity: women may be selected or may self-select into different marital or fertility states on the basis of unmeasured characteristics that are correlated with wages (e.g. "career orientation"), even if marriage or fertility are not directly responsive to wages. Finally, bias could result if, among married women or women with children, those with high wages tend to select into employment (i.e. the standard problem of sample selection bias).

Previous researchers have recognized some of these potential problems in interpreting cross-sectional relationships between wages, marriage, and children, but have not attempted to evaluate the empirical importance of each of them in a single data set. This chapter presents evidence on the magnitudes of these biases, assesses the sensitivity of the estimated effects to alternative approaches to eliminating bias, and attempts to arrive at unbiased estimates of the effects of marriage and children on wages.

The effects of marriage and motherhood on wages are of particular interest due to their relation to male–female wage differentials. For example, Becker (1985) has hypothesized that a portion of male–female wage differentials is attributable to gender-role specialization by married women and men. In particular, he has argued that the "hourly earnings of single women [should] exceed those of married women even when both work the same number of hours and have the same market capital because child care and other household responsibilities induce married women to seek more convenient and less energy intensive jobs" (p. S54).[1] Therefore, the empirical analysis of wage differentials between single and married women, and women with and without children, can shed light on the wage effects of gender-role specialization.

Empirical studies of marriage, children, and women's wages

Using the 1976 Panel Study of Income Dynamics, in multiple regression analysis with a standard set of human capital controls, Hill (1979) finds that married, white women with a spouse present earn more than their never-married counterparts, but less than divorced, separated, or widowed women. However, these differences are small and not statistically significant. Controlling for marital status, the number of children present is significantly negatively related to earnings. But when Hill adds detailed measures of labor force attachment and interruptions, the negative association between children and wages becomes small and insignificant (less than 1 percent per child).[2,3]

Focusing exclusively on the association between children and wages, Moore and Wilson (1982) examine a cross-section of married women aged 35–49 in 1972 who were full-time workers, from the National Longitudinal Survey (NLS) Mature Women file. Controlling for a wide variety of worker characteristics, they find that married women with three or more children earn about 11 percent less per hour than married women without children, but that there are small and statistically insignificant differences among women with zero, one, or two children.

Goldin and Polachek (1987) examine the 1/1,000 Public Use Sample of the 1980 US Census of Population and find substantial and significant annual earnings differentials favoring never-married women. However, substituting a variable called the "Expected Human Capital Stock" (which varies across individuals with differences in expected lifetime labor force participation) for education and experience variables reduces the marriage differential to about 38 percent of its original size.[4] Goldin and Polachek argue, *à la* Becker (1985), that much of the remaining differential "probably owes to the problem of controlling for intensity of work among individuals with greater home responsibilities" (p. 149).

Three English studies provide further evidence on the relationship between marital status and wages. Greenhalgh (1980), analyzing repeated cross-sections of British women from the General Household Surveys of 1971 and 1975 finds mean hourly earnings differentials favoring single women of 45 and 42 percent in 1971 and 1975, respectively. But estimates of separate wage equations by marital status leave only 3–12 percent of these differentials "unexplained" by differences in the characteristics of workers or jobs.

Siebert and Sloane (1981), using wage surveys of four English establishments, find roughly 10–25 percent unadjusted (i.e. mean) annual earnings differentials favoring single women in three establishments, and an 11 percent differential favoring married women in the fourth. Controlling for worker attributes (typically experience, tenure, and education) lowers the differential substantially in one establishment, but raises or leaves unchanged the others. Siebert and Sloane also report that the presence of children under age 12 is unrelated to wages for married women who worked in the one establishment that collected information on children.

Dolton and Makepeace (1987) estimate the association between marriage, children, and wages using the (English) 1970 Survey of Graduates. The coefficient of a marriage variable from an ordinary least squares (OLS) log wage equation is −0.02 (with a standard error of 0.02) for women with no children, and −0.03 for those with children.[5] Correcting for selectivity into employment leads to a negligible change in the coefficient estimates.

In summary, these findings suggest that marriage has little or no association with women's wages,[6] while children appear to reduce wages primarily "indirectly," by reducing labor force participation and the accumulation of human capital, rather than "directly," by lowering the productivity of otherwise similar women. However, all of these studies take children and marital status, as well as experience and tenure, to be exogenous determinants of wage rates, and only one study (Dolton and Makepeace) attempts to account for employment selectivity.

Data and empirical findings

Data

The data analyzed are from the National Longitudinal Survey of Young Women. Most of our cross-sectional specifications are estimated using the 1982 wave of the survey, when the respondents were aged 28–38. This period covers an age range that captures both post-schooling labor market experience and marital status and fertility transitions that are needed for longitudinal estimation. From the original sample of 5,159 in 1968, attrition, nonmissing data requirements, and the restriction of the sample to white women reduce the sample size to 1,207 women working for a wage as of the 1982 survey. To perform longitudinal analyses, we need repeated wage observations; much of our longitudinal analysis focuses on the 911 women who worked for a wage in 1980 and 1982. We will address the influence of selection into the sample of women working in 1982, as well as the smaller sample working in both 1980 and 1982.

In order to estimate a direct effect of marriage and children on wages—apart from an indirect effect that may operate through reduced human capital accumulation—good controls for labor market experience and tenure are needed. Experience and tenure are constructed from job history questions that were asked over the entire range (1968–82) of the data set. Experience is measured as year-equivalents of actual weeks worked, while tenure simply counts the number of years for which a respondent reports working for the same employer.

Table 2.1 Mean log wages and changes in log wages, for white working women classified by marital status, number of children, and changes in marital status and number of children[a]

	Married, spouse present	Divorced or separated	Never married	No children	One child	Two + children
Status as of 1982						
1982 sample						
(1) Log wage	6.39	6.45	6.60	6.59	6.48	6.32
(1982)	(0.01)	(0.03)	(0.04)	(0.02)	(0.03)	(0.02)
N	787	262	158	371	234	602
1980–2 sample						
(2) Log wage	6.46	6.47	6.59	6.60	6.53	6.37
(1982)	(0.02)	(0.03)	(0.04)	(0.02)	(0.03)	(0.02)
(3) Change in						
log wage	0.20	0.21	0.22	0.22	0.19	0.19
(1980–2)	(0.01)	(0.02)	(0.02)	(0.02)	(0.02)	(0.02)
N	576	194	141	316	190	405
Status entered 1980–2						
1980–2 sample						
(4) Change in						
log wage	0.17	0.21			0.25	0.18
(1980–2)	(0.06)	(0.05)			(0.05)	(0.04)
Number of changers	46	53			33	26

Note

a Standard errors of means are reported in parentheses. Sample weights were not used in computing estimates. The 1980 data are reported only for observations with wages and other variables used in wage regressions available for 1982. Wages are nominal values, with levels coded in cents.

A first look at wage levels and changes

The upper panel of Table 2.1 reports mean log hourly wages (with wages measured in cents) for women with different marital statuses, and different numbers of children, as well as the distribution of women across these categories. Row (1) covers the sample of women working for a wage in 1982. On average, never-married women earn wages 15 percent higher than divorced or separated women who, in turn, earn slightly more than women who are married with a spouse present.[7] More pronounced differences appear between women with different numbers of children. The greatest wage differential (about 27 percent) is found between childless women and those with two or more children.

Although such differentials suggest that marriage and children lower a woman's wage, they may also reflect other differences (observable or unobservable) among women. One approach to this heterogeneity problem is to examine how wages change as a woman changes marital status or has children. Rows (3) and (4) provide a first pass at this first-difference analysis. Row (4) reports mean changes in log wages between 1980 and 1982 for women who changed marital or fertility status. These changes can be compared to the figures in row (3), which are the mean changes in log hourly earnings for all women.

The mean change in the log wage is lower for women who marry between 1980 and 1982 (0.17 in row (4)) than for women who remain single in 1982 (0.22, row (3)). However, the mean change is only slightly lower for women who have a second child (0.18, row (4)) compared to women with one child as of 1982 (0.19, row (3)), and is actually relatively high for women who have a first child between 1980 and 1982 (0.25, row (4)). Thus, wage growth appears unaffected by changes in marital status or number of children, raising the possibility that the cross-sectional differences in wages by marital status or number of children may be mostly due to heterogeneity, observable or not.

However, the first-difference approach may be flawed because *recent* changers (e.g. women who had a first birth between 1980 and 1982) who worked in 1982 may be a select group. In addition, because they are aged 28–38 in 1982, these recent changers are also relatively "late" child bearers, who tend to be relatively high earners (Bloom, 1987; Blackburn *et al.*, 1990). Finally, as mentioned, the marital status and fertility transitions may to some extent reflect *responses to* wages. These potential problems underscore the need for multivariate analysis that explicitly account for heterogeneity, employment selectivity, and endogeneity of marital status and number of children.

OLS regression estimates

Table 2.2 reports estimates from OLS cross-sectional log wage regressions. Never-married women and childless women are the reference categories. Column (1) reports the regression of log wages on the marital status and number of children variables. As the estimates show, when dummy variables for number of children are included in the equation, the negative associations of marriage or divorce with wages (apparent in Table 2.1) disappear, while children (especially two or more) are associated with significantly lower wages. When years of education completed and dummy variables for living in the South and in an SMSA are added in columns (2) and (3), the coefficients of the number of children dummy variables are reduced by about one-half; only the coefficient of the two or more children dummy variable remains statistically significant. In column (4) experience and tenure are included, reducing the magnitude of the coefficients of the number of children variables even further.[8] These results are consistent with the findings of many of the studies reviewed in the section "Empirical studies of marriage, children, and women's wages": after controlling for experience and tenure, marriage and children have relatively little association with wages.[9,10]

Bias in OLS regression estimates

As discussed in the introduction, there are many potential sources of bias in the cross-sectional estimates presented in Table 2.2. The previous subsection touched on biases that could be addressed by the inclusion of better measures

Table 2.2 Wage equation estimates for white working women, 1982, OLS (dependent variable: natural logarithm of hourly earnings)[a]

	(1)	(2)	(3)	(4)
Married, spouse present	−0.02	0.01	0.02	0.05
	(0.05)	(0.04)	(0.04)	(0.04)
Divorced or separated	−0.00	0.05	0.05	0.10
	(0.05)	(0.05)	(0.05)	(0.04)
One child	−0.13	−0.05	−0.05	−0.04
	(0.04)	(0.04)	(0.04)	(0.04)
Two + children	−0.30	−0.18	−0.18	−0.07
	(0.03)	(0.03)	(0.03)	(0.03)
Education	—	0.06	0.06	0.07
		(0.01)	(0.01)	(0.01)
South	—	—	−0.05	−0.05
			(0.02)	(0.02)
Urban	—	—	0.15	0.15
			(0.03)	(0.02)
Experience	—	—	—	0.02
				(0.004)
Tenure	—	—	—	0.03
				(0.003)
F-test[b]	0.00	0.00	0.00	0.03
R^2	0.10	0.19	0.23	0.33

Notes
a There are 1,207 observations. Standard errors are reported in parentheses. Sample weights were not used in computing estimates. Observations are included only if the wage reported is for a job at which the respondent is currently working. Never married and no children are the reference categories. Single-year age dummy variables are included in all specifications.
b *p*-value for joint test of significance of marital status and fertility variables.

of observed characteristics. This section considers sources of bias associated with unobservables: endogeneity; heterogeneity arising from selection into different categories of marital status and number of children on the basis of unmeasured characteristics correlated with wages; and selection into employment.

Endogeneity bias and instrumental variables estimates

Table 2.3 reports estimated coefficients and standard errors from equations in which marital status and number of children, as well as experience and tenure, are treated as potentially correlated with the wage equation error. The table also reports test statistics for the exogeneity of these variables with respect to the wage equation error (Hausman, 1978). The instrumental variables, described in detail in the footnotes to Table 2.3, fall into two categories: family background variables and measures of attitudes and expectations. Exclusion restrictions to identify coefficients necessarily involve untestable assumptions. In this section, the maintained assumption is that family background measures are valid instruments.

Table 2.3 Wage equation estimates for white working women, 1982, two-stage least squares (dependent variable: natural logarithm of hourly earnings)[a]

	Experience, tenure, marital status, and fertility endogenous				Experience and tenure endogenous	
	(1)	(2)	(3)	(4)	(5)	(6)
Coefficients						
Married, spouse present	0.40	−0.02	−0.07	−0.14	0.04	0.04
	(0.51)	(0.30)	(0.31)	(0.19)	(0.05)	(0.05)
Divorced or separated	0.75	0.16	—	—	0.07	0.08
	(0.59)	(0.30)			(0.07)	(0.06)
One child	−0.59	−0.44	—	—	−0.04	−0.04
	(0.69)	(0.41)			(0.04)	(0.04)
Two + children	−0.38	−0.40	—	—	−0.20	−0.19
	(0.43)	(0.24)			(0.08)	(0.06)
Children	—	—	−0.27	−0.33	—	—
			(0.36)	(0.20)		
Experience	−0.03	−0.03	−0.02	−0.03	−0.03	−0.03
	(0.05)	(0.02)	(0.04)	(0.02)	(0.03)	(0.02)
Tenure	0.03	0.03	0.01	0.03	0.03	0.03
	(0.06)	(0.03)	(0.04)	(0.03)	(0.04)	(0.02)
F-test[b]	0.59	0.07	0.49	0.01	0.02	0.00
Family background variables used as IVs[c]	Yes	Yes	Yes	Yes	Yes	Yes
Expectational/attitudinal variables used as IVs[d]	No	Yes	No	Yes	No	Yes
Specification tests (p-values)						
Experience and tenure exogenous[e]	0.23	0.00	0.09	0.00	0.09	0.00
Marital status exogenous[e]	0.38	0.79	0.80	0.49	—	—
Fertility status exogenous[e]	0.59	0.27	0.54	0.07	—	—
Expectational/attitudinal variables excluded[f]	0.74	—	0.74	—	0.36	—

Notes

a There are 1,207 observations. Standard errors are reported in parentheses. Sample weights were not used in computing estimates. Observations are included only if the wage reported is for a job at which the respondent is currently working. Single-year age dummy variables were included in all specifications. Never married and no children are the reference categories. Other independent variables are the same as those in Table 2.2, column (3).

b p-value for joint test of significance of marital and fertility status variables.

c Variables include: father's education; mother's education; parents' educational goal for respondent at age 14; number of siblings; a dummy variable equal to one if the respondent's mother worked when respondent was age 14; a dummy variable equal to one if the respondent lived with both a father and mother at age 14, and dummy variables corresponding to each of these variables, equal to one when the variable was missing (in which case the variables were set equal to zero).

d Variables include a dummy variable set equal to one if respondent disagreed or strongly disagreed with statement that it is alright for a woman to work even if her husband disagrees, asked in 1971; a dummy variable set equal to one if respondent agreed or strongly agreed with this statement, in 1971; ideal age at marriage reported by respondent at age 14 (set equal to zero, with a dummy variable set equal to one if response was never to marry); expected number of children, in 1970; educational expectations, in 1970; educational goal, in 1970; and dummy variables corresponding to each of these variables, equal to one when the variable was missing (in which case the variables were set equal to zero).

e p-value for joint significance of coefficients of the residuals from least squares regression of these variables on instruments and exogenous variables, when these residuals are added to wage equation.

f p-value for asymptotic F-test for exclusion of variables from wage equation.

Researchers using sibling pairs to identify wage equation parameters have shown that, once ability and schooling are taken in account, family background does not have an independent effect on earnings or wages (Griliches, 1979). These findings suggest using family background measures as instruments. Conditional upon the maintained assumption that family background variables are valid instruments, the exclusion of measures of attitudes and expectations from the wage equation can be tested as over-identifying restrictions.

Instrumental variables (IV) estimates of the specifications from Table 2.2, column (4)—using family background variables as instruments for experience, tenure, marital status and number of children—are reported in column (1) of Table 2.3. There is no statistical evidence that experience, tenure, marital status, or number of children are correlated with the wage equation error; in the bottom panel of the table, the p-values for the exogeneity tests are all greater than 0.05.[11] As the last entry in column (1) indicates, when the equation was re-estimated including measures of attitudes and expectations, the exclusion of these measures from the wage equation could not be rejected. Hence, column (2) adds attitudes and expectations to the instrument list. In this specification there is also no evidence that marital status or children are correlated with the wage equation error; the p-values for the exogeneity tests are 0.79 and 0.27, respectively. But the exogeneity of experience and tenure is rejected.

To examine the sensitivity of these conclusions to alternative specifications, in columns (3) and (4) we specify a simpler wage equation that includes a dummy variable for married, spouse present only (so that never-married *or* divorced or separated is the reference category), and a dummy variable for whether the woman has any children. Repeating the analysis of columns (1) and (2) with this simpler specification, our conclusions are unchanged (using a 5 percent significance level). However, the correlation between children and the wage equation error is stronger; the p-value for the exogeneity test in column (4) is 0.07.

The instrumental variables methods do not lead to a rejection of the exogeneity of marital status and children, and yield imprecise estimates of their effects. Consequently, in columns (5) and (6) we treat experience and tenure (only) as potentially correlated with the wage equation error. We continue to reject the exogeneity of experience and tenure, and their coefficients are not significantly different from zero. For tenure this is solely because the standard error increases, while for experience the point estimate changes considerably (although a negative coefficient seems implausible).[12] More importantly, the coefficients of the marital status and children variables are very similar to the OLS coefficients in column (3) of Table 2.2, in which experience and tenure were omitted. Of course, this finding stands in contrast to OLS estimates that include experience and tenure, in which the negative association between children and wages is attenuated or eliminated.

As long as the error is uncorrelated with the instruments, the instrumental variables methods used in Table 2.3 are sensitive to any source of correlation between the right-hand-side variables and the wage equation error. If the source of correlation is a fixed effect, then first-difference methods provide an alternative estimation strategy that may be preferable to IV methods for two reasons. First of all, first-difference methods do not rely on untestable exclusion restrictions.

Second, if there are fixed effects that, for example, influence both wages and fertility, IV methods require not only an exclusion restriction, but an additional assumption that the excluded variable(s) are orthogonal to the fixed effect.

Unobserved heterogeneity bias and fixed-effects estimates

We use first differences estimated for 1980 and 1982 to eliminate potential biases from fixed, unmeasured characteristics on the basis of which women select into different marital or fertility states. Although we exclude experience and tenure from these specifications, this exclusion has virtually no effect on estimates of the marital status and children coefficients. This is because a short first difference implicitly controls for experience and tenure by using a sample of women employed in two consecutive survey years (e.g. 1980 and 1982). For women employed in two consecutive years, having a child, for example, does not lead to much reduction in experience and tenure, relative to childless women.[13]

For comparison with what follows, the first row of Table 2.4 reports OLS coefficient estimates for the subset of the sample for which 1980 and 1982 data are available.[14] The second row of the table reports estimates from the 1980 and 1982 change equation.[15] None of the marital status or children coefficients is significantly different from zero, nor are these variables jointly significant (the

Table 2.4 Wage equation estimates for white working women, first-difference specifications (dependent variables: levels and changes of natural logarithm of hourly earnings)[a]

	Married, spouse present	Divorced or separated	One child	Two + children	Early[b] wage	F-test[c]	N
1980–2 data							
(1) 1982	0.05	0.05	−0.01	−0.15	—	0.00	911
	(0.04)	(0.05)	(0.04)	(0.04)			
(2) 1982–80[d] change	−0.06	−0.04	0.05	0.02	—	0.76	911
	(0.08)	(0.08)	(0.05)	(0.07)			
Specification test							
(3) 1982–80 change	−0.05	−0.01	−0.00	−0.03	0.04	0.62	728
	(0.07)	(0.08)	(0.05)	(0.07)	(0.03)		
Early difference							
(4) 1973	0.05	0.06	0.01	−0.09	—	0.11	543
	(0.03)	(0.06)	(0.04)	(0.05)			
(5) 1973–71[d] change	0.03	0.07	−0.02	−0.02	—	0.70	543
	(0.03)	(0.06)	(0.06)	(0.11)			

Notes

a Standard errors are reported in parentheses. Sample weights were not used in computing estimates. Observations are included only if the wage reported is for a job at which the respondent is currently working. Single-year age dummy variables were included in all specifications for wage levels. Other independent variables are the same as those in Table 2.2, column (3). Right-hand-side variables are levels in rows (1) and (4), and first differences in all other rows. In the cross-sectional specifications, never married and no children are the reference categories.

b 1978 log wage.

c *p*-value for joint test of significance of marital status and fertility variables.

d Standard fixed-effects estimator.

p-value from the F-test is 0.76). The coefficients of marital status fall considerably and become negative, while the coefficients of the number of children variables actually become positive. The fixed-effects estimates suggest that cross-sectional estimates are biased by unmeasured heterogeneity. In other words, women with wage-enhancing characteristics (net of observables) appear less likely to have (two or more) children.

Heckman and Hotz (1989) have proposed an "overidentification test" of the fixed-effect assumption. This test asks whether early wage levels are associated with later wage growth, indicating selection into different marital or fertility states based on wage *growth*, in contrast to the fixed-effects assumption of selection on wage *levels*. To perform this test, we retain an earlier (1978) wage, and estimate

$$(w_{82} - w_{80}) = (X_{82} - X_{80})b_{82} + w_{78}d + (e_{82} - e_{80}).$$

An estimated d significantly different from zero indicates a violation of the fixed-effects assumption. The results reported in row (3) indicate that $\hat{d}$ is not significantly different from zero, so we do not reject the fixed-effects specification.[16]

Despite the results of the specification test, two problems may arise from using 1980–2 first differences, because the effects of marital status and number of children are identified from women who changed states between 1980 and 1982. First, because they are *recent* changers (i.e. they had a birth between 1980 and 1982), those who chose to work in 1982 might be changers with particularly high wages. This is the standard problem of selection into employment, but it may be particularly severe for recent changers (Solon, 1988). We examine the problem of selectivity of recent changers in the following subsection.

Second, the women in our sample were aged 26–36 in 1980, which suggests that the changers are relatively late marriers or child bearers who may have higher than average wages following first births or marriage (perhaps because they are more able to afford child care), leading to upward-biased estimates in the first-difference specifications. To address the problem of "late changer" bias, we estimated an early first difference (1971–3), when the women were 17–29 years old.[17] The results, also reported in Table 2.4, differ little from the 1980–2 first-difference estimates, indicating that there is no serious bias from using late marriers and child bearers.

One approach to the problem of "recent changer" bias would be to use a longer first difference, in which effects of children and marriage are identified from women who change states, even if they are not employed in the years immediately following the change. However, equality of the wage equation coefficients for 1973 and 1982 (the long difference we examined) was rejected ($p = 0.02$). Moreover, the fixed-effects specification was rejected according to the overidentification test described earlier. Thus, we could not use long differences to correct for selectivity among recent changers. In the following section we use alternative methods to test and correct for employment selectivity.

Employment selectivity bias and sample selection corrections

We first selectivity-correct the 1980–2 first-difference estimates, applying Heckman's (1979) sample-selection correction techniques to first differences, assuming jointly normally distributed errors. Before turning to these estimates, OLS and selectivity-corrected estimates of the 1982 cross-sectional wage equation are reported in the first two columns of Table 2.5.[18] Since recent changers influence the cross-sectional estimates, some selectivity bias in the cross-sectional estimates is expected. Indeed, the estimates of the number of children coefficients become more negative when account is taken of selectivity, although the changes are small. The coefficient of the inverse Mills' ratio (lambda) is marginally significant, with a t-statistic of 1.86.

Table 2.5 Wage equation estimates for white working women, sample selectivity-corrected (SSC) estimates (dependent variables: levels and changes of natural logarithm of hourly earnings)[a]

	1982 OLS (1)	1982 SSC[b] (2)	1982–80 OLS[c] (3)	1982–80 SSC[d] (4)
Status in 1982				
Married, spouse present	0.02	0.01	−0.05	−0.07
	(0.04)	(0.04)	(0.08)	(0.08)
Divorced or separated	0.05	0.07	−0.04	−0.05
	(0.05)	(0.05)	(0.08)	(0.08)
One child	−0.05	−0.07	0.04	0.05
	(0.04)	(0.04)	(0.05)	(0.06)
Two + children	−0.18	−0.22	0.04	0.05
	(0.03)	(0.04)	(0.07)	(0.09)
Lambda	—	0.13	—	—
		(0.07)		
Lambda–80	—	—	—	−0.04
				(0.05)
Lambda–82	—	—	—	−0.06
				(0.07)
F-test[e]	0.00	0.00	0.83	0.75
N	1,181	1,181	888	888

Notes
a Standard errors are reported in parentheses. Sample weights were not used in computing estimates. Observations are included only if the wage reported is for a job at which the respondent is currently working. Single-year age dummy variables were included in all specifications for wage levels. Other independent variables are the same as those in Table 2.2, column (3). In the cross-sectional specifications, never married and no children are the reference categories.
b Variables in the employment probit include 1982 values of all variables included in wage equation specification in Table 2.2, column (3), as well as dummy variables indicating whether a respondent changed marital or fertility states between 1980 and 1982 (a different dummy variable is used for each of the four categories). Finally, measures of husband's income and weeks husband spent unemployed in 1982 (both set to zero for unmarried women), and the sum of income from alimony and child support (set to zero for never-married women), are included.
c Standard fixed-effects estimator.
d A bivariate probit model is used for the selectivity correction. Variables included in probits for 1982 and 1980 are values for corresponding year of all variables included in wage equation specification in column (3) of Table 2.2, values of husband's income and weeks husband spent unemployed (both set to zero for unmarried women), the sum of income from alimony and child support (set to zero for never-married women), and—for 1982—dummy variables indicating whether a respondent changed marital or fertility states between 1980 and 1982 (a different dummy variable is used for each of the four categories).
e *p*-value for joint test of significance of marital status and fertility variables.

In columns (3) and (4) we apply a similar technique to the 1980–2 first difference, using a bivariate selectivity criterion for employment in 1980 as well as 1982.[19] The coefficient estimates are unaffected by the selectivity correction, and the estimated coefficients of the lambda terms (one for each year) do not indicate the presence of sample selectivity.

As an alternative test for selectivity bias from recent changers—one that does not require the specification of employment equations—we estimate a wage regression for all women who worked in 1980 (whether or not they worked in 1982). In this wage regression for 1980, we include dummy variables indicating whether a woman changed into one of the marital or fertility states between 1980 and 1982, as well as interactions between these variables and a variable indicating whether the woman was employed in 1982. The coefficients of the interaction terms measure, for example, the wage in 1980 of a woman who had her first child between 1980 and 1982 *and worked in 1982*, relative to the wage of a similar woman who had her first child between 1980 and 1982, but was *not employed in 1982*. If high

Table 2.6 Wage equation estimates for white working women, survey year prior to change in marital status or number of children (dependent variable: natural logarithm of hourly earnings)[a]

	Became married, spouse present	Became divorced or separated	Had first child	Had second child
1980 wage regression				
(Change in marital or fertility	0.02	0.24	0.05	−0.03
status) × (worked in 1982)[b]	(0.15)	(0.27)	(0.12)	(0.15)
Number worked 1980 and 1982[c]	50	57	38	30
Number worked 1980 only[d]	7	2	15	8
1971 wage regression				
(Change in marital or fertility	0.02	−0.17	0.14	−0.11
status) × (worked in 1973)[b]	(0.05)	(0.11)	(0.08)	(0.11)
Number worked 1971 and 1973[c]	111	20	21	9
Number worked 1971 only[d]	65	9	51	21

Notes

a There are 833 observations for the 1971 regression, and 1,091 observations for the 1980 regression. Standard errors are reported in parentheses. Sample weights were not used in computing estimates. For each year, observations are included if the wage reported is for a job at which the respondent is currently working. Single-year age dummy variables were included in all specifications for wage levels. All independent variables listed in Table 2.2, column (3) are included. In addition, dummy-variable indicators of changes in marital status and numbers of children are included.

b Estimated coefficients of variables defined as the 1982 (1973) marital status or number of children variable, times a dummy variable equal to one if the woman changed into the category between 1980 and 1982 (1971 and 1973), times a dummy variable equal to one if the woman remained in the workforce in 1982 (1973).

c Number of women who changed into the indicated marital status or number of children category between 1980 and 1982 (1971 and 1973), and worked for a wage in 1982 (1973).

d Number of women who changed into the indicated marital status or number of children category between 1980 and 1982 (1971 and 1973), and did not work for a wage in 1982 (1973).

earners among recent changers select into employment, then a woman who had a child between 1980 and 1982 and who worked in 1982, should earn relatively higher wages *in 1980* than a woman who had a child between 1980 and 1982 but did not work in 1982.

Table 2.6 reports results for these specifications for both 1971 and 1980, to examine the importance of selectivity bias in the 1971–3 and 1980–2 first differences. We find no evidence of selectivity bias from recent changers. None of the coefficients of the recent changer interactions is statistically significant. These conclusions do not differ from the tests based on the more standard selectivity-correction methods.

Conclusions

We have explored the consequences of a number of potential problems with drawing causal inferences from cross-sectional relationships between marriage, motherhood, and wages. These problems include: endogeneity of marriage and motherhood, and experience and tenure; heterogeneity; and selectivity into employment.

We have three main findings to report. First, introducing experience and tenure into wage equations estimated by OLS attenuates but does not eliminate the large negative relationship between children and wages. Instrumental variables techniques and the accompanying tests suggest that marital status and number of children are exogenous variables in wage equations. However, IV results also suggest that experience and tenure are not exogenous. This finding is important because the size and statistical significance of the wage effects of children in cross-sections are sensitive to the exclusion of experience and tenure controls, and to their estimated coefficients. Instrumenting for experience and tenure yields estimated effects of marital status and number of children that are similar to OLS estimates when experience and tenure are *excluded*; in particular, the negative effects of having two or more children appear to be large.

Second, first-difference specifications suggest that fixed unobservables bias cross-sectional estimates of the effects of children on wages. Short first differences (estimated over a two-year period) indicate no negative effects of motherhood on wages.

Finally, standard sample-selection corrections, as well as selectivity tests that do not depend upon specifying an employment equation, provide no evidence of selectivity bias from using a sample of recent changers (women who are employed despite recent changes of marital or fertility states).

Like many previous cross-sectional estimates, the first-difference estimates do not support the contention that marriage or motherhood lower women's wages. However, the IV results call into question specifications that include controls for experience and tenure, either explicitly (as in cross-sections) or implicitly (as in first differences). Estimates from such specifications are likely to understate the *direct* effects of children on wages, because the lower experience and tenure associated with marriage and motherhood may arise as an endogenous response to lower wages. In other words, the IV results suggest that children lower wages "directly," and women respond to these lower wages by curtailing their labor supply and hence the accumulation of labor market experience and tenure. This conclusion contrasts with the more standard conclusion—suggested by our fixed-effects estimates and by estimates from earlier studies—that children lower wages primarily "indirectly" by lowering attachment to the labor force, or experience and tenure. If the standard conclusion is correct, then by remaining employed women would experience no adverse wage effects from having children. On the other hand, the IV estimates suggest that high labor force attachment alone will not prevent child bearing and child rearing from having an effect on women's wages. The sensitivity of the principal conclusions to the treatment of experience and tenure, therefore, highlights the need for continued research on the more general question of whether experience and tenure should be treated as exogenous variables in wage equations for women.

Acknowledgments

The authors thank McKinley Blackburn. David Bloom, Richard Freeman, Claudia Goldin, Lawrence Katz, Bruce Meyer, anonymous referees, and seminar participants at the National Bureau of Economic Research Labor Studies Program, Princeton University, and the University of South Carolina for helpful comments, and Elaina Rose for research assistance.

Notes

1 Fuchs (1988) makes a similar argument.
2 Although we focus on white women, we note that Hill finds positive associations between both marriage and children and the earnings of black women.
3 Suter and Miller (1973) discuss unreported regression estimates from a cross-sectional sample of women aged 30–44 drawn from the 1967 NLS Mature Women's file that lead them to essentially the same conclusion as Hill: "It appears that once a woman's occupational status and work experience are known, learning that she is married and has children does not significantly improve our ability to predict her income" (p. 192).
4 Goldin and Polachek also note (p. 149) that their results confirm those of an earlier study by Polachek (1975) using 1960 Census data.
5 This last coefficient comes from an interactive specification; its standard error cannot be computed from the information given in the paper.
6 For a review of the evidence for men see Korenman and Neumark (1991).
7 The category "divorced or separated" includes a few widows as well as a few women who are married with no spouse present.
8 When potential experience (defined as age—schooling—six) is used in place of actual experience and tenure, the marital status coefficients are unchanged, while the children coefficients are very close to those in column (3) of Table 2.2. This is expected because potential experience overstates actual labor market experience the most for women with many labor force interruptions, who are likely to be those with children.
9 We explored the sensitivity of the coefficients reported in column (4) of Table 2.2 to the inclusion of controls for, in turn, years married and years divorced or separated; the number of preschool-age children; and age of the mother at first birth. The results do not differ qualitatively from those in Table 2.2: adding years married and years divorced or separated reduces the coefficients of the dummy variables for marital status, although only the coefficient of the years divorced or separated variable is significant, and there is no negative effect of marital status in any year of marriage; the effect of young children is slightly positive, but insignificant; finally, the effect of children on wages varies with

maternal age at first birth, but the marital status and number of children coefficients are essentially unchanged.

10 Perhaps the most direct interpretation of Becker's hypothesis is that the joint effect of marriage (or divorce) and children is to lower wages. The p-values for the F-statistics for the joint significance of the marital status and number of children variables in the regressions in Table 2.2 indicate that these variables are jointly significant. However, in most of the specifications the coefficient of the married variable is *positive*. Indeed, in column (4) the point estimate of the summed effect of marriage and children is close to zero: -0.02 for women with two or more children, and 0.01 for women with one child.

11 This test involves: (i) regressing the potentially correlated variables on the set of instrumental variables and exogenous variables; (ii) including the residuals from these regressions in the wage equation estimated by OLS; and (iii) testing the joint significance of the constructed residuals.

12 These results contrast with Heckman (1980) and Mincer and Polachek (1974), who find no evidence of endogeneity of experience in wage regressions estimated for the NLS Mature Women sample. They do not include tenure, and use a different and more limited set of instrumental variables (including the number of young children).

13 An implication of the fact that a short difference implicitly controls for experience and tenure is that a short difference cannot be used to obtain an estimate of the direct *plus* the indirect effect of marriage and motherhood on wages (i.e. effects that do not control for experience and tenure).

14 We also carried out the analyses in Tables 2.2 and 2.3 using this smaller subsample, with no changes in the conclusions.

15 The p-value for the asymptotic F-test of equality of coefficients across the 1980 and 1982 cross-sections—using the SUR estimator to account for cross-year correlations in the residuals—was 0.93.

16 A similar specification test of the fixed-effects assumption (Heckman and Robb, 1986), which uses information for two years prior to 1980 and prior to marriage and childbearing, also did not lead to rejection of the fixed-effects specification.

17 The p-value for the test of equality of coefficients in the 1971 and 1973 cross-sections was 0.40. In addition, the 1971–3 first-difference specification was also not rejected according to the overidentification test described in the text.

18 Variables included in the employment probit, but excluded from the wage equation, include: husband's income; income from alimony or child support; weeks the husband spent unemployed in the year preceding the 1982 survey; and indicators of changes in marriage or fertility states. The sample is reduced slightly because these additional variables used in the employment probit were occasionally unavailable.

   While these variables should affect the reservation wage, and not the offer wage, they are correlated with marital status, and may therefore provide little independent information. However, because under the normality assumption the selection model is identified without these exclusion restrictions (Olsen, 1980), the restrictions were tested by including these variables in the wage equation and testing their significance; the p-value for the F-test of the joint significance of these three variables in the wage equation was 0.59.

19 Details are given in the footnotes to Table 2.5. The exclusion restriction of husband's income, income from alimony or child support, and weeks unemployed (of the husband) was not rejected ($p = 0.78$).

References

Becker, G. S. 1981. *A Treatise on the Family*. Cambridge: Harvard University Press.
——. 1985. "Human Capital, Effort, and the Sexual Division of Labor." *Journal of Labor Economics* 3(1, Part 2): S33–58.
Blackburn, M. L., D. E. Bloom and D. Neumark. 1990. "Fertility Timing, Wages, and Human Capital." NBER Working Paper.

Bloom, D. E. 1987. "Fertility Timing, Labor Supply Disruptions, and the Wage Profiles of American Women." *1986 Proceedings of the Social Statistics Section of the American Statistical Association*, pp. 49–63.

Butz, W. P. and M. P. Ward. 1979. "The Emergence of Countercyclical US Fertility." *American Economic Review* 69(3): 318–28.

Dolton, P. and G. Makepeace. 1987. "Marital Status, Child Rearing and Earnings Differentials in the Graduate Labour Market." *The Economic Journal* 97(388): 897–922.

Easterlin, R. A. 1980. *Birth and Fortune: The Impact of Numbers on Personal Welfare.* New York: Basic Books, Inc.

Fuchs, V. 1988. "Women's Quest for Economic Equality." *Journal of Economic Perspectives* 3(1): 25–41.

Goldin, C. and S. Polachek. 1987. "Residual Differences by Sex: Perspectives on the Gender Gap in Earnings." *American Economic Review* 77(2): 143–51.

Greenhalgh, C. 1980. "Male–Female Wage Differentials in Great Britain: Is Marriage an Equal Opportunity?" *The Economic Journal* 90(360): 751–75.

Griliches, Z. 1979. "Sibling Models and Data in Economics: Beginnings of a Survey." *Journal of Political Economy* 87(5, Part II): S74–103.

Hausman, J. A. 1978. "Specification Tests in Econometrics." *Econometrica* 46(6): 1251–71.

Heckman, J. J. 1979. "Sample Selection Bias as a Specification Error." *Econometrica* 47(1): 153–61.

——. 1980. "Sample Selection Bias as a Specification Error with an Application to the Estimation of Labor Supply Functions." In *Female Labor Supply*, ed. J. P. Smith, 206–48. Princeton: Princeton University Press.

Heckman, J. J. and V. J. Hotz. 1989. "Choosing Among Alternative Nonexperimental Methods for Estimating the Impact of Social Programs: The Case of Manpower Training." *Journal of the American Statistical Association* 84(408): 862–74.

Heckman, J. J. and R. Robb. 1986. "Alternative Identifying Assumptions in Econometric Models of Selection Bias." *Advances in Econometrics* 5: 243–87.

Hill, M. 1979. "The Wage Effects of Marital Status and Children." *The Journal of Human Resources* 14(4): 579–94.

Korenman, S. and D. Neumark. 1991. "Does Marriage Really Make Men More Productive?" *Journal of Human Resources* 26(2): 282–307.

Mincer, J. and S. Polachek. 1974. "Family Investments in Human Capital: Earnings of Women." In *Economics of the Family*, ed. T. W. Schultz, 397–429. Chicago: University of Chicago Press.

Moore, W. and R. Wilson. 1982. "The Influence of Children on the Wage Rates of Married Women." *Eastern Economic Journal* 3(3): 197–210.

Olsen, R. 1980. "A Least Squares Correction for Selectivity Bias." *Econometrica* 148(7): 815–20.

Polachek, S. 1975. "Differences in Post-School Investment as a Determinant of Market Wage Differentials." *International Economic Review* 16(2): 451–70.

Siebert, W. and P. Sloane. 1981. "The Measurement of Sex and Marital Status Discrimination at the Workplace." *Economica* 48(190): 125–41.

Solon, G. 1988. "Self-Selection Bias in Longitudinal Estimation of Wage Gaps." *Economics Letters* 28(3): 285–90.

Suter, L. E. and H. P. Miller. 1973. "Income Differences Between Men and Career Women." *American Journal of Sociology* 78(4): 962–75.

3 Sources of bias in women's wage equations

Results using sibling data

(with Sanders Korenman)

Introduction

Wage equations estimated for samples of women are used frequently in labor economics. Often the wage equation estimates are the direct objects of interest. Examples include: estimating wage discrimination via "decomposition" techniques; documenting and explaining the rise in women's earnings relative to men's; testing theories explaining wage differentials between men and women; and estimating effects of demographic decisions or outcomes on wages.[1] In addition, estimates of women's wage equations are used as initial inputs in studying other questions. Examples include: constructing instrumental variables for wages to estimate labor supply parameters (e.g. Nakamura and Nakamura, 1985a; Mroz, 1987); computation of wage values in microanalytic simulation models (e.g. Orcutt and Glazer, 1980); and legal applications regarding pay discrimination or computations of potential earnings (e.g. Bloom and Killingsworth, 1982).

Much of this research uses standard Ordinary Least Square (OLS) estimates of variants of the human capital earnings function. But much of this research also recognizes the potential for biases from endogeneity of the regressors, and from unobserved heterogeneity associated with the regressors. Different researchers address alternative sources of bias, using varying identifying assumptions. At the same time, some research papers in this area continue to use OLS estimates of wage equations for women (e.g. O'Neill and Polachek, 1993). In general, our reading of the literature on women's wage equations, summarized in the section on Past research: an overview, suggests that there is no consensus regarding the empirical importance of these various sources of bias, nor the validity of the assumptions used to attempt to correct for them; as a consequence, there is no consensus regarding the treatment of these alternative sources of bias.

In this chapter, we utilize data on sisters in an attempt to provide a more unified analysis of sources of bias in women's wage equations. Data on sisters offer advantages for estimation of wage equations correcting for endogeneity and heterogeneity bias; these advantages are spelled out in the section on Advantages of using sibling data. The chapter shows how the estimated effects of marital status, number of children, labor market experience, and schooling differ depending on the source of bias considered, and the identifying assumptions used to correct for the bias. It also exploits the sibling data to test a variety of overidentifying assumptions. Our goal is to contribute toward building a much-needed consensus in the statistical approaches to estimating women's wage equations.

Sources of bias in women's wage equations

Past research on women's wage equations has considered three principal sources of potential bias: heterogeneity bias, endogeneity bias, and bias from selection into employment. In this chapter, we focus on the first two sources of bias, based on our past research (Korenman and Neumark, 1992) showing that heterogeneity and endogeneity bias are important in estimates of women's wage equations. We assume that wages are influenced by characteristics that may reflect human capital investment (such as schooling and experience), household specialization or time allocation decisions (such as marital status and number of children), and cost-of-living differentials (residence in the South and an SMSA). Of course, these characteristics may be correlated with the wage equation error. On the other hand, we assume that there are some variables that can be plausibly excluded from the wage equation, and hence serve as instruments. In many of our estimations, we assume that family background variables can be excluded. This assumption parallels earlier work on the returns to schooling in which family background variables have a large influence on an individual's level of schooling, but not a direct influence on the wage (see, for example Griliches, 1979).[2] Alternative identifying assumptions are considered below.

The wage equation we are interested in estimating takes the general form

$$w_i = X_i \beta + Y_i \gamma + \varepsilon_i, \tag{1}$$

where w is the log wage, X is a vector of exogenous control variables, and ε is a stochastic normally distributed error uncorrelated with X, assumed to be i.i.d. Y is the vector of variables on which attention is focused. For the purposes of exposition, we will assume that Y contains a single variable; for concreteness in providing examples, we will suppose this variable is the number of children.

Heterogeneity bias may arise if the true wage equation also includes an unmeasured variable, denoted A, which is correlated with Y.[3] For example, A may represent unobserved characteristics that raise market productivity relative to home productivity, and therefore increase wages, and (via substitution effects) reduce childbearing. A standard approach is fixed-effects estimation, which makes the identifying assumption that A is fixed over time, with a constant coefficient. Then, for repeated observations on individuals, the true wage equation is

$$w_{it} = X_{it} \beta + Y_{it} \gamma + A_i + \varepsilon_{it}, \tag{2}$$

where t indexes time.[4] Because there are repeated observations on each unit i, individual-specific dummy variables can be included to control for the unobservable A, yielding consistent estimates of γ; this is the fixed-effects estimator.[5]

Endogeneity bias may arise if childbearing is simultaneously determined along with wages. For example, a draw of a high-wage residual (i.e. a high wage net of observables) may lead, via substitution effects, to lower childbearing. In this case, though, the bias comes from a contemporaneous correlation between ε and Y, so that a fixed-effects estimator does not solve the problem. The only potential correction for this type of bias is to assume that there is an instrumental variable Z, which is correlated with Y, but does not itself enter the wage equation. In principle, then, there is an equation for Y of the form

$$Y_i = Z_i \delta + X_i \beta' + \eta_i, \tag{3}$$

where η also satisfies the standard assumptions. Under these assumptions, two-stage least squares can be used to obtain consistent estimates of γ. This procedure amounts to estimating equation (3) by OLS, substituting the fitted values from (3) for Y_i in equation (1), and estimating equation (1) by least squares (correcting the standard errors); the estimation is done in a single step using all of the exogenous variables as instruments.

Past research: an overview

As we pointed out in the Introduction, we are not the first to consider these sources of bias. Table 3.1 provides a chronological survey of this literature. As noted in the Introduction, different researchers address alternative sources of bias, most frequently focusing on a single source of bias (such as endogeneity bias), in a limited set of variables (such as experience). Second, different researchers invoke alternative identifying assumptions to address the same source of bias (e.g. compare Mincer and Polachek, 1974, to Wright and Ermisch, 1991). Finally, some recent work continues to use OLS estimates of wage equations for women. The lack of consensus is apparent.

In Korenman and Neumark (1992), we conducted an analysis of the sensitivity of wage equation estimates for women to heterogeneity and endogeneity bias (as well as selection bias), considered individually. Our principal concern was with wage differences associated with marital status and number of children, which turn out to be closely related to returns to labor force attachment (experience and tenure); these coefficients are the focus of much of the research cited earlier. Our results offer one reason why no consensus has emerged regarding the treatment of these biases. Specifically, the resulting coefficient estimates are sensitive to the source of bias addressed; details are summarized in the section on Heterogeneity bias. The other reason that no consensus has emerged may be skepticism regarding the identifying assumptions needed to correct for these biases. In Korenman and Neumark (1992) we provide tests of the overidentifying assumptions whenever possible, but a priori identifying assumptions are always required, the validity of which must necessarily remain untested.[6] The sibling data set that we use in this chapter offers numerous advantages relative to earlier research by ourselves and others.

Table 3.1 Estimators and identifying restrictions in existing research on women's wages (a partial summary)[a]

Paper	Source of bias[b]	Estimator[c]	Dataset	Identifying restrictions
Oaxaca (1973)	—	OLS	1967 SEO	—
Mincer and Polachek (1974)	Endogenous experience	2SLS	NLS Mature Women	Husband's education and number of children excl. from wage eqn.
Sandell and Shapiro (1978)	Endogenous experience and hometime	2SLS	NLS Mature Women	Husband's education, number of children, and potential experience excluded from wage eqn.
Corcoran and Duncan (1979)	—	OLS	PSID	—
Hill (1979)	—	OLS	PSID	—
Corcoran *et al.* (1983)	Heterogeneity, selection	First difference, SSC first difference	PSID	Education, experience, non-labor income, number of children, number of young children in household, and marital status (at time of first wage observation) excluded from wage change eqn.
Cox (1984)	—	OLS	1973 CPS-SSA Match File	—
O'Neill (1985)	—	OLS	NLS Young Women and Mature Women	—
Dolton and Makepeace (1987)	Selection, heterogeneity	SSC longitudinal	Early Careers of 1970 Graduates (UK)	Marital status, number of children, age, occupational status of job, and interactions of these excluded from wage eqn in some specifications.
Goldin and Polachek (1987)	—	OLS	1980 Census	—
Neumark (1988)	—	OLS	NLS Young Men and Young Women	—
Lundberg and Plotnick (1990)	Endogeneity of fertility/ marriage states	SSC earnings equations for different fertility/marriage groups	NLSY	Husband's unemployment, fraction of year woman married, spouse's income, local labor market conditions, number of children, number of children under age 6 excluded from initial wage equation, included in employment eqn. Age at menarche, religion, and attendance at religious services excluded from potential earnings eqn, included in fertility/marriage eqn.

Study	Sources of bias	Method	Data	Exclusion restrictions
Blackburn et al. (1993)	Heterogeneity, selection	Longitudinal, SSC	NLS Young Women	Husband's income, husband's weeks unemployed, and income from alimony and child support excluded from wage eqn.
Kim and Polachek (1991)	Heterogeneity, endogeneity of experience and schooling	2SLS Within	PSID	Race, age, father's education, mother's education, and occupation dummy variables excluded from wage eqn.
O'Neill and Polachek (1993)	—	OLS	CPS, PSID	—
Wright and Ermisch (1991)	Endogeneity of experience and tenure, selection	2SLS, SSC	1980 Women and employment Survey (U.K.)	2SLS and SSC: Wife's age, housing tenure, number and age of children, local unemployment rate, husband's employment, nonlabor income, husband's age, husband's education, husband's social class, and wife's age at marriage excluded from wage equation.[d]
Korenman and Neumark (1992)	Heterogeneity, endogeneity, selection	First difference, 2SLS, SSC first difference	NLS Young Women	2SLS: Father's education, mother's education, parents' educational goal, number of siblings, mother worked, and lived with father and mother excluded from wage eqn.[e] SSC: Husband's income, husband's weeks employed, income from alimony and child support, and changes in marital or fertility status excluded from employment eqn for each year.

Notes

a When OLS analysis of cross-sectional data was included along with an analysis of a source of bias, only the latter approach is described in the table.

b This refers to the three sources of bias considered in this chapter: heterogeneity bias, endogeneity bias, and sample selection bias. It does not refer to the numerous attempts made to reduce omitted variable bias or measurement error bias by introducing new or improved variables into wage equations. Many of these latter types of studies were omitted from the table.

c "OLS" implies that cross-sectional data were used. All fixed-effects estimators difference across individuals over time. "Longitudinal" refers to including an early wage or early wage residual.

d Wright and Ermisch also consider the endogeneity of experience and home time in the employment probit.

e These are the a priori identifying restrictions; other overidentifying restrictions are tested.

Advantages of using sibling data

Estimation

We can best highlight the potential advantages of using sibling data to study sources of bias in women's wage equations by referring to our earlier work (Korenman and Neumark, 1992), which used standard cross-sectional and longitudinal panel data. We attempted to correct for heterogeneity bias in the estimated effects of marriage and children by differencing data on individuals over time (over a two-year interval). We recognized the danger that such an estimator may implicitly control for experience and tenure if there is little variation in these variables among women who work in both years.[7] Consequently, it may have been difficult to untangle the independent roles of labor force attachment and heterogeneity bias in generating wage differentials associated with children. In contrast, sibling data allow us to difference across sisters rather than across time; differencing across sisters should not implicitly control for labor force attachment. Of course, sister differences remove heterogeneity bias only under the assumption that such bias results from unmeasured attributes that are common to sisters, such as, for example, unmeasured (and equal) parental investment in their daughters' human capital.[8]

Second, we assumed that family background and attitudes/expectations variables that are fixed over time (in contrast to contemporaneous or lagged variables that change over time) can be excluded from the wage equation, and hence provide the identifying information for instrumental variables estimation. Because these instruments are fixed over time, repeated observations on individuals do not permit estimation of wage equations that simultaneously account for heterogeneity and endogeneity. Sibling data, however, allow us to jointly address heterogeneity bias and endogeneity bias, using these fixed family background and attitudes/expectations variables as instruments.

Econometrically, it is straightforward to study heterogeneity bias and endogeneity bias simultaneously. Let the wage equation be given by equation (2), where Y is now a potentially endogenous variable, and A is an unmeasured, time-invariant variable potentially correlated with Y. Assume that there is a set of instrumental variables Z that identify the parameters of equation (2), such that

$$Y_{it} = Z_{it}\delta + X_{it}\beta' + A_i\phi + \eta_{it}, \tag{4}$$

where η also satisfies the standard assumptions. Equation (4) parallels equation (3), but also includes the fixed effect A, to reflect the fact that there can be endogeneity bias and heterogeneity bias at the same time. Nonetheless, the same two-stage least squares procedure can be used to recover consistent estimates of the wage equation. The only change is that individual fixed effects (dummy variables) are included in the list of instruments. (Equivalently, in the two-step version of the estimator, the fixed effects are included in both the first- and second-stage regressions, and hence the fixed effects in equation (4) must be estimated to construct the fitted values of Y.)

In principle, instrumental variables estimation is sufficient to solve the endogeneity and the heterogeneity problem without repeated observations (and hence without the estimation of individual-specific intercepts). This estimation requires instruments that are uncorrelated with A as well as ε (see, e.g. Heckman and Robb, 1986). Such instruments are unlikely to exist, except in instances of the occurrence of "natural experiments" (e.g. Angrist and Krueger, 1991). For example, family background variables such as parents' education may be correlated with the individual's schooling and uncorrelated with the nonsystematic part of the error structure ε, but are likely to be correlated with the individual-specific component, A (see Griliches, 1979).

Assuming that repeated observations are required to account for heterogeneity bias, the difficulty with using fixed family background or attitudes/expectations variables as instruments in a standard longitudinal data set is that they are fixed over time for an individual. This difficulty is not a matter of data availability, but instead reflects our belief that it is unlikely that there exist contemporaneous or lagged (changing) variables that provide valid instruments in wage equations. The problem can be seen easily from equation (4); if Z is time-invariant for an individual, it is perfectly collinear with the individual fixed effect A, and hence provides no identifying information. (Equivalently, if we difference equation (2) and equation (4), the instrument set Z drops out.) Thus, given the restriction to time-invariant instrumental variables, endogeneity cannot be addressed in the context of the longitudinal within specification.

An alternative approach is to use data on sisters, attempting to eliminate the heterogeneity bias by computing within-*family* estimates. The assumption here is that the source of heterogeneity bias is something common to sisters. In this case, A_i indicates a family-specific fixed effect, the "i" in the subscripts indexes families, and the "t" indexes sisters within families. We assume that only the family-specific component of the unobservable determinants of wages is correlated with the regressors. The advantage of panel data of this type, conditional on the validity of the assumptions, is that the instrumental variables are not necessarily constant across the repeated observations (i.e. sisters in the same family). Consequently, with sibling data, we can carry out the two-stage least squares procedure accounting for heterogeneity, described earlier.

The family background variables used as initial instruments are: father's and mother's education; parents' educational goal for respondent at age 14; and dummy variables for whether the respondent's mother worked at age 14, and whether the respondent lived with both a father and mother at age 14. In addition, taking these family background variables as a priori valid instruments, we consider the use of a set of instruments measuring respondents' gender-role attitudes and expectations regarding fertility, marriage and education, that were asked generally more than ten years prior to the period to which wages and labor market characteristics pertain. (Details are given in the footnotes to Table 3.3.) What information identifies the model in the presence of fixed family effects? Because there are fixed family effects in the wage equation, these fixed effects also appear in the first-stage reduced-form regressions for the potentially endogenous variables.[9] The implication is that within-family differences in the family background and attitudes/expectations variables provide the identifying information. While within-family differences in some of these variables—such as parents' education—may reflect measurement error, within-family differences in other variables—such as expected number of children, or household structure at age 14—are likely to be real. However, while these sibling differences formally identify the model, it remains a reasonable concern whether they provide sufficient variation and influence to yield informative instrumental variables estimates.

There are at least two alternative approaches to jointly addressing heterogeneity and endogeneity biases, both of which involve introducing alternative identifying assumptions. The first, in the context of either longitudinal or sibling data, is to use a woman's own lagged characteristics (experience, number of children, etc.) as instruments for contemporaneous values. However, it seems plausible that, for example, the pattern of accumulation of experience, or the pattern of past child-bearing, may have an effect on wages independently of the contemporaneous value of experience or number of children; this is precisely the point of the intermittent labor force participation literature developed by Polachek and others.

Second, as Table 3.1 indicates, spouse's income and spouse's unemployment (or employment) have sometimes been used as instruments; these instruments could in principle be used with longitudinal or sibling data. But models of family specialization (Becker, 1985; Killingsworth, 1990) suggest that a wife's wage may be influenced by her husband's wages, labor supply, etc.[10]

More generally, however, the sibling approach offers a potentially better means of controlling for heterogeneity—differencing across sisters rather than across a short interval of time—by not implicitly controlling for labor force attachment, and therefore not removing a potentially important source of covariation between number of children and wages.

Identification

In addition to the identifying assumptions mentioned in the previous section, a sister's fertility, experience, etc., would seem to be valid instruments for a respondent's own values of these variables, since the sister's value may reflect other unobservable characteristics of the family that affect the respondent's characteristics that are not captured in the observable instrumental variables, yet have no independent effect on the respondent's wage.[11,12] Unfortunately, in the fixed family effects specifications, the sibling's value of the endogenous variable cannot be used as an instrument, since controlling for the fixed family effect, the sibling value provides a near-perfect prediction of the endogenous variable.[13] However, we do carry out an alternative heterogeneity experiment in which we can use the sibling values as instruments. We can then make the a priori identifying assumption that sibling values of the potentially endogenous variables are excluded from the wage equation, and test the exclusion of the family background and attitudes/expectations variables from the wage equation.[14] We also extend the analysis to consider the validity of identifying assumptions used by other researchers to correct for endogeneity, as described in Table 3.1. In particular, with the sibling data in hand, we can test, as overidentifying restrictions, some typical identifying assumptions invoked by other researchers.

Empirical results for sibling data analyses

The data

The Young Women's cohort of the NLS contains over one thousand women who have at least one sister in the survey. A sample of sisters was constructed in two steps. First, data on wages, labor market characteristics, and the instrumental variables were extracted, looking first in 1982, but if data were missing (perhaps because of nonemployment), then taking data from 1980, 1978, 1977, 1975, or 1973, if available, but always drawing data from the latest year possible. All combinations of sisters in the resulting extract were matched. This yielded a final sample of 766 observations. Of these, there are 518 whites and 248 blacks;[15] it turns out, as reported later, that there is statistical evidence against pooling these two samples. Descriptive statistics for the white and black samples used for the panel data analysis are reported in Appendix Table 3.A1.[16]

Heterogeneity bias

In Chapter 2, OLS estimates of women's wage equations excluding experience and tenure suggested large negative effects of children, but controlling for actual experience and tenure lowered the estimated effects considerably, consistent with the findings of, for example, Hill (1979). These estimates suggested that the effects of children were primarily "indirect," reducing wages by reducing mothers' labor force attachment. But our estimates were sensitive to corrections for heterogeneity or endogeneity bias. Longitudinal within estimates excluding experience and tenure revealed no effect of children on wages, in contrast to the negative association found in the cross-sectional OLS estimates. On the other hand, when we treated labor market experience and tenure as endogenous variables, instrumenting with family background and attitudes/expectations variables, we found that the overall return to time in the labor force was near zero, and that children were associated with substantial negative effects on wages. Thus, the longitudinal estimates suggested that unobserved heterogeneity generates the cross-sectional negative association between children and wages (women who would earn low wages tend to have children), while the instrumental variables estimates suggested a "true" negative effect of children, whether because of discrimination or productivity, which was understated by OLS estimates.[17,18]

Table 3.2, columns (1)–(4), reports OLS and fixed family effects estimates of a log wage equation specification similar to that used in Korenman and Neumark (1992). We have simplified the specification by using a single "married, spouse present" category, a linear specification for the number of children variable, and including only experience (omitting tenure).[19] The estimates are reported for specifications first excluding, and then including, experience, for white women.

Table 3.2 OLS and fixed-effects wage equation estimates for sibling sample, white women (dependent variable: natural logarithm of hourly earnings)[a]

	OLS		Family fixed effect (FE)		OLS	FE
	(1)	*(2)*	*(3)*	*(4)*	*(5)*	*(6)*
Coefficients						
Married, spouse	0.062	0.039	0.069	0.058	0.029	0.052
present	(0.039)	(0.038)	(0.054)	(0.053)	(0.034)	(0.049)
Number of children	−0.089	−0.074	−0.071	−0.050	−0.052	−0.039
	(0.018)	(0.017)	(0.024)	(0.024)	(0.016)	(0.022)
Experience	—	0.030	—	0.035	0.020	0.021
		(0.006)		(0.008)	(0.005)	(0.008)
Schooling	0.054	0.066	0.058	0.070	0.051	0.056
	(0.008)	(0.008)	(0.013)	(0.013)	(0.007)	(0.012)
Lagged own wage[b]	—	—	—	—	0.518	0.436
					(0.046)	(0.062)
$\bar{R}^2$	0.494	0.521	0.546	0.573	0.617	0.641
Heterogeneity bias						
p-value[c]	—	—	0.610	0.464	—	—

Notes

a There are 518 observations. Standard errors are reported in parentheses. Observations are included only if the wage reported is for a job at which the respondent is currently working. Observations were drawn from 1982 if possible, and otherwise from 1980, 1978, 1977, 1975, or 1973; observations were always selected from the latest year possible. Other variables included were: years of schooling; dummy variables for residence in the South and in an SMSA; and dummy variables for the year from which the observation was drawn.

b Wage from previous survey. A dummy variable was included for a missing lagged wage.

c *p*-value from Hausman specification test of statistical significance of the difference between the OLS and FE estimates of the coefficients reported in the table.

The OLS estimates are similar to our earlier estimates. With experience excluded, in column (1), there is a large and statistically significant negative coefficient on the number of children variable. On the other hand, there is no statistically significant effect of marriage. When experience is added to the equation, in column (2), the coefficient on the number of children variable falls by about one-fifth, but remains statistically significant.

Columns (3) and (4) report estimates from specifications that allow a fixed family effect. In the previous chapter we were cautious in interpreting our longitudinal (or fixed individual-effects) results because we used a short (two-year) first difference that may have implicitly controlled for labor force attachment. Among women working in both 1980 and 1982, there was relatively little variation in accumulated experience. As a result, the first-difference estimates of the effects of children that excluded experience (and tenure) controls may have been biased toward zero.

The within-family estimates reported in columns (3) and (4) are consistent with this suspicion. When experience is omitted from the model, the negative association between wages and children persists in the fixed-effects estimates (column (3)), whereas in our previous chapter it fell to zero. These results suggest two differences with respect to our earlier work. First, the heterogeneity bias detected using longitudinal data, even in specifications excluding labor force attachment controls, was overstated, and at least partially reflected the effect of implicitly controlling for this attachment.[20] Compared to our earlier results, these estimates suggest that differences in labor force attachment are a more important determinant of wage differentials associated with children, even after accounting for heterogeneity; when experience is included in the model, in column (4), the negative association between wages and children falls by about one-third. Second, a statistically significant negative association between children and wages persists in the fixed-effects estimates. However, as in our previous work, in either the OLS or fixed-effects estimates there is no evidence to support a negative effect of marriage that a simple interpretation of Becker's (1985) model of specialization within marriage might lead one to predict.

An alternative reason for the differences we have found between individual and family fixed-effects estimates of the effects of children on wages is that the two estimators may remove different fixed effects; in particular, the family fixed effect may not capture all of the individual heterogeneity that potentially biases the estimates. While there is no way to address this question definitively, in columns (5) and (6) of Table 3.2 we offer some evidence. We reestimated the OLS and family fixed-effect wage equation adding the individual's lagged wage. One interpretation of a significant coefficient on the individual's lagged wage in the family fixed-effects estimates is that the family fixed effect does not sufficiently capture the heterogeneity.[21] The significant, positive coefficient of the lagged wage is consistent with this interpretation. However, this evidence is only suggestive, since the relevant question is whether the family fixed effect controls for the heterogeneity that is correlated with the included variables, not whether the lagged individual's wage has explanatory power once the family effect is included. To shed light on this question, we can ask whether the inclusion of the family fixed effect or the lagged individual wage appears to have more impact on the coefficient estimates, relative to the OLS estimates. With respect to the number of children coefficient, the inclusion of the family fixed effect has a larger impact than adding the lagged wage. While this suggests that the family fixed effect may remove much of the bias, we cannot rule out the possibility that the family fixed effect does not adequately remove heterogeneity bias.

Endogeneity bias in the estimated effects of experience, marital status, number of children, and schooling

In Table 3.3 we present results from specifications in which we address endogeneity of experience, marital status, number of children, and schooling, along with heterogeneity bias. Chapter 2 indicated that endogeneity bias in the estimated returns to experience and tenure had serious consequences for the estimated effects of children on wages. A Hausman test led us to reject the joint hypothesis of the exogeneity of experience and tenure, and IV estimates led to overall returns to labor force attachment that were near zero. Because women with children have lower

Table 3.3 Two-stage least squares, fixed-family effects estimates of wage equation for sibling sample, alternative endogenous variables, white women (dependent variable: natural logarithm of hourly earnings)[a]

	(1)	(2)	(3)	(4)	(5)
Coefficients					
Married, spouse present	0.049	0.463	0.117	0.061	0.534
	(0.053)	(0.217)	(0.078)	(0.055)	(0.254)
Number of children	−0.056	−0.104	−0.149	−0.075	−0.039
	(0.027)	(0.038)	(0.087)	(0.031)	(0.085)
Experience	0.028	0.032	0.027	0.028	0.038
	(0.022)	(0.010)	(0.011)	(0.010)	(0.024)
Schooling	0.081	0.063	0.066	0.020	0.055
	(0.019)	(0.015)	(0.023)	(0.059)	(0.023)
Variables used as instruments[b]					
Family background	Yes	Yes	Yes	Yes	Yes
Attitudes/expectations	No	Yes	No	No	Yes
Endogeneity tests					
Experience residual[c]	0.007	—	—	—	−0.003
	(0.024)				(0.022)
Married, spouse present residual[c]	—	−0.437	—	—	−0.508
		(0.202)			(0.223)
Number of children residual[c]	—	—	0.105	—	−0.005
			(0.088)		(0.076)
Schooling residual[c]	—	—	—	0.071	0.035
				(0.060)	(0.027)
p-value[d]	0.759	0.031	0.232	0.096	0.102
Exclusion restrictions in wage equation[e]					
Attitudes/expectations	0.050	0.206	0.055	0.099	0.482

Notes
a See Table 3.2 for details. Family background variables include: father's education; mother's education; parents' educational goal for respondent at age 14; number of siblings; a dummy variable equal to 1 if the respondent's mother worked when respondent was age 14; a dummy variable equal to 1 if the respondent lived with both a father and mother at age 14. Attitudes/expectations variables include: a dummy variable set equal to 1 if respondent disagreed or strongly disagreed with statement that it is alright for a woman to work even if her husband disagrees, asked in 1971 (nontraditional sex-role attitude); a dummy variable set equal to one if respondent agreed or strongly agreed with this statement, in 1971 (traditional sex-role attitude); ideal age at marriage reported by respondent at age 14 (set equal to zero, with a dummy variable set equal to 1 if response was never to marry); expected number of children, in 1970; educational expectations, in 1970; educational goal, in 1970. For both sets of instruments, dummy variables corresponding to each of these variables were also included, equal to 1 when the variable was missing (in which case variables were set equal to zero).
b When attitudes/expectations variables are not used as instruments, they are included in wage equation.
c Coefficient of residual from regression of potentially endogenous variable on instruments and exogenous variables, included in log wage equation estimated with least squares.
d *p*-value from (joint) test of significance of residual coefficient(s).
e *p*-value from Wald test of joint significance of set of instruments in wage equation, in unrestricted model.

experience and tenure than women without children, we found that the reduction in the return to time in the labor force in turn led to a much stronger negative association between children and wages than suggested by the OLS estimates.

In column (1) of Table 3.3 we report specification tests and final estimates of the wage equation with family fixed effects, and endogenous experience. We use the data on sisters to account for heterogeneity while also instrumenting for experience. We began by estimating an unrestricted specification in which the attitudes/expectations variables were included in the wage equation. The identifying assumption is that the family background variables are excluded from the wage equation.[22] (In the section on Testing the exclusion of the family background variables from the wage equation, we use the sibling data coupled with an alternative heterogeneity experiment to explore the validity of excluding the family background variables from the wage equation.) We then tested the exclusion of the attitudes/expectations variables from the wage equation; this exclusion is rejected at the 5-percent significance level, as indicated by the p-value in the last row of the table.[23] Consequently, for endogenous experience we report estimates of the less restricted model. The estimates reveal little change relative to the fixed-effects estimates in Table 3.2; the return to experience declines slightly, and the negative effect of children grows slightly (from -0.050 to -0.056). But the exogeneity of experience is not rejected; the p-value is 0.759.[24]

We also estimated models to examine the possible endogeneity of other determinants of women's wages, in particular, marital status, number of children, and schooling. The results are reported in Table 3.3, columns (2)–(4), where again we first estimated the unrestricted model, including the attitudes/expectations variables in the wage equation, and then tested the exclusion of these variables from the wage equation. We report coefficient estimates for the model that survives this procedure. The benchmark for comparison is the fixed-effects specification reported in column (4) of Table 3.2.[25]

In the specification treating marital status as endogenous, in column (2) of Table 3.3, the exclusion of the attitudes/expectations variables from the wage equation is not rejected at the 5-percent significance level, so the restricted model is reported. Instrumenting for marital status leads to a sharp increase in the coefficient on the marital status dummy, resulting in a statistically significant positive effect of marriage on women's wages. This may reflect downward bias in the estimated coefficient of marital status in the pure fixed-effects specification; while a point estimate of 0.463 seems dubiously high, it is plausible that there is downward bias in the estimate treating marital status as exogenous, if women with low contemporaneous wage draws are more likely to become married. (Alternatively, the bias may be generated by individual heterogeneity that is unrelated to the fixed family effect, such that low wage women, net of observables and the fixed family effect, tend to marry.) Furthermore, this result was replicated in alternative specifications. We computed IV/FE estimates adding a second dummy variable for divorced or separated, and alternatively did and did not treat the divorced or separated dummy variable as endogenous; the point estimate of the married, spouse present variable remained positive and statistically significant, and the p-values for tests of exogeneity were 0.01. Also, this result is not attributable to the instability of the estimated effects of marriage and children; in a specification excluding the number of children, the coefficient (standard error) of the married, spouse present dummy variable was 0.55 (0.26), and the p-value for the exogeneity test was 0.01.[26] On the other hand, pure instrumental variables estimates (without fixed effects) led to no change in the marital status coefficient, and no evidence against its exogeneity, implying that heterogeneity is important.[27,28]

In contrast to the results for marital status, instrumenting for the number of children has no significant effect on the estimated effect of the number of children, and exogeneity is not rejected. The results for the schooling coefficient are suggestive of upward endogeneity bias; the p-value for the Hausman specification test (0.096) indicates that exogeneity is rejected at the 10-percent level. The point estimate of the schooling coefficient, 0.020, has a high standard error, since it comes from the unrestricted wage equation; we report this specification in the table since there was evidence, at the 10-percent significance level, against the exclusion of the attitudes/expectations variables from the wage equation. Nonetheless, the results were qualitatively similar in the restricted model; the coefficient (standard error) of schooling was 0.049 (0.019), and the p-value for the exogeneity test was 0.12.[29]

Finally, in column (5) these three variables as well as experience are allowed to be endogenous. Overall, the specification test nearly rejects exogeneity of the entire set of variables at the 10-percent level. Not surprisingly, the estimated standard errors are large relative to the fixed-effects estimates or the estimates instrumenting for one variable at a time. A significant positive effect of marriage persists, whereas the estimated schooling coefficient returns to a value nearer to the pure fixed-effects estimate, as does the return to experience.

Wage equation estimates for black women

Table 3.4 summarizes the key specifications estimated for black women. For purposes of comparison, in columns (1) and (2) of Table 3.4 we report OLS and fixed-effects estimates of the wage equation. A comparison with columns (1) and (2) of Table 3.3 reveals lower returns to schooling (in fixed-effects estimates) and to experience for black women, and no discernible negative effect of children.[30] These differences are statistically significant. In OLS and fixed-effects estimates in which the coefficients of the five variables reported in the table (and the intercept for OLS) differed, the equality of coefficients across black and white women was rejected at the 5-percent level.

The fixed-effects estimation leads to a sizable reduction in the estimated return to schooling (from 0.070 to 0.036).[31] The overall evidence of heterogeneity bias is statistically significant, as indicated by the p-value from the Hausman specification test (0.014). Columns (3)–(7) report IV/FE estimates corresponding to those estimated for white women in Table 3.3. In all cases we report results for the restricted specification in which the attitudes/expectations variables (as well as the family background variables) are excluded from the wage equation; the exclusion of this set of variables from the wage equation could not be rejected in any of the columns. In contrast to the results for white women, there is no statistically significant evidence of endogeneity bias in the estimated coefficients of marital status, number of children, schooling, or experience.

Table 3.4 Alternative estimates of wage equation for sibling sample, black women (dependent variable: natural logarithm of hourly earnings)[a]

	OLS	Family fixed effect (FE)	IV/FE				
	(1)	*(2)*	*(3)*	*(4)*	*(5)*	*(6)*	*(7)*
Coefficients							
Married, spouse present	0.013	0.017	0.023	−0.077	0.004	0.012	−0.055
	(0.044)	(0.053)	(0.056)	(0.101)	(0.059)	(0.054)	(0.111)
Number of children	0.008	−0.003	−0.010	0.009	0.019	−0.006	0.033
	(0.017)	(0.024)	(0.026)	(0.027)	(0.049)	(0.025)	(0.061)
Experience	0.016	0.011	−0.023	0.011	0.011	0.010	−0.028
	(0.007)	(0.010)	(0.024)	(0.010)	(0.010)	(0.010)	(0.027)
Schooling	0.070	0.036	0.031	0.033	0.039	0.027	0.035
	(0.011)	(0.015)	(0.016)	(0.015)	(0.016)	(0.025)	(0.032)
$\bar{R}^2$	0.544	0.657	—	—	—	—	—
Heterogeneity bias							
p-value	—	0.014	—	—	—	—	—
Variables used as instruments							
Family background	—	—	Yes	Yes	Yes	Yes	Yes
Attitudes/expectations	—	—	Yes	Yes	Yes	Yes	Yes
Endogeneity tests							
Experience residual	—	—	0.042	—	—	—	0.046
			(0.026)				(0.028)
Married, spouse present residual	—	—	—	0.132	—	—	0.109
				(0.118)			(0.121)
Number of children residual	—	—	—	—	−0.029	—	−0.043
					(0.057)		(0.064)
Schooling residual	—	—	—	—	—	0.015	0.007
						(0.031)	(0.035)
p-value	—	—	0.108	0.264	0.611	0.622	0.379
Exclusion restrictions in wage equation							
Attitudes/expectations	—	—	0.996	0.968	0.958	0.978	0.972

Note
a There are 248 observations. See Table 3.2 for details regarding sample and variables. See Table 3.3 for details regarding specifications and test statistics.

Testing the exclusion of the family background variables from the wage equation

To this point, the maintained identifying assumption in the instrumental variables fixed-effects estimation has been that the family background variables can be excluded from the wage equation. While the sibling values of the endogenous variables may provide better a priori valid instruments, for reasons explained in the section "Advantages of using sibling data" we cannot use these values as instruments in specifications with fixed family effects. In Table 3.5 we report results from an alternative statistical experiment in which we attempt to account for heterogeneity by including the sibling's wage in the wage equation.[32] This experiment may

Table 3.5 Two-stage least squares estimates of wage equation for sibling sample, using sibling's wage residual to control for heterogeneity, white women (dependent variable: natural logarithm of hourly earnings)[a]

	OLS	2SLS				
	(1)	(2)	(3)	(4)	(5)	(6)
Coefficients						
Married, spouse present	0.039	0.042	−0.007	0.052	0.041	−0.014
	(0.038)	(0.038)	(0.175)	(0.052)	(0.037)	(0.170)
Number of children	−0.072	−0.074	−0.065	−0.090	−0.076	−0.085
	(0.017)	(0.018)	(0.029)	(0.058)	(0.018)	(0.060)
Experience	0.030	0.027	0.031	0.030	0.030	0.027
	(0.005)	(0.014)	(0.006)	(0.006)	(0.006)	(0.015)
Schooling	0.063	0.062	0.064	0.060	0.059	0.056
	(0.008)	(0.009)	(0.008)	(0.012)	(0.010)	(0.012)
Sibling's wage[b]	0.088	0.088	0.088	0.086	0.091	0.088
	(0.039)	(0.039)	(0.039)	(0.040)	(0.039)	(0.041)
$\bar{R}^2$	0.525	—	—	—	—	—
Variables used as instruments						
Family background	—	Yes	Yes	Yes	Yes	Yes
Attitudes/expectations	—	Yes	Yes	Yes	Yes	Yes
Endogeneity tests						
Experience residual	—	0.004	—	—	—	0.004
		(0.015)				(0.016)
Married, spouse present residual	—	—	0.049	—	—	0.055
			(0.181)			(0.176)
Number of children residual	—	—	—	0.020	—	0.016
				(0.062)		(0.063)
Schooling residual	—	—	—	—	0.012	0.015
					(0.016)	(0.018)
p-value	—	0.777	0.786	0.741	0.447	0.932
Exclusion restrictions in wage equation						
Family background	—	0.574	0.643	0.946	0.639	0.992
Attitudes/expectations[c]	—	0.659	0.763	0.790	0.823	0.648

Notes
a There are 518 observations. See Table 3.2 for details regarding sample and variables. See Table 3.3 for details regarding specifications and test statistics.
b Residual from regression on year dummy variables.
c These come from specifications excluding the family background variables from the wage equation.

provide a less adequate means of controlling for heterogeneity, since it does not control for differences across siblings in the right-hand-side variables (in contrast to fixed-effects estimates).[33] On the other hand, it does allow us to use the sibling values of the potentially endogenous variables as instruments, and to test the exclusion of the family background variables from the wage equation.

The estimates reported in column (1) show that the sibling's wage is significantly related to the respondent's wage. But the point estimates of the other coefficients are closer to the OLS estimates in column (2) of Table 3.2 than to the fixed-effects estimates in column (4) of that table, implying that this is not an equivalent means of controlling for heterogeneity. Nonetheless, it is the best we can do with respect to testing the identifying assumptions. The last two rows of the table report the tests of the exclusion restrictions. In none of the specifications is there evidence against the exclusion of the family background variables from the wage equations. In addition, in contrast to Table 3.3, there was no evidence against the exclusion of the attitudes/expectations variables, conditional on excluding the family background variables.

Testing identifying assumptions used in previous research

Table 3.1 highlighted the wide variety of identifying assumptions that researchers have used to attempt to correct for endogeneity bias. Earlier, we presented a priori arguments for our identifying assumptions. In this section, we continue to use these identifying assumptions, and based on them, test as overidentifying restrictions some of the identifying assumptions used by others. We focus on a limited subset used to correct for endogeneity of experience and childbearing. These overidentification tests may prove useful to researchers who have available as instruments only the variables that, in our data set (and with our assumptions), provide overidentification.

In columns (1) and (2) of Table 3.6, we report tests of exclusion restrictions of three variables commonly used to instrument for experience and fertility, based on our preferred specifications from the IV/FE analysis in Table 3.3. Three common choices of instruments for experience are husband's weeks unemployed (in a year), husband's income, and number of children. (Of the papers cited in Table 3.1, see Mincer and Polachek, 1974; Sandell and Shapiro, 1978; and Wright and Ermisch, 1991.) As reported in column (1), we do not reject the exclusion of husband's unemployment from the wage equation, but do reject the exclusion of either husband's income or number of children. In column (2) we report results treating the number of children as endogenous (see Lundberg and Plotnick, 1989). Again, we do not reject the exclusion of husband's unemployment, but do reject the exclusion of husband's income. In columns (3) and (4) we repeat the analysis for the specifications considered in Table 3.5, in which we include the sibling's wage residual instead of the family fixed effect. The conclusions with respect to the exclusion restrictions are virtually unchanged, although strictly speaking the exclusion of husband's income is rejected at significance levels slightly higher than 5 percent.

Finally, the results reported in columns (1)–(4) are based on specifications with some attempt made to control for heterogeneity, whereas other researchers may have available only cross-sectional data. Since the test results may differ without the heterogeneity controls, we also use the sibling data to test the validity of these same identifying assumptions used in other research on a cross-sectional sample constructed from our data set, including sibling values of the potentially endogenous variables. To construct the data set for this analysis, we randomly sampled one individual from each family, to eliminate any error components structure to the data.[34] Results are reported in columns (5) and (6) of Table 3.6; the conclusions are largely unchanged.

Table 3.6 Results from overidentification tests for alternative instruments[a]

	Endogenous variables					
	Table 3.3 Specifications[b] (IV/FE)		Table 3.5 Specifications[c] (IV with sibling residual)		"Cross section"[d]	
	Experience (1)	Number of children (2)	Experience (3)	Number of children (4)	Experience (5)	Number of children (6)
Weeks husband unemployed[e]	0.478	0.286	0.478	0.464	0.175	0.176
Husband's income	0.036	0.022	0.060	0.057	0.027	0.041
Number of children[f]	0.034	—	0.000	—	0.001	—

Notes

a p-values from tests of exclusion restrictions of indicated variables are reported. Each of the alternative instruments is added to the model specification individually. Dummy variables for missing weeks husband unemployed or husband's income are included, in which case the variables were set to zero. See Tables 3.2, 3.3, and 3.5 for further details.

b Family background variables are excluded from wage equation, and used as instruments, while attitudes/expectations variables are included in wage equation, based on tests of exclusion restrictions in Table 3.3.

c Family background and attitudes/expectations variables are excluded from wage equation, and used as instruments, based on tests of exclusion restrictions in Table 3.5.

d Based on subsample of one woman randomly sampled from each sibship. Family background and attitudes/expectations variables are excluded from wage equation, and used as instruments, based on overidentification tests identical to those carried out in Table 3.5.

e For 1973, this is restricted to weeks husband collected unemployment compensation.

f This parallels earlier work (see Table 3.1) excluding number of children from the wage equation, and using it as an instrument for experience.

Conclusions

In this chapter we report results from the analysis of heterogeneity and endogeneity bias in women's wage equations, using data on siblings both to estimate models with fixed family effects, and to provide instrumental variables. The small samples of sisters available for the statistical experiments carried out in this chapter may seem to preclude rejecting any restrictions. But indeed numerous restrictions are rejected.

To summarize our results, we find evidence of statistically significant biases (at the 10-percent level or less) in OLS estimates of wage equations for white and black women, in coefficients that have attracted attention in the literature on women's wages (marital status, number of children, experience, and schooling). There is evidence of significant downward bias in the estimated effect of marital status on wages of white women. Estimates of the parameter are insignificantly different from zero in OLS estimates in our sample as well as others (Korenman and Neumark, 1992), but positive after accounting for heterogeneity and endogeneity. There is also evidence, for white women, of upward endogeneity bias in the estimated return to schooling.[35] Finally, there is evidence of significant upward heterogeneity bias in the estimated return to schooling for black women.

A question of equal importance is whether researchers can correct for biases in such estimates with the data typically available. We do find that some of the exclusion restrictions used to identify parameters in instrumental variables estimation of women's wage equations in cross-sectional data are not rejected; generally speaking, this is true for family background variables but not for attitudes/expectations variables. We also find that some of the exclusion restrictions that have been used in instrumental variables estimation are rejected in overidentifying tests using sibling data to obtain identification. Furthermore, while there appear to be valid instruments available in standard cross-sectional labor market surveys, the evidence of heterogeneity bias for white women (in estimates in which we simultaneously instrument) and for black women (more generally) suggests that panel data may be required to obtain unbiased estimates. Unfortunately, in this particular context, using repeated observations on individuals to control for heterogeneity may be problematic.

We close by pointing out some implications for the uses or applications of women's wage equations discussed in the Introduction. In constructing predicted wages for studies of other labor market variables with which wages may be endogenously determined, the incorrect treatment of wage equation regressors as exogenous may lead to misleading results. Mroz (1987) provides a striking example, showing that estimates of women's labor supply elasticities are considerably larger (positive) when experience is included in the reduced form wage equation; in contrast, when experience is treated as endogenous, the estimated labor supply elasticity is near zero (see his table VI).

Our findings are also relevant to estimates of discrimination based on decomposing sex differences in wages into discriminatory and non-discriminatory components. First, in most samples, OLS estimates indicate higher returns to schooling for women than for men (e.g. Oaxaca, 1973, table 3; Corcoran and Duncan, 1979; Neumark, 1988). Upward bias in the estimated return to schooling for women would lead to underestimates of gender-based wage discrimination. Second, the same decomposition techniques treat the positive wage premium paid to married men, coupled with the absence of a premium for women, as a wage differential attributable to discrimination.[36] But our endogeneity-corrected estimates of the effect of marital status on women's wages suggest that the premium for women may be as large as that paid to married men. Estimates in Neumark (1988) suggest that wage equation decompositions based on equal wage premiums for married men and women would reduce the estimate of discrimination by about one-third, compared to decompositions based on OLS estimates. Finally, the lower estimates of the return to schooling for black women would contribute to a larger estimate of the discriminatory component of within-sex race differences in wages.

A third use of women's wage equations is in testing theories of wage differences between men and women. For example, one explanation of the positive effect of marriage on men's wages (Korenman and Neumark, 1991) is that married men specialize in market production and human capital investment, while women specialize in the home (Becker, 1985). A positive effect of marriage on women's wages, especially in specifications that do not control for children, would undermine this hypothesis.

Finally, estimates of the effects of demographic decisions on wages are interesting for numerous reasons, including estimating the opportunity costs of these decisions (e.g. Lundberg and Plotnick, 1990). For white women our results provide a more conclusive answer regarding the effects of children on wages than did our previous research; while the effect is not significant in all specifications, it is unambiguously negative. On the other hand, our estimates for black women, which are generally as precise as those for white women, provide no compelling evidence that wages are reduced by having children. It remains to be seen whether additional (and alternative) approaches to untangling causal effects of demographic decisions on wages and earnings will provide explanations for variation in demographic behavior across individuals and time. In our view, this is likely to be an area in which research on women's wage equations will yield high returns.

Appendix

Table 3.A1 Descriptive statistics for panel data sample

	White women	Black women
Distribution of sibships		
Two sisters	223	96
Three sisters	24	17
Five sisters	0	1
Means (standard deviations)		
Log wage	6.177	5.992
	(0.537)	(0.485)
Married, spouse present	0.680	0.536
Number of children	1.002	1.641
	(1.117)	(1.430)
Experience	5.806	5.695
	(3.556)	(3.465)
Schooling	13.463	12.359
	(2.323)	(2.233)
South	0.266	0.633
Urban	0.685	0.746
1982	0.527	0.516
1980	0.098	0.077
1978	0.154	0.165
1977	0.029	0.032
1975	0.058	0.040
1973	0.133	0.169
Correlation with sibling values[a]		
Married, spouse present	0.154	0.003
Number of children	0.140	0.286
Experience	0.181	0.317
Schooling	0.447	0.397
Sample size	518	248

Note

a For sibships with more than two members, this is the average over the other siblings.

Table 3.A2 First-stage regressions for instrumental variables/fixed effects estimation,[a] coefficients of instruments in first-stage regressions[b]

Coefficients	Experience	Married, spouse present	Number of children	Schooling
	(1)	(2)	(3)	(4)
Father's education	−0.324	0.001	−0.067	−0.022
	(0.124)	(0.022)	(0.046)	(0.064)
Mother's education	−0.174	−0.019	−0.018	0.089
	(0.194)	(0.033)	(0.072)	(0.100)
Parents' educational goal	0.085	0.001	0.027	0.062
	(0.051)	(0.009)	(0.019)	(0.026)
Number of siblings	0.293	−0.019	0.040	0.005
	(0.132)	(0.023)	(0.050)	(0.069)
Mother worked	−2.358	0.170	−0.691	0.133
	(0.587)	(0.104)	(0.221)	(0.312)
Lived with father and mother	−1.412	0.017	−0.464	−0.461
	(1.010)	(0.174)	(0.377)	(0.521)
Nontraditional sex-role attitude	—	0.068	—	—
		(0.084)		
Ideal age at marriage	—	0.001	—	—
		(0.012)		
Expected number of children	—	0.002	—	—
		(0.019)		
Educational expectations	—	0.025	—	—
		(0.029)		
Educational goal	—	−0.031	—	—
		(0.026)		
R^2	0.545	0.221	0.359	0.717
Joint significance[c]	0.000	0.815	0.017	0.288

Notes
a See Tables 3.2 and 3.3 for details regarding sample and variables.
b These correspond to the specifications in Table 3.3, columns (1)–(4). Coefficients are reported for variables excluded from wage equation and used as instruments; coefficients of other variables included in wage equation (including family dummy variables), and dummy variables for missing instruments, are not reported.
c *p*-value from F-test of joint significance of coefficients reported in table.

Acknowledgments

We thank McKinley Blackburn, William Even, Michael Keane, Alice Nakamura, Mark Rosenzweig, Ken Wolpin, and an anonymous referee for helpful comments. Elaina Rose provided research assistance.

Notes

1 Representative examples of this research are listed in Table 3.1, discussed in the section on Past research: an overview.
2 Admittedly, though, this is more likely to be true when controls for unobserved ability, such as test scores, are included.

3 Because this is a study of bias in women's wage equations, we do not explore random effects estimation.

4 Another implicit assumption, which can be relaxed, is that the other coefficients (β and γ) are constant across time.

5 This estimator may be problematic if the researcher is interested in the effect of a variable for which changes are potentially endogenous (Solon, 1988). Gibbons and Katz (1992) provide a good discussion of this problem in the context of controlling for unobserved labor quality in estimating industry wage differentials in wage equations, and show how isolating exogenous changes (in their case, by studying displaced workers) may be beneficial.

6 In estimates correcting for heterogeneity, the test is based on Heckman and Hotz (1989). For the instrumental variables estimates, we report tests of overidentifying restrictions, given a priori assumptions regarding exclusion restrictions that secure identification.

7 Although a first-difference estimator computed over a long interval ought to mitigate this problem, specification tests (from Heckman and Hotz, 1989) indicated that only a first-difference estimator computed over a short interval could be used.

8 Previous research suggests sister–sister correlations in wage equation residuals on the order of 0.2 (e.g. Shackett, 1981). We give more direct evidence on family vs. individual fixed effects later.

9 Because these first-stage regressions are reduced forms, we do not know whether the fixed family effects represent common family influences on wages, which in turn affect the potentially endogenous variables, or instead represent direct common influences on the endogenous variables.

10 Yet another possibility is that the wage equation (2) could be differenced across time, with levels of the family background and attitudes/expectations variables used as instruments for the changes in the potentially endogenous variables. In order for this approach to be valid the following equation must hold:

$$\Delta Y_{it} = Z_i \delta + \Delta X_{it} \beta' + \Delta \eta_{it},$$

that is, Z_i must remain in the differenced equation for Y. The implication is that the variable $Z_i \delta \cdot t$ must appear in the (level) equation for Y. This specification may not be unreasonable for, say, experience, since it implies that the growth rate of Y is related to Z, but it does seem an inappropriate specification for marital and fertility status. Furthermore, we want to consider the potential endogeneity of schooling, which drops out in this approach. Finally, there may be considerably less scope for endogeneity of experience in a short first difference than in a cross-section.

11 Of course, no argument justifying an identifying assumption is fool-proof. It could be argued that a respondent may choose a low-wage job because her sister has high schooling and experience, and therefore a high actual or potential wage, some of which may be transferred to the respondent. However, in the 1985 wave of the NLS Young Women's survey, only 16 out of 3,708 women reported transfers from siblings (brothers or sisters), so this seems an unlikely problem.

12 If we had repeated observations on sibling values of the endogenous variables, we could in principle use these as instruments while correcting for heterogeneity in longitudinal data for individuals, since these sibling values can change over time. But to the extent that the sibling values reflect omitted *fixed* characteristics, variation over time in the sibling values does not provide any identifying information (in contrast, say, to the mean of the sibling values over many periods).

13 In a sample containing pairs of siblings only, the family-specific dummy variable and the sibling's value of the endogenous variable provide a perfect fit for the respondent's value of the endogenous variable. This is nearly, but not exactly so, in a sample with triplets of siblings as well as pairs, as we have in our sample.

14 This analysis has some parallels in earlier research on men by Chamberlain and Griliches (1977), using a sibling's ability test score to instrument for test scores in wage equations.

15 For expository ease, we refer to "non-blacks" as "whites." The Young Women's NLS did not distinguish Hispanics and other non-whites.

16 For sibships of more than two members, "sibling value" refers to the average over the other siblings. We maintain this definition throughout the chapter.

The relatively smaller numbers of observations from particular years (1975, 1977, and 1980) reflect the need to construct the number of children variable from retrospective information for these years.

17 This difference in the instrumental variables and first difference results may also reflect our concerns, noted in the section "Advantages of using sibling data," regarding using instrumental variables estimation to account for heterogeneity.

18 In contrast to these findings, there was no evidence of bias from selective employment in either the cross-sectional or longitudinal estimates.

19 OLS and fixed-effects results reported for this specification in the remaining tables were qualitatively unchanged by using the specification in Korenman and Neumark (1992), including both "married, spouse present" and "divorced or separated" dummy variables, dummy variables for one and for two or more children, and including both experience and tenure. Experiments with this richer specification revealed that serious multicollinearity plagued estimates instrumenting for both experience and tenure (especially when fixed-family effects were included). Nonetheless, the instrumental variables estimates indicated no change in the estimated effect of children on wages, just as in the results reported in the paper using experience only.

20 Consistent with this, the Hausman specification test does not reject the exclusion of fixed effects (and hence the use of OLS) from the specification either including or excluding experience. Of course, this result does not necessarily imply an absence of heterogeneity bias in estimates accounting for endogeneity, so we retain the family fixed effects in the instrumental variables estimation that follows.

21 This parallels the test of the fixed-effect assumption in longitudinal data on individuals proposed by Heckman and Hotz (1989), entailing including earlier values of the dependent variable in first-difference specifications.

22 These assumptions regarding the instruments are identical to those used in Chapter 2.

23 In all cases, we report the results from the joint test of significance of the instruments themselves, not including in the test the coefficients of the dummy variables indicating missing data for the potential instruments.

24 The absence of any change in the return to labor force attachment contrasts with the results from our earlier paper (Korenman and Neumark, 1992). However, results not reported in the tables reveal that the difference in results is not attributable to the omission of tenure, nor is it attributable to the inclusion of family fixed effects. The remaining candidate explanation is changes in the sample, which is necessarily much smaller in the present chapter. Given the large standard errors of the instrumental-variables estimates of the returns to experience (or tenure), it is not surprising that the point estimates are fragile.

25 Strictly speaking, depending on the results of the tests of the exclusion restrictions, the IV/FE estimates should perhaps be compared with fixed-effects estimates including the attitudes/expectations variables. But the coefficients reported in Table 3.2 were little changed by including these variables.

26 The pure fixed-effects estimate was 0.02 (0.05).

27 However, there is not a straightforward Hausman-type test of the IV vs. the IV/FE specification, since the inclusion of the fixed family effects in the first-stage regressions of the IV/FE estimation can (and does) make the IV/FE estimates more efficient than the IV estimates.

28 In all cases, a linear probability model was used for marital status, given that fixed effects cannot be consistently estimated in dichotomous choice models.
29 Appendix Table 3.A2 reports the coefficients of the family background and attitudes/expectations variables from the first-stage regressions corresponding to Table 3.3, columns (1)–(4).

Nakamura and Nakamura (1985b) show that the power of Hausman exogeneity tests falls as the R^2 values from these first-stage regressions fall. In fact, the adjusted R^2 for the "ever married" and tenure regressions, reported in Table 3.A2, are relatively low, while the evidence against exogeneity is strongest for these variables. This has two implications: first, the likelihood that the power of the exogeneity test for marital status was low gives added credibility to the rejection of exogeneity of marital status; and second, the fact that we can reject exogeneity, in this sample, even for variables for which the instruments have relatively little explanatory power, means that our results from this sample are informative.
30 Estimates of the effects of children were also near zero in specifications excluding experience. The OLS and fixed-effects estimates (standard errors) were 0.001 (0.017), and −0.005 (0.024).
31 Results for the test of whether the family fixed effect adequately removes the heterogeneity were similar to the results for white women.
32 This is the residual from an OLS regression of the sibling's wage on the year dummy variables. Extracting the residual from an OLS regression on all of the control variables would ignore potential biases in the OLS estimates.
33 Furthermore, this approach does not increase the attractiveness of panel data on individuals across time (rather than across families) because the same problem of reducing or eliminating variation in experience or tenure if we condition on the availability of two wage observations arises as with fixed-effects estimation.
34 While random effects could be used to account for such a structure, the random-effects estimator can be interpreted as a weighted average of the OLS and fixed-effects estimator, in which case the experiment would not replicate that faced by a researcher using a single cross section of data.
35 This contrasts with results for men in which there is some evidence of downward endogeneity bias in the return to schooling (Griliches, 1977).
36 Our findings in Korenman and Neumark (1991), however, suggest that the wage differential paid to married men may represent higher productivity.

References

Angrist, Joshua D. and Alan B. Krueger. 1991. "Does Compulsory School Attendance Affect Schooling and Earnings?" *Quarterly Journal of Economics* 106: 979–1014.
Becker, Gary S. 1985. "Human Capital, Effort, and the Sexual Division of Labor," *Journal of Labor Economics* 3(1, Part 2): S33–58.
Blackburn, McKinley L., David. E. Bloom, and David Neumark. 1993. "Fertility Timing, Wages, and Human Capital." *Journal of Population Economics* 6(1): 1–30.
Bloom, David E. and Mark R. Killingsworth. 1982. "Pay Discrimination Research and Litigation: The Use of Regressions." *Industrial Relations* 21: 318–39.
Chamberlain, Gary and Zvi Griliches. 1977. "More On Brothers." In *Kinometrics: Determinants of Socioeconomic Success Within and Between Families*, ed. P. Taubman, Amsterdam: North-Holland Publishing Company.
Corcoran, Mary and Gregory J. Duncan. 1979. "Work History, Labor Force Attachment, and Earnings Differences between the Races and Sexes." *Journal of Human Resources* 14: 3–20.

Corcoran, Mary, Gregory J. Duncan, and Michael Ponza. 1983. "A Longitudinal Analysis of White Women's Wages." *Journal of Human Resources* 28(4): 497–520.

Cox, Donald. 1984. "Panel Estimates of the Effects of Career Interruptions on the Earnings of Women." *Economic Inquiry* 22(3): 386–403.

Dolton, P. J. and G. H. Makepeace. 1987. "Marital Status, Child Rearing and Earnings Differentials in the Graduate Labour Market." *The Economic Journal* 97: 897–922.

Gibbons, Robert and Lawrence Katz. 1992. "Does Unmeasured Ability Explain Inter-Industry Wage Differentials?" *Review of Economic Studies* 59: 515–35.

Goldin, Claudia and Solomon Polachek. 1987. "Residual Differences by Sex: Perspectives on the Gender Gap in Earnings." *American Economic Review* 77(2): 143–51.

Griliches, Zvi. 1977. "Estimating the Returns to Schooling: Some Econometric Problems." *Econometrica* 45: 1–22.

——. 1979. "Sibling Models and Data in Economics: Beginnings of a Survey." *Journal of Political Economy* 87(Part 2): S37–64.

Heckman, James J. and V. Joseph Hotz. 1989. "Choosing Among Alternative Nonexperimental Methods for Estimating the Impact of Social Programs: The Case of Manpower Training." *Journal of the American Statistical Association* 84: 862–74.

Heckman, James J. and Richard Robb. 1986. "Alternative Identifying Assumptions in Econometric Models of Selection Bias." *Advances in Econometrics* 5: 243–87.

Hill, Martha. 1979. "The Wage Effects of Marital Status and Children." *Journal of Human Resources* 14(4): 579–94.

Killingsworth, Mark R. 1990. "Marriage, Labor Supply and Wage Rates: Estimates from a New Econometric Framework." Mimeograph.

Kim, Moon-Kak and Solomon W. Polachek. 1991. "Panel Estimates of the Effects of Labor Market Intermittency on Market Wages." Mimeograph.

Korenman, Sanders and David Neumark. 1991. "Does Marriage Really Make Men More Productive?" *Journal of Human Resources* 26(2): 282–307.

——. 1992. "Marriage, Motherhood, and Wages." *Journal of Human Resources* 27(2): 233–55.

Lundberg, Shelly and Robert Plotnick. 1990. "Earnings Losses Caused by Teenage Premarital and Marital Childbearing." Mimeograph.

Mincer, Jacob and Solomon Polachek. 1974. "Family Investments in Human Capital: Earnings of Women." *Journal of Political Economy* 82: S76–108.

Mroz, Thomas. 1987. "The Sensitivity of an Empirical Model of Married Women's Hours of Work to Economic and Structural Assumptions." *Econometrica* 55: 765–800.

Nakamura, Alice and Masao Nakamura. 1985a. *The Second Paycheck: A Socioeconomic Analysis of Earnings*. Orlando, FL: Academic Press, Inc.

——. 1985b. "On the Performance of Tests by Wu and by Hausman for Detecting the Ordinary Least Squares Bias Problem." *Journal of Econometrics* 29: 213–27.

Neumark, David. 1988. "Employers' Discriminatory Behavior and the Estimation of Wage Discrimination." *Journal of Human Resources* 23(3): 279–95.

Oaxaca, Ronald. 1973. "Male–Female Wage Differentials in Urban Labor Markets." *International Economic Review* 14(3): 693–709.

O'Neill, June. 1985. "The Trend in the Male–Female Wage Gap in the United States." *Journal of Labor Economics* 3(1, Supplement): S91–116.

O'Neill, June and Solomon Polachek. 1993. "Why the Gender Gap in Wages Narrowed in the 1980s." *Journal of Labor Economics* 11(1, Part 1): 205–28.

Orcutt, Guy H. and A. Glazer. 1980. "Microanalytical Modeling and Simulation." In *Micro Simulation-Models, Methods and Applications*, eds Barbara Bergman, Gunnar Eliasson, and Guy Orcutt. IUI Conference reports, 1980:1. Stockholm: Almquist and Wilksell International.

Sandell, Steven and David Shapiro. 1978. "The Theory of Human Capital and the Earnings of Women: A Rexamination of the Evidence." *Journal of Human Resources*, 13(1): 103–17.

Shackett, Joyce. 1981. "Experience and Earnings of Young Women." Unpublished PhD dissertation, Harvard University.

Solon, Gary. 1988. "Self-Selection Bias in Longitudinal Estimation of Wage Gaps." *Economics Letters* 28: 285–90.

Wright, R. E. and J. F. Ermisch. 1991. "Gender Discrimination in the British Labour Market: A Reassessment." *The Economic Journal* 101: 508–22.

4 Fertility timing, wages, and human capital

(with McKinley L. Blackburn and David E. Bloom)

Introduction

Between 1970 and 1983, the first birth rate in the United States declined by 19 percent. In addition, according to survey data collected by the Census Bureau, the proportion of childless women increased substantially between 1976 and 1985 in the age groups 25–29, 30–34, and 35–39 (see Table 4.1). An extensive body of previous research has established that these trends reflect both (1) an increased tendency to permanently forego childbearing and (2) an increasing tendency to delay the initiation of childbearing, among those women who do ultimately bear children (see Bloom, 1982, 1984, 1987; Bloom and Pebley, 1982; Bloom and Trussell, 1984; O'Connell, 1985; Rindfuss et al., 1988). In addition, after many years of remarkable stability, the female/male wage ratio also began to increase in the 1980s (from 0.59 in 1980 to 0.67 in 1987). There is some evidence that this latter change is associated with increasing human capital accumulation on the part of women (see Smith and Ward, 1984; O'Neill, 1985).

This chapter develops some explicit theoretical linkages concerning the relationship between women's fertility-timing behavior and their human capital acquisition and wage profiles. By simplifying the nature of the fertility/work decision, we are able to describe the conditions under which women who prefer (and therefore expect) to be delayed childbearers will invest more heavily in their human capital than women who prefer to have an early first birth. The model suggests that these conditions are fairly general: if the discount rate is greater than the economy-wide

Table 4.1 Percentage of childless women, 1976–85 (by age)

Age group	1976	1980	1982	1984	1985
18–24	69.0	70.0	72.2	71.4	71.4
25–29	30.8	36.8	38.8	39.9	41.5
30–34	15.6	19.8	22.5	23.5	26.2
35–39	10.5	12.1	14.4	15.4	16.7
40–44	10.2	10.1	11.0	11.1	11.4

Source: US Bureau of the Census, Current Population Reports, Series P-20, No. 406: Fertility of American women (June 1985). US Government Printing Office, Washington, DC, 1986.

growth rate of wages for workers who are not human capital investors, then delayers will be more likely to invest in human capital. Our empirical analysis provides some support for this theoretical model. There exists a strong positive relationship between several proxies for human capital investment and the age at which women bear their first child. However, the empirical analysis does not support the proposition that the usual proxies for human capital represent more intensive investment by women who choose to delay their childbearing.

Stylized facts

Our empirical analysis uses the National Longitudinal Survey (NLS) of Young Women. This NLS has been conducted every year (or every other year in some periods) since 1968, when it started with 5,159 women aged 14–24. The main purpose of this survey has been to gather information on the labor market experiences of young women. Questions on ages of children in various years of the survey enabled us to calculate age at first birth. We have used the NLS data through 1982 to construct a data set with wage, labor market, and fertility timing data for a sample of working women aged 28–38 in 1982. Like many longitudinal data sets, the NLS Young Women's Cohort has suffered from sample attrition over time; still, the 1982 reinterview includes roughly 70 percent of the original respondents. The NLS data offer a number of advantages compared to other data sets used to study the correlates of fertility timing. For one, the longitudinal structure provides a method of accounting for unobserved heterogeneity. More importantly, perhaps, the richness of the NLS data permits us to construct typically unavailable measures of several key determinants of earnings. The variables used in this study whose construction relies on data from a large section of women's work lives (in many cases their entire career to date) include actual labor market experience,[1] tenure, and occupational training.

Table 4.2 reports statistics descriptive of wages, human capital, and other characteristics of white women[2] classified into four groups on the basis of the age at which they bore their first child: (1) women who had their first birth before the survey in which they were age 22 ("early" childbearers); (2) women who had their first birth between ages 22 and 26 (inclusive); (3) women who first gave birth after age 26 ("late" childbearers); and (4) women who had not given birth by the time of the 1982 survey ("childless" women).[3] Only individuals with no missing data for any variables (except the training, occupation, and early wage variables) are used to compute the statistics reported in Table 4.2.[4] The statistics are reported separately for women who were currently employed on the data surveyed in 1982, and for women who were not employed at that time; the differences in the reported statistics across age-at-first-birth categories tend to be very similar for these two samples. With the exception of the early wage variable, all values are for 1982.

Table 4.2 reveals a cross-sectional pattern of increases in the 1982 wage, and in all of the human capital measures, as age at first birth increases; childless women tend to have values of these variables that are close to those of the late childbearers. These are raw means, of course, and therefore do not control for the influence of

Table 4.2 Wages and other characteristics of white working women aged 28–38, by age at first birth (NLS of Young Women: 1982)[a]

	Currently working women, age at first birth				Non-working women, age at first birth			
	<22	22–26	27+	Childless	<22	22–26	27+	Childless
Wage[b]	5.75	6.59	8.23	7.93	—	—	—	—
	(0.11)	(0.20)	(0.32)	(0.18)				
Education[c]	11.96	13.55	15.01	14.66	11.20	13.25	14.00	12.71
	(0.08)	(0.13)	(0.21)	(0.12)	(0.12)	(0.16)	(0.26)	(0.50)
Experience[d]	7.00	7.85	8.09	7.77	2.67	4.06	5.95	4.96
	(0.17)	(0.25)	(0.33)	(0.18)	(0.19)	(0.19)	(0.31)	(0.51)
Tenure[e]	4.69	5.27	5.50	6.04	—	—	—	—
	(0.16)	(0.27)	(0.37)	(0.23)				
Age	33.39	33.35	33.06	31.77	33.16	32.46	33.34	32.14
	(0.14)	(0.20)	(0.27)	(0.15)	(0.21)	(0.22)	(0.28)	(0.36)
Number of children	2.31	1.90	1.37	—	2.90	2.28	1.64	—
	(0.04)	(0.05)	(0.05)		(0.07)	(0.06)	(0.07)	
% in occupations[f]								
Manager	0.08	0.07	0.11	0.14	0.03	0.03	0.06	0.07
Professional	0.11	0.29	0.45	0.41	0.05	0.21	0.32	0.15
Administrative	0.48	0.41	0.26	0.28	0.29	0.46	0.40	0.31
Service	0.17	0.13	0.11	0.11	0.25	0.17	0.12	0.22
Blue collar	0.15	0.10	0.06	0.07	0.31	0.12	0.10	0.14
No occupation reported	—	—	—	—	0.07	0.01	0.00	0.11
Early wage[g]	4.32	5.26	5.98	5.66	3.82	5.02	5.78	4.86
	(0.14)	(0.14)	(0.21)	(0.13)	(0.19)	(0.15)	(0.19)	(0.23)
Training[h]	0.15	0.15	0.25	0.17	0.10	0.07	0.13	0.26
	(0.02)	(0.02)	(0.06)	(0.02)	(0.02)	(0.02)	(0.03)	(0.07)
N[i]	467	256	115	372	252	192	104	59

Notes

a Standard errors of means are reported in parentheses. Sample weights were not used in computing the estimates.

b The hourly wage is constructed from reported rates and time units of pay.

c Highest grade completed.

d Actual experience is constructed from a combination of sample period and retrospective job history questions.

e For each year in the survey, the respondent indicates whether or not she is with the same employer as in the previous survey. This information is combined with occasional questions on when the respondent began her last job to construct a measure of years with the current employer. Tenure is reset to zero when a woman is not working at the time of the survey.

f For the nonworking women, this is occupation of last job, for those who report an occupation.

g First available observation prior to 1982 when woman was childless. Adjusted for inflation and productivity to 1982 base using PCE fixed-weight index and index of nonfarm business productivity. Available for sample of 701 women working for a wage, and 290 women not working for a wage, for whom this observation could be constructed.

h Constructed from survey questions on duration of occupational and on-the-job training. Measured in year-equivalents (units of 2,000 hours). Available for 1,133 observations on women working for a wage, and 583 women not working for a wage.

i Cell sizes are smaller for early wage and training measures.

some of the variables in the table on others. For example, an explanation for the positive association between wages and age at first birth may be that educational attainment is positively related to age at first birth.[5] Also, the small experience and tenure differences in Table 4.2 actually do represent a substantially more intensive rate of investment in experience- and tenure-related human capital for delayed childbearers, since their greater investment in education leaves them with relatively less potential time for accumulating experience and tenure.[6] The training measure does not follow as consistent a pattern as education, tenure, and experience, but it does reveal a weak tendency to increase with age at first birth. Finally, later childbearers and childless women are more likely to be in professional and managerial occupations than earlier childbearers, who are more likely to be in administrative, service and blue collar occupations.

The early wage variable reported in Table 4.2 represents an attempt to measure the hourly rate of pay at which women begin their labor market career following the completion of their schooling. In selecting this variable, we found the earliest wage (in 1968 or later) for each woman in a year in which she was not in school, and had not previously had her first birth. We were able to measure such a wage for 991 of the 1,817 women in our sample.[7] The differences in the average level of the early wage across age-at-first-birth categories are similar in pattern to those for the 1982 wage. However, the differences tend to be somewhat larger with the 1982 wage. For example, the average early wage of "late" childbearers is 37 percent higher than the average early wage for "early" childbearers, while the 1982 wage for late childbearers is 43 percent higher than the 1982 wage for early childbearers. For the childless compared to the early childbearers, the difference grows from 31 percent in the early wage to 38 percent in the 1982 wage.[8]

Some of the relationships revealed in these descriptive statistics replicate results in other studies. Previous analyses of the covariates of age at first-birth uniformly reveal that educational attainment varies positively and strongly with first-birth timing and the likelihood of being childless (Bloom, 1982, 1984; Bloom and Trussell, 1984). A related literature documents and studies the relationship between teen childbearing and schooling (e.g. Furstenberg, 1976; Hofferth, 1984; Furstenberg *et al.*, 1987; McCrate, 1989; Upchurch and McCarthy, 1990; Geronimus and Korenman, 1992). However, there is considerably less research on the direct relationship between women's wages or earnings and the timing of their childbearing.[9] Bloom (1987) finds that in the younger of two cohorts analyzed in the June 1985 CPS, there is a positive relationship between age at first birth and wages, even controlling for schooling, time out of the labor force, and other determinants of earnings. While much has been written about the impact on wages of interruptions in labor force attachment for childbearing and childrearing, this research has not focused on the timing of these interruptions (e.g. Polachek, 1975; Mincer and Ofek, 1982; Corcoran *et al.*, 1983; O'Neill, 1985).

One line of research that does explore specific links between wages and fertility timing is the "business cycle" work of Butz and Ward (1979). The idea underlying this work is that working women will tend to have children when real wages are relatively low, as during a recession. This theory could also have implications for the cross-section relationship between fertility timing and wages, although there have been few attempts to test these implications.[10]

What appears to be lacking in the existing literature is a model that explains the key relationships in Table 4.2 in a reasonably unified manner. In the next section we offer a theoretical model in which human capital and fertility timing decisions are made jointly. Our model suggests that women who prefer to delay the initiation of childbearing will invest more in human capital than women who prefer to begin their childbearing earlier. After presenting this model, the sections "Wage equation estimates and fertility timing" and "The relationship between human capital and fertility timing," explore more fully some of its empirical implications.

Theoretical model

The key defining feature of the standard human capital model is that individuals have the opportunity to invest in training that enhances their productivity but that is costly to obtain. Workers find it desirable to obtain training when its benefits— higher wages after the training is completed—outweigh its costs. In this section, we extend a simple human capital model to allow childbearing to affect the human capital investment decision through the effect that withdrawal from the labor force after childbearing has on the benefits of the human capital investment. The key implication of the model is that relatively late childbearing is associated with greater human capital investment; factors that lead to relatively late childbearing also lead to greater human capital investment, and vice versa.

In analyzing the human capital/fertility-timing decision for women, we make several simplifying assumptions.[11] First, we assume that all women are equally productive in the labor market at the start of their working career. Second, all women bear one, and only one, child. Third, all women work from time 0 to time R, except for a period of length τ following childbirth when women leave the work force and have no earnings; women must choose to have their child at some time between time 0 and time $R - \tau$. Fourth, all women have the option of investing in one type of human capital which increases a woman's productivity (and thus her wage), at the rate s, while she is working; the cost of the human capital investment is C (at time 0) and is the same for all women. Finally, the only source of income for a woman is her own earnings.

We also assume that a woman's lifetime utility depends on the present value of her lifetime income and on the time period in which she has her child, that is, $U = U(Y, T)$ where Y is the present value of lifetime income and T is the time period of childbirth; women prefer both higher incomes and earlier periods of childbearing (i.e. we assume $U_Y > 0$ and $U_T < 0$). For tractability, we use a linear utility function, $U = Y - aT$, with $a > 0$.[12] Women differ in their preferences toward early childbearing, so that a varies across women.

At the start of her working career, a woman has two choices to make: first, whether she should invest in human capital; and, second, when she should have her first child. We seek a description of these two choices in the following way: first, we derive an expression for the optimal age at first birth conditional on either investment (with optimal age T_I^*) or non-investment (T_N^*); second, given that the woman is optimizing in her choice of time of childbirth, we ask whether her lifetime utility would be higher under investment or under non-investment.

The complete details of the solution for these two decisions are quite cumbersome (due to the possibility of boundary solutions for time of birth) and therefore are presented in the Appendix. Here we highlight the nature of the solution by focusing on the case where all women choose an interior solution for time of birth (i.e. $0 < T^* < R - \tau$). If a woman chooses to invest in human capital, then the present value of her lifetime income is

$$Y_I = \int_0^T we^{(s+q-r)t}\,dt + \int_{T+\tau}^R we^{(q-r)t}e^{s(t-\tau)}\,dt - C,$$

where w is the initial wage, q is the economy-wide rate of growth of wages, and r is the discount rate. $U(Y_I, T)$ is maximized with respect to T, for which the first-order condition for a utility extremum is

$$MB_I(T) \equiv we^{(s+q-r)T}[1 - e^{(q-r)\tau}] = a. \tag{1}$$

The left-hand side of equation (1) represents the marginal benefit from delaying childbirth, and equals the present value of the wage received prior to childbirth minus the present value of the wage received when returning to the labor market after childbirth. The right-hand side of equation (1) is the marginal cost of delaying. It follows that the marginal benefit of delaying will only be positive if $q < r$, which we assume throughout. The condition will represent a maximum if $s + q - r < 0$, which we also presently assume. (If $s + q - r > 0$, the optimal time for the birth will be either 0 or $R - \tau$; this case is discussed in the Appendix.)

If the woman chooses not to invest in human capital, lifetime income is

$$Y_N = \int_0^T we^{(q-r)t}\,dt + \int_{T+\tau}^R we^{(q-r)t}\,dt.$$

The condition for a utility extremum is

$$MB_N(T) \equiv we^{(q-r)T}[1 - e^{(q-r)\tau}] = a, \tag{2}$$

which is also the condition for a maximum when $q < r$. The left-hand side of equation (2) represents the marginal benefit of delaying for a non-investor.

It follows from equations (1) and (2) that a woman who has invested in human capital will choose to delay her childbearing more than if she had not invested in human capital. This fact is illustrated in Figure 4.1, which graphs the marginal benefit and marginal cost functions for both investors and non-investors. While the two marginal benefit functions are equal when $T = 0$, at any time T the slope of the investor's marginal benefit function is larger (less negative) than the slope of the non-investor's function. As a result, $T_I^* > T_N^*$ must hold. As a decreases (as in the fall from a_0 to a_1 in Figure 4.2), the larger slope of the investor's marginal benefit function implies that the difference between T_I^* and T_N^* will increase, as long as T_I^* has not reached $R - \tau$, the upper boundary for childbearing ages.[13]

The next step in our analysis of the decision process is the human capital investment decision. Given that the woman will be optimizing on her fertility timing once she has chosen whether or not to invest, we can derive the indirect utilities of the two choices as functions of the parameters of the problem, that is,

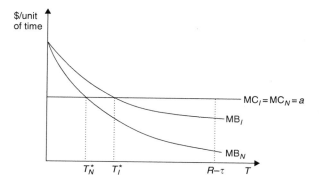

Figure 4.1 Marginal benefit and marginal cost functions for investors and non-investors.

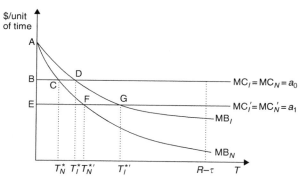

Figure 4.2 Effect of difference in preferences for delayed childbearing.

$V_j = V_j(w, q, r, a, s, C)$, $j = I, N$. Then a woman will choose to invest in human capital if $V_I > V_N$. As is demonstrated in the Appendix, the indirect utility from investing grows more quickly as a declines than does the indirect utility from not investing; this means that women with weaker preferences for early childbearing are more likely to find $V_I > V_N$ to be true than women with stronger preferences for an early birth.

This result is illustrated in Figure 4.2 for the case where both investors and non-investors choose an interior solution for T^*. Define the surplus from delaying childbearing as the total additional benefits associated with delaying childbearing past $T = 0$ minus the total additional (utility) costs. For instance, with childbearing preference parameter $a = a_0$, the surplus from delaying for non-investors is $S_N(a_0) = \text{area}(ABC)$ in Figure 4.2, and the surplus for investors is $S_I(a_0) = \text{area}(ABD)$. While it is obvious that $S_I(a_0) > S_N(a_0)$, a woman with utility parameter a_0 will choose to invest only if

$$S_I(a_0) - S_N(a_0) > -(V_I - V_N)|_{T^*=0}, \tag{3}$$

that is, if the additional surplus associated with investing is greater than minus the difference in indirect utility between investors and non-investors if both were to have their child at time 0. $(V_I - V_N)|_{T^*=0}$ does not depend on the value of a (see case 1 of the Appendix).[14]

Consider another woman with utility parameter $a = a_1$, where $a_1 < a_0$. Her surplus from delaying will be $S_N(a_1) = $ area(AEF) if she does not invest, and $S_I(a_1) = $ area(AEG) if she does. Going from a_0 to a_1, the change in both surpluses will be positive, that is $\Delta S_I = S_I(a_1) - S_I(a_0) = $ area(BEGD) and $\Delta S_N = S_N(a_1) - S_N(a_0) = $ area(BEFC) are both greater than zero. But as is clear from Figure 4.2, $\Delta S_I > \Delta S_N$, implying that it is more likely for a woman with the lower value of a to find investing optimal than for a woman with the higher value, since the left-hand side of equation (3) increases as a decreases but the right-hand side remains unchanged.

What does this imply for the earnings of women who choose to delay childbearing? As discussed earlier, we expect women with lower values for a to delay their childbearing more, while we also except them to be more likely to invest in human capital. With human capital investment increasing the wages of investors relative to non-investors at all times after $T = 0$, we expect to observe delayed childbearers having higher wages than otherwise similar women (in terms of initial productivity) who choose to bear their child earlier. It also follows that the difference in the wages of delayed and early childbearers will grow over time due to the higher rate of human capital investment among delayed childbearers.

While the model has been discussed in terms of variation in the taste parameter a being the only difference between women, it is also true that increases in s, or decreases in C, make it more likely both that women will delay childbearing and that they will invest in human capital. Furthermore, slight changes in the model do not alter the basic conclusions. For example, if the model is changed to reflect the fact that women have more difficulty continuing their investment in human capital after having their first child, so that wages grow at the rate q (and not at the rate $q + s$) after returning from childbirth even for women who were earlier investing in human capital, our primary conclusions still hold. Likewise, if there is depreciation of human capital while a woman is out of the labor force, delayers will still invest more in human capital, as depreciation merely increases the difference between the leaving and returning wages and so "swings out" the $MB_I(T)$ curve.

Differential investment in human capital is not the only reason why delayed childbearers might be expected to have higher wages. Suppose there were no possibility of investing in human capital, and that all women had the same value for the childbearing utility parameter a. Instead, women differ in their initial level of productivity (and so their wage) at the time they enter the labor force. From equation (2) we know that a higher initial wage will shift upwards the marginal benefit curve, as from MB_N to MB'_N in Figure 4.3. As a result, women with higher initial wages will more often choose to delay, and so delayed childbearing will be associated with higher wages at all points in the woman's lifetime. Differences in initial wages may also be part of the explanation for the fact, discussed in the previous section, that more educated women tend to delay their childbearing more after completing their schooling.[15]

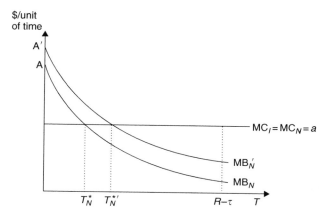

Figure 4.3 Effect of wage difference.

The empirical implications of our model are that women who choose to delay childbearing will accumulate more education, and, to the extent that labor market experience and tenure represent human capital investment, will also accumulate more experience and tenure. This greater investment will raise the relative earnings of later childbearers. We might expect two additional findings, because we may not be able to perfectly measure human capital investment, but rather must regard variables such as education, experience, tenure, and even our training measure as proxies. First, we may find that fertility timing has an effect on wages after controlling for measurable human capital, though such residual effects could also be due to unobserved heterogeneity in the initial productivity of workers. Second, we may find higher returns to education, experience, and tenure, for delayed childbearers, in wage regressions. We explore these possibilities in the next section.

Wage equation estimates and fertility timing

It is difficult if not impossible to measure human capital directly. As a result, labor economists often interpret wage variation associated with variation in certain observable factors as resulting from differences in investment in human capital, relying on a theoretical structure that relates the observable variables to human capital investment. One famous example is Mincer's interpretation of labor market experience as representing investments in on-the-job training (see Mincer, 1974). In the present context, this approach suggests including age-at-first-birth variables in a wage regression as potentially reflecting differences in human capital investment not captured by other human capital proxies that are included in the regression. In this section, we consider this approach, as well as more explicit tests of the human capital model.

Table 4.3 presents least squares estimates of log wage equations for the NLS sample of working women considered in Table 4.2. The wage variable is the reported hourly wage and salary income usually earned in the respondent's primary job at the time of the survey. In all of our regressions, we include as independent variables dummy variables for the same classification of age at first birth as was used for Table 4.2; age at first birth less than 22 is the omitted category.[16] In column (1), we report coefficient estimates from a least-squares regression of the natural logarithm of the wage on these timing dummy variables, as well as dummy variables for living in the South and living in an SMSA (crude controls for cost-of-living differentials). In addition, we include as regressors age at the time of the survey, and dummy variables for whether the woman was married with spouse present, or was instead divorced, widowed or living apart from her spouse (never married is the omitted category).[17] Since the number of children to which

Table 4.3 Wage equation estimates for white working women, OLS (dependent variable: natural logarithm of hourly earnings)[a]

	(1)	*(2)*	*(3)*	*(4)*
Age at first birth				
22–26	0.10	0.01	−0.03	−0.03
	(0.03)	(0.03)	(0.03)	(0.03)
27+	0.32	0.14	0.07	0.06
	(0.05)	(0.05)	(0.04)	(0.04)
Childless	0.30	0.14	0.07	0.06
	(0.04)	(0.04)	(0.04)	(0.04)
Joint significance (*p*-value)[b]	0.00	0.00	0.05	0.06
Years of education	—	0.06	0.07	0.06
		(0.01)	(0.01)	(0.01)
Post-college dummy variable	—	−0.07	−0.05	−0.06
		(0.04)	(0.04)	(0.04)
Experience	—	—	0.02	0.02
			(0.003)	(0.003)
Tenure	—	—	0.05	0.05
			(0.01)	(0.01)
Tenure[b] $\times 10^{-2}$	—	—	−0.16	−0.15
			(0.05)	(0.04)
R^2	0.16	0.23	0.34	0.36
Occupation dummy variables included[c]	No	No	No	Yes

Notes

a There are 1,210 observations. Standard errors of estimates are reported in parentheses. Controls included in all specifications include: dummy variables for two children and three or more children; dummy variables for marital status (married, spouse present and divorced, widowed, or separated); and dummy variables for residence in the South and in an SMSA. Regressions in columns (1) and (2) also include age entered as a linear variable; the estimated coefficient of a quadratic term was statistically insignificant, as were the estimated coefficients of the linear and quadratic terms in columns (3) and (4). The estimated coefficient of a quadratic term in experience was statistically insignificant in columns (3) and (4), and was omitted.

b Computed from standard F-test.

c The occupation categories in Table 4.2 are used to define dummy variables for occupation.

a woman has given birth is correlated with her age at first birth (see Table 4.2), we also include dummy variables for two children, and for three or more children, as independent variables. The choice of omitted category for the number of children classification implies that the childless coefficient measures the difference between childless women and early childbearers with one child. As the estimates in Table 4.3 make clear, substantial wage differentials by age at first birth persist once these controls are added. Women with age at first birth between 22 and 26 earn on average 10 percent more than early childbearers, and these differentials rise to about 30 percent for late childbearers and childless women.

Because few (if any) controls for human capital investment are included in the specification in column (1), these estimates of wage differentials due to age at first birth may reflect differences in the observable proxies for human capital such as education and experience. In column (2), we add education to the to the regression.[18] Not surprisingly, the wage differentials by age at first birth fall. Nonetheless, sizable and statistically significant differentials remain for late childbearers and childless women, consistent with differences in human capital investment above and beyond education.

Human capital investment may also occur on the job. In column (3) we add experience, tenure, and its square to the regression.[19] The coefficient estimates for experience and tenure are statistically significant, and of the expected sign and magnitude. The age-at-first-birth coefficients are further reduced by the inclusion of experience and tenure, and though individually are statistically insignificant, remain significant in a joint F-test. Inclusion of occupational dummy variables—which may reflect human capital investment differences—further reduces the coefficient for "late" childbearers, leaving the age-at-first-birth dummy coefficients significant only at the 0.06 level.

The estimates in Table 4.3 support two important findings. First, differences in observed proxies for human capital investment (schooling, experience, and tenure) can explain a sizable portion of wage differentials associated with fertility timing. Second, wage differentials remain once account is taken of these proxies, consistent with there being differences in unobserved human capital investment (although the statistical evidence on this point is not strong). We next ask whether these remaining fertility-timing effects actually reflect further differences in human capital investment.

Including dummy variables for fertility timing may be a crude way to estimate effects of differential human capital investment that remain once our proxies are included. A better specification may be to let the coefficients of these proxies vary with age at first birth. These types of effects could arise if the education of women who intend to delay childbearing is associated with more intensive human capital investment per year of schooling (thus giving rise to higher returns to education), or if later childbearers invest more per unit of labor market experience or tenure. In column (1) of Table 4.4, we let the coefficient on the years of schooling variable differ for late childbearers and childless women by including interactions of education with the 27+ and childless dummies.[20] In column (2), we let the linear experience and tenure coefficients vary by age-at-first-birth category, while

Table 4.4 Wage equation estimates for white working women, interactive specifications and incorporating training measures, OLS (dependent variable: natural logarithm of hourly earnings)[a]

	Interactive specifications			Training specifications	
	(1)	(2)	(3)	(4)	(5)
Age at first birth					
22–26	−0.02	−0.03	−0.02	−0.03	−0.03
	(0.03)	(0.03)	(0.03)	(0.03)	(0.03)
27+	0.04	0.07	0.05	0.08	0.07
	(0.05)	(0.04)	(0.05)	(0.04)	(0.04)
Childless	0.07	0.07	0.07	0.06	0.06
	(0.04)	(0.04)	(0.04)	(0.04)	(0.04)
Joint significance (p-value)[b]	0.17	0.04	0.12	0.06	0.08
Years of education	0.05	0.05	0.05	0.06	0.06
	(0.01)	(0.01)	(0.01)	(0.01)	(0.01)
Post-college dummy variable	−0.08	−0.06	−0.08	−0.04	−0.04
	(0.04)	(0.04)	(0.04)	(0.04)	(0.04)
Experience	0.02	0.02	0.02	0.02	0.02
	(0.003)	(0.004)	(0.004)	(0.003)	(0.003)
Tenure	0.05	0.05	0.05	0.05	0.05
	(0.01)	(0.01)	(0.01)	(0.01)	(0.01)
Tenure[b] $\times 10^{-2}$	−0.15	−0.13	−0.13	−0.17	−0.17
	(0.04)	(0.05)	(0.05)	(0.05)	(0.05)
Training	—	—	—	—	0.05
					(0.03)
Age at first birth $\times$ education					
27+	0.029	—	0.027	—	—
	(0.017)		(0.019)		
Childless	0.014	—	0.011	—	—
	(0.011)		(0.012)		
Joint significance (p-value)[b]	0.17	—	0.31	—	—
Age at first birth $\times$ experience					
27+	—	−0.014	−0.007	—	—
		(0.011)	(0.012)		
Childless	—	−0.004	−0.003	—	—
		(0.007)	(0.008)		
Joint significance (p-value)[b]	—	0.41	0.83	—	—
Age at first birth $\times$ tenure					
27+	—	0.013	0.013	—	—
		(0.010)	(0.010)		
Childless	—	−0.010	−0.010	—	—
		(0.006)	(0.006)		
Joint significance (p-value)[b]	—	0.06	0.05	—	—
R^2	0.37	0.37	0.37	0.37	0.37
N	1,210	1,210	1,210	1,133	1,133

Notes

a Standard errors of estimates are reported in parentheses. Controls included in all specifications include: dummy variables for two children and three or more children; dummy variables for marital status (married, spouse present and divorced, widowed, or separated); dummy variables for residence in the South and in an SMSA; and occupation dummy variables. The education, experience, and tenure interactions are products of the age at first birth dummy variables and the respective variable minus its sample mean; thus, for example, the coefficient on years of education continues to measure the effect of education on log wages evaluated at the sample means.

b Computed from standard F-test.

in column (3) we let the returns to all three human capital proxies vary. Focusing on column (3), we see that the point estimates of the education interactions are consistent with greater human capital investment for each year of education for later childbearers. For example, the return to education is almost 60 percent higher for the late childbearers (27+) relative to the <22 category.[21] But these differences are not statistically significant. While the point estimates for the experience interactions are small and insignificant, the tenure interactions are jointly significant. The tenure coefficient estimates suggest that late childbearers receive a higher return to tenure, but also provide the anomalous result that childless women receive lower returns to tenure (this latter inference supported by a marginally significant *t*-statistic). Overall, the patterns in these interactions do not support the proposition that our human capital measures represent more human capital investment per unit of education and experience for women who delay their childbearing than for early childbearers.

As a final attempt to better capture human capital differences, we utilize the training measure presented in Table 4.2 as a more direct measure of human capital investment. In column (4) of Table 4.4 we repeat the estimation of the specification in column (4) of Table 4.3 using the smaller sample with nonmissing training. Then, in column (5), we add to this specification the training measure. The estimates suggest that each additional year of training leads to a 5 percent increase in wages. However, inclusion of training does not affect the fertility timing coefficient estimates, or the coefficient estimates for experience and tenure.[22]

Our next step in the empirical work is to explore whether these conclusions are affected by the failure to control for two other potential influences on the relationship between wages and fertility timing: the effect of fertility timing on labor force participation; and the direct effect of wages on fertility timing.

Since the estimates in Tables 4.3 and 4.4 are based on samples of women that exclude those women not working in 1982, inferences from these estimates may suffer from sample selection bias (see Heckman, 1979). The nature of our sample definition implies that our estimates are conditional on women working, and so may not correspond to the population of all women. In particular, it seems plausible that the age-at-first-birth coefficients may be affected by our sample selection, since from Table 4.2 there are clear differences in the proportion of women working across age-at-first-birth categories. (This proportion varies from 53 percent among the late childbearers to 86 percent among the childless.) This difference may be due to reservation wages varying systematically by women's ages at first birth, so that late childbearers have higher reservation wages, and childless women lower reservation wages, than earlier childbearers.[23] If so, then we would expect equations estimated with the complete population (i.e. not conditional on working in 1982) to exhibit larger differences in wages between early childbearers and the childless, and smaller differences between the early childbearers and the later childbearers, than we observed in earlier tables.

To study the influence of selectivity on our wage equation estimates, we re-estimated specification (2) in Table 4.3—where education, but not experience and tenure are included—using a maximum-likelihood procedure for the two-equation model suggested in Heckman (1979).[24] In column (1) of Table 4.5, we present estimates from a model where several variables are included as determinants of working status (husband's income and unemployment, alimony and child support, and several family background variables) but are assumed not to belong in the wage equation specification. Compared to Table 4.3, these results suggest that—consistent with our expectations—the 27+ effect was overstated in our earlier estimates, while the childless effect was understated; but the changes in the coefficients due to the selection correction are not very large. Since it is also possible to correct for selectivity without imposing the restriction that the additional variables (mentioned earlier) be excluded form the wage equation, we re-estimated our selection model without imposing these restrictions.[25] These alternative estimates are presented in column (2). In contrast to the previous results, with this specification the 27+ coefficient estimate is unchanged while the childless coefficient drops, relative to the least-squares estimates. However, there are two reasons to prefer the estimates in column (1): first, the likelihood-ratio statistic ($\chi^2 = 14$, with 13 degrees of freedom) for testing the exclusion restrictions in column (1) is not significant; and, second, the positive sign of the error correlation in column (1) is more plausible.[26]

The idea that wages may directly affect fertility timing was illustrated in the discussion of Figure 4.3 in the previous section. This discussion suggested that fixed omitted variables in a wage equation (e.g. ability, aggressiveness, and "spunk"), which would tend to increase starting wages, should also lead to delayed childbearing.[27] We consider this possibility in two ways. First, we attempt to control for the fixed wage effect that may be correlated with age at first birth in estimating our wage equations for 1982. We do this by including as a regressor the residual from a regression of the early (log) wage on characteristics of women at the time of the early wage observation.[28] In column (4) of Table 4.5, we re-estimate the specification reported in column (4) of Table 3 using the smaller sample for which the early wage variable was available. In column (5) of Table 4.5, we add the early wage residual.[29] The results suggest that there is some persistence in wages over time, as the coefficient estimate for the early wage residual (which is measured, on average, eleven years prior to 1982) is 0.23. The coefficient estimates for the fertility timing dummy variables fall when the early wage residual is included, although the decline in the coefficients is small relative to the standard errors of the coefficient estimates. The implication is that heterogeneity in initial wages does not affect to any great extent the measured relationships between wages and fertility timing. In column (3), we report coefficient estimates for the age-at-first-birth dummies when they are included as regressors in the early wage equation. These estimates also reveal a weak correlation between starting wages and the timing of (later) fertility once the effects of human capital on wages are removed.[30]

Our second method for handling the potential correlation between age at first birth and wages is to instrument for the age-at-first-birth dummies. This method is potentially more useful because it can correct for such a correlation arising from heterogeneity or endogeneity. We estimate linear probability models for each of the three first-birth dummies, using family background variables available in the NLS (as well as the exogenous variables in the wage equation) as independent variables. We then use predicted probabilities from these estimated models as instruments for the first-birth dummies in the 1982 wage equation (see Heckman, 1978). As experience and tenure might also be endogenous in the wage equation, we estimate a wage equation that excludes these variables. We also exclude other demographic variables (marital status and number of children), allowing age at first birth to capture all possible demographic effects. However, we include the early wage residual as a regressor; if this residual captures unobserved ability, it should be valid to exclude family background variables from the wage equation (see Griliches, 1979). The results in column (6) of Table 4.5 are OLS estimates for this equation, while column (7) reports our instrumental variables estimates.[31] The IV estimation increases the coefficient estimates for the first-birth dummies, but also leads to considerably less precise estimates. Results from a Hausman test—performed by including the residuals from the linear probability models as additional regressors—suggest that we cannot reject the hypothesis that the fertility timing variables are exogenous. (The p-value for the joint significance of these residuals is 0.51.)

We also estimated the variant of our wage equation model that includes experience and (linear) tenure, treating these two variables as potentially endogenous in the wage equation. Given the results of the Hausman test for column (7) of Table 4.5, we treat age at first birth as exogenous in this estimation, and include the other demographic controls. Identifying instruments include the family background variables as well as nonlabor income and husband's income. Column (8) provides the OLS estimates for the specification and sample used, while column (9) provides the estimates instrumenting for experience and tenure. The Hausman test suggests that there is clear evidence that experience (though not tenure) is endogenous in the wage equation; indeed, the experience coefficient is (insignificantly) negative in the IV results. These results also suggest larger effects of age at first birth on wages than the corresponding OLS estimates.[32]

The relationship between human capital and fertility timing

The results in the previous section indicate that wages are higher for delayed childbearers largely because they have greater accumulation of observable proxies for human capital. As mentioned, this is consistent with our model of joint human capital and fertility-timing decisions. In this section, we explore the alternative possibility that the correlation between human capital and fertility timing is spurious, in the sense that human capital and timing appear to be related because both are primarily determined by women's family background.[33]

We would like to be able to disentangle the structural relationship between timing and human capital, but the exclusion restrictions necessary to identify such a model, given our data, would be so arbitrary that an interpretation of the results as valid structural estimates would be highly dubious.[34] Instead, we focus

Table 4.5 Wage equation estimates for white working women, biases from selection, heterogeneity, and endogeneity (dependent variable: natural logarithm of hourly earnings)[a]

	Sample-selectivity correction[b]		Heterogeneity correction[c]			Endogeneity corrections[d]			
			Early	1982	1982	OLS	Endogenous age at first birth	OLS	Endogenous experience and tenure
	(1)	(2)	(3)	(4)	(5)	(6)	(7)	(8)	(9)
Age at first birth									
22–26	−0.01	0.02	0.01	−0.05	−0.06	−0.02	0.20	−0.06	0.03
	(0.03)	(0.04)	(0.04)	(0.05)	(0.05)	(0.05)	(0.92)	(0.05)	(0.07)
27+	0.10	0.14	0.01	0.05	0.04	0.11	0.24	0.03	0.18
	(0.05)	(0.06)	(0.05)	(0.06)	(0.06)	(0.06)	(0.59)	(0.06)	(0.10)
Childless	0.15	0.11	0.02	0.08	0.06	0.11	0.51	0.05	0.16
	(0.04)	(0.05)	(0.04)	(0.06)	(0.06)	(0.05)	(0.64)	(0.06)	(0.08)
Joint significance	0.00	0.01	0.94	0.04	0.05	0.00	0.22	0.07	0.05
Experience	—	—	0.04	0.02	0.02	—	—	0.014	−0.050
			(0.01)	(0.004)	(0.005)			(0.005)	(0.032)
Tenure	—	—	0.05	0.05	0.05	—	—	0.024	0.047
			(0.01)	(0.01)	(0.01)			(0.004)	(0.031)
Early wage residual			—	—	0.23	0.28	0.29	0.22	0.27
					(0.04)	(0.04)	(0.05)	(0.04)	(0.06)
Estimation method	MLE	MLE	OLS	OLS	OLS	OLS	IV	OLS	IV
Corresponding OLS estimates	Table 4.3, column (2)	Table 4.3, column (2)	—	—		—	column (6)	—	column (8)
Rho	0.33	−0.13							
	(0.14)	(0.43)							
Log-likelihood	−1552.4	−1548.5							
Hausman tests (separate regressions)									
Age at first birth							−0.22	—	—
22–26 residual							(0.88)		

Age at first birth 27+ residual	—	—	-0.14 (0.56)	—	—	—
Childless residual	—	—	-0.40 (0.61)	—	—	—
Joint significance			0.51			
Experience residual	—	—	—	—	—	0.09 (0.03)
Tenure residual	—	—	—	—	—	-0.01 (0.03)

Notes

a Asymptotic standard errors of estimates are reported in parentheses.

b Based on 1,817 observations, with 1,210 working women. Controls included in wage equation and employment probit include: age; dummy variables for two children and three or more children; dummy variables for marital status (married, spouse present and divorced, widowed, or separated); dummy variables for residence in the South and in an SMSA; years of education and a dummy variable for post-college education. In column (2) the following family background variables are included in both equations: husband's income (set to zero for unmarried women); the sum of income from alimony and child support (set to zero for never married women); father's education; mother's education; number of siblings; a dummy variable equal to 1 if the respondent's mother worked when respondent was age 14; a dummy variable equal to 1 if the respondent lived with both a father and a mother at age 14; and dummy variables corresponding to each of these variables, equal to 1 when the variable was missing (in which case the variables were set equal to zero). In column (1) these variables were excluded from the wage equation.

c Based on 701 observations. Controls included in columns (3)–(5) include: years of education and a post-college dummy variable; tenure squared; dummy variables for marital status; dummy variables for residence in the South and in an SMSA; and occupation dummy variables. In each case, the years from which these controls are drawn are indicated in the column heading. The age-at-first-birth variables, however, are always as defined in 1982. In column (3) dummy variables for the year from which the early wage are drawn are included. The early wage residual is computed from the early wage regression excluding age-at-first-birth variables.

d Based on 701 observations. Controls included in columns (6) and (7) include: age; years of education and a post-college dummy variable; and dummy variables for residence in the South and in an SMSA. Additional controls included in columns (8) and (9) are: dummy variables for two children and three or more children; and dummy variables for marital status. The square of tenure was excluded. Instrumental variables used in column (7) were: father's education; mother's education; number of siblings; a dummy variable equal to 1 if the respondent's mother worked when respondent was age 14; a dummy variable equal to 1 if the respondent lived with both a father and a mother at age 14; and dummy variables corresponding to each of these variables, equal to 1 when the variable was missing (in which case the variables were set equal to zero). Instruments for experience and tenure in column (9) include these variables, as well as: husband's income (set to zero for unmarried women); the sum of income from alimony and child support (set to zero for never married women). Residuals reported in last five rows of table for columns (6)–(9) are from regressions of potentially endogenous variables on all exogenous variables and instruments. These residuals are then included in the OLS regression, and their coefficients (standard errors) are reported. Statistically insignificant coefficient estimates imply that exogeneity cannot be rejected.

on the "equilibrium" relationship between fertility timing and human capital. In particular, we consider whether the positive relationships between age at first birth and human capital variables in Table 4.2 are to any extent due to unobserved heterogeneity associated with family background. We estimate regressions of education, experience, and tenure on the same set of age-at-first-birth dummy variables used earlier. We then add an extensive set of family background variables available in the NLS.[35] We do not assert that these variables capture all sources of unobserved heterogeneity. Indeed, if we find that the inclusion of these variables partially reduces the association between fertility timing and human capital, we would have to allow for the possibility that a more complete set of variables could explain the entire relationship. However, if we find no diminution in fertility-timing effects once we control for background, it seems reasonable to conclude that heterogeneity does not underlie the results.

The first two columns of Table 4.6 report results with education as the dependent variable. In column (1) the background variables are excluded, while in column (2) they are included. When these variables are added, the coefficients of the fertility timing dummy variables decline by 20–25 percent. Thus, we cannot decisively

Table 4.6 Years of education, experience, and tenure regressions for white working women, ordinary least squares[a]

	Years of education		Experience		Tenure	
	(1)	*(2)*	*(3)*	*(4)*	*(5)*	*(6)*
Age at first birth						
22–26	1.59	1.26	0.98	0.97	0.50	0.47
	(0.16)	(0.15)	(0.39)	(0.39)	(0.56)	(0.56)
27+	3.06	2.30	1.90	1.98	1.01	1.01
	(0.22)	(0.20)	(0.44)	(0.44)	(0.63)	(0.64)
Childless	2.78	2.19	2.00	2.06	1.73	1.74
	(0.15)	(0.14)	(0.37)	(0.37)	(0.53)	(0.53)
Years of education	—	—	−0.69	−0.67	−0.25	−0.19
			(0.07)	(0.07)	(0.09)	(0.10)
Early wage residual[b]	—	—	—	0.39	—	0.84
				(0.32)		(0.46)
R^2	0.27	0.39	0.36	0.37	0.09	0.11
N	1,210	1,210	701	701	701	701
Family background variables included[c]	No	Yes	No	Yes	No	Yes

Notes
a Standard errors of estimates are reported in parentheses. Age is included in all regressions.
b This is constructed from a wage regression including: years of education and a post-college dummy variable; dummy variables for marital status; dummy variables for residence in the South and in an SMSA; and dummy variables for the year from which the observation was drawn.
c Family background variables include: father's education; mother's education; number of siblings; a dummy variable equal to 1 if the respondent's mother worked when respondent was age 14; a dummy variable equal to 1 if the respondent lived with both a father and a mother at age 14; and dummy variables corresponding to each of these variables, equal to 1 when the variable was missing (in which case the variables were set equal to zero).

reject the view that the education/fertility-timing differentials reflect unobserved heterogeneity rather than human capital investment choices.

In columns (3) and (4) we estimate regressions with experience as the dependent variable, and with education included as an independent variable. The equation is identified by assuming that the errors of the education and experience equations are uncorrelated.[36] In the equation for experience in column (4), we also add the early wage residual, to allow for the possibility that delayed childbearers accumulate more experience because they start off with (and possibly continue to have) higher wages. The addition of the early wage residual and the family background variables leaves the estimated age-at-first-birth effects on experience unaltered. In columns (5) and (6) we use tenure rather than experience as the dependent variable; with tenure, inclusion of family background and the early wage residual reduces the age-at-first-birth coefficient estimates by 10 percent or less.[37]

We are therefore comfortable concluding that heterogeneity related to family background does not explain the estimated experience and tenure differences associated with fertility timing. Our theoretical model of the relationship between fertility timing and human capital investment offers an explanation for these differences. It may also partially explain the correlation between education and fertility timing, although our results suggest that this empirical relationship is at least partly due to heterogeneity associated with family background characteristics.

Conclusions

This chapter has developed a model of a woman's optimal human capital investment behavior over the life cycle conditional on her preferences over the timing of her first birth. In the context of this model we show that late childbearers will tend to invest more heavily in human capital than early childbearers. Our model also suggests that women with higher initial wages will choose to delay their childbearing more. Our empirical analysis explores the validity of these theoretical linkages between fertility timing and the wages that women earn while in their late twenties and thirties. Fertility timing is strongly associated with differences in wages, as well as differences in education, experience, and tenure. The wage differences are largely explained by differences in these latter variables, which appear to be good proxies for human capital. We find that the positive relationship between human capital and age at first birth can be only partly attributed to underlying heterogeneity. Thus, the human capital differences seem to explain an important component of the overall relationship between labor market outcomes and fertility timing.

We wish to emphasize that our results are consistent with the human capital hypothesis, but cannot be said decisively to confirm this hypothesis. In fact, what may be a stronger test of our theory—that the usual human capital proxies represent greater investment for delayers—receives little support from the data. Still, our model does provide a unified explanation of the relationships we observe between human capital and fertility timing. We take it as a challenge for future research to develop and test alternative, encompassing models to explain these same empirical relationships.

Appendix

An age-at-first-birth/wage model with endogenous fertility timing

Notation

Y_I = present value of lifetime income for a woman who invests in human capital

Y_N = present value of lifetime income for a woman who does not invest in human capital

w = wage received at beginning of work career

T = point in time at which woman bears her first (and only) child

τ = length of period spent out of the labor force after childbirth

R = time of retirement

s = growth rate of (real) wages due to investment in human capital

q = growth rate in wages due to general wage growth

r = discount rate

Assumptions

(i)   all women are identical (in terms of productivity-related characteristics) at the start of their working career;

(ii) all women work from time 0 to time R, except for the period of length τ following childbirth. τ is the same for all women; in particular it does not depend on T;

(iii) all women have identical discount rates;

(iv) all women have the option of investing in one type of human capital by paying C (at time 0) and receiving a higher growth rate of their wage over time, with the difference in the growth rate of wages between investors and non-investors equaling s;

(v)   a woman's lifetime utility depends only on the present value of her lifetime income (i.e. her lifetime earnings) and the age at which she has her first child, that is, $U = U(Y,T)$, with $\partial U/\partial Y > 0$ and $\partial U/\partial T < 0$. In particular, we assume $U = Y - aT$, with $a > 0$.

Fertility-timing decisions

(*1*) *Optimal timing for human capital investors.*   From text equation (1), we know that the first-order condition for a utility extremum conditional on a woman investing in human capital is:

$$\mathrm{MB}_I(T) \equiv we^{(s+q-r)T}[1 - e^{(q-r)\tau}] = a. \tag{A1}$$

Note that if $q < r$, the optimal timing is always $T^* = 0$. For there to be an interior solution for T^*, it is necessary that (A1) represent the conditions for a maximum and not a minimum. This will be the case if

$$\frac{\partial MB_I(T)}{\partial T} = w(s + q - r)e^{(s+q-r)T}[1 - e^{(q-r)\tau}] < 0,$$

that is, if $s + q < r$. If $s + q > r$, then either $T^* = 0$ or $T^* = R - \tau$.

Assuming $s + q < r$, we have the following description of T^* for investors:

$$T_I^* = \begin{cases} 0 & \text{if } \dfrac{a}{w[1 - e^{(q-r)\tau}]} \geq 1 \\[4mm] \dfrac{1}{(s + q - r)} \log\left[\dfrac{a}{w[1 - e^{(q-r)\tau}]}\right] & \text{if } 1 > \dfrac{a}{w[1 - e^{(q-r)\tau}]} \\[4mm] & \qquad > e^{(s+q-r)(R-\tau)} \\[4mm] R - \tau & \text{if } e^{(s+q-r)(R-\tau)} \geq \dfrac{a}{w[1 - e^{(q-r)\tau}]}. \end{cases}$$

The condition for $T_I^* = 0$ is that $MB(0) \leq a$; the condition for $T_I^* = R - \tau$ is that $MB(R - \tau) \geq a$. Note that $\partial T_I^*/\partial a \leq 0$, that is, the lower the preference for early childbearing the longer the delay before first birth. If $s + q > r$, then the woman chooses to delay until $R - \tau$ as long as $\int_0^{R-\tau} MB_I(s)ds \geq a(R - \tau)$. This leads to the optimal timing decision:

$$T_I^* = \begin{cases} 0 & \text{if } \dfrac{a}{w[1 - e^{(q-r)\tau}]} > \dfrac{e^{(s+q-r)(R-\tau)} - 1}{(s + q - r)(R - \tau)} \\[4mm] R - \tau & \text{otherwise.} \end{cases}$$

The upper boundary for T_I^* will hold for lower values of a. (Notice that when $a = w[1-e^{(q-r)\tau}][e^{(s+q-r)(R-\tau)} - 1]/[(s + q - r)(R - \tau)]$, the woman is indifferent between choosing $T^* = 0$ or $T^* = R-\tau$, since the utility of both choices is equal.)

(2) *Optimal timing for non-investors.* The first-order condition for a utility extremum (text equation (2)) is

$$we^{(q-r)T}[1 - e^{(q-r)\tau}] = a. \tag{A2}$$

The second-order condition for a maximum is satisfied if:

$$w(q - r)e^{(q-r)T}[1 - e^{(q-r)\tau}] < 0,$$

which holds under the assumption $q < r$. The description of the age at first birth choice is:

$$T_N^* = \begin{cases} 0 & \text{if } \dfrac{a}{w[1 - e^{(q-r)\tau}]} \geq 1 \\[4mm] \dfrac{1}{(q - r)} \log\left[\dfrac{a}{w[1 - e^{(q-r)\tau}]}\right] & \text{if } 1 > \dfrac{a}{w[1 - e^{(q-r)\tau}]} > e^{(q-r)(R-\tau)} \\[4mm] R - \tau & \text{if } e^{(q-r)(R-\tau)} \geq \dfrac{a}{w[1 - e^{(q-r)\tau}]}. \end{cases}$$

As with $T_I^*, \partial T_N^*/\partial a \leq 0$. The condition for $T_N^* = 0$ is the same as for $T_I^* = 0$ (assuming $s + q < r$); however, $T_N^* = R - \tau$ is less likely than $T_I^* = R - \tau$. The expression for the difference in optimal fertility times between investors and non-investors (assuming an interior solution for both) is:

$$T_I^* - T_N^* = \left[\frac{-s}{(s + q - r)(q - r)} \right] \log \left[\frac{a}{w[1 - e^{(q-r)\tau}]} \right] > 0,$$

so that investors will wait longer until their first birth. In addition, $T_I^* = R - \tau$ is more likely than $T_N^* = R - \tau$, which also supports the idea that investors are more likely to delay. It also follows that $\partial (T_I^* - T_N^*)/\partial a < 0$, so that changes in timing preferences have a larger effect on investors' timing decisions than on non-investors'.

Human capital investment decision

Given that boundary solutions to the age-at-first-birth decision are possible, it is necessary that we analyze the investment decision under several cases (corresponding to whether or not an investor or non-investor would be at one or the other boundary). There are five separate cases that are exhaustive of the possibilities. (Again, throughout this section we will assume that $q < r$.) Under each case, we derive the following: one, the conditions under which the case holds; and two, an expression for the difference in the indirect utilities $V_j = V_j(w, q, r, a, s, C), j = I, N$, between investors and non-investors. The discussion assumes that the only characteristic that varies across women is the value for a in the utility function.

Case (1): $T_I^* = 0; T_N^* = 0$.
Conditions: (A) if $s + q < r$, then this case holds if

$$\frac{a}{w[1 - e^{(q-r)\tau}]} \geq 1;$$

or (B) if $s + q > r$, then this case holds if

$$\frac{a}{w[1 - e^{(q-r)\tau}]} > \frac{e^{(s+q-r)(R-\tau)} - 1}{(s + q - r)(R - \tau)}.$$

Difference in indirect utilities:

$$V_I = \int_\tau^R w e^{(q-r)t} e^{s(t-\tau)} dt - C$$

$$V_N = \int_\tau^R w e^{(q-r)t} dt; \quad \text{so}$$

$$V_I - V_N = \frac{w e^{-s\tau}}{s + q - r} [e^{(s+q-r)R} - e^{(s+q-r)\tau}]$$

$$- \frac{w}{(q - r)} [e^{(q-r)R} - e^{(q-r)\tau}] - C.$$

The difference in utilities does not depend on a, but lower values of a make this case less likely.

Case (2): $T_I^* = R - \tau; T_N^* = 0.$
Conditions: (A) $s + q > r$

and (B) $1 \leq \dfrac{a}{w[1 - e^{(q-r)\tau}]} \leq \dfrac{e^{(s+q-r)(R-\tau)} - 1}{(s + q - r)(R - \tau)}.$

Note that $(e^x - 1)/x > 1$ as long as $x > 0$ (the proof follows from L'Hôpital's Rule and the fact that $d[(e^x - 1)/x]/dx > 0$ when $x > 0$), so that this case is possible if $s + q > r$.
Difference in indirect utilities:

$$V_I - V_N = \frac{w}{(s + q - r)}[e^{(s+q-r)(R-\tau)} - 1]$$
$$- \frac{w}{(q - r)}[e^{(q-r)R} - e^{(q-r)\tau}] - a(R - \tau) - C.$$

It follows that $\partial(V_I - V_N)/\partial a < 0.$

Case (3): $0 < T_I^* < R - \tau; 0 < T_N^* < R - \tau$
Conditions:
This is the case where neither investors nor non-investors would be at a boundary. This happens if $s + q < r$, and if

$$1 > \frac{a}{w[1 - e^{(q-r)\tau}]} > e^{(s+q-r)(R-\tau)}.$$

Difference in indirect utilities:

$$V_I - V_N = \frac{we^{-s\tau}}{(s + q - r)}\left[e^{(s+q-r)R} - \frac{ae^{(s+q-r)\tau}}{w[1 - e^{(q-r)\tau}]}\right]$$
$$- \frac{w}{(q - r)}\left[e^{(q-r)R} - \frac{ae^{(q-r)\tau}}{w[1 - e^{(q-r)\tau}]}\right]$$
$$+ \frac{sw}{(s + q - r)(q - r)}\left[1 - \frac{a}{w[1 - e^{(q-r)\tau}]}\right]$$
$$+ \frac{sa}{(s + q - r)(q - r)}\log\left[\frac{a}{w[1 - e^{(q-r)\tau}]}\right] - C.$$

The difference in indirect utilities increases as a decreases, since:

$$\frac{\partial(V_I - V_N)}{\partial a} = \frac{s}{(s + q - r)(q - r)}\log\left[\frac{a}{w[1 - e^{(q-r)\tau}]}\right] < 0.$$

Case (4): $T_I^* = R - \tau; 0 < T_N^* < R - \tau$

This can happen under one of two sets of conditions:

(A) if $s + q < r$, and $e^{(q-r)(R-\tau)} < \dfrac{a}{w[1 - e^{(q-r)\tau}]} \leq e^{(s+q-r)(R-\tau)}$; or

(B) if $s + q > r$, and $e^{(q-r)(R-\tau)} < \dfrac{a}{w[1 - e^{(q-r)\tau}]} < 1.$

The difference in indirect utilities is:

$$V_I - V_N = \frac{w}{(s+q-r)}[e^{(s+q-r)(R-\tau)} - 1] - \frac{w}{(q-r)}[e^{(q-r)R} - 1]$$
$$- \frac{a}{(q-r)}\left\{1 - \log\left[\frac{a}{w[1 - e^{(q-r)\tau}]}\right]\right\} - a(R - \tau) - C.$$

Again, lower values for a will be associated with a greater likelihood of investment in human capital, since:

$$\frac{\partial(V_I - V_N)}{\partial a} = \frac{1}{(q-r)}\log\left[\frac{a}{w[1 - e^{(q-r)\tau}]}\right] - (R - \tau) < 0.$$

Case (5): $T_I^* = R - \tau; T_N^* = R - \tau$

Condition: $\dfrac{a}{w[1 - e^{(q-r)\tau}]} \leq e^{(q-r)(R-\tau)}.$

Difference in indirect utilities:

$$V_I - V_N = \frac{w}{(s+q-r)}[e^{(s+q-r)(R-\tau)} - 1] - \frac{w}{(q-r)}[e^{(q-r)(R-\tau)} - 1] - C.$$

Conditional on this case holding, the likelihood of investing does not depend on a.

Summary

Combining cases where appropriate, it follows that there will exist a single value for $a = a^*$ such that women with $a > a^*$ will choose not to invest in human capital while those women with $a \leq a^*$ will choose to invest. The Table 4.A1 summarizes how the difference in indirect utilities is affected by changes in a. The value for a such that $V_I - V_N = 0$ will be a^*; with lower values of a making

Table 4.A1 Effect of change in utility parameter a on differences in indirect utility

Case	$s + q < r$	$s + q > r$
(1)	$\partial(V_I - V_N)/\partial a = 0$	$\partial(V_I - V_N)/\partial a = 0$
(2)	—	$\partial(V_I - V_N)/\partial a < 0$
(3)	$\partial(V_I - V_N)/\partial a < 0$	—
(4)	$\partial(V_I - V_N)/\partial a < 0$	$\partial(V_I - V_N)/\partial a < 0$
(5)	$\partial(V_I - V_N)/\partial a = 0$	$\partial(V_I - V_N)/\partial a = 0$

higher-numbered cases more likely, it follows that as a is decreasing below a^*, $V_I - V_N$ must be nonnegative and nondecreasing, while as a increases and is greater than a^*, $V_I - V_N$ must be nonpositive and nonincreasing.[38] Lower values of a will thus be associated with more delaying and greater investment in human capital.

Acknowledgments

Helpful comments were provided by Claudia Goldin, Paul Taubman, by seminar participants at Baruch College, CUNY Graduate Center, Queens College, Rutgers University, and the University of Pennsylvania, and anonymous referees.

Notes

1 This is preferable to potential experience, usually approximated as age minus education minus 5, which is known to be a poor indicator of actual experience for women (see Garvey and Reimers, 1980).
2 The sample excludes all nonwhites. Initial investigations suggested that the estimated effect of age at first birth on wages in wage regressions for blacks was very different from the estimated effect for whites. Also, the percentage of blacks who delayed childbearing past the age of 26 was very small.
3 Many of the women who are classified as childless in 1982 will eventually become late childbearers. We would like to separate these women from those who will remain permanently childless, but cannot do so with our data.
4 The training variable is missing for some individuals, and otherwise seemed to contribute little independent information. Consequently, we retained observations for which this variable could not be constructed.
5 While it is not noted in Table 4.2, it is also true that later childbearers are not delaying simply because they spend more years in school. In fact, higher education is associated with more delaying net of the extra years spent in school. This follows from calculations that show that the difference between age at first birth and the age at completion of schooling is greater for women with more education.
6 This is clear from the fact that educational attainment increases with age at first birth, while the average age in each age-at-first-birth category is roughly the same (except for the childless, for whom it is the lowest).
7 Since this variable is from different years for different women, we make corrections for differences in the price level and the level of labor productivity across the years.
8 These comparisons are made using the early wage averages for the part of the sample that was working in 1982.
9 To our knowledge, the only prior empirical studies of this subject are Trussell and Abowd (1980), Bloom (1987), and Lundberg and Plotnick (1989). Both Lundberg and Plotnick, and Trussell and Abowd, focus on the effects of teenage childbearing only.
10 Macunovich and Lillard (1989) attempt to apply the Butz and Ward model to micro-data. In contrast to fertility responses to aggregate wage movements, however, they identify effects of wages on fertility timing from cross-section wage variation and time-series wage changes in a panel data set. It seems that a complete test of the Butz and Ward model using micro-data should distinguish expected from unexpected wage changes, and examine the effects of unexpected changes.
11 A related but simpler model, due to Edlefsen (1980), is presented in Montgomery and Trussell (1986). Happel *et al.*, (1984), Razin (1980), and Cigno and Ermisch (1989)

also present economic models of fertility timing decisions, but only Cigno and Ermisch have treated human capital accumulation as determined jointly with fertility timing.

12　The important aspect of this assumption for the analysis of this chapter is that utility be strongly separable in the woman's labor income and fertility timing.

13　Note also that as s increases, the investor's marginal benefit function will grow less steep (swinging out to the right but keeping the same y-intercept), which increases T_I^*, and the difference between T_I^* and T_N^*.

14　This difference may be positive, though in this case all women would end up choosing to make the human capital investment.

15　Cigno and Ermisch (1989) suggest that post-marital investments in human capital will be larger for delayed childbearers. In their model, higher pre-marital investments in human capital increase a woman's tempo of fertility, but reduce completed family size.

16　In unreported results, we experimented with linear, quadratic, and other specifications of age-at-first-birth effects. A linear specification was clearly inadequate, and the dummy variable specification is more readily interpretable than other nonlinear specifications that appeared to fit the data equally well.

17　Women's marital status has been linked theoretically to differential human capital investment (Becker, 1985), though Korenman and Neumark (1992) find some empirical evidence to the contrary.

18　The education variables are years of schooling, and a dummy for post-college (i.e. more than sixteen years of schooling). Specifications including dummy variables for high school and college degrees were also estimated, but the coefficient estimates were statistically insignificant and small.

19　Coefficient estimates for experience squared were insignificant; excluding this variable has little effect on other coefficient estimates. We also exclude age at survey in specifications that include experience and tenure.

20　An interaction for the 22–26 category was not included because the estimates in Table 4.3 provided no evidence that these women earn higher wages than early childbearers once observable human capital proxies are included in the wage regression.

21　In unreported results, we verified that these differences do not simply reflect nonlinearities in education effects entailing higher returns to the higher levels of education of later childbearers.

22　One interpretation of these results is that much of the human capital investment undertaken by delayed childbearers does not occur in the formal settings captured by the training variable.

23　Reservation wages would follow this pattern if the presence of children (and especially young children) raised the opportunity cost of market time for women.

24　Experience and tenure were not included in the wage equation or the probit equation for working in our selection-corrected estimations. Tenure could not be included, since it is zero if and only if the woman is not working, while past labor market experience is very likely to be correlated with the error term in the probit equation for currently working.

25　In this specification, identification comes from the nonlinearity associated with the assumption of bivariate normality for the error terms.

26　The negative correlation coefficient found in specification (2) suggests that low-wage women are more likely to be working than high-wage women, all else the same. Given that exogenous income variables are included in the probit equation, this seems unlikely.

27　The presence of fixed effects in the wage equation error is a plausible explanation for why there may be a correlation between the wage equation error and the age-at-first-birth variables, leading to biased coefficient estimates. However, since current wages should have little direct effect on past childbearing behavior, a correlation between the current wage and the age-at-first-birth variables is unlikely to arise from a correlation between age at first birth and the current-period innovation in the wage equation error.

28 We cannot estimate a standard fixed-effects model because the age-at-first-birth dummy variables are fixed over time.

29 The age-at-first-birth dummies were not included in the early wage regressions used to generate the early wage residuals.

30 Although not reported in the table, we also estimated the interactive specifications reported in Table 4.4 correcting for selectivity or heterogeneity; the results of these specifications were unaffected by these corrections (see Blackburn *et al.*, 1990).

31 We also computed estimates paralleling those in column (7) in which we constructed instruments for the age-at-first-birth dummy variables by estimating an ordered probit for these dummy variables. We used the ranking: age at first birth at age 21 or less; at ages 22–26; at age 27 or higher; and childless. (With age included as a control variable, this seemed the most appropriate ranking for childless.) We used the ordered probit estimates to predict the most likely outcome, and used these expected age-at-first-birth dummies as instruments for the actual first-birth dummies. This procedure (and the procedure described in the text) should lead to consistent estimates and standard errors. However, the estimated standard errors for the age-at-first-birth variables were considerably larger using the ordered probit. The Hausman test also did not reject exogeneity in this specification (*p*-value = 0.91).

   Given the imprecision of the IV estimates, we also experimented with a simpler specification that combined the 27+ and childless as one first-birth category (since their OLS coefficient estimates were quite similar), and dropped the 22–26 dummy. Combining the 27+ and childless categories also allows us to ignore the fertility-timing distinction that might be most directly affected by the current wage error. The OLS coefficient estimate for this group, in a specification corresponding to column (6), was 0.13 (0.03), while the IV estimate (using linear probability instruments) was 0.35 (0.17). However, exogeneity was again not rejected (*p*-value = 0.18).

32 Some skepticism might be attached to the IV estimate of a negative return to experience for women. However, it could be argued that the estimates suggest that for women there is no return to experience. Dropping experience as a regressor in the relevant specifications in Tables 4.3 and 4.4 had negligible effects on the other estimates, and no effects on the statistical conclusions.

33 Lundberg and Plotnick (1989), McCrate (1989), and Geronimus and Korenman (1992) have considered this possibility for education.

34 One possibility would be to use family background variables as instruments for age at first birth (as at the end of the previous section) in regressions with human capital measures as dependent variables. However, we find it particularly difficult to believe that schooling decisions are not directly affected by family background. We are also doubtful that labor–market ties (such as experience and tenure) are not determined partly by family background.

35 Geronimus and Korenman (1992) take this a step further by looking at differences in schooling completion, conditional on whether or not a teen birth occurred, for a sample of siblings. By looking at within-family differences, they may be able to control more thoroughly for differences in family background and other sources of heterogeneity.

36 With this restriction, our two-equation model follows the classical recursive-system form. Qualitatively similar results were found using reduced-form experience equations, although the changes in the coefficient estimates when the family background variables are added are more difficult to interpret in this case.

37 While we are suspicious of the identifying restrictions, we did estimate experience and tenure equations that excluded the family background variables from the set of regressors, and used them as instruments for the first-birth dummies. The results of Hausman tests suggest that the exogeneity of age at first birth again could not be rejected, with *p*-values of 0.23 for the experience equation and 0.64 for the tenure equation. The

validity of these test results, though, does depend on the appropriateness of the exclusion restrictions.

38 For this reasoning to hold, it is also necessary that $V_I - V_N$ not experience discrete downward jumps when moving from one case to another. Continuity of $V_I - V_N$ rules out any such discrete downward jumps. If $s + q < r$, we know $V_I - V_N$ is a continuous function of a, since T_I^* and T_N^* are continuous functions of a, and V_I and V_N are continuous functions of T_I^* and T_N^*. If $s + q > r$, T_I^* is no longer a continuous function of a; but since the indirect utility of $T^* = 0$ and $T^* = R - \tau$ is the same at the point where the investor switches from case (1) to case (2), it follows that V_I is still a continuous function of a.

References

Becker, G. S. 1985. "Human Capital, Effort, and the Sexual Division of Labor." *Journal of Labor Economics* 3: S33–58.

Blackburn, McK. L., D. E. Bloom, and D. Neumark. 1990. "Fertility Timing, Wages, and Human Capital." NBER Working Paper No. 3422.

Bloom, D. E. 1982. What's Happening to the Age at First Birth in the United States? A Study of Recent Cohorts. *Demography* 19: 351–70.

Bloom, D. E. 1984. "Delayed Childbearing in the United States." *Population Research and Policy Review* 3: 103–39.

Bloom, D. E. 1987. "Fertility Timing, Labor Supply Disruptions, and the Wage Profiles of American Women." Proceedings of the Social Statistics Section of the American Statistical Association, 1986, pp. 49–63.

Bloom, D. E. and A. R. Pebley. 1982. "Voluntary Childlessness: A Review of the Evidence and Implications." *Population Research and Policy Review* 1: 203–24.

Bloom, D. E. and J. Trussell. 1984. "What are the Determinants of Delayed Childbearing and Permanent Childlessness in the United States?" *Demography* 21: 591–611.

Butz, W. P. and M. P. Ward. 1979. "The Emergence of Countercyclical US Fertility." *American Economic Review* 69: 318–28.

Cigno, A. and J. Ermisch. 1989. "A Microeconomic Analysis of the Timing of Births." *European Economic Review* 33: 737–60.

Corcoran, M., G. J. Duncan, and M. Ponza. 1983. "A Longitudinal Analysis of White Women's Wages." *Journal of Human Resources* 18: 497–520.

Edlefsen, L. 1980. "The Opportunity Costs of Time and the Numbers, Timing and Spacing of Births." Mimeograph.

Furstenberg, F. 1976. *Unplanned Parenthood*. New York: Free Press.

Furstenberg, F., J. Brooks-Gunn, and S. P. Morgan. 1987. *Adolescent Mothers in Later Life*. Cambridge: Cambridge University Press.

Garvey, N. and C. Reimers. 1980. "Predicted vs. Potential Work Experience and Earnings Functions for Young Women." In *Research in Labor Economics*, ed. R. Ehrenberg. Greenwich, CT: JAI Press.

Geronimus, A. T. and S. Korenman. 1992. "The Socioeconomic Consequences of Teen Childbearing Reconsidered. *Quarterly Journal of Economics* 107: 1187–214.

Griliches, Z. 1979. "Sibling Models and Data in Economics: Beginnings of a Survey." *Journal of Political Economy* 86: S37–64.

Happel, S. K., J. K. Hill, and S. A. Low. 1984. "An Economic Analysis of the Timing of Childbirth." *Population Studies* 38: 299–311.

Heckman, J. J. 1978. "Dummy Endogenous Variables in a Simultaneous Equation System." *Econometrica* 46: 931–59.

Heckman, J. J. 1979. "Sample Selection Bias as a Specification Error." *Econometrica* 47: 153–61.

Hofferth, S. L. 1984. "Long-term Economic Consequences for Women of Delayed Childbearing and Reduced Family Size." *Demography* 21: 141–56.

Korenman, S. and D. Neumark. 1992. "Marriage, Motherhood, and Wages." *Journal of Human Resources* 27: 233–55.

Lundberg, S. and R. D. Plotnick. 1989. "Teenage Childbearing and Adult Wages." Mimeograph.

Macunovich, D. J. and L. A. Lillard. 1989. "Income and Substitution Effects in the First Birth Interval in the US, 1967–1984." Mimeograph.

McCrate, E. 1989. "Returns to Education and Teenage Childbearing." Mimeograph.

Mincer, J. 1974. *Schooling, Experience and Earnings.* New York: National Bureau of Economic Research.

Mincer, J. and H. Ofek. 1992. "Interrupted Work Careers: Depreciation and Restoration of Human Capital." *Journal of Human Resources* 17: 3–24.

Montgomery, M. and J. Trussel. 1986. "Models of Marital Status and Childbearing." In *Handbook of Labor Economics*, eds O. Ashenfelter and R. Layard, pp. 205–271. Amsterdam: North-Holland.

O'Connell, M. 1985. "Measures of Delayed Childbearing from the Current Population Survey, 1971–1983." Unpublished paper presented at the 1985 Annual Meetings of the Population Association of America.

O'Neill, J. 1985. "The Trend in the Male–Female Wage Gap in the United States." *Journal of Labor Economics* 3: S91–116.

Polachek, S. W. 1975. "Differences in Expected Post-School Investment as a Determinant of Market Wage Differentials." *International Economic Review* 16: 451–69.

Razin, A. 1980. "Number, Spacing and Quality of Children: A Microeconomic Viewpoint." *Research in Population Economics* 2: 279–93.

Rindfuss, R. S., S. P. Morgan, and G. Swicegood. 1988. *First Births in America.* Berkeley, CA: University of California Press.

Smith, J. P. and M. P. Ward. 1984. "Women's Wages and Work in the Twentieth Century." Rand Report No. R-3119-NICHD.

Trussell, J. and J. Abowd. 1980. "Teenage Mothers, Labor-Force Participation, and Wage Rates." *Canadian Studies in Population* 7: 33–48.

Upchurch, D. M. and J. McCarthy. 1990. "The Timing of a First Birth and High-School Completion." *American Sociological Review* 55(2): 224–34.

US Bureau of the Census. 1986. "Fertility of American Women: June 1985." Current Population Reports, Series P-20 No. 406. Washington, DC: US Government Printing Office.

5 Relative income concerns and the rise in married women's employment

(with Andrew Postlewaite)

Introduction

What are the important factors in the decision to work? The standard neoclassical model provides an explanation as to why such factors as the wage rate, education, age and past work experience, spouse's income, as well as other personal and household characteristics can affect the decision. This model has been extremely useful in understanding labor supply decisions, but—not surprisingly—there are some cases in which it falls short of providing compelling explanations. We are particularly interested in the rise in the employment of married women in the United States in the twentieth century. Empirical estimates of the simple neoclassical model of married women's labor force participation suggest that positive substitution effects outweigh negative own and husbands' income effects, with the consequence that rising real wages draw women into the labor market (Mincer, 1962; Smith and Ward, 1985). But there is ample evidence that this simple model fails to fully explain the rise in the employment of married women in the United States.

The theme of this chapter is that there may be important variables in women's decisions to enter the work force that are omitted from standard neoclassical models. We specifically focus on the possibility that a woman's decision whether to be in the workforce may be affected by the decisions of other women in ways not captured by standard models. Other women's decisions may affect a particular woman's decision in many ways. For example, other women's decisions will affect the "quality" of remaining out of the workforce if there are positive externalities among women who remain at home. Perhaps most importantly (although this remains an open question), to the extent that people care about their relative income position, a given woman's employment decision can be influenced by other women's employment decisions.

In this chapter we develop a model that augments the simple neoclassical framework by introducing relative income concerns into women's (or families') utility functions. In this model, the entry of some women into paid employment can spur the entry of other women, independently of wage and income effects. We show that relative income concerns can help to explain why, over some periods, women's employment rose faster than can be accounted for by the simple neoclassical model.[1]

We test the model by asking whether women's decisions to seek paid employment depend on the employment or incomes of other women with whom relative income comparisons might be important, independently of standard variables affecting the employment decision. A natural peer or reference group, which has the advantage of being exogenously given, is a woman's siblings. We first test whether women's employment is affected by the employment of their sisters-in-law; we use sisters-in-law rather than sisters because, with the former, unobserved heterogeneity is much less likely to bias the results in favor of the relative income hypothesis. We also test whether women's employment is affected by the income of their husbands relative to the income of their sisters' husbands, a test that is more directly motivated by the theoretical model of relative income concerns that we develop. Both tests support the predictions of the model.

The rise in married women's employment: evidence and explanations

The twentieth century was characterized by rapid increases in women's employment in the United States, especially that of married women. There was a slow acceleration of women's employment prior to 1940, concentrated among younger women. From 1940 to 1960 employment exploded for women aged 35 and over, with participation rates doubling for women aged 45–54 (to about 47 percent) and women aged 55–64 (to about 35 percent), and increasing by about 50 percent for women aged 35–54 (Smith and Ward, 1985, table 1). After 1960 the employment of younger women accelerated, while the employment of older women held steady or declined, with the participation rate of women aged 25–34 rising two percentage points a year in the 1970s.[2]

Mincer (1962) developed the basic neoclassical model of married women's labor supply to attempt to explain the increased employment of married women. In this model, women's employment is influenced by two potentially offsetting factors. Rising real wages act through the husband's income to exert a negative income effect on employment. But rising real wages also act through the wife's market wage, with opposing income and substitution effects. Mincer estimated a cross-section model of women's employment, using 1950 Census data on SMSA averages to focus on permanent components of earnings. He found that the compensated substitution effect via the wife's wage dominated the income effect, and the positive uncompensated substitution effect dominated the negative income effect through the husband's wage. Consequently, rising real wages over time predict rising employment of married women.

Mincer then used the cross-sectional estimates, along with time-series data on full-time earnings of men and women, to ask whether the neoclassical model could explain the time-series changes in women's employment. He found that the cross-section estimates overpredicted the increase in married women's employment for 1919–29, accurately predicted the increase for 1929–39, and underpredicted the increase for 1939–59 (1962, table 10). His cross-section model explained 77 percent of the increase for 1939–49, and 68 percent of the increase for 1949–59.

Later work by Bowen and Finegan (1969) strengthened the conclusion that the neoclassical model cannot adequately explain the rise in married women's employment, finding, for example, that the neoclassical model can explain only 25 percent of this rise in the two decades following the Second World War.[3]

Of course no one would expect the simple neoclassical model to explain all of the increase in married women's employment. Researchers have also identified rising education levels and the growth of the clerical sector as potentially partly exogenous factors spurring this increase. Fertility declines over the twentieth century (the baby boom excepted) may also have contributed, although fertility is probably best treated as jointly determined with employment. Researchers have also pointed to the effects of the Second World War in bringing women into the workforce, although Goldin (1991) presents evidence that the War had little permanent effect on women's employment, based on sample evidence that only about 20 percent of women working in 1950 had entered the labor force during the War, and about half of the wartime entrants left the labor force after the War (p. 755).[4]

An alternative argument is that changes in income and substitution effects led to a faster rise in women's employment than is predicted by a stable set of cross-sectional estimates. Mincer (1962) argued that substitutability between home-produced and market-bought goods has increased over time. With low substitutability, an increase in income goes into increased consumption of goods produced in the home (as well as leisure). With increased substitutability, the increase in income is more likely to go partly into increased consumption of goods purchased in the market, hence leading to less of a reduction in market hours of work. Similarly, the declining income effect would increase the uncompensated effect of the wage on women's employment. These changes in income and substitution effects would lead Mincer's (1962) time-series experiment with stable cross-section estimates to overpredict the growth of employment early in his sample period, and to underpredict it later, given rising income of both husbands and wives.

Goldin (1990) examines this hypothesis by assembling cross-section estimates at various points of time, also based on cross-city variation. Consistent with Mincer's conjecture, she finds that income elasticities appear to have declined consistently throughout the century. But uncompensated wage effects appear to have increased through 1950 (see also Goldin, 1994, for a discussion of increases in substitution effects over this period), and then fallen again, in contrast to Mincer's conjecture.[5]

To summarize, our reading of this literature suggests that the simple neoclassical model helps to explain the rise in married women's employment. However, the model cannot fully explain the rise. In the next section, we develop a formal model that can explain the "faster than expected" growth in married women's employment, via peer- or reference-group effects driven by relative income comparisons. The incorporation of concerns over relative income has become popular in other models, especially in labor economics, to attempt to explain behavior that is difficult to fully reconcile or explain with the neoclassical model (Duesenberry, 1949; Akerlof, 1982; Frank, 1985; Summers, 1988). We are interested in exploring whether such concerns may also help to explain the rise in married women's employment.

A relative income model of women's employment

The neoclassical world

We begin with a neoclassical model that, on the one hand, replicates Mincer's (1962) finding that the positive uncompensated substitution effect of general wage increases on women's employment dominates the negative income effect through the husband's wage, and on the other hand, is easily extended to incorporate ranking concerns. There is a continuum of couples, each consisting of a man and a woman. Each woman is characterized by an ability level denoted by a, and each man is characterized by an ability level denoted by b. We assume that $a \in (0, A]$ and $b \in (0, B]$, $A, B < \infty$. A person who works earns w (>0) per unit of ability. We assume all men work. We want to capture the idea that there is an opportunity cost to a woman working, which we interpret for now to represent lost household production. In theory this opportunity cost might depend on a number of variables including family income, the woman's ability, the number and ages of the children the couple might have, and so on. For our purposes, we will assume that the opportunity cost depends only on the husband's income, that is, there is a function $v(i)$ that specifies the value of the woman's home production.[6]

If the wage rate is w, a couple whose abilities are represented by (b, a) will have utility $(a + b) \times w$ if the woman works and $b \times w + v(b \times w)$ if she does not. We assume $v' > 0$, that is, that higher-income families put higher value on the home production of the woman. A consequence of this form for the opportunity cost is that of the women matched with men of the same ability level b, it is those women with the highest ability who will work, since women work if $a > v(b \times w)/w$. Figure 5.1 illustrates the set of possible characteristics of couples, with the set divided into two components: those couples with (b, a) such that $a > v(b \times w)/w$, in which utility is higher if the woman works; and those for whom the reverse holds.

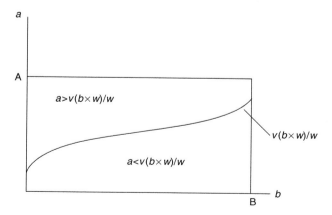

Figure 5.1 The neoclassical employment decision of women.

We are interested in the effect of an increase in the wage rate, w, on women's employment.[7] If we fix the ability of the man at level b, a woman with ability a who is matched to this man, where a is such that $a \times w = v(b \times w)$, is indifferent between employment and nonemployment, while any woman with higher ability married to a man of this ability will strictly prefer employment. In other words, the marginal woman matched with a man of ability b has ability $a = v(b \times w)/w$. If we differentiate this with respect to w, we find $\partial a/\partial w = (v' \times b - a)/w$. $\partial a/\partial w$ will be negative if $v'(b \times w) \times b < a$; that is, if v does not increase too quickly, increases in the wage rate will result in increased women's employment. We assume that this holds for all values of a, b, and w.

We can see from Figure 5.1 what the effect of an increase in the wage would be on women's employment. As mentioned here, the woman in a couple with abilities (b, a) will work if $a \times w > v(b \times w)$. Suppose a woman does not work when the wage rate is w but enters the workforce when the wage increases to w^*. It must be the case then that $a \times w < v(b \times w)$ and $a \times w^* > v(b \times w^*)$. If we let $a' = (w^*/w) \times a$ and $b' = (w^*/w) \times b$, then $a \times w^* > v(b \times w^*)$ if and only if $a' \times w > v(b' \times w)$. That is, the increase in the wage rate from w to w^* will cause the woman to enter the workforce if and only if a proportional increase in their abilities that resulted in the same wages would cause the woman to enter the workforce. Alternatively, if one wished to predict whether the woman in the couple with abilities (b, a) would work when the wage increased by a specified amount, one could check whether a woman in a couple with higher abilities in proportion to the wage increase works at wage w. Thus, the assumption made at the end of the previous paragraph assures that in our model the positive uncompensated substitution effect of general wage increases on women's employment dominates the negative income effect through the husband's wage.

The effect of ranking concerns

The phenomenon that we are interested in is a particular externality between couples. The externality is one in which when the woman in one couple enters the workforce, this decreases the reservation wage for the woman in the comparison couple. There are a number of reasons that might underlie such a concern. For example, if in all the couples with whom one socializes, the wives begin to work, then dinner outings, cocktail parties, etc., may become more expensive. To the extent that we believe that a couple's utility may depend on the probability of retaining and socializing with their friends, a woman's reservation wage will naturally be affected by other women's decisions to work. One can think of this story as explaining how the indirect utility for money in a reduced form model might depend on the labor supply decisions of acquaintances. Alternatively, there are natural ways in which the opportunity cost associated with a woman's working might depend on other women's labor supply decisions. The reservation wage for a given woman is the utility a woman gets when at home rather than in the workforce. This may well be affected by whether a close friend is at home or working. Besides the pure recreational value of that person's company, it may be possible to share child care responsibilities or other work only when both are out of the workforce.

While there are many ways in which the optimal employment decision for a woman may depend on the decisions of other women, we will simply assume that couples are concerned with their relative income position. There is a broad array of specific forms such a concern might take, such as a concern with how far one is from the top of the income distribution, how far from the bottom, or one's percentile rank in the distribution. While we believe that it is perfectly plausible that there is a concern with relative position, we are not confident about the precise form. It is quite reasonable to believe that the specific form varies from couple to couple and often is some composite of a number of different aspects like those mentioned. For our purposes, we will assume a simple form of the concern that has two advantages. First, it provides clear and unambiguous predictions about the effect of ranking concerns on women's employment decisions, and second, it is relatively easily translated into empirical tests. However, the qualitative characteristics of the equilibrium with which we are most interested are not driven by the particular form of the relative income concern; how the results of our model might change as we vary the form of the ranking concern is discussed in the section "Discussion of model."

We assume that each couple is concerned with its relative position *vis-à-vis* a particular comparison couple. That is, the set of all couples is broken into pairs with members of each pair of couples comparing themselves with the other couple in the pair. We assume that the benefit of being the higher income family generates an increase in utility equal to $c > 0$. The increase c is independent of the size of the difference in incomes.[8] We will further assume for now that c is greater than the opportunity cost of the home production value of a woman's time, that is, $c > v(b \times w)$ for all $b < B$. We assume that couples are matched randomly so that for any given couple, the distribution over the characteristics of couples with whom they compare themselves is the same as the unconditional distribution over couples' characteristics. As with the form of the concern, our assumptions about the size and determinants of the benefit and the couples with whom a given couple will compare themselves are made primarily for reasons of tractability. We will discuss later how alternative assumptions would affect the nature of our results.

To see how the concern with relative position affects women's employment decisions, we first note that for those couples (b, a) with $a \times w > v(b \times w)$, women will work. That is, if women were better off working than not when ignoring ranking concerns, the inclusion of the ranking consideration will not cause them to leave the workforce. Any effects of the ranking consideration will show up in the decisions of those women who in the absence of ranking concerns would decide not to work.

To see how the inclusion of ranking considerations might affect a woman's decision to enter the workforce, consider a couple (b, a) in which the woman would not be working in the absence of ranking considerations, depicted in Figure 5.2. The set of couples who have the same combined ability as the given couple is shown by the straight line (with slope -1) through the point (b, a). If both the man

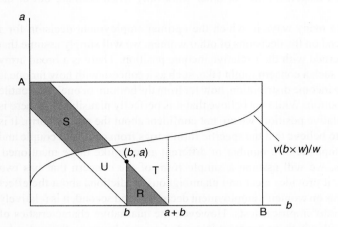

Figure 5.2 The employment decision of women with relative income concerns.

and the woman in the couple whose characteristics are on this line work, they will have higher combined income than any couple whose characteristics are below the line. In addition, they will have higher income than any family with characteristics (b', a') with $b' < b$ such that the woman does not work. If the woman in the couple with characteristics (b, a) does not work, the couple will have higher income than those families with characteristics below the line with horizontal intercept b and slope -1, plus those couples in which the man's ability is less than b and the woman does not work.

We are most interested in those comparison couples whose incomes would be higher than (b, a)'s income if the woman in (b, a) does not work, but lower if she works, even if the woman in the comparison couple works. This is precisely the set of couples who will be "jumped over" if the woman in (b, a) decides to work. The shaded regions in Figure 5.2 represent these comparison couples. In the lower (right-hand) shaded region (R), the woman in the comparison couple is not working, but the comparison couple would have lower income even if she did work. Although the ability of the husband in the comparison couple, b', is greater than the ability of the husband in the given couple, this is more than offset by the lower ability of the woman in the comparison couple (a'). For any couple in the upper left-hand shaded region (S), the woman in the comparison couple is already working, and if the wife in couple (b, a) works, this couple earns higher income than the comparison couple. Thus, for the sets of couples in these shaded regions, we need not be concerned with possible reactions of the comparison couple in determining the incentives facing the woman in our given couple (b, a).

The issue of the comparison couple's reaction does arise, however, with respect to comparison couples that could revert to earning higher income if the wife responds by also going to work. Consider a couple (b', a') with $a' + b' > a + b > b'$ and $a' \times w < v(b' \times w)$. In Figure 5.2, such a couple would be represented by a point in the region (T) formed by the vertical line through $a + b$ on the horizontal axis, the diagonal through (b, a), and the curve $v(b \times w)/w$. The last inequality implies that in the absence of ranking concerns, the woman in this couple (as the woman in our given couple) would not work. A consequence of the first inequality, however, is that starting from a position in which neither woman is working, the couple (b, a) can jump over the couple (b', a') if the wife goes to work, but if the woman in (b', a') also enters the workforce, the ranking reverts to the original order.

Our exclusion of couples in region T from the set which would represent a reversal of the two couples' ranks warrants a brief discussion. We have not specified precisely the game form representing the strategic interaction of the couples, and will avoid doing so. It is straightforward to construct numerous such game forms for which the outcome we are focusing on—that in situations such as those above, neither woman enters the workforce—is an equilibrium. More importantly, however, for many such game forms the only equilibrium outcomes will be the ones on which we are focusing. Suppose the game is a sequential game in which there is no "last mover," that is, whenever the woman in one couple enters the workforce the woman in the comparison couple can respond to that decision by entering herself. For such a game, a best response for a couple whose characteristics satisfy the inequalities in the above paragraph would be for the woman to enter the workforce if the woman in the couple (b, a) entered. Thus, in any Nash equilibrium, the woman in couple (b, a) entering the workforce would always be followed by the woman in the comparison couple entering as well. Thus, for equilibria of such game forms, it is appropriate to exclude those couples in region T.

Essentially the same issue arises with respect to a couple with characteristics satisfying $a + b > a' + b' > b$, $b' < b$, and $a' \times w < v(b' \times w)$. Couples (b', a') satisfying these inequalities are those in the unshaded trapezoidal region (U) in Figure 5.2. For a couple represented by a point in this region, because of ranking concerns the woman in (b', a') would work if the woman in (b, a) did not, but the couple (b, a) could jump back ahead if the woman in this couple worked.

What then is the female labor supply with this ranking effect added? First, as mentioned above, all women in couples with characteristics above $v(b \times w)/w$ will work. In addition, some women in couples below that line will work, namely those for whom the comparison couple for that couple lies in the shaded regions. Thus, we see that for any characteristics below the line $v(b \times w)/w$, the proportion of the women in a couple with those characteristics who are in the workforce is equal to the proportion of women in the shaded regions. It is straightforward to see that the probability that a woman married to a man with ability b works is an increasing function of her ability.

"Cross-section" predictions of "time-series" increases in employment

To see that this model may explain why married women's employment rose faster than predicted by the simple neoclassical model, consider what predictions we might make about the effects of wage changes on employment if we fail to take account of ranking considerations. If we look at a couple (b, a) as making a decision independent of those made by other couples, an increase in the wage rate will have two effects: the extra income the woman can earn goes up because of her own ability; and the opportunity cost goes up because of her husband's increased income. We can think about generating the analogue to the usual cross-section estimate of the effect of the wage on the proportion of women working from differences in the proportion of women working between couples with different levels of ability. For example, since the choice the couple (b, a) makes depends on the potential income of the woman and the actual income of the man, we can find existing couples whose potential and actual incomes today are precisely the same as those the couple (b, a) would be faced with given any hypothetical wage increase. Our prediction would then be that the proportion of the women in couples (b, a) who will be in the workforce when the wage rate goes up by this amount is equal to the proportion of those higher ability couples for which women are working today. For the interesting case of women who would not work in the absence of ranking concerns, this proportion is represented by the two shaded regions in Figure 5.3.[9] These are comparable to the shaded regions R and S in Figure 5.2, but shifted to the right.

For our model, this would be an accurate estimate of the probability that the woman in the couple (b, a) would work if the wage increased for this couple only. If this is a general wage increase that affects all workers, however, this analysis will miss an important effect. We are assuming that the nature of the function v is such that when the wage rate goes up, women's employment goes up for purely economic reasons (i.e. excluding ranking considerations). But this increases the set of couples for whom the ranking will be reversed if the woman in this couple enters

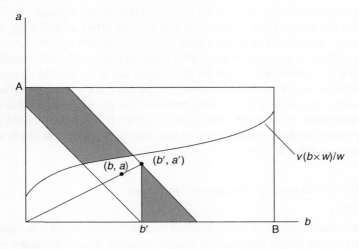

Figure 5.3 The "cross-sectional" effects of the wage on women's employment.

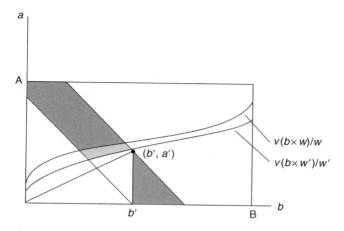

Figure 5.4 The effect of general ("time-series") wage increases on women's employment.

the workforce. In Figure 5.4, the increase in the set of comparison couples that would induce the woman in (b, a) to enter the workforce, after the wage increase to w', is shown by the lightly shaded region. Thus, the wage increase causes a "purely economic" increase in women's employment, which in turn amplifies the incentives for women to enter for ranking considerations.[10]

To sum up, our estimate from cross-section covariation between employment and wages of the proportion of women who will enter the workforce in response to a wage increase ignores the increased incentive for women to enter the workforce, which imparts a downward bias (toward zero) to the estimated effect of a general wage increase. Thus, the model with ranking concerns may help to explain why cross-section estimates of women's employment equations fail to fully predict the time-series increase in women's employment.[11]

Discussion of model

Naturally our model incorporates a number of simplifying assumptions. While we take these assumptions to be plausible, we want to point out that they have been made for reasons of tractability and do not drive the main qualitative result in which we are interested, namely that the use of cross-section data to estimate the elasticity of female employment with respect to wages may result in estimates that are biased toward zero if ranking considerations are not taken into account. We now discuss briefly the nature of the various assumptions and how changes would affect our main conclusions.

We assumed that the opportunity cost of a woman's working was a function of the man's income only. This assumption allows us to focus on the effects of general wage increases on women's employment, and in particular how these increases cause a secondary effect due to the entrance of women into employment because the woman in the comparison couple entered the workforce. We would expect a similar effect even if the opportunity cost was a more complicated function that depended also on the number and ages of children, the woman's ability, etc. As long as wage increases lead to increased female employment excluding ranking considerations, including ranking considerations will amplify the employment increase. It would be more difficult, however, to make a simple argument that cross-section estimates of the effects of wages on employment are biased downward, because it would be significantly more difficult to trace through the model the effects of wage increases.

We also assumed that the wage rate per ability unit is the same for men and for women. If women earn some fixed percentage of what men earn, this could be incorporated into the abilities; that is, one could simply multiply women's abilities by this fixed percentage. What this assumption does not allow for is varying rates of wage increases for men and women. One could easily write down an extension of our model to allow for such differences, and one would expect the same qualitative conclusion that estimates of wage elasticities from individual wage variation would yield downward biased estimates of the effects of general wage increases. This is for essentially the same reason as mentioned just above; the bias comes from the amplification of the employment effect due to ranking considerations.

We assumed that the couples were paired randomly with respect to the ranking comparison. This is likely the least plausible of our simplifying assumptions. We might believe that there is substantial homogeneity in the characteristics of couples in comparison groups. At first pass, we can say the same thing as in the previous two comments; this will not alter the fact that wage increases lead to increased female employment for purely economic reasons, and hence the ranking considerations will amplify the effect. Here, however, we will speculate a bit about the magnitude of the effects. We are only interested in the model if the size of the bias is not trivial. It could be that the amplification that we have identified is negligible. This would be the case if the probability that a given couple could jump over its comparison couple changed little when the wage rate increased. But if couples compare themselves to other couples with similar characteristics, this probability should be higher than in the case we considered. Thus, although one has to be careful about how one made the comparison relation more realistic, one would expect the effect we are focusing on to become more important.

We also assumed that the benefit of "beating" the comparison couple generated a fixed utility increment c that was greater than the opportunity cost of any woman's working. It is clear that allowing the benefit to differ across couples will have only a quantitative effect, not a qualitative one. Furthermore, given the discussion above, we might expect the comparison couples to be similar. But this implies that when a woman enters employment for purely economic reasons, the woman in the comparison couple may prefer not to work, but the decision will be close. Hence, a small increment c may send her to work.

Allowing the increment c to depend in a more sophisticated way on the ranking might raise one difficulty. If the increment depended on the amount by which a couple's income exceeded the comparison couple's, then in light of the previous suggestion that comparison couples have similar characteristics, a woman who would otherwise not have wanted to work will gain little by working since the amount by which incomes will differ if both women work will be small. On the other hand, if we allowed c also to be negatively related to the amount by which you "lost" the income race, the situation would be more or less as in our analysis.

Probably more significant than the detailed assumptions we made within our model are several that are embedded within the basic structure of the model. First, we have assumed that couples care whether they have higher income than their comparison couple. While we are convinced of the plausibility of such concerns, it is of interest to understand the basis of them. At the simplest level, it can be posited that these are the preferences of people (Frank, 1989). However, many economists are more comfortable with explanations that can be derived from standard utility functions (e.g. Becker, 1976, ch. 1), rather than alternative assumptions about tastes. We discussed at the beginning of this section how our concern for ranking might arise as a reduced form of models in which there was no direct concern for ranking, but rather that relative ranking affects some nonmarket decisions (e.g. the social opportunities mentioned earlier).[12]

A second defense of our approach is that it generates testable restrictions. The model does not automatically lead to the conclusion that cross-sectional estimates of the elasticity of female employment will be biased downward. For small enough gains from being the higher income couple or for large enough opportunity costs of entering the workforce, there will be no relative income effects on women's employment. Further, the model can be extended in simple ways so as to generate secondary and tertiary implications of the central ideas that can themselves be tested. For example, if we were to allow other shocks to a family's income such as shocks to the man's income or bequests from the man's family, such shocks should have an effect on the labor supply decisions of the woman in the comparison couple. The central idea of the model—that relative income matters—is specified in sufficient detail at the micro level that we need not be concerned that we cannot test the hypothesis.

We argued earlier that the important aspect of our model is that there be an externality associated with a woman's decision to work. One of the examples illustrating how an externality might arise centered on the decrease in utility a nonworking woman might suffer when a close friend or relative entered the work-force. The utility decrease might lower the reservation wage for such a woman. One can slightly alter our model to allow a utility increment c only if both the woman herself and the woman in the comparison couple are not working. The analysis and conclusions are essentially unchanged, with one exception. The sort of pure externality described earlier might lead to a utility loss to a woman who enters the workforce when the woman in the comparison couple is out of the work-force. This could lead to a situation with multiple equilibria; it could be optimal for each woman in a pair of matched couples to be out of the workforce if the other woman is, yet be optimal to be in the workforce if the other woman is.[13] A model that is similar to ours but based on such externalities rather than income comparisons could then have an "inertial" property that entry initially is slower than would occur in the absence of the externality. We say "could" because there would be delay in one of the multiple equilibria. Despite the possibility of the initial delay, once entry starts to occur, it would occur more rapidly than would be expected in the absence of the externality for much the same reason as in our model; one woman's entry into the workforce lowers the reservation wage for the woman in the comparison couple.[14]

Another feature of the model that should be discussed is the built-in assumption that the externality, or the comparison group for relative income concerns, is confined to two couples. There are several things to be said about extending our model to larger comparison groups. First, the basic logic of our model should carry over with little change. As more women become employed for purely economic reasons, this provides an additional incentive for other women not employed to become so. Second, extending the model does not present many technical difficulties. However, in discussing the effect of wage increases when ranking matters, we mentioned one difficulty that arose, namely that for a woman contemplating entering the workforce to know what the net benefit would be, she needed to predict the reaction of the woman in the comparison group. We made the simplifying assumption that the second woman would enter if doing so restored her to first place. This assumption simplified the analysis of the first woman's decision whether to work. Any extension to larger groups would exacerbate the problem of forecasting the decisions of other women in a comparison group.

Empirical analysis

The empirical approach

The model developed in the previous section suggests that women's employment decisions may depend not only on the individual-level variables included in standard employment equations, but also on the employment decisions or incomes of other women or couples with respect to whom relative income comparisons are made. This suggests that we might want to incorporate into a standard employment equation information on the employment status or income of such women or couples. In principle, surveys could elicit information on the employment status or incomes of women's peers, although we are not aware of any surveys that do so. A potential problem with such data, however, would be that individuals may subjectively define their peer groups so that their relative income is high compared to that of their peers. That is, the definition of one's peer group could be contaminated by relative income concerns. Thus, we instead focus on what we might think of as "objectively determined" peers, namely family members.

First, we look at the relationship between women's employment and that of their sisters-in-law, asking whether women's employment decisions depend on the employment decisions of their sisters-in-law, independently of standard variables suggested by the neoclassical model of the employment decision. We obtain data on sisters and sisters-in-law from the National Longitudinal Survey of Youth (NLSY).

Theoretical and empirical results on assortative mating suggest that common unobserved components may be much less important for sister/sister-in-law pairs than for sister/sister pairs. Thus, estimates for sister/sister-in-law pairs are much less likely to generate spurious evidence in favor of the relative income hypothesis. Becker (1981) derives theoretical conditions for positive or negative assortative mating on given traits. The general result is that we expect negative sorting on wages (as marriage markets generate a sex-based division of labor), and positive sorting on non-wage characteristics. Behrman *et al.* (1994) use data on twins and their spouses to study explicitly the relationship between earnings endowments (i.e. unobserved ability that affects earnings) of men and schooling of their wives. They find evidence of a negative relationship, which they interpret as evidence of negative sorting on wage-related characteristics, because schooling is positively related to the propensity to work. Assuming that brothers and sisters have positively correlated unobserved propensities to work (because of similarities in motivation or ability), then this negative sorting suggests that the unobserved propensities to work of sisters and their sisters-in-law should be negatively correlated, if anything. Based on this result, our evidence from sisters matched to sisters-in-law is not biased in favor of the relative income hypothesis. We also present additional findings using our data that confirm negative sorting on unobserved propensities to work of sisters and their sisters-in-law.

To begin, we posit a standard equation for the propensity to work

$$E_{it}^* = X_{it}\beta + \varepsilon_{it}. \tag{1}$$

E_{it} is an observed dummy variable equal to one for woman i in period t if $E_{it}^* > 0$ and she is therefore employed, and X_{it} is a set of standard control variables. For the most part, the variables in X are assumed to be determinants either of the market wage or the value of home production. Thus, the argument made in the previous section regarding cross-section estimates of wage effects on employment carries over to the effects of most of the variables in X. We estimate equation (1) as a logit model.

Evidence on whether women's employment decisions are affected by the employment decisions of their sisters-in-law speaks to the general types of externalities we discussed in the section "A relative income model of women's employment." But it is also directly related to relative income concerns, because the sister-in-law's employment decision affects the income of the comparison couple. To see this, note that in Figure 5.2, a woman's employment decision should be unaffected by her sister-in-law's employment (denoted E') unless her sister-in-law and her brother fall in regions R or S. If they fall in region R or S, the woman works even though she would not have worked in the absence of relative income concerns. Thus, a positive estimated relationship between E and E' arises from the fraction of women whose sisters-in-law (and their husbands) are in region S. On the other hand, the figure indicates that for women whose sisters-in-law are in region R, a negative relationship between E and E' is predicted. Thus, taking the figure literally, the model only predicts a positive relationship between E and E' when the fraction of sisters-in-law in S exceeds the fraction in R. Nonetheless, a positive estimate of the effect of E' on E is consistent with the relative income model, but not the standard neoclassical model.

We therefore add to the employment equation the observed employment status of the sister-in-law, E'

$$E_{it}^* = X_{it}\beta + E_{it}'\gamma + \varepsilon_{it}.^{15} \tag{2}$$

To examine whether the results for equation (2) are influenced by heterogeneity bias—possibly, as the negative assortative mating argument above suggested, biasing the estimate of γ downward—we also estimate a specification including the woman's own lagged employment in the equation.[16]

After looking at the relationship between the employment of sisters-in-law, we turn to a test that is more directly motivated by the relative income model we developed in the previous section, and for which the model makes more precise predictions. The test is most easily explained by looking at Figure 5.2, where the comparison is now made with the sister's family, since in this empirical exercise we will not be studying directly the employment of women and their sisters. First, if a woman's sister is not employed, the woman should be more likely to work if her sister's husband earns more than her own husband. To see this, note that if her sister is not employed, then her sister (and her husband) lie somewhere below the $v(b \times w)/w$ locus. The woman has no incentive to work if her sister's husband's ability is less than b (her own husband's ability), but does have an incentive to work if her sister's husband's ability is greater than b. This makes intuitive sense; if the sister's husband earns less than a woman's own husband, and the sister does not work, then the woman does not need to work in order for her family's income to be higher. However, if the sister's husband earns more than her own husband, and her sister does not work, then by going to work, the woman may be able to "win" the income race. She will be able to do so precisely when her sister lies in the region R. So a positive estimated relationship between the woman's employment and her sister's husband's relative income arises from the fraction of women with comparison couples in region R. By the same token, if her sister is employed, then the woman's employment should be *negatively* related to her sister's husband's relative income. In this case, the sister (and her husband) lie above the $v(b \times w)/w$ locus. The only case in which a woman's working changes the outcome—enabling her to "win" the income race—is if her sister (and her husband) lie in the region S, giving rise to a negative relationship between the woman's employment and her sister's husband's relative income.

Therefore, we also estimate the equation

$$E_{it}^* = X_{it}\beta + \text{RI}_{it}\gamma + \varepsilon_{it}, \tag{3}$$

where RI is a dummy variable equal to 1 if the sister's husband's income exceeds the woman's own husband's income. The model predicts that the estimate of γ should be positive if the sister is nonemployed, and negative if the sister is employed. We regard the evidence from this test as stronger for three reasons: first, the variable RI is more closely related to the specific model we have developed; second, it is likely to be less prone to remaining biases from common contemporaneous unobservables affecting sisters' employment; and third, for the test using relative income of husbands, the model makes more specific predictions, depending on the employment of the sister.

We do not interpret the equations we estimate as representing structural relationships obtained from the model. Specifying such structural relationships would require strong assumptions regarding functional form, the game facing women in their employment decisions, the nature of the rankings, etc., as well as data related to husbands' and wives' abilities or productive capacities. Rather, we view the empirical exercise primarily as testing the plausibility of a model that augments the neoclassical model with relative income concerns or externalities among women with respect to their employment decisions.

The data

The data are extracted from the NLSY. The survey contains many multiple-respondent households, consisting of individuals in the age range of the initial sample (14–22) in 1979 who were living in the same household. We excluded women in the NLSY's military subsample. We then matched up all sister/brother pairs, for the sister/sister-in-law equation, and all sister/sister pairs, for the relative income equation. When there was more than one possible match (because, for example, there were three or more sisters), we randomly paired up individuals, until all members of the sibship were matched, without using data on any individual in more than one pair in a particular sample.[17] For each woman respondent in these samples, we identified the first observation after which she had left school, which means that she did not re-enroll in subsequent years of the survey (which extends through 1990 for the data used in this chapter). We then extracted information on employment status in each year after leaving school, as well as standard control variables typically used in employment equations (education, number of children, marital status, husband's income, other nonlabor income, etc.).

Because of the strong persistence in married women's participation and employment (Goldin, 1991), we view the relative income hypothesis primarily as an explanation of why some women choose to work, and others do not, rather than as an explanation of year-to-year transitions into and out of employment. Consequently, we use the earliest possible data on women, and do not utilize the full longitudinal structure of the NLSY. In particular, for the sister/sister pairs we selected data for the first two contiguous years on each sister in each pair for which both sisters were out of school and married. For the sister/sister-in-law pairs this requirement was imposed for the woman and her brother (although the woman was only required to be ever married). These restrictions led to 140 pairs of currently married sisters, and 305 sister/sister-in-law pairs. Descriptive statistics are reported in columns (1) and (2) of Table 5.1.

Results

Logit estimates of the basic employment equation (1) are reported in column (3) of Table 5.1.[18] The specification includes controls for husband's income and other income, the woman's level of education, which is a proxy for her wage, the local unemployment rate, demographic controls, and a dummy variable for whether the husband was unemployed and collected unemployment compensation

Table 5.1 Descriptive statistics and basic employment equation[a]

| | Descriptive statistics | | Basic employment logit[c] |
	Sister/sister-in-law pairs (1)	Currently married sister/sister pairs[b] (2)	(3)
Currently employed	0.820	0.678	—
Husband's income/$1,000	12.761	16.902	−0.005
	(12.770)	(14.241)	(−2.396)
Other income/$1,000	0.276	0.686	−0.005
	(0.992)	(3.257)	(−0.229)
Years of education	12.682	12.789	0.038
	(2.107)	(2.119)	(2.816)
Local unemployment rate	7.617	7.225	−0.016
	(3.585)	(3.270)	(−2.640)
Husband unemployed during year	0.059	0.079	0.049
			(0.594)
Urban	0.751	0.757	0.057
			(1.195)
Black	0.184	0.143	−0.039
			(−0.672)
Hispanic	0.170	0.132	0.040
			(0.533)
Age	24.954	25.389	0.016
	(3.127)	(3.042)	(1.782)
Number of children	1.082	1.050	−0.084
	(1.024)	(1.060)	(−3.427)
Number of children aged 1 year or less	0.236	0.250	0.079
	(0.448)	(0.442)	(1.731)
Divorced, widowed, separated, or spouse absent	0.161	—	−0.101
			(−1.684)
Number of individuals	305	280	305

Notes

a Standard deviations are reported in parentheses in columns (1) and (2), and asymptotic t-statistics in column (3). Data from the second year on each woman are used. Husband's income and own income refer to labor income, and all income measures refer to the past calendar year. The income measures are top-coded. Because the top-codes vary across the years in the NLSY, sometimes rising and sometimes falling across the years, the smallest nominal top code for each income measure was chosen. The CPI was used to create a nominal top code for the other years of the survey, and the data were then treated as top-coded at those values. Finally, the income measures were deflated by the CPI. Husband's income and unemployment variables are set to zero for women not currently married with spouse present.

b The sister/sister data set is constructed to contain one record for each woman in the sample. Thus, there are two observations for each sibling pair, one with one sister as the unit of observation whose employment is to be explained (perhaps partly by her sister's employment), and another with the other sister as the unit of observation.

c Estimates are reported for women respondents in sister/sister-in-law sample. Most of the estimates were similar for the women in the sister/sister sample. Partial derivatives of the probability of employment evaluated at the sample means are reported, with the asymptotic t-statistic for the corresponding coefficient reported in parentheses.

during the past calendar year.[19] The estimated signs of the coefficients of the income variables (negative), education (positive), and the local unemployment rate (negative) are as expected. Children appear to have significant negative effects on women's employment, although the estimated effect of young children is positive, which is unexpected, although late child bearers (who have younger children, controlling for age) do have higher wages, possibly because of greater human capital investment (Blackburn *et al.*, 1993).

The first test of the model entails adding to the employment equation the employment status of the sister-in-law, as in equation (2). Estimates are reported in column (1) of Table 5.2. The estimate of γ, the coefficient of the sister-in-law's employment, is positive and nearly statistically significant at the 10-percent level. The estimates imply that women with employed sisters-in-law are about seven percentage points more likely to be employed, when the probability expressions are evaluated at the sample means. The other estimated coefficients—some of which are reported in the table—are little changed from those in column (3) of Table 5.1.

To examine whether the estimate of γ is influenced by unobservables, in column (2) we add a dummy variable for the woman's own lagged employment status, which is strongly positively related to her current employment status. The estimated effect of sister-in-law's employment rises, and becomes significant at the 5-percent level. The increase in the estimate of γ suggests that the residual in equation (1) is negatively correlated with the sister-in-law's employment status, which is consistent with the negative assortative mating on propensities to work that motivated the sister/sister-in-law test.[20]

The model described in the section "A relative income model of women's employment" refers to married couples. The estimates in columns (1) and (2) are based on samples that include divorced, separated, or widowed women, and married women with absent spouses. This was done partly to boost sample sizes,

Table 5.2 Logit estimates of sister/sister-in-law employment equations[a]

	(1)	(2)	(3)
Sister-in-law employed	0.067	0.072	0.059
	(1.612)	(2.001)	(1.522)
Own employment, lagged one year	—	0.259	0.247
	—	(6.473)	(5.668)
Husband's income/$1,000	−0.005	−0.002	−0.003
	(−2.400)	(−1.611)	(−1.571)
Other income/$1,000	−0.005	0.003	0.006
	(−0.232)	(0.185)	(0.227)
Years of education	0.035	0.019	0.014
	(2.573)	(1.627)	(1.169)
Currently married respondents only	No	No	Yes
Sample size	305	305	256

Note

a Partial derivatives of the probability of employment evaluated at the sample means are reported, with the asymptotic *t*-statistic for the corresponding coefficient reported in parentheses. The other control variables are the same as in column (3) of Table 5.1.

partly because we are interested in feedback effects that stem from sources other than relative income concerns, such as other externalities, and partly because there is no reason to believe that relative income concerns are relevant only for currently married women. To gauge the sensitivity of the results to the inclusion of previously married women, column (3) reports estimates using only the subset of currently married women (the sisters-in-law are always currently married, or there would not be any data on them, since their husbands are sampled). The estimate of γ falls only slightly, remaining positive and marginally significant.

Finally, we turn to evidence on the test that is more directly linked to the model described in the section "A relative income model of women's employment," and report estimates of equation (3). This equation provides a more direct test of the model by isolating the impact of relative income concerns on women's employment decisions. However, this test entails smaller samples, as we must use the sample of currently married sisters, split into subsamples with employed and nonemployed sisters.

The results are reported in Table 5.3. Panel A reports results for the sample of women whose sisters are not employed. In columns (1) and (2), for logit estimates of the employment equation, the estimated effect of the husband's relative income variable is positive, as predicted; note that this arises even though the level of the husband's income is already included as a control variable. The estimated coefficient is significant at the 5-percent level when we exclude lagged own employment, and marginally significant when lagged own employment is included. The estimates indicate that—for women with nonemployed sisters—when sisters' husbands' incomes are relatively higher, women's own employment probability is boosted by 16–25 percentage points. Panel B reports results for the sample of women whose sisters are employed. In columns (1) and (2) the estimated effect is negative, also as predicted, and the estimated coefficient is nearly significant at the 10-percent level when lagged own employment is included.[21] Overall, then, the evidence is consistent with the predictions of the relative income model

Table 5.3 Logit estimates of relative income employment equations[a]

	(1)	*(2)*	*(3)*
A. Sister nonemployed (N = 90)			
Sister's husband's income greater	0.254	0.158	0.126
than own husband's income	(2.515)	(1.495)	(1.441)
B. Sister employed (N = 190)			
Sister's husband's income greater	−0.089	−0.085	−0.097
than own husband's income	(−1.490)	(−1.611)	(−1.772)
Other control variables included in Panels A and B			
Lagged own employment	No	Yes	Yes
Age of sister	No	No	Yes

Note
a Partial derivatives of the probability of employment evaluated at the sample means are reported, with the asymptotic *t*-statistic for the corresponding coefficient reported in parentheses. The other control variables are the same as in column (3) of Table 5.1.

that we developed in the section "A relative income model of women's employment," although perhaps because of the small samples, the results are not strongly significant.

We also consider the possibility that the results in Table 5.3 stem from life cycle developments that bias the results in the direction of the predicted effects. In particular, the sample in Panel A might tend to include women who are younger than their sisters. These women may still be employed, while their sisters are nonemployed, in part because the latter's (generally older) husbands have attained higher earnings. Thus, there may be positive upward bias. In Panel B, the opposite might hold. The sample could be weighted toward older sisters who might be nonemployed while the younger sister is employed, in part because the older sister's husband earns more, also creating positive bias, and hence strengthening the evidence of a negative effect in columns (1) and (2) of Panel B.[22] We explore this in column (3) by adding sister's age as a control variable. In Panel A, the effect of sister's husband's relative income falls slightly, consistent with this source of bias. Similarly, in Panel B the estimated effect strengthens, becoming significant at the 10-percent level. The estimates in both panels, and especially in Panel B, remain consistent with the relative income hypothesis.

Conclusions

The striking rise in the employment of married women can be partially but not fully explained by a neoclassical model including variables capturing individual women's market opportunities, home productivity, other sources of income, and taste shifters such as demographic controls. In this chapter, we propose a "relative income" model of women's employment decisions which implies that, in addition to the variables identified by the neoclassical model, the employment decisions and incomes of other women may affect a woman's own employment decisions. We test the prediction of this model that a woman's employment decision depends on the employment or incomes of her peers in two ways.

First, we look at the interrelationship between the employment decisions of women and their sisters-in-law. Consistent with the model, we find that there is a positive effect of sister-in-laws' employment on women's own employment, after taking account of the explanatory variables suggested by the neoclassical model.

We also look at evidence on whether women's employment responds to the income of their husbands relative to that of their sisters' husbands, as the specific form of our model predicts. This evidence is largely consistent with the model's predictions. In particular, women with nonworking sisters are more likely to be employed if their husbands earn less than their sisters' husbands; this result is consistent with women's employment decisions being partly driven by relative income concerns, because women with relatively low-earning husbands and nonworking sisters may be able to attain higher relative family income if they work. In addition, women with working sisters are less likely to be employed if their husbands earn less than their sisters' husbands; this is also consistent with the relative income model, since such women are unlikely to be able to attain higher relative family income by working.

In our view, the weight of the evidence, combined with the theoretical results, suggests that relative income concerns can help to explain women's employment decisions, and in particular why married women's employment in the United States rose faster than can be explained by the standard neoclassical model.

Finally, while this chapter considers expanding the standard neoclassical model to include relative income comparisons in order to help illuminate a particular issue—the rapid rise in married women's employment—the general strategy of expanding the neoclassical model in this way opens up some interesting theoretical and empirical questions. First, if we take seriously the idea that individuals take into account relative position when making economic decisions, it seems clear that the comparison group could be quite wide. For example, in our particular context, a woman could be affected not only by the employment decisions of her sister-in-law, but also by the decisions of other friends and acquaintances. Our model incorporating relative comparisons is a particularly simple model that, as we pointed out, gives a woman substantially less ability to alter the comparison set than possible alternative models. An interesting and more realistic model would endogenously determine the comparison relationships as well as the employment decisions. Both the theoretical development and the testing of such a model would be extremely difficult, however.

Second, there are other interesting implications of an individual's employment decision being affected by the employment status of a comparison group. One is that small exogenous shocks to the economy will be amplified. A new plant opening in a town might employ a relatively small number of people. But if those people are treated as comparisons by others, the marginal willingness to work for those others may be increased. If, as a consequence, some of those others decide to work, still others who compare themselves to this new group will have their willingness to work increased. The ripple effects of the direct employment increase will result in greater employment increases than a standard neoclassical model would suggest. There would be an analogous multiplier effect in the case of decreases in employment. A plant shutdown reduces the income for some group, and hence decreases the willingness to work for those who compare their incomes to that group. In general, the existence of the type of income externality we have presented would lead to larger responses to economic shocks than would occur in the absence of such externalities.

Acknowledgments

We would like to thank Andrew Foster, George Mailath, Steve Matusz, Mark Rosenzweig, Robert Topel, Ken Wolpin, and seminar participants at Michigan State University, the University of Michigan, and the University of Pennsylvania for helpful comments and suggestions, and Sadiq Currimbhoy for research assistance. Postlewaite's research was partially supported by the National Science Foundation.

Notes

1 Goldin (1994) considers how another non-neoclassical factor may influence changes in married women's participation over time, specifically the social stigma against married women's employment in manufacturing.

2 These increases were concentrated among married women, as single women had high employment rates at the beginning of the century. Participation rates among black women display similar trends to those of white women, but started at much higher levels, and declined during the Depression (Goldin, 1990).

3 Smith and Ward (1985) reach a qualitatively similar conclusion from a more sophisticated empirical analysis of the neoclassical model.

4 Bowen and Finegan (1969) also discount the importance of the War *per se*, finding that standard income, wage, and shadow wage variables are particularly powerful predictors of married women's employment for the 1940–50 period. Cain (1966) reached a similar conclusion, focusing in particular on the decrease in family income owing to drafting of husbands, and the decline in the demand for women's household services.

5 Goldin offers two reasons why the uncompensated wage effect may have fallen. First, for women work has become less solely a way to earn money, and more a means of seeking purpose and status in life. Thus, the decision to work has become less responsive to the wage. Second, with women gaining access to better jobs, work at one point in the life cycle may increase earnings at other points in the life cycle via, for example, training. This also would diminish the response of employment to wages.

6 The subsection "Discussion of model" discusses the possible implications of relaxing this specification of the opportunity cost.

7 Because we are most interested in relative income concerns, we focus on employment, not participation, although we recognize that employment depends on a labor supply decision as well as a labor demand decision.

8 We should point out that there are naturally (at least) two distinct components of a concern for relative position. We discussed above why families might want their incomes to be similar to those of families with whom they socialize. This concern would properly be labeled "conformism" while our model might be thought of as closer to competition or emulation. For the problem we address, the distinction will not be important.

9 Note that we are showing the proportion of women at (b', a') who work, not the difference between the proportion of those working at (b', a') vs. those working at (b, a).

10 This result does not speak to the question raised in the section "The rise in married women's employment: evidence and explanations" regarding changes over time in cross-section estimates of the effects of changes in women's and men's wages. Nor does it speak to changes in relative income effects over time. Without further restrictions on functional forms, our model makes no predictions as to how income and substitution effects or relative income effects would vary as, for example, the proportion of women working rises. (See Vendrik, 1996, for an approach to such questions.)

11 We have attempted to distinguish between wage effects in which relative income concerns do not play a role (because the wage increase only occurs for one couple, paralleling the effect we would identify using micro-level data), and wage effects in which they do play a role (because the wage increase is general, as in time-series data). Mincer's (1962) estimates use cross-city variation, which may partially reflect general wage variation or at least wage variation that also affects the comparison group. However, as this section demonstrates, in that case the estimated "neoclassical" wage effects are likely biased upward, strengthening the conclusion that—based on his estimates—the neoclassical model fails to fully explain the rise in married women's employment.

Kapetyn and Woittiez (1990) use panel data to estimate a model with interdependent preferences in which the effects of variation grow over time because of interdependencies in labor supply decisions. Additional econometric work incorporating relative income concerns, along the lines of the research by Kapetyn and Woittiez that tries to embed such concerns in a fully specified family labor supply model, would be valuable.

12 Cole *et al.* (1992) analyze a model in which no agents care directly about their relative income position, but in equilibrium relative income matters because nonmarket decisions (children's marriage prospects in that model) might be affected by relative income position. They discuss in more detail how reduced form utility functions may depend on relative wealth when direct utility functions do not.

13 A model in a similar spirit is provided in Becker (1991), in which because of social interactions, individual demands for some goods depend on the aggregate market demand. In our case, women's labor supply depends to some extent on the labor supply of other women.

14 This type of phenomenon could, in principle, explain why the neoclassical model appears to fall short of explaining the rise in married women's labor force participation only in the latter part of this century.

15 Note that it is the dummy variable representing the sister-in-law's employment, rather than the latent variable underlying E'_{it}, that enters the equation. Heckman (1978) discusses models with mixed latent variable and dummy variable structures. He identifies cases in which sensible statistical models do not exist, as when the dummy variable for an event enters into the equation for the latent variable underlying that dummy variable. However, this is not the case here, since it is the *sister-in-law's* dummy variable that enters the equation for the woman's unobserved propensity to work.

16 In addition, if the true value of γ is positive, there may be upward endogeneity bias in the estimate of γ because there is a parallel equation to (2) for the sister-in-law. However, endogeneity cannot alone explain a positive estimate of γ.

17 Siblings are identified in the NLSY sample if they were coresident in surveyed households in 1979. The issue of biases from this nonrandom selection of the sample has been raised in research using sister data to estimate the socioeconomic effects of teenage childbearing (Geronimus and Korenman, 1993; Hoffman and Michael Foster, 1993). However, this concern is less important in the current context for two reasons. First, the issue originally arose for the NLS Young Women's sample, in which sisters had to be coresident between ages 14 and 24. There may be biases from this selection rule for 22–24 year-olds, among whom those remaining at home are likely to be nonrandom sample (Hoffman and Michael Foster, 1993). In contrast, the NLSY age range was 14–21 in 1979. Second, the teenage childbearing literature is concerned with outcomes that are directly related to household formation, for which selection rules related to household structure seem most likely to create problems.

18 Throughout, we report the implied partial derivatives of the probability of employment, evaluated at the sample means. The t-statistic for the corresponding coefficient is reported in parentheses.

19 Child support and alimony are other measures of exogenous income. However, data on these variables were not available for many years in the NLSY, and therefore could not be used.

We use education rather than an imputed wage to avoid having to impute wages for nonworking women. Without knowing the form of the employment equation (which is the issue this paper addresses), we cannot confidently impute wages for non-working women.

The unemployment rate is for the standard metropolitan statistical area (SMSA), for those residing in an SMSA, and for the non-SMSA population of the state of residence otherwise. The only measure of husband's unemployment that is consistently available across the years in the NLSY is that based on receipt of unemployment compensation. Controls such as marital status and number and age of children are potentially endogenous variables. The results reported were qualitatively similar, although the statistical evidence was sometimes a bit weaker, when these variables were excluded.

20 In contrast, in a preliminary version of this study (Neumark and Postlewaite, 1995), we found that for sister/sister pairs the estimate of γ falls toward zero when own lagged

employment status is included, consistent with a positive correlation among sisters in unobserved propensities to work, and implying that studying the relationship between employment decisions of sisters is likely to lead to spurious evidence in favor of the relative income hypothesis if we cannot fully control for unobserved heterogeneity.

21 If women's employment is negatively related to their husbands' income, either because husband's income responds endogenously to women's employment, or because of negative assortative mating on wage-related characteristics, there may be positive upward endogeneity bias in the estimated coefficient of the relative income variable (since husband's income appears in the denominator). This suggests that in Panel B there may be some bias against the hypothesis being tested, and in Panel A some bias in its favor. For this reason, and others discussed, we regard the evidence in Panel B as more compelling.

22 Although the inclusion of the level of husband's income as a control variable may partially control for these life cycle effects, it may not fully do so because husband's income also influences the relative income variable.

References

Akerlof, George A. 1982. "Labor Contracts as Partial Gift Exchange." *Quarterly Journal of Economics* 97: 543–69.

Becker, Gary S. 1991. "A Note on Restaurant Pricing and Other Examples of Social Influences on Price." *Journal of Political Economy* 99(5): 1109–16.

———. 1981. *A Treatise on the Family*. Cambridge: Harvard University Press.

———. 1976. *The Economic Approach to Human Behavior*. Chicago: University of Chicago Press.

Behrman, Jere R., Mark R. Rosenzweig, and Paul Taubman. 1994. "Endowments and the Allocation of Schooling in the Family and in the Marriage Market: The Twins Experiment." *Journal of Political Economy* 102: 1131–74.

Blackburn, McKinley, David E. Bloom, and David Neumark. 1993. "Fertility Timing, Wages, and Human Capital." *Journal of Population Economics* 6: 1–30.

Bowen, William G. and T. Aldrich Finegan. 1969. *The Economics of Labor Force Participation*. Princeton: Princeton University Press.

Cain, Glen. 1966. *Married Women in the Labor Force*. Chicago: University of Chicago Press.

Cole, Harold, George Mailath, and Andrew Postlewaite. 1992. "Social Norms, Savings Behavior and Growth," *Journal of Political Economy* 100: 1092–125.

Duesenberry, James S. 1949. *Income, Savings, and the Theory of Consumer Behavior*. Cambridge, MA: Harvard University Press, Cambridge.

Frank, Robert H. 1989. "Frames of Reference and the Quality of Life." *American Economic Review* 79(2): 80–5.

———. 1985. *Choosing the Right Pond: Human Behavior and the Quest for Status*. New York: Oxford University Press.

Geronimus, Arline T. and Sanders Korenman. 1993. "The Costs of Teenage Childbearing: Evidence and Interpretation." *Demography* 30(2): 281–90.

Goldin, Claudia D. 1990. *Understanding the Gender Gap: An Economic History of American Women*. New York: Oxford University Press.

———. 1991. "The Role of World War II in the Rise of Women's Employment." *American Economic Review* 81(4): 741–56.

———. 1994. "The U-Shaped Female Labor Force Function in Economic Development and Economic History." NBER Working Paper No. 4707.

Heckman, James J. 1978. "Dummy Endogenous Variables in a Simultaneous Equation System." *Econometrica* 46(6): 931–59.

Hoffman, Saul D. and E. Michael Foster. 1993. "Reevaluating the Costs of Teenage Childbearing: Response to Geronimus and Korenman." *Demography* 30(2): 291–5.

Kapetyn, Arie and Isolde Woittiez. 1990. "Preference Interdependence and Habit Formation in Family Labor Supply." In *Microeconometrics: Surveys and Applications*, eds Jean-Pierre Florens, Marc Ivaldi, Jean-Jacques Laffont, and Francois Laisney, pp. 231–63. Oxford: Basil Blackwell.

Mincer, Jacob. 1962. "Labor Force Participation of Married Women: A Study of Labor Supply." In *Aspects of Labor Economics*, ed. H. Gregg Lewis, pp. 63–97. Princeton: Princeton University Press.

Neumark, David and Andrew Postlewaite. 1995. "Relative Income Concerns and the Rise in Married Women's Employment." NBER Working Paper No. 5044.

Smith, James P. and Michael P. Ward. 1985. "Time-Series Growth in the Female Labor Force." *Journal of Labor Economics* 3(1, Supplement): S59–90.

Summers, Lawrence H. 1988. "Relative Wages, Efficiency Wages, and Keynesian Unemployment." *American Economic Review* 78(2): 383–88.

Vendrik, C. M. Maarten. 1996. "Bandwagon and Habit Effects on Female Labor Force Participation." Manuscript, Maastricht University.

Part II

Testing for discrimination

6 Employers' discriminatory behavior and the estimation of wage discrimination

Introduction

This chapter considers the linkage of empirical estimates of wage discrimination between two groups, as introduced by Oaxaca (1973), to a theoretical model of employers' discriminatory behavior. Oaxaca's widely used empirical technique estimates wage discrimination by determining how much of the wage differential between two groups is due to differences in coefficients of separately estimated wage regressions. (For examples, see Blinder, 1973; Malkiel and Malkiel, 1973; Corcoran and Duncan, 1979; Ferber and Green, 1982.) The more general basis of this technique is a comparison of the wage structures for the two groups—captured in coefficients from separately estimated regressions—to an estimate of the wage structure that would prevail in the absence of discrimination (Reimers, 1983). The component of the wage differential due to differences between the existing and the "no-discrimination" wage structure is attributed to discrimination. The remainder, which is due to differences in characteristics, is interpreted as nondiscriminatory.[1]

The chapter argues that the no-discrimination wage structure used in this approach should be derived from a theoretical model of discriminatory behavior, and shows how this can be done using an extension of Becker's (1957) and Arrow's (1972a) model of employer discrimination. The particular focus is on the relationship between the form of employers' discriminatory tastes and the resulting estimate of wage discrimination. It is shown that under different assumptions about these tastes, embodied in particular characteristics of employers' utility functions, Oaxaca's estimators of wage discrimination can be derived. That the approach is more generally useful is demonstrated by deriving an alternative estimator of wage discrimination based on a different assumption about these tastes, specifically that within each type of labor (e.g. unskilled, skilled) the utility function is homogeneous of degree zero with respect to labor inputs from each group. This alternative estimator is applied to data from the Young Men and Young Women samples of the National Longitudinal Survey (Center for Human Resources Research, 1984), and the results are compared to those produced by Oaxaca's estimators.

The next section briefly reviews Oaxaca's approach to estimating wage discrimination, and shows that it uses two special cases of a more general decomposition of the wage differential. The section "The relationship between employers' discriminatory tastes and the no-discrimination wage structure" develops the theoretical model of employer discrimination, and shows how different assumptions about employers' discriminatory tastes lead to Oaxaca's estimators, as well as to the alternative estimator of this chapter. The section "An empirical application" implements this alternative estimator, and compares its behavior to Oaxaca's estimators. The final section concludes the chapter.

Oaxaca's approach to estimating wage discrimination

Let $\ln(\overline{w}_m)$ and $\ln(\overline{w}_f)$ be the means of the (natural) logs of male (m) and female (f) wages. (Any two groups could be used; the application to gender differentials in earnings is simply an example.) If the standard log wage model is estimated separately for males and females, then since regression lines pass through the means of the variables

$$\ln(\overline{w}_m) - \ln(\overline{w}_f) = \overline{X}'_m b_m - \overline{X}'_f b_f, \tag{1}$$

where $\overline{X}_m$ and $\overline{X}_f$ are vectors containing the means of the variables for males and females, respectively, and b_m and b_f are the estimated coefficients.

Given this result, the log wage differential can be decomposed in two ways. Letting

$$\Delta \overline{X}' = \overline{X}'_m - \overline{X}'_f, \text{ and } \Delta b = b_m - b_f,$$

equation (1) can be written as:

$$\ln(\overline{w}_m) - \ln(\overline{w}_f) = \Delta \overline{X}' b_m + \overline{X}'_f \Delta b, \tag{2}$$

or

$$\ln(\overline{w}_m) - \ln(\overline{w}_f) = \Delta \overline{X}' b_f + \overline{X}'_m \Delta b. \tag{3}$$

The first term of either equation (2) or (3) is the part of the log wage differential due to different (average) characteristics of males and females, and the second term is the part of the differential due to different coefficients, or different wage structures. If in the absence of discrimination males and females would receive identical returns for the same characteristics, and differences in wages would therefore be due only to differences in pay-related characteristics, then this second term can be interpreted as the part of the log wage differential due to discrimination. This is the essence of Oaxaca's approach. A critical assumption, maintained in this chapter as well, is that labor supply and individual characteristics are fixed, and would not respond to the changes in wages that would result from the elimination of discrimination (Butler, 1982).

The question arises as to which of the two equations (2) and (3) to use in empirical work. In general they will yield different answers, and in some cases they are far apart. For example, in Oaxaca's original article, using data on whites, equation (2) yields an estimate of 52.9 percent of the male–female log wage differential as due to discrimination, while equation (3) yields an estimate of 63.9 percent. A much larger discrepancy arises in Ferber and Green (1982), in a study of pay discrimination for a sample of university professors, in which equation (2) gives an estimate of 2 percent of the wage differential as due to discrimination, while equation (3) gives an estimate of 70 percent.[2]

To understand the source of these differences, consider the assumptions made in using equation (2) or (3). In equation (2) it is assumed that in the absence of discrimination the male wage structure would prevail, since in estimating the wage differential that would then exist, the coefficients of the male wage structure are used to weight the differences in characteristics. Conversely, in equation (3) it is assumed that the female wage structure would prevail. While Oaxaca characterizes the choice of a no-discrimination wage structure as "the familiar index number problem" (1973, p. 697), a principal goal of this chapter is to show that the choice actually hinges on the nature of discriminatory behavior. This, in turn, suggests that b_m and b_f need not be the only no-discrimination wage structures considered.

To see most clearly how the estimate of wage discrimination depends on the choice of a no-discrimination wage structure, consider a more general decomposition of the wage differential.

$$\ln(\overline{w}_m) - \ln(\overline{w}_f) = \Delta \overline{X}' b + \left[\overline{X}'_m (b_m - b) - \overline{X}'_f (b_f - b) \right], \tag{4}$$

where b is the no-discrimination wage structure.[3] In this decomposition, as before, the first term can be interpreted as the part of the log wage differential due to differences in characteristics. The second term, similarly, can be interpreted as the part due to discrimination.[4] If it is assumed that in the absence of discrimination the current male wage structure would prevail, then $b = b_m$, and the decomposition in equation (4) is identical to (2). If instead it is assumed that $b = b_f$, then equation (4) reduces to (3). Thus Oaxaca's estimators are two special cases of this more general decomposition. More generally, this points out that the critical issue is the choice of b, the no-discrimination wage structure.[5]

In the next section, a theoretical model of employer discrimination is developed, and the relationship between particular assumptions about employers' discriminatory tastes and the choice of the no-discrimination wage structure is explored. The assumptions that justify using either b_m or b_f as the no-discrimination wage structure, as in Oaxaca's approach, are clarified. Based on a different assumption about employers' discriminatory tastes, an alternative, easily estimable no-discrimination wage structure is derived.

The relationship between employers' discriminatory tastes and the no-discrimination wage structure

The model used to explore this question is an extension of the employer discrimination model of Arrow (1972a) and Becker (1957). For expositional purposes most of what follows extends this previous work by allowing for two types of labor; the empirical implementation, however, is based on a generalization to any number of different types of labor.

An economy of identical firms produces output with the technology $f(A, B)$, where A and B are two types of labor (e.g. unskilled and skilled, or blue-collar and white-collar); $f(\cdot, \cdot)$ is strictly concave and increasing. A and B labor may have different productivities, but within each type males and females are homogeneous inputs. Due to the possibility of discrimination, four labor prices exist, $w_{M_A}, w_{M_B}, w_{F_A}$, and w_{F_B}, where w_{M_A} is the price of type A male labor, etc. The price of output is normalized to 1. Letting M_A, M_B, F_A, and F_B be the inputs of each type of labor, differentiated by gender, profits of each firm are

$$\pi = f(M_A + F_A, M_B + F_B) - w_{M_A}M_A - w_{F_A}F_A$$
$$- w_{M_B}M_B - w_{F_B}F_B. \tag{5}$$

Discrimination arises because employers derive utility not only from profits, but also from the gender-composition of their labor force. Employers have identical, strictly concave utility functions

$$U(\pi, M_A, F_A, M_B, F_B) \tag{6}$$

with $U_{M_A} \geq 0, U_{M_B} \geq 0, U_{F_A} \leq 0$, and $U_{F_B} \leq 0$. At least one of these must hold with strict inequality to capture discrimination against women and/or nepotism toward men.

Assume that the supplies of each type of labor, for each gender, are fixed (as in the empirical estimation of wage discrimination) and that firms are at interior solutions. Then the equilibrium quantities of labor in each firm are the total supplies divided by the number of firms. Indexing types of labor by $j = A, B$, the first-order conditions for each firm's optimum are

$$U_\pi(f_j - w_{M_j}) + U_{M_j} = 0$$
$$U_\pi(f_j - w_{F_j}) + U_{F_j} = 0. \tag{7}$$

Letting

$$d_{M_j} = \frac{-U_{M_j}}{U_\pi} \qquad d_{F_j} = \frac{-U_{F_j}}{U_\pi}, \tag{8}$$

the first-order conditions can be rewritten as

$$w_{M_j} = f_j - d_{M_j}$$
$$w_{F_j} = f_j - d_{F_j}, \tag{9}$$

d_{M_j} and d_{F_j} are similar to Becker's (1957) "discrimination coefficients," differing only in that they are not constant, but instead are functions of the partial derivatives of the utility function. Given the signs of the first derivatives of the utility function, equation (9) implies that

$$w_{M_j} \geq f_j \geq w_{F_j}, \tag{10}$$

with strict inequality holding at least once.

Having developed the general model, different assumptions about the structure of employers' discriminatory tastes, and their different implications for the no-discrimination wage structure, can be explored. First, suppose $d_{M_A} = d_{M_B} = 0$, so that there is no nepotism toward males, but only discrimination against females. Then

$$w_{M_j} = f_j,$$
$$w_{F_j} = f_j - d_{F_j}. \tag{11}$$

Males are therefore receiving their marginal products. Thus if discrimination were eliminated their wages would not change at all, while wages of females (within each type of labor) would rise to those of males.

To apply this result to data on earnings and characteristics, in order to obtain a no-discrimination wage structure in terms of a set of wage regression coefficients, identify types of labor by different sets of values for the independent variables. Then in the pure discrimination case captured in equation (11), letting a type j worker be identified by a given set of characteristics X_j, and generalizing to any number of types of labor, implies that the current male wage structure, b_m, is the appropriate no-discrimination wage structure to use in estimating wage discrimination.

The polar opposite case is when there is no discrimination against females, but only nepotism toward males. Then

$$w_{M_j} = f_j - d_{M_j},$$
$$w_{F_j} = f_j. \tag{12}$$

In this case male employees take the whole gain from employers' discriminatory behavior, and in its absence their wages would fall to female wages. This characterizes the situation in which it is appropriate to use the current female wage structure, b_f, as the no-discrimination wage structure.

Whether one should accept b_m, b_f, or some other set of coefficients as the no-discrimination wage structure, and if so which one, therefore depends on the nature of employers' discriminatory behavior. The true nature of discrimination may be empirically indiscernible. Previous work by Arrow (1972b) and Goldberg (1982) considers whether discrimination or nepotism is the more likely cause of wage differentials, the central focus being their long-run sustainability.[6]

While the issue remains unresolved, the alternative no-discrimination wage structure derived in this chapter is generated by an assumption about employers' discriminatory tastes that imposes neither pure discrimination nor pure nepotism.

Instead, it is assumed that employers can be both nepotistic toward males and discriminatory toward females. This avoids a strong asymmetry in employers' tastes such that, for example, they require higher profits to compensate for hiring females, but are not willing to accept lower profits to hire males. Thus d_{M_A} and d_{M_B} can be negative, and d_{F_A} and d_{F_B} can be positive, implying that in the absence of discrimination wages of males would fall, while those of females would rise.

The cost of relaxing the pure nepotism or pure discrimination assumption is that some other restriction must be imposed on employers' tastes in order to derive an estimable no-discrimination wage structure. The restriction imposed on the utility function is that, within each type of labor, it is homogeneous of degree zero with respect to male and female labor inputs. Equivalently, if the numbers of male and female workers of a given type are increased or decreased proportionately, the employer's utility is unchanged. Intuitively, this means that employers care only about the relative proportions of males and females, and not absolute numbers. The assumption is less restrictive than it may seem, though, since homogeneity of degree zero must hold only within each type of labor, so that the employer's utility is affected by the distribution of workers, by gender, across types of labor.

Given this assumption, the alternative no-discrimination wage structure and its estimator are derived in three steps. First, a theoretical implication of the assumed form of the utility function of employers is derived. Second, as above, a method of applying this result to data on the earnings and characteristics of workers, in order to estimate the no-discrimination wage structure as a set of coefficients in a wage regression, is presented. Third, it is shown that implementation of this estimator is often simple, requiring only the estimation of the log wage regression for the full sample.

Under the assumed form of the utility function, an expression for the no-discrimination wage structure, in terms of wages in the presence of discrimination, emerges. Homogeneity of degree zero for each type of labor implies, by Euler's Theorem, that for each j

$$U_{M_j} \cdot M_j + U_{F_j} \cdot F_j = 0. \tag{13}$$

Dividing through by $-U_\pi$ yields

$$d_{M_j} \cdot M_j + d_{F_j} \cdot F_j = 0. \tag{14}$$

Using the first-order conditions in equation (9), this implies

$$(f_j - w_{M_j})M_j + (f_j - w_{F_j})F_j = 0 \tag{15}$$

or

$$f_j = \frac{w_{M_j} M_j + w_{F_j} F_j}{M_j + F_j}. \tag{16}$$

But f_j, the marginal product of a type j worker (of either gender) is, of course, equal to the no-discrimination wage. This shows that, for each type of labor j, the no-discrimination wage can be expressed as the weighted average of the wages for males and females of that type in the presence of discrimination.

An appealing feature of this result is that changes in wages in going from the discriminatory to the nondiscriminatory wage structure are sensitive to the gender-composition of each type of labor. This is clear from equation (16). Thus the no-discrimination wage for a type of labor that is predominantly female will be relatively closer to the current wage for women, and vice versa. With Oaxaca's method, in contrast, the no-discrimination wage structure is insensitive to these numbers.[7]

To apply this result to data on earnings and characteristics, consider first a simplified case, in which there are only two types of workers, with type A workers described by the vector X_A, and type B workers X_B. While for each gender the wage of a worker with given X may vary, due to the usual causes of residual variation in a wage equation, the most obvious way to estimate, say, the wage for a type A, male worker, is to use the fitted value from the wage regression for the male sample, at $X = X_A$. This leads to four fitted wages, $\hat{w}_{M_A}, \hat{w}_{F_A}, \hat{w}_{M_B}$, and $\hat{w}_{F_B}$. In this simple example the no-discrimination wage structure could be constructed by finding the two points w_A and w_B (or equivalently f_A and f_B) that satisfy equation (16). (Actually, to preserve linearity, the wage model should be in terms of log wages; this issue is taken up below.) If there are J types of workers instead, each described by X_j, and receiving a (fitted) wage $\hat{w}_{M_j}$ or $\hat{w}_{F_j}$, a similar procedure could be followed. The problem is that there is no reason for the J wages similar to equation (16) to lie on a line. A reasonable approach is to adopt a least-squares criterion in fitting a line to these J points, weighting by the number of workers of each type.

The rationale for using this procedure to estimate the no-discrimination wage structure is as follows. Equation (16) gives the wage for each type of labor that would prevail in the absence of discrimination. As in the Oaxaca decompositions, the implicit simplifying assumption is that individual characteristics are fixed, and would not change if discrimination were eliminated. As long as the form of the standard wage equation would still hold in the absence of discrimination, then it makes sense to estimate the coefficients of this equation in the usual way, by minimizing the sum of squared residuals of the predicted wages around the surface generated by the independent variables.[8]

A minor point that requires discussion is that the desired specification of the wage regression is log-linear, while the theoretical result in equation (16) is in terms of wages. Taking the logarithm of the no-discrimination wage derived in equation (16) gives

$$\ln(w_j) = \ln \left[\frac{M_j \cdot w_{M_j} + F_j \cdot w_{F_j}}{M_j + F_j} \right]. \tag{17}$$

What is needed instead is

$$\ln(w_j) = \frac{M_j \cdot \ln(w_{M_j}) + F_j \cdot \ln(w_{F_j})}{M_j + F_j}. \tag{18}$$

By Jensen's inequality, the first expression is greater than the second. For reasonable ranges of the data, though, these numbers are very close. Further, the constant component of this approximation error gets loaded onto the constant term of the wage structure. But equation (4) shows that the constant term does not affect the decomposition, so that only biases in the slope coefficients are relevant.

It turns out that this estimator of the no-discrimination wage structure can be implemented simply, as the coefficients estimated from the log wage regression for the whole sample, using fitted wages from the separate wage regressions as the dependent variable. To see this, let there be J types of workers, indexed by $j = 1, \ldots, J$, with each type of labor defined by a unique K-vector X_j. Then expressions similar to equation (16) can be derived for each type of labor j. To determine the wage structure that the fitting procedure described above produces, let M_j and F_j be the number of workers of each gender of type j, $\ln(w_{M_j})$ and $\ln(w_{F_j})$ their respective log wages, and $\ln(\hat{w}_{M_j})$ and $\ln(\hat{w}_{F_j})$ their fitted wages. Denote by Λ the J-vector with jth element

$$\Lambda_j = \left[\frac{M_j}{M_j + F_j} \right] \cdot \ln(\hat{w}_{M_j}) + \left[\frac{F_j}{M_j + F_j} \right] \cdot \ln(\hat{w}_{F_j}) \tag{19}$$

and by X the $(J \times K)$ matrix describing each type of worker. Lastly, let $\Omega = diag(M_1 + F_1, \ldots, M_J + F_J)$. Under the least squares criterion discussed above the function to be minimized in estimating the no-discrimination wage structure β is

$$(\Lambda - X\beta)' \Omega (\Lambda - X\beta). \tag{20}$$

Minimizing this with respect to β yields the solution

$$b = (X'\Omega X)^{-1}(X'\Omega\Lambda). \tag{21}$$

Consider instead the simpler approach in which the fitted wages from the separate regressions are regressed on X for the individual workers in this model. Type j workers are still characterized by the same "bundle" of characteristics X_j, but indexing by $i = 1, \ldots, N$ for individual workers, the minimand becomes

$$\sum_{i=1}^{N} (\ln(\hat{w}_i) - X_i \beta)^2. \tag{22}$$

Given that X_i is equal across all workers of the same type and $\ln(\hat{w}_i)$ is equal across same-gender workers of the same type, this is equivalent to

$$\underset{\text{men } j=1}{\sum^{J}} M_j (\ln(\hat{w}_{M_j}) - X_j \beta)^2 + \underset{\text{women } j=1}{\sum^{J}} F_j (\ln(\hat{w}_{F_j}) - X_j \beta)^2. \tag{23}$$

Letting Λ_M and Λ_F be J-vectors of fitted male and female log wages for each type of labor, $\Omega_M = diag(M_1, \ldots, M_J)$, and similarly for Ω_F, this can be written as

$$(\Lambda_M - X\beta)'\Omega_M(\Lambda_M - X\beta) + (\Lambda_F - X\beta)'\Omega_F(\Lambda_F - X\beta). \tag{24}$$

Minimizing this with respect to β yields

$$b_{LS} = \left[(X'\Omega_M X) + (X'\Omega_F X)\right]^{-1}\left[(X'\Omega_M \Lambda_M) + (X'\Omega_F \Lambda_F)\right]. \tag{25}$$

It turns out, however, that b and b_{LS} are identical. To see this, note that the first matrices of (21) and (25) are equivalent by inspection. The kth element of the second matrix (which is a vector) in (25) is

$$\sum_{j=1}^{J}(X_{jk}M_j \cdot \ln(\hat{w}_{M_j}) + X_{jk}F_j \cdot \ln(\hat{w}_{F_j})). \tag{26}$$

The kth element of the second matrix in (21) is

$$\sum_{j=1}^{J} X_{jk}\left(M_j + F_j\right)\left[\frac{M_j \cdot \ln(\hat{w}_{M_j})}{M_j + F_j} + \frac{F_j \cdot \ln(\hat{w}_{F_j})}{M_j + F_j}\right]$$

$$= \sum_{j=1}^{J}(X_{jk}M_j \cdot \ln(\hat{w}_{M_j}) + X_{jk}F_j \cdot \ln(\hat{w}_{F_j})), \tag{27}$$

which is identical to (26).[9]

Finally, it is straightforward to show that unless sample weights are being used, identical coefficient estimates result from using actual log wages for individuals instead of fitted values from the separate regressions, so that the no-discrimination wage structure is simply the set of coefficients from the pooled regression. Thus, given the assumed form of the utility function, the model leads to an alternative, easily estimable no-discrimination wage structure to use in estimating wage discrimination.

An empirical application

In this section the alternative estimator of wage discrimination is applied to data from the National Longitudinal Survey of Young Men and Young Women (NLS). It turns out that this alternative estimator yields a lower estimate of discrimination than either of the Oaxaca decompositions. The reason for this lies in the implications of the different assumptions underlying the various estimators of wage discrimination.

Most of the data are taken from the 1980 questionnaires of the NLS, with work history data from earlier surveys also used to construct a measure of actual work experience. Four factors result in final sample sizes of 1,819 men and 1,505 women: (1) attrition from the sample, (2) missing data on some subset of the independent variables, (3) deletion of self-employed and others not working for a wage, and

(4) missing wage due to not working or working without pay. The detailed results that follow are given for the data uncorrected for sampling weights. Final estimates of wage discrimination, however, are also given (in Table 6.3) for data using sampling weights in the NLS, as well as an adjustment for gender-specific attrition rates.

Table 6.1 presents descriptive statistics and variable definitions. The log wage differential of 0.502 is typical, translating, at the means, into female wages being 61 percent of male wages. The mean values for schooling and experience are higher for males, which is, however, partly due to males being more than 1.5 years older because of the earlier starting date for men in the NLS. This age difference is also probably reflected in the higher proportion married in the male sample. These figures also reflect oversampling of blacks, leading to a relatively high proportion non-white and from the South.

Table 6.2 presents regression results for one specification of the log wage equation.[10] At the bottom of the table these results are combined with those of Table 6.1, to estimate wage discrimination based on the two Oaxaca decompositions (denoted b_f and b_m) and the alternative decomposition of this chapter (denoted b_{LS}).

The alternative decomposition produces considerably lower estimates of the percentage of the wage differential due to discrimination. Using b_m as the no-discrimination wage structure, it is estimated that 70 percent of the log wage differential between men and women is due to discrimination, while using b_f

Table 6.1 Descriptive statistics

Variable	Mean (Standard deviation)			Variable definition
	Full sample (N = 3,324)	Female sample (N = 1,505)	Male sample (N = 1,819)	
LNWAGE	6.467 (0.515)	6.192 (0.434)	6.694 (0.464)	Natural logarithm of hourly wage
SCHOOL	13.146 (2.565)	12.793 (2.353)	13.437 (2.694)	Highest grade completed
EXPER	8.469 (4.767)	6.763 (3.458)	9.881 (5.218)	Post-schooling actual work experience
AGE	31.670 (3.264)	30.753 (3.073)	32.429 (3.224)	
URBAN	0.696 (0.460)	0.694 (0.461)	0.698 (0.459)	Dummy variable = 1 if lived in SMSA
SOUTH	0.415 (0.493)	0.429 (0.495)	0.403 (0.491)	Dummy variable = 1 if lived in South
UNION	0.321 (0.467)	0.277 (0.448)	0.358 (0.480)	Dummy variable = 1 if wages set by collective bargaining
MST	0.701 (0.458)	0.630 (0.483)	0.760 (0.427)	Dummy variable = 1 if married, spouse present
WHITE	0.749 (0.433)	0.710 (0.454)	0.782 (0.413)	Dummy variable = 1 if white

Table 6.2 Regression estimates and wage differential decompositions[a]

Variable	Full sample	Female sample	Male sample
CONSTANT	4.418	5.173	4.817
	(0.083)	(0.113)	(0.109)
	[−1.247]	[−1.034]	[−1.006]
SCHOOL	0.088	0.072	0.062
	(0.003)	(0.004)	(0.004)
	[−0.517]	[−0.398]	[−0.369]
EXPER	0.033	0.034	0.011
	(0.002)	(0.003)	(0.002)
	[−0.791]	[−0.661]	[−0.440]
AGE	0.008	−0.009	0.015
	(0.003)	(0.003)	(0.003)
	[2.697]	[2.323]	[2.144]
URBAN	0.175	0.129	0.205
	(0.016)	(0.021)	(0.020)
	[0.185]	[0.154]	[0.149]
SOUTH	−0.077	−0.092	−0.070
	(0.016)	(0.021)	(0.020)
	[0.033]	[0.027]	[0.028]
UNION	0.172	0.138	0.134
	(0.016)	(0.021)	(0.020)
	[−0.015]	[−0.005]	[−0.004]
MST	0.100	−0.001	0.153
	(0.016)	(0.020)	(0.022)
	[0.364]	[0.340]	[0.274]
WHITE	0.169	0.106	0.218
	(0.018)	(0.023)	(0.024)
	[0.291]	[0.255]	[0.225]
R^2	0.360	0.292	0.317
Coefficients used in decomposition	b_{LS}	b_f	b_m
Percent due to characteristics	0.43	0.31	0.30
Percent due to discrimination	0.57	0.69	0.70

Note

a Standard errors are in parentheses. For the full sample estimates the standard error and R^2 are for the regression using actual log wages, not fitted values. Proportional contributions to the discriminatory component of the log wage differential, as estimated using coefficients in the column as the no-discrimination wage structure, are given in square brackets.

leads to an estimate of 69 percent. But when the decomposition based on b_{LS} is used, the estimate drops to 57 percent.

Table 6.3 gives summary results for other specifications, and for the weighted analysis. Quantitatively and qualitatively, the results are very similar. In both the weighted and unweighted analyses, when industry and occupation dummy variables are added, the estimate of discrimination falls. This is not surprising, given that there is some tendency for women to be concentrated in lower-paying industries, and a strong tendency for the same to be true across occupations. The question of whether industry or occupation dummy variables should be included

Table 6.3 Estimates of wage discrimination for alternative specifications, and after adjustment for sample weights[a]

Coefficients used in decomposition	b_{LS}	b_f	b_m
Unweighted			
Industry dummy variables included			
Percent due to characteristics	0.59	0.41	0.44
Percent due to discrimination	0.41	0.59	0.56
Industry and occupation dummy variables included			
Percent due to characteristics	0.69	0.47	0.52
Percent due to discrimination	0.31	0.53	0.48
Weighted			
Specification as in Table 6.2			
Percent due to characteristics	0.47	0.32	0.32
Percent due to discrimination	0.53	0.68	0.68
Industry dummy variables included			
Percent due to characteristics	0.63	0.40	0.49
Percent due to discrimination	0.37	0.60	0.51
Industry and occupation dummy variables included			
Percent due to characteristics	0.72	0.46	0.54
Percent due to discrimination	0.28	0.54	0.46

Note
a Industry and occupation dummy variables are for one-digit 1960 *SIC* and *SOC* codes.

in regressions to estimate wage discrimination hinges on the extent to which the distribution of men and women across industries and occupations is itself a result of discrimination. The range of results indicates that, together with the choice of the no-discrimination wage structure, the answer to this question has a strong effect on the ultimate estimate of wage discrimination.

The explanation of the lower estimates of discrimination produced by the alternative decomposition of this chapter lies in the effects of the distribution of characteristics on the no-discrimination wage structure. The implication of the assumption that leads to the alternative decomposition, as equation (16) shows, is that the effect of discrimination is to redistribute wages only within each type of labor. Thus, the resulting estimate of wage discrimination is sensitive to differences in the distribution of characteristics across men and women. The no-discrimination wage structures used in Oaxaca's decompositions, however, are insensitive to these differences. The relevance of this to the resulting estimates of wage discrimination can be demonstrated explicitly for the simple case of a model with one explanatory variable, X, and a constant which is the same for men and women. In this case it can be shown that whenever the more highly paid group has the greater endowment of X, the alternative estimator of the no-discrimination wage structure produces a higher coefficient of X than the coefficient in either of the regressions estimated separately for males and females, and hence a lower estimate of wage discrimination than either of Oaxaca's estimators.[11]

The theoretical material developed above suggests that one should not adopt the estimate provided by the alternative estimator simply because it yields an unambiguous answer, as opposed to Oaxaca's approach. At the same time, the empirical results show that one should not accept the two estimates produced by the Oaxaca decompositions as "a range of possible values" (Oaxaca, 1973: p. 697) for the "true" answer. Jointly, the results demonstrate that decomposing the wage differential between two groups to estimate wage discrimination should not be considered an algebraic exercise independent of the nature of the underlying discriminatory behavior.

Conclusions

This chapter has considered the problem of linking empirical estimates of wage discrimination to a theoretical model of discriminatory behavior by employers, by deriving implications of the nature of this behavior for the structure of wages that would prevail in the absence of discrimination. It utilized a simple model of employer discrimination to show how particular assumptions about employers' discriminatory tastes can, in this framework, justify Oaxaca's widely used estimators. But it also showed that different assumptions about these tastes can lead to different estimators of wage discrimination. Furthermore, the application demonstrates that the implications for estimates of wage discrimination are empirically substantial. The application of the general approach to other models of discrimination, and to other assumptions about employers' discriminatory tastes, will be taken up in future research.

At this stage, the only possible conclusion is that there is some arbitrariness in using decompositions of wage differentials to estimate wage discrimination. While it was demonstrated that different estimates can be linked to theoretical models of employer discrimination, the choice of the theoretical model to use remains an open question. But there is no reason for this state of affairs to last. Empirical as well as theoretical explorations of the various models should be pursued. The dependence of these empirical measures of wage discrimination on the underlying model provides an important motivation for doing so.

Acknowledgments

The author would like to thank McKinley Blackburn, David Bloom, John Bound, Ronald Ehrenberg, Zvi Griliches, Reuven Gronau, George Johnson, Lawrence Katz, and an anonymous referee for helpful comments and suggestions. He takes responsibility for any remaining errors.

This material is based upon the first essay of the author's dissertation, for which he gratefully acknowledges the support of a National Science Foundation Graduate Fellowships.

Notes

1 A related application of the comparison between current and "no-discrimination" wage structures is to the analysis of the effects of comparable worth (Gregory and Ho, 1985; Johnson and Solon, 1986; Ehrenberg and Smith, 1987).
2 They write, "The results show that under the male reward structure women would earn $15,199, on average, instead of the $15,101 they actually earn. Men on the other hand, would earn only $16,463 according to the female wage structure, although they actually earn $19,699" (p. 557). I am grateful to David Bloom for pointing out this finding. which provided the initial motivation for this research.
3 The decomposition in equation (4) holds as long as equation (1) holds. This requires only that b_m and b_f are least-squares estimates of the log-wage model for the separate samples.
4 The weights on the differences between the coefficients of the discriminatory and the no-discrimination wage structures are more natural in equation (4) than in Oaxaca's decompositions in which another "index number problem" arises.
5 This issue was raised by Reimers (1983), who used $b = 0.5 \cdot b_m + 0.5 \cdot b_f$ as the no-discrimination wage structure.
6 Goldberg (1982) concludes that only nepotism is sustainable, since there is a utility gain from staying in business that compenstates the employer for the pecuniary costs of his discriminatory behavior.
7 This problem with Oaxaca's method was raised by Chiplin (1979), who suggested that since there were more males in the labor force, b_m should be used as the no-discrimination wage structure.
8 A slightly different approach is to minimize this sum over types of labor, rather than individuals, in which case there would be no need to weight by the number of workers of each type. This could lead to somewhat different results if some individuals have identical X vectors.
9 This proof could only be carried out using a characterization of different types of workers that is an oversimplification, in associating with each type of worker the "bundle" of characteristics X_j. But the result implies that the technique can be applied to actual data in which the regression cannot feasibly be estimated for workers assigned to each of J categories.
10 For all of the specifications considered, the hypothesis that a single regression could be fitted to the data for males and females was rejected at the 1-percent significance level. When quadratic terms in *EXPER* and *AGE* were included, they did not have a statistically significant effect, probably due to the relative youth of the sample.
11 This analytical result does not hold for the multiple regression model, since each coefficient of the estimated alternative no-discrimination wage structure depends on all of the coefficients from the separate regressions. But experimentation with more parsimonious specifications than the model in Table 6.2 shows that it tends to hold empirically.

References

Arrow, Kenneth. 1972a. "Some Mathematical Models of Race Discrimination in the Labor Market." In *Racial Discrimination in Economic Life*, ed. Anthony Pascal, pp. 187–203. Lexington: D. C. Heath.

——. 1972b. "Models of Job Discrimination." In *Racial Discrimination in Economic Life*, ed. Anthony Pascal, pp. 82–101. Lexington: D.C. Heath.

Becker, Gary S. 1957. *The Economics of Discrimination*. Chicago: University of Chicago Press.

Blinder, Alan S. 1973. "Wage Discrimination: Reduced Form and Structural Estimates." *Journal of Human Resources* 8(4): 436–55.

Butler, Richard. 1982. "Estimating Wage Discrimination in the Labor Market." *Journal of Human Resources* 17(4): 606–21.

Center for Human Resources Research. 1984. *The National Longitudinal Survey Handbook.* Columbus: Ohio State University.

Chiplin, Brian. 1979. "The Evaluation of Sex Discrimination: Some Problems and a Suggested Reorientation." In *Women in the Labor Market*, eds Cynthia B. Lloyd, Emily Andrews, and Curtis L. Gilroy, pp. 246–70. New York: Columbia University Press.

Corcoran, Mary and Greg J. Duncan. 1979. "Work History, Labor Force Attachment, and Earnings Differences Between the Races and the Sexes." *Journal of Human Resources* 14(1): 3–20.

Ehrenberg, Ronald and Robert S. Smith. 1987. "Comparable-Worth Wage Adjustments and Female Employment in the State and Local Sector." *Journal of Labor Economics* 5(1): 43–62.

Ferber, Marianne A. and Carole A. Green. 1982. "Traditional or Reverse Sex Discrimination? A Case Study of a Large Public University." *Industrial and Labor Relations Review* 35(4): 550–64.

Goldberg, Matthew S. 1982. "Discrimination, Nepotism, and Long-Run Wage Differentials." *Quarterly Journal of Economics* 97(2): 307–19.

Gregory, Robert G. and Vivian Ho. 1985. "Equal Pay and Comparable Worth: What Can the U.S. Learn from the Australian Experience?" The Australian National University Centre for Economic Policy Research Discussion Paper No. 123.

Johnson, George and Gary Solon. 1986. "Estimates of the Direct Effects of Comparable Worth Policy." *American Economic Review* 76(5): 1117–25.

Malkiel, Burton G. and Judith A. Malkiel. 1973. "Male–Female Pay Differentials in Professional Employment." *American Economic Review* 63(4): 693–705.

Oaxaca, Ronald. 1973. "Male–Female Wage Differentials in Urban Labor Markets." *International Economic Review* 14(3): 693–709.

Reimers, Cordelia W. 1983. "Labor Market Discrimination Against Hispanic and Black Men." *The Review of Economics and Statistics* 65(4): 570–9.

7 Sex discrimination and women's labor market outcomes

(with Michele McLennan)

Introduction

The central tenet of the human capital explanation of sex differences in wages is that, because of specialization in household production, women intend to work in the labor market more intermittently than men, and therefore invest less. Because much human capital investment is unobserved, it is argued that this lower investment leads to lower wages, even after controlling for observable variables that affect wages (Mincer and Polachek, 1974; Polachek, 1975; Becker, 1985). Numerous studies show that women accumulate less actual experience and job tenure than men (e.g. O'Neill, 1985). Moreover, the evidence originally presented by Mincer and Polachek (1974) is consistent with the human capital explanation of sex differences in wages. In log wage regressions the coefficients on experience tend to be higher for never married women and women without children than for women with children. Other researchers have presented related supporting evidence (e.g. Sandell and Shapiro, 1980), including evidence partially consistent with the human capital model's hypotheses regarding the effects of household specialization on men's and women's wages (Korenman and Neumark, 1991, 1992). On the other hand, empirical evidence against the human capital explanation has also been garnered, focusing on estimation of the returns to experience (Sandell and Shapiro, 1978; Blau and Ferber, 1992), and on the role of depreciation of human capital during labor market withdrawals (Corcoran, 1979).

An alternative "feedback" hypothesis that is consistent with these findings is that women experience labor market discrimination—partly reflected in lower wage levels and wage growth—and respond with career interruptions associated with specialization in household production. These interruptions may in turn lower subsequent wage growth. The competing explanations of sex differences in wages have been tested in recent work by Gronau (1988) and Blau and Ferber (1991), and in previous work surveyed in Blau and Ferber (1992, chapter 7). The papers by Gronau, and by Blau and Ferber focus explicitly on distinguishing between the human capital and feedback hypotheses, by addressing the joint causality running from women's labor market intermittency to lower wages, and from lower wages (presumably attributable in part to discrimination) to intermittency. Both papers do this by invoking sufficient identifying assumptions to estimate simultaneous equations models with wages and future labor market separations as the jointly dependent variables. Gronau's results with respect to the human capital model are ambiguous. He finds evidence that future separations lower current wages, once account is taken of the effect of such separations on on-the-job training.[1] But he does not find evidence that future separations reduce the skill requirements of women's jobs. Furthermore, consistent with the feedback hypothesis, he finds that lower wages lead to labor market separations. Blau and Ferber tend to find no evidence supporting either the human capital model or the feedback hypothesis, with no effect of expected years of full-time work on expected earnings growth (conditional on continuous employment), nor of expected earnings growth on planned years of work. However, the validity of the findings in these papers hinges in large part on identifying assumptions in the form of exclusion restrictions, which are somewhat arbitrary (as Gronau acknowledges).

The goal of this chapter is to pursue an alternative empirical approach to studying the feedback hypothesis. Rather than attempting to untangle the joint determination of wages and labor market interruptions, this chapter looks at the relationship between women's self-reports of sex discrimination on the job and future labor market outcomes, including labor market interruptions, employer changes, demographic changes, and wage growth. A variety of approaches to estimating these relationships are considered, to account for numerous possible biases arising from the use of self-reported discrimination data.

Thus, this approach differs in two ways from the existing research. First, since reported discrimination is presumably not a choice variable of the individual (in contrast to wage levels or growth rates, which, according to the human capital hypothesis, are partly choice variables), there is not an inherent simultaneity problem. That is, self-reported discrimination may provide a more exogenous measure of discrimination experienced by women than does the wage. Second, in contrast to previous research, this approach focuses on the effects of discrimination *per se*, in contrast to the effects of wages paid. Thus, it is potentially a more direct test of the hypothesis that sex discrimination contributes to women's labor market interruptions. While these are advantages of the approach, the disadvantage is that self-reports of discrimination are subjective measures. We view it as a goal for future research to further assess the validity of such subjective measures, and to better integrate the use of objective and subjective measures in the study of discrimination.

The data

This chapter utilizes self-reported data on sex discrimination in the National Longitudinal Survey of Young Women. In 1972, 1978, 1980, 1982, 1983, and 1988 women were asked whether they had experienced sex discrimination on the job. In particular, in all of these years but one, women were asked, for a period ranging over the past two to five years, "so far as work is concerned, have you been in any way discriminated against because of race, religion, sex, age, nationality, or for any other reason?" Respondents could then indicate all applicable reasons (e.g. sex and race). In the 1972 survey, respondents were asked explicitly if they had ever experienced sex discrimination on the job. There is relatively little information on the nature of discrimination experienced, for the years for which we use the self-reports. In 1978, 1980, 1982, and 1983 no information on the nature of discrimination experienced was elicited from those reporting discrimination. In 1972, respondents indicated whether the discrimination was in the form of hiring, promotion/assignment, demotion or layoff, or "general" discrimination. Only in 1988 was pay discrimination included as a possible response for the nature of discrimination. But because we require data following the discrimination report for our analysis of the feedback hypothesis, and because we want to capture the effects of discrimination early in the career, we do not use the 1988 reports for this analysis. Nonetheless, toward the end of the chapter we use the 1988 data to attempt to understand some of the findings related to self-reported discrimination. For the main analysis we simply use a discrete variable indicating whether or not a woman reported sex discrimination.

In addition to the self-reported discrimination data, variables measuring actual labor market experience (in years, not hours-weighted) and tenure were constructed using information on work histories and current employment in each year. The other variables used are quite standard. Our samples include black and non-black women, unless otherwise indicated. For each set of estimates that follow, we selected the largest sample available for analysis. The sample selection criteria do not require that women are continuously in the sample (or continuously employed), but, as the ensuing discussion clarifies, do require a number of observations on each woman, at some of which she must be employed.

The empirical approach

The chapter focuses on three broad categories of dependent variables. The first is labor market attachment, measured by the accumulation of actual labor market experience, and by employer changes.[2] The second is demographic changes, including changes in the number of children, incidence of first births, and marriage, all of which may be associated with direct breaks in labor market attachment, as well as less effort on the job or lower human capital investment because of increased specialization in household production. Finally, the consequences of sex discrimination for wage growth are also examined.

The question regarding sex discrimination was generally asked of all respondents. However, for nonworking women a response of no discrimination may simply reflect the fact that they were not working. Thus, only the data collected from working women are useful. We focus on the relationship between discrimination reported by currently working women, and future labor market behavior. In general, equations are estimated of the form:

$$(y_{it''} - y_{it'}) = \alpha + (x_{it''} - x_{it'})\beta + D_{it}\delta + \varepsilon_{it'}, \quad t'' > t', \quad t' \geq t. \tag{1}$$

D_{it} is a dummy variable equal to 1 if respondent i reported sex discrimination in an interval preceding the survey at time t, and x represents a (row) vector of control variables. Changes in various dependent variables (y) are studied from some time beginning with or following the self-report on discrimination (which occurs at time t), to some future date t''. For example, in the first set of specifications reported, $(y_{it''} - y_{it'})$ is the change in actual experience measured from period t—the time of the discrimination report—to the last available observation. (If we measured these changes over the period covered by the discrimination report, we would have no way of knowing whether the change occurred before or after the reported discrimination.) As a shorthand, equation (1) will be written

$$\Delta y_{it'} = \alpha + \Delta x_{it'}\beta + D_{it}\delta + \varepsilon_{it'}.$$

$\Delta y_{it'}$ will sometimes be a dichotomous variable, in which case logit estimates of equation (1) are reported.

The key parameter of interest in equation (1) is δ. For example, when $\Delta y_{it'}$ is the change in experience, a negative estimate of δ would suggest that discrimination reduces the future accumulation of labor market experience. This would provide support for the hypothesis that discrimination causes, at least in part, weaker labor market attachment.

Note that in contrast to the research by Gronau (1988) and Blau and Ferber (1991), there is not an inherent simultaneity problem in equation (1), if the self-reported discrimination data accurately reflect discrimination experienced by women that is exogenous to their own decisions. In contrast, their research substitutes the wage level (or wage growth) for D_{it} in equation (1), a variable that is clearly jointly determined under the human capital hypothesis. Nonetheless, while there is no inherent simultaneity problem, the use of self-reported discrimination data may cast doubt on the assumption that D_{it} is uncorrelated with the error term in equation (1).

Potential biases from using discrimination self-reports

One source of bias from using discrimination self-reports may be heterogeneity in the propensity to report sex discrimination. There is evidence of such heterogeneity in research by Kuhn (1987), who finds that women who are *least* underpaid based on conventional wage equation decompositions are *most* likely to report sex discrimination. One explanation of this finding is that women who report discrimination experience relatively little wage discrimination, and relatively more nonwage discrimination (such as sexual harassment and lower benefits). An alternative hypothesis, though, is that women who are in jobs experiencing relatively small amounts of wage discrimination are also women who are more likely to report sex discrimination. The fact that relatively young, more educated women in Kuhn's samples are more likely to report sex discrimination, controlling for measured discrimination (based on wage equation decompositions), seems consistent with heterogeneity in the propensity to report discrimination. These women may be more aware of or attuned to sex discrimination, and hence more likely to report it independently of measured wage discrimination, or perhaps despite lower measured wage discrimination (Kuhn, 1990). Such heterogeneity may also influence our results. In particular, if women more attached or committed to the labor market are more likely to report sex discrimination, then there is a bias against finding evidence favoring the feedback hypothesis, as those reporting discrimination may have fewer career interruptions and higher wage growth.

To address this heterogeneity bias, we control for a fixed propensity to report sex discrimination by focusing on the subsample of women reporting no sex discrimination at the time of their first valid report. D_{it} (in equation (1)) is then defined to indicate women among this subsample who report sex discrimination at the time of their *second* report, and the changes in dependent and control variables are defined as changes subsequent to the second report. The estimated coefficient of D_{it} for this subsample should be relatively free of heterogeneity bias, because it is identified solely from women who initially reported no sex discrimination, and then switched to reporting discrimination.[3]

Biases may also arise because discrimination self-reports are subjective. In particular, we might be concerned that women who experience negative outcomes on the job or in the labor market, independent of sex discrimination, may nonetheless report sex discrimination. Because women may respond to such outcomes just as they would to true discrimination—for example, by changing employers or reducing human capital investment—we may be led to overstate the effects of discrimination. On the other hand, when wage growth is the dependent variable, there may be a bias in the opposite direction; if the negative outcome is reflected in low *current* wages, then regression to the mean may create a spurious positive correlation between reported discrimination and wage *growth*. While there is no fully satisfactory solution to the general problem of subjective assessments reflecting negative outcomes, when we look at wage growth, we can at least minimize the latter problem by defining wage growth from the first observation *following* the report of discrimination to the last available observation.

Biases from the reflection of negative outcomes in self-reports of discrimination may be exacerbated by the fact that a woman's past labor market behavior may influence the negative outcomes that are perceived as discriminatory. For example, for specifications in which $\Delta y_{it'}$ is the change in experience, consider a woman who has a job history of short spells of employment interrupted frequently by spells out of the labor market. An employer may respond by paying a lower wage, or granting fewer promotions. This may be perceived as sex discrimination by the woman, and, assuming that the intermittent employment pattern persists into the future, generate a spurious negative correlation between self-reported discrimination and future accumulation of labor market experience (i.e. spurious evidence in favor of the feedback hypothesis).

Such biases are addressed in two ways. First, period t is defined as the *first* observation at which a woman is working for a wage and a discrimination self-report is available, to minimize as much as possible the influence of past labor market behavior on employer decisions. Second, for changes in marital status and childbearing, results are contrasted for the first occurrence of an event—for which there can be no "track record" influencing employer decisions—and the general incidence of these events.[4]

Empirical results

Table 7.1 provides descriptive statistics classified by discrimination self-reports. The first two columns classify the observations by whether or not women report sex discrimination at the first labor market observation with a self-report. The last three columns classify observations by changes in self-reported discrimination from the first to the second observation. In all cases, means and standard errors are reported for the variables at the time of the first observation, in order to focus on characteristics associated with reporting discrimination; information on outcomes that might ensue from experiencing discrimination is provided in the tables that

Table 7.1 Descriptive statistics at first observation on self-report of discrimination[a]

	First self-report		First self-report/second self-report		
	No disc.	Disc.	No disc./ no disc.	No disc./ disc.	Disc./ disc.
	(1)	(2)	(3)	(4)	(5)
Log real wage	1.85	2.00	1.85	1.89	1.99
	(0.01)	(0.03)	(0.01)	(0.04)	(0.05)
Schooling	12.93	14.13	12.96	13.57	14.53
	(0.06)	(0.20)	(0.06)	(0.23)	(0.28)
Experience	4.93	5.24	4.99	4.88	5.48
	(0.07)	(0.20)	(0.07)	(0.28)	(0.32)
Tenure	2.87	2.93	2.95	2.44	3.15
	(0.07)	(0.22)	(0.07)	(0.25)	(0.36)
Age	25.91	26.79	26.10	26.00	26.86
	(0.09)	(0.25)	(0.09)	(0.33)	(0.34)
Year	1975.25	1976.50	1975.45	1975.76	1976.93
	(0.08)	(0.21)	(0.08)	(0.31)	(0.27)
Black	0.27	0.13	0.28	0.18	0.12
	(0.01)	(0.03)	(0.01)	(0.04)	(0.04)
Married, spouse present	0.60	0.47	0.60	0.55	0.49
	(0.01)	(0.04)	(0.01)	(0.05)	(0.06)
Divorced, widowed, or separated	0.13	0.17	0.13	0.14	0.07
	(0.01)	(0.03)	(0.01)	(0.04)	(0.03)
Number of children	0.99	0.63	1.04	0.76	0.38
	(0.03)	(0.07)	(0.03)	(0.10)	(0.08)
Union	0.24	0.21	0.24	0.25	0.18
	(0.01)	(0.03)	(0.01)	(0.05)	(0.05)
Urban	0.74	0.81	0.73	0.80	0.84
	(0.01)	(0.03)	(0.01)	(0.04)	(0.04)
South	0.42	0.34	0.43	0.31	0.36
	(0.01)	(0.04)	(0.01)	(0.05)	(0.06)
Sample size	1,517	156	1,296	91	73

Note

a Standard errors are reported in parentheses. In columns (3)–(5) descriptive statistics are reported for the sample with available data on all of the variables in the table. An additional eighty-three women reported discrimination in the first self-report but not the second.

follow. Columns (1) and (2) reveal quite large differences associated with reporting discrimination at the first report. The wages of those who report discrimination are 15 percent higher than those who do not, and those reporting discrimination have a schooling advantage of more than one year, and have slightly higher (although not significantly so) experience and tenure. They are also less likely to be married, and have fewer children on average. These results may indicate that higher-paying jobs are associated with more sex discrimination. An alternative interpretation, however, is that women in these jobs are more likely to report discrimination, independently of actual experiences of discrimination.

The proposed solution to this heterogeneity problem will be successful to the extent that changes in reported discrimination are exogenous with respect to unobserved characteristics. Columns (3)–(5) attempt to shed some light on the plausibility of this assumption, providing descriptive statistics based on changes in self-reports of discrimination. Along many dimensions—wages, schooling, experience, tenure, marital status, and number of children—the differences between columns (3) and (4) are considerably smaller than those between columns (1) and (2), and sometimes become statistically insignificant or change sign. Since changes in reported discrimination are considerably less strongly related to the observables than are first reports of discrimination, it seems likely that the heterogeneity bias is considerably reduced by identifying the effects of discrimination from these changes. Finally, column (5) reports means for those reporting discrimination in both periods. The fact that wages and wage-related observables are considerably higher than in either columns (3) or (4) gives further credence to the presence of heterogeneity in the propensity to report sex discrimination.

Next, estimates of the equations measuring the relationships between reported discrimination and subsequent labor market outcomes are reported in Tables 7.2–7.4. The results are presented for three categories of dependent variables: measures of labor market attachment; demographic changes; and wage growth. For each set of variables, equation (1) is first estimated with D_{it} defined as a dummy variable for self-reported discrimination in the first report (in column (1) of the tables). These estimates measure the association between self-reported discrimination at an early labor market observation and subsequent behavior. For each dependent variable, the maximum number of observations with available data is used. In each case, estimates of this association are reported first with no controls, then adding exogenous factors such as the time elapsed between observations (and sometimes age), and finally adding as additional controls variables that may themselves be influenced by reported discrimination, some of which therefore appear as dependent variables in other tables; because of potential simultaneity biases, these latter estimates must be interpreted cautiously.

Results are then reported for the equations using the changes in self-reported discrimination, for the subset of women reporting no discrimination at the first observation, again with various sets of control variables (in column (3) of the tables). One potentially confounding influence in these estimates is the sample selection criteria imposed because there have to be two observations at which women are working for a wage and provide self-reports on discrimination, as well as data on subsequent behavior. Another confounding influence is that the dependent variable now measures changes following the second self-report, rather than the first. To gauge the separate influences of the sampling rule and variable construction, on the one hand, and the heterogeneity experiment, on the other, we report an intermediate set of results (in column (2) of the tables) which parallel the first analysis in looking only at the initial report of discrimination, but for the dependent variable and subsample of women used in the heterogeneity experiment. The differences between the final results and these intermediate results isolate the influences of the heterogeneity bias. The discussion focuses on the final (column (3)) results, and only briefly touches on the other results to assess the evidence regarding heterogeneity bias.

Labor market attachment

Table 7.2 reports results from regressions for changes in experience, and logits for employer changes. The changes in experience or changes of employer are measured from the time of the discrimination report to the last available observation. Estimates of the coefficient of the dummy variable indicating reported sex discrimination are reported in the table; each entry reports the estimate from a separate regression or logit. Panel A reports results for the change in experience. The sample consists of all women working at the time of the discrimination report. The first row reports results with no controls. The estimates in column (3) are for discrimination at the second self-report, for the subsample reporting no discrimination at the first self-report. They indicate no relationship between reported discrimination and subsequent accumulation of actual labor market experience, in contrast to the feedback hypothesis. The estimates are small, never indicating a difference of more than a fraction of a year in accumulated experience, and are statistically insignificant.[5]

Panel B carries out a similar analysis, restricting the sample to women working for a wage at the last observation, and measuring the change in experience to that point. If one response to discrimination is to drop out of the labor market, then smaller responses might be expected in Panel B than in Panel A. On the other hand, discrimination may be relatively more important for women who are more attached to the labor market. Results for this subsample are also potentially important because, by focusing on women who remain at work, they speak to the question of wage differences among employed women (and employed women and men). The results in Panel B are somewhat more supportive of the feedback hypothesis. The coefficient estimates in column (3) are negative, suggesting that women who change to reporting discrimination subsequently accumulate less experience, although the effects are not statistically significant. Note that, in contrast, the estimates in columns (1) and (2) are positive, suggesting mild heterogeneity bias such that the propensity to report discrimination is positively related to subsequent accumulation of experience. However, the differences between the alternative estimates are small relative to the standard errors.

Table 7.2 Change in experience and employer regression (logit) coefficients[a]

	Full sample, changes measured from first observation on discrimination report to last available observation	Sample with two discrimination reports, changes measured from second observation on discrimination report to last	
	Coefficient: discrimination first period (1)	Coefficient: discrimination first period (2)	No discrimination at first report, coefficient: discrimination second period (3)
A. Dependent variable: change in actual experience			
No controls	0.17	-0.07	-0.22
	(0.32)	(0.20)	(0.27)
Add years between observations	-0.01	0.03	-0.03
	(0.15)	(0.13)	(0.18)
Add changes in marital status and number of children	-0.02	0.05	0.10
	(0.15)	(0.13)	(0.18)
Sample size	1,776	1,532	1,370
B. Dependent variable: change in actual experience, women working for a wage at last available observation			
No controls	0.43	0.08	-0.53
	(0.37)	(0.22)	(0.30)
Add years between observations	0.02	0.03	-0.13
	(0.15)	(0.13)	(0.17)
Add changes in marital status and number of children	-0.01	0.03	-0.07
	(0.15)	(0.13)	(0.17)
Sample size	1,437	1,239	1,113
C. Dependent variable: change of employer			
No controls	0.44	0.28	0.53
	(0.18)	(0.16)	(0.21)
	[0.10]	[0.07]	[0.13]
Add years between observations	0.47	0.28	0.55
	(0.18)	(0.16)	(0.21)
	[0.10]	[0.07]	[0.13]
Add changes in marital status and number of children	0.48	0.28	0.52
	(0.18)	(0.16)	(0.21)
	[0.10]	[0.07]	[0.13]
Sample size	2,027	1,791	1,611

Note

a Employer change equations are estimated as logits. Standard errors are reported in parentheses. For the logits, partial derivatives of the probability of an employer change with respect to the discrimination dummy variable, evaluated at sample means, are reported in square brackets. Each entry reports the coefficient estimate of the discrimination dummy variable for one regression or logit. In column (1) sample is restricted to women working for a wage at the time of the first observation on the self-reported discrimination question; in columns (2) and (3) sample is restricted to women working for a wage at the time of the first and second observations on the self-reported discrimination question.

Panel C focuses on an alternative dependent variable—whether a woman who reports sex discrimination subsequently changes employers. This analysis also restricts attention to women who are working at some later date, since only for such women can an employer change be defined.[6] The estimates ranging from 0.52 to 0.55 reported in column (3), corresponding to a partial derivative of 0.13, indicate that women who report discrimination are more likely subsequently to change employers. This result holds with and without the alternative control variables, and is statistically significant. Also, the estimates are larger than those in column (2), suggesting that there is heterogeneity bias against the feedback hypothesis in the cross-section estimates; the bias, again, is consistent with those more attached to the labor market (their current employer, in particular) having a greater propensity to report discrimination.

Demographic changes

Table 7.3 reports results for changes in marriage and childbearing. We might expect the effects of these demographic changes to be partly reflected in the results for experience and tenure reported in Table 7.2. However, the direct effects of reported discrimination on marriage and childbearing are of independent interest because marriage and childbearing are likely to be associated with greater specialization in household production, and hence may affect human capital investment, and therefore wages, independently of their effects on experience and tenure (Polachek, 1975; Becker, 1985). But in contrast to the human capital explanation, the feedback hypothesis suggests that the greater household specialization entailed by marriage and childbearing is partly a response to discrimination.

Panel A reports results for the change in the number of children following the second self-report on discrimination. The estimates in column (3) are positive and significant, regardless of the set of control variables included, indicating that women who switch to reporting discrimination subsequently have more children. Panel B instead focuses on the probability of having a first birth, for the subset of women who are childless at the time of the second self-report on discrimination. The coefficient estimates are again positive, and significant unless changes in marital status are included (in which case the estimate is still significant at the 10-percent level). The estimates excluding marital status imply that reported discrimination is associated with a 0.13 increase in the probability of a first birth. A comparison of the column (3) estimates with those in column (2) again suggests heterogeneity in the propensity to report discrimination that is positively associated with labor market attachment, this time in the form of less childbearing; only when we control for this heterogeneity do we observe significant positive effects of reported discrimination on childbearing.[7]

Panels C and D focus on marital status transitions. In Panel C, the dependent variable is whether never married women marry for the first time, while in Panel D it is whether unmarried women marry subsequently. In both cases, the estimated coefficient of the discrimination dummy variable is positive, and for the larger sample of all unmarried women it is statistically significant with or without controls.

Table 7.3 Change in number of children, first birth, and marital status regression (logit) coefficients[a]

	Full sample, changes measured from first observation on discrimination report to last available observation	Sample with two discrimination reports, changes measured from second observation on discrimination report to last available observation	
	Coefficient: discrimination first period (1)	Coefficient: discrimination first period (2)	No discrimination at first report, coefficient: discrimination second period (3)
A. Dependent variable: change in number of children			
No controls	−0.04	0.04	0.26
	(0.07)	(0.05)	(0.07)
Add years between observations and age at time of self-report	−0.01	0.02	0.23
	(0.06)	(0.05)	(0.07)
Add changes in marital status	−0.02	0.01	0.22
	(0.06)	(0.05)	(0.07)
Sample size	2,046	1,829	1,645
B. Dependent variable: first birth			
No controls	0.08	0.29	0.61
	(0.20)	(0.23)	(0.30)
	[0.02]	[0.06]	[0.13]
Add years between observations and age at time of self-report	0.18	0.38	0.61
	(0.21)	(0.24)	(0.31)
	[0.04]	[0.08]	[0.13]
Add changes in marital status	0.18	0.31	0.55
	(0.21)	(0.24)	(0.32)
	[0.04]	[0.07]	[0.11]
Sample size	893	645	547
C. Dependent variable: first marriage			
No controls	−0.10	0.20	0.81
	(0.28)	(0.33)	(0.44)
	[−0.02]	[0.04]	[0.15]
Add years between observations and age at time of self-report	0.17	0.39	0.59
	(0.29)	(0.35)	(0.46)
	[0.04]	[0.07]	[0.10]
Sample size	549	365	314
D. Dependent variable: marriage			
No controls	0.06	0.45	0.71
	(0.22)	(0.22)	(0.29)
	[0.01]	[0.10]	[0.15]
Add years between observations and age at time of self-report	0.22	0.53	0.72
	(0.23)	(0.23)	(0.30)
	[0.05]	[0.12]	[0.15]
Sample size	823	727	631

Note
a First birth and marriage equations are estimated as logits. Standard errors are reported in parentheses. See footnote to Table 7.2 for additional details.

Wage growth

Table 7.4 reports results on the relationship between self-reported discrimination and wage growth. If discrimination causes career interruptions, and career interruptions lead to lower human capital investment, then there should be a negative relationship between self-reported discrimination and subsequent wage growth. In principle, this should be strongest if account is not taken of these interruptions, since then differences in wage growth reflect both the interruptions and differences in returns to time in the labor market. In contrast, once controls for these interruptions are included in the regressions, the discrimination dummy variables should reflect only differences in returns to time in the labor market.

Panel A uses wage growth subsequent to the discrimination report as the dependent variable, where the change is measured from the first observation *following* the discrimination report, to a later date, in order to avoid a possible negative relationship between contemporaneous wages and self-reported discrimination. In contrast to what might be expected if discrimination reduces human capital investment, the estimates in column (3) indicate that women reporting sex discrimination do not subsequently have lower wage growth. The point estimates are actually positive, although insignificant. The larger positive estimates in columns (1) and (2) are consistent with women more attached to the labor force being more likely to report sex discrimination.

However, there are two reasons why the estimates in column (3) may be biased against finding lower subsequent wage growth for women who switch to reporting discrimination. First, women who report discrimination are more likely to change employers. This may entail a one-time reduction in wages as accumulated tenure is lost, but these women may then, at their new employers, invest at rates higher than other women.[8] To examine this possibility, Panel B focuses on women who do not subsequently change employers. Partially consistent with this source of bias, in column (3), where the sample is restricted to women who did not change employers, the estimated association between reported discrimination and subsequent wage growth becomes negative, although not statistically significant.

A second source of bias may be selectivity with respect to continuing to work after experiencing discrimination. In particular, among those who report discrimination, only women with particularly high wage growth may work in subsequent years. This selection may bias the coefficient estimates of the discrimination dummy variable upward. On the other hand, if women working while reporting discrimination are those earning particularly high *current* wages, estimates of the effects of reported discrimination on wage *growth* may be biased downward, owing to regression to the mean in wages.

To study this bias, the standard selection correction is used (Heckman, 1979). The present context, however, differs from the usual cross-sectional setup. First, the "employment" equation is a single equation indicating whether a woman worked for a wage in at least two periods after the discrimination report. Second, for working women the changes in union status, age, and the other control variables

Table 7.4 Wage change regression coefficients, based on first self-report of discrimination[a]

	Full sample, changes measured from first observation after first discrimination report to last available observation		Sample with two discrimination reports, changes measured from first observation after second discrimination report to last available observation			
	Coefficient: discrimination first period	λ	Coefficient: discrimination first period	λ	No discrimination at first report, coefficient: discrimination second period	λ
	(1)	(1')	(2)	(2')	(3)	(3')
A. Dependent variable: annual change in log wage						
No controls	0.012 (0.005)		0.011 (0.008)		0.006 (0.011)	
Add changes in union, urban, South, age, and schooling	0.012 (0.005)		0.011 (0.008)		0.004 (0.011)	
Add changes in experience and tenure	0.013 (0.005)		0.012 (0.008)		0.005 (0.011)	
Add changes in marital status and number of children	0.013 (0.005)		0.013 (0.008)		0.006 (0.011)	
Sample size	1,211		1,134		1,014	
B. Dependent variable: annual change in log wage, for women working at same employer						
No controls	0.001 (0.007)		0.002 (0.009)		−0.018 (0.013)	
Add changes in union, urban, South, age, and schooling	0.001 (0.007)		0.001 (0.009)		−0.017 (0.013)	
Add changes in experience and tenure	0.001 (0.007)		0.002 (0.009)		−0.017 (0.013)	
Add changes in marital status and number of children	0.001 (0.007)		0.002 (0.009)		−0.018 (0.013)	
Sample size	443		549		497	

C. Selectivity-corrected estimates[b]

Dependent variable: annual change in log wage

	(1)	(1′)	(2)	(2′)	(3)	(3′)
OLS	0.013 (0.005)	—	0.013 (0.008)	—	0.016 (0.012)	—
Selectivity corrected, probit also includes marital status and husband's income	0.007 (0.007)	-0.043 (0.033)	0.002 (0.012)	-0.064 (0.052)	0.011 (0.014)	-0.052 (0.052)
Selectivity corrected, number of children, urban, South, schooling, and age added to probit	0.007 (0.006)	-0.050 (0.022)	0.004 (0.010)	-0.052 (0.024)	0.011 (0.013)	-0.056 (0.025)
Selectivity corrected, second discrimination self-report added to probit	—	—	0.003 (0.010)	-0.058 (0.024)	—	—
Selectivity corrected, experience added to probit	0.007 (0.006)	-0.051 (0.019)	0.006 (0.010)	-0.043 (0.022)	0.012 (0.013)	-0.041 (0.023)
Sample size for wage regression	1,174		1,054		940	
Sample size for probit	1,597		1,690		1,534	

Notes

a Standard errors are reported in parentheses. Each entry reports the coefficient estimate of the self-reported discrimination dummy variable for one regression. In column (1) sample is restricted to women working for a wage at the time of the first discrimination question; in columns (2) and (3) sample is restricted to women working for a wage at the time of the first and second observations on the self-reported discrimination question. In Panels A and B the sample is further restricted to women working for a wage for at least two observations after the first (column (1)) or second (columns (2) and (3)) discrimination self-reports.

b The wage equation control variables (changes) used in Panels A and B are omitted in this panel, because the changes cannot be defined over comparable periods for women for whom there are not two observations working for a wage after the discrimination self-report. The two-stage selection correction was used. Variables included in the employment probit are defined as of the first discrimination self-report in all three columns (with the exception of the dummy for self-reported discrimination in column (2)). All probits also include the discrimination self-report dummy variable that is included in the wage regression. Sample sizes for the wage regression are smaller than in Panel A because of missing data on the variables included in the probits. In columns (3) and (3′), both the employed and nonemployed samples are conditioned on not reporting discrimination at the first self-report.

are defined over an interval covering observations at which women are employed. For nonworking women, however, there is no comparable way to define such an interval. We therefore specify a simpler model, in which the wage equation includes only the dummy variable for the discrimination self-report, and the employment equation includes this same dummy variable, as well as other controls defined at the time of the discrimination self-report. Thus, the wage change equation is

$$(w_{it''} - w_{it'}) = \alpha + D_{it}\delta + \varepsilon_{it'}, \tag{2}$$

where w_{it} is the log wage. The wage change $(w_{it''} - w_{it'})$ is observed if $P_{it'}^*$, a latent variable describing the propensity to be employed after the discrimination report, satisfies

$$P_{it'}^* > \gamma + Z_{it}\pi + \eta_{it'}, \tag{3}$$

where Z_{it} is a vector of control variables defined at the time of the discrimination self-report, including D_{it}. ε and η are assumed to have a bivariate normal distribution.

Columns (3) and (3') of Panel C first report OLS estimates for the smaller samples with nonmissing data on the variables included in Z. The estimated coefficient of the discrimination variable is 0.016, slightly higher than in Panel A, but still insignificant. The second row of Panel C reports selectivity-corrected estimates using only the discrimination dummy variable, marital status, and husband's income in the employment probit. As expected, the estimated coefficient of the discrimination dummy variable falls. However, the estimates clearly do not become negative, as would be predicted by the feedback hypothesis. The results are very similar in the next row of the table, which adds urban, South, schooling, number of children, and age to the employment probit.

We might also be interested in whether later discrimination induces women to leave the labor market. In column (2), we can introduce a dummy variable for the second discrimination report into the employment probit to capture this effect. (We cannot do this for the first column, because women in that sample need not be working at the time of the second discrimination report. We also cannot do this for the third column, since we are already using the second discrimination report.) As the table shows, this has virtually no effect on the estimates.

Finally, in the last row of the table, labor market experience at the time of the discrimination report is added to the employment probit, although this is undoubtedly correlated with η. The inclusion of experience also has little effect on the estimates. Thus, the selectivity-corrected wage growth equation estimates provide no more support for the feedback hypothesis than do the OLS estimates.[9]

The nature of self-reported sex discrimination

Kuhn's (1987) findings that women who report sex discrimination earn relatively high wages (net of observables), and the findings in the previous section suggesting that, in general, women more attached to the labor force are more likely to report discrimination, raise the question of what is indicated by a self-report of discrimination. In this section, we turn to information from the 1988 wave of the NLS on the type of sex discrimination reported, to attempt to shed some light on this issue.

One possibility is that women may be reporting discrimination unrelated to wages, such as sexual harassment, lower benefits, or failure to get desirable assignments or promotions, that are somewhat independent of wages.[10] The first row of Panel A of Table 7.5 reports the proportion of women reporting each type of discrimination in that year. The figures are consistent with considerable nonwage discrimination, revealing that nearly three-fourths of those reporting sex discrimination report that it is unrelated to pay. Panel A also reports the proportions indicating each type of discrimination unrelated to pay.[11]

Second, other factors associated with higher wages (or wage growth) may also be associated with greater perceived discrimination, which would lead to an upward-biased estimate of the relationship between wage growth and reported discrimination. For example, women who work alongside males may perceive or experience more discrimination, but also earn higher wages than otherwise similar women. Panel A also reports the mean percent female in women's three-digit occupations. The figures suggest that women reporting discrimination, especially discrimination unrelated to pay, are more likely to be in occupations with a lower percent female. Panel B of Table 7.5 carries this analysis further, reporting logit estimates for reported discrimination as a function of the percent female in the occupation, controlling for other individual characteristics (listed in the footnote to the table). The estimates show that the probability of reporting discrimination related to pay is not significantly related to the percent female, but that the probability of reporting discrimination unrelated to pay is significantly higher in occupations with a low percent female.[12]

If a lower percent female is also associated with higher wages (among women), then the negative relationship between the percent female and reported discrimination may help to "explain" why women who report discrimination earn higher wages relative to otherwise similar women. We investigate this issue in Panel C. As a preliminary, column (1) reports estimated coefficients of dummy variables for pay and other discrimination, from a standard log wage equation. Paralleling Kuhn's findings, reported discrimination (pay-related or not) is associated with about 12–15 percent higher wages. In column (2), we add the percent female to the equation. Paralleling other findings in the literature (e.g. Sorenson, 1987) the estimated coefficient of this variable is significant and negative, indicating that a 10-percent increase in the percent female is associated with a 2 percent reduction in wages. As expected, the estimated coefficients of the discrimination dummy variables decline. However, the decline is small, and a strong positive association between wages and reported sex discrimination persists. This remains true if we use a set of dummy variables corresponding to different ranges of the percent female.

Finally, columns (3) and (4) of Panel C report estimates of the same wage equations correcting for selectivity into employment. Because women who experience

Table 7.5 Evidence from 1988 self-reports of discrimination[a]

A. Descriptive statistics

	No disc. (1)	Pay disc. (2)	Non-pay disc. (3)
Proportion reporting	88.2	3.3	8.5
Percent female, 3-digit occupation	69.9	62.1	53.7

Types of non-pay discrimination

	Not hired/interviewed (1)	Not promoted (2)	Job performance (3)	Co-workers (4)	Supervisor (5)	Demoted/laid off (6)	Company disc. (7)	General disc. (8)	Other (9)
Proportion reporting	0.2	3.1	0.5	0.7	0.7	0.2	0.2	0.4	2.4
Percent female, 3-digit occupation	45.2	52.4	57.1	62.7	51.1	19.4	73.6	41.5	56.3

B. Logits for reported discrimination

Dependent variables

	Any disc. (1)	Pay disc. (2)	Other disc. (3)
Percent female	−1.76	−0.73	−1.97
(std. error)	(0.30)	(0.57)	(0.34)
[partial derivative]	[−0.16]	[−0.02]	[−0.14]

C. Log wage regressions

Log wage

	(1)	(2)	(3)	(4)
Reported pay disc.	0.121	0.109	0.128	0.116
	(0.062)	(0.061)	(0.075)	(0.076)
Reported other disc.	0.153	0.123	0.154	0.124
	(0.040)	(0.040)	(0.040)	(0.041)
Percent female	—	−0.195	—	−0.190
		(0.043)		(0.048)
Estimation	OLS	OLS	SSC	SSC

Note
a The sample in Panel A is restricted to 721 women working for a wage in 1988, for whom data on the variables used in Panels B and C are also available. Percent female in the occupation was based on percentages female in three-digit occupations in the outgoing rotation group file of the 1987 CPS. In Panel B, the other controls include years of schooling, age, experience, number of children ever born, and dummy variables for South, SMSA, and marital status. Partial derivatives are reported in square brackets. In Panel C standard errors are reported in parentheses. In Panel B are included as controls. For the SSC estimates, additional variables included in the employment probit are husband's income, child support, and alimony. The sample of women not employed in 1988 is restricted to those with some work experience between 1983 and 1988, the period referred to by the discrimination self-report. In addition to the 721 women included in the wage equation, there were 153 nonemployed women used to estimate the employment probit.

discrimination and nonetheless remain employed may be particularly high earners (net of observables), selectivity may create a spurious positive association between wages and reported discrimination. The estimates in columns (3) and (4) indicate, however, that correcting for selectivity bias (as best we can) has little effect on the estimates. As in columns (1) and (2), the estimated coefficient of the "other discrimination" dummy variable declines slightly when the percent female is added. But the positive association between wages and reported discrimination persists.

We think the evidence that many women report discrimination unrelated to pay, and that reported discrimination is higher for women working alongside more men, bolsters the validity of the self-reports of discrimination, despite Kuhn's findings. But we are still left with the puzzle of why higher-wage women have a greater tendency to report discrimination. Whether this reflects heterogeneity in the propensity to report discrimination, unmeasured dimensions of true discrimination, or misperceptions of discrimination, remains an open question.

Differences by race and sex

To this point, we have focused on the estimated impacts of reported sex discrimination on women. To further assess the validity of data on self-reported discrimination, and to examine whether the discrimination indicated by the self-reports is likely to generate sex differences in labor market outcomes, in this section we consider additional evidence on women's responses to sex, race, and other discrimination, and we contrast men's and women's responses to reported discrimination. We focus on the effect of reported discrimination on leaving one's employer, because this outcome was strongly linked to reported discrimination for women, and ought to exhibit a similar response for men (in contrast to marriage or childbearing). For women, we utilize the information on discrimination described earlier, but now also consider self-reported discrimination along the lines of race and other dimensions. For men, we utilize 1971 and 1976 data on self-reported discrimination in the National Longitudinal Survey of Young Men (the only years for which such data are available).

Panel A of Table 7.6 reports estimates of the same employer change logit specifications as in Table 7.2, Panel C, column (3), which condition on reporting no discrimination at the time of the first self-report. Column (1) repeats the estimates from Table 7.2. Column (2) reports estimates of the impact of reported sex discrimination for non-black women only. The estimated effects are very similar to those in column (1). Column (3) instead restricts attention to the effects of reported sex discrimination for black women. The estimated effects are very similar to those for non-black women, although the standard errors are more than twice as large, so the effects are not statistically significant. Finally, column (4) continues to look at black women only, but considers the effects of any reported discrimination. As the table shows, most of the discrimination that identifies the effects in this column is race discrimination; more than half of those switching to reporting discrimination indicate race discrimination. The estimated effects of reported discrimination on employer changes are similar to those in column (3), for sex discrimination only,

Table 7.6 Change in employer logit coefficients for black women vs. all women, and men vs. women[a]

	(1)	(2)	(3)	(4)
A. Non-black vs. black women, all years				
	All women, sex discrimination	Non-black women, sex discrimination	Black women, sex discrimination	Black women, any discrimination
Dependent variable: proportion changing employer				
No controls	0.53	0.54	0.41	0.46
	(0.21)	(0.24)	(0.46)	(0.29)
	[0.13]	[0.13]	[0.10]	[0.11]
Add years between	0.55	0.54	0.52	0.45
observations	(0.21)	(0.24)	(0.47)	(0.29)
	[0.13]	[0.13]	[0.13]	[0.11]
Add changes in marital	0.52	0.52	0.47	0.43
status and number	(0.21)	(0.24)	(0.47)	(0.29)
of children	[0.13]	[0.12]	[0.12]	[0.11]
Sample size	1,611	1,175	436	407
Number changing to reporting:[b]				
Sex discrimination	109	88	21	19
Race discrimination	67	17	50	39
Age discrimination	11	8	3	1
Other discrimination	66	48	18	13

B. Men vs. women, 1971 and 1976 (men), 1972 and 1978 (women)			
	All women, sex discrimination	All men, any discrimination	Black men, any discrimination
Dependent variable: proportion changing employer			
No controls	0.72	0.02	0.45
	(0.39)	(0.15)	(0.29)
	[0.18]	[0.004]	[0.11]
Add years between	0.74	0.01	0.45
observations	(0.39)	(0.15)	(0.29)
	[0.18]	[0.004]	[0.11]
Sample size	584	1,612	373
Number changing to reporting:			
Sex discrimination	33	1	0
Race discrimination	15	95	46
Age discrimination	3	27	3
Other discrimination	20	93	9

Notes

a Coefficient estimates are reported by race, sex, and type of discrimination for the same specifications as in Table 7.2, Panel C, column (3). In Panel B, the discrimination reports come only from the years 1972 and 1978 for women, and 1971 and 1976 for men. See footnote to Table 7.2 for additional details.

b This is the number as of the second observation on the discrimination self-report. The samples exclude those reporting discrimination as of the first report. Individuals may report more than one type of discrimination, although we have redefined "other discrimination" to equal one only when no other type of discrimination is specified.

but now the estimates are more precise and marginally significant. These estimates suggest that, for women, reported sex discrimination has effects similar to reported race discrimination.

The second panel of Table 7.6 turns to sex differences in the estimated effects of reported discrimination. We restrict attention to the 1972 and 1978 discrimination self-reports for women, to correspond as closely as possible to the years for which similar data are available for men. Column (1) reports estimates of the same specification in column (1) of Panel A, but for the subsample of women whose discrimination reports come from these two years. The estimated effects are similar to those using all years, although the estimates are significant only at the 10-percent level. Column (2) reports results for men (switching to) reporting any discrimination. The estimated effects are essentially zero. Only one man reports sex discrimination, but many report other types of discrimination. Thus, these results suggest that discrimination, at least as it is perceived by men and women, increases turnover among women but not among men. On the other hand, as column (3) shows, when we restrict attention to black men only, for whom we identify the effects of discrimination mainly from self-reports of race discrimination, we obtain results similar to those for women, and nearly identical to those for black women in Panel A. Overall, the results in this section provide evidence of consistent effects of reported sex and race discrimination, and also provide evidence that sex discrimination generates sex differences in turnover.

Conclusions

This chapter provides some evidence that sex discrimination in labor markets plays a role in labor market outcomes for women that may be related to lower wages. There is a statistically significant effect of reported discrimination on the probability that women change employers. In addition, women who report sex discrimination at work are significantly more likely subsequently to have children and to marry.

However, there is not direct, statistically significant evidence for those implications of the feedback hypothesis that most sharply challenge the human capital model. While working women who report discrimination subsequently accumulate somewhat less labor market experience than otherwise similar women, this effect is small and is not statistically significant. In addition, the relationship between self-reported discrimination and subsequent wage growth is only negative for the subsample of women who remain with the same employer, and even then is not statistically significant. It remains an open question whether there are other biases, for which the procedures used in the chapter fail to correct, which obscure evidence in favor of the feedback hypothesis.

There also may be coherent explanations of feedback effects such that discrimination leads to labor market interruptions, but not to lower returns to time in the labor market. First, there may be a statistical inference problem on the part of employers. They may know that women, on average, are more likely to experience discrimination, and hence are more prone to career interruptions than men, but cannot discern which women are more likely to experience interruptions; hence, they shy away from specific human capital investments in all women. This could lead to lower wage growth for women generally, but no differences in wage growth among women based on the experience of discrimination. At the same time, the general statistical discrimination problem of discerning which women are likely to stay in the labor force may help to explain why women who are more committed to the labor force appear to be more likely to report sex discrimination.

An alternative explanation is that women hold similar *ex ante* probabilities of experiencing sex discrimination and the ensuing labor market interruptions. Since human capital investments are largely based on expected interruptions, if women hold similar expectations regarding discrimination and interruptions there may be small differences, *ex post*, in the human capital investment of those women who do and do not experience discrimination. In this case, cross-section variation in the experience of discrimination may not identify the effects of discrimination. At the same time, we would expect those who experience discrimination to respond by, for example, changing employers.

If either of these explanations is correct, then evidence that reported sex discrimination leads to outcomes related to lower wages suggests that sex discrimination may also be part of the reason for women's lower wages compared with men, even if reported sex discrimination explains little of the variation in wages among women.

Acknowledgments

Fran Blau, Hank Farber, Andrew Foster, Mark Killingsworth, Tom Kneisner, an anonymous referee, and participants in the NBER Labor Studies Program provided helpful comments.

Notes

1 Given that workers in his sample have an average age of 36, and are therefore largely past the overtaking age, the human capital model predicts that future separations associated with lower investment should be negatively related to wages.
2 We study employer changes rather than changes in tenure. Changes in tenure generate asymmetric distributions because tenure can only increase by the number of years elapsed between surveys, whereas it can decrease by the whole amount of accumulated tenure.
3 A parallel approach is to use all women, specifying an equation including dummy variables for all possible combinations of reported discrimination on the first and second self-reports. We verified that for all of the specifications estimated in this chapter, the estimated effects of changing from initially reporting no discrimination to reporting discrimination were nearly identical using this approach. (We did not test whether there is a symmetric but opposite-signed effect of switching *from* reporting discrimination, since the initial experience of discrimination may affect subsequent behavior.)
4 An alternative approach would be to study "changes in changes," estimating the equation

$$\Delta y_{it'} - \Delta y_{is} = (\Delta x_{it'} - \Delta x_{is})\beta + D_{it}\delta + \varepsilon_{it'},$$

where Δy_{is} and Δx_{is} are changes *prior to* the self-report of discrimination. In this equation, δ measures the relationship between reported discrimination and the *change in*, for example, the rate of accumulation of labor market experience. However, this approach precludes focusing on the earliest available self-report on discrimination. Also, if past labor market outcomes influence self-reported discrimination, D_{it} may be endogenously related to Δy_{is}. Finally, it demands considerably more data, requiring two observations on labor market behavior both before and after the discrimination self-report.

5 Most of the equations are estimated for all women. The inclusion of a race dummy variable has virtually no effect on any of the estimates. Also, estimates computed for the subsample of non-black women are very similar to those reported in the tables. Estimates for black women are qualitatively similar, although because of smaller sample sizes, they are less precise; Table 7.6 (p. 180) provides some limited results.

6 The sample is larger than in Panels A and B because the construction of the experience measure used in those panels requires job history and employment data that are frequently missing for some year(s), while the construction of the tenure variable is less demanding.

7 It is possible that pregnant women experience (or perceive) sex discrimination related to their pregnancy, and that the estimated effects of reported discrimination on childbearing in Table 7.3 reflect this, rather than effects of discrimination on subsequent childbearing. To examine this possibility, the models in Table 7.3 were re-estimated defining changes in number of children (or incidence of a first birth) beginning one year (or one survey) after the second discrimination report, to exclude births by women who may have been pregnant at the time of the report. The effects are qualitatively similar, although the estimates are less precise because some observations are lost by requiring data for the survey year following the second report. For the estimates corresponding to Panel A, for the change in the number of children, the estimates corresponding to column (3) are around 0.25, and remain statistically significant. For the estimates corresponding to Panel B, for first births, the column (3) estimates remain positive, although their statistical significance declines somewhat.

8 The regressions control for the change in tenure, but not the level.

9 Even in column (3) the estimates of equations (2) and (3) are somewhat anomalous, as the negative estimate of the coefficient of λ implies that the covariance between ε and η is negative, and the estimated effects of reported discrimination on employment (not shown in the table) are positive although insignificant. These anomalies may be attributable to the limited wage equation specification that we are forced to use.

10 Currie (1993) reports that the "gender gap" in the incidence of health insurance and pension benefits is not higher for higher-wage women, but does not present evidence on the value of these benefits.

11 As discussed in the section "The data", there is also information on type of discrimination in the 1972 wave of the NLS, although the possible responses do not include pay discrimination. We re-estimated the specifications in column (1) of Tables 7.2–7.4, distinguishing by type of discrimination reported, using the 1972 data. (With only one report including information on the type of discrimination, only the column (1) specifications can be estimated.) We were unable to detect consistently different effects of different types of reported discrimination, although this may be partly because the cell sizes were very small.

12 As in Kuhn (1987), we find that education is significantly positively related to reporting discrimination.

References

Becker, Gary S. 1985. "Human Capital, Effort, and the Sexual Division of Labor." *Journal of Labor Economics* 3(Supplement, 1): S33–58.

Blau, Francine D. and Marianne A. Ferber. 1991. "Career Plans and Expectations of Young Men and Women." *The Journal of Human Resources* 26(4): 581–607.

184   *Testing for discrimination*

———. 1992. *The Economics of Women, Men and Work.* Englewood Cliffs: Prentice-Hall.

Corcoran, Mary E. 1979. "Work Experience, Labor Force Withdrawals, and Women's Wages: Empirical Results Using the 1976 Panel of Income Dynamics." In *Women in the Labor Market*, eds C. B. Lloyd, E. Andrews and C. Gilroy, pp. 216–45. New York: Columbia University Press.

Currie, Janet. 1993. "Gender Gaps in Benefit Coverage." NBER Working Paper No. 4265.

Gronau, Reuben. 1988. "Sex-related Wage Differentials and Women's Interrupted Labor Careers—the Chicken or the Egg." *Journal of Labor Economics* 6(3): 277–301.

Heckman, James J. 1979. "Sample Selection Bias as a Specification Error." *Econometrica* 47(1): 153–61.

Korenman, Sanders and David Neumark. 1991. "Does Marriage Really Make Men More Productive?" *The Journal of Human Resources* 26(2): 282–307.

———. 1992. "Marriage, Motherhood, and Wages." *The Journal of Human Resources* 27(2): 233–55.

Kuhn, Peter J. 1987. "Sex Discrimination in Labor Markets: The Role of Statistical Evidence." *The American Economic Review* 77(4): 567–83.

———. 1990. "Sex Discrimination in Labor Markets: The Role of Statistical Evidence: Reply." *The American Economic Review* 80(1): 290–97.

Mincer, Jacob. 1962. "Labor Force Participation of Married Women." In *Aspects of Labor Economics*, ed. H. G. Lewis, pp. 63–73. Princeton: Princeton University Press.

Mincer, Jacob and Solomon Polachek. 1974. "Family Investments in Human Capital: Earnings of Women." *Journal of Political Economy* 82(Part II, 2): S76–108.

O'Neill, June. 1985. "The Trend in the Male–Female Wage Gap in the United States." *Journal of Labor Economics* 3(Part II, 1): S91–116.

Polachek, Solomon. 1975. "Potential Biases in Measuring Male–Female Wage Discrimination." *The Journal of Human Resources* 10(2): 205–29.

Sandell, Steven H. and David Shapiro. 1978. "An Exchange: The Theory of Human Capital and the Earnings of Women." *The Journal of Human Resources* 13(1): 103–17.

———. 1980. "Work Expectations, Human Capital Accumulation, and the Wages of Young Women." *The Journal of Human Resources* 15(3): 335–53.

Sorenson, Elaine. 1987. "Effect of Comparable Worth Policies on Earnings." *Industrial Relations* 26(3): 227–39.

8 Sex discrimination in restaurant hiring

An audit study

Introduction

The overall sex gap in wages can be broken into an across-occupation and a within-occupation component. The sex gap related to across-occupation segregation has alternatively been attributed to human capital investment (Polachek, 1981), preferences (Daymont and Andrisani, 1984), and employment discrimination (Beller, 1982; Bergmann, 1974). The sex gap that remains within occupations may reflect pure pay discrimination between men and women working alongside one another. It may also reflect segregation across high- and low-wage firms (Blau, 1977; Groshen, 1991), or segregation across jobs within occupations and perhaps also within firms (Seiling, 1984). This "vertical" segregation may arise for any of the reasons used to explain segregation across occupations.

In this chapter we investigate the role of discrimination in vertical segregation among waiters and waitresses. There is a sizable sex gap in wages even in this narrow occupation. In the 1993 outgoing rotation group files of the Current Population Survey (CPS), the ratio of mean weekly earnings of waitresses to mean weekly earnings of waiters is 0.71, and the ratio of median weekly earnings is 0.75. Restricting attention to full-time workers, the corresponding ratios are 0.75 and 0.73. Finally, in a log weekly earnings regression estimated for full-time waitpersons, including the usual controls, the estimated coefficient of the dummy variable for waitresses is −0.18 (standard error 0.04).[1]

Along what dimensions might vertical segregation among waiters and waitresses contribute to this earnings gap? Although there is no existing hard evidence on this point, researchers of sex differences in labor markets have suggested that males are favored in high-price, formal restaurants, where wages and tips are higher.[2] In *Pink Collar Workers* Howe (1977) writes that in "the heart of Manhattan's most expensive restaurant district, there were only a relative handful of 'tablecloth restaurants' that hired women for anything but hat-checking. At the same time further uptown and downtown, farther west and east, throughout the other boroughs . . . the overwhelming majority of those serving food were women" (p. 104). Howe also cites the 1972–3 US Department of Labor *Occupational Outlook Handbook* noting that "Jobs for waiters tended to be concentrated in those restaurants, hotel dining rooms, private clubs, and other establishments where meal service was formal," and she claims that wages and tips are highest in precisely those jobs in which waiters are concentrated (p. 104). Similarly, Bergmann (1986) claims that friction between waitresses and other male employees in restaurants leads to the segregation of waiters into high-price restaurants, and waitresses into low-price restaurants. She writes that, "In American restaurants that offer fine food and/or a luxurious setting, the size of the check allows for tips big enough to attract male waiters. In cheaper restaurants, the owners put up with the friction rather than supplement the tips to an extent necessary to be able to have male waiters" (p. 99n). Furthermore, Bergmann claims that "Many of the restaurants that employ . . . male waiters have never hired a waitress" (p. 124), and if they do, they have "assigned them to different parts of the restaurant or different shifts, with the males getting the assignments in which the tips are higher" (p. 124n).[3]

To investigate the potential role of sex discrimination in vertical segregation among waiters and waitresses, we conducted a small-scale "audit study" patterned on studies of race discrimination in hiring pioneered by researchers at the Urban Institute (Cross *et al.*, 1990; Turner, *et al.*, 1991; Kenney and Wissoker, 1994). Specifically, as part of a research project in an undergraduate economics research seminar, we sent two male and two female college students to apply for jobs as waiters and waitresses at sixty-five restaurants in Philadelphia. We divided the restaurants into high-, medium-, and low-price categories, with the goal of estimating sex differences in the receipt of job offers in each price category. We designed the study so that a male and female pair applied for a job at each restaurant, and so that, on paper at least, the male and female candidates were on average identical.

The purpose of an audit study is to provide much more direct evidence on discrimination than is provided by other empirical methods. For example, inferences regarding sex discrimination in hiring are sometimes drawn from an estimated sex difference in employment rates controlling for the sex composition and other observed characteristics of the applicant pool. Such estimates (which are common in hiring discrimination lawsuits) may lead to incorrect conclusions if there are differences between men and women that are unobserved by the econometrician.[4] Incorrect conclusions may also be reached if the rates at which men and women apply for jobs differ.[5] The audit methodology offers a potentially powerful means of overcoming both of these problems. Unobservable differences between men and women are eliminated, at least in principle, by matching their characteristics, and differences in application rates are eliminated because outcomes for a male and female applicant to the same employer are compared. Nonetheless, audit studies are not without their potential pitfalls, which we discuss in later sections.

Our findings provide strong evidence of discrimination against women in high-price restaurants, and weaker evidence of discrimination in women's favor in low-price restaurants. Of the 13 job offers from high-price restaurants, 11 were made to men. In contrast, of the 10 job offers from low-price restaurants, 8 were made to women. In addition, information gathered from restaurants included in the study suggests that earnings are substantially higher in high-price restaurants, so that the apparent hiring discrimination we find has implications for sex differences in earnings among waitpersons. The following sections describe the study fully, and provide a statistical analysis of the data we collected.

The Urban Institute audit studies, which focused on discrimination against black and Hispanic men, also tended to find evidence of hiring discrimination, although not as pronounced as the evidence in this chapter. For example, Kenney and Wissoker (1994) report that in 22 percent of their cases only Anglos received job offers, while in 8 percent of cases only Hispanics received offers. Turner *et al.* (1991), report that in 15 percent of cases only white applicants received offers, whereas in 5 percent of cases only black applicants received offers. The comparable summary figures for this study indicate that, in high-price restaurants, 43 percent of cases resulted in only males receiving offers, vs. 4 percent of cases in which only females received offers. The greater disparity in this study may reflect more pronounced discrimination against women than against minorities, or unique features of the particular labor market studied.

Among the possible sources of the discrimination that we find are employer discrimination and customer discrimination.[6] According to the EEOC's interpretation of Title VII of the Civil Rights Act of 1964, both types of discrimination are illegal. Title VII permits employers to hire based on sex only when it is a "bona fide occupational qualification reasonably necessary to the normal operation of that particular business or enterprise." The EEOC interprets the bona fide exception very narrowly; Section 1604.2 of the Code of Federal Regulations specifies that the exception does not apply to "The refusal to hire an individual because of the preferences of coworkers, the employer, clients or customers" unless it is "necessary for the purpose of authenticity or genuineness . . . e.g., an actor or actress." Epstein argues that the EEOC and the courts "look with considerable hostility on any explicit sex classification, save perhaps those that are based on the need to accommodate the personal privacy of clients and customers in certain intimate situations involving bodily functions, hygiene, and the like" (1992, p. 288).

Although uncovering the source of discrimination is generally not the purpose of an audit study, it is nonetheless of interest to attempt to identify the primary source of hiring discrimination against women in high-price restaurants. We therefore also present some additional evidence showing that the proportion male among the waitstaff is significantly positively related to the proportion male among the clientele, both overall and (more so) within the high- and medium-price restaurant categories. At the same time, the proportion male among the waitstaff is not positively related to whether hiring decisions are made by male owners and managers. While not definitive, this evidence is inconsistent with a preference on the part of male owners and managers for male employees. On the other hand, it is consistent with preferences of male customers for the types of restaurants that tend to hire male waitpersons.

The study

We are interested in whether a job applicant's sex affects the likelihood of receiving either a job interview or a job offer. Formally, denote the unobserved probability of either of these outcomes as P^*. The relationship we estimate is

$$P_{ij}^* = \alpha + \beta F_{ij} + \varepsilon_{ij}, \tag{1}$$

where i refers to the individual, j refers to the restaurant, and equation (1) is estimated separately for each price category of restaurant. We can estimate β a number of ways, including estimating equation (1) as a probit model or a linear probability model. In the latter case, **b**, the estimate of β, measures the amount by which the probability that a female receives an interview or offer differs from the probability for a male. Also, so long as no other variables affect the outcome in equation (1), β can be estimated, and the statistical significance of **b** can be obtained, from a simple comparison of the difference between the proportions of women and men receiving a job interview or offer. This is the "paired difference-of-means" test.[7]

If we simply drew observations from real-world job applicants and outcomes, there is a variety of reasons—such as differences in human capital investment, past work experience, etc.—to expect F to be correlated with ε. If it is, then **b** is a biased estimator of the sex difference in outcomes for workers identical in every respect except sex, a difference that would be interpreted as discrimination. The estimate of β would still be more informative than simply comparing the numbers of men and women who receive job offers because, by taking account of who applied for jobs, it would control for differences in job application rates of men and women.

However, the audit study methodology seeks to go considerably farther, and remove sources of correlation between sex and other determinants of the job application outcome (i.e. between F and ε). The principle underlying the methodology in our particular context was to try to get as close as possible to the following experiment: send pairs of men and women, who are identical in every respect except their sex, to apply for jobs at restaurants in different price categories, and observe whether there are any statistically significant differences between the sexes in the receipt of job offers. In this ideal experiment, by matching characteristics of men and women, we remove any correlation between F and ε. By observing differences between male and female applicants to the same restaurant, we eliminate the influence of different application rates (as well as any restaurant-specific effects). If we can approach this experimental ideal, then **b** provides an estimate of discrimination. We took numerous steps to get as close to this ideal experiment as possible.

The first step was to make the male and female applicants (or "testers") identical on paper. To do this, we created a set of three resumes that were quite similar in terms of personal history and past work experience. Although the resumes were designed to be similar, to avoid sex differences in outcomes that might be attributable to differences in the impressions potential employers gained from the resumes, the resumes were rotated among the job applicants over the course of the study. Specifically, over the three-week period during which the resumes were dropped off at restaurants, each of the two men and two women used each resume for one week.[8]

Each resume indicated that the applicant had some experience in both local restaurants and national chains. To boost the likelihood of job offers from restaurants in the high-price category, where we suspected offers might be harder to obtain, each resume was designed to convey the type of experience and knowledge that might make an applicant attractive to such restaurants. Thus, two of the resumes indicated some involvement in restaurant-related activities (such as wine tasting), while the third emphasized the high quality and range of the applicant's previous experience. In addition to restaurant and restaurant-related experience, each resume also indicated some general retail experience, a high-school education, some involvement in social action, and personal interests that were not strongly sex-typed (since men and women had to use the resumes). Finally, in order to minimize employers checking references, possibly through personal contacts with other restaurant owners in Philadelphia, each resume indicated that the candidate had come from another city, and acquired their work experience in that city.[9] The three resumes are reproduced in the Appendix.

The second step was to minimize the effects of differences in personality or appearance that might affect job offers, and that might be related to sex. Three elements of the research design address this concern. First, two men and two women were used to search for jobs, rather than just one of each sex.[10] This should help to reduce the effect of personality characteristics that are unique to any individual tester. Of course, to the extent that there are personality differences that differ systematically by sex, and that are valued differently by restaurant owners, even an infinitely large sample of testers will not help.[11] All that the researcher can do in this case is to attempt to eliminate sex-related personality differences that might influence employers' decisions. Even if we eliminate observed personality differences, employers might nonetheless prefer to hire one sex or the other because of stereotypical views of personality differences between the sexes. However, under EEOC guidelines, hiring based on such preferences would be illegal. The same regulations cited in the Introduction explicitly bar "The refusal to hire an individual based on stereotyped characterizations of the sexes." Thus, as long as we have eliminated observed personality differences, a finding indicating preferences for hiring men points to discrimination as defined by the law.

As a second means of attempting to eliminate the influence of differences in personality, or of experimenter effects, the testers were instructed to maintain an even demeanor throughout all contacts with the restaurants, and to dress similarly. However, because these data were collected as part of a research seminar, the testers did not receive the type of professional training used in the well-funded Urban Institute studies (Cross *et al.*, 1990; Turner *et al.*, 1991), nor were the testers ignorant of the questions raised in the study (as in Ayres and Siegelman, 1995). Because of these limitations, the case for assuming that any influence of personality or of experimenter effects was eliminated is weaker than in these other studies. However, it is important to emphasize that there is probably no foolproof method of avoiding these types of effects.

Because of these limitations on the training of testers and the number of testers, we employed a second means of minimizing (and perhaps eliminating) effects of differences in personality and appearance, as well as experimenter effects. While hiring decisions were based on interviews in which personality and appearance can play a role, we endeavored to get employers to make a decision regarding whether or not to interview an applicant based solely on the information in the resumes. In particular, when the job applicants stopped into restaurants, the strategy they followed was to give their resume to the first employee they encountered. This was frequently a host, or a waitperson or busperson setting up, since we tried to have applicants stop into restaurants during times when business was slow, such as the late morning. The applicant requested that this employee give the resume to the owner or manager, with instructions to call if there was any possibility of being interviewed for the job. Because interviews are therefore based almost solely on the information from the resumes, a comparison of results for receipt of interviews and job offers can be used to gauge the role of differences in personality or appearance. If there are no differences in outcomes by sex for interviews, but there are for job offers, then it is possible that personality or appearance differences affect the outcomes. However, sex differences in outcomes at the interview stage cannot be attributed to personality or appearance differences.[12]

Because we were interested in differential treatment of men and women in restaurants in different price categories, we used *Zagat's Philadelphia Restaurant Guide* to identify three price categories: high-price (average meal price over $30); medium-price ($15–$30); and low-price (less than $15).[13] We did not restrict attention to restaurants advertising for positions, since some initial "trial runs" of our job application procedure revealed that restaurants hired on a fairly continual basis, generally without advertising. We avoided strictly ethnic restaurants since we suspected they might prefer to hire members of the same ethnic group, although this, of course, might be regarded as discriminatory.

Over a three-week period in the spring of 1994, pairs of male and female job applicants dropped off resumes at sixty-five restaurants (just over twenty per week). In each week, applications were made to restaurants in all three price categories. The pairings of males and females and the order in which the resumes were dropped off (male or female first) were alternated from restaurant to restaurant, to attempt to avoid any systematic biases in the estimated outcomes by sex. Of the 130 job applications, as of approximately one month after we completed dropping off the resumes, 54 resulted in job interviews, and 39 of those interviews resulted in job offers. (No job offers were made without interviews.)

Given the data we collected, we first estimate β for each price category of restaurant, and test for statistical evidence of discrimination, using the paired difference-in-means test that allows for correlated outcomes at the same restaurant. This test statistic is

$$\frac{[\overline{y}_m - \overline{y}_f]}{\sqrt{\text{var}(y_m) + \text{var}(y_f) - 2\text{cov}(y_m, y_f)}}, \tag{2}$$

where y_m is equal to 1 if the male applicant to a restaurant received an offer (or interview), and y_f is a similar variable for the female applicant to the same restaurant.[14] Equation (2) yields the same estimate as the random effects linear probability estimator that allows a correlation between the errors for job applicants at the same restaurant (Yinger, 1986).

We also compute the "symmetry test" proposed by Heckman and Siegelman (1993). This test is based on the difference between the number of audits in which the male received an offer (or interview), and the female did not (N_m), and the number in which the female received an offer and the male did not (N_f). Let P_m and P_f equal the probabilities of each of these outcomes. Then the null hypothesis of symmetric treatment is $P_m/(P_m + P_f) = 1/2$. The likelihoods under the null and the alternative, from which a likelihood ratio test can be constructed, are easily calculated from the multinomial distribution.[15]

Finally, when we want to test whether other factors (such as the resume used) affect the outcome, we estimate equation (1) as a linear regression.[16]

Results

Descriptive statistics and basic tests

Table 8.1 reports on the outcomes for job offers and job interviews for each price category of restaurants, and reports tests of the null hypothesis of no discrimination by sex. Panel A covers high-price restaurants. The first row reports evidence on job offers. Males received job offers in 48 percent of the cases, whereas females received offers only in 9 percent. The paired-differences test rejects the null hypothesis of no sex discrimination at better than the 5 percent level (the p-value is 0.01), in favor of the hypothesis of discrimination against women.[17] Panel A also reveals that in 43 percent of the cases an offer was made only to the male applicant, while only in 4 percent of cases was an offer made only to the female applicant. The symmetry test results in a test statistic for the difference in these proportions. This test similarly rejects the null hypothesis of no discrimination, with a p-value of 0.01.

The second row of Panel A looks at the receipt of interviews in high-price restaurants. Recall that one of the main purposes of studying interviews is to attempt to eliminate the effects of personality differences or experimenter effects that are correlated with sex. The results for interviews, however, are very similar to those for job offers, indicating that such factors do not drive the job offer results. Males received interviews in 61 percent of the cases, whereas females received interviews only in 26 percent. The paired-differences test rejects the null hypothesis of no sex discrimination (p-value $= 0.04$), as does the symmetry test (p-value $= 0.02$).

Panel B reports results for medium-price restaurants. The outcomes for both job offers and interviews again favor males. Men received job offers in 48 percent of the cases, compared with 29 percent for women. They received interviews in 62 percent of the cases, compared with 43 percent for women. However, the results of the paired-difference and symmetry tests indicate that the evidence for medium-price restaurants is considerably weaker. The evidence against the null of no discrimination is not significant for either test, for either job offers or interviews.

Table 8.1 Descriptive statistics and basic tests[a]

	# Audits	No offers/ interviews	Offer/interview to both	Offer/interview to male only	Offer/interview to female only	Male success	Female success	Test statistics h_0: no discrimination (p-value)	
								Paired difference	Symmetry
	(1)	(2)	(3)	(4)	(5)	(6)	(7)	(8)	(9)
A. High-price									
Offers	23	0.48	0.04	0.43	0.04	0.48	0.09	0.01	0.01
Interviews	23	0.26	0.13	0.48	0.13	0.61	0.26	0.04	0.02
B. Medium-price									
Offers	21	0.43	0.19	0.29	0.10	0.48	0.29	0.18	0.11
Interviews	21	0.29	0.33	0.29	0.10	0.62	0.43	0.18	0.11
C. Low-price									
Offers	21	0.62	0.10	0.00	0.29	0.10	0.38	0.01	0.02
Interviews	21	0.52	0.10	0.10	0.29	0.19	0.38	0.18	0.11

Note

a p-values are reported for two-sided tests. (In the paired-difference tests, when the covariance is ignored, the p-values are slightly higher.)

Finally, Panel C reports results for low-price restaurants. In contrast to the preceding results, the outcomes for both job offers and interviews at low-price restaurants favor females. Men received job offers in only 10 percent of the cases, compared with 38 percent for women. They received interviews in 19 percent of the cases, compared with 38 percent for women. With respect to hiring, the evidence against the null of no discrimination is significant for either test. However, with respect to interviews the evidence against this null is not significant.

To summarize, for low-price restaurants the job offer evidence suggests statistically significant evidence of discrimination against men. However, the interview evidence is not statistically significant, so we cannot rule out the possibility that the job offer results for low-price restaurants are influenced by personality differences or experimenter effects. However, the evidence does indicate hiring discrimination against women in high-price restaurants, as the evidence is statistically significant for both job offers and interviews.

Heckman and Siegelman (1993) also focus on whether it is appropriate to pool observations across pairs of job applicants, which essentially asks whether subsets of pairs of applicants drive the results, possibly because the degree of "match" between male and female testers varies across pairs of applicants. For example, if in a particular pairing of male and female testers the male always creates a more favorable impression than the female, but in other pairs this is not the case, then results may be driven by the first pair. Because we alternated the pairings of males and females, tests for pooling are complicated by the fact that observations from different pairs are not independent. However, the possibility with which we are most concerned is that the results are driven by pairs in which males were matched to female 2, since female 2 was Asian, and may have experienced differential treatment for this reason. The non-Asian (female 1) had a higher job offer rate at the medium-price restaurants (0.45 vs. 0.10), while female 2 had a higher rate at the low-price restaurants (0.56 vs. 0.25). The same pattern of outcomes occurred for interviews. However, neither female had much success at the high-price restaurants; each received just one job offer and three interviews. When the tests in Table 8.1 were recalculated using only pairs involving the non-Asian woman, the evidence of discrimination against women in high-price restaurants remained statistically significant. For offers, both the paired-difference test and the symmetry test led to a *p*-value of 0.01. The corresponding *p*-values for interviews were 0.05 for both tests. The evidence of discrimination against men in low-price restaurants was not statistically significant for offers or interviews, reflecting the higher success rate of the Asian woman at low-price restaurants.[18]

Multivariate analyses

Table 8.2 reports estimates of linear probability models, which allow us to test the statistical strength of the relationships in Table 8.1 once we control for some other potential influences on the job offer and interview decisions. As the table footnotes describe, the results were the same using probit estimates, and estimating the linear probability models with correlated errors across observations on the same

Table 8.2 Tests of discrimination in job offers and interviews, with control variables[a]

	High price		Medium price		Low price	
	Offer (1)	Interview (2)	Offer (3)	Interview (4)	Offer (5)	Interview (6)
A. Paired difference						
Female–male	−0.39	−0.35	−0.19	−0.19	0.29	0.19
	(0.13)	(0.16)	(0.14)	(0.14)	(0.11)	(0.14)
B. Regression estimates with control variables						
Female	−0.46	−0.46	0.08	0.14	0.11	0.02
	(0.16)	(0.21)	(0.24)	(0.22)	(0.16)	(0.18)
Resume 2	−0.05	−0.20	0.01	0.14	0.02	0.12
	(0.14)	(0.16)	(0.16)	(0.16)	(0.16)	(0.17)
Resume 3	0.02	0.02	0.11	0.20	0.05	0.14
	(0.15)	(0.18)	(0.18)	(0.17)	(0.12)	(0.14)
Paired with female 2	0.00	0.01	−0.13	−0.11	0.25	0.23
	(0.11)	(0.18)	(0.18)	(0.16)	(0.24)	(0.25)
Paired with male 2	−0.13	−0.23	0.03	−0.07	0.03	0.06
	(0.21)	(0.19)	(0.22)	(0.21)	(0.14)	(0.17)
Female 2	−0.00	−0.01	−0.37	−0.63	0.15	0.16
	(0.11)	(0.18)	(0.17)	(0.16)	(0.25)	(0.26)
Sample size	46	46	42	42	42	42

Note
a Panel A reports paired-difference estimates, with the standard errors in parentheses; these are the estimates used in column (8) of Table 8.1. Panel B reports linear probability model estimates. Heteroskedasticity-consistent standard errors are reported in parentheses. An intercept was included in all specifications. Female 2 is the Asian female. The conclusions in Panel B were unchanged in probit estimates, and in linear models estimated with random effects (allowing a correlation between audits of the same restaurant). For the latter, in an LM test for each specification, the null hypothesis of no correlation between errors for observations on the same restaurant could not be rejected (or, in one case, the estimated variance component was not positive).

restaurant (random effects). In the latter case, the data did not reject the restriction of no correlated errors.[19]

Columns (1) and (2) of Table 8.2 report estimates for high-price restaurants. Panel A reports the paired-difference estimates (used to obtain the *p*-values in Table 8.1). As already reported, for both offers and interviews, females did significantly worse than males, with a 0.39 (0.35) lower probability of an offer (interview).

Panel B reports the corresponding regression estimates when some control variables of interest are added.[20] First, the resumes were designed to provide impressions of job applicants that were roughly equivalent. In addition, as mentioned earlier, the resumes were rotated among job applicants, so that each resume was used approximately the same number of times by men and women. Nonetheless, to assess whether the distribution of the resumes affects the results, dummy variables for the resume that the job applicant used are added. Second, we examine the pooling problem raised by Heckman and Siegelman (1993), by asking whether the results are driven by particular pairings of applicants. To explore this question, we include dummy variables for the possible pairings of males and females. Finally, as discussed earlier, female 2 (who is Asian) had relatively more success in low-price restaurants, relatively less success in medium-price restaurants, and lower success overall. Thus, to obtain estimates that identify sex differences only from comparisons between the two males and female 1, we add a dummy variable for female 2.

Turning to the regression results for high-price restaurants, the estimated effects of the resume dummy variables on the probability of either a job offer or an interview are small and statistically insignificant, as was intended in the design of the resumes and the experiment. The estimates also indicate that the effects of the pairings are small and statistically insignificant. Finally, the estimated coefficient of the dummy variable for female 2 is effectively zero (reflecting the fact that in high-price restaurants, the two females had nearly identical outcomes). More importantly, the estimated difference in outcomes between males and females is unchanged by the inclusion of these control variables. The estimate in the first row of Panel B indicates that, net of these variables, the probability that females received either offers or interviews was significantly lower than that for men, by 0.46.

Columns (3) and (4) repeat this analysis for the medium-price restaurants. As for high-price restaurants, the estimated effects of the resumes and the pairings are insignificant. The only significant coefficient for the control variables is that for the dummy variable for female 2, who had much less success at the medium-price restaurants. Nonetheless, the main finding of no significant differences between the treatment of males and females at medium-price restaurants holds up in the regression analysis.

Finally, columns (5) and (6) report results for the low-price restaurants. In this case, none of the estimated coefficients for the resumes or pairings, or female 2, are significant. However, a number of the estimated coefficients are a bit larger in absolute value, with the result that the estimated advantage for females in receiving job offers becomes smaller and statistically insignificant, when the control variables are added.

To summarize, the regression analysis provides confirming evidence of hiring discrimination against women in high-price restaurants. It also bolsters the validity of the study design, especially for the high-price restaurants, by showing that factors (such as resumes, pairings, and individual characteristics) that were intended to be uncorrelated with sex do not generate biases in the estimated sex differences in outcomes.

Earnings differences

The audit results indicate hiring discrimination against women in high-price restaurants. However, as discussed in the Introduction, there is no existing hard evidence that earnings are higher in high-price restaurants than in low- or medium-price restaurants, although this has typically been assumed. If such earnings differences do not exist, then the pattern of hiring discrimination that we have uncovered may be unimportant from the perspective of explaining the sex gap in earnings among waitpersons.

While this question was not the principal focus of this project, we did gather some informal survey evidence via telephone interviews with the restaurants in our sample some time following the audit study. We telephoned the restaurants during non-peak hours, and attempted to talk with a manager, telling them that we were engaged in a small-scale research project on earnings in entry-level jobs. We generally reached a manager, but were occasionally put in touch with a waitperson. We asked for that person's best estimate of the hourly earnings of waitpersons (wages plus tips). In general, there was a great deal of reluctance to discuss tip income, since the IRS works rather hard to monitor compliance with tax payments on tip income.[21] In addition, even among those respondents willing to talk, some refused to be pinned down to any earnings estimates, and others did so only after being assured that we were only seeking their best estimate, and understood that earnings of waitpersons could be highly variable, and that tip earnings were often unknown to managers. Other restaurants were unwilling to talk for other reasons, and a few had closed.

Table 8.3 reports summary statistics. For each price category of restaurants we report the average minimum, maximum, and midpoint of hourly earnings using the figures reported directly, the averages when we fill in the missing minimum and maximum (and sometimes midpoint) with the available data, and the averages

Table 8.3 Information on hourly earnings by restaurant price category[a]

	Minimum/hr.	*Midpoint/hr.*	*Maximum/hr.*
A. High price (N = 10)			
Average	$16.24	$21.79	$21.81
Average filling in all cells	$19.67	$20.56	$21.47
Average filling in all cells, deleting high and low values	$17.49	$18.57	$19.69
B. Medium price (N = 9)			
Average	$10.43	$12.53	$13.94
Average filling in all cells	$11.27	$12.53	$13.90
Average filling in all cells, deleting high and low values	$11.22	$12.61	$13.82
C. Low price (N = 9)			
Average	$8.62	$10.65	$11.31
Average filling in all cells	$9.84	$10.65	$11.45
Average filling in all cells, deleting high and low values	$10.15	$11.08	$12.02

Note

a Respondents sometimes gave a range of hours and a range of earnings, and sometimes reported only a minimum figure. Minimum, maximum, and midpoint hourly earnings estimates were constructed from these, using midpoints of wage or earnings ranges and midpoints of ranges of hours per shift to construct the midpoint estimate. "Average filling in all cells" is computed after filling in missing minimums and maximums with midpoints, and after filling in midpoints and maximums with minimums when only the latter are reported.

when we drop the high and low values for each category. Regardless of how we calculate average hourly earnings, the data indicate large positive earnings differentials in high-price restaurants relative to both medium- and low-price restaurants, and smaller positive differentials in medium-price relative to low-price restaurants. For example, using the averages for the mid-points deleting the highest and lowest values, average hourly earnings in high-price restaurants ($18.57) are 47 percent higher than earnings in medium-price restaurants ($12.61), and 68 percent higher than earnings in low-price restaurants ($11.08). The same qualitative conclusion emerges from comparisons of any of the other averages. Thus, the hiring advantage that men seem to enjoy in high-price restaurants translates into substantial earnings advantages.

The nature of discrimination

While the audit study was designed solely to test for hiring discrimination in the restaurant industry, it is nonetheless of interest to attempt to understand the nature or source of the discrimination that we find. As discussed in the Introduction, two likely candidates are employer discrimination—presumably in the form of a preference of male owners/managers for male waitpersons—and customer discrimination—presumably in the form of a preference of male customers for restaurants that tend to hire male waitpersons.

To attempt to assess the role of each of these, we collected additional evidence (subsequent to the audit study) from a sample of restaurants included in the audit study, on (i) the proportion of the waitstaff that is male, (ii) the proportion of the clients that is male, and (iii) the sex of the owner(s) and the person(s) most responsible for hiring. We collected the data by having two research assistants (a male and female couple) visit each restaurant, remaining for about an hour while having a drink or dessert, always visiting during dinnertime hours on weekdays. During this time, the research assistants obtained their best estimate of the proportion male among the waitstaff and the clientele by observation. They also informally interviewed one or more waitpersons, obtaining their estimates of these proportions, as well as information on the sex of the owner(s) and person(s) most responsible for hiring. Given the time and expense required to obtain this information, and given some restaurant closings and difficulties with getting these data from some restaurants, data were obtained from roughly one-half of the restaurants in the audit study (with a slightly higher proportion of high- and medium-price restaurants). Also, because we had two (presumably noisy) estimates of the proportions male among the waitstaff and the clientele, we averaged these estimates.[22]

Table 8.4 reports information from these data. Panel A provides descriptive statistics. The figures show that the proportion of the waitstaff that is male rises monotonically with the price category, from 0.39 in the low-price restaurants to 0.72 in the high-price restaurants. The proportion of clients that is male is essentially the same in low- and medium-price restaurants, and is about 0.1 higher in high-price restaurants (0.62). Finally, we coded two variables indicating whether

Table 8.4 Information on sex of waitstaff, clients, owners, and managers[a]

	High price (1)	Medium price (2)	Low price (3)
A. Descriptive statistics			
Proportion waitstaff male	0.72 (0.07)	0.51 (0.08)	0.39 (0.10)
Proportion adult clients male	0.62 (0.02)	0.52 (0.03)	0.53 (0.04)
Only males responsible for hiring	0.83 (0.12)	0.50 (0.16)	0.67 (0.18)
Only females responsible for hiring	0.08 (0.09)	0.33 (0.15)	0.22 (0.16)

B. Regression for proportion waitstaff male, across price categories	High price (1)	Medium price (2)	Percent clients male (3)	Only females hire (4)	R^2 (5)
	0.28 (0.11)	0.10 (0.10)	0.94 (0.43)	0.26 (0.10)	0.44

C. Regressions for proportion waitstaff male, within price categories	Percent clients male (1)	Only females hire (2)	R^2 (3)
High price	1.49 (0.73)	—	0.29
	1.58 (0.69)	0.30 (0.20)	0.44
Medium price	1.63 (0.79)	—	0.30
	1.67 (0.74)	0.19 (0.13)	0.44
Low price	−0.33 (0.87)	—	0.02
	0.03 (0.98)	0.30 (0.24)	0.23

Note

a There are data on twelve high-price, twelve medium-price, and nine low-price restaurants. Panel A reports means, and standard errors of means are in parentheses. Panels B and C report OLS regression coefficients, and standard errors in parentheses. The variable "only males responsible for hiring" indicates that the person(s) most directly responsible for hiring was (were) male, and the owners—if reported—was (were) male. The corresponding variable for females is defined in the same way. (The two variables are not exhaustive because there may have been more than one person "most directly responsible for hiring," or this person(s) and the other owners(s) may have been different sexes.) The estimated coefficients of the "only males" variable were never significant, so specifications are reported excluding this variable; this had no qualitative effect on the results.

the owner(s) and person(s) most responsible for hiring were either all male or all female. Panel A indicates that the relationship between these variables and the price category is not monotonic, although the proportion in which only males hire is highest in high-price restaurants.

Next, in Panel B we report the estimated regression of the proportion of the waitstaff that is male on dummy variables for price category and for whether females (only) are responsible for hiring, as well as the proportion of the clientele that is male. The estimated coefficients for the dummy variables indicating the sex of those responsible for hiring are not consistent with employer discrimination. The estimated coefficient (not reported) of the variable indicating that males only were responsible was small (-0.03) and insignificant, while the estimated coefficient for the corresponding variable for females is positive and significant.[23] On the other hand, the proportion of the clientele that is male is significantly positively related to the proportion of the waitstaff that is male, with an estimated coefficient near 1. Thus, the results are consistent with customer discrimination, but not employer discrimination (unless, of course, female owners/managers prefer male employees).[24] Nonetheless, customer preferences do not explain a large part of the variation across price categories in the proportion of the waitstaff that is male. The estimated coefficient of the dummy variable for high-price restaurants shows that the estimated proportion of the waitstaff that is male is 0.28 higher in high-price than in low-price restaurants after introducing the control variables in Panel B, compared with the average difference in Panel A of 0.33.

Finally, Panel C reports estimated regressions within price categories. These estimates provide stronger evidence that the proportion male among the clientele is positively associated with the proportion male among the waitstaff, although this relationship appears only for high- and medium-price restaurants. Furthermore, the estimated coefficients of the dummy variables indicating the sex of those responsible for hiring are never significant in these regressions. These estimates suggest that customer discrimination may play somewhat more of a role in influencing whether men or women get hired than is indicated by the pooled regression in Panel B.

Overall, the results in Table 8.4 indicate that customer discrimination may be partially responsible for discrimination against women in restaurant hiring. We tend to think that this customer discrimination is not a direct preference of male clients for male waitpersons, but rather a preference of male clients for the types of restaurants that hire male wait staff, perhaps because such hiring signals "traditional" or "prestigious" restaurants. Such restaurants may be particularly appealing to business clients, who are more likely to be male, and whose expense accounts may cushion them from the higher costs generated by discrimination.

Conclusions

Our results for job offers and interviews provide statistically significant evidence of sex discrimination against women in high-price restaurants. In high-price restaurants, job applications from women had an estimated probability of receiving a job offer that was lower by about 0.4, and an estimated probability of receiving an interview that was lower by about 0.35.

As discussed in the Introduction, occupational segregation has alternatively been attributed to differences in human capital investment, preferences, and discrimination. The research design used in this audit study isolates the effect of discrimination. We control for the effects of self-selection based on preferences or anticipated human capital investments by sending male and female job applicants to all restaurants, and we control for past human capital investment (and any other past differences) by presenting equivalent resumes to potential employers. Thus, we are quite confident in interpreting our results as reflecting discrimination.

The audit study does not address the question of the nature of the discrimination. Two plausible candidates are taste discrimination on the part of employers and on the part of customers. Some relatively crude evidence suggests that customer discrimination—in the form of preferences of male clients for restaurants that tend to hire male waitstaff—partly underlies the discrimination that we find, but does not appear to be the complete explanation.

Another candidate is statistical discrimination. If employers have to invest in their workers, and believe that women are likely to quit sooner than men, they may be reluctant to hire women. Conceivably, such investment could be more important in high-price restaurants, where service, knowledge, and formality may be more important. We speculate, however, that such considerations are relatively unimportant in explaining our results. First of all, some job history is provided on the resumes, and by design the applications from women show the same past persistence on the job, on average, as do the applications from men. Second, the relative ease with which job offers were obtained, and the near equality of job offer rates (for both sexes combined) in the high- and low-price restaurants, suggests that there is relatively high turnover in all price categories of restaurants, and that turnover is not lower in the high-price restaurants that tend to hire men.[25]

Our audit results indicate hiring discrimination against women in high-price restaurants. In addition, our less formal survey evidence suggests that wage and tip earnings are substantially higher in high-price restaurants. Therefore, the pattern of hiring discrimination that we have uncovered may go a long way toward explaining the sex gap in earnings among waiters and waitresses.

Finally, while our findings provide strong evidence of discrimination, we caution against drawing overly strong conclusions based solely on the findings of this study. Audit studies offer important advantages relative to other approaches to studying discrimination, and perhaps even provide the only way of drawing convincing inferences regarding discrimination. But they also suffer from the potential disadvantage that the data they use are generated by the researcher and influenced by the precise methods used, and hence are more idiosyncratic than studies using data from publicly available secondary data sources.[26] This is by no means a fatal flaw of such studies, but it does imply that findings from audit studies should be interpreted cautiously until similar results emerge from related audit studies that address similar questions, but that vary in the methods of implementation. In other words, like other empirical studies, the findings of audit studies should be assessed in terms of their robustness across replication studies that vary the precise design of the experiment.

Appendix: Resumes[27]

Resume #1

Employment Objective
A full or part-time position as a food server.

Education
Lebanon High School, Lebanon, PA 17104.

Activities: Active in Lebanon YMCA youth outreach program. Mt. Hope Wine Group—a group organized to sample and critique the world's wines.

Experience
Stallions Bar and Grill: Front waiting in moderate to upscale dining institution. Responsible for food prep, dining room setup, and late night cocktail waiting, May 1993–February 1994. 1290 Front End Blvd, Harrisburg, PA.

Cesare Place: Front and back waiting in fine dining institution with a continental menu. Occasional work for Cesare Catering. Experience includes buffet service. Headwaiter for last three months of employment and weekly hosting shift, January 1991–May 1993. 509 Washington Rd, Harrisburg, PA.

Red Lobster: Busperson and waitperson, June 1990–May 1991. West Valley Shopping Plaza, Harrisburg, PA.

Boscov's Department Store: Worked summers and Christmas as extra sales staff and cashier. Worked primarily in toys and sporting goods, June 1989–December 1990.

Personal
Basic understanding of retail computing systems and IBMs. Personal hobbies include exercise, reading, and piano playing.

Resume #2

Employment Objective
A full or part-time position as a food server/waitperson.

Education
Kennedy High School, Chicago, IL.

Activities: Volunteer for the Urban Adult Literacy Program for the homeless. Big Brother/Big Sister program of Chicago.

Experience
Cafe Carlos: Wait position in fine dining institution (front waiting only). Via catering also had experience in bartending, buffet setup, interior design and food preparation, August 1992–February 1994. 1245 Front St., Chicago, IL.

Connections Restaurant and Bar: Lunch waitperson (back and front waiting), host and food prep. Summer only 1991–3. 19 Broadway, Chicago, IL.

Ground Round: Wait position and busperson, February 1990–August 1991. Cherry Creek Mall, Chicago, IL.

Ritz Camera: Retail sales of photography equipment and photo developing. Experience with darkroom equipment and 1-Hour photo developing machinery. Cherry Creek Mall, Chicago, IL.

Personal

Basic use of Macintosh and IBM personal computing systems. Personal interests include photography, DJ'ing, and current affairs.

Resume #3

Employment Objective

A full or part-time position as a waitperson.

Education

Cedar Crest High School, Denver, CO.

Activities: Volunteer as senior companion in Silver Springs nursing home. Active in Denver's restaurant review guild.

Experience

Fleur: Waitperson in fine dining. Began as a busperson but worked up the ranks to headwaiter within two years. In addition to fine dining wait skills and extensive wine knowledge, also had experience with scheduling, data analysis and catering, July 1991–February 1994. Westpoint Mall, Denver, CO.

Jody's Grill and Bar: Front and back waiting with food prep. Also did cocktail waiting on an outdoor deck, March 1991–July 1991. Englewood, CO.

Perkins Restaurant: Busperson for fast paced family restaurant, summers and weekends, June 1989–July 1990. 578 Bridgeport Rd, Englewood, CO.

Safeway Supermarkets: Checkout teller in supermarket. Extensive customer service skills and computerized checkout system, January 1989–June 1989. Walnut Hill Rd, Englewood, CO.

Personal

Excellent in use of data systems, computers, and registers. I enjoy reading, exercising, and fishing.

Acknowledgments

I am grateful to Wendy Stock for outstanding research assistance, to Susan Tsu and Charles Gassenheimer for assistance with the study, and to James Heckman, Harry Holzer, Lawrence Katz, Paul Menchik, and an anonymous referee for helpful comments.

This paper was written with the assistance of Roy J. Bank and Kyle D. Van Nort, students in an undergraduate research seminar who were instrumental in the planning and implementation of this project.

Notes

1 The regression estimates are based on a sample of 1,012 individuals. The controls include race, marital status, union membership, schooling, age, and its square, SMSA, and Census region

2 There is no large-scale data set of which we are aware that would permit the comparison of earnings of waitpersons in high- and low-price restaurants.

3 Bergmann does suggest, however, that "Recently, some restaurants have started using males and females interchangeably" (1986, p. 124n).

4 The same is also true of wage regression estimates used to draw inferences regarding wage discrimination against women based on "residual" wage differentials between men and women.

5 In fact, in a *Newsweek* article discussing an early version of this study, one restaurant owner explained the lack of waitresses in his upscale restaurant as "a question of us seeing an endless number of male applicants and few female applicants" (*Newsweek* April 10, 1995). The issue of whether the differential job application rate itself stems from discrimination is sometimes raised in hiring discrimination suits.

6 Employee discrimination cannot, by itself, explain segregation of women by price category, whereas the other two forms of discrimination can, depending on the distribution of employers and customers across restaurants in different price categories.

7 The paired difference-of-means test results in the same estimate **b** as does the linear probability model (Yinger, 1986).

   This test can also take account of correlation between outcomes for individuals at the same restaurant (i.e. a restaurant-specific component μ_j of the error term ε_{ij}). This common error component can be similarly handled in the linear probability or probit model by introducing random effects (as in Kenney and Wissoker (1994)). Once we introduce covariates other than F into equation (1), one of these latter two methods is required, if we are to obtain a single estimate of β for each price category.

8 Of course, the name and telephone number of the applicant at the top of the resume was changed to correspond to the person using the resume. One of the female testers had a name that was sex-neutral. Since (for reasons discussed) we wanted potential employers to know the sex of the job applicant based solely on information from the resume, this person used a different, traditionally female name for the course of the study.

9 We received no indication from any of the potential employers that they had checked on the job references on the resumes. Even if they did so, the effects should have been sex-neutral.

10 In fact, one potential problem arose because one of the female students in the research seminar who served as a job applicant was Asian. Thus, when we test for sex differences in outcomes we ask if the results differ when we compare outcomes for both men and both women, or just for both men and the non-Asian woman.

11 One might argue that we reduce this problem by looking for sex differences in the receipt of job offers in different price categories of restaurants. If males or females turn out to be relatively favored in all three price categories, perhaps because one of the testers simply came across as more or less impressive than the rest, then an interpretation based on differences in personality or appearance might be difficult to refute. However, if males are favored in one price category (such as high-price restaurants), and females in another category, then such an interpretation is less tenable, although it is still possible that different characteristics of personality or appearance are valued in restaurants in different price categories.

12 This principle is also exploited in a study by McIntyre, *et al.* (1980), who compare differential responses of companies to fictitious resumes made comparable by randomizing across the entries on the resume, and then randomly indicating sex or race. This study found significant evidence of more favorable responses to men than to women.

13 According to *Zagat's*, these prices are based on dinner including an appetizer, main course, and one drink excluding the tip.

14 This statistic is normally distributed in large samples, and has a t distribution in small samples if ε is normally distributed.

15 This is a large sample test. Heckman and Siegelman (1993) also discuss small sample "conditional sign" tests that tend to reject the null of no discrimination (symmetric treatment) somewhat more frequently.

16 We initially estimate the model with random effects, to allow for the same correlation between outcomes at the same restaurant as the paired difference-in-means test allows.

17 Unless otherwise noted, from this point on statements regarding statistical significance refer to the 5 percent significance level in two-sided tests.

18 In the multivariate analysis that follows, we also control for the pooling problem by including dummy variables for the male–female pair on which each observation is based.

19 We also estimated random effects probit models. The estimated correlations between errors for observations on the same restaurant were insignificant, with asymptotic t-statistics near or below one, so the random effects specification again was not needed.

20 Recall that the regression estimate without controls is identical to the paired-difference estimate.

21 See, for example, the Internal Revenue Service's *Tip Income Study* (1990).

22 There was one case where the interviewee actually took the data from the payroll sheets; in this case we simply used this estimate of the proportion male among the waitstaff. Overall, the means of the alternative estimates were relatively close (within 0.04 for all but the proportion male among the waitstaff in the low-price restaurants). The correlation between the two measures for the waitstaff was 0.74. However, the correlation for the two measures for clients was lower, at 0.39; this was driven by significant clustering of interview responses for the proportion of clients male at 0.5 (16 of 33 observations). The results were qualitatively similar using data only based on observation, or only from the interviews.

23 The reported specification excludes the former variable.

24 Other research takes a more direct approach to testing for customer discrimination. For example, Nardinelli and Simon (1990) test for customer discrimination in sports markets by looking at race effects on the value of baseball cards. Consistent with the evidence presented here, they find evidence of customer discrimination.

25 This also suggests that the earnings differentials in Table 8.3 do not reflect tenure effects. The similar offer rates for low- and high-price restaurants may also be attributable to the resumes being more appropriate for the latter.

26 As an example, Heckman and Siegelman (1993) compare the Urban Institute studies and a study of the Denver labor market by James and DelCastillo (1991). They conclude that despite following quite similar procedures, the studies appear to lead to different conclusions.

   Along the same lines, a referee was concerned that the resumes we used were more appropriate for high-price than low-price restaurants. We have no way of assessing whether this affected the outcome, but the concern helps emphasize the issue that a variety of idiosyncrasies of audit studies may influence the results.

27 In the study, each of the three different resumes was produced with a different font and presentation style. Also, each resume included a name, telephone number, and address.

References

Ayres, Ian and Peter Siegelman. 1995. "Race and Gender Discrimination in Bargaining for a New Car." *American Economic Review* LXXXV: 304–21.

Beller, Andrea H. 1982. "Occupational Segregation by Sex: Determinants and Changes." *Journal of Human Resources* XVII: 371–92.

Bergmann, Barbara. 1974. "Occupational Segregation, Wages and Profits When Employers Discriminate by Race or Sex." *Eastern Economic Journal* I: 103–10.

——. 1986. *The Economic Emergence of Women*. New York, NY: Basic Books, Inc.

Blau, Francine D. 1977. *Equal Pay in the Office*. Lexington, MA: Lexington Books.

Cross, Harry, Genevieve Kenney, Jane Mell, and Wendy Zimmerman. 1990. *Employer Hiring Practices: Differential Treatment of Hispanic and Anglo Job Seekers*, Urban Institute Report 90–4. Washington, DC: The Urban Institute.

Daymont, Thomas N. and Paul J. Andrisani. 1984. "Job Preferences, College Major, and the Gender Gap in Earnings." *Journal of Human Resources* XIX: 409–28.

Epstein, Richard A. 1992. *Forbidden Grounds: The Case Against Employment Discrimination Laws*. Cambridge, MA: Harvard University Press.

Groshen, Erica L. 1991. "The Structure of the Female/Male Wage Differential." *Journal of Human Resources* XXVI: 457–72.

Heckman, James J. and Peter Siegelman. 1993. "The Urban Institute Audit Studies: Their Methods and Findings." In *Clear and Convincing Evidence: Measurement of Discrimination in America*, eds Michael Fix and Raymond J. Struyk, pp. 187–258. Washington, DC: The Urban Institute.

Howe, Louise Kapp. 1977. *Pink Collar Workers*. New York, NY: G. P. Putnam's Sons.

Internal Revenue Service, Department of the Treasury. 1990. *Tip Income Study*. Publication 1530.

James, F. and S. W. DelCastillo. 1991. "Measuring Job Discrimination by Private Employers against Young Black and Hispanic Males Seeking Entry Level Work in the Denver Metropolitan Area." Denver: University of Colorado.

Kenney, Genevieve M. and Douglas A. Wissoker. 1994. "An Analysis of the Correlates of Discrimination Facing Young Hispanic Job-Seekers." *American Economic Review* LXXXIV: 674–83.

McIntyre, Shelby, Dennis J. Moberg, and Barry Z. Posner. 1980. "Preferential Treatment in Preselection Decisions According to Sex and Race." *Academy of Management Journal* XXIII: 738–49.

Nardinelli, Clark and Curtis Simon. 1990. "Customer Racial Discrimination in the Market for Memorabilia: The Case of Baseball." *Quarterly Journal of Economics* CV: 575–96.

Polachek, Solomon W. 1981. "Occupational Self-Selection: A Human Capital Approach to Sex Differences in Occupational Structure." *Review of Economics and Statistics* LVIII: 60–9.

Seiling, Mark S. 1984. "Staffing Patterns and the Gender Pay Gap." *Monthly Labor Review* 29–33.

Turner, Margery Austin, Michael Fix, and Raymond J. Struyk. 1991. *Opportunities Denied, Opportunities Diminished: Racial Discrimination in Hiring*, Urban Institute Report 91–9. Washington, DC: The Urban Institute.

Yinger, John. 1986. "Measuring Racial Discrimination with Fair Housing Audits: Caught in the Act." *American Economic Review* LXXVI: 881–93.

9 Wages, productivity, and worker characteristics

Evidence from plant-level production functions and wage equations

(with Judith K. Hellerstein and Kenneth R. Troske)

Introduction

The existence of wage differentials across workers in different demographic groups has been documented in many empirical studies. Three types of differences across workers and the reasons behind them have received a great deal of attention and are the focus of this chapter. First, estimates of wage differentials associated with age or experience are used to examine implications of human capital models of wage growth. Second, estimates of wage differentials associated with sex or race are used to test for wage discrimination. Third, estimates of wage differentials associated with marriage have been interpreted as reflecting productivity effects. Additional areas of inquiry include wage differentials by union status, education, and industry.

The problem with the traditional approach of estimating wage regressions to test theories of wage determination is that, without independent measures of worker productivity, it is difficult to determine whether wage differentials associated with worker characteristics reflect productivity differentials or some other factor, such as discrimination. For example, with data only on wages and worker characteristics over the life cycle, it is difficult to distinguish human capital models of wage growth (such as Ben-Porath, 1967; Becker, 1975; Mincer, 1974) from incentive-compatible models of wage growth (Lazear, 1979) or forced-saving models of life-cycle wage profiles (Loewenstein and Sicherman, 1991; Frank and Hutchens, 1993). Typical wage regression results report positive coefficients on age, conditional on a variety of covariates, but these positive coefficients neither imply that older workers are more productive than younger ones, nor that wages rise faster than productivity. Similarly, without direct measures of the relative productivity of workers, discrimination by sex, race, or marital status cannot be established based on significant coefficients on sex, race, or marital status dummy variables in standard wage regressions, since the usual individual-level wage regression controls may not fully capture productivity differences (e.g. Becker, 1985).

The major contribution of this chapter is to use a unique new data set that combines data on individual workers with data on their employers to estimate relative marginal products for various groups of workers, which we then compare with relative wages. This employer–employee data set, the Worker Establishment Characteristics Database (WECD), matches long-form respondents to the 1990 Decennial Census of Population to data on their employers from the Longitudinal Research Database (LRD). These data are a major improvement over previously available data sources because they combine detailed demographic information on workers in a sample of plants with information on plant-level inputs and outputs.[1] We use these data to estimate production functions in which workers with different demographic characteristics have potentially different marginal products, thereby obtaining estimates of these relative marginal productivities. In addition, we explore numerous issues regarding the estimation of these production functions in an attempt to obtain reliable estimates of these productivity differentials. For the most part, we find that our estimates of marginal productivity appear relatively robust and reasonable, although, not surprisingly, they do change somewhat as we vary our specification and sample.

Because we have information on plant labor costs, we also specify and estimate plant-level earnings equations. These plant-level earnings equations represent the aggregation of individual-level earnings equations over workers employed in a plant, and hence are the plant-level counterparts to the individual-level wage regressions that motivate this research. By simultaneously estimating the production functions and earnings equations at the plant level, we can compare the relative marginal products and relative wages of workers distinguished by various demographic characteristics.[2,3] Thus, the data and empirical framework we develop supply the independent productivity measures needed to draw more decisive conclusions on numerous topics regarding the determination of wages, including race and sex discrimination in wages, the causes of rising wages over the life cycle, and the returns to marriage.

The relationship between wages and productivity

In order to motivate the approach we take in this chapter, we first present the simplest model illustrating the relationship between wages and productivity under perfect competition. Consider an economy consisting of plants that produce output Y with a technology that utilizes two different types of perfectly substitutable labor inputs, L_1 and L_2. The production function of these plants is

$$Y = F(L_1 + \phi L_2), \tag{1}$$

where ϕ is the marginal productivity of L_2 relative to L_1. These plants are assumed to operate in perfectly competitive spot labor markets, and labor supply is assumed to be completely inelastic. The price of the output Y is normalized to equal 1. Wages of workers of types L_1 and L_2 are w_1 and w_2, respectively. Define the relative wage rate (w_2/w_1) to be λ. Given this setup, the proportional mix of the two types of labor in each plant will be determined by the relationship between ϕ and λ. If $\phi = \lambda$, then under profit maximization or cost minimization plants will be indifferent to the proportional mix of the two types of labor in the plant. If there is a wedge between the relative marginal product and relative wage so that $\phi \neq \lambda$, then profit-maximizing or cost-minimizing plants will be at a corner solution, hiring either only workers of type L_1 (if $\phi < \lambda$) or only workers of type L_2 (if $\phi > \lambda$). The only equilibrium in this model is when wages adjust so that $\phi = \lambda$, and plants are indifferent between the two types of labor.

Evidence that $\phi \neq \lambda$ is inconsistent with the assumption that we are observing profit-maximizing or cost-minimizing plants in a competitive spot labor market.[4] This chapter can be interpreted as providing empirical tests of this characterization of labor markets. We estimate variants of the plant-level production function in equation (1) simultaneously with plant-level wage equations in order to obtain estimates of parameters corresponding to ϕ and λ for various types of workers. We interpret cases where we cannot reject the equality of ϕ and λ as evidence consistent with competitive spot labor markets. Cases in which we reject the equality of ϕ and λ indicate some deviation from this characterization of labor markets, such as long-term incentive contracts or discrimination.

The data

The WECD, constructed at the US Census Bureau, links information for a subset of individuals responding to the long form of the 1990 Decennial Census of Population with information about their employers in the 1989 LRD. Long-form Census of Population respondents report the location of their employer in the prior week, and the type of business or industry in which they work. The Census Bureau then assigns a code for the location of the employer, corresponding to a unique city block for densely populated areas, or corresponding to a unique place for sparsely populated areas. The Census Bureau also classifies workers into industries using Census industry codes so that respondents can be assigned to a unique industry-location cell. In addition, the Census Bureau maintains a complete list of all manufacturing establishments operating in the United States in a given year, along with location and industry information for these establishments that is similar to the data available for workers. Thus, it is possible to assign all plants in the United States to an industry-location cell. The WECD is constructed by first selecting all manufacturing establishments in operation in 1990 that are unique in an industry-location cell. Then all workers who are located in the same industry-location cell as a unique establishment are matched to that establishment. This results in a data set consisting of 199,558 workers matched to 16,144 plants.

To obtain data on a worker's employer, these data must be matched to the plant-level data in the LRD. The LRD is a compilation of plant responses to the Annual Survey of Manufacturers (ASM) and Census of Manufacturers (CM). The CM is conducted in years ending in a 2 or a 7, while the ASM is conducted in all other years for a sample of plants. The LRD contains plant data from every CM since 1963 and every ASM since 1971. Data in the LRD are of the sort typically used in production function estimation, such as output, capital stock, materials expenditures, and number of workers. In addition, the LRD contains information on total salaries and wages and total non-salary compensation paid by the plant in a given year (McGuckin and Pascoe, 1988).

Since worker earnings and labor force information in the Decennial Census of Population refer to 1989, we match the worker data to the 1989 plant data in the LRD. Since 1989 is an ASM year, data are only available for a sample of plants. Furthermore, since plant-level capital stock information is only available in CM years, we require all plants to be in the LRD in both 1989 and 1987.[5] Finally, to increase the representativeness of the sample of workers in each plant, we require plants in our data set to have at least 20 employees in 1989 (as reported in the LRD), and at least 5 percent of their workforce contained in the WECD. Our final sample contains data on 3,102 plants and 128,460 workers. Summary statistics for plant-level data are given in Table 9.1. The average plant has 353 employees, and on average 12 percent of a plant's workforce is matched to the plant.[6] Troske (1998) concludes that workers are matched to their correct plants—based on the match rate and on high correlations between variables available in the two data sets—with approximately 5 percent of manufacturing workers from the Census of Population long-form represented in the WECD. The matching process does not, however, yield a representative sample of workers, as non-black, male, married workers are over-represented in the WECD. In the following sections we discuss some of the implications of this for our empirical results.

Estimating marginal productivity differentials

Basic approach

To estimate parameters corresponding to ϕ—the relative marginal productivities of various types of labor—we estimate a translog production function in which the value of output Y is a function of capital K, materials M, and a quality of labor aggregate QL.[7] In logs, this is

$$\ln(Y) = \ln(A) + \alpha \ln(K) + \beta \ln(M) + \gamma \ln(QL) + g(K, M, QL) + \mu, \qquad (2)$$

where $g(K, M, QL)$ is the second-order terms in the production function (Jorgenson *et al.*, 1973), and μ is an error term.

For each plant in our data set, we have demographic information on a sample of the workforce from the WECD. We assume that in the quality of labor aggregate QL, workers with different demographic characteristics are perfectly substitutable inputs with potentially different marginal products.[8] For example, assume that workers are distinguished only by sex. Then QL would be defined as

$$QL = L \left(1 + (\phi_F - 1)\frac{F}{L} \right), \qquad (3)$$

where L is the total number of workers in the plant, F is the number of women in the plant, and ϕ_F is the marginal productivity of women relative to men. Substituting equation (3) into equation (2), we obtain a production function with which we can estimate ϕ_F, using plant-level data on output, capital and materials inputs, and the number of workers and sex composition of the workforce.

Table 9.1 Descriptive statistics for matched establishments[a]

LRD Data	Mean (1)	Standard deviation (2)	Census of Population Data	Mean (3)	Standard deviation (4)
Log output ($1,000)	10.19	1.33	Log estimated wages and salaries ($1,000)	8.38	1.17
Log value added ($1,000)	9.34	1.39	Proportion of LRD employment matched	0.12	0.08
Log capital ($1,000)	8.82	1.53	Proportion with 2–5 workers matched	0.14	
Log cost of materials ($1,000)	9.43	1.51	Proportion with 6–10 workers matched	0.18	
Log wages and salaries ($1,000)	8.40	1.17	Proportion with 11–20 workers matched	0.24	
Log compensation costs ($1,000)	8.62	1.18	Proportion with 21–40 workers matched	0.21	
			Proportion with 41+ workers matched	0.24	
Employment	353.0	846.8			
			Proportions:		
Establishment size			Female	0.30	0.23
1–75 employees	0.22		Black	0.07	0.12
76–150 employees	0.25		Aged 34 or less	0.39	0.20
151–350 employees	0.29		Aged 35–54	0.48	0.18
351+ employees	0.25		Aged 55 or more	0.13	0.12
Industry			Some college	0.36	0.21
Food products and tobacco products	0.16		Ever married	0.84	0.14
			Managerial/professional workers	0.15	0.15
Textile mill products, apparel, and leather and leather products	0.07		Technical, sales, administrative, and service workers	0.20	0.15
Lumber and wood products and furniture fixtures	0.04		Precision production, craft, and repair workers	0.20	0.15
Paper and allied products and printing and publishing	0.16		Operators, fabricators, and laborers	0.45	0.22
Chemicals and petroleum refining	0.10				
Rubber and plastics	0.05				
Stone/clay/glass/concrete	0.04				
Primary metals	0.08				
Fabricated metal products	0.08				
Machinery/computer equipment	0.06				
Electrical/electronic equipment	0.06				
Transportation equipment	0.06				
Instruments/clocks/optical goods and miscellaneous manufacturing	0.03				
Region					
Northeast	0.29				
Midwest	0.44				
South	0.23				
West	0.05				
Multiple-establishment unit	0.82				

Note

a There are 3,102 establishment-level observations, and 128,460 matched individuals from the Census of Population. The sample is restricted to those establishments with total employment of twenty or more, for which at least 5 percent of employees are matched.

We actually define QL to assume that workers are distinguished not only by sex but also by: race (black and non-black); marital status (ever married); age (divided into three broad categories—under 35, 35–54, 55 and over); education (defined as having attended at least some college); and occupation (divided into four groups—(1) operators, fabricators, and laborers (unskilled production workers), (2) managers and professionals, (3) technical, sales, administrative, and service, and (4) precision production, craft, and repair). A firm's workforce can then be fully described by the proportions of workers in each of 192 possible combinations of these demographic characteristics.

To reduce the dimensionality of the problem, for much of our work we impose two restrictions on the form of QL. First, we restrict the relative marginal products of two types of workers within one demographic group to be equal to the relative marginal products of those same two types of workers within another demographic group. For example, the relative marginal productivity of black women to black men is restricted to equal the relative marginal productivity of non-black women to non-black men. Similarly, the race difference in marginal productivity is restricted to be the same across the sexes. Second, we restrict the proportion of workers in an establishment defined by a demographic group to be constant across all other groups; for example, we restrict blacks to be equally represented in all occupations, education levels, marital status groups, etc. We impose these restrictions due to data limitations. For each establishment, we do not have data on the actual number of workers in each of the 192 possible combinations of demographic characteristics, but instead estimate that number using our sample of workers matched to the plant. It is likely, therefore, that we cannot obtain accurate estimates of the representation of workers in narrowly defined sets of demographic groups. Our restrictions on QL reduce the number of sample estimates based on small numbers of workers, as well as the number of parameters.

With these assumptions, the log of the quality of labor term in the production function becomes

$$
\ln(QL) = \gamma \ln \left[(L + (\phi_F - 1) F) \left(1 + (\phi_B - 1) \frac{B}{L} \right) \left(1 + (\phi_R - 1) \frac{R}{L} \right) \right.
$$
$$
\times \left(1 + (\phi_G - 1) \frac{G}{L} \right) \left(1 + (\phi_P - 1) \frac{P}{L} + (\phi_O - 1) \frac{O}{L} \right)
$$
$$
\left. \times \left(1 + (\phi_N - 1) \frac{N}{L} + (\phi_S - 1) \frac{S}{L} + (\phi_C - 1) \frac{C}{L} \right) \right], \quad (4)
$$

where B is the number of black workers, R is the number of workers ever married, G is the number of workers who have some college education, P is the number of workers in the plant between the ages of 35 and 54, O is the number of workers who are 55 or older, and N, S, and C are the numbers of workers in the second through fourth occupational categories defined above.[9] Note that the way QL is defined, productivity differentials between groups are indicated when the estimate of the relevant ϕ is significantly different from one (rather than zero). For example, a finding of $\phi_R = 1.3$ would imply that ever-married workers are 30 percent more productive than never-married workers.[10]

We also allow productivity to vary by size of plant (see Lucas, 1978; Baily *et al.*, 1992), industry, region, and whether or not the plant is part of a multi-plant firm, by adding controls for these plant-level characteristics to the production function.[11,12]

Assessing the robustness of the relative marginal productivity estimates

To this point, we have described the basic approach to the estimation of productivity differentials across workers in different demographic groups. Because the estimation of relative marginal productivities is the central contribution of this chapter, we carry out a number of additional analyses relaxing various assumptions imposed on the production function estimation, to assess the robustness of the estimates.

Among the endogeneity biases that might be most troubling is the potential endogeneity of materials. We first address this issue by estimating a value-added version of the production function, using $\ln(Y - M)$ as the dependent variable, since the value-added specification finesses the endogeneity issue by avoiding estimation of a coefficient on materials. There are also other potential virtues of a value-added specification, as Griliches and Ringstad (1971) discuss. The value-added specification enhances comparability of data across industries and across establishments within industries, when industries or establishments differ in their degree of vertical integration. In addition, the value-added specification can be derived from quite polar production function specifications: one in which the elasticity of substitution between materials and value added is infinite (i.e. $Y = f(K, QL) + M$); and one in which this elasticity of substitution is zero (so that materials have to be used in a fixed proportion to output). The second approach to the endogeneity problem is instrumental variables estimation of the output specification of the production function, treating materials as endogenous and using data on materials usage in the 1987 CM to form an instrument for current materials use. The specifics of the approach are discussed in the empirical section.

As explained earlier, the way that labor enters the production function is restrictive in two senses.[13] First, the relative marginal productivities of two types of workers within one demographic group are restricted to equal the relative marginal productivities of those types of workers within another demographic group. Second, the proportion of workers defined by one demographic group is restricted to be constant across all other groups. We do, however, present estimates relaxing some of these assumptions to see if they have a substantive effect on the estimates. To explain how we relax these assumptions, consider the approach used for one specific set of estimates in which we relax both types of restrictions with regard to marriage, race, and sex.[14] In the production function, this yields a quality of labor term of the form:

$$
\begin{aligned}
QL = {} & (L + (\phi_F - 1)WFS + (\phi_R - 1)WMR + (\phi_B - 1)BMS \\
& + (\phi_R \cdot \phi_B - 1)BMR + (\phi_R \cdot \phi_F \cdot \phi_{FXR} - 1)WFR \\
& + (\phi_F \cdot \phi_B \cdot \phi_{FXB} - 1)BFS \\
& + (\phi_F \cdot \phi_B \cdot \phi_R \cdot \phi_{FXR} \cdot \phi_{FXB} - 1)BFR) \\
& \times \left(1 + (\phi_G - 1)\frac{G}{L}\right)\left(1 + (\phi_P - 1)\frac{P}{L} + (\phi_O - 1)\frac{O}{L}\right) \\
& \times \left(1 + (\phi_N - 1)\frac{N}{L} + (\phi_S - 1)\frac{S}{L} + (\phi_C - 1)\frac{C}{L}\right),
\end{aligned}
\tag{5}
$$

where WFS denotes the number of non-black, never-married females in the plant, WMR the number of nonblack married males, BMS the number of black, never-married males, etc. Introducing these variables relaxes the equiproportionate restriction regarding the distribution of workers. The term ϕ_{FXR} is the coefficient on the interaction for being female and married. A finding that $\phi_{FXR} = 1$ would indicate that the marriage productivity premium for women is no different than that for men. The term ϕ_{FXB} is the interaction coefficient for black females, where $\phi_{FXB} = 1$ would imply that the productivity differential between men and women does not vary by race. Introducing these parameters relaxes the equal relative productivity restriction.[15]

Empirically, when we estimate this augmented specification we first estimate the unrestricted model, using the expression for QL in equation (5). We then re-estimate the equations retaining only the "interaction" coefficients (such as ϕ_{FXR}) that are significantly different from one. We report the latter (restricted) set of estimates. However, we always use the disaggregated estimates of the distribution of workers (WFS, WMR, etc.).

In addition to the specific case considered here, we carry out estimations relaxing both types of restrictions for the following combinations of variables: sex and occupation; sex and age; and age and education. The sex by occupation restrictions are natural to question because the occupational distribution differs markedly by sex. The sex by age restrictions are natural to question because younger cohorts of women are likely to be quite different (relative to men) from older cohorts. Because of the limitations of the Census of Population we do not have data on experience (or tenure), but instead use age as a proxy. Younger cohorts of women are likely to have more continuous experience than older women, so that for them age should be a better proxy; by comparing sex differences by age cohort, we can assess the sensitivity of the estimates to this measurement issue. Finally, relaxing the age by education restrictions is appealing because rising education levels have generated much higher education levels for younger cohorts.

To this point, the production function has been specified so that workers of different types have different marginal products, but are perfectly substitutable. Because this specification may be too restrictive, we also consider evidence from estimates of a production function in which workers are imperfect rather than perfect substitutes. It seems to us most natural to separate labor inputs along occupational lines. We therefore estimate a production function of the form

$$\ln(Y) = \ln(A) + \alpha \ln(K) + \beta \ln(M) + \gamma_P \ln(QL_P) + \gamma_{NP} \ln(QL_{NP})$$
$$+ g(K, M, QL_P, QL_{NP}) + \mu, \tag{6}$$

where the subscripts "P" and "NP" denote production and non-production workers, respectively, and $g(K, M, QL_P, QL_{NP})$ represents the higher-order terms in the translog production function.[16] The QL terms in equation (6) are of the same form as equation (4), but defined for the two subsets of workers.[17] We assume that the relative marginal productivities (and wages) are the same for workers in different demographic groups within each of these broad occupational groups, which permits us to focus on the consequences of relaxing the perfect substitutes assumption.

To preview the production function results, we find that the methods described in this subsection indicate that the productivity estimates are relatively robust. This suggests that we have obtained reliable estimates of marginal productivity differentials across different types of workers. Because we can supply robust estimates of the marginal productivity differentials, we can accomplish the central goal of this chapter, which is to compare estimated marginal productivity differentials with estimated wage differentials.

Finally, there is one fundamental identification issue regarding the estimation of plant-level production functions. As the preceding equations make clear, identification of productivity differentials associated with demographic characteristics of workers comes from covariation *across* plants in the demographic composition of the workforce and output. If we find evidence suggesting that, for example, women are less productive than men, the plant-level data do not enable us to determine whether the estimated lower productivity of women comes from the segregation of women into low-productivity plants,[18] with the productivities of women and men within plants roughly the same, or instead from the lower productivity of women relative to men within plants. However, when it comes to wages or earnings (for which precisely the same question arises), we can assess evidence on this question, since we have data on earnings at both the individual and plant level. We return to this point at the end of the next section when we describe our estimation of earnings differentials among workers.

Earnings differentials among workers

The goal of this chapter is to estimate the relative marginal products of different types of workers and then to compare these estimates with estimated relative wage differentials. There are a number of ways one could obtain the relative wage differentials. One possibility would be to use the estimates of wage differentials from some of the many papers filled with wage regressions. We prefer instead to use wage regression estimates computed from the sample of workers matched to plants in the WECD, in order to obtain the most comparable estimates of relative wages and relative productivity. To do this, we estimate wage differentials using plant-level (rather than individual-level) earnings equations. We have chosen to focus on plant-level earnings equations (although we verify that these estimates are not at odds with individual-level wage equation estimates) for three reasons. First, we are ultimately interested in testing the equality of wage and marginal productivity differentials. Focusing on plant-level wage equations allows us to jointly estimate the production function and wage equations, yielding straightforward statistical tests of the equality of relative wages and relative marginal products. Second, the labor cost measure from the Census of Population (the only one available at the individual level) refers to all jobs worked in the year, and therefore may not reflect earnings worked at the plant to which the worker is matched. Thus, the plant-level labor cost measure from the LRD is a more reliable earnings measure to use for estimating wage differentials to compare to our plant-level productivity differentials. Third, there may be some unobservables in the production function and wage equation. However, as long as we estimate both of these at the plant level, any biases from these unobservables ought to affect the estimated productivity and wage differentials similarly, at least under the null hypothesis, thus minimizing their impact on tests of the equality of relative marginal products and relative wages.

To establish a baseline for comparison with other data sets, Table 9.2 reports individual-level earnings regression estimates using the individual workers in the WECD. These regressions obviously use the Census of Population earnings measure, which is earnings on all jobs in the year. The first column reports estimates from a standard earnings regression. The estimates display results common to numerous other data sets. There is a significant wage gap between men and women, and a smaller but still significant wage gap between blacks and nonblacks.[19] The estimated life-cycle wage profile has the usual quadratic shape and the positive marriage premium (of 14 percent) parallels that found elsewhere.

As explained earlier, to get more reliable estimates of the demographic composition of plants' workforces, in the plant-level estimation we define workers' demographic characteristics more broadly than is typical for individual-level wage equations. In order to provide direct comparability between individual-level wage equations and the plant-level equations we discuss below, column (2) of Table 9.2 reports the results of the individual-level regression using the more aggregated forms of these characteristics including using cells for age ranges and establishment size, and using more limited education, occupation, and industry controls. The only major qualitative difference is that the magnitude of the estimated marriage premium increases. Other than that, the estimated coefficients of race and sex scarcely change, and the estimated age coefficients broadly reflect the quadratic shape from column (1).

To obtain a plant-level wage equation, for most of the analysis we retain the equiproportionate distribution restriction made in defining QL in the production function. We also (again paralleling the production function) restrict the relative wages of workers within a demographic group to be constant across all other demographic groups. Furthermore, we assume that all workers within each unique set of demographic groupings are paid the same amount, up to a plant-specific multiplicative random error. Under these assumptions, total log wages in a plant

Table 9.2 Individual-level Census of Population log earnings regressions[a]

	Specifications with usual individual-level controls (1)	Specifications with variables used in plant-level analysis (2)	Fixed plant effects (3)
Individual-level variables			
Female	−0.35	−0.38	−0.32
	(0.003)	(0.003)	(0.003)
Black	−0.05	−0.03	−0.08
	(0.01)	(0.01)	(0.01)
Age	0.08	—	—
	(0.001)		
Age$^2 \times 10^{-2}$	−0.08	—	—
	(0.001)		
Age 35–54	—	0.24	0.19
		(0.003)	(0.003)
Age 55+	—	0.23	0.18
		(0.005)	(0.004)
Ever married	0.14	0.28	0.25
	(0.004)	(0.004)	(0.004)
Highest degree attained			
High-school diploma	0.14	—	—
	(0.004)		
Some college/no degree	0.19	—	—
	(0.004)		
AA degree	0.22	—	—
	(0.01)		
BA or BS degree	0.37	—	—
	(0.01)		
Advanced degree	0.47	—	—
	(0.01)		
Some college or higher	—	0.15	0.11
		(0.003)	(0.003)
MSA	0.13	—	—
	(0.003)		
Log establishment employment	0.08	—	—
	(0.001)		
Dummy variables included for			
Region (4)	Yes	Yes	—
Occupation (one-digit)	Yes	No	No
Occupation (4)	No	Yes	Yes
Industry (two-digit)	Yes	No	—
Industry (13)	No	Yes	—
Establishment size (4)	No	Yes	—
R^2	0.48	0.39	—

Note

a The dependent variable is log earnings. Standard errors of the estimates are reported in parentheses. The sample size is 128,460. The sample includes all individuals matched to the establishments used in the analysis in the following tables. Less than high-school diploma is the omitted education category.

can be written as

$$\ln(w) = a' + \ln \left\{ [L + (\lambda_F - 1) F] \left[1 + (\lambda_B - 1) \frac{B}{L} \right] \left[1 + (\lambda_R - 1) \frac{R}{L} \right] \right.$$

$$\times \left[1 + (\lambda_G - 1) \frac{G}{L} \right] \left[1 + (\lambda_P - 1) \frac{P}{L} + (\lambda_O - 1) \frac{O}{L} \right]$$

$$\left. \times \left[1 + (\lambda_N - 1) \frac{N}{L} + (\lambda_S - 1) \frac{S}{L} + (\lambda_C - 1) \frac{C}{L} \right] \right\} + \varepsilon, \quad (7)$$

where a' is the log wage of the reference group (nonblack, never married, male, no college, young, unskilled production worker) and the λ terms represent the relative wage differentials associated with each characteristic. To see that this plant-level equation can be interpreted as the aggregation over workers in the plant of the individual-level wage equation, consider a simpler version of the wage equation involving only men and women. The total wage bill in levels implied by equation (7) is

$$w = w_M (L - F) + w_F F, \qquad (8)$$

where w_M and w_F are the average wages of men and women. This can be rewritten as

$$w = w_M (L - F) + \lambda_F w_M F = w_M (L + (\lambda_F - 1) F),$$

which in logs is

$$\ln w = a' + \ln(L + (\lambda_F - 1) F),$$

as in equation (7), where $a' = \ln(w_M)$.

Next, consider the individual-level wage equation in levels

$$w_i = w_M M_i + w_F F_i, \qquad (9)$$

where M_i and F_i are dummy variables for men and women, respectively. Clearly, the aggregation of this equation over all workers in the plant yields equation (8), from which, as we have shown, equation (7) can be derived.

We interpret equation (7) not as a behavioral equation but simply a definitional one. It assumes that all plants are wage takers in a competitive labor market so that wages do not vary systematically across plants.[20] In order to relax this assumption somewhat, in the empirical analysis we allow wages to vary systematically with industry and plant size.[21]

We actually have three compensation measures available in our data set: the plant's total annual wage and salary bill as reported in the LRD; the plant's total annual wage and salary bill plus expenditures on nonwage compensation as reported in the LRD; and an estimate of the plant's total annual wage and salary bill derived from Census of Population data on the sample of workers matched to the establishment, which, as noted above, refers to all jobs worked in the year. For simplicity, in the following discussion we refer to each of these measures as the plant's total wages. We examined results with each of the compensation measures, although our preferred measure is the plant's wages and salaries from the LRD, as this measure avoids the problems with using Census of Population earnings and is closer to the measures used in the vast literature on individual-level wage or earnings regressions than is the total labor cost measure.

As we noted at the end of the previous section, we cannot examine within-plant productivity differentials across groups of workers. However, we can use the Census of Population earnings to look at within-plant earnings differentials. We do this in column (3) of Table 9.2 by adding plant fixed effects to the individual-level earnings equation. The estimates indicate that most of the estimated wage differentials (with the exception of those associated with race) are largely *within* plants.[22] Given this, it seems valid to interpret the plant-level wage equation as the plant-level aggregation of the equation for individual wages. In contrast, if the wage differentials were largely between plants, we could not confidently interpret our estimates as measuring differences between demographic groups. In the absence of measures of productivity for individual workers, we cannot test whether estimated productivity differentials also reflect primarily within-plant differentials. However, given the evidence from the within-plant wage regressions, it is reasonable to assume this to be the case.

Measurement issues

Before turning to the results, we note that two additional measurement issues arise with respect to the demographic composition of the workforce. First, we measure the percentages of labor input from each demographic group as the percentages of workers in each demographic group in the sample of workers matched to each plant. However, if workers in different demographic groups work different numbers of hours, then we will mismeasure the proportion of labor supplied by workers in different groups. For example, if women on average work fewer hours per week than men, then we will overstate the female labor input and will underestimate the relative productivity of female labor (ϕ_F).[23] An alternative is to calculate the percentage of labor supplied by each type of worker using data on weeks worked and usual hours worked per week, as reported in the Census of Population, to construct annual hours estimates. In results not reported in the tables, when we measure the percentages of labor input for each demographic group using annual hours we obtain the expected result: women have higher estimated relative marginal products and relative earnings than when we do not use hours data to measure labor inputs. However, the Census of Population data measure weeks and hours on all jobs worked in the year. Because men are much more likely than women to hold multiple jobs, the annual hours estimate we construct from the Census of Population may go too far in adjusting hours supplied to the plant. Indeed, there is some evidence that this is occurring. Plant-level estimates of the male–female wage difference that we obtain when we use earnings data from the Census of Population are larger than those we obtain when we use the plant-level earnings measure from the LRD. This suggests that men's earnings in the Census of Population come partly from hours worked in jobs other than those in the plants to which we match these men. As a result, we have chosen to maintain the measurement of demographic composition using simply the number of workers of each type employed at the plant. We note, however, that with respect to the questions of substantive interest—such as whether there is a difference between the relative marginal product and relative earnings of women—the hours corrections did not affect our conclusions.

The second measurement problem arises because we treat the percentages of workers in each demographic group as known for the purposes of estimation, although they are in fact estimated from a sample. This measurement error may bias the estimated productivity and wage differentials. The measurement error in the estimates of the percentage of workers in each demographic group is likely to affect both the productivity and wage equations, however, and it is the comparison between corresponding coefficients in the two equations that is of primary interest.[24] Nonetheless, to the extent that productivity differentials across workers may be of independent interest, and to the extent that measurement error may under some circumstances bias coefficients differently in the wage and productivity equations, it is an issue that merits consideration. To explore the consequences of measurement error, we carry out a Monte Carlo simulation that essentially mimics the sampling we do in constructing the WECD. The precise methods are described in the following section. To preview our results, we find what we regard as relatively small biases in the estimated productivity (and wage) differentials, which do not affect the qualitative conclusions.

Plant-level estimates of marginal productivity and wage differentials

Up to this point we have described our methods of estimating relative marginal productivities in detail, and have also explained how we estimate corresponding relative wages. With these estimates in hand, it is straightforward to test whether relative wages across workers in different demographic groups reflect differences in marginal productivity. Because the production functions and wage equations are estimated jointly and because we test for differences between them, we present the production function estimates and wage equation estimates together in each of the next four tables.

Our main results are presented in Tables 9.3–9.6. Each table presents joint estimates of equation (4) and equation (7), for alternative specifications of the production function and, when appropriate, corresponding differences in the specification of the earnings equation. The parameters are estimated using nonlinear least squares. In each case, we present p-values for Wald tests of the equality of the estimates of the ϕ's (the productivity differentials) with the corresponding estimates of the λ's (the wage differentials).

Table 9.3 begins by reporting basic results of the joint estimation of the wage and productivity equations. In this table, we use LRD wages and salaries to measure earnings. We first discuss the production function estimates. The coefficient for

Table 9.3 Joint production function and wage equation estimates: translog output production function, using LRD wages and salaries[a]

	Log (output) (1)	Log (wages and salaries) (2)	p-*value,* col. (1)= col. (2) (3)
Demographic characteristics			
Female	0.84	0.55	0.00
	(0.06)	(0.02)	
Black	1.18	1.12	0.63
	(0.14)	(0.05)	
Aged 35–54	1.15	1.19	0.71
	(0.11)	(0.04)	
Aged 55+	1.19	1.18	0.95
	(0.15)	(0.05)	
Ever married	1.45	1.37	0.68
	(0.21)	(0.07)	
Productive inputs			
Log capital	0.05	—	
	(0.01)		
Log capital × log capital	0.021	—	
	(0.008)		
Log capital × log materials	−0.03	—	
	(0.01)		
Log capital × log labor quality	0.014	—	
	(0.009)		
Log materials	0.59	—	
	(0.02)		
Log materials × log materials	0.15	—	
	(0.01)		
Log materials × log labor quality	−0.12	—	
	(0.01)		
Log labor quality	0.34	—	
	(0.02)		
Log labor quality ×log labor quality	0.11	—	
	(0.02)		
Other worker controls			
Some college	1.67	1.43	
	(0.16)	(0.04)	
Managerial/professional	1.13	1.00	
	(0.14)	(0.04)	
Technical, sales, administrative and service	1.27	1.11	
	(0.12)	(0.04)	
Precision production, craft, and repair	1.06	1.02	
	(0.12)	(0.04)	

Note

a Standard errors of the estimates are reported in parentheses. The sample size is 3,102. Estimates of the intercept are not reported. Test statistics are from Wald tests. The excluded occupation is operators, fabricators, and laborers. Other control variables included in the production function are: industries (13); size (4 categories); region (4); and establishment part of multi-plant firm. Other control variables included in the wage equation are: industries (13); size (4 categories); and region (4). These control variables were selected by estimating the production function and wage equation jointly without the demographic controls, and retaining those sets of control variables that were jointly significant. The model is estimated with the data transformed so that output is homogeneous of degree S in the inputs, where S is the sum of the coefficients of the linear terms for the production function inputs. For variables that enter linearly, we use deviations from the means. For variables that enter nonlinearly, we first estimate the model using the data in levels, and then take deviations from the means of the nonlinear terms. This two-step procedure is valid because the estimated coefficients of all of the nonlinear terms are invariant to the deviations from the mean transformation.

females indicates that women are somewhat less productive than men, with an estimate of ϕ_F of 0.84, which is significantly less than 1. The estimates indicate that blacks are if anything slightly more productive than nonblack workers, as the estimate of ϕ_B is 1.18, although this estimate is not significantly different from one. The estimated age profile suggests that productivity increases somewhat with age, although the differences are not statistically significant. Finally, the estimates indicate that married workers are considerably more productive than unmarried workers, with an estimated relative marginal productivity of 1.45, which is significantly different from 1.

The other estimates are of some interest. The estimated coefficients on the capital, materials, and labor inputs provide evidence against a Cobb–Douglas specification of the production function, since many of the estimated coefficients on the higher-order terms are significantly different from zero. The estimated coefficients of the relative marginal productivity of more-educated workers and workers in higher-skilled occupations (the omitted occupation is operators, fabricators, and laborers, or unskilled blue-collar workers) are in line with expectations, as all of these exceed 1, some significantly.

The estimates of relative wage differentials are reported in column (2). The estimates indicate that women's wages are 45 percent lower than men's, a difference that is strongly statistically significant and is consistent with the individual-level regression results in Table 9.2. The estimates also indicate significantly higher wages for workers aged 35–54, aged 55+, and for married workers. In addition, although we do not focus as much on these results, paralleling the productivity results the estimated wage differential for workers with more education is strongly positive, and the wage differentials for the three excluded occupations are positive or non-negative.

Comparing the estimated wage and marginal productivity differentials shows that for most groups of workers, the estimated differentials are statistically indistinguishable. For the age categories, marital status, and race, the p-values for the tests of the equality of the estimated wage and productivity differentials range from 0.63 to 0.95. Moreover, the point estimates of the marginal productivity and wage differentials are very close, particularly for the age estimates.[25] Thus we fail to reject the hypothesis that the wage differentials reflect differences in marginal products for these workers. This is also true for our occupational groupings. Our estimates do suggest, however, that for educated workers the difference between the estimated productivity and wage differential is marginally statistically significant (with a p-value of 0.11).[26]

The sharp departure from these results is the evidence for sex differences. The production function estimates indicate that women's marginal productivity is somewhat lower than men's, as the estimate of ϕ_F is 0.84. However, the wage equation estimates point to a larger wage gap, with an estimate of λ_F of 0.55. The p-value of 0.00 shows that we strongly reject the hypothesis of equality of productivity and wage gaps. The results imply that, on average, women's wages fall short of men's by considerably more than can be explained by their lower marginal productivity. This is consistent with the standard wage discrimination hypothesis.

The plant-level wage equation results for blacks showing that blacks earn slightly *higher* wages than nonblacks conflicts with the individual-level wage regressions reported in Table 9.2 (and the commonplace finding) showing a small negative, but statistically significant, wage differential between blacks and non-blacks. The reason for this difference is probably due to upward bias in our estimates of ϕ_B and λ_B, which arises for two reasons. First, as discussed in the section "The data," our sample of workers underestimates the number of blacks working in manufacturing. The under-representation of blacks would cause the estimates of both λ_B and ϕ_B to be biased away from 1. However, since we are testing for the difference between λ_B and ϕ_B, our test of the equality of the wage and productivity differentials is still valid under the null hypothesis that $\phi_B = \lambda_B$.[27] Second, the fixed-plant-effects estimate of the wage differential between blacks and nonblacks in the WECD is a bit larger (-0.08) than the cross-section differential (-0.05), indicating that within plants, blacks earn less than nonblacks, but that blacks work in slightly higher-paying plants (see also Carrington and Troske, 1998). This suggests that the production function and wage equation estimates—which use cross-plant variation—mask lower relative wages paid to blacks. Nonetheless, our results should be biased toward finding no evidence of discrimination only if blacks tend to work in plants that pay relatively higher wages, but in which productivity is not relatively higher. Given that we cannot measure within-plant productivity differentials between workers, all we can conclude is that our results from the between-plant estimates are not consistent with discrimination against black workers.

The finding of equal changes in relative marginal productivity and relative wages with age is most consistent with the general human capital model of investment, in which wages rise lock-step with productivity (Mincer, 1974). In contrast, these results are less consistent with models in which wages rise faster than marginal product over the life cycle (Lazear, 1979), or, as in some models of specific human capital investment, more slowly. The equality of relative marginal productivity and wages of married workers shows that the marriage wage premium reflects an underlying productivity differential and is not attributable to discrimination in favor of married workers. However, the result does not help sort out whether marriage increases the productivity of men or whether high productivity men are selected into marriage (see Korenman and Neumark, 1991).[28]

We now turn to numerous analyses of the robustness of the results reported to this point, focusing in particular on alternative estimates of the production function from which the estimated marginal productivity differentials are obtained. Table 9.4 examines the issue of the potential endogeneity of materials in the production function, reporting estimates from the value-added specification, and IV estimates of the output production function. In the value-added estimates, reported in columns (1)–(3), most of the estimated productivity differentials are very similar to the results in Table 9.3. The only differences are that the estimated relative productivity of married workers rises, and that of workers aged 55 and over falls (to a bit below 1, although not significantly). Instrumental variables estimates are reported in columns (4)–(6). Since the production function and wage equations are nonlinear, there is no clear choice of instruments because identification can be achieved with both linear and nonlinear combinations of the exogenous variables in the equations and the excluded variables (in this case, the log of lagged materials). We used as our instrument list the most obvious choice given the production function and wage equation: all demographic characteristics and dummy variables, and linear and second-order combinations (squares and interactions) of log(capital), log(lagged materials), and log(total employment). We do not emphasize the IV estimation elsewhere in the chapter because if there are omitted plant fixed effects that are correlated with materials, then lagged materials is not a valid instrument (the instrument is valid, however, if the output differences over time are due to serially uncorrelated period-specific effects). However, the results reported in columns (4)–(6) in Table 9.4 are similar to those in Table 9.3, with two exceptions. First, the estimated marginal productivity of women relative to men rises to 1.01, indicating no difference in productivity. Since the estimate of relative earnings is unchanged, this only strengthens the evidence that women's relative earnings are less than their marginal products. Second, the estimated relative marginal productivity of more-educated workers falls somewhat to 1.61 and becomes less precise, so that the deviation between relative marginal products and relative earnings of these workers shrinks and is no longer significant (with a p-value of 0.55). Overall, although the value-added and IV estimation results vary somewhat from the results found in Table 9.3, these changes are generally not large, and do not affect the substantive conclusions. In particular, regardless of our specification we find evidence consistent with sex discrimination.

In Panels A–D of Table 9.5, we report results based on estimations for which we drop the restrictions of equiproportionate distributions of workers across demographic groups, and equiproportionate productivity restrictions. In the estimation in Panel A we define the proportions of female, married workers and female, unmarried workers directly, rather than assuming that the proportion of females is the same among both married and unmarried workers. Similarly, we relax the restriction that the marginal productivity of female married workers relative to male married workers equals that of female unmarried workers to male unmarried workers. We also relax the corresponding restrictions by race. In this panel, for neither wages nor productivity were any of the estimated interaction coefficients significantly different from 1. We therefore report the fully restricted model, but without imposing the equiproportionate restriction on the data.[29] The estimates and test results closely parallel the corresponding estimates in Table 9.3. Thus, the imposition in Table 9.3 of the equiproportionate assumption on the data—at least for the demographic categories that we have considered here—has little or no effect on the estimates.

In Panel B we carry out a similar exercise, but relax the restrictions with regard to sex and occupation, allowing the proportion of the workforce in each occupation to vary by sex, and wage and productivity differentials to vary by sex, across occupations. Our primary interest is in the sensitivity of estimated wage and productivity differentials by sex to these restrictions—especially the restriction that the occupational distribution by sex is the same. In the unrestricted model, the

Table 9.4 Joint production function and wage equation estimates: translog value-added production function, and instrumental variables estimates of translog output production function, using LRD wages and salaries[a]

	Translog value-added production function, NLLS			Translog output production function, IV		
	Log (value added) (1)	Log (wages and salaries) (2)	p-value, col. (1) = col. (2) (3)	Log (output) (4)	Log (wages and salaries) (5)	p-value, col. (4) = col. (5) (6)
Demographic characteristics						
Female	0.83 (0.07)	0.56 (0.02)	0.00	1.01 (0.10)	0.55 (0.02)	0.00
Black	1.13 (0.15)	1.12 (0.05)	0.92	1.19 (0.18)	1.12 (0.05)	0.66
Aged 35–54	1.25 (0.12)	1.20 (0.04)	0.65	1.23 (0.21)	1.20 (0.04)	0.87
Aged 55+	0.93 (0.14)	1.18 (0.05)	0.07	1.17 (0.20)	1.18 (0.05)	0.94
Ever married	1.72 (0.29)	1.37 (0.07)	0.22	1.48 (0.29)	1.39 (0.07)	0.73
Productive inputs						
Log capital	0.16 (0.01)	—		0.07 (0.02)	—	
Log capital × log capital	0.04 (0.01)	—		0.06 (0.01)	—	
Log capital × log materials	—	—		−0.030 (0.014)	—	
Log capital × log labor quality	−0.027 (0.019)	—		−0.04 (0.03)	—	
Log materials	—	—		0.60 (0.05)	—	
Log materials × log materials	—	—		0.17 (0.01)	—	
Log materials × log labor quality	—	—		−0.14 (0.02)	—	
Log labor quality	0.82 (0.04)	—		0.32 (0.13)	—	
Log labor quality ×log labor quality	0.03 (0.04)	—		0.19 (0.08)	—	
Other worker controls						
Some college	1.73 (0.17)	1.44 (0.04)		1.61 (0.29)	1.44 (0.04)	
Managerial/ professional	0.86 (0.12)	0.99 (0.04)		1.19 (0.17)	0.99 (0.04)	

Table 9.4 Continued

	Translog value-added production function, NLLS			Translog output production function, IV		
	Log (value added) (1)	Log (wages and salaries) (2)	p-value, col. (1) = col. (2) (3)	Log (output) (4)	Log (wages and salaries) (5)	p-value, col. (4) = col. (5) (6)
Technical, sales, administrative and service	1.13 (0.12)	1.11 (0.04)		1.28 (0.17)	1.11 (0.04)	
Precision production, craft, and repair	1.00 (0.12)	1.02 (0.04)		1.02 (0.15)	1.02 (0.04)	

Note

a See footnotes to Table 9.3 for details. NLLS: nonlinear least squares. For the IV estimation, since the production function and wage equation are nonlinear, there is no clear choice of instruments because identification can be achieved with both linear and nonlinear combinations of the exogenous variables in the equations and the excluded variables (in this case, the log of lagged materials). We used as our instrument list the most obvious choice given the production function and wage equation: all demographic characteristics and dummy variables, and linear and second-order combinations (squares and interactions) of log(capital), log(lagged materials), and log(total employment).

interactions for managerial/professional workers and technical, sales, etc., workers were significant for either the production function or the wage equation (or both), so the specification retaining these is reported in Panel B. In this case, the coefficients for female in the top panel refer to unskilled workers (operators, fabricators, and laborers) and precision production, craft, and repair workers. Among these workers, the relative wage of women is less than their relative marginal productivity (0.49 vs. 0.71), and the estimates are significantly different from each other (p-value $= 0.00$). The last two rows of the panel report sex differences in wages and productivity for the other two occupational categories.[30] The sex gap in wages exceeds that in productivity for both occupations, but only for technical, sales, etc., workers, is the difference significant. For female managerial/professional workers, although we find that relative earnings fall short of relative marginal products (0.70 vs. 0.89), the difference between productivity and wages is insignificant. The extra information that we obtain from Panel B of Table 9.5, then, is that the evidence consistent with sex discrimination comes from the nonmanagerial and nonprofessional occupations, in which 86 percent of the women in the sample work.

Panels C and D, in turn, relax these restrictions for sex differentials by age, and age differentials by education. In both cases, the interactions on the wage differentials are significantly different from 1, so we report these richer specifications in the table. Looking first at Panel C, we find that the relative marginal productivities and relative wages of older cohorts of women are lower than for

Table 9.5 Joint production function and wage equation estimates: translog output production function, using LRD wages and salaries, dropping equiproportionate restrictions on means and parameters, and relaxing perfect substitutes assumption, estimated coefficients of demographic characteristics[a]

	A. Drop restrictions on marriage, sex, and race			B. Drop restrictions on sex and occupation			C. Drop restrictions on sex and age			D. Drop restrictions on age and education			E. Prod. and Non-Prod. Workers as Imperfect Substitutes		
	Log (output)	Log (wages and salaries)	p-value, (1) = (2)	Log (output)	Log (wages and salaries)	p-value, (4) = (5)	Log (output)	Log (wages and salaries)	p-value, (7) = (8)	Log (output)	Log (wages and salaries)	p-value, (10) = (11)	Log (output)	Log (wages and salaries)	p-value, (13) = (14)
	(1)	(2)	(3)	(4)	(5)	(6)	(7)	(8)	(9)	(10)	(11)	(12)	(13)	(14)	(15)
Female	0.84 (0.06)	0.55 (0.02)	0.00	0.71 (0.07)	0.49 (0.02)	0.00	0.99 (0.15)	0.65 (0.04)	0.02	0.84 (0.06)	0.55 (0.02)	0.00	0.90 (0.07)	0.56 (0.02)	0.00
Black	1.18 (0.14)	1.13 (0.05)	0.70	1.22 (0.14)	1.13 (0.05)	0.51	1.18 (0.14)	1.11 (0.05)	0.62	1.19 (0.14)	1.12 (0.05)	0.59	1.43 (0.17)	1.16 (0.05)	0.10
Aged 35–54	1.15 (0.11)	1.19 (0.04)	0.73	1.15 (0.11)	1.20 (0.04)	0.65	1.25 (0.14)	1.26 (0.04)	0.96	1.22 (0.16)	1.26 (0.05)	0.80	1.22 (0.12)	1.17 (0.04)	0.70
Aged 55+	1.19 (0.15)	1.18 (0.05)	0.93	1.17 (0.14)	1.18 (0.05)	0.93	1.23 (0.18)	1.22 (0.06)	0.97	1.16 (0.20)	1.31 (0.07)	0.45	1.19 (0.15)	1.16 (0.05)	0.84
Ever married	1.46 (0.21)	1.38 (0.06)	0.68	1.47 (0.21)	1.38 (0.07)	0.64	1.45 (0.21)	1.36 (0.06)	0.66	1.48 (0.21)	1.39 (0.07)	0.64	1.48 (0.22)	1.51 (0.09)	0.88
Female × managerial/professional	—	—		1.26 (0.32)	1.42 (0.15)		—	—		—	—		—	—	
Female × technical, sales, administrative, and service	—	—		1.81 (0.38)	1.42 (0.12)		—	—		—	—		—	—	
Female × aged 35–54	—	—		—	—		0.75 (0.17)	0.77 (0.07)		—	—		—	—	
Female × aged 55+	—	—		—	—		0.88 (0.26)	0.83 (0.11)		—	—		—	—	
Aged 35–54 × some college	—	—		—	—		—	—		0.86 (0.16)	0.87 (0.05)		—	—	
Aged 55+ × some college	—	—		—	—		—	—		0.96 (0.26)	0.72 (0.07)		—	—	

Relative marginal product and wage of women within occupations			
Managerial/professional	0.89	0.70	0.33
Technical, etc.	1.29	0.70	0.01
Relative marginal product and wage of women within age groups			
Aged 35–54	0.74	0.50	0.01
Aged 55+	0.87	0.54	0.10
Relative marginal product and wage of workers aged 35–54 with some college	1.05	1.10	0.71
Relative marginal product and wage of workers age 55+ with some college	1.11	0.94	0.38

Note

a See footnotes to Table 9.3 for details. In Panels A–D, we dropped the equiproportionate restriction in estimating the proportion of workers in each demographic group, and the corresponding restriction on the parameters, and estimated the unrestricted model. We then re-estimated the model imposing those parameter restrictions that were not rejected at the 5 percent significance level; if either the productivity or wage interaction was significant, we retained both. The bottom rows report estimated productivity and wage differentials for pairings of demographic groups for which parameter restrictions were not rejected. In Panel E, the sample size is 2,883. It is slightly smaller than in the previous tables because plants with either no production workers or no nonproduction workers in the matched sample of workers had to be dropped. In these specifications, the relative wages and marginal productivity of production and nonproduction workers are allowed to differ, but separate occupational differentials within the production and nonproduction groups are not included.

the youngest cohort. This could occur because age overstates experience more for older cohorts, so that conditional on age older women are less productive (and paid less). For the youngest and prime-aged cohort, the evidence that the sex gap in wages exceeds the productivity gap remains very strong, with *p*-values of 0.01 or less. For the oldest workers the estimates point in the same direction, but because the marginal productivity differential is imprecisely estimated, the *p*-value rises to 0.10. Panel D introduces interactions of age and education, to allow for educational differences across age cohorts. For the oldest group the point estimates suggest wage profiles rising faster than marginal productivity for the less-educated group (with relative earnings of 1.31, vs. relative marginal productivity of 1.16), and the opposite for the more-educated group (with relative earnings of 0.94, vs. relative marginal productivity of 1.11). However, the estimates of this richer model are sufficiently imprecise that the statistical conclusion is unchanged, as we fail to reject the equality of changes in relative marginal products and wages with age, for either education level.[31]

The estimates in Panel E are for the specification of the production function in which production and nonproduction workers are imperfect substitutes. This has relatively little impact on the estimated relative marginal products of different types of workers. The estimated marginal productivity of women rises slightly to 0.90. The corresponding estimate rises more for blacks, but this estimate is relatively imprecise. The estimated productivity differentials for older and married workers are similar to those in Table 9.3 in which perfect substitutability is imposed. Although not reported in the table, it is of interest that for this specification the estimated relative marginal product of more-educated workers falls to 1.43, virtually the same as the estimated relative earnings of these workers (1.44). Thus, the differential between relative marginal products and earnings for more-educated workers appears due to the perfect substitutes production function specification. On the other hand, this panel shows that imposing the perfect substitutes assumption has little effect on the estimated relatively marginal products and earnings for the groups of workers in which we are most interested.

The WECD only contains information on a cross-section of plants and workers. Because of this, we are unable to account formally (say, through a fixed-effects analysis) for differences across plants in unobservables that may be correlated with the demographic characteristics of a plant. If these unobservable plant-level characteristics affect the productivity of workers in the plant (and also perhaps wages), then we would expect the omission of these plant-level characteristics to bias our estimates of productivity (and wage differences) across different types of workers.[32] While we obviously cannot account for all unobservable plant-level differences, we can try to get a sense of the magnitude of this problem by breaking up the sample along dimensions in which we think plants may differ. This should account for at least some differences across plants that may be related to their demographic composition.

In Panel A of Table 9.6, we divide the sample into plants with above- and below-median percentages female in the workforce, for two reasons. First, the nature or extent of sex discrimination may differ in plants with varying proportions of female workers. Second, women may disproportionately work in plants with

Table 9.6 Joint production function and wage equation estimates: translog output production function, using LRD wages and salaries, estimated coefficients of demographic characteristics, subsamples of the data set[a]

	Log (output) (1)	Log (wages and salaries) (2)	p-value, col. (1) = col. (2) (3)	Log (output) (4)	Log (wages and salaries) (5)	p-value, col. (4) = col. (5) (6)
A. High and low percent female						
	Plants above median (25%) percent female (N = 1,508)			Plants at or below median percent female (N = 1,594)		
Female	1.01 (0.15)	0.56 (0.03)	0.00	1.13 (0.24)	0.74 (0.07)	0.10
Black	1.41 (0.22)	1.12 (0.07)	0.17	0.83 (0.18)	1.10 (0.06)	0.11
Aged 35–54	1.05 (0.16)	1.13 (0.06)	0.63	1.27 (0.14)	1.18 (0.05)	0.50
Aged 55+	1.29 (0.24)	1.15 (0.08)	0.53	1.04 (0.17)	1.17 (0.06)	0.44
Ever married	1.56 (0.34)	1.42 (0.11)	0.67	1.34 (0.23)	1.26 (0.07)	0.72
B. High and low employment						
	Above median (166) employment (N = 1,551)			At or below median employment (N = 1,551)		
Female	1.11 (0.14)	0.53 (0.02)	0.00	0.73 (0.07)	0.61 (0.03)	0.05
Black	1.04 (0.21)	1.15 (0.06)	0.57	1.30 (0.17)	1.10 (0.07)	0.24
Aged 35–54	1.76 (0.36)	1.51 (0.08)	0.48	1.05 (0.10)	1.05 (0.04)	0.92
Aged 55+	1.03 (0.35)	1.22 (0.10)	0.58	1.20 (0.15)	1.13 (0.06)	0.60
Ever married	1.65 (0.63)	1.90 (0.24)	0.68	1.34 (0.18)	1.27 (0.07)	0.69

Note
a See footnotes to Table 9.3 for details.

different technologies than plants which employ mostly men. Some of the estimates vary quite a bit across these two subsamples—in particular, the estimated relative marginal productivity of blacks, and of workers aged 35–54 and 55+. However, the estimates are not sufficiently precise that the statistical conclusions regarding these groups are affected. The estimated relative marginal productivity of women is approximately 1 in both subsamples, but relative earnings are estimated to be a bit higher in plants with a lower percent female. This fact, coupled with the imprecision of the relative marginal productivity estimate, means that we cannot strongly reject the hypothesis of the equality of relative marginal products and relative wages (p-value $= 0.10$) for women in these plants. One particular hypothesis regarding technological differences and the percent female is that the percent female is highest in plants that have adopted technology that conserves on (generally male) production labor.[33] This would bias upward our estimates of ϕ_F because high percent female plants would also tend to be highly productive, technically sophisticated plants. However, as long as these plants take wages as given, relative wages will not be affected, hence potentially leading to spurious evidence of discrimination in the tests we report in the earlier tables. If our previous estimates of ϕ_F were biased upward because of this cross-plant variation in labor-saving technology coupled with a positive covariation between such technology and the percent female, then when we split the sample into plants with relatively higher or lower percentages of women, the estimate of ϕ_F should fall, as we effectively condition on this technology.[34] In fact, however, the estimate of ϕ_F rises in both subsamples.[35]

In Panel B we disaggregate the plants into those with employment levels above and below the median. These results may provide some indication of possible differences in the extent of discrimination between large and small plants. The estimated degree of discrimination against women (measured by the estimate of $\phi_F - \lambda_F$) is much smaller in the smaller plants. These results suggest that smaller firms are less able to indulge in sex discrimination, which may be in part because they have less market power (Becker, 1971). Some of the other estimates vary quite a bit between the two subsamples, but only in cases in which the estimates become imprecise; the qualitative conclusions are not affected.

Overall, the disaggregated estimates indicate that the estimates of relative marginal products of workers in different demographic groups are somewhat sensitive to the sample composition. However, the qualitative nature of the evidence from the separate subsamples is consistent, indicating that the full-sample estimates of the relative marginal products of different types of workers are relatively robust. In our view, the stability of these estimates across the various specifications we present provides strong evidence that we are obtaining parameter estimates of marginal productivity differentials that can be meaningfully compared with estimated earnings differentials, to test alternative theories of wage differences between these types of workers. We would not argue, however, that additional research utilizing the approach we pursue in this chapter could not generate more reliable estimates of variations in marginal productivity across different types of workers.

The role of measurement error from matched samples of workers

As mentioned earlier, although we only have estimates of the percentage of workers with each set of demographic characteristics in each plant, until now we have treated these percentages as known for the purposes of estimation. In this section, we explore more fully the potential effects of measurement error that arises from estimating these percentages. Specifically, we quantify the magnitudes of measurement error biases with a Monte Carlo simulation.[36]

Consider the production function and wage equations given by equations (2), (4), and (7).[37] From the data, we know the true values of Y, K, M, and L for each plant. All of the remaining variables (F/L, R/L, etc.) are estimated from the sample of T workers within each plant. We simulate the effects of measurement error by creating a synthetic workforce of L workers for each plant. We do this by creating L/T (rounded to the nearest integer) synthetic workers for each of the T workers in the sample. With this new synthetic workforce of L workers, we sample randomly without replacement T workers, and use this simulated sample to estimate the proportions of workers in each demographic group.[38] Finally, we use these simulated estimates of these proportions to jointly estimate the production function and wage specifications in columns (1) and (2) of Table 9.3, obtaining new estimates of the productivity and wage differentials (the ϕ's and λ's) across demographic groups. We repeat this process 1,000 times, yielding 1,000 different values for each of the ϕ's and λ's. This procedure enables us to assess the impact on our results of measurement error in the estimated proportions of workers in each demographic group, by comparing model estimates based on the simulated data to model estimates based on the WECD data, which we treat as true. In other words, we assess the impact of measurement error on the estimated ϕ's and λ's by adding sampling error to the estimated proportions of workers in each demographic group, and re-estimating these parameters.[39]

Summary results of the 1,000 simulations are reported in columns (3) and (4) of Table 9.7, and can be compared to the results from Table 9.3 (repeated in columns (1) and (2)) to assess the magnitude of the biases caused by estimating the demographic proportions. The results indicate measurement error biases that, as expected, pull the estimated coefficients toward 1, and are greater in magnitude the farther from 1 is the true value. For example, the mean estimate of ϕ_F in the

Table 9.7 Measurement error simulation results[a]

	Estimated productivity differential (1)	*Estimated wage differential* (2)	*Simulated mean productivity differential* (3)	*Simulated mean wage differential* (4)
Female	0.84	0.55	0.87	0.63
	(0.06)	(0.02)	(0.03)	(0.01)
Aged 35–54	1.15	1.19	1.12	1.15
	(0.11)	(0.04)	(0.06)	(0.02)
Aged 55+	1.19	1.18	1.14	1.14
	(0.15)	(0.05)	(0.07)	(0.03)
Ever married	1.45	1.37	1.23	1.21
	(0.21)	(0.07)	(0.08)	(0.03)

Note

a The estimated productivity and wage differentials in columns (1) and (2) are from Table 9.3, columns (1) and (2). The standard errors of the estimates, and the standard deviations of the simulated values, are reported in parentheses.

simulations is 0.87, and the estimate using the actual data is 0.84; the mean estimate of λ_F in the simulations is 0.63, and the estimate using the actual data is 0.55. These results show that the effect of measurement error is to bias us toward finding no discernable productivity or wage differentials across workers, and toward finding no differences between the relative productivity and wage estimates for a given type of worker (since estimates of parameters that are further from 1 have larger absolute biases toward 1). Thus, the power of the tests of the equality of wage and productivity differentials is somewhat reduced because of measurement error.

We therefore conclude from the simulation that our earlier estimates indicating significant estimated gaps between relative wages and productivity for women are robust to the measurement error problem. On the other hand, we consistently found evidence of the equality of relative wages and relative marginal products for married workers and for workers of different ages, using the actual data. However, the closeness of the point estimates of these premia, the relatively large estimated standard errors of the productivity differentials, and the similarity between the distributions of the simulated estimates for the wage and productivity premia in Table 9.7, lead us to believe that even in the absence of measurement error, we would still find no significant difference between the relative wages and relative marginal products for married workers or for workers in different age categories.[40]

Conclusions

Using evidence on wage differentials among different types of workers to test theories of wage determination is one of the most common avenues of research in labor economics. Often, the alternative theories being considered are "productivity-based" vs. "nonproductivity-based," such as in the discrimination literature. What is almost invariably missing from these studies, however, is an independent measure of productivity. Most studies instead use observable individual-level characteristics that are presumed to be proxies for productivity.

This chapter uses plant-level data on inputs and outputs matched with individual-level data on workers to estimate relative marginal products of workers with different demographic characteristics. Although production function estimation is a complicated task, and even more so in our case where we are adding labor quality terms that distinguish among many types of workers, we obtain relatively robust (and seemingly reasonable) estimates of these relative marginal products. We then compare these estimates of relative marginal products to estimates of relative earnings and address many of the same questions that have previously been addressed without the advantage of an independent productivity measure.

With one major exception, our basic results indicate that for most groups of workers wage differentials do, in fact, match productivity differentials. Workers who have ever been married are paid more than never-married workers and the wage premium they receive reflects a corresponding productivity premium. This suggests that the marriage premium does not simply reflect discrimination against unmarried workers, but reflects actual productivity differences. However, our data do not allow us to distinguish between the hypothesis that marriage reflects an unobservable variable associated with higher wages, and the hypothesis that marriage makes workers more productive.

We find that for prime-aged workers (aged 35–54) and older workers (aged 55 and over) productivity and earnings rise at the same rate over the life cycle. Although the estimated productivity differentials by age are not very precise, they are very close to the estimated earnings differentials. This evidence is most consistent with models in which wages rise lock-step with productivity, such as the general human capital model.

We find no evidence consistent with discrimination against blacks in manufacturing. In addition, there does not appear to be any productivity differential between blacks and nonblacks which might be attributable to pre-market discrimination or other unobserved characteristics, although we are less confident in our separate estimates of the race gap in wages and the race gap in productivity than in our estimates of the difference between them.

Finally, in contrast, in nearly all of our specifications and samples, we find that women's marginal product is perhaps somewhat below that of men. But we find that women are paid significantly less than men, with the wage differential between men and women generally much larger than the productivity differential. These results are strongest for women who are not managers (most of the sample), women who work in plants that employ a lot of women, and larger plants. The statistical evidence is strong enough to reject the null hypothesis that relative marginal products and relative wages are equal, which would be implied by a spot labor market with no sex discrimination. Although there is probably no single decisive test for discrimination in labor markets, we regard this evidence—based on independent estimates of relative marginal products to compare with relative earnings—to be considerably more convincing than the evidence produced by the typical wage regression discrimination study.

Acknowledgments

We are grateful to Joe Altonji, Zvi Griliches, Bruce Meyer, Chris Robinson, Dek Terrell, an anonymous referee, and seminar participants at the University of Chicago, Hebrew University, Michigan, Michigan State, Northwestern, NYU, UCLA, UCSD, the FTC, the Census Bureau, and the NBER for helpful comments, and to Kim Bayard and Daniel Hansen for research assistance. The opinions expressed herein are solely those of the authors and do not in any way reflect the views of the US Census Bureau. This research was supported by NSF grant SBR95-10876. Neumark's research was also supported by NIA grant K01-AG00589.

The main data used in this chapter were collected under the provisions of Title 13 US Code and are only available at the Center for Economic Studies, US Census Bureau. To obtain access to these data, contact the Center for Economic Studies, US Census Bureau, Rm. 211/WPII, Washington, DC, 20233.

Notes

1 However, they are somewhat limited in that they are only cross-sectional, only cover the manufacturing sector, and are weighted toward large plants.
2 The WECD is a very rich and useful data set, and has so far been utilized only in a few other studies (Troske, 1999; Carrington and Troske, 1998). There are clearly many important issues which these data may be able to address; we limit this chapter solely to the analysis of the relationship between the productivity and wage differentials among workers with different demographic characteristics.
3 This chapter builds on the framework used in Hellerstein and Neumark (1995 and 1999), to analyze Israeli manufacturing data (although the WECD offers numerous advantages over the Israeli data), and it represents a departure from most of the existing empirical literature on wage determination. As discussed in those two papers, there is little existing research comparing productivity and wage data, and even less using firm-level data. Brown and Medoff (1978) estimate a production function using state-by-industry level data to test whether the union wage premium is associated with higher productivity of union labor. Leonard (1984) uses similar data over time to examine the impact of Affirmative Action laws on productivity in the United States. One firm-level productivity and wage study examines evidence of sex discrimination using data from the nineteenth-century French textile industry (Cox and Nye, 1989). Studies applied to more narrowly defined industries have been pursued in the union literature (Clark, 1980; Allen, 1984). Other research has used proxies for productivity, including using piece-rate pay to measure productivity in time-rate work (Foster and Rosenzweig, 1993) and performance ratings (Medoff and Abraham, 1980; Holzer, 1990; Korenman and Neumark, 1991).
4 Labor supply could be less than completely inelastic; as long as market wages remain above reservation wages, the conclusions are unchanged.
5 Total capital in the plant is measured as the sum of the end-of-year book value of buildings and machinery in 1987.
6 We have no fewer than two workers per plant. Table 9.1 also reports the distribution of plants based on number of workers matched.
7 The results reported in the chapter were very similar when a Cobb–Douglas production function was used.
8 Issues relating to this specification of the labor input are discussed in Rosen (1983). In the subsection on Assessing the robustness of the relative marginal productivity estimates, we report some estimates dropping the perfect substitutes assumption.
9 For example, suppose workers are distinguished by race and sex. Then the unrestricted quality of labor term is

$$QL = L + (\phi_F - 1)WF + (\phi_B - 1)BM + (\phi_F \cdot \phi_B \cdot \phi_{FXB} - 1)BF,$$

where WF is the number of white females, BM the number of black males, and BF the number of black females. The restriction of equal relative marginal productivities implies $\phi_{FXB} = 1$. The equiproportionate distribution restriction implies $BF = B \cdot (F/L)$, $BM = B(1 - (F/L))$, and $WF = F(1 - (B/L))$. Substituting, we obtain

$$QL = L + (\phi_F - 1)F(1 - (B/L)) + (\phi_B - 1)B(1 - (F/L))$$
$$+ (\phi_F \cdot \phi_B \cdot \phi_{FXB} - 1)B(F/L),$$

which reduces to

$$QL = (L + (\phi_F - 1)F)(1 + (\phi_B - 1)(B/L)),$$

paralleling equation (4).

10 In the text of the chapter, we sometimes report the estimate of ϕ, and whether it is significantly different from 1, and sometimes refer to the implied percentage differential $(\phi - 1)$, and whether it is statistically significant (i.e. significantly different from zero). The tables report estimates of the ϕ's.

11 As Griliches and Ringstad (1971) point out, estimates of the first-order terms in the translog production function are not invariant to the units of the data. We therefore de-mean the (log of) capital, materials, and labor quality inputs prior to estimating the production function, so that the coefficients on the productive inputs in the production function are estimated at the mean of the sample. Following Crepon and Mairesse (1993), we de-mean the log quality of labor term, $\ln(QL)$, by first estimating the translog production function without demeaning, constructing plant-level estimates of $\ln(QL)$, and then taking the mean over the sample of the estimated values of $\ln(QL)$. This allows us to measure the returns to scale parameter by adding up the coefficients on the linear terms.

12 We initially also entered controls for age of plant in the production function (and wage equation). However, the estimated coefficients on these variables were individually and jointly insignificant, and their exclusion had little effect on the other estimated coefficients.

13 The same restrictions are imposed in the plant-level wage equation estimation described in this section, and in the empirical section the restrictions are relaxed in the same manner described here.

14 One motivation for this is evidence from wage equations that the marriage wage premium for men does not carry over to women and that the race differential is larger for men than for women (e.g. Corcoran and Duncan, 1979).

15 One way to see that the formulation in equation (5) is correct is to impose these restrictions on the parameters, impose the equiproportionate assumption on the data (e.g. $WMR = (R/L) \cdot (1 - \{F/L\}) \cdot (1 - \{B/L\}))$, and note that the original quality of labor term in equation (4) results.

16 Production workers include the two blue-collar occupations, and nonproduction workers include the other two occupations. With this form of the production function, output is zero for any plants without workers in an occupation category. We had to drop 219 plants with either no production workers or no nonproduction workers in the matched sample of workers. Had we entered all four occupations as imperfectly substitutable labor inputs, we would have had to drop many more observations.

17 In the wage equation that is estimated jointly with this production function, described in the section "Earnings differentials among workers," we also break out production and nonproduction workers.

18 This could parallel evidence that women are crowded into low-wage employers (e.g. Blau, 1977).

19 A race–wage gap of this magnitude (5 percent) is standard in manufacturing and suggests that we may be unable to detect significant differences between blacks and nonblacks in plant-level estimates of wage equations (and production functions).

20 As discussed in the section "The relationship between wages and productivity," this is the correct assumption to make given that we are testing the null hypothesis of competitive spot labor markets.

21 We also report some results estimating the wage equation and production function for various subsets of the data, in which case wage differentials across workers are not constrained to be equal in all plants.

22 Groshen (1991) finds a larger role for between-plant wage variation in the male–female wage gap. However, her results are not very comparable to ours. First, she has much finer controls for occupation, and second, she studies only five detailed industries, three of which are not in manufacturing.

23 The same problem will arise in the plant-level wage equation.

24 In the textbook linear model, the measurement error bias is proportional to the signal to signal-plus-noise ratio, and therefore under the null of equality of relative marginal products and wages, the bias would be the same in the two equations.

25 This parallels results for Israeli manufacturing reported in Hellerstein and Neumark (1995).

26 The estimated productivity and wage differentials by education are, unfortunately, of no help in distinguishing among the two major theories of the positive association between wages and education—the human capital and signalling models. In either model, workers with more education are more productive.

27 Because, white, male, and married workers are overrepresented in the WECD, the same argument may apply to the estimated ϕ's and λ's for women and marital status, although the problem will be most severe with respect to blacks since they make up such a small percentage of the workforce in the WECD.

28 We carried out two other robustness checks that are largely unrelated to the estimation of marginal productivity differentials. First, we estimated the equations using LRD total compensation costs, and also using Census of Population earnings. In the former case, the results were very similar to those using LRD wages and salaries. Using LRD compensation costs led to slightly higher estimates of relative earnings than with LRD wages and salaries for workers aged 35–54 (1.24) and 55+ (1.26); however, these are only about 0.07–0.09 greater than the estimated relative marginal productivities of these workers, and the p-values for the tests of equality are high (0.36 for ages 35–54, and 0.61 for ages 55+). The finding that total compensation costs are relatively higher for older workers than wage and salary costs is not surprising, since these workers are more likely to receive costly benefits such as health insurance. Using Census of Population wages and salaries, estimated wage growth over the life cycle is considerably higher than we found using LRD earnings measures, with relative earnings of 1.43 for 35–54 year-olds, and 1.32 for those aged 55 and over. In addition, for the 35–54 group, this estimate was significantly higher than the estimate of relative marginal productivity. However, relative earnings of prime-age workers in the Census of Population (relative to the LRD) are likely to be overstated if prime-age workers have a greater tendency to report earnings from more than one job. Second, we estimated the specifications in Table 9.3 including controls for capital and materials usage of the plant in the wage equation. These variables may help capture unobservable worker quality. Including these variables did not affect the qualitative conclusions. Some of these results are reported more fully in the working paper version of this study (Hellerstein *et al.*, 1996).

29 Manipulation of the equations in note 9 shows that this leads to a different specification from the fully restricted version.

30 We obtain these by multiplying the parameter estimates for the reference group by the estimated interaction parameters. For example, the marginal productivity of managerial/professional women (relative to managerial/professional men) is $0.71 \times 1.26 = 0.89$.

31 Interestingly, the marginal productivity and wage differentials by education are quite different by age group. For the young and prime-aged group, the differences between these differentials fall to 0.20 and 0.15, respectively, compared with 0.24 in Table 9.3; neither of these is statistically significant, with p-values around 0.4. But for the oldest group the estimated relative marginal product is 1.70, and the estimate of relative earnings is 1.13, with the p-value falling to 0.14.

32 If these unobservables affect productivity and wages similarly, however, they should not affect the tests of equality of relative marginal products and relative wages.

33 For evidence that technological change has reduced the proportion of production worker employment, see Berman *et al.* (1994) and Dunne *et al.* (1997).

34 This bias will arise if such technological change is not fully accounted for in the book value of capital (and we would not expect it to be). This problem would not arise if technological change is capital augmenting, and is correctly captured in capital price

deflators. While these desirable circumstances seem unlikely to hold exactly, Baily *et al.* (1992) find that results for total factor productivity regressions are the same using book value of capital and a more carefully constructed capital series based on initial capital stocks and annual investment data.

35 In Hellerstein *et al.* (1996) we examine additional evidence on this question. For a subset of industries we have independent information on technological innovation from the Census Bureau's 1988 Survey of Manufacturing Technology (see Doms *et al.*, 1997). This survey covered over 10,000 establishments in SIC industries 34–38 (which are high-technology industries). Over 350 establishments in the WECD can be matched to establishments in this survey. The results indicate that there is no evidence that these advanced technologies are associated with fewer production workers, and that the percent female tends to be lower, rather than higher, in plants using the advanced technologies. Thus, for this subset of industries at least, there is no evidence suggesting that the estimated relative marginal productivity of women is biased upward because the percent female tends to be higher in plants that have installed technology that saves on male production labor, or on male labor generally.

36 Although we know the number of workers sampled in each plant, we do not implement a formal correction for the measurement error bias that results from sampling error. This correction would require a consistent estimate of the variance of the measurement error, which varies by plant depending on the true proportion of workers in any particular category. (For example, at one extreme, in a plant with no female workers the variance of the measurement error in the proportion female is zero.) In other contexts, measurement-error corrections of this type (with nonhomogeneous error variances across observations) result in near-singular covariance matrices, because of a high ratio of error variance to total variance (Cockburn and Griliches, 1987).

37 In this section we do not estimate a separate coefficient for blacks versus nonblacks. The simulation requires repeated sampling of workers within a plant, and there are too few blacks in the sample to successfully estimate a race coefficient for many of the simulations.

38 For example, suppose in the WECD we have four men and six women matched to a plant ($T = 10$), and we know from the LRD that there are 100 workers in the plant ($L = 100$). We then create a simulated sample of 40 men ($4 \times 100/10$) and 60 women ($6 \times 100/10$). Finally, we sample 10 members of this sample, and obtain a new estimate of the proportion female.

39 Because the estimated proportions of workers in each category that we treat as known for our simulation are overdispersed relative to the true population distribution, the extent of measurement error bias indicated by our simulation method is a lower bound for the magnitude of measurement error in the real data.

40 For example, for the estimates for married workers the distribution of the productivity premium bounds that of the wage premium. Below the median, the productivity premium is slightly below the wage premium; above the median, the productivity premium is greater than the wage premium. The magnitude of the estimated standard error on the marriage productivity premium in Table 9.3 alone suggests that measurement error would have to be reducing the gap between the wage and productivity premia by a factor of 5 before we would reject equality of the wage and productivity marriage premia. For the age coefficients, this factor would have to be about the same for the 35–54 group, and even larger for the 55+ group, before we would reject equality.

References

Allen, Steven G. 1984. "Unionized Construction Workers Are More Productive." *Quarterly Journal of Economics* 91: 543–69.

Baily, Martin Neil, Hulten, Charles, and Campbell, David. 1992. "Productivity Dynamics in Manufacturing Plants." *Brookings Papers on Economic Activity: Microeconomics* 187–249.

Becker, Gary S. 1971. *The Economics of Discrimination*. 2nd ed. Chicago: The University of Chicago Press.

——. *Human Capital*. 2nd ed. 1975. Chicago: The University of Chicago Press.

Becker, Garry S. 1985. "Human Capital, Effort, and the Sexual Division of Labor." *Journal of Labor Economics* 3: S33–58.

Ben-Porath, Yoram. 1967. "The Production of Human Capital and the Life Cycle of Earnings." *Journal of Political Economy* 75: 352–65.

Bergmann, Barbara R. 1974. "Occupational Segregation, Wages, and Profits When Employers Discriminate by Race and Sex." *Eastern Economic Journal* 1–2: 103–10.

Berman, Eli, Bound, John, and Griliches, Zvi. 1994. "Changes in the Demand for Skilled Labor within U.S. Manufacturing: Evidence from the Annual Survey of Manufacturing." *Quarterly Journal of Economics* 109: 367–98.

Blau, Francine D. 1977. *Equal Pay in the Office*. Lexington, MA: Lexington Books.

Brown, Charles and Medoff, James L. 1978. "Trade Unions in the Production Process." *Journal of Political Economy* 84: 355–78.

Carrington, William and Troske, Kenneth. 1998. "Interfirm Racial Segregation." *Journal of Labor Economics* 16: 231–60.

Clark, Kim. 1980. "The Impact of Unionization on Productivity: A Case Study." *Industrial and Labor Relations Review* 33: 451–69.

Cockburn, Ian and Griliches, Zvi. 1987. "Industry Effects and Appropriability Measures in the Stock Market's Valuation of R & D and Patents." NBER Working Paper No. 2465.

Corcoran, Mary, and Duncan, Greg J. 1979. "Work History, Labor Force Attachment, and Earnings Differences Between Races and Sexes." *Journal of Human Resources* 14: 3–20.

Cox, Donald and Nye, John V. 1989. "Male–Female Wage Discrimination in Nineteenth-Century France." *Journal of Economic History* XLIX: 903–20.

Crepon, Bruno and Mairesse, Jacques. 1993. "Productivite, Recherche-Developpement et Qualifications." *INSEE-Methodes* 37–38: 181–200.

Doms, Mark, Dunne, Timothy, and Troske, Kenneth R. 1997. "Workers, Wages, and Technology." *Quarterly Journal of Economics* 112: 253–90.

Dunne, Timothy, Haltiwanger, John, and Troske, Kenneth. 1997. "Technology and Jobs: Secular Change and Cyclical Dynamics." *Carnegie-Rochester Conference Series on Public Policy* 46: 107–78.

Foster, Andrew D. and Rosenzweig, Mark R. 1993. "Information, Learning, and Wage Rates in Low-Income Rural Areas." *Journal of Human Resources* 28: 759–90.

Frank, Robert H. and Hutchens, Robert M. 1993. "Wages, Seniority, and the Demand for Rising Consumption Profiles." *Journal of Economic Behavior and Organization* 21: 251–76.

Griliches, Zvi and Ringstad, Vidar. 1971. *Economies of Scale in the Form of the Production Function*. Amsterdam: North-Holland Publishing Company.

Groshen, Erica. 1991. "The Structure of the Female/Male Wage Differential: Is it Who You Are, What You Do, or Where You Work?" *The Journal of Human Resources* 26: 457–72.

Hellerstein, Judith K. and Neumark, David. 1995. "Are Earnings Profiles Steeper than Productivity Profiles? Evidence from Israeli Firm-Level Data?" *Journal of Human Resources* 30: 89–112.

——. 1999. "Sex, Wages, and Productivity: An Empirical Analysis of Israeli Firm-Level Data." *International Economic Review* 40: 95–123.

Hellerstein, Judith K., Neumark, David, and Troske, Kenneth R. 1996. "Wages, Productivity, and Worker Characteristics: Evidence from Plant-Level Production Functions and Wage Equations." NBER Working Paper No. 5626.

Holzer, Harry J. 1990. "The Determinants of Employee Productivity and Earnings." *Industrial Relations* 29: 403–22.

Jorgenson, Dale W., Christensen, Laurits R., and Lau, Lawrence J. 1973. "Transcendental Logarithmic Production Frontiers." *Review of Economics and Statistics* 55: 28–45.

Korenman, Sanders, and Neumark, David. 1991. "Does Marriage Really Make Men More Productive?" *Journal of Human Resources* 26: 282–307.

Lazear, Edward P. 1979. "Why Is There Mandatory Retirement?" *Journal of Political Economy* 87: 1261–84.

Leonard, Jonathan S. 1984. "Anti-Discrimination or Reverse Discrimination: The Impact of Title VII, Affirmative Action and Changing Demographics on Productivity." *Journal of Human Resources* 19: 145–74.

Loewenstein, George and Sicherman, Nachum. 1991. "Do Workers Prefer Increasing Wage Profiles?" *Journal of Labor Economics* 9: 67–84.

Lucas, Robert E., Jr. 1978. "On the Size Distribution of Business Firms." *Bell Journal of Economics* 9: 508–23.

McGuckin, Robert and Pascoe, George. 1988. "The Longitudinal Research Database (LRD): Status and Research Possibilities." *Survey of Current Business*: 30–7.

Medoff, James L. and Abraham, Katherine G. 1980. "Experience, Performance, and Earnings." *Quarterly Journal of Economics* 95: 703–36.

Mincer, Jacob. 1974. *Schooling, Experience, and Earnings.* New York: Columbia University Press.

Rosen, Sherwin. 1983. "A Note on Aggregation of Skills and Labor Quality." *Journal of Human Resources* 18: 425–31.

Troske, Kenneth R. 1998. "The Worker-Establishment Characteristics Database." In *Labor Statistics Measurement Issues*, eds John Haltiwanger, Marilyn Manser, and Robert Topel, pp. 371–404. Chicago: University of Chicago Press.

——. 1999. "Evidence on the Employer Size-Wage Premium for Worker-Establishment Matched Data." *Review of Economics and Statistics* 81: 15–26.

Part III

Testing models of discrimination

10 Wage differentials by race and sex

The roles of taste discrimination and labor market information

Introduction

Labor economists agree on the existence of persistent wage differentials by race and sex in the US labor market, but disagree on the source of these differentials. There are two dominant explanations of these wage differentials that are the basis for most empirical research on this topic. The first is that employers discriminate against women or minorities in some fashion that results in lower wages for them even when they are equally productive. The second is that women or minorities come to the market with productivity shortfalls.

Typical empirical studies of these alternative explanations proceed by estimating regressions of log wages on race or sex variables controlling for variables that are proxies for human capital, which in turn is assumed to determine productivity.[1] However, although wage differentials by race and sex usually survive such exercises (although they are smaller), their interpretation is not conclusive, because one can always argue that there are remaining productivity differences between, say, blacks and whites, which are not captured by the included proxies. Improving on this typical exercise, this chapter considers the relationship between starting wages, race, and sex, in a data set in which performance ratings are also available. The performance ratings afford the opportunity to better control for productivity differences than in the typical wage regression with human capital proxies. The chapter first documents that gaps in starting wages by race and sex persist even when we account for measured performance on the job.

This difference in starting wages could reflect taste discrimination, as in Becker's seminal work (1957) in which minorities or women are paid less because of employers' distastes for hiring from these groups. However, if employers base starting wages on expected productivity or performance, and average performance is lower for minority workers (as it is in these data), then these estimated differentials could reflect simple statistical discrimination. From a policy perspective, whether taste discrimination or statistical discrimination plays a major role in race and sex differences in wages is significant. If taste discrimination accounts for the unexplained lower wages of women and minorities, then anti-discrimination legislation may be the only appropriate response. On the other hand, if statistical discrimination is important, especially in conjunction with some other factor that leads to group discrimination, then better means of assessing workers' productivity—including apprenticeships, skill certification, job testing, etc.—may contribute to the reduction of discrimination at the individual or group level. The goal of differentiating between these two forms of discrimination is the reason this chapter focuses on starting wages. Starting wages can potentially reflect either of the two types of discrimination—taste discrimination and statistical discrimination—in a fairly simple way, and an analysis of starting wages leads to some straightforward tests of these alternative models of discrimination.

Statistical discrimination

In general, the statistical discrimination model, originally developed by Phelps (1972), has received relatively little empirical attention with regard to wage differentials by race and sex.[2] The reason is that in a simple statistical discrimination model in which the distribution of productivity in subpopulations of white men, women, and minorities is the same, the inability of employers to accurately predict or measure an individual worker's productivity does not generate average wage differentials among these subgroups. As Cain (1986) emphasizes, average wage differentials only emerge if there are average productivity differentials, in which case the average wage differentials do not reflect "group discrimination." Thus, without extensions of the simple model, statistical discrimination is not thought to provide a compelling theory of wage discrimination against particular groups in the labor market.

However, there are extensions of statistical discrimination models that generate group discrimination. For example, Aigner and Cain (1977) show that if a minority group has a less reliable signal, and employers are risk averse, then the minority group will earn a lower average wage despite identical average productivity. Rothschild and Stiglitz (1982) obtain a similar result by positing a production function in which productivity depends on the quality of the match of the worker to the job. Another line of research considers "self-fulfilling prophecies" in statistical discrimination models, in which initially incorrect prior beliefs of lower productivity for a group result in lower human capital investment among that group, hence rationalizing and perpetuating the prior beliefs (Farmer and Terrell, 1996).

Whether or not some form of statistical discrimination leads to group discrimination, in all of these models imperfect information implies that the most productive members of a group with lower actual or assumed average productivity (e.g. a minority group) will be paid less than equally able members of the nonminority group. Even though the minority group as a whole may not be treated unfairly, there is an obvious sense in which highly productive individuals suffer from discrimination—in that they are paid less by virtue of identification with that group—although the least-able members of this group (and any group) likely benefit from statistical discrimination. Of course, if there is group discrimination then the implications are even more apparent.

This chapter assesses evidence on imperfections in employer information about new workers, and their role in generating wage differentials by race and sex.

The methods used borrow heavily from research by Foster and Rosenzweig (1993, hereafter FR) that studied statistical vs. taste discrimination in developing countries, applying their methods to data from the United States that might be informative with respect to some of the same questions they consider. In addition, the chapter presents some innovations relative to their methods. The analysis of the role of information—which follows the presentation of some basic findings on wages, sex, race, and performance ratings—proceeds in three steps. First, using FR's methods directly, evidence is presented on whether wage differences between apparently equally productive white and minority workers are better characterized as reflecting taste discrimination or statistical discrimination. As noted earlier, even in the simple statistical discrimination model, minority workers who are as productive as white workers will receive lower wages than comparable white workers if average productivity of minority workers is lower—where "comparability" is determined based on actual productivity, rather than expected productivity which determines starting wages in the statistical discrimination model. Thus, evidence that looks like taste discrimination may stem solely from statistical discrimination. Second, extending FR's methods, the empirical analysis attempts to distinguish between imperfect information on the part of employers and measurement error in the productivity proxies available to econometricians, which have similar empirical implications for the test of taste discrimination vs. statistical discrimination, but quite different implications for modeling wage setting and for policy. Finally, evidence is presented on whether employers have better information about some groups of workers than others. As suggested by the Rothschild–Stiglitz model, worse information about a particular group could lead not only to the usual statistical discrimination result, but also to group discrimination, so that average wage differentials exceed average productivity differentials.

Statistical vs. taste discrimination

The empirical approach to testing for employer taste discrimination vs. statistical discrimination was originally developed by FR. The discussion here is geared more closely toward the data used in the present chapter, as discussed fully in the section "The data." Suppose that data are available on starting wages (w_s), race (R, a dummy variable defined as 1 for minorities and 0 otherwise), and (marginal) productivity (P).[3] It is assumed that P is constant over the time horizon considered by the employer (ruling out human capital investment), and that there are no incentive considerations (as in Lazear, 1979) that lead wages to diverge from productivity. According to the simple statistical discrimination model, w_s is set equal to the expected value of P when the worker begins the job, denoted P_s^*, and defined as

$$P_s^* = E(P|I_s),\qquad(1)$$

where I_s is all information about the worker available to the employer when the starting wage is set.[4] Under the null hypothesis of no race discrimination, in the regression

$$w_s = \alpha P_s^* + R\beta + \varepsilon, \tag{2}$$

we should find that $\beta = 0$. However, we do not have data on expected productivity, but only on actual productivity P, where because of equation (1),

$$P = P_s^* + \eta_s, \eta_s \perp P_s^*.^5 \tag{3}$$

Thus, the estimated equation is

$$w_s = \alpha P + R\beta + \varepsilon - \alpha\eta_s. \tag{4}$$

Clearly, the OLS estimate of α (a_{OLS}) will be biased downward. In particular, the attenuation bias in the OLS estimate of α is given by

$$\text{plim}(a_{OLS}) = \alpha\{\text{Var}(P_s^*)/\text{Var}(P)\}, \tag{5}$$

where $\text{Var}(P_s^*)/\text{Var}(P)$ is the reliability of the information available on new hires.

Now suppose that P and R are negatively correlated, which would occur if minorities were on average less productive. In this case, the OLS estimate of β (b_{OLS}) would also be biased downward. As a result, OLS estimates of equation (4) may lead to evidence that taste discrimination generates race differences in wages, because controlling for productivity, minorities are paid lower starting wages. But the downward bias in the estimate of β implies that β could nonetheless equal zero, with starting wages conditional on *expected* productivity not reflecting any race differential.

What is required to correct the estimates of equation (4) for the bias from using P instead of P_s^* is a variable that is correlated with productivity but uncorrelated with η_s, and that does not appear in equation (2). Because η_s is orthogonal to the information set I_s, any variable that is in I_s and correlated with productivity satisfies the first two criteria. However, to satisfy the third criterion, this variable has to be unrelated to starting wages conditional on expected productivity. Given that the null hypothesis is that there is taste discrimination, only variables that measure characteristics not subject to taste discrimination are valid instruments. The instruments considered include education, age, and training or experience requirements. Age is potentially objectionable, given that there may well be age discrimination in the workplace (e.g. Johnson and Neumark, 1997). However, this is unlikely to be an issue in the present context, both because the sample consists of relatively young workers, and because most age discrimination claims concern discharges, layoffs, and hiring, rather than wage discrimination.[6]

Under statistical discrimination, a minority worker will earn less than an equally productive white worker, as long as average productivity for minority workers is lower. But a minority and white worker with identical *expected* productivity will earn the same starting wage. Taste discrimination, on the other hand, implies that even with equal expected productivity, the minority worker will be paid less. Therefore, at the one extreme of pure taste discrimination, the IV and OLS estimates of

β will be identical, while at the other extreme of pure statistical discrimination, the IV estimate of β (b_{IV}) will fall in absolute value to zero. Thus, a statistical test of whether race differences in wages reflect taste or statistical discrimination is obtained from a Hausman test for bias in the OLS estimate of the coefficient of R, which is a test of the null hypothesis of pure taste discrimination.[7] A statistical test of the broader question of whether employers have accurate information about workers on which they base starting wages is obtained from a Hausman test for the "exogeneity" of P in equation (4), which is a test of the null hypothesis of complete information (under which the IV estimate of α (a_{IV}) equals a_{OLS}).

An additional important component of the empirical analysis, which is described following the discussion of the results testing for taste vs. statistical discrimination, concerns whether the differences between a_{OLS} and a_{IV} indicated by the data stem from imperfect information, or simply from measurement error in the performance rating available in the data set as a measure of true, *known* productivity. This is potentially important because the latter type of measurement error could generate evidence of statistical discrimination, despite employers (but not econometricians) having perfect information about workers.[8]

Is labor market information better for some demographic groups?

An additional issue relating to labor market information and race and sex differences in wages is whether employers have better information about white workers than about minority or female workers. This informational advantage enjoyed by white or male workers could stem from more word-of-mouth references, better communication (Lang, 1986), or less difficulty on the part of employers in discerning true signals.[9] The tests described in the previous section may not indicate that imperfect information gives rise to statistical discrimination, which in turn leads to evidence looking like taste discrimination, if expected productivity is the same across groups. Nonetheless, information problems that are more severe for minority or female workers could help to explain their lower wages. For example, in the Rothschild–Stiglitz model of statistical discrimination, less accurate information about minorities can lead to group discrimination—that is, an average wage gap that is larger than the average productivity gap (which could equal zero). Thus, this model explains why groups of workers with identical *expected* productivity could earn different wages, and therefore provides yet another reason why labor market information may generate wage differences between similar workers. This is perhaps most pertinent for sex differences in wages, because women do not, on average, receive lower performance ratings than men. While simple statistical discrimination therefore cannot explain women's lower wages, such extensions of the statistical discrimination model, coupled with worse information about women, can generate group discrimination against women.

To this point, a single reliability ratio for information regarding new hires is estimated. The question of differential information, however, hinges on whether the reliability ratio differs across groups. This question can be addressed by estimating the regression

$$w_s = \alpha P + \varepsilon \tag{6}$$

for each subgroup, obtaining both OLS and IV estimates.

The reliability of information on new workers can be estimated as the ratio of the OLS estimate of α (a_{OLS}) to the IV estimate (a_{IV}), since

$$\text{plim}(a_{OLS}/a_{IV}) = \text{Var}(P^*)/\text{Var}(P).^{10} \tag{7}$$

To carry out a statistical test for differences in this estimated ratio across demographic groups, an estimate of the variance of this ratio is required. A first-order Taylor-series expansion of (a_{OLS}/a_{IV}) yields an approximation for the variance

$$\text{Var}(a_{OLS}/a_{IV}) \approx (1/\alpha_{IV}^2)\text{Var}(a_{OLS}) + (\alpha_{OLS}^2/\alpha_{IV}^4)\text{Var}(a_{IV})$$

$$- 2 \cdot (\alpha_{OLS}/\alpha_{IV}^3)\text{Cov}(a_{IV}, a_{OLS}).^{11} \tag{8}$$

The covariance term in equation (8) is straightforward to estimate, since both a_{IV} and a_{OLS} are linear estimators. In particular,

$$\text{Cov}(a_{IV}, a_{OLS}) = \text{Cov}(e_{OLS}, e_{IV})(P'P)^{-1} = \text{Var}(e_{OLS})(P'P)^{-1}, \tag{9}$$

where e_{OLS} and e_{IV} are the OLS and IV residuals. In fact, equation (6) ends up being estimated for more than one demographic group, in which case P in equation (9) is simply the matrix including the performance rating as well as the dummy variables for demographic subgroups. The estimates from each demographic group (or set of groups) can be treated as coming from independent samples, making it easy to test for differences in the estimated ratios a_{OLS}/a_{IV} across groups.

There is no way to determine how much differences in labor market information would shift average wages for a group. Nonetheless, evidence of differences would suggest that better information about particular groups of workers could raise their average wages.

The data

These questions are studied using an employer data set stemming from the Multi-City Study of Urban Inequality (MCSUI).[12] This data set contains information on starting and current wages, worker characteristics, and employers' performance ratings of employees. The information available in the MCSUI conforms quite closely to the data required to implement the tests described in the previous section, with some exceptions discussed here.

The data are from a survey that was administered to about 800 establishments in each of four metropolitan areas: Atlanta, Boston, Detroit, and Los Angeles. The survey was administered between June of 1992 and May of 1994. It was administered over the phone, and averaged roughly 35 minutes in length. The sample of establishments was drawn from two sources: (1) a listing of establishments and their phone numbers provided by Survey Sampling, Inc. (SSI), which is drawn primarily from local phone directories and supplemented by other sources; and (2) the establishments of employment of respondents in household surveys that were also administered in each of these four metropolitan areas. For the establishments in the SSI part of the sample, the main respondent to the survey is the person who is responsible for hiring noncollege workers. The interviews for this part of the sample focused only on hiring for jobs not requiring a college degree. For the sample drawn from the household survey, the respondent is the person responsible for hiring into the occupation of the household respondent.[13] The sample was constructed to permit pooling data from these two sources, as both were designed to generate employee-weighted samples of establishments, when sample weights are used. The overall response rate for the survey was 67 percent for establishments that were successfully screened.[14] This response rate compares favorably with other phone surveys of employers (e.g. Kling, 1995). Additional discussion of the data set is provided in Holzer (1995, 1996a,b).

Respondents are asked about the last worker hired, whether or not that worker is still with the employer. The recorded characteristics of the last worker hired include race/ethnicity, sex, age, educational attainment, starting and current wages, and job requirements. In addition, a supervisor's performance rating of the worker is also provided, measured on a scale of 1–100.[15] These ratings are used to measure productivity (P).

There are both conceptual and measurement issues that arise with respect to the performance ratings. First, the performance ratings do not provide an explicit productivity measure. In contrast, FR used time-rate pay as their measure of the wage, and piece-rate pay for the same worker to measure productivity. Nonetheless, it seems reasonable to assume that rated performance is monotonically positively related to productivity. We therefore use alternative positive monotonic transformations of the performance rating, specifically linear and log forms.

Second, if the performance ratings were the product of a formal evaluation procedure used to set wages and determine promotions, the ratings might be influenced by discrimination in the same way as are data on wages (as employers might feel constrained to manipulate performance ratings to back up their wage decisions). In this case, performance ratings might "explain" wage differentials by race or sex, but not because they reflect true differences in productivity. However, these ratings are informal and not explicitly related to actual pay and promotion decisions. In addition, survey respondents were promised full confidentiality. Therefore, the ratings seem likely to provide an unbiased measure of a worker's true job performance.[16]

Finally, the performance ratings pose some pure measurement problems, because they may vary for reasons other than the worker's actual performance. In particular, the ratings that particular respondents provide may vary for random reasons, with some tending to give higher and some lower ratings for equally productive workers.[17,18] This case may be interpreted as one of pure measurement error in the performance rating. Unfortunately, in this case the instrumental variables procedure may be correcting for this pure measurement error, rather than that which arises in the imperfect information story because of discrepancies between actual and expected productivity. Because the IV procedure may simply correct for standard measurement error bias, it could lead to spurious evidence in favor of the statistical discrimination model, with a_{IV} larger in absolute value than a_{OLS}, and b_{IV} falling in absolute value relative to b_{OLS}.[19] Nonetheless, if there is taste discrimination, b_{IV} should still be significantly different from zero, as opposed to the case of pure statistical discrimination. While this implies that a test of whether b_{IV} differs from zero provides a test for taste discrimination, a significant difference between b_{IV} and b_{OLS} would not necessarily imply that there is statistical discrimination. As a result, considerable effort is devoted to distinguishing between the statistical discrimination and pure measurement error interpretations of the findings.

Aside from these potential problems with the productivity proxy, the MCSUI data offer some advantages for this study. First, the wage measure is a starting wage, which, according to the statistical discrimination model, is the wage that should be set equal to expected productivity. On the other hand, the performance rating is current, and workers in this data set have median tenure of about two to three months, so that we would expect actual productivity to differ from expected productivity. Thus, the time frame to which the data refer are precisely what is required for the tests this chapter considers.[20]

The data set includes three types of variables that can be potentially used as predictors of productivity that do not themselves (i.e. independently of productivity) affect wages: age, education, and job requirements.[21] The information on job requirements comes from survey questions asking the employer whether specific experience, general experience, and vocational education or formal training are "absolutely required, strongly preferred, mildly preferred, or does not matter." It seems reasonable to suppose that if these are absolutely required of a hire, then that hire must possess these qualifications, and the data are used in this manner. In fact, this supposition could be checked using another question on whether a high school diploma was required and corresponding information on the reported actual education of the worker hired; only 1.4 percent of those hires for which a high school diploma was absolutely required (27 percent of the hires in the sample) did not actually have a high school diploma.[22,23]

Finally, because of measurement problems attention is restricted to the bulk of the sample (about 70 percent) paid hourly wages.[24] This addresses the problem that the only hours information available comes from a question regarding how many hours per week are usually worked, with no distinction between the time periods referring to the starting wage and the current wage. Consequently, there is no way to accurately construct an hourly starting wage for those paid on a nonhourly basis. This is likely to be further complicated by differences between hourly and nonhourly workers in the value of nonwage compensation.[25]

Basic results on starting wages, race, sex, and performance ratings

Table 10.1 reports descriptive statistics on log starting wages, performance ratings, and log performance ratings.[26] The wage differences between race and ethnic

Table 10.1 Sample means for hourly wages and productivity proxies[a]

	Men			Women		
	White	Black	Hispanic	White	Black	Hispanic
Log starting wage	2.12	1.93	2.04	1.98	1.79	1.94
	(0.42)	(0.33)	(0.36)	(0.41)	(0.28)	(0.36)
Performance rating	78.10	74.43	73.48	79.29	76.66	78.37
	(13.24)	(16.16)	(13.08)	(14.58)	(15.23)	(12.48)
Log performance rating	4.34	4.28	4.28	4.35	4.31	4.35
	(0.19)	(0.30)	(0.20)	(0.23)	(0.24)	(0.17)
N	345	158	155	359	164	110

Note

a Standard deviations are reported in parentheses. Sample is restricted to those earning hourly wages. Estimates are weighted.

groups are similar for men and women, with whites earning about 19 percent more than blacks, and 4–8 percent more than Hispanics.[27] The difference in starting wages between men and women is about 10–14 percent, toward the lower figure for Hispanics. These sex-related differentials are somewhat small compared with representative samples of the US workforce, but the data here refer to starting wages of relatively young workers (29.5 years old, on average); existing work with other data sets documents lower sex differences in wages for workers early in their careers (e.g. Light and Ureta, 1995).

The performance ratings—which of course are measured after workers have accumulated some time with the employer—reveal that women in each race or ethnic group receive higher scores than men, on average, using either levels or logs. This implies, of course, that differences in performance ratings do not account for the sex difference in wages. On the other hand, within sexes, whites generally receive higher ratings than blacks or Hispanics.

The possibility that statistical discrimination generates evidence that looks like taste discrimination—which is the motivation for the test of statistical vs. taste discrimination—requires lower average productivity of the lower-paid group. Since this does not apply to male–female differentials, the test for statistical vs. taste discrimination is carried out only for race/ethnic differences for each sex considered separately. However, the second test regarding the quality of information about each demographic group is still pertinent; women could have higher average productivity, but if labor market information about them is worse, and mismatches costly, they could receive lower wages.

Table 10.2 turns to estimates of log wage equations that parallel typical wage regressions, followed by an exploration of the consequences of adding controls for performance ratings. Columns (1) and (5) report OLS estimates of a standard log wage regression (for starting wages) without any information on performance ratings, with controls for education, age, job requirements, and race/ethnicity. In both the male and female samples, wages of blacks are significantly lower by about 14 percent, while wages of Hispanics are not significantly lower (with the point

Table 10.2 OLS estimates of log starting hourly wage regressions[a]

	Men				Women			
	(1)	*(2)*	*(3)*	*(4)*	*(5)*	*(6)*	*(7)*	*(8)*
Performance rating	—	0.0044 (0.0011)	0.0034 (0.0009)	—	—	0.0014 (0.0011)	−0.0007 (0.0010)	—
Log performance rating	—	—	—	0.222 (0.055)	—	—	—	−0.058 (0.061)
Black	−0.143 (0.032)	—	−0.132 (0.032)	−0.130 (0.032)	−0.136 (0.036)	—	−0.137 (0.036)	−0.137 (0.036)
Hispanic	−0.039 (0.030)	—	−0.025 (0.030)	−0.026 (0.030)	−0.010 (0.037)	—	−0.009 (0.038)	−0.009 (0.038)
Schooling = 12	0.120 (0.042)	—	0.117 (0.042)	0.118 (0.042)	0.090 (0.056)	—	0.093 (0.056)	0.095 (0.056)
Schooling = 13–15	0.093 (0.049)	—	0.086 (0.049)	0.086 (0.049)	0.173 (0.059)	—	0.179 (0.060)	0.181 (0.060)
Schooling = 16+	0.436 (0.054)	—	0.427 (0.053)	0.424 (0.053)	0.227 (0.066)	—	0.234 (0.066)	0.235 (0.066)
Age	0.050 (0.007)	—	0.050 (0.007)	0.051 (0.007)	0.035 (0.009)	—	0.035 (0.009)	0.035 (0.009)
$Age^2 \times 10^{-2}$	−0.061 (0.010)	—	−0.063 (0.010)	−0.063 (0.010)	−0.040 (0.012)	—	−0.039 (0.013)	−0.039 (0.013)
General experience required	0.026 (0.031)	—	0.030 (0.031)	0.031 (0.031)	−0.036 (0.039)	—	−0.037 (0.039)	−0.037 (0.039)
Specific experience required	0.122 (0.034)	—	0.117 (0.034)	0.115 (0.034)	0.132 (0.042)	—	0.133 (0.042)	0.133 (0.042)
Vocational education/ training required	0.264 (0.039)	—	0.271 (0.039)	0.271 (0.039)	0.233 (0.044)	—	0.234 (0.044)	0.234 (0.044)
R^2	0.384	0.024	0.398	0.399	0.228	0.003	0.228	0.229

Note
a There are 658 observations for men and 633 observations for women. Standard errors of estimates are reported in parentheses. All estimates are weighted.

estimates indicating wage gaps of 1–4 percent).[28] These results are not fully consistent with other estimates of racial and ethnic wage differentials, where it is more common to find a smaller race difference among women than among men (Blau and Beller, 1992), and Hispanic–white differences are often larger than black–white differences (Reimers, 1983). However, this sample is somewhat unique in covering four specific metropolitan areas, and the wage measure studied here is the starting wage. The starting wage differentials associated with schooling appear relatively similar to those observed in other data sets for contemporaneous wages, although the considerably higher wage premium for male college graduates compared with female college graduates is unusual.[29] The relationship between age and starting wages also parallels the usual relationship. Among the job requirements, both specific experience and training are associated with significantly higher wages, while general experience is not.

The remaining columns explore whether differences in performance ratings help to account for these wage differences by race and ethnicity. Columns (2) and (6) report OLS estimates of regressions of log wages on performance ratings only. For men, the estimated coefficient of the performance rating is positive and statistically significant. Using the standard deviations from Table 10.1, a 1 standard deviation increase in the performance rating (a weighted average across the demographic groups of 13.90) is associated with a 6 percent increase in the wage, which is about one-sixth of the standard deviation of log wages. Thus, the estimated coefficient on the performance variable appears quite small. For women, the estimated coefficient (in column (6)) is even smaller, and not statistically significant.

Next, columns (3) and (7) report estimates obtained from including all of the standard control variables as well as the performance ratings. For men, the estimated coefficient of the productivity proxy falls a bit (to 0.0034), but does not differ much from column (2). More significantly, the estimated wage differentials for blacks and Hispanics are only a shade smaller than in column (1), suggesting that performance or productivity differences between white, black, and Hispanic men do not explain the differences between them in starting wages. For women, once the controls and performance ratings are included together, in column (7), the estimated coefficient on the performance rating is essentially zero (-0.0007, and not significant). Not surprisingly, then, the estimates of the race/ethnicity differentials are similar to those excluding the performance rating. Finally, in columns (4) and (8) these estimates are repeated using the log of the performance rating, with very similar results. Clearly the persistence of the starting wage differentials (here, between blacks and whites, in particular) upon including performance ratings is consistent with taste discrimination, paralleling the conclusions of many wage regression studies that do not benefit from the availability of data on performance ratings. However, as discussed in the previous section, including a measure of performance in a regression for starting wages is not necessarily the same as controlling for productivity, so these results need not reflect taste discrimination. The next section therefore considers evidence on the roles of taste discrimination vs. statistical discrimination.

Testing the alternative interpretations

Statistical vs. taste discrimination

Tables 10.3 and 10.4 report the results for the test of statistical vs. taste discrimination, for men and women. In each case, as in Table 10.2 estimates are presented for specifications with performance ratings entered linearly as well as in logs. Before proceeding to the IV estimation, a decision had to be made regarding which instrumental variables to use, choosing among the age, education, and job requirements variables, thus leading to different "baseline" wage regressions from those reported in Table 10.2. The maintained assumption is that at least one set of

Table 10.3 Tests of statistical vs. taste discrimination, men[a]

	OLS (1)	IV (2)	OLS (3)	IV (4)	IV (5)
A. Using linear performance rating					
Performance rating	0.0035	0.009	0.0038	0.035	0.027
	(0.0009)	(0.009)	(0.001)	(0.015)	(0.011)
Black	−0.126	−0.106	−0.178	−0.062	−0.091
	(0.033)	(0.047)	(0.029)	(0.081)	(0.064)
Hispanic	−0.006	0.020	−0.066	0.080	0.043
	(0.031)	(0.053)	(0.034)	(0.089)	(0.067)
Schooling = 12	0.187	0.184	—	—	—
	(0.042)	(0.044)			
Schooling = 13–15	0.152	0.142	—	—	—
	(0.050)	(0.054)			
Schooling = 16+	0.549	0.533	—	—	—
	(0.053)	(0.060)			
General experience required	0.043	0.051	—	—	—
	(0.032)	(0.035)			
Specific experience required	0.158	0.147	—	—	—
	(0.035)	(0.040)			
Vocational education/training required	0.292	0.303	—	—	—
	(0.040)	(0.045)			
R^2	0.347	—	0.054	—	—
p-value from *F*-test of instruments in first-stage regression					
Age variables only	0.03	—	—	—	—
Education variables only	0.58	—	—	—	—
Job requirement variables only	0.47	—	—	—	—
Instruments	—	Age	—	Age	Age, education, job requirements
F-statistic on instruments in first-stage regression	—	3.39	—	3.81	1.50
Overidentifying restrictions *p*-value	—	—	—	—	0.00
Bias in OLS estimates, *p*-value from Hausman test					
Performance rating	—	0.55	—	0.04	0.03
Black	—	0.56	—	0.11	0.09
Hispanic	—	0.56	—	0.07	0.06
B. Using log performance rating					
Performance rating	0.220	0.034	0.252	2.012	1.899
	(0.057)	(0.657)	(0.068)	(1.025)	(0.689)
Black	−0.124	−0.136	−0.175	−0.059	−0.067
	(0.033)	(0.053)	(0.039)	(0.088)	(0.070)
Hispanic	−0.008	−0.020	−0.068	0.043	0.036
	(0.030)	(0.052)	(0.036)	(0.082)	(0.065)
p-value from *F*-test of instruments in first-stage regression					
Age variables only	0.09	—	—	—	—
Education variables only	0.32	—	—	—	—
Job requirement variables only	0.40	—	—	—	—
F-statistic on instruments in first-stage regression	—	2.47	—	2.92	1.51
Overidentifying restrictions, *p*-value	—	—	—	—	0.00
Bias in OLS estimates, *p*-value from Hausman test					
Performance rating	—	0.78	—	0.09	0.02
Black	—	0.78	—	0.14	0.06
Hispanic	—	0.78	—	0.13	0.06

Note

a There are 658 observations. Standard errors of estimates are reported in parentheses. Hausman tests are calculated based on individual coefficient estimates. Specifications in Panel B correspond to those in Panel A, although only selected coefficient estimates are reported. All estimates are weighted. Choice of instruments used in column (2) are based on *F*-statistics from first-stage regression for the productivity score, as reported in the table. Instruments are the same in Panels A and B. R^2 for Panel B were almost identical to Panel A.

Table 10.4 Tests of statistical vs. taste discrimination, women[a]

	OLS (1)	IV (2)	OLS (3)	IV (4)	OLS (5)	IV (6)	IV (7)
A. Using linear performance rating							
Performance rating	−0.0001	0.027	0.0004	0.034	0.0010	0.041	0.047
	(0.0010)	(0.009)	(0.0010)	(0.010)	(0.0010)	(0.010)	(0.011)
Black	−0.156	−0.101	−0.172	−0.089	−0.185	−0.081	−0.065
	(0.036)	(0.057)	(0.037)	(0.066)	(0.039)	(0.075)	(0.083)
Hispanic	−0.042	−0.026	−0.062	−0.026	−0.041	−0.004	0.001
	(0.037)	(0.056)	(0.038)	(0.065)	(0.040)	(0.073)	(0.081)
Age	0.039	0.037	—	—	—	—	—
	(0.009)	(0.013)					
Age$^2 \times 10^{-2}$	−0.044	−0.047	—	—	—	—	—
	(0.012)	(0.019)					
General experience required	−0.033	−0.015	−0.030	−0.006	—	—	—
	(0.039)	(0.058)	(0.040)	(0.068)			
Specific experience required	0.135	0.091	0.181	0.103	—	—	—
	(0.043)	(0.066)	(0.043)	(0.077)			
Vocational education/training required	0.247	0.207	0.255	0.205	—	—	—
	(0.044)	(0.068)	(0.046)	(0.079)			
R^2	0.204	—	0.148	—	0.037	—	—
p-value from F-test of instruments in first-stage regression							
Age variables only	0.17	—	—	—	—	—	—
Education variables only	0.00	—	—	—	—	—	—
Job requirement variables only	0.69	—	—	—	—	—	—
Instruments	—	Education	—	Education, age	—	Education, age	Education, age, job requirements
F-statistic on instruments in first-stage regression	—	5.00	—	3.98	—	4.44	2.95
Overidentifying restrictions, p-value	—	—	—	0.75	—	0.95	0.20
Bias in OLS estimates, p-value from Hausman test							
Performance rating	—	0.00	—	0.00	—	0.00	0.00
Black	—	0.21	—	0.13	—	0.11	0.10
Hispanic	—	0.70	—	0.50	—	0.55	0.55

(*Table 10.4 continued*)

Table 10.4 Continued

	OLS (1)	IV (2)	OLS (3)	IV (4)	OLS (5)	IV (6)	IV (7)
B. Using log performance rating							
Performance rating	−0.021	1.623	0.006	2.184	0.041	2.627	3.028
	(0.062)	(0.613)	(0.063)	(0.642)	(0.067)	(0.704)	(0.764)
Black	−0.156	−0.108	−0.173	−0.096	−0.186	−0.090	−0.075
	(0.036)	(0.055)	(0.037)	(0.066)	(0.039)	(0.076)	(0.084)
Hispanic	−0.042	−0.044	−0.062	−0.051	−0.042	−0.033	−0.031
	(0.037)	(0.054)	(0.038)	(0.065)	(0.040)	(0.073)	(0.081)
p-value from F-test of instruments in first-stage regression							
Age variables only	0.21	—	—	—	—	—	—
Education variables only	0.00	—	—	—	—	—	—
Job requirement variables only	0.82	—	—	—	—	—	—
F-statistic on instruments in first-stage regression	—	4.58	—	3.60	—	3.94	2.56
Overidentifying restrictions, p-value	—	—	—	0.52	—	0.84	0.12
Bias in OLS estimates, p-value from Hausman test							
Performance rating	—	0.01	—	0.00	—	0.00	0.00
Black	—	0.25	—	0.16	—	0.14	0.13
Hispanic	—	0.96	—	0.82	—	0.88	0.88

Note

a There are 633 observations. Standard errors of estimates are reported in parentheses. Hausman tests are calculated based on individual coefficient estimates. Specifications in Panel B correspond to those in Panel A, although only selected coefficient estimates are reported. All estimates are weighted. Choice of instruments used in column (2) are based on F-statistics from first-stage regression for the productivity score, as reported in the table. Instruments are the same in Panels A and B. R-squares for Panel B were almost identical to Panel A.

these variables can be excluded from the starting wage equation. The question that can be addressed empirically, however, is which set of instruments provides the most predictive power for the performance rating in the first-stage regression. To assess this, the first-stage regression was estimated using each set of instruments separately. For men, only the age variables were jointly significant in the first-stage regression; as reported in column (1), for the levels specification the p-value for the test of joint significance was 0.03 for the age variables, 0.58 for the education variables, and 0.47 for the job requirement variables, with qualitatively similar results for the log specification. Thus, for men the first set of instruments considered is the age variables. For women, only the education coefficients were jointly significant, with p-values of 0.00 in both the levels and log specifications.

However, the p-values for the age variables are also relatively low (0.17 and 0.21 in the two specifications); consequently, specifications using education and age as instruments are also reported for women.[30]

Turning first to the results for men, columns (1) and (2) of Table 10.3 report OLS estimates and IV estimates of the wage equation, using age and its square as instruments, in this case including the other variables (education and job requirements) in the wage equation. The OLS estimates of α, the coefficient of the productivity proxy, are similar to those in Table 10.2. The IV estimate rises to 0.009 in the levels specification, but with the increased standard error becomes insignificant; in the log specification the IV estimate of α actually falls, also becoming insignificant. However, although the education and job requirements variables enter significantly in both the OLS and IV estimations, this model may be misspecified, and these variables may simply capture productivity differentials that would otherwise be captured in the performance rating.

Thus, columns (3) and (4) omit the education and job requirement controls, retaining only the productivity proxy and the race/ethnicity variables that may, because of taste discrimination, affect wages independently of productivity. This seems the most appropriate specification of the starting wage equation with which to test for statistical vs. taste discrimination. In the OLS regression, the R^2 is considerably lower than in the earlier specifications. Of course, this may be partly attributable to the discrepancy between the performance rating P and expected productivity P_s^*. Note that the F-statistic for the joint significance of the instruments in the first-stage regression is reasonably high (3.81 in the levels specification, and 2.92 in the log specification), indicating that small sample biases toward the OLS estimates are unlikely to be severe. The IV estimates of α are considerably higher than the OLS estimates, rising by a factor of 8 or 9, and in both the linear and log specifications these estimates are statistically significant. As reported in the table, for both the levels and log specification the null hypothesis of no bias in the estimated coefficient of the actual performance rating is rejected (at the 5-percent level in the levels specification, and the 10-percent level in logs). For the linear specification, a 1 standard deviation in the performance rating is associated with an increase of 0.49 in the log wage, a bit higher than 1 standard deviation of the log wage. For the log specification, a 1 standard deviation in the performance rating is associated with a 0.44 increase in the log wage, approximately the same result. Thus, these IV estimates appear to generate estimated coefficients of the productivity proxy that map into wages relatively well.

Turning to the question of substantive interest, the estimated wage shortfalls for blacks and Hispanics in the OLS estimates of the levels specification are -0.178 and -0.066 respectively, with the latter only significant at the 10-percent level. However, instrumenting for the performance rating causes the differential for blacks to fall to -0.062, and that for Hispanics to change sign; both estimated differentials become statistically insignificant. Qualitatively, these reductions in the wage shortfalls for black and Hispanic men are consistent with a substantial part of these shortfalls being attributable to statistical discrimination rather than taste discrimination. The results are similar for the log specification. Hausman tests to gauge the statistical significance of the differences are reported in the last two rows of each panel. In the levels specification, the p-values for the test of the null of pure taste discrimination—implying no bias in the OLS estimates of the race/ethnicity wage differentials—are 0.11 for blacks and 0.07 for Hispanics. In the log specification, the corresponding p-values are 0.14 and 0.13. Thus, there is some evidence against the lower wages paid to blacks and Hispanics reflecting solely taste discrimination, although it is not overwhelming.[31]

Finally, column (5) repeats the IV estimation, but now using education and job requirements as instruments as well. The estimates are more precise as we would expect, leading to lower p-values from the tests of the null of taste discrimination (in the 0.06–0.09 range). However, the overidentifying restrictions are rejected, and the full set of instruments has relatively weak predictive power for the performance rating, as reflected in the F-statistics of 1.50 or 1.51. Thus, this column probably does not provide very reliable evidence.

Having discussed the various specifications and analyses for men in detail, the results for women can be discussed more succinctly. In the levels specification in column (1) of Table 10.4, the OLS estimate of α is actually negative (-0.0001) but insignificant. The estimates of the race/ethnicity differentials are similar to those excluding the performance rating. Instrumenting for the performance rating with the education variables, in column (2), causes the estimate of α to rise to 0.027 and become statistically significant. A similar result holds for the log specification. Columns (3) and (4) instead use the age variables along with education as instruments, with similar results. The overidentifying restrictions are not rejected for this specification, with p-values of 0.75 in the levels specification, and 0.52 in logs. Thus, these estimates are preferable. Note also that the F-statistics for the instruments in the first-stage regression are high for all of the specifications discussed so far. As for men, the model in columns (3) and (4) may be misspecified by including the job requirements variables, so columns (5) and (6) report specifications excluding these variables. The results are little changed. Finally, in column (7) the job requirements variables are also used as instruments. The overidentifying restrictions are not rejected, although the p-values are relatively low (0.20 for the levels specification, and 0.12 for the log specification). Thus, the specifications in columns (5) and (6) are the preferred ones, and the remaining results are discussed in reference to them; nonetheless, the qualitative conclusions are the same for the other specifications.

The IV estimate of α is considerably higher than the OLS estimate in both the linear and log specifications, and the IV estimates are statistically significant. For both the levels and log specification the null hypothesis of no bias in the estimated coefficient of the performance rating is rejected, with p-values of 0.00. For the linear specification, a 1-standard deviation in the performance rating is associated with an increase of 0.49 in the log wage. For the log specification, a 1 standard deviation in the performance rating is associated with a 0.55 increase in the log wage. Again the IV estimates appear to generate estimated coefficients of the productivity proxy that map into wages relatively well.

Turning to the question of most interest, the estimated wage shortfalls for blacks and Hispanics in the OLS estimates of the levels specification are -0.185 and -0.041, respectively, with the latter insignificant. Instrumenting for the performance rating causes the differential for blacks to fall by more than half, to -0.081, and that for Hispanics to fall to zero. Similar results occur for the log specifications, although the changes are a bit smaller. Like for men, these reductions in the wage shortfalls for black and Hispanic women are consistent with a substantial part of these shortfalls being attributable to statistical discrimination rather than taste discrimination. The Hausman tests indicate that the change for Hispanic women is not statistically significant, while for black women the p-values for the test of the null of pure taste discrimination are 0.11 in the levels specification, and 0.14 in the log specification.

Overall, then, for black and Hispanic men and for black women there is some evidence that imperfect information is partly responsible for the lower starting wages they receive, compared with white workers with identical performance ratings. The point estimates of the shortfalls in starting wages experienced by black and Hispanic workers fall substantially once account is taken of statistical discrimination via an instrumental variables procedure, generally by more than half for blacks, and disappearing altogether for Hispanic men. The null hypothesis that these starting wage differentials are solely attributable to taste discrimination is rejected—for the specifications that fit the data—at the 0.07–0.14 significance level, evidence that is not overly strong, but which nonetheless suggests that the evidence against the null of pure taste discrimination should not be dismissed.[32]

Statistical discrimination vs. pure measurement error in the performance rating

The evidence to this point is consistent with statistical discrimination being partly responsible for the lower starting wages of minority workers relative to equally productive white workers. However, as discussed earlier, some caution is in order because the same contrast between the OLS and IV estimates could arise if there is no information problem—that is, employers know a worker's productivity when the worker is first hired—but the performance rating measures this known productivity with error. In this scenario, the results would have no implications with respect to labor market information, but would nonetheless tend to weaken evidence from studies claiming discrimination based on results in which race or sex differences in wages persist when error-ridden proxies for productivity are included in wage regressions.

There is some information that can be used to assess these alternative interpretations of the data. Specifically, the MCSUI data set includes information on whether there was a probation period for the most recently hired employee. Presumably, a probationary period is used when it is difficult to assess the worker's productivity prior to hiring. Thus, using the same reasoning as discussed in the section "Statistical discrimination" in relation to the test for different quality of labor market information about different demographic groups, the ratio a_{OLS}/a_{IV} can be compared for the subsample subject to a probationary period and the subsample not subject to one. If in fact labor market information plays a role in driving down the OLS estimate of α relative to the IV estimate, this ratio should be lower for those who are subject to a probationary period.[33]

Results for the nonprobationary and probationary subsamples are reported in Table 10.5. Columns (1) and (2) present results for men and women combined, using age and education as instruments, and columns (3) and (4) present results for men only, using age as the instrument.[34] The proportion subject to probation is 0.79, with the proportions very close among men and women.[35] The results in Table 10.5 suggest that labor market information drives the differences between the OLS and

Table 10.5 Estimates of quality of labor market information for nonprobationary and probationary workers[a]

	Men and women combined		Men only	
	Nonprobationary (1)	*Probationary* (2)	*Nonprobationary* (3)	*Probationary* (4)
A. Using linear performance rating				
a_{OLS}	0.0017	0.0026	0.0062	0.0032
	(0.0018)	(0.0008)	(0.0025)	(0.0012)
a_{IV}	0.020	0.079	0.021	0.050
	(0.008)	(0.023)	(0.020)	(0.029)
a_{OLS}/a_{IV}	0.089	0.033	0.294	0.065
	(0.093)	(0.014)	(0.295)	(0.043)
Instruments	Age, education		Age	
First-stage regression				
F-statistic on instruments	3.80	2.46	1.31	1.79
p-value	0.00	0.03	0.27	0.17
N	274	1021	135	524
B. Using log performance rating				
a_{OLS}	0.128	0.153	0.434	0.219
	(0.124)	(0.051)	(0.181)	(0.072)
a_{IV}	1.349	4.744	1.349	2.579
	(0.591)	(1.459)	(1.423)	(1.783)
a_{OLS}/a_{IV}	0.095	0.032	0.322	0.085
	(0.093)	(0.014)	(0.349)	(0.064)
Instruments	Age, education		Age	
First-stage regression				
F-statistic on instruments	3.37	2.24	1.28	1.31
p-value	0.01	0.05	0.28	0.27

Note
a Standard errors of estimates are reported in parentheses. All regressions exclude age, education, and job requirement variables from the wage equation. All estimates are weighted.

IV estimates of α. For both samples, the ratio a_{OLS}/a_{IV} is considerably higher for the nonprobationary sample for which initial labor market information should be better, although this ratio is estimated imprecisely for the smaller nonprobationary subsamples.

Thus, based on the distinctions between probationary and nonprobationary workers, the OLS and IV estimates of α correspond to what would be expected if there is imperfect information in labor markets. Although the evidence is not statistically strong, it suggests that the changes in estimates of α that result from instrumenting reflect errors of measurement on the part of employers in the reported performance rating relative to initial expected productivity, rather than perfect information on the part of employers with the measurement error reflecting only errors in the reported (to the researcher) performance rating relative to true, known productivity.

Another way this result should manifest itself is in the changes in the estimated race gaps in wages for the alternative subsamples. In particular, when statistical discrimination is likely to be more important (i.e. for the probationary workers) the estimates should indicate that a larger fraction of estimated race gaps in wages are attributable to statistical discrimination. Table 10.6 reports these results, providing the estimated race coefficients corresponding to the specifications in Table 10.5 for the male-only sample.[36] The results for both blacks and Hispanics are consistent with expectations. Simply using the point estimates, the estimated proportion of the wage gap attributable to statistical discrimination is higher for the probationary workers. Indeed, for the probationary workers the IV estimates of the race/ethnicity gaps in wages are non-negative, whereas for the nonprobationary workers the IV estimates of these gaps are about three-fourths as large as the OLS estimates. In results for women not reported in the table, the same conclusion emerged. For black–white differences (there are essentially no Hispanic–white differences for women, as shown in Tables 10.2 and 10.4), the estimated proportion of the wage gap due to statistical discrimination was 0.06–0.13 for the nonprobationary sample, compared with 0.43–0.51 for the probationary sample. Thus, in general, the findings for tests of statistical vs. taste discrimination are consistent with the IV results being driven by imperfect information on the part of employers.

As discussed in the Introduction, the appropriate policy response to statistical discrimination might be quite different from the appropriate policy response to taste discrimination. In particular, an important role for statistical discrimination suggests that better labor market information—perhaps in the form of skills certification or job testing—might help to boost starting wages of minorities and women. However, we do not, in fact, know much about how to convey useful information about employees to potential employers; research on the consequences of using alternative methods for doing this (skills certification, job testing, etc.) would therefore be very useful. Nonetheless, the results in Table 10.6 help to highlight the potential from such policies. One can interpret the jobs with a probationary period as jobs in which employers, at the outset at least, do not have much information on workers' productivity. The estimates suggest that for these jobs the black–white wage gap in starting wages is entirely due to statistical discrimination.[37] While not

Table 10.6 Estimates of degree of statistical discrimination depending on quality of labor market information, men[a]

	Nonprobationary (1)	Probationary (2)
A. Using linear performance rating		
OLS Estimates		
Black	−0.283	−0.148
	(0.093)	(0.043)
Hispanic	−0.194	−0.039
	(0.097)	(0.039)
IV Estimates		
Black	−0.213	0.010
	(0.142)	(0.129)
Hispanic	−0.149	0.167
	(0.125)	(0.148)
Proportion of wage gap due to statistical discrimination		
Black	0.25	1.0
Hispanic	0.23	1.0
B. Using log performance rating		
OLS Estimates		
Black	−0.287	−0.144
	(0.093)	(0.043)
Hispanic	−0.192	−0.040
	(0.098)	(0.038)
IV Estimates		
Black	−0.233	0.014
	(0.132)	(0.141)
Hispanic	−0.147	0.099
	(0.127)	(0.125)
Proportion of wage gap due to statistical discrimination		
Black	0.19	1.0
Hispanic	0.23	1.0

Note

a Estimates in columns (1) and (2) are from the specifications in columns (3) and (4) of Table 10.5. See notes to Tables 10.2–10.5 for details. The proportion of the wage gap due to statistical discrimination is recorded as 1.0 when the IV estimated is greater than or equal to zero, consistent with statistical discrimination explaining all of the wage gap. All estimates are weighted.

demonstrating that we can, in fact, successfully improve labor market information, these results hint at the potential value from doing so.

Is labor market information better for some demographic groups?

The evidence from the preceding sections suggests that labor market information problems may partially account for the lower wages paid to minority workers, among both women and men. This subsection turns to the question of whether employer information is better about some demographic groups than others. If mismatches lower productivity, then worse information about women or minorities can lower that group's average wage, providing another channel for labor market information to lead to lower wages for such groups. In addition, even if the type of test from the preceding section does not point to information problems as a source of unexplained wage differences between equally productive workers in different demographic groups, the test in this subsection can. This is potentially most pertinent to sex differences in wages, which cannot be explained as stemming from simple statistical discrimination, given that women's performance ratings are on average at least as high as men's.

The analysis initially proceeded by estimating the wage equation separately for each demographic group. However, for some of the smaller groups the estimates of α (particularly the OLS estimates, but one IV estimate as well) were negative. Consequently, the estimates are computed for two comparison groups, men vs. women and whites vs. nonwhites. Since the latter results in pooling men and women, for whom different instruments appeared to perform well, estimates for this comparison are reported using first just the age variables, and then the age and education variables as instruments. The results are reported in Table 10.7.

Columns (1) and (2) look at sex differences, grouping workers of each race and ethnicity, of the same sex, together, and including race and ethnicity dummy variables in the regression. For both the linear and log specifications, the ratio a_{OLS}/a_{IV} is considerably higher for men (0.12–0.13) than for women (0.02–0.03). The lower estimate of α_{OLS} for women implies that women's starting wages are much more weakly related to their performance rating—which is measured after they have accumulated some time with the employer—than are men's. On the other hand, the estimates of α_{IV} are if anything higher for women, implying that their starting wages are at least as strongly related to *expected* productivity as are men's. Together, this evidence suggests that employers have considerably worse information about new female employees than about new male employees. However, the standard errors of the estimated ratios of α_{OLS}/α_{IV} are relatively large, so the t-statistics for testing the null hypothesis of equality of these ratios for men and women are in the 1.4–1.5 range, implying that the evidence of a lower ratio for women is not statistically strong.

Turning to the results for whites vs. nonwhites, there is no evidence that employers have better information on white workers. In particular, in all of the specifications the estimate of the ratio α_{OLS}/α_{IV} is a bit lower for white than for minority workers, indicating if anything slightly worse information about white workers, although the differences are nowhere near significant.[38]

Conclusions

In the data set analyzed in this chapter, OLS regressions of starting wages on current performance—which is measured some time after the beginning of employment—indicate that minority workers are paid lower starting wages than white workers

Table 10.7 Estimates of quality of labor market information for different demographic groups[a]

	Men (1)	Women (2)	White (3)	Nonwhite (4)	White (5)	Nonwhite (6)
A. Using linear performance rating						
a_{OLS}	0.0039	0.0010	0.0017	0.0034	0.0017	0.0034
	(0.0011)	(0.0010)	(0.0011)	(0.0010)	(0.0011)	(0.0010)
a_{IV}	0.034	0.041	0.046	0.081	0.045	0.068
	(0.015)	(0.010)	(0.017)	(0.048)	(0.013)	(0.021)
a_{OLS}/a_{IV}	0.115	0.025	0.037	0.042	0.038	0.049
	(0.058)	(0.026)	(0.027)	(0.027)	(0.026)	(0.020)
Instruments	Age	Age, education	Age		Age, education	
First-stage regression						
F-statistic on instruments	3.82	4.36	4.87	1.43	3.18	2.16
p-value	0.02	0.00	0.01	0.24	0.01	0.06
B. Using log performance rating						
a_{OLS}	0.253	0.041	0.093	0.212	0.093	0.212
	(0.067)	(0.066)	(0.073)	(0.058)	(0.073)	(0.058)
a_{IV}	1.886	2.631	2.779	5.815	2.481	4.401
	(0.985)	(0.712)	(1.167)	(3.842)	(0.791)	(1.417)
a_{OLS}/a_{IV}	0.134	0.016	0.034	0.036	0.038	0.048
	(0.076)	(0.025)	(0.029)	(0.026)	(0.031)	(0.020)
Instruments	Age	Age, education	Age		Age, education	
First-stage regression						
F-statistic on instruments	2.93	3.84	4.06	1.13	3.06	1.96
p-value	0.05	0.00	0.02	0.32	0.01	0.08

Note

a Standard errors of estimates are reported in parentheses. All regressions exclude age, education, and job requirement variables from the wage equation. All estimates are weighted.

with the same eventual performance, among both men and women. The inclusion of a performance measure—in contrast to typical wage regression studies of discrimination—might be thought to bolster the case that these wage differences reflect taste discrimination.

However, if employers base starting wages on expected productivity or performance, and average performance is lower for minority workers (as it is in these data), then these estimated differentials could reflect simple statistical discrimination. Minority workers and white workers may each receive average starting wages equal to average performance, but a minority worker who turns out to be a high performer will end up getting a lower starting wage than a white worker who turns out to be a low performer, even if these workers turn out to have the same performance. A test of statistical vs. taste discrimination, and a test of statistical discrimination vs. pure measurement error, provide some evidence for both men and women that statistical discrimination is partly to blame for these differences in starting wages between minority and white workers, although the evidence is not very strong statistically.

Average performance of women in the sample studied in this chapter is if anything higher than that of men, so simple statistical discrimination cannot explain the lower starting wages that women receive. However, more complex models of statistical discrimination suggest that worse labor market information about a particular group can lead to lower demand for that group (even conditional on the same average performance or productivity), and hence generate wage differentials. A test of the quality of labor market information regarding male and female employees suggests that employers have better information about male workers, which may partly explain the lower starting wages paid to women, although again the evidence is not strong.

Together, these findings provide some reasons to believe that better labor market information about minority or female employees (and, in fact, all employees) might help to boost starting wages of minorities and women. However, these conclusions should be treated cautiously for four reasons. First, the evidence reported in the chapter is not overwhelmingly strong from a statistical standpoint. Second, it is difficult to distinguish fully between the statistical discrimination hypothesis and the hypothesis that the performance ratings studied in this chapter are simply prone to classical measurement error, although evidence reported in the chapter suggests that the problem of labor market information is real. Third, the empirical methods rely on identifying assumptions that are obviously open to debate; alternative identifying assumptions that can be pursued using other data sets would clearly be of interest. Finally, relatively little is known about how to convey useful information about employees to potential employers. Direct examination of the consequences of using alternative methods (skills certification, job testing, etc.) would also be necessary to evaluate whether wage differentials by race and sex can be partly addressed via better labor market information.

Acknowledgments

I am very grateful to Harry Holzer for supplying the data, to Kathleen Beegle for outstanding research assistance, to an anonymous referee and Dan Mitchell for helpful comments, and to Harry Holzer, Peter Schmidt, and Jeff Wooldridge for helpful discussions. This research was supported by a grant from the Office of Educational Research and Improvement of the US Department of Education to the National Center for Postsecondary Improvement.

Notes

1 Examples of research on wage differences by race and sex include: Bergmann (1989); Neumark (1996); Oaxaca (1973); Fix and Struyk (1993); Becker (1985); Neal and Johnson (1996); and Smith and Ward (1989). An extensive compendium of this research is provided in Darity (1995).
2 See Oettinger (1996) and Altonji and Pierret (1997) for recent applications of this model.
3 In the empirical implementation, a set of dummy variables for race and ethnicity is used.

4   P does not have an "s" subscript, indicating that it is measured some time after the starting wage is set.

5   Note that this is different from what is typically assumed in statistical discrimination models, in which the observed signal available to the employer is equal to true productivity plus orthogonal noise (Cain, 1986). Rather, starting wages are set based on P_s^*, but P (which is true productivity) is a noisy signal of P_s^*.

6   For example, in 1994 out of 19,571 total charges under the Age Discrimination in Employment Act filed with the EEOC, in 5.7 percent of cases wages were an issue, vs. 9.1 percent for race discrimination charges and 10.2 percent for sex discrimination charges (United States Equal Employment Opportunity Commission, 1994).

7   One could imagine trying to distinguish between taste discrimination and statistical discrimination based on the statistical significance of the IV estimates of β; this is equivalent to treating the null as statistical discrimination, and testing for evidence against it. But a small reduction in the absolute value of the estimate of β from instrumenting could be enough to make the estimate insignificant, while representing little change from the OLS estimate of β. In addition, given the focus in the literature on taste discrimination, it seems appropriate to treat this hypothesis as the null in research testing for alternative forms of discrimination.

8   FR do not consider this issue.

9   For example, Cain (1986) notes that women may have difficulty signalling their long-term commitment to the labor market.

10 FR also estimate this reliability ratio (although differently, given their data), but do not contrast it across groups to compare reliability of labor market information.

11 The expansion is taken around the plims of a_{OLS} and a_{IV}, denoted $(\alpha_{OLS}, \alpha_{IV})$.

12 These data were generously supplied by Harry Holzer. The employer data set from the MCSUI has many parallels to the earlier Employment Opportunity Pilot Project (EOPP). Although the MCSUI includes other data sets, in this chapter the employer data set is referred to as the MCSUI data.

13 Other than education, most characteristics of workers and jobs do not differ significantly across the samples of establishments generated by the two data sources.

14 Successfully screened establishments were those where the correct establishment and the person responsible for new hiring into the relevant types of positions were contacted.

15 A similar variable is used in the EOPP Survey (e.g. Barron *et al.*, 1989) and a more recent, similar survey of members of the National Federation of Independent Businesses (Bishop, 1993). Since the main survey respondent was the person responsible for hiring, in small- and medium-sized companies the performance rating was typically elicited from this respondent, who was likely to be a manager or owner, and who should therefore be able to speak knowledgeably about a worker's job performance. In large companies, these functions are more likely to be separated. As a result, in these cases the interviewer generally elicited the performance rating from a supervisor.

16 The piece-rate data used by FR as a proxy for productivity are not immune to the influence of discrimination. For example, tasks, equipment, or work sites may be allocated in such as way as to affect the output of specific groups (such as men vs. women).

17 The scale should be the same, however, as respondents are instructed to regard a rating of 50 as average, although employers' perceptions of "average" are likely to vary.

18 In other work using these data (Holzer and Neumark, 1999), the performance rating standardized by the supervisor's rating of the typical new hire into the job was used. However, the analysis in that paper concerned within-job differences in performance. In this chapter, in contrast, the performance rating should distinguish between a highly productive worker in a demanding job and a less-productive worker in an undemanding job, when both have fairly typical performance for workers in those jobs, by assigning a higher rating to the former.

19 Moreover, as long as there is some pure measurement error of this variety, the results are biased in the direction of rejecting the null of pure taste discrimination.

20 One could argue that OLS regressions using current wages—which are available in this data set—coupled with performance ratings, would provide a clean test of taste discrimination uncontaminated by statistical discrimination. However, there is no reason to believe that wages adjust continuously to realized performance. Indeed, in the data set used in this chapter, it is more likely that no adjustment has occurred by the time the current wage is recorded. The tenure of a typical worker in this data set is very low, since the survey covers companies' most recent hires, and for 56 percent of the observations that we use, recorded current and starting wages are identical.

21 The MCSUI offers little else in the way of potential instruments for the performance rating, since most of the questions included in the survey relate to firm characteristics or hiring and recruiting procedures, rather than workers.

22 In contrast, the percentage was 4.8 when a high school diploma was strongly preferred, 14.1 when it was mildly preferred, and 24.9 when it did not matter.

23 However, some measurement error may be introduced because some individuals in jobs in which these qualifications are not absolutely required may still possess them; of course, in jobs in which these qualifications are unimportant, workers who possess them may not be more productive.

24 About 7 percent are paid a weekly or monthly rate, and 23 percent an annual salary.

25 In the data, a considerably higher fraction of nonhourly workers receive health, dental, and pension benefits (the differences in the proportions of nonhourly and hourly workers receiving these benefits are 0.23, 0.22, and 0.26, respectively).

26 Because of the sampling scheme described in the previous section, all estimates are weighted.

27 The MCSUI does not include separate race and ethnicity variables. Rather, the survey elicits the "racial or ethnic background" of the new employee, which is then coded as either white, black, Hispanic, Asian, or other. (Individuals in the latter two categories are dropped from the analysis.)

28 Unless otherwise specified, statements about statistical significance refer to the 5-percent level.

29 The educational classification available in the MCSUI is actually somewhat more detailed. But the results for these specifications as well as the IV estimations reported later were qualitatively similar using the richer classification, so the simpler results are reported here.

30 These results are similar if only one set of possible instruments at a time is included in the first-stage regression; the only difference is that the p-values for the age variables for women were lower, although again not as low as those for the education variables.

31 As noted earlier, one could test the null hypothesis of statistical discrimination based on whether the IV estimates of the coefficients of the race/ethnicity dummy variables are significantly different from zero. The estimates in column (4) indicate a failure to reject this null, and the same result occurs for women, discussed later. However, as mentioned earlier, it is probably preferable to treat taste discrimination as the null hypothesis.

32 This range of p-values refers to the tests for bias in the OLS estimates of the race/ethnicity differentials in the preferred specifications in Table 10.3 (columns (3) and (4)) and Table 10.4 (columns (5) and (6)).

33 This test is based on the assumption that the bias from pure measurement error would be no different for the probationary and nonprobationary samples; this assumption seems reasonable given that the measurement error would be attributable solely to errors in the reported performance rating relative to productivity that is known to the employer.

34 In unreported estimates for men and women combined using only the age instruments, the IV estimates of the coefficients of the productivity scores in the nonprobationary sample were small and insignificant, and the F-statistics for the instruments in the first-stage regression were much lower than when age and education were used as instruments. In unreported estimates for women only using age and education as instruments, the OLS estimates of the coefficients of the productivity scores in the nonprobationary sample were negative and insignificant.

35 This is relevant because, later, results are presented indicating that the ratio a_{OLS}/a_{IV} is smaller for women than for men. The similar demographic compositions of the nonprobationary and probationary groups implies that this sex difference does not drive those results.

36 As explained earlier, the samples pooling men and women are not suitable for testing statistical vs. taste discrimination.

37 The wage gap is larger for nonprobationary jobs, but the estimates nonetheless imply that the average starting wage gap would decline with better information.

38 This is true looking at the ratio α_{OLS}/α_{IV} or the difference between α_{OLS} and α_{IV}. The ratio is more relevant to the test, because a given difference between a_{OLS} and a_{IV} could be consistent with ratios close to 1 (e.g. $a_{OLS} = 0.8$ and $a_{IV} = 0.9$) and close to 0 (e.g. $a_{OLS} = 0.02$ and $a_{IV} = 0.12$), and hence consistent with widely varying reliability of the employer's labor market information.

References

Aigner, Dennis J. and Glen C. Cain. 1977. "Statistical Theories of Discrimination in the Labor Market." *Industrial and Labor Relations Review* 30: 175–87.

Altonji, Joseph G. and Charles R. Pierret. 1997. "Employer Learning and Statistical Discrimination." Working Paper No. 6297. Cambridge, MA: National Bureau of Economic Research.

Barron, John, Mark Berger, and Dan Black. 1989. "Job Matching and On-the-Job Training." *Journal of Labor Economics* 7: 1–19.

Becker, Gary S. 1957. *The Economics of Discrimination*. Chicago: University of Chicago Press.

———. 1985. "Human Capital, Effort, and the Sexual Division of Labor." *Journal of Labor Economics* 3 (Supplement): S33–58.

Bergmann, Barbara R. 1989. "Does the Market for Women's Labor Need Fixing?" *Journal of Economic Perspectives* 3: 43–60.

Bishop, John. 1993. "Improving Job Matches in the U.S. Labor Market." *Brooking Papers on Economic Activity: Microeconomics* 1: 335–90.

Blau, Francine and Andrea Beller. 1992. "Black–White Earnings over the 1980s: Gender Differences in Trends." *Review of Economics and Statistics* 74: 276–86.

Cain, Glen C. 1986. "The Economic Analysis of Labor Market Discrimination: A Survey." In *Handbook of Labor Economics*, eds Orley Ashenfelter and Richard Layard, pp. 693–786. Amsterdam: North Holland.

Darity, William, Jr, ed. 1995. *Economics and Discrimination*. Aldershot: Edward Elgar Publishing Limited.

Farmer, Amy and Dek Terrell. 1996. "Discrimination, Bayesian Updating of Employer Beliefs, and Human Capital Accumulation." *Economic Inquiry* 34: 204–19.

Fix, Michael and Raymond Struyk. 1993. *Clear and Convincing Evidence*. Washington, DC: Urban Institute Press.

Foster, Andrew D. and Mark R. Rosenzweig. 1993. "Information, Learning, and Wage Rates in Low-Income Rural Areas." *Journal of Human Resources* 28: 759–90.

Holzer, Harry J. 1995. "Employer Skill Needs and Labor Market Outcomes Across Groups." Working Paper. New York: Russell Sage Foundation.

——. 1996a. *What Employers Want: Job Prospects for Less-Educated Workers*. New York: Russell Sage Foundation.

——. 1996b. "Employer Hiring Decisions and Antidiscrimination Policy." In *Generating Jobs: How to Increase Demand for Less-Skilled Workers*, eds Richard Freeman and Peter Gottschalk, pp. 223–57. New York: Russell Sage Foundation.

Holzer, Harry, and David Neumark. 1999. "Are Affirmative Action Hires Less Qualified? Evidence from Employer–Employee Data on New Hires." *Journal of Labor Economics* 17: 534–69.

Johnson, Richard J. and David Neumark. 1997. "Age Discrimination, Job Separations, and Employment Status of Older Workers: Evidence from Self Reports." *Journal of Human Resources* 32: 779–811.

Kling, Jeffrey. 1995. "High Performance Work Systems and Firm Performance." *Monthly Labor Review* 118: 29–36.

Lang, Kevin. 1986. "A Language Theory of Discrimination." *Quarterly Journal of Economics* 101: 363–82.

Lazear, Edward P. 1979. "Why Is There Mandatory Retirement?" *Journal of Political Economy* 87: 1261–84.

Light, Audrey and Manuelita Ureta. 1995. "Early-Career Work Experience and Gender Wage Differentials." *Journal of Labor Economics* 13: 121–54.

Neal, Derek A. and William R. Johnson. 1996. "The Role of Premarket Factors in Black–White Wage Differences." *Journal of Political Economy* 104: 869–95.

Neumark, David. 1996. "Sex Discrimination in Restaurant Hiring: An Audit Study." *Quarterly Journal of Economics* 111: 915–42.

Oaxaca, Ronald. 1973. "Male–Female Wage Differentials in Urban Labor Markets." *International Economic Review* 14: 693–709.

Oettinger, Gerald. 1996. "Statistical Discrimination and the Early Career Evolution of the Black–White Wage Gap." *Journal of Labor Economics* 14: 52–78.

Phelps, Edmund S. 1972. "The Statistical Theory of Racism and Sexism." *American Economic Review* 52: 659–61.

Reimers, Cordelia. 1983. "Labor-Market Discrimination Against Black and Hispanic Men." *Review of Economics and Statistics* 65: 570–9.

Rothschild, Michael and Joseph E. Stiglitz. 1982. "A Model of Employment Outcomes Illustrating the Effect of the Structure of Information on the Level and Distribution of Income." *Economics Letters* 10: 231–6.

Smith, James P. and Michael Ward. 1989. "Women in the Labor Market and in the Family." *Journal of Economic Perspectives* 3: 9–24.

United States Equal Employment Opportunity Commission. 1994. *EEOC Fiscal Year 1994 Annual Report*.

11 Market forces and sex discrimination

(with Judith K. Hellerstein and Kenneth R. Troske)

Introduction

The residual wage gap between men and women has been documented in an extensive body of research. Some view the residual wage gap as evidence of sex discrimination in wages, arguing that if a gap remains after controlling for variables measuring workers' productivity, it must reflect discrimination. This interpretation of the evidence comes directly from Becker's (1971) classic model of employer discrimination, in which discrimination is reflected in a gap between wages and marginal products. Others, citing the same model, focus on Becker's conclusion that under sufficiently competitive conditions discriminatory employers will fail to thrive, and will eventually be competed out of existence; since the sex–wage differential has persisted, it must reflect unobserved productivity differences rather than discrimination (Fuchs, 1988; O'Neill, 1994). In this chapter, we report new evidence on both of these issues: whether sex discrimination exists, and whether competitive market forces act to reduce or eliminate discrimination. Specifically, we use plant- and firm-level data to examine short-run profitability and longer-run growth and ownership changes, in relation to the sex composition of a plant's or firm's workforce, and we explore how these relationships vary with the strength of product market competition.

In our view, this evidence is far more informative than what we can learn from analyzing wage regressions. Given that the individual-level data sets used to estimate unexplained or residual wage gaps between men and women contain only proxies for workers' productivity, it is difficult to refute the argument that the residual wage gap reflects unobserved productivity differences. Furthermore, because we do not know how quickly nondiscriminatory sources of the residual sex–wage gap might be changing, evidence on changes in the sex–wage gap over time may not be particularly informative regarding the role of competition in eliminating or reducing discrimination.

We begin with a simple test for sex discrimination. If there is no discrimination against women, then there should be no cross-sectional relationship between profitability and the sex composition of the workforce. Any sex difference in wages must reflect only observed or unobserved productivity differentials between men and women, and firms or plants that employ more women should earn no higher profits. Evidence that plants or firms that employ relatively more women earn higher profits, in contrast, would be consistent with sex discrimination. We determine which of these hypotheses holds empirically by estimating the cross-sectional relationship between plant or firm profitability and the sex composition of the workforce.

Next, we explore the more direct static implication of Becker's model that discrimination is likely to exist only where there is product market power, and conversely that product market competition hinders discrimination. We test whether—as the Becker model predicts—there is a positive short-run relationship between profitability and the sex composition of the workforce only among plants with product market power, because only among such plants are there positive economic profits that may be exploited to indulge the discriminatory tastes of some employers.

This evidence is arguably more decisive than that obtained from wage regressions with individual-level controls, because firm or plant profitability, unlike wages, is a direct measure of performance, obviating the need to find proxies for workers' productivity. In addition, the results incorporating market power are informative about the role of competitive market forces, which Becker's model highlights.

However, higher profits at a point in time in plants or firms employing more women (possibly only where there is product market power) does not contradict the dynamic implication of Becker's model that market forces may eliminate discrimination over the longer run. Market forces may undermine discrimination in different ways, depending on the nature of product market competition, barriers to entry, transferability of assets, and the form of employers' discriminatory tastes. We use longitudinal data on the plants in our data set to test the dynamic implications of Becker's model, asking whether nondiscriminatory plants—those which, according to the cross-sectional evidence, employ more women and earn higher profits—grow faster or are less likely to undergo a change of ownership, compared with discriminatory plants. The combined static and dynamic evidence provides us with a better understanding of sex discrimination in labor markets, and the role of competitive market forces in reducing or eliminating this discrimination, than can be obtained from conventional wage equation approaches to discrimination, or even from more convincing cross-sectional tests for discrimination (such as audit studies), which cannot say anything about the dynamic implications of Becker's model.[1]

This evidence is complementary to and builds upon our research testing whether wage differences between men and women are larger than productivity differences (Hellerstein *et al.*, 1999). In that research, we specify a plant-level production function, with explicit assumptions about its functional form, including the role of male and female labor inputs in production. Conditional on those assumptions, we estimate the relative marginal products of men and women, and compare them with relative wages.[2] This chapter differs in two fundamental ways. First, the results do not hinge on the specification of a structural production function. More importantly, we present new evidence on competitive market forces and discrimination, allowing richer tests of Becker's model of discrimination.

The Becker model

Our empirical work is framed by the Becker (1971) model of employer discrimination. Consider a wage-taking firm with a production function Y that uses two inputs: the labor of men, M, and the labor of women, F. Employers have a distaste for hiring female workers, and do not maximize profits but rather maximize utility defined as

$$U(\pi, M, F) = P \cdot Y(M, F) - w_M M - w_F F - d \cdot (F/M), \tag{1}$$

where d is the discrimination coefficient capturing this distaste, P is output price, and w_M and w_F are the market wages of men and women respectively. Short-run utility maximization then implies

$$MRP_M + d \cdot (F/M^2) = w_M, \quad MRP_F - d/M = w_F. \tag{2}$$

The marginal revenue product of male labor is set below its input price, because male labor increases the employer's utility, while the marginal revenue product of female labor is discounted by the non-pecuniary cost of discrimination to the employer, and hence is above the input price of female labor. The discrimination coefficient d will lead the firm in the short run to hire fewer women and more men than profit maximization would dictate.[3] In other words, Becker models discrimination as a price differential needed to induce employers to hire women, which in turn leads to employment differences between men and women that would not exist absent the discrimination.

The discrimination coefficient d is assumed to vary across firms. Firms with weaker discriminatory tastes (smaller d) will tend to hire relatively more women and relatively fewer men, and vice versa. Thus, tastes provide the exogenous source of variation in the proportion female across otherwise identical plants or firms that is the basis of our empirical tests. Since males are paid more than their marginal revenue product, and women less, plants or firms that hire relatively more men and relatively fewer women are less profitable, *ceteris paribus*, motivating our basic test for discrimination.

Becker then goes on to show that with this type of employer utility function, under some conditions market forces will cause discrimination to disappear in the long run. If product markets are perfectly competitive, then discrimination will disappear over time through competition in product markets if there are sufficient potential employers with nondiscriminatory tastes. If product markets are not perfectly competitive but some entry is possible, then discrimination will be competed away if there are nondecreasing returns to scale and at least one potential employer has nondiscriminatory tastes. In the case of total barriers to entry in product markets, even with decreasing returns to scale, if businesses are transferable and there is a potential nondiscriminating employer, discrimination may disappear through competition in the market for firms. Although Becker's model was not inherently dynamic, the implication of discriminatory tastes in each of these cases is that discriminating employers not only give up current profits to indulge their tastes for discrimination, but also sacrifice future profits, since they will earn lower profits in the future because of reduced market share. Finally, Becker (1971) notes that if employers' tastes are nepotistic rather than discriminatory, then discrimination will not be eliminated by competition in the market for firms, although product market competition may still suffice. In our view the conditions for competition to eliminate discrimination have been glossed over by those who interpret the Becker model as implying that discrimination cannot persist, which is another motivation for testing these implications empirically.

In addition to the employer discrimination model, Becker (1971) also develops models of employee discrimination and customer discrimination. It is of interest to ask whether evidence consistent with the employer discrimination model—that plants employing more women are more profitable—is equally consistent with either of these other two models, or instead points explicitly to employer discrimination. In a fundamental sense, these alternative models do not predict a relationship between employment of women (or whatever group bears the brunt of discrimination) and profitability; because employers do not have discriminatory tastes, it is not they who are willing to pay a pecuniary cost to avoid contact with women. For example, in the simplest employee discrimination model firms are completely segregated, with no effect on profits. Discrimination also has no effect on profits in a richer model of employee discrimination with supervisory inputs in which complete desegregation does not occur (Arrow, 1972). In Becker's model of customer discrimination, the effects on prices of customers' tastes regarding transactions with particular groups should be fully reflected in wages of workers involved in these transactions, so that profitability should be unaffected by such discrimination. We do not claim that one cannot construct a model with discriminatory tastes on the part of employees or customers that affect both the proportion female and profitability. However, we interpret the evidence we ultimately find of a positive relationship between profitability and the proportion female (among plants with product market power) as consistent primarily with employer discrimination.

Data

Our data come from the Worker Establishment Characteristics Database (WECD) and the Longitudinal Research Database (LRD).[4] The WECD is based on the 1990 Sample Edited Detail File (SEDF), which includes all household responses to the 1990 Decennial Census long form, and the 1990 Standard Statistical Establishment List (SSEL), a complete list of all establishments in the United States. In the first step, manufacturing workers in the SEDF are matched to establishments in the SSEL using the detailed location and industry information available in both data sets. To help ensure that we have a representative sample of workers in a plant, we only keep plants with at least three workers matched to the plant; the average number of workers matched to a plant is around thirty. To form the WECD, these records are then linked to the LRD, a longitudinal panel of establishments drawn from each Census of Manufacturers (CM) conducted since 1963 (1963, 1967, 1972, 1977, 1982, 1987) as well as the 1973–93 Annual Survey of Manufacturers (ASM).[5] Since much of the labor market information in the Decennial Census refers to 1989, we link the worker records to establishments in the LRD in 1989 for our main cross-sectional analysis.

The matched worker data are used to construct the proportion female, as well as the proportions of the workforce in each of a number of other categories (age, education, race, marital status, and occupation). The plant-level data are used to construct a number of controls for plant-level characteristics that may be related to profitability and growth, such as plant age and industry.

Finally, we define two measures of performance that we use as proxies for profitability. The first is operating income (sales + inventory accumulation−labor costs−material costs) divided by inventory-adjusted sales (i.e. current year sales plus the change in inventories). The second also subtracts out from the numerator purchased business services or overhead costs (such as purchased electricity, legal services, advertising, and repairs). These firm performance measures used as proxies for profitability are essentially price cost-margins (see, for example, Domowitz *et al.*, 1986).[6] The one obvious omission from this performance measure is that the numerator does not subtract off the costs of capital flow expenditures. In CM years, the Census Bureau collects detailed data on the book value of capital of each plant, but there is no straightforward method to transform this book value measure into a capital flow measure, or to recover the rental rate of capital (see Caballero *et al.*, 1995). Instead, we control for the ratio of book value of capital to shipments on the right-hand side of the regressions when appropriate, providing some accounting for the variation across plants in capital expenditures. Using 1987 data to construct the capital/shipments variable should mitigate endogeneity bias.

Since the Becker model of employer discrimination is based on the actions of owners, focusing solely on plants could be somewhat misleading if decision making is done at the firm level. The Census Bureau focuses on plants in its data collection, but in CM years we can link together all plants that belong to the same parent firm, and obtain information on employment and costs at the nonproduction facilities of these firms. We therefore also construct a firm-level data set paralleling our 1989 plant-level data set, by matching workers in the WECD to plants in the 1987 CM, and combining data on all establishments belonging to the same firm. Because information on the demographic characteristics of the workforces of these firms comes from the Census of Population, we are forced to assume that the demographic composition of each firm's workforce was the same in 1987. We also use these firm-level data to estimate cross-sectional profitability regressions.

Because of difficulties in defining and tracking firms over time, in our dynamic analysis we study only plants. Moreover, we cannot follow changes in workforce characteristics over time with the WECD. We can, though, study growth in plants (in terms of both employment and shipments) by matching plants in the WECD to the 1990 and 1995 ASMs. We also look at the issue of plant ownership changes by identifying plants in the 1990 ASM that have a different owner in 1995. Because the Census Bureau drew a new ASM sample for 1994, some plants are not in the 1995 ASM simply because they were not included in the new sample; these plants are omitted from this analysis. Finally, we note that the period 1990–5 may represent a window that is short relative to the long run that is the focus of Becker's model; but 1995 is the most recent year of data available.

Table 11.1 presents descriptive statistics. Column (1) covers the full sample of 3,089 plants in the 1989 ASM that appear in the WECD. Column (2) covers the sample of 2,578 firms constructed by linking plants together with units from the same firm, using the 1987 CM. Column (3) again reports statistics on data from plants in 1989, but only for the subsample of 2,634 plants for which we also have data in the 1995 ASM.[7] The similarities between columns (1) and (3) suggest that our analysis of plant growth and ownership change between 1990 and 1995 does not suffer from sample selection bias attributable to changes in the ASM sample. Finally, we note that the proportion female varies widely across plants, and the data do not reflect complete or near-complete segregation. In particular, in 49 percent of the plants 0–25 percent of the workers are female (in 14 percent 0–5 percent are female), in 32 percent of the plants 25–50 percent are female, in 15 percent of the plants 50–75 percent are female, and in 5 percent of the plants 75–100 percent are female.

Empirical approach and results

We first examine the relationship between profitability and the proportion female. We include as controls other demographic characteristics of the workforce, and plant or firm characteristics that are likely to be associated with profitability, such as age, industry, and measures of market power. The controls for plant age are particularly important, as women are on average newer entrants and hence may work in newer plants, which are more profitable. As discussed earlier, we also control for the ratio of capital to shipments, since the profit rate measures do not account for capital expenditures. In the idealized case in which the data reflect perfect competition in the long run, our measures of profitability would be unrelated to all of these variables except the capital/shipments variable as long as these measures capture economic profits rather than accounting profits, or if divergences between accounting and economic profits are unrelated to these variables. On the other hand, if some employers are discriminating against women, those that employ more women should earn higher profits.

In fact, the more direct implication of the Becker model is that the relationship between profitability and the proportion female should be particularly strong among plants or firms that have product market power. For such plants or firms, competitive market forces may play less of a role in punishing discriminating employers, at least in the short run. Thus, after presenting the simple regressions of profitability on the proportion female, we proceed to what we regard as the most convincing cross-sectional test of the Becker model, asking whether market power strengthens the positive relationship between profitability and the proportion female.

Table 11.1 Descriptive statistics[a]

	Plants, 1989 (1)	Firms, 1987 (2)	Plants in 1995 ASM, 1989 (3)
Operating income/sales	0.229 (0.201)	0.238 (0.154)	0.235 (0.206)
(Operating income − overhead costs)/sales	0.213 (0.206)	—	0.219 (0.210)
Proportional growth in shipments, 1990–5	—	—	0.131 (1.03)
Proportional growth in employment, 1990–5	—	—	−0.134 (0.472)
Changed ownership, 1990–5	—	—	0.159
Proportion female	0.286 (0.226)	0.312 (0.246)	0.288 (0.225)
Proportion black	0.078 (0.132)	0.071 (0.135)	0.079 (0.131)
Proportion married	0.863 (0.125)	0.841 (0.141)	0.866 (0.121)
Proportion aged 35–54	0.509 (0.186)	0.476 (0.187)	0.513 (0.183)
Proportion aged 55+	0.137 (0.128)	0.142 (0.136)	0.134 (0.123)
Proportion some college	0.370 (0.211)	0.353 (0.211)	0.375 (0.211)
Proportion managerial	0.155 (0.155)	0.158 (0.157)	0.156 (0.155)
Proportion sales	0.197 (0.144)	0.201 (0.150)	0.197 (0.143)
Proportion craft	0.208 (0.146)	0.201 (0.153)	0.207 (0.144)
Capital/shipments, 1987	0.470 (2.23)	0.358 (2.53)	0.492 (2.41)
Output share in 4-digit industry, 1987	0.017 (0.035)	—	0.018 (0.036)
Birth year of plant	1955 (20.6)	—	1955 (20.8)
N	3,089	2,578	2,634

Note
a Standard deviations are reported in parentheses. Observations with extreme values of the dependent variables (less than 1 percent of the sample) are deleted here and in subsequent tables. The variable in the second row is constructed using overhead costs for 1987, since these are available for ASM establishments only in CM years. For multi-plant firms in column (2) we aggregate the variables used to construct profits across all establishments in the firm. These data are available only for CM years, along with a separate survey of nonproduction sites. Data on capital/shipments and output share are also from 1987 (capital and output share are not available for 1989).

Following this analysis, we turn to the question of the longer-run prospects of plants that appear to discriminate by hiring fewer women, compared with those that do not. For the subsample of plants that do not change ownership between 1990 and 1995, we estimate models of growth in output or employment, as functions of the same plant and workforce characteristics used in the profitability regressions. Plants that fail during this period are included in the sample, assigned shipments and employment growth (measured as the proportional change) of −1, and no ownership change. We do not include plants that changed ownership in the growth regressions, because the mechanism by which discrimination is potentially competed away for these plants is through the market for plants, not the product market. We also take all the plants for which we have data in 1990 and 1995 and estimate ownership-change models using the same covariates.

Our empirical tests have some potential limitations that bear consideration. First, while our tests (and data) are well suited to testing for employer discrimination, and testing other implications of Becker's model, they are not well suited to unraveling the mechanism by which discrimination arises, since they do not permit any sort of detailed look at firm hiring practices or the availability of applicants for different positions. Second, there may be unobservable determinants of productivity (such as physical strength) that are correlated with sex. As we noted in the Introduction, however, if wages adjust to reflect unobservable productivity differences, then there should be no relationship between profitability and the proportion female. On the other hand, if there are constraints on paying men and women different wages despite these productivity differences (because of equal pay laws), then firms using more women will be less, rather than more profitable. There is bias in the direction of a positive relationship between profitability and the employment of women only if the unobservables are positively correlated with female labor. This is the opposite of what is often claimed by researchers studying the sex wage gap, who assume that productive attributes of workers are negatively correlated with female labor. Third, as usual there are other potential explanations of our findings. For example, plants or firms that are doing badly may have contracted recently, and if they have discriminatory tastes against women may have fired women first, generating a positive association between the proportion female and profitability. This scenario still entails discrimination, but not necessarily differences in discriminatory tastes across employers. As an empirical matter, we cannot rule out this scenario. However, we regard it as a less plausible interpretation of our evidence for two reasons. First, it implies that the firms that are doing the worst engage in the behavior that is most damaging to profits—discriminating against women—which seems an unlikely response. Second, it assumes that the labor supply curve of men to the plant is upward sloping, which is why the plant cannot continually hire more men as it grows.

Profitability and the proportion female

Table 11.2 reports OLS estimates of the cross-sectional relationship between profitability and the proportion female. Columns (1) and (2) report regressions using the full sample, and column (3) using the subsample of plants in 1989 for which we also have data in 1995. The specifications include four-digit industry dummy variables, to control as well as possible for unobserved heterogeneity across plants. This is potentially important because plant-level characteristics may be associated

Table 11.2 Profitability regressions, plant and firm level[a]

	Plants			Firms
	Operating income/sales, 1989	*(Operating income − overhead costs)/sales, 1989*	*Plants in 1995 ASM, (operating income − overhead costs)/sales, 1989*	*Operating income/ sales, 1987*
	(1)	*(2)*	*(3)*	*(4)*
Proportion female	0.047	0.046	0.056	0.088
	(0.021)	(0.022)	(0.025)	(0.014)
Proportion black	−0.029	−0.030	−0.049	−0.016
	(0.029)	(0.029)	(0.033)	(0.022)
Proportion married	−0.024	−0.033	−0.036	−0.005
	(0.031)	(0.032)	(0.036)	(0.023)
Proportion aged 35–54	0.016	0.018	0.011	−0.004
	(0.022)	(0.022)	(0.025)	(0.018)
Proportion aged 55+	−0.061	−0.065	−0.078	−0.046
	(0.030)	(0.031)	(0.036)	(0.023)
Proportion some college	−0.032	−0.037	−0.040	0.014
	(0.024)	(0.024)	(0.028)	(0.019)
Proportion managerial	−0.022	−0.031	−0.037	0.056
	(0.033)	(0.034)	(0.038)	(0.025)
Proportion sales	0.088	0.081	0.068	0.029
	(0.028)	(0.029)	(0.033)	(0.022)
Proportion craft	0.022	0.014	−0.019	0.031
	(0.029)	(0.030)	(0.034)	(0.022)
Multi-plant firm	−0.011	−0.009	−0.005	0.038
	(0.014)	(0.014)	(0.019)	(0.007)
Capital/shipments	−0.0025	−0.0026	−0.0024	−0.018
	(0.0014)	(0.0015)	(0.0015)	(0.012)
2nd output share quartile	0.045	0.047	0.054	—
	(0.010)	(0.011)	(0.012)	
3rd output share quartile	0.096	0.103	0.112	—
	(0.012)	(0.012)	(0.014)	
4th output share quartile	0.159	0.168	0.182	—
	(0.013)	(0.014)	(0.015)	
Plant 11–20 years old	−0.024	−0.024	−0.022	—
	(0.014)	(0.015)	(0.016)	
Plant 21–30 years old	−0.037	−0.039	−0.034	—
	(0.013)	(0.014)	(0.015)	
Plant 31–40 years old	−0.053	−0.055	−0.052	—
	(0.014)	(0.014)	(0.015)	
Plant 41–50 years old	−0.051	−0.053	−0.053	—
	(0.019)	(0.019)	(0.021)	
Plant 51+ years old	−0.051	−0.054	−0.049	—
	(0.015)	(0.016)	(0.017)	
R^2	0.374	0.370	0.395	0.135
N	3,089	3,089	2,634	2,578

Note

a Four-digit industry dummy variables (in columns (1)–(3)) and three Census region dummy variables are also included.

with the proportion female. In addition, we use output share as a measure of market power, which is likely to be a more reliable measure within finely disaggregated industries, in which other factors influencing market power (such as transportation costs) are more homogeneous. The results indicate that, whether or not we subtract overhead costs from income, and irrespective of the sample, the proportion female in a plant's workforce is significantly positively related to profitability. For example, the point estimate in column (2) indicates that a 10 percentage point increase in the proportion female raises the profit rate by 0.46 percentage point.

To get some sense of the magnitudes of these estimates, consider the following simple example of an upper-bound estimate of how increasing the proportion female could change profitability. Suppose men and women are equally productive, so that the entire 30 percent market wage differential (in these data) arises solely because of discrimination. Suppose further that output is constant, that men and women are perfect substitutes in production, and that labor's share in total sales is 75 percent (also an upper bound, since this figure is closer to labor's share in total costs). Assume a discriminating plant is forced to increase the proportion female in its workforce by 10 percentage points while decreasing the proportion male by 10 percentage points (therefore holding the total labor input fixed). This would lead to an increase in the profit rate of 2.3 percentage points, about five times what we find.

Aside from the findings for the proportion female, the results in the first three columns of Table 11.2 provide little evidence of other workforce variables that are significantly related to profitability. Of the other demographic characteristics, only the proportion of workers aged 55 and over is consistently significantly related to profitability. This is unlikely to reflect plant life cycle effects, because we have included detailed plant age dummy variables. Rather, we suspect it reflects shocks to plants' profitability; for example, a negative shock would reduce hiring and lead to an older work force, more so if there are seniority rules regarding layoffs. The absence of any positive relationship between profitability and the proportion black in the workforce is consistent with no discrimination against blacks. Of the variables representing the proportion of workers in different occupations, only the proportion of the workforce in sales is significantly related to profitability. However, in the firm-level specification this estimate becomes small and insignificant, suggesting that the estimates in columns (1)–(3) may be attributable to higher measured profitability in the plants (within firms) in which sales workers are based. The absence of any systematic relationship between profitability and so many of the demographic characteristics suggests that there are not large problems with unobservable characteristics of workers biasing our results for the proportion female, since if there were we would expect many unobservables that were correlated with the proportion female also to be correlated with other worker characteristics.

Turning to the plant-level controls, the estimated coefficient of the capital/shipments ratio, while statistically insignificant, is negative. This is not the sign one would expect, but capital is measured as book value, which is a non-depreciated measure of past capital investments. This is one motivation for the inclusion of a set of dummy variables for the age of the plant; plant age is negatively and significantly correlated with profitability.

We also include in the first three columns of Table 11.2 a measure of the market power of a plant in its output market. The question of how best to measure market power is an old one, and, in the context of cross-industry studies such as this one, comes down to whether one wants to use an industry-based measure of concentration, such as the four-firm concentration ratio or Herfindahl index, or a firm- or establishment-based measure, such as output share.[8] An establishment-based measure of market power is preferable in this case. First, we want to be able to control for industry characteristics aside from market power at a detailed level, by including disaggregated industry dummy variables. This precludes estimating effects of market power defined at the same level of disaggregation as the industry dummy variables. Second, from a theoretical perspective, we want to investigate profitability differences among plants competing in the same industry, since the Becker model points to the potential role of competition from firms or plants in the same industry in eliminating or reducing discrimination. We therefore use the output market share of an establishment within its industry as a proxy for market power. This can be rationalized theoretically. For example, in a Cournot model of competition, a firm's price-cost margin is proportional to the industry output share of that firm (Tirole, 1989). To construct this measure we use the 1987 CM to calculate the share of shipments produced in 1987 by a plant, relative to total shipments in 1987 in the four-digit industry.[9] A potential problem is that this market power measure may be endogenously determined with profitability, but there are two reasons why the potential endogeneity of market power is mitigated. First, the output share variable is based on lagged data from 1987. Second, we do not use a continuous measure of output share directly in the regression. Instead we use industry-specific rankings of the output share of plants in our sample to form dummy variables for the quartile in which the plant is located. The use of these dummy variables also allows profitability to be nonlinearly related to output share.

In columns (1)–(3) of Table 11.2, the estimated coefficients of the dummy variables for the quartile of the plant's industry-specific output share distribution are monotonically increasing across the quartiles and highly significant. These results indicate that plants with higher output shares earn higher profit rates than plants with lower shares of output relative to other plants in their four-digit industries, suggesting that output share is a good proxy for product market power. As the included four-digit industry dummy variables should capture industry-based market power, the relationship between output share and profitability in these specifications points to variation in market power across plants within an industry. Finally, we note that when we experimented with using the four-firm concentration ratio as our measure of market power (and removed the industry dummy variables), its relationship to profitability was not monotonically positive, and the overall strength of the relationship was weak.

The estimates in column (2) use overhead costs in the profitability measure, with nearly identical results to those in column (1), while those in column (3) use the smaller subsample. The similarity of the latter results to those in column (2) again suggests that we do not have a sample selection problem resulting from the selection of a new sample of plants in 1994 that is used for the dynamic analysis that follows. In the rest of our cross-section analyses using 1989 data, we therefore only report results for the full sample of 3,089 plants, the sample represented in the first two columns of Table 11.2.

In column (4), we present results for the sample of firms (rather than plants) that we constructed by aggregating together plants in the 1987 CM that belong to the same firm. Because firms produce in a variety of four-digit industries, we cannot define or construct a firm-level market power measure analogous to the output share categories we used in the plant-level regressions. We therefore report results using a specification that excludes market power measures. Nonetheless, the point estimates of the coefficients of variables for which we can construct firm-level data are quite similar to the plant-level results (and are also similar to plant-level results excluding the output share dummy variables, which we do not report). In particular, the coefficient on the proportion female is 0.088 with a standard error of 0.014, implying a 0.88 percentage point increase in a firm's profit rate from a 10 percentage point increase in the proportion of workers who are female in the firm. The similarity of the plant-level and firm-level results suggests that examining plant-level data is not biasing our results.

The results in Table 11.2 indicate that plants that employ a higher proportion of women are more profitable, consistent with sex discrimination in the labor market. But this evidence cannot identify the mechanism by which this discrimination occurs. In Table 11.3, we provide some limited evidence on this issue, and on the robustness of the results to differences in specification or sample. First, the linear specification constrains the effect of proportion female on profitability to be constant. Column (1) of Table 11.3 reports estimates where we add a quadratic term in the proportion female to the specification. The estimated coefficient on the linear term rises (to 0.100), remaining statistically significant at the 5-percent level. The estimated coefficient of the quadratic term is negative, although insignificant. The data are therefore consistent with a diminishing effect, although a linear model cannot be rejected.[10]

The evidence can also be further examined in light of research based on the human capital model suggesting that the sex wage gap results in large part from specialization within marriage, leading to lower human capital investment among married women so that the shortfall in women's wages emerges (and grows) within marriage (e.g. Mincer and Polachek, 1974). In column (2) of Table 11.3, we augment the specification by adding a variable measuring the proportion of females that are married. This results in insignificant coefficient estimates for the proportion female variable as well as this new variable. However, the point estimates are consistent with little or no relationship between profitability and the proportion of unmarried females, but higher profitability when the proportion of married females is high. If the estimates were statistically significant, this would be consistent with discrimination against married women, in contrast to the human capital hypothesis, which implies that both wages and productivity of married women are lower.[11]

Table 11.3 Profitability regressions, plant level, robustness checks[a]

	Nonlinearities (1)	Marriage interaction (2)	Urban vs. nonurban (3)	Higher cutoff for matched workers/plant (4)
Proportion female	0.100	−0.030	0.051	0.064
	(0.051)	(0.061)	(0.025)	(0.029)
Proportion female squared	−0.076 (0.065)	—	—	—
Proportion female and married	—	0.089 (0.067)	—	—
Proportion female × urban	—	—	−0.016 (0.038)	—
Urban	—	—	−0.003 (0.012)	—
Proportion black	−0.031	−0.027	−0.027	−0.023
	(0.029)	(0.029)	(0.030)	(0.037)
Proportion married	−0.033	−0.059	−0.035	0.001
	(0.032)	(0.037)	(0.032)	(0.047)
Proportion aged 35–54	0.018	0.019	0.019	−0.005
	(0.022)	(0.022)	(0.022)	(0.030)
Proportion aged 55+	−0.064	−0.064	−0.061	−0.126
	(0.031)	(0.031)	(0.032)	(0.044)
Proportion some college	−0.038	−0.037	−0.036	−0.045
	(0.024)	(0.024)	(0.024)	(0.034)
Proportion managerial	−0.035	−0.029	−0.028	−0.015
	(0.034)	(0.033)	(0.034)	(0.047)
Proportion sales	0.076	0.082	0.084	0.119
	(0.029)	(0.029)	(0.029)	(0.040)
Proportion craft	0.013	0.015	0.014	−0.017
	(0.030)	(0.030)	(0.030)	(0.041)
R^2	0.256	0.371	0.370	0.420
N	3,089	3,089	3,089	2,426

Note

a Columns (1)–(3) use all plants, while column (4) uses the subsample of plants to which we matched at least seven workers. With the exception of the added interactive variables, the specifications and dependent variable are the same as in column (2) of Table 11.2. However, only the estimated coefficients of the worker characteristics are reported. Results were very similar using operating income/sales.

We conducted three additional robustness checks. First, we tested whether there are any differences in the relationship of the proportion female to profitability between rural and urban plants, which may arise if employers in isolated locations have monopsony power over female employees. However, the urban–rural difference in the estimated effect of the proportion female, reported in column (3), is very small (0.016) and insignificant. Second, as noted in the section "Data," we imposed a low cutoff (three) on the number of workers that had to be matched to a plant for the plant to be included. To reduce the potential measurement error from using a sample of matched workers, we re-estimated the basic specification for the subsample with seven or more matched workers. As column (4) shows, the estimated coefficient of the proportion female becomes more strongly positive. Finally, because the newest plants may have qualitatively different technology, which could be correlated with the proportion female and profitability, we divided up the younger plant age category more finely, breaking out plants aged 0–5 years. Although not reported in the table, this had essentially no effect on the estimated coefficient of the proportion female. Thus, our basic test for sex discrimination provides a robust finding of a positive relationship between employment of women and profitability.

Market forces and discrimination, a cross-sectional test

As discussed earlier, the Becker model predicts that product market power can inhibit the influence of competitive forces in eliminating discrimination (although competition in the market for firms may still exert such influence over the long run). This implies that for plants with considerable product market power there will be a positive relationship between employment of women and profitability, whereas for plants with little market power, the relationship will be nonexistent or at least weaker. (Ashenfelter and Hannan (1986) and Cavalluzzo *et al.* (1999) study the relationship between market power and discrimination, but not profitability.)

We first test this prediction in column (1) of Table 11.4, where we report results from a plant-level profitability regression adding interactions between the output share dummy variables and the proportion female in the plant. Compared with Table 11.2 (column (2)), the linear coefficient on proportion female is smaller (0.024), and is statistically insignificant. The second quartile interaction is negative and also statistically insignificant. More importantly, the third and fourth quartile interactions indicate a strengthening relationship between profitability and the proportion female at higher output shares, with the fourth quartile interaction large (0.136) and strongly significant. Adding together the linear and interactive variables, the implied effects of the proportion female in the first through fourth quartiles are 0.024, −0.029, 0.086, and 0.160, respectively. The *p*-value for the test of a constant effect of the proportion female in the lower three quartiles is approximately 0.05. On the other hand, the equality of the effect of proportion female across all four quartiles is strongly rejected, with a *p*-value of 0.001. Especially coupled with the results in column (2) (discussed more later), for which the *t*-statistic for the proportion female × third quartile interaction is 1.6, we read our estimates as indicating no relationship between profitability and the proportion female over the lower half of the market share distribution, and then a strengthening positive relationship, which becomes strongly significant in the fourth quartile. Using the same calculation as before, for plants with the most market power the estimated coefficients imply that a 10 percentage point increase in the proportion female raises the profit rate by 1.60 percentage points (10 × {0.024 + 0.136}). This can be compared to the example discussed earlier, which indicated that a 2.3 percentage point increase is a reasonable upper-bound estimate.

This positive relationship between the proportion female and profitability among plants with high output share is consistent with the predictions of the Becker model

Table 11.4 Profitability regressions, plant level, effects of proportion female at different points of output share distribution[a]

	Interactions of proportion female with output share (1)	Interactions of all demographic variables with output share (2)
Proportion female	0.024	0.019
	(0.033)	(0.034)
× 2nd output share quartile	−0.053	−0.051
	(0.044)	(0.046)
× 3rd output share quartile	0.062	0.079
	(0.047)	(0.049)
× 4th output share quartile	0.136	0.135
	(0.050)	(0.055)
p-value for restriction of equal effects across quartiles	0.001	0.003
Proportion black	−0.029	−0.000
	(0.029)	(0.054)
Proportion married	−0.036	−0.063
	(0.032)	(0.051)
Proportion aged 35–54	0.022	0.016
	(0.022)	(0.038)
Proportion aged 55+	−0.062	−0.042
	(0.031)	(0.053)
Capital/shipments	−0.0026	−0.0025
	(0.0015)	(0.0015)
2nd output share quartile	0.061	0.040
	(0.016)	(0.070)
3rd output share quartile	0.085	−0.005
	(0.016)	(0.078)
4th output share quartile	0.127	0.051
	(0.020)	(0.089)
Number of coefficient estimates significant at 10-percent level, 2nd–4th output share quartiles		
× proportion black	—	1
× proportion married	—	0
× proportion aged 35–54	—	0
× proportion aged 55+	—	1
× proportion some college	—	0
× proportion managerial	—	0
× proportion sales	—	0
× proportion craft	—	0
R^2	0.374	0.379

Note

a There are 3,089 observations. With the exception of the added interactive variables, the specifications and dependent variable are the same as in column (2) of Table 11.2. Results were very similar using operating income/sales. Because the output share quartile dummy variables are interacted with many variables in column (2), the estimated coefficients of the quartile dummy variables are not comparable to those in column (1).

relating discrimination to market power.[12] In plants that operate in a competitive output market, there is no performance advantage to hiring women; since discriminatory employers are unable to indulge their tastes for discrimination, wages in this sector are quickly bid to equality with marginal products. But in (typically larger) plants where there is market power and where plants can discriminate if they wish, at least in the short run, those that do not discriminate and hire more women—who cost less—achieve better performance. We discuss how these different behaviors can coexist within industries in the next subsection.

We report one other analysis in Table 11.4. If the proportion female is a proxy for other unobservable characteristics of the plant (including its workforce) that may affect profitability differently for plants with different levels of market power, it is reasonable to think that other demographic characteristics of the plant's workforce might also be proxies for such unobservables. This suggests that we should include in the regression a full set of interactions between the output share quartile dummy variables and all the demographic characteristics of workers in a plant, and verify whether the results for the proportion female-market power relationship hold up. We do this in column (2). The first thing to note is that the coefficients on the third and fourth quartile interactions between output share and the proportion female are similar to those in column (1), although, as noted above, larger for the third quartile interaction. Second, at the bottom of the columns we report some results for the interactions of the output share quartiles with the other demographic characteristics; of all the interactions estimated, only one interaction with black and one with age are significant at the 10-percent level. The fact that so few of these interactions are significant, and that the proportion female results persist, suggest to us that the results for the proportion female are not being driven primarily by unobservables. It appears to be specifically the hiring of women among plants with market power that is associated with higher profitability.[13]

To summarize, while there is no clear evidence of a relationship between profitability and proportion female for plants falling into the bottom part of the output share distribution, there is clear evidence of a positive relationship between profitability and a more female workforce for plants with considerable market power. We interpret this evidence as being most consistent with Becker's model of employer taste discrimination, where plants that have market power are able to indulge their discriminatory tastes against women, but forfeit profits as a result.

Interpreting the cross-sectional results

It is worth discussing in the context of our results the market forces in Becker's model relating market power to discrimination. If wages are set competitively,[14] plants that do not discriminate will hire men and women until the ratio of marginal revenue products between men and women is equal to the ratio of market wages, regardless of whether the plant has product market power. In plants with technologies where men and women are perfect substitutes in production, the ratio of marginal revenue products is determined exogenously by the technology, and competition in the labor market will work to equate the ratio of wages to that of marginal revenue products. In that case, nondiscriminatory employers will be indifferent between hiring men and women. If men and women are not perfect substitutes, the ratio of relative marginal products will be a function of the sex mix of the plant's workforce, and will therefore be a decision variable for the plant. Once again, however, labor market competition will determine the relative wages of men and women.

We interpret our cross-sectional results as suggesting that among the set of plants with product market power—which are typically larger plants—some exploit the supra-competitive profits stemming from their product market power to indulge in discriminatory behavior against women. Higher profitability among those plants in the less-competitive sector that have a higher proportion female must imply a gap between relative marginal products and relative wages of women in this less-competitive sector. Similarly, the fact that profitability is unrelated to the proportion female among plants in the more-competitive sector must imply that this gap does not exist in this sector. Evidence presented in our earlier work (Hellerstein *et al.*, 1999) is consistent with this, as the gap between relative wages and relative marginal products of women and men is much smaller among small plants than large plants.

Given that wages are set by the market, we do not expect the wage gap between men and women to differ between the less- and more-competitive sectors. Rather, a larger gap between relative wages and relative marginal products in the less-competitive sector would have to reflect higher relative productivity of women in the less-competitive sector, possibly because of technological differences (the perfect substitutes case), or because fewer women are employed than would be the case in the absence of discrimination (in the imperfect substitutes case) in this sector. The data are consistent with these predictions. In our earlier research, we found no productivity gap between men and women among larger firms, but we found that in smaller firms women were less productive than men. Moreover, wage regressions using plant-level data indicate that the relative wage of women is not particularly low among plants in the less-competitive sector that employ a high proportion female (the estimated coefficients of interactions between output share and the proportion female were small and insignificant).

Finally, this scenario is consistent with labor market equilibrium. As long as plants in the less-competitive sector compete for workers with plants in the more-competitive sector, and as long as the latter sector is large enough, the market wage ratio between men and women will be determined in the more-competitive sector and will be equal to the relative marginal products of men and women in the more-competitive sector. Then, despite discrimination against women by some employers in the less-competitive sector, women have no incentive to switch sectors. This equilibrium will persist unless or until competitive forces in the product market or in the market for firms begin to work and eventually bid up the wages of women in the less-competitive sector. The question then is whether, and how quickly, the competitive process works to undermine discrimination. We turn to evidence on this question in the next section.

Market forces and discrimination, dynamic tests

The preceding cross-sectional results suggest that plants or firms can indulge their discriminatory tastes only when they enjoy product market power. Nonetheless, market forces may reduce or eliminate discrimination as the more profitable plants or firms among those with market power grow relative to the less profitable ones, or as discriminating employers are bought out by nondiscriminating employers. Because in our cross-sectional analysis the relationship between profitability and the proportion female is large and statistically significant only for plants in the fourth quartile of the market power measure, and because the test of equality of all four quartile coefficients is strongly rejected, we focus on these fourth quartile plants in the analysis of plant dynamics. Specifically, for plants in the top quartile of the output share distribution, we estimate regressions for growth of both employment and shipments, and probits for ownership change, as functions of, among other things, the proportion female in a plant's workforce. This should make it more likely that we find evidence, if there is any, consistent with the dynamic implications of Becker's model, since we focus on the plants for which we are most likely to see growth or ownership change related to the proportion female.

In columns (1) and (2) of Table 11.5 we examine whether discrimination is eliminated through competition in the product market, by asking whether plants that initially employ more women and earn higher profits grow faster than otherwise similar plants. We examine two different measures of changes in performance—growth in employment and growth in shipments—from 1990 to 1995, using the same covariates as in the first cross-section profitability regressions. The only exception is that we do not include as a regressor the capital/shipments ratio, since the dependent variable no longer suffers from a missing measure of the return to capital.

All the estimated coefficients on the proportion female are small and statistically insignificant.[15] There is therefore no evidence that sex discrimination in wages is reduced or eliminated by market forces that cause nondiscriminatory plants to expand relative to discriminatory plants. We also examined the relationships between growth of both shipments and employment and the proportion female for other quartiles of the output share distribution. Given that we found no significant cross-sectional relationship between the proportion female and profitability for plants in these quartiles in the cross-section, we would not have expected to find such a relationship in the growth results if the relationship between growth and the proportion female is being driven by market forces affecting discrimination. Indeed, the results from the other quartiles (not reported) also show no relationship between the proportion female and growth, with the estimated coefficients small and insignificant.

In column (3) of Table 11.5 we analyze the effect of higher relative employment of women in the base year on the probability of changing ownership between 1990 and 1995, again for plants in the top quartile of the output share distribution. Becker's model predicts that in the case of discriminatory tastes on the part of

Table 11.5 Growth and ownership change regressions (1990–5), plant level, effects of proportion female in fourth quartile of output share distribution[a]

	Shipments growth (1)	Employment growth (2)	Change in ownership (3)
Proportion female	−0.036	0.027	−0.203
	(0.218)	(0.170)	(0.240)
Proportion black	−0.180	−0.044	−0.048
	(0.281)	(0.220)	(0.302)
Proportion married	−0.106	−0.033	0.376
	(0.347)	(0.271)	(0.442)
Proportion aged 35–54	−0.462	−0.426	0.002
	(0.217)	(0.170)	(0.269)
Proportion aged 55+	−0.826	−0.434	−0.202
	(0.324)	(0.253)	(0.376)
Proportion some college	−0.093	−0.011	−0.592
	(0.261)	(0.204)	(0.323)
Proportion managerial	0.146	−0.301	−0.160
	(0.367)	(0.286)	(0.450)
Proportion sales	−0.255	−0.199	−0.283
	(0.315)	(0.246)	(0.376)
Proportion craft	0.196	−0.244	0.049
	(0.299)	(0.234)	(0.324)
Multi-plant firm	−0.132	−0.008	−0.115
	(0.183)	(0.143)	(0.192)
Plant 11–20 years old	0.017	0.040	−0.094
	(0.131)	(0.102)	(0.158)
Plant 21–30 years old	0.028	0.136	0.040
	(0.128)	(0.100)	(0.180)
Plant 31–40 years old	0.067	0.064	0.038
	(0.118)	(0.092)	(0.171)
Plant 41–50 years old	0.068	−0.008	−0.081
	(0.143)	(0.112)	(0.169)
Plant 51+ years old	−0.006	−0.050	0.096
	(0.128)	(0.100)	(0.179)
R^2	0.518	0.535	0.140
N	605	605	319

Note

a The results in columns (1) and (2) are from OLS regressions, and contain data from plants that do not change ownership between 1990 and 1995. The results in column (3) are from probits, with partial derivatives of the probability of a change in ownership with respect to each variable reported, and standard errors rescaled to match t-statistics on probit coefficient estimates. The sample size reported in column (3) only includes the 319 plants in four-digit industries for which there were both plants that did and did not change ownership, to avoid perfect predictions. The pseudo R^2 is reported in that column. All specifications include four-digit industry dummy variables and three Census region dummy variables.

employers (as opposed to nepotistic tastes), plants with discriminatory owners who hire too few women will tend to be bought out by nondiscriminating owners. We test whether the data are consistent with this prediction of the model by estimating probits in which the dependent variable is 1 if the plant changed ownership and 0 otherwise. The point estimate of the effect of the proportion female is negative, consistent with plants employing fewer women being more likely to change ownership, as predicted by Becker's model. However, the relationship is not statistically significant.

Overall, the results in Table 11.5 provide little evidence of market forces that bid away the sex discrimination reflected in the cross-sectional relationship between profitability and the proportion female for plants with product market power. We emphasize, however, that these results on growth and ownership change are derived from five-year changes, and it is possible that this is not a long enough period of time to be able to measure the effect of competitive market forces on discriminatory practices. To put this in perspective, the wage gap between men and women has persisted (although it has narrowed) for decades. Of course, at the level of individual plants or firms, we might expect market forces to have effects that are manifested more quickly.

A retrospective look at growth

To get some sense of whether examining growth and ownership change over the period 1990–5 is sufficient to draw conclusions about long-term competitive market forces, one can think retrospectively about how competitive market forces during the 1980s may have impacted a plant's choices about the composition of its labor force in 1990.[16] First, if competitive forces were working in the 1980s to reduce discrimination, we would expect that by 1990 nondiscriminating employers would have a higher proportion of female employees and, as a result of their profitable nondiscriminatory behavior, would have a relatively larger market share. This pattern is confirmed in the cross-sectional data for 1990. The correlation between the proportion female variable and the fourth quartile output share dummy is positive (0.05) and statistically significant, whereas the correlations between the proportion female and the first three output share quartile dummies are negative (-0.01, -0.03, and -0.01 for the first, second, and third quartile dummies).

Second, if competitive market forces in the 1980s were bidding away discrimination, one would expect that, all else equal, plants that by 1990 had a higher proportion of female workers were those that should have grown the most during the 1980s. We cannot conduct a formal test of this hypothesis, since it is impossible for us to hold "all else equal" and examine the relationship between growth in the 1980s and the proportion female in a plant in 1990. For example, we have no data on the characteristics of workers in plants prior to 1990. However, a positive relationship between growth in the 1980s and the proportion female in 1990 is at least consistent with the hypothesis that market forces in the 1980s were working to reduce discrimination.

To see whether this relationship holds, we have constructed data on proportional growth in employment and shipments from 1982 to 1987 for the subset of 1968 plants in the WECD that existed in 1982, using data on these plants from the 1982 and 1987 CMs. We use these lagged growth measures to examine whether lagged growth is at all related to the characteristics of plants in 1990. In Table 11.6, we report results from regressions of lagged growth in both shipments and employment from 1982 to 1987 on the same set of characteristics of plants in 1990 that we used

Table 11.6 Lagged shipments and employment growth regressions (1982–7), plant level, continuing plants not changing ownership[a]

	Shipments (1)	Employment (2)
Proportion female	0.947	0.606
	(0.338)	(0.189)
Proportion black	0.140	−0.238
	(0.437)	(0.244)
Proportion married	1.45	0.734
	(0.497)	(0.278)
Proportion aged 35–54	−1.30	−0.775
	(0.351)	(0.196)
Proportion aged 55+	−1.14	−0.611
	(0.469)	(0.262)
Proportion some college	0.141	−0.071
	(0.381)	(0.213)
Proportion managerial	−0.661	−0.040
	(0.528)	(0.295)
Proportion sales	1.08	0.861
	(0.438)	(0.244)
Proportion craft	0.352	−0.242
	(0.470)	(0.262)
Multi-plant firm	−0.162	−0.171
	(0.199)	(0.111)
2nd output share quartile	−0.562	−0.175
	(0.162)	(0.090)
3rd output share quartile	−0.741	−0.245
	(0.188)	(0.105)
4th output share quartile	−0.902	−0.309
	(0.214)	(0.120)
Plant 11–20 years old	−0.744	−0.175
	(0.232)	(0.129)
Plant 21–30 years old	−1.23	−0.426
	(0.224)	(0.125)
Plant 31–40 years old	−1.10	−0.392
	(0.225)	(0.126)
Plant 41–50 years old	−1.07	−0.386
	(0.308)	(0.172)
Plant 51+ years old	−0.112	−0.465
	(0.248)	(0.139)
R^2	0.240	0.184

Note

a There are 1,968 observations. Four-digit industry dummy variables and three Census region dummy variables are also included. We construct the output share quartile dummies using data from the 1982 CM.

in Table 11.2. The results in Table 11.6 indicate that employment and shipments growth between 1982 and 1987 were positively and statistically related to the proportion female in 1990. The magnitudes of the coefficients on proportion female in these regressions are very large (with large standard errors), but we emphasize that they do not have any causal interpretation. Rather, we interpret the positive and significant relationship between lagged growth and proportion female in 1990 as simply suggesting that one may need to look over a longer period than just 1990–5 in order to observe whether the dynamics of competition are eliminating discrimination.

Conclusions

We find that among plants with high levels of product market power, those that employ relatively more women are more profitable. No such relationship exists for plants with apparently low levels of market power. This is consistent with sex discrimination in wages in the short run in markets where plants have product market power. We also find a positive relationship at the firm level between profitability and the proportion of the workforce that is female.

We then turn to evidence on the longer-run effects of market forces on discrimination, asking whether discriminatory employers with market power as evidenced in the cross-sectional results are punished over time through lower growth than nondiscriminatory employers, or whether discriminatory employers are bought out by nondiscriminators. We find little conclusive evidence that this occurs over a five-year period, as growth and ownership change for plants with market power are generally not significantly related to the sex composition of a plant's workforce. Indeed, evidence on the wage gap coupled with suggestive results in our data indicate that it is possible that market forces combating discrimination may have been stronger in the period preceding the five-year period we analyze to test for longer-run effects of market forces.

Overall, the results are consistent with the short-run implications of Becker's model of employer discrimination. There is evidence of discrimination in the short run for plants with product market power, which indicates that market power may be a prerequisite to the exercise of discriminatory tastes by employers. The evidence does not allow us to reject the hypothesis that market forces do not punish those discriminatory employers with market power in ways that tend to drive them from the market, or at least to shrink them relative to the market. This longer-run evidence is therefore not consistent with the dynamic or long-run implications of Becker's model for discriminatory employers, which, as Becker explained, would hold under only some conditions regarding barriers to entry, returns to scale, and the nature of discriminatory tastes. Our analysis does not identify which of these conditions might be violated, nor does it assess other possible explanations for the failure of competitive market forces to discipline discriminatory employers in the long run. This is obviously an important unanswered question, and is probably related to the same factors that lead to a persistent relationship between market power and profitability in the first place.[17] Of course, we only have data to test for the effect of market forces over a specific five-year period, and it is quite possible that this window of time was too short for these market forces to have been detectable in our data. In addition, failure to reject no effect of the proportion female on longer-run growth or changes in ownership does not necessarily imply that these relationships do not exist, but may instead reflect an inability to detect significant relationships. Nonetheless, this evidence does not provide support for the conclusion that market forces tend to eliminate discrimination by punishing discriminatory employers.

Empirical evidence on the role of competitive market forces in eliminating or reducing discrimination—such as that presented in this chapter—is critical in assessing government policies to combat discrimination. The direct tools at the government's disposal are equal pay or employment legislation and Affirmative Action. If market forces reduce or eliminate discrimination, then these direct tools may be unnecessary, and efforts to enhance competition may represent better policies. The results in this chapter suggest that product market competition deters discrimination, in that plants and firms with relatively little market power appear not to discriminate, while discrimination only occurs among those plants or firms that are large relative to the market. The evidence also suggests that competitive market forces are unlikely to be completely sufficient to eliminate discrimination among these large plants or firms. In particular, there is little evidence that, among employers with product market power, longer-run product market competition or competition in the market for ownership acts to undermine or eliminate discrimination. As long as the government is unlikely to enact policies that substantially reduce the product market power of the largest plants or firms, direct government intervention in the labor market may be required if the goal is to eliminate discrimination entirely.

Acknowledgments

We are grateful to Kim Bayard, Nicole Nestoriak, and Gigi Foster for outstanding research assistance, and to Bob Frank, anonymous referees, and seminar participants at Carnegie-Mellon, Cornell, Johns Hopkins, the University of Maryland, Michigan State, the University of Missouri, Wharton, and the NBER Summer Institute for helpful comments.

This research was supported by NSF grant SBR95—10876 through the NBER. All opinions, findings, and conclusions are those of the authors and do not in any way reflect the views of the US Census Bureau. The main data used in this chapter were collected under the provisions of Title 13 US Code and are only available at the Center for Economic Studies, US Census Bureau. To obtain access to these data, contact the Center for Economic Studies, US Census Bureau, Rm. 211/WPII, Washington, DC, 20233.

Notes

1 There is virtually no existing work attempting to draw conclusions regarding discrimination from data on profitability. One exception is Hersch (1991), who studies the effects of charges of EEO violations on the equity value of firms, finding that these charges reduce firm value. This evidence is indirect at best, as EEO charges may bring about not only a reduction in discrimination, but also high legal and settlement costs.

2 Hellerstein and Neumark (1999) also implement the production function approach using data on Israeli manufacturing plants. In those data, in contrast to the US data, the pay and productivity gaps are of similar magnitude, consistent with no discrimination. There is no obvious explanation for the differences across the two countries, although the institutional, legal, and cultural environments are arguably quite different.

3 This formulation comes from Arrow (1973). In Becker's original model d simply multiplies F in the employer's utility function, which generates complete sex segregation across all but the marginal employer. The utility function based on the relative number of female workers generates an equilibrium less at odds with observed employment patterns.

4 This section provides a brief discussion of the data; for more details see Hellerstein *et al.* (1999).

5 Each CM is a complete census of manufacturing establishments, and the ASM is a probability sample of establishments, surveyed over a five-year period including CM years. A new ASM sample is drawn two years after a CM, with the probability of an establishment being included in the ASM increasing with its total employment in the previous CM. Establishments with more than 250 employees in the previous CM are in the ASM with certainty.

6 Beginning in 1987, the book value of capital is only collected in the CM, so we use 1987 capital data. In addition, overhead costs are only collected in the ASM sample in CM years, so the overhead costs we use are from the 1987 ASM. Because not all plants in the 1989 ASM appear in the 1987 ASM, we lose some observations as a result of this linkage. We experimented with the full sample of observations from 1989, using the profitability measure that does not include overhead costs; the results were very similar to those obtained for the restricted sample for which we have data in 1987.

7 Plants in the 1989 WECD are those that were in both the 1989 and 1987 ASMs, since we use overhead costs from the 1987 ASM. Therefore WECD plants in 1989 are disproportionately selected into ASMs as certainty selections, so many of them appear again in the 1995 ASM.

8 For a review of studies on the relationship between profitability and market power, see Salinger (1990).

9 When output share was included in these specifications, the estimated effects of plant size (defined in terms of employment) became small and insignificant, so size variables are excluded. Of course, size and output share are positively correlated.

10 The coefficients imply that the relationship is positive up to a proportion female of 0.66. However, it is hard to identify the curvature accurately because there is not much data at the right-hand tail of the distribution of the proportion female.

11 We also attempted to include in our specifications the proportion of the workforce that is female in each of the occupation categories, to attempt to isolate the "location" of the discrimination, and hence perhaps learn more about its nature (e.g. a "glass ceiling" restricting women's access to managerial positions). However, this yielded imprecise estimates, in part because we construct these proportions only from the sample of workers that we match to a plant.

12 These results are also consistent with tabulations from the 1940 Census reported by Becker, indicating that relative to firms operating in competitive industries, firms operating in monopolistic industries appear to engage in discriminatory behavior (1971, Table 2, p. 48); Becker's results, however, refer to hiring of non-whites.

13 Because of the counterintuitive negative coefficient on the ratio of book value of capital to shipments, we experimented with including this variable nonlinearly in the regression; the results were not qualitatively affected. We also re-ran the regressions restricting the coefficient on the book value of capital to be positive (0.06, at the suggestion of Caballero *et al.*, 1995). The results for the proportion female effects were unchanged. This is not surprising, given that the correlation between book value of capital and proportion female is only −0.03.

14 The Becker model presumes that wages are set competitively and that there is therefore one market wage differential between men and women. Our data are consistent with this; when we estimate individual-level wage regressions, the estimated coefficient of the female dummy variable remains large when plant fixed effects are included.

15 In fact, the only significant coefficients in column (1) are for the worker age variables, which are negative. As mentioned earlier, we interpret such results as reflecting plant-specific shocks.

16 There is evidence that the wage gap between men and women shrank during the 1980s but not during the 1990s (Blau *et al.*, 1997). This is consistent with the notion that competitive market forces were bidding away discrimination during the 1980s, but that these market pressures weakened in the 1990s.

17 Some recent research points to two potential barriers to competitive pressures that might otherwise discipline discriminatory employers, while also indicating that in some cases it may be possible to increase these pressures. Looking at the banking sector, Black and Strahan (2001) find that the wages of women relative to men rose when deregulation increased competitive pressures on banks. Similarly, Black and Brainerd (1999) report that increased product market competition via international trade raised the relative wages of women in manufacturing industries.

References

Arrow, Kenneth J. 1972. "Some Mathematical Models of Race Discrimination in the Labor Market." In *Racial Discrimination in Economic Life*, ed. A. H. Pascal, pp. 187–204. Lexington, MA: D.C. Heath.

——. 1973. "The Theory of Discrimination." In *Discrimination in Labor Markets*, eds Orley Ashenfelter and Albert Rees, pp. 3–33. Princeton, NJ: Princeton University Press.

Ashenfelter, Orley and Timothy Hannan. 1986. "Sex Discrimination and Product Market Competition: The Case of the Banking Industry." *Quarterly Journal of Economics* 101(1): 149–73.

Becker, Gary S. 1971. *The Economics of Discrimination*. Chicago: University of Chicago Press.

Black, Sandra E. and Elizabeth Brainerd. 1999. "Importing Equality? The Effects of Increased Competition on the Gender–Wage Gap." Working Paper. New York: Federal Reserve Bank of New York.

Black, Sandra E. and Phillip E. Strahan. 2001 "The Division of Spoils: Rent Sharing and Discrimination in a Regulated Industry." *American Economic Review* 91(4): 814–31.

Blau, Francine D., Marianne A. Ferber, and Anne E. Winkler. 1997. *The Economics of Men, Women, and Work*, 3rd edn. Englewood Cliffs, NJ: Prentice-Hall.

Caballero, Ricardo, John Haltiwanger, and Eduardo Engel. 1995. "Plant-Level Adjustment and Aggregative Investment Dynamics." *Brookings Papers on Economic Activity* 2: 1–39.

Cavalluzzo, Ken, Linda Cavalluzzo, and John Wolken. 1999. "Competition, Small Business Financing, and Discrimination: Evidence from a New Survey." Mimeograph. Washington, DC: Georgetown University.

Domowitz, Ian, R. Glenn Hubbard, and Bruce C. Peterson. 1986. "Business Cycles and the Relationship Between Concentration and Price-Cost Margins." *Rand Journal of Economics* 1(17): 1–17.

Fuchs, Victor R. 1988. *Women's Quest for Economic Equality*. Cambridge, MA: Harvard University Press.

Hellerstein, Judith K. and David Neumark. 1999. "Sex, Wages, and Productivity: An Empirical Analysis of Israeli Firm-Level Data." *International Economic Review* 40(1): 95–123.

Hellerstein, Judith K., David Neumark and Kenneth R. Troske. 1999. "Wages, Productivity, and Worker Characteristics: Evidence from Plant-Level Production Functions and Wage Equations." *Journal of Labor Economics* 17(3): 409–46.

Hersch, Joni. 1991. "Equal Employment Opportunity Law and Firm Profitability." *Journal of Human Resources* 26(1): 139–53.

Mincer, Jacob and Solomon Polachek. 1974. "Family Investment in Human Capital: Earnings of Women." *Journal of Political Economy* 82(2, Part II): S76–108.

O'Neill, June. 1994. "Discrimination and Income Differences." In *Race and Gender in the American Economy*, ed. Susan F. Feiner, pp. 13–7. Englewood Cliffs, NJ: Prentice-Hall, Inc.

Salinger, Michael. 1990. "The Concentration–Margins Relationship Reconsidered." *Brookings Papers on Economic Activity, Microeconomics*, Special Issue: 287–335.

Tirole, Jean. 1989. *The Theory of Industrial Organization*. Cambridge, MA: The MIT Press.

Part IV

Evaluating policy responses to sex differences and sex discrimination

12 New evidence on sex segregation and sex differences in wages from matched employer–employee data

(with Kimberly Bayard, Judith K. Hellerstein, and Kenneth R. Troske)

Introduction

Women have consistently earned lower wages than men in US labor markets, although this gap has narrowed in recent decades (Blau, 1998). Understanding the sources of sex differences in wages is vital to determining why the wage gap between men and women persists. Previous research has focused on the impact of the occupational segregation of men and women on the wage gap (e.g. Macpherson and Hirsch, 1995), the effect of industry segregation (e.g. Fields and Wolff, 1995), and, to a lesser extent, on the segregation of men and women into different employers (Blau, 1977; Bielby and Baron, 1984; Carrington and Troske, 1998). These studies all find evidence that the wage gap falls considerably after accounting for segregation.

Evidence on the contribution to the wage gap of within-establishment, within-occupation segregation is far harder to find. Indeed, we are not aware of any empirical work on this issue that uses large data sets representative of a wide array of industries. The reason for this is the paucity of data sets containing detailed demographic information for multiple workers in the same establishment. As a result, studies of the effects of establishment and occupation-establishment segregation have used unusual, quite narrow data sets. For example, the best-known study is by Groshen (1991), which uses surveys of wages for a subset of occupations in five specific industries included as part of the Bureau of Labor Statistics (BLS) Industry Wage Surveys (IWS). In earlier work, Blau (1977) used the BLS Area Wage Surveys to provide a decomposition of the sex gap in wages, including evidence on the importance of an individual's sex within occupation, establishment, and job cell. Her data covered subsets of three broad occupations in three large northeastern cities.

The focus in these studies on a handful of industries or occupations provides something closer to a set of case studies, with the lack of representativeness limiting their usefulness in assessing the forces at work in generating the sex wage gap in the United States. Our goal in this chapter is to use a much broader and more nationally representative data set to estimate the contributions of sex segregation by industry, occupation, and occupation-establishment cell (job cell) to the sex wage gap. For our analysis, we construct and use an extended version of the Worker Establishment Characteristics Database (WECD) to decompose the source of male–female wage differentials. Like the WECD, this data set uses the US Census Bureau's Standard Statistical Establishment List (SSEL) to identify the employers of individuals who responded to the long form of the 1990 Decennial Census. However, whereas the WECD is limited to manufacturing plants, this new data set (the New WECD, or NWECD) includes workers and establishments from all sectors of the economy and all regions.[1] Nonetheless, because of the constraints imposed by matching employees to employers, some nonrepresentative characteristics of the data set are unavoidable.

Using the NWECD, we provide new estimates of the role of various dimensions of sex segregation in generating sex differences in wages. Although in some respects our evidence may be viewed as complementary to that in the earlier studies, in our view the NWECD, while having some shortcomings, is clearly better suited to characterizing the effects of sex segregation in US labor markets. Our results indicate that a sizable fraction of the sex gap in wages is accounted for by the segregation of women into lower-paying occupations, industries, establishments, and occupations within establishments. We also find, however, that a very substantial part of the sex gap in wages remains attributable to the individual's sex.

The data

The data used in this study come from a match between worker records from the 1990 Sample Edited Detail File (SEDF) to establishment records in the 1990 SSEL. The 1990 SEDF consists of all household responses to the 1990 Decennial Census long form. As part of the Decennial Census, one-sixth of all households receive a "long-form" survey, which asks a number of questions about each member of the household ("person questions") as well as about the housing unit ("housing questions"). Those receiving the long form are asked to identify each employed household member's (1) occupation, (2) employer location, and (3) employer industry in the previous week. The Census Bureau then assigns occupational, industrial, and geographic codes to long-form responses. Thus, the SEDF contains the standard demographic information for workers collected on the long form of the Decennial Census, along with detailed location information and a three-digit Census industry code for each respondent's place of work.

The SSEL is an annual list of business establishments maintained by the US Census Bureau. The SSEL contains detailed location information and a four-digit SIC code for each establishment, along with a unique establishment identifier that is common to other Census Bureau economic surveys and censuses. It also includes information on total payroll expenses, employment, and whether or not the establishment is part of a multi-establishment firm.

We matched workers and establishments using the detailed location and industry information available in both data sets. We did this because we did not actually have the employer name available on both establishment and worker records. Briefly, the first step in the matching process was to keep only establishments unique to an industry-location cell. Next, all workers indicating that they work in the same industry-location cell as a retained establishment were linked to the establishment. The matched data set is the NWECD. Because the SEDF contains only a sample of workers, and because not all workers are matched, the matched data set includes a sample of workers at each establishment. Complete details of the matching procedure are provided in the Appendix.

In our matched sample, we impose some restrictions on both individuals and establishments. We include only individuals who report usually working between 30 and 65 hours per week, and 30 or more weeks in the last year (1989). These restrictions on hours and weeks are intended to pick out full-time, full-year workers who are less likely to have changed jobs in the past year, as well as those whose hours are so high that they may have held multiple jobs. We make these restrictions for three reasons. First, because the Decennial Census collects data on earnings from all jobs, rather than wages on the current job, we need to try to eliminate variation in wages that stems from multiple job-holding at a point in time or during the previous calendar year.[2] Second, because the 1990 Decennial Census asks workers to report the address of the establishment where they worked in the previous week, while the earnings data are for the previous calendar year, job changing may lead to inaccurate measurement of earnings in the matched data. Imposing restrictions that get us closer to full-year, full-time workers should disproportionately eliminate workers who have changed jobs.[3] Finally, the IWS data, with which we eventually are interested in drawing some comparisons, cover only full-time workers. We also restrict the sample to workers aged 18–65, with a constructed hourly wage ((annual earnings/weeks worked)/usual hours worked per week) in the range $2.50–$500, and exclude those working in establishments in public administration (in order to restrict our focus to the private sector).

We also require that establishments have total employment of at least twenty-five, for two reasons: first, when we compared average establishment-level worker earnings in the matched observations in the SEDF with average payroll expenses in the SSEL, these corresponded much more closely for establishments with twenty-five or more workers; second, the IWS industry samples included mainly establishments with twenty-five or more workers. In addition, to ensure that we have a reasonable basis for estimating the characteristics of an establishment's workforce, we required that the number of matched workers be least 5 percent of employment as reported in the SSEL. Finally, we eliminated the less than 0.1 percent of establishments that reported earnings exceeding more than $600,000 per worker.

Table 12.1 documents the effects of these various matching rules and exclusion restrictions on the sample size, the number of matched workers, and average earnings and employment calculated from both the SSEL and SEDF data. We define measures of establishment earnings per worker from data in both the SSEL and the SEDF. For the SSEL, earnings per worker are constructed as Total Annual Payroll/Total Employment. For the SEDF, establishment earnings per worker are created by averaging the annual wages and salaries of all workers matched to the establishment.[4] The table shows that 7 percent of establishments can be assigned

Table 12.1 Construction of NWECD[a]

	Number of establishments (SSEL)	Number of workers (SEDF)	Average number of matched workers	Average establishment employment from SSEL data	Average establishment earnings/worker from SSEL data	Average establishment earnings/worker from SEDF data	Average earnings/worker from SEDF data
	(1)	(2)	(3)	(4)	(5)	(6)	(7)
A. Establishments in SSEL with positive employment	5,593,379	—	—	21.10 (0.45)	19,310.37 (10.98)	—	—
B. Establishments in unique industry-location cells	388,787	—	—	41.17 (2.30)	17,102.78 (28.97)	—	—
C. Workers among long-form respondents in SEDF	—	17,311,211	—	—	—	—	20,977.51 (6.75)
D. Respondents matched to establishments in B	201,944	1,720,423	8.52 (0.08)	66.46 (4.43)	18,123.98 (205.00)	17,094.00 (38.83)	20,831.89 (17.28)
E. Discard matches with imputed industry or location, or number of matched workers greater than SSEL employment; discard workers with zero or missing earnings, or working outside United States	156,332	1,117,424	7.15 (0.07)	83.24 (5.72)	18,218.33 (181.34)	19,416.60 (47.81)	22,582.18 (21.21)
F. Exclude workers with hours < 30 or > 65, weeks in 1989 < 30, age < 18 or > 65, wage < $2.50 or > $500, public administration	129,021	845,036	6.55 (0.07)	83.59 (6.70)	19,224.23 (218.75)	23,112.66 (53.66)	25,611.43 (23.88)
G. Discard establishments with employment < 25, number of matched workers < 5% of SSEL employment, and earnings outliers; final sample	32,931	637,718	19.37 (0.26)	180.84 (2.68)	20,983.40 (63.64)	23,327.76 (71.73)	25,978.52 (26.58)

Notes

a Standard errors of means are reported in parentheses.

NWECD: New Worker Establishment Characteristics Database; SEDF: Sample Edited Detail File; SSEL: Standard Statistical Establishment List.

to unique industry-location cells. These establishments are nearly twice as large as those in the overall sample (with an average of 41.17 workers, vs. 21.10 for the full SSEL sample), but have average earnings that are lower by about $2,200. This does not contrast with standard size-wage effects (Brown and Medoff, 1989), since there are no controls for industry, etc., and the ability to assign establishments to unique industry-location cells is not random with respect to these characteristics.

The next three rows (C–E) provide information on the observations on workers in the SEDF. Out of a total of 17,311,211 workers, we match 1.1 million, or 6.5 percent, to establishments, once we discard unreliable matches or workers without earnings data. There are, of course, numerous establishments to which no workers are matched, reflected in the decline in the number of matched establishments from 388,787 to 201,944 based on the simple match, and 156,332 once other restrictions are imposed. Naturally, the establishments to which workers in the SEDF are matched tend to be larger, with average employment of 83.24. The last three columns compare earnings data. Average establishment earnings per worker reported in the SSEL are about $1,200 lower than the corresponding figure estimated from the SEDF ($18,218 vs. $19,416); this is presumably in part attributable to the fact that in the SEDF individuals can report earnings from more than one job. We also find, comparing columns (6) and (7) of row E, that average earnings per worker in the SEDF data are about $3,170 higher than average establishment earnings estimated from the same (matched) data. These numbers can differ because the earnings per establishment figures are not weighted by the number of matched workers in estimating average establishment earnings per worker; thus, this result likely stems from the concentration of higher-earning workers in larger establishments. Row F drops workers based on the restrictions on hours, weeks, age, wages, etc., with little impact except to drop those with lower earnings.

The final sample is described in row G, which we obtain after dropping establishments with fewer than twenty-five employees, with an insufficiently small percentage of matched employees, and with earnings outliers. We end up with a sample of 637,718 workers matched to 32,931 establishments. These establishments are of course much larger than those represented in the previous rows, and have an average of 19.37 workers matched to them. We also find that in this subset of larger establishments, average establishment earnings estimated from the SSEL and the SEDF are considerably closer ($20,983 vs. $23,328).

Descriptive statistics for the matched sample are reported in column (1) of Table 12.2. The sample is approximately 47 percent female and 7 percent black, with an average age of 40. The percentage currently married is 71. With respect to education, 21.1 percent have a bachelor's degree or higher, and 50 percent report no college education. Column (2) reports descriptive statistics for the entire SEDF file, with the weeks and hours restrictions imposed. Most of the demographic characteristics are quite close in the matched and full sample. Geographically, individuals living in MSA's are less likely to be in the matched sample, presumably because in urban areas individuals are less likely to work in unique industry-location cells. Turning to occupation, laborers are overrepresented in the matched sample, and support occupations are underrepresented. Similarly, the

Table 12.2 Descriptive statistics for NWECD and full 1990 SEDF, full-time full-year workers[a]

	Women and men combined		Women		Men	
	NWECD (1)	SEDF (2)	NWECD (3)	SEDF (4)	NWECD (5)	SEDF (6)
Annual earnings	25,978.52	27,259.79	19,512.50	19,931.10	31,674.73	32,735.24
	(21,227.38)	(29,275.13)	(13,696.45)	(15,477.93)	(24,759.25)	(35,330.59)
Log hourly wage	2.349	2.336	2.150	2.148	2.525	2.476
	(0.539)	(0.600)	(0.493)	(0.528)	(0.516)	(0.612)
Demographics						
Female	0.468	0.428	—	—	—	—
Age	39.589	38.440	39.423	38.230	39.735	38.598
	(10.979)	(11.272)	(10.986)	(11.239)	(10.970)	(11.295)
Black	0.070	0.077	0.082	0.094	0.059	0.064
Currently married	0.712	0.661	0.647	0.596	0.769	0.710
High school degree	0.369	0.325	0.359	0.334	0.378	0.319
Some college	0.191	0.216	0.190	0.229	0.191	0.207
Associate's degree	0.095	0.078	0.121	0.091	0.071	0.069
Bachelor's degree	0.128	0.159	0.129	0.157	0.127	0.160
Advanced degree	0.083	0.085	0.078	0.078	0.088	0.091
Location						
MSA	0.575	0.764	0.549	0.762	0.597	0.765
New England	0.044	0.056	0.042	0.058	0.046	0.056
Mid-Atlantic	0.143	0.153	0.148	0.152	0.139	0.155
East North Central	0.273	0.195	0.259	0.189	0.285	0.200
West North Central	0.122	0.092	0.123	0.093	0.121	0.091
South Atlantic	0.137	0.165	0.147	0.174	0.128	0.159
East South Central	0.083	0.059	0.085	0.061	0.081	0.058
West South Central	0.086	0.095	0.088	0.095	0.084	0.094
Mountain	0.038	0.050	0.036	0.049	0.039	0.051
Pacific	0.075	0.134	0.072	0.130	0.078	0.137
Occupation						
Manager	0.270	0.281	0.308	0.310	0.238	0.260
Support	0.230	0.306	0.338	0.432	0.134	0.213
Service	0.086	0.088	0.115	0.122	0.060	0.063
Farming	0.004	0.016	0.001	0.005	0.007	0.024
Production	0.145	0.135	0.042	0.028	0.236	0.215
Laborer	0.265	0.173	0.196	0.104	0.326	0.225
Industry						
Agriculture	0.004	0.018	0.002	0.009	0.006	0.026
Mining	0.006	0.009	0.001	0.003	0.011	0.014
Construction	0.0001	0.067	0.00003	0.015	0.0002	0.106
Manufacturing	0.517	0.239	0.349	0.176	0.666	0.286
Transportation	0.062	0.085	0.036	0.054	0.086	0.108
Wholesale	0.012	0.052	0.007	0.034	0.017	0.065
Retail	0.039	0.139	0.051	0.152	0.029	0.129
FIRE	0.007	0.076	0.011	0.109	0.003	0.052
Business services	0.004	0.043	0.004	0.033	0.005	0.050
Personal services	0.002	0.023	0.003	0.034	0.002	0.014
Entertainment services	0.002	0.010	0.001	0.009	0.002	0.011
Professional services	0.343	0.238	0.535	0.373	0.175	0.138
N	637,718	10,830,247	298,677	4,631,357	339,041	6,198,890

Note
a Means are reported, with standard deviations in parentheses.

industry composition of the sample is heavily weighted toward manufacturing, with 52 percent of workers in this industry, vs. 24 percent in the full sample, while retail is grossly underrepresented, presumably because many retail establishments are in locations in which similar establishments are located (such as malls). In the empirical analysis, we address the potential consequences of the overrepresentation of manufacturing establishments. The remaining columns of Table 12.2 compare the descriptive statistics for the NWECD and SEDF separately by sex. The patterns of overrepresentation and underrepresentation are similar, with manufacturing overrepresented for both men and women, retail underrepresented, etc. In addition, the sex differences look similar across the two samples. For example, women's earnings are 61.6 percent of men's in the NWECD, compared with 60.9 percent in the SEDF.

We noted earlier (p. 303) that small establishments (those with fewer than twenty-five employees) are dropped from the sample. If women are overrepresented in smaller establishments, then given that smaller establishments also pay lower wages, we may understate the contribution of establishment segregation to the wage gap. To examine this question, we looked at information on the representation of women in establishments of different sizes, using the May 1988 CPS Survey of Employee Benefits Supplement. Across all industries, women are not overrepresented in smaller establishments. The percent female in establishments with fewer than twenty-five employees is just over 43 percent, compared with 44.6 percent overall. However, there are slight differences across the manufacturing and nonmanufacturing sectors, with women somewhat underrepresented in the smaller establishments in the manufacturing sector (26.1 percent female in establishments with fewer than twenty-five employees, compared with 32.2 percent overall), and only slightly underrepresented in these smaller establishments in the nonmanufacturing sector (45 percent, compared with 48.7 percent overall). On the other hand, only a small proportion (2.9 percent) of the manufacturing workforce is employed in plants with fewer than twenty-five employees. The magnitudes suggest that it is unlikely that our establishment-size cutoff has much impact. At any rate, the underrepresentation of women in smaller establishments, coupled with lower wages in smaller establishments, suggest if anything upward bias in our estimate of the contribution of establishment segregation.

The fact that the NWECD does not comprise a representative sample of US workers is not surprising given the requirements for a match, and given the size restrictions imposed on matched establishments. For our purposes, however, the most important question is whether the NWECD is not representative in ways that will bias the wage regressions we estimate. To partially answer this question, we report in Table 12.3 estimates from basic wage regressions with and without industry and occupation controls. Columns (1) and (2) provide benchmark estimates from wage regressions, first with no controls, and then with the basic demographic and human capital controls, but without industry and occupation controls, using workers from the SEDF. These are followed by specifications including interactions between the female dummy variable and age and its square, and then adding in the industry and occupation controls.

Table 12.3 Regressions for log wages for SEDF and NWECD workers[a]

	SEDF workers					NWECD workers				
	(1)	(2)	(3)	(4)	(5)	(6)	(7)	(8)	(9)	(10)
Female	-0.328	-0.316	-0.317	-0.238	-0.240	-0.375	-0.362	-0.364	-0.230	-0.234
	(0.0004)	(0.0003)	(0.0003)	(0.0004)	(0.0004)	(0.001)	(0.001)	(0.001)	(0.001)	(0.001)
Age	—	0.063	0.076	0.049	0.061	—	0.060	0.074	0.046	0.058
		(0.0001)	(0.0001)	(0.0001)	(0.0001)		(0.0003)	(0.0005)	(0.0003)	(0.0004)
$Age^2/100$	—	-0.062	-0.073	-0.047	-0.058	—	-0.059	-0.071	-0.043	-0.055
		(0.0001)	(0.0001)	(0.0001)	(0.0001)		(0.0004)	(0.001)	(0.0004)	(0.001)
Black	—	-0.078	-0.079	-0.034	-0.037	—	-0.091	-0.094	-0.051	-0.053
		(0.001)	(0.001)	(0.001)	(0.001)		(0.002)	(0.002)	(0.002)	(0.002)
Currently married	—	0.097	0.086	0.065	0.057	—	0.076	0.066	0.049	0.042
		(0.0003)	(0.003)	(0.001)	(0.001)		(0.001)	(0.001)	(0.001)	(0.002)
High school degree	—	0.186	0.186	0.114	0.116	—	0.163	0.162	0.107	0.108
		(0.0005)	(0.0005)	(0.0004)	(0.0004)		(0.002)	(0.002)	(0.002)	(0.002)
Some college	—	0.297	0.291	0.172	0.170	—	0.264	0.260	0.157	0.156
		(0.001)	(0.001)	(0.001)	(0.0005)		(0.002)	(0.002)	(0.002)	(0.002)
Associate's degree	—	0.377	0.370	0.207	0.203	—	0.410	0.405	0.209	0.206
		(0.001)	(0.001)	(0.001)	(0.001)		(0.002)	(0.002)	(0.002)	(0.002)
Bachelor's degree	—	0.585	0.576	0.360	0.355	—	0.555	0.548	0.342	0.338
		(0.001)	(0.001)	(0.001)	(0.001)		(0.002)	(0.002)	(0.002)	(0.002)
Advanced degree	—	0.762	0.754	0.520	0.514	—	0.681	0.674	0.498	0.495
		(0.001)	(0.001)	(0.001)	(0.001)		(0.002)	(0.002)	(0.003)	(0.003)
MSA	—	0.215	0.214	0.175	0.175	—	0.162	0.160	0.125	0.124
		(0.0003)	(0.0003)	(0.001)	(0.0003)		(0.001)	(0.001)	(0.001)	(0.001)
Female × age	—	—	-0.026	—	-0.024	—	—	-0.027	—	-0.024
			(0.0002)		(0.0002)			(0.001)		(0.001)
Female × $(age^2/100)$	—	—	0.022	—	0.021	—	—	0.023	—	0.022
			(0.0002)		(0.0002)			(0.001)		(0.001)
Industry and occupation controls	No	No	No	Yes	Yes	No	No	No	Yes	Yes
R^2	0.073	0.356	0.363	0.466	0.470	0.121	0.400	0.407	0.533	0.537

Note
a Standard errors of regression estimates are reported in parentheses. The industry and occupation controls include dummy variables for the full set of three-digit Census industry and occupation codes. There are 10,830,247 observations in the SEDF regressions, and 637,718 observations in the NWECD regressions. In columns (3), (5), (8), and (10) the interactions of the female dummy variable and the age variables are created using the age variables minus their sample means, so the estimated coefficient of the female dummy variable measures the sex difference evaluated at the sample means of the control variables.

Not surprisingly, the results from the SEDF are very similar to those from other large, nationally representative data sets (such as the CPS). The male–female wage gap in column (2) is 31.6 percent, but falls to 23.8 percent in column (4) when we control for broad occupation and industry categories. Similarly, the black–white wage gap is significant in both regressions, but it is considerably smaller in column (4). The estimates show evidence of quadratic age profiles and positive returns to education, although the returns to education are smaller in column (4). The specifications with the female–age interactions in columns (3) and (5) indicate slower wage growth with age for women over most of the age range; this is expected, and is likely attributable to age overstating experience and tenure more for women than for men, and perhaps also lower human capital investment per unit of time in the labor market among women. Columns (6)–(10) replicate the specifications of columns (1)–(5), but use the NWECD data. The male–female wage gap in column (7) is 36.2 percent, which is somewhat larger than that in the SEDF (31.6 percent), but the difference in the male–female wage gap between the two data sets is virtually eliminated once we control broadly for industry and occupation (23.8 percent in the SEDF vs. 23.0 percent in the NWECD). The same is true in the specifications that include the female–age interactions. It makes sense that the estimates would match better after controlling for industry and occupation, because of the overrepresentation of some industries and occupations, and the underrepresentation of others, in the NWECD. Looking across the columns of Table 12.3, there are some other minor differences between the two data sets, but for the most part the wage regression results from the NWECD come close to replicating those from the SEDF, particularly once controls for industry and occupation are added. Note that in the empirical work in the following section, we always include some sort of controls for industry and occupation since one of our interests is in the effects of industry and occupation segregation on male–female wage differences.

Therefore, while the NWECD data are not representative of the underlying population of US workers, this data set represents a substantial improvement over existing data sources used to study the role of sex segregation along a number of dimensions in the workplace. The NWECD covers essentially the entire array of industries, occupations, locations, etc., in the US economy. Moreover, wage regression estimates from the NWECD do not differ substantively from those obtained from a representative sample of the US population of workers. Nonetheless, it remains to future work to attempt to construct even more representative samples of matched employer–employee data.

Methods

In our initial empirical work, we assume that the wage gap between men and women is a function of individual human capital characteristics and characteristics of the "femaleness" of where a worker works, as represented by the percent female in a worker's occupation, industry, establishment, and occupation within an establishment (job cell). That is, we estimate wage regressions of the following form:

$$w_{poiej} = \alpha + \beta F_p + \gamma \text{OCC\%}F_o + \delta \text{IND\%}F_i + \lambda \text{EST\%}F_e + \theta \text{JOB\%}F_j$$
$$+ X_{poiej}\Phi + \varepsilon_{poiej}, \tag{1}$$

where w is the log hourly wage, F is a dummy variable equal to 1 if individual p is female, $\text{OCC\%}F$ is the percent female in occupation o, $\text{IND\%}F$ is the percent female in industry i, $\text{EST\%}F$ is the percent female in establishment e, and $\text{JOB \%}F$ is the percent female in job cell j. A vector of control variables is represented by X.

With the estimated coefficients of equation (1) in hand, we can construct a wage decomposition expressing the difference in average log wages between women and men as follows:

$$w_f - w_m = \beta' + \gamma'(\text{OCC\%}F_f - \text{OCC\%}F_m) + \delta'(\text{IND\%}F_f - \text{IND\%}F_m)$$
$$+ \lambda'(\text{EST\%}F_f - \text{EST\%}F_m) + \theta'(\text{JOB\%}F_f - \text{JOB\%}F_m)$$
$$+ (X_f - X_m)\Phi', \tag{2}$$

where primes on the coefficients indicate estimates, and f and m subscripts on the variables indicate means for women and men, respectively. This decomposition gives the proportion of the wage gap due to: segregation of women into particular (generally lower-wage) occupations ($\gamma'[\text{OCC\%}F_f - \text{OCC\%}F_m]$), industries ($\delta'[\text{IND\%}F_f - \text{IND\%}F_m]$), establishments ($\lambda'[\text{EST\%}F_f - \text{EST\%}F_m]$), and job cells ($\theta'[\text{JOB\%}F_f - \text{JOB\%}F_m]$); differences in other observable characteristics ($[X_f - X_m]\Phi'$); and, most important, sex differences in wages controlling for segregation along all four dimensions (and therefore implicitly within job cells), as well as these other characteristics, captured in β'. These decompositions can therefore be thought of as traditional Oaxaca (1973) decompositions, imposing the restriction that the coefficients are the same for men and women. We present most of our results imposing this restriction, but as we discuss later, we also repeated the basic analysis using the unrestricted decomposition and did not find qualitative differences in the results.

While establishments are well defined, industry and occupation can be defined at a variety of levels of disaggregation. Since the question of primary concern is within- vs. across-job wage differences, we are interested in trying to use narrow occupational classifications. If, however, we use highly disaggregated occupations, we may end up with very small job cells (establishment-occupation cells), particularly since we only have a sample of workers in each plant, which may cause measurement error problems. Consequently, we report evidence from specifications using a variety of levels of occupational disaggregation, beginning with 13 broad Census occupations, and then using successive levels of disaggregation of occupations used by the Census Bureau, down to the finest level of disaggregation into 501 occupations (of which 491 are represented in our data). Each detailed Census occupation code corresponds generally to a mix of three-digit and four-digit Standard Occupation Classification (SOC) codes, often combining two or three four-digit occupations into a Census occupation.[5] To preview the results, we find that while using different levels of occupational disaggregation does change the quantitative results, the qualitative conclusion is not strongly affected by the level of occupational detail that we use.

The percent-female variables in equation (1) are all estimated directly from the data. The percentages female in the occupation and industry are estimated from the full SEDF sample, so measurement error is likely to be minimal. However, the percentages female in the plant and job cell are estimated by necessity from the matched data in the NWECD. On average 19.37 workers are matched to a plant, so job-cell estimates, in particular, are often based on a small number of observations. In order to eliminate potential measurement error, we also report results in which we estimate the coefficient on the female dummy variable, β, controlling for fixed occupation, industry, establishment, and job-cell effects, rather than controlling for the percent female in each of these categories; this amounts, of course, to putting in job-cell dummy variables, since these absorb occupation, industry, and establishment effects. In the absence of bias stemming from measurement error in the percent-female variables, we would not expect estimates of β obtained using these fixed effects to differ much from estimates using the percent-female variables if the percent-female variables do a reasonable job of characterizing how wages are affected by the sorting of workers into different industries, occupations, establishments, and job cells. Using job-cell dummies, however, avoids the measurement error inherent in the percent-female variables, and therefore should provide more reliable estimates of the within-job-cell sex difference in wages (β).[6] Nonetheless, most of the results we report use the percent-female variables, both to follow some of the earlier literature, and because the estimated effects of the percent-female variables are of interest in their own right—for example, in inferring the potential effects of a policy of comparable worth (Johnson and Solon, 1986).

Results using the NWECD

Basic analysis

Table 12.4 begins by reporting results of wage regression estimations using thirteen broad occupation categories. Panel A reports results with no control variables. We report results from this simple specification for two reasons. First, it allows us to focus on the effects of segregation and to see how much of the sex gap in wages can be eliminated by controlling solely for measures of segregation. Second, no information on other characteristics of workers is available in the IWS, so this specification provides the closest comparison. However, to better contrast these estimates with standard wage regression estimates in other studies, Panel B reports results adding the same basic set of human capital and other control variables used in the previous table. Finally, to provide a comparison with most other studies of sex segregation—in which data only on the percent female in the industry and occupation are available (e.g. Johnson and Solon, 1986;

Table 12.4 Estimated log wage differentials by sex and proportion female in occupation, industry, establishment, and job cell[a]

	Coefficient estimate (1)	Coefficient estimate (2)	Mean difference, women−men (3)	Absolute contribution to wage gap, (2) × (3) (4)	Relative contribution to wage gap (5)
A. Full decomposition, no controls					
Female	−0.375 (0.001)	−0.244 (0.002)	1.00	−0.244	0.651
Proportion female in occupation	—	0.180 (0.013)	0.180	0.032	−0.087
Proportion female in industry	—	0.122 (0.026)	0.248	0.030	−0.081
Proportion female in establishment	—	−0.188 (0.019)	0.338	−0.064	0.170
Proportion female in job cell	—	−0.243 (0.008)	0.536	−0.130	0.347
R^2	0.121	0.140			
B. Full decomposition, with basic controls					
Female	−0.375 (0.001)	−0.193 (0.002)	1.00	−0.193	0.514
Proportion female in occupation	—	−0.103 (0.006)	0.180	−0.019	0.050
Proportion female in industry	—	−0.171 (0.018)	0.248	−0.043	0.113
Proportion female in establishment	—	−0.173 (0.014)	0.338	−0.059	0.156
Proportion female in job cell	—	−0.098 (0.004)	0.536	−0.053	0.141
R^2	0.121	0.432			

C. Limited decomposition, no controls

Female	−0.375	−0.341	1.00	−0.341	0.910
	(0.001)	(0.002)			
Proportion female in occupation	—	0.086	0.180	0.016	−0.041
		(0.003)			
Proportion female in industry	—	−0.198	0.248	−0.049	0.131
		(0.003)			
R^2	0.121	0.126			

D. Limited decomposition, with basic controls

Female	−0.375	−0.241	1.00	−0.241	0.643
	(0.001)	(0.002)			
Proportion female in occupation	—	−0.143	0.180	−0.026	0.069
		(0.005)			
Proportion female in industry	—	−0.395	0.248	−0.098	0.261
		(0.012)			
R^2	0.121	0.427			

Note

a The sample size is 637,718. Standard errors of regression estimates are reported in parentheses; all standard errors are adjusted for non-independence of residuals within establishments. In this table, thirteen occupational categories are used. In Panels B and D the control variables listed in Table 12.3, columns (2) and (7), are included.

Sorensen, 1989; Fields and Wolff, 1995; Macpherson and Hirsch, 1995)—
Panels C and D report results using only these segregation measures.

Beginning with Panel A, column (1) simply reports the estimate of the raw
wage gap from a regression of log hourly wages on the female dummy variable;
the raw gap in these data is −0.375.[7] Column (2) then reports wage regression
estimates introducing the four percent-female variables; we divide the percent-
female variables by 100, and therefore in the tables and accompanying discussion
refer instead to the proportion female. Controlling for segregation by industry,
occupation, establishment, and job cell, the sex gap in wages falls by about one-
third, to −0.244. Wages are lower in establishments with a higher proportion
female, and within establishments they are lower in occupations with a higher
proportion female (the job-cell effect). In this specification without other controls
(notably education), occupational and industry segregation have the opposite of
the usual effects, with wages higher in occupations and industries with a higher
proportion female. However, as Panel B shows, this result is reversed when
individual-level controls are added. In addition, as just noted, most studies of
sex segregation do not control for segregation at the level of the establishment and
job cell. Thus, these studies no doubt overstate the role of occupational and/or
industry segregation *per se*. This is demonstrated in Panel D; when the establishment and job-cell segregation variables are dropped, and the basic controls are
included, the negative effects of occupation and especially industry segregation
are stronger.[8]

The decomposition of the sex gap in wages requires not only the regression
coefficients, but also the mean differences between women and men of the right-
hand-side variables, which are reported in column (3) of each panel. Women,
of course, are in occupations, industries, establishments, and job cells with a
higher proportion female. Columns (4) and (5) present the decomposition results.
Column (4) reports the absolute contribution of each variable to the wage gap,
and column (5) the relative contribution. In Panel A, the estimates in column (5)
indicate that nearly two-thirds (65.1 percent) of the wage gap is attributable to
sex differences in wages that remain after accounting for segregation by occupation, industry, establishment, and job cell. Just over one-third (34.7 percent)
is due to segregation into lower-paying occupations within establishments. Upon
including the basic controls, in Panel B, the estimated coefficient of the female
dummy variable declines by about 20 percent in absolute value (from −0.244
to −0.193), while the estimated coefficient of the proportion female in the job
cell declines more sharply (from −0.243 to −0.098). In terms of the decomposition, after accounting for the effects of sex segregation by occupation, industry,
establishment, and job cell, the sex difference in wages remains large, contributing approximately one-half of the sex gap (51.4 percent). The fact that this figure
is smaller than in Panel A, without the basic controls, implies some differences
in observables between men and women, conditioning on the segregation measures; this raises the possibility, which we of course cannot address directly, that
some unobservable differences remain. The contribution of establishment segregation remains about the same, while the contribution of segregation within jobs

within establishments falls by over half (to 14.1 percent). Finally, Panels C and D indicate that controlling for establishment and job-cell segregation is important, as the share of the sex wage gap accounted for by an individual's sex is higher when segregation along these dimensions is ignored.

Our basic results therefore suggest that while segregation does explain a substantial fraction of the sex gap in wages, a large proportion of the sex wage gap is still attributable to the sex of the worker. We now turn to evaluating the robustness of these results.

The effects of the degree of occupational disaggregation

The results in Table 12.4 are based on thirteen highly aggregated occupations. Because sex segregation (reflected in the mean difference in the proportion female in women's vs. men's occupations) is likely to be more severe at a more-detailed occupational level, the decomposition results may be sensitive to the level of occupational aggregation used. To explore this question, in columns (1)–(3) of Table 12.5 we report results for increasing degrees of occupational disaggregation. From this point on, we report the results from specifications including the control variables, to provide the most reliable estimates of the decomposition. Column (1) replicates the key results from Table 12.4 (corresponding to Panel B, columns (2), (3), and (5)). In the second column, we increase the number of occupational classifications to 72, which amounts to disaggregating each of the 13 original occupations into anywhere from 2 to 14 distinct occupations. In the third column, we disaggregate as much as our data allow and use the most-detailed Census occupation codes.

The first two rows of the table show, as we would expect, that given the greater degree of sex segregation in more-detailed occupations, the mean sex difference in the proportion female by occupation and job cell is larger in each successive column. (The figures for industry and establishment are unchanged, of course.) Turning to the wage regression estimates, the estimated coefficient of the female dummy variable, or the effect of an individual worker's sex, declines a bit as more-detailed occupations are used, from −0.193 in column (1) to −0.151 in column (3), with the corresponding relative contribution to the wage gap falling from 51.4 to 40.2 percent. Nonetheless, a sizable sex wage gap persists. Among the segregation measures, the contributions of establishment and job-cell segregation are most affected by the level of occupational disaggregation. The percentage of the sex gap accounted for by establishment segregation rises from 15.6 to 17.7 percent, and the percentage accounted for by job-cell segregation rises from 14.1 to 23.9 percent.

Not-elsewhere-classified occupations

It turns out that workers in the Census are often assigned to not-elsewhere-classified (n.e.c.) occupations, when there is not a detailed occupational classification in which it seems appropriate to classify a worker. Such "residual" occupations are likely to be more heterogeneous and less sex segregated than standard occupations,

Table 12.5 Estimated log wage differentials by sex and proportion female in occupation, industry, establishment, and job cell, varying degrees of occupational disaggregation[a]

	All occupations			Excluding n.e.c. occupations
	(1)	(2)	(3)	(4)
Number of occupations	13	72	491	451
Mean differences, women–men				
Proportion female in occupation	0.180	0.340	0.396	0.418
Proportion female in job cell	0.536	0.657	0.744	0.746
Coefficient estimates				
Female	−0.193	−0.164	−0.151	−0.143
	(0.002)	(0.002)	(0.002)	(0.002)
Proportion female in occupation	−0.103	−0.011	−0.041	−0.042
	(0.006)	(0.005)	(0.004)	(0.005)
Proportion female in industry	−0.171	−0.187	−0.171	−0.138
	(0.018)	(0.018)	(0.018)	(0.018)
Proportion female in establishment	−0.173	−0.169	−0.196	−0.218
	(0.014)	(0.014)	(0.014)	(0.014)
Proportion female in job cell	−0.098	−0.142	−0.120	−0.116
	(0.004)	(0.003)	(0.003)	(0.004)
Age	0.056	0.056	0.056	0.056
	(0.001)	(0.001)	(0.001)	(0.001)
$Age^2/100$	−0.054	−0.054	−0.054	−0.055
	(0.001)	(0.001)	(0.001)	(0.001)
Black	−0.084	−0.083	−0.083	−0.080
	(0.004)	(0.004)	(0.004)	(0.004)
Currently married	0.074	0.074	0.074	0.070
	(0.001)	(0.001)	(0.001)	(0.002)
High school degree	0.164	0.161	0.164	0.155
	(0.002)	(0.002)	(0.002)	(0.002)
Some college	0.281	0.275	0.276	0.264
	(0.003)	(0.003)	(0.003)	(0.003)
Associate's degree	0.460	0.456	0.458	0.460
	(0.005)	(0.005)	(0.005)	(0.005)
Bachelor's degree	0.604	0.595	0.596	0.583
	(0.005)	(0.005)	(0.005)	(0.005)
Advanced degree	0.769	0.757	0.758	0.755
	(0.006)	(0.006)	(0.006)	(0.006)
MSA	0.150	0.148	0.148	0.148
	(0.005)	(0.005)	(0.005)	(0.005)
Relative contribution to wage gap				
Female	0.514	0.438	0.402	0.406
Proportion female in occupation	0.050	0.010	0.043	0.050
Proportion female in industry	0.113	0.124	0.114	0.098
Proportion female in establishment	0.156	0.153	0.177	0.210
Proportion female in job cell	0.141	0.249	0.239	0.245
N	637,718	637,718	637,718	567,965

Note
a Other than the level of occupational disaggregation, the specifications are the same as in Panel B, Table 12.4. Column (1) reproduces results from Panel B, columns (2), (3), and (5), of Table 12.4. Standard errors of regression estimates are reported in parentheses; all standard errors are adjusted for nonindependence of residuals within establishments. "n.e.c." refers to not-elsewhere-classified.

because they presumably lump together many jobs. If so, and if these occupations are quantitatively important, the estimated coefficient of the dummy variable for females may overstate the within-job-cell wage gap, because for n.e.c. occupations the female dummy variable may capture, to some extent at least, a wage gap across jobs within n.e.c. occupations.[9]

To explore this issue, column (4) of Table 12.5 reports estimates after dropping workers in the n.e.c. occupations. As the table indicates, a fairly high proportion of workers are in these occupations (10.9 percent). In addition, estimated segregation—captured by the mean differences between women and men in the proportion female in the occupation or job cell—is higher once these workers are excluded. However, the differences are small. Finally, the wage equation estimates indicate a slightly lower effect of sex *per se* on the wage gap, with the estimated coefficient falling (in absolute value) from -0.151 to -0.143, although the relative contribution of sex to the wage gap actually rises slightly from 40.2 to 40.6 percent. Thus, the n.e.c. occupations do not in any way drive the results.[10]

The effects of other forms of disaggregation

The results reported thus far follow much of the literature in using a single wage regression for men and women, with a dummy variable for women. A more flexible decomposition procedure is to use separate wage regressions for men and women, following Oaxaca (1973). Using this less restrictive decomposition (whether we use the male or female wage structure as the "no-discrimination wage structure," as explained in Neumark (1988)), we found some differences in the estimated coefficients on the proportion-female variables between men and women. Although the apparent differences in the effects of segregation for men and women are of independent interest and bear further exploration, for the purposes of this chapter the important point is that using separate wage equations for men and women did not eliminate the significant role of an individual's sex in determining wages, conditional on all of the segregation measures. Compared with single-equation estimates, the estimated overall effect of an individual's sex was as large (in absolute value) using the female wage structure, and larger using the male wage structure.

Another potential disaggregation issue is the difference between urban and nonurban labor markets. For example, there may be some monopsony power in nonurban markets, and this may particularly influence women's wages, although the relative influences of monopsony power on the various components of the sex wage gap are not obvious. We re-estimated the specifications separately for establishments located in MSAs and those located outside of MSAs. The results were qualitatively similar in the two subsamples. Using the most disaggregated occupations, an individual's sex accounted for 42.5 percent of the sex wage gap in the MSA subsample, and 39.6 percent in the non-MSA subsample. In both subsamples, job-cell segregation contributed the second largest share, and establishment segregation the third largest share.

Earlier, we noted that the sample of establishments in the NWECD is disproportionately weighted toward manufacturing. If the effects of sex segregation or an individual's sex are different in manufacturing and nonmanufacturing industries, then in order to obtain unbiased estimates of population parameters, one might want to weight the data to make them more representative. Of course, many other factors influence selection into the NWECD sample, some of which may be related to unobservable characteristics, making it unclear how the weights might be constructed. We explored the most salient nonrepresentativeness—the preponderance of manufacturing plants—by estimating the equations and decomposition separately for the manufacturing and nonmanufacturing sectors. There are some differences between the two sectors. In general, there is more segregation in the nonmanufacturing sector except at the job-cell level; this may reflect the greater variety of industries comprising this sector. There are some differences in the relative contributions to the wage gap of occupation, industry, establishment, and job-cell segregation, as well as sex *per se*. In particular, the contribution of job-cell segregation is larger in nonmanufacturing (25.5 vs. 15.8 percent), while the contribution of establishment segregation is larger in manufacturing (16.2 vs. 9.2 percent). Furthermore, the sex gap that remains conditional on the various segregation measures is a bit larger in nonmanufacturing than in manufacturing (42.1 vs. 35.2 percent). However, the estimates are relatively close, and the key finding that the individual's sex accounts for a large share of the wage gap persists in both sectors. Thus, the most pronounced source of nonrepresentativeness has little influence on the qualitative findings.

The effects of eliminating measurement error

As discussed in the previous section, sampling error in the estimates of the percent or proportion female in the establishment and job cell may be quite severe. One approach that eliminates any role of measurement error in the proportion female variables is to include in place of the segregation measures a full set of job-cell dummy variables, which capture occupation, industry, establishment, and of course job-cell fixed effects. This specification has the added benefit that, unlike the wage decompositions used to this point, it does not impose a particular functional form on the way segregation affects wages, although it sacrifices estimates of the effects of sex segregation.

These estimates are reported in Table 12.6. Panel A reports results excluding the other controls, and Panel B including them. In Panel A, using the job-cell dummy variables, the estimated effect of the individual's sex is only slightly smaller than in Table 12.5, at each level of disaggregation of occupations.[11] The last row of the panel reports the ratio of the estimated coefficient of the female dummy variable using fixed effects to that using the segregation variables. While below 1, the estimates range from 0.96 to 0.91, decreasing as we disaggregate occupations further. Because the female dummy is positively correlated with the mismeasured proportion female in establishment and job-cell variables, attenuation bias in these latter coefficients would tend to bias the estimated coefficient of the female dummy variable away from zero. This bias should be larger the more severe the measurement error is, which is consistent with a smaller ratio using more disaggregated

Table 12.6 Estimated log wage differentials by sex, with fixed occupation, industry, establishment, and job-cell effects, alternative sets of control variables[a]

	(1)	(2)	(3)
A. No controls			
Number of occupations	13	72	491
Estimated coefficient of female dummy variable	−0.235	−0.196	−0.180
	(0.002)	(0.003)	(0.003)
Relative contribution to wage gap	0.628	0.524	0.481
Estimate relative to specification using proportion female variables	0.96	0.93	0.91
B. Basic controls			
Estimated coefficient of female dummy variable	−0.205	−0.176	−0.162
	(0.001)	(0.002)	(0.002)
Relative contribution to wage gap	0.548	0.469	0.433
Estimate relative to specification using proportion female variables	1.06	1.07	1.07

(*Table 12.6 continued*)

Table 12.6 Continued

C. Fully interactive specifications, augmented controls, most disaggregated occupations only

Race	Black	Nonblack			
	−0.121 (0.007)	−0.164 (0.003)			
Age	Age ≤ 25	Age 26–35	Age 36–45	Age 46–55	Age ≥ 56
	−0.081 (0.007)	−0.123 (0.004)	−0.174 (0.004)	−0.217 (0.005)	−0.221 (0.007)
Marriage/children	Single, no children	Married, no children	Married, with children		
	−0.092 (0.005)	−0.162 (0.004)	−0.198 (0.003)		
Region	Northeast	North Central	South	West	
	−0.169 (0.007)	−0.160 (0.005)	−0.157 (0.005)	−0.161 (0.008)	
Industry	Agriculture	Mining	Construction	Manufacturing	TCU	Wholesale
	−0.132 (0.062)	−0.158 (0.047)	−0.143 (0.006)	−0.169 (0.004)	−0.181 (0.013)	−0.234 (0.048)
			Retail	FIRE	Services	
			−0.249 (0.016)	−0.344 (0.050)	−0.142 (0.005)	

Note

a In Panel C, the specification includes: the basic controls substituting age group dummy variables for the linear and quadratic age variables. For each subpanel in Panel C, a separate specification is estimated that also includes the female dummy variable interacted with the listed variables, and it is those interactions that are reported; thus, the panel reports the within-job-cell sex wage gap for each of the indicated categories.

occupations. Of course as more control variables are added, any such predictions of the effects of measurement error become less definitive. Thus, in Panel B, in which the specifications include the other control variables, the estimated coefficients of the dummy variable for females are actually a shade larger than the corresponding estimates in Table 12.5.

The key finding, however, is that a large share of the wage gap remains within job cells (or, alternatively, attributable to an individual's sex).[12] The finding in the earlier tables was not a spurious result stemming from mismeasurement of the segregation variables.[13] Note also that in this table, adding the basic controls has less of an impact on the relative contribution of the within-job-cell sex wage gap to the overall gap than was the case using the segregation measures. This is natural, as the very large set of dummy variables for each job cell is likely to capture far more heterogeneity than the limited set of direct segregation measures. Finally, the results in Table 12.6 also indicate that the finding of a sizable within-job-cell sex difference in Table 12.5 is not attributable to the functional form used to estimate the impact of segregation on wages.

One potential objection to the estimates with fixed job-cell effects is that different individuals identify the coefficient of the female dummy variable than in the specifications using the segregation measures. In particular, in the former only women and men in integrated job cells contribute identifying information; clearly if all women and men were in completely sex-segregated job cells, the coefficient on the female dummy variable would be unidentified. However, we re-estimated the specification using the segregation measures, but including only individuals in integrated job cells. The key result is unchanged; for example, for the specification corresponding to column (3) of Table 12.5 (using the most disaggregated occupations), the within-job-cell sex gap in wages remains large (−0.147, compared with −0.151 in Table 12.5).

Control variables and results for different types of women and men

Finally, the sex wage gap may vary with measured human capital characteristics and other controls, even within job cells. To examine how this affects the conclusions, Panel C reports results from specifications with fixed job-cell effects where we augment the set of control variables to allow the within-job-cell sex wage gap to differ by race, age, and marital/childbearing status, by interacting the sex dummy variable with these controls.[14] We include each of these interactions in separate regressions because including a full set of interactions between sex and the other variables in one regression makes it difficult to evaluate the results.

The results in the first row of Panel C come from a regression where we include interactions between race and sex, and indicate that there is a significant within-job-cell sex gap in wages for both blacks and nonblacks. Consistent with the findings in other studies, though, the sex gap in wages is smaller for blacks than for non-blacks (see, Bayard *et al.*, 1999). The results in the second row indicate that there is a sex gap in wages that is significant at all ages, with a low of 8.1 percent for the youngest age category that rises monotonically to a high of 22.1 percent for the oldest age category. In the next row, we report results from a regression where we allow the effects of an individual's sex to differ by marital status and past childbearing. In this specification, in which we are trying to capture the effects of marriage and childbearing, we also include a dummy variable measuring whether a woman has ever had children.[15] We do this because the Decennial Census does not have any direct information on experience or tenure, and for women, past childbearing is negatively associated with wages, especially in the absence of experience or tenure controls (Korenman and Neumark, 1992). The within-job-cell sex wage gap for single, childless women is 9.2 percent, and is much larger for married women whether or not they have children. Finally, the last two sets of estimates disaggregate the results by region and industry. While the within-job-cell sex wage gaps are quite stable across regions, they vary considerably across industries, although all are positive and sizable.

A fundamental question that arises with regard to interpreting within-job-cell sex wage gaps is whether they could be due solely to unmeasured human capital differences. We read the evidence in Panel C as providing some support for a role for human capital in determining sex wage gaps. For example, the widening of the sex gap in wages with age is consistent with a cumulative widening of the human capital gap between men and women over time. This widening gap stems from the smaller positive impact of age on women's wages than men's wages (see Table 12.3), which could be interpreted as lower human capital investment, or as reflecting more intermittent accumulation of experience among women. Similarly, the smaller gap for single women with no children compared with married women with children is consistent with models of human capital investment based on household specialization, and the gap between single and married childless women could reflect planned or expected future labor market interruptions for the latter, as in the Polachek model (1975). Nonetheless, all of the results in Panel C still indicate that a statistically significant sex gap in wages exists, even within job cells and within categories of workers defined by race, age, and marital/childbearing status. While we cannot rule out a human capital explanation for the remaining sex gap in wages, it is important to emphasize again that this gap exists even after we have controlled for a potentially huge set of job-related characteristics, presumably including skill requirements, with the inclusion of the job-cell dummy variables. Indeed we may want to interpret the within-job-cell sex differences for the youngest women, or single childless women, as lower-bound estimates of within-job wage discrimination, estimates that are on the order of 8–9 percent.

Comparison with Groshen's estimates

The findings from the NWECD indicating that occupational segregation is quantitatively unimportant, and that within-job-cell sex differences in wages contribute a large (in fact, the largest) share of the sex wage gap, contrast sharply with Groshen's (1991) findings. Using IWS data from the 1970s and 1980s on five specific industries (Miscellaneous Plastic Products, Nonelectrical Machinery, Life Insurance, Banking, and Computer and Data Processing), she reports that within-job-cell sex differences account for only −1.0 to 6.6 percent of the wage gap, while the effect of job-cell segregation ranges from explaining −2.7 to 32.5 percent of the wage gap, with the percentage above 20 for 3 of the 5 industries. The proportion female in the occupation accounts for the largest share, ranging from 40.6 to 74.8 percent. The estimated contributions of job-cell segregation are not very different from ours, but the estimated contributions of occupational segregation and within-job-cell sex differences contrast strongly.[16]

There is a natural explanation for the difference in the estimated role of within-job-cell sex wage gaps. In particular, the IWS data may indicate a much smaller role for within-job-cell sex differences in wages because occupation classifications in the IWS are much more narrowly defined than Census occupation codes, and are even industry specific. As an example, in the Miscellaneous Plastics Products industry, there are separate occupation codes for "Compression-Molding Machine Operators," "Extrusion Press Operators," "Injection-Molding Machine Operators," "Preform-Machine Operators," and "Vacuum-Plastics-Forming Machine Operators," all of which get aggregated into one three-digit Census occupation (719, "Molding and Casting Machine Operators"). If it is only at the level of disaggregation of the IWS occupations that the within-job-cell sex wage gap disappears, then the results using the NWECD and IWS might coincide if they were based on the same level of occupational disaggregation. In this section, we explore this possibility by aggregating IWS occupation categories into Census occupations (at the most detailed level of Census occupation codes), using in-house BLS documentation.[17] We then perform the decompositions using the IWS data based on these broader occupations and compare the results to those in the NWECD.

To carry out this exercise, we obtained from the BLS the original IWS data that Groshen studied. To establish a baseline, we first verified that we could replicate Groshen's results using the IWS data. Having done this, to draw a sharper comparison we drew subsamples in our NWECD data set for the five IWS industries, and restricted our analysis to 3 of the 5 industries (Miscellaneous Plastics Products, Nonelectrical Machinery, and Banking) for which we have reasonable-sized samples in the NWECD.[18] We also used the original IWS documentation to determine which classes of occupations the IWS covered, and further restricted our NWECD sample to workers in these occupations. Even restricting the NWECD data to the industries and occupations covered by Groshen's IWS analysis, the differences between the two data sets remain sharp. In the two manufacturing industries, 41–49 percent of the wage gap is due to occupational segregation in the IWS, compared with 6–17 percent in the corresponding NWECD data. In Banking, the IWS estimates indicate an even larger role for occupational segregation, contributing 71 percent of the sex gap in wages, compared with 36 percent in the NWECD data. And for two of the three industries the NWECD results replicate the finding from the full NWECD that the sex gap within job cells accounts for a large share of the wage gap—41.4 percent in Nonelectrical Machinery and 43.7 percent of this gap in Banking based on the NWECD, compared with −1 and 2.4 percent, respectively, in the IWS data. For Plastics, the estimated contributions are closer, but still larger by a factor of 3 in the NWECD data (13.5 vs. 4.7 percent). Thus, the NWECD data assign a much *less* prominent role to occupational segregation, and a much *more* prominent role to sex wage gaps within establishments and occupations.

Having established the differences in the results using comparable industries and occupations in the two data sets, we next turn to the evidence on the role of occupational disaggregation. The results are reported in Table 12.7. In columns (1) and (2) we report (for comparison purposes) the estimated coefficients and relative contributions of each component of the decomposition to the wage gap in the IWS using IWS occupation definitions. In columns (3) and (4) we report the same set of results, except using the IWS occupations aggregated up to the same Census occupations that we use in the NWECD. Finally, in columns (5) and (6), we report estimated coefficients and relative contributions using the NWECD data for workers in these occupations in each of the three IWS industries.

The results for Plastics are given in Panel A. The coefficient on the female dummy using IWS data aggregated into Census occupations is −0.033, as reported in column (3). This is slightly larger than the estimated coefficient of −0.011 in column (1), based on IWS occupation classifications, and raises the relative contribution of the female dummy to the total sex wage gap from 4.7 to 13.8 percent, as reported in columns (2) and (4). The estimated coefficient on the female dummy variable for the NWECD is −0.026, which is similar to the IWS result, as is the estimated relative contribution of an individual's sex (13.5 percent, which closely matches the aggregated IWS estimate of 13.8 percent). This is a relative contribution, however, so it is partially driven by the fact that in the NWECD, the proportion female in the establishment contributes virtually nothing to the wage gap. But while the results for Plastics do suggest that aggregation has an effect on relative wage gaps, the effect of an individual's sex in the NWECD in Plastics is a small fraction of what it is in the other two industries.

The IWS and NWECD comparisons for Nonelectrical Machinery appear in Panel B. Comparing columns (1) and (3), we see that aggregation changes the coefficient on the female dummy variable in the IWS from 0.003 to −0.022. This, of course, changes both the sign and the magnitude of the relative contribution of an individual's sex, from −1.0 to 7.3 percent. In column (5), however, the estimated coefficient on the female dummy variable in the NWECD sample is −0.123, much larger than that in the IWS for the same level of occupational disaggregation (−0.022). The relative contribution of an individual's sex in the NWECD is also much larger, 41.4 percent, as reported in column (6). So while aggregation does change the estimated contribution of an individual's sex in the IWS, its contribution is still much smaller than we find in the NWECD.

The results in Banking, reported in Panel C, are equally stark. The coefficient on the female dummy variable in Banking in the IWS rises (in absolute value) from −0.009 to −0.026 with occupational aggregation, which raises the relative contribution from 2.4 to 7.0 percent. However, the coefficient on the female dummy variable in the NWECD is −0.301, and the relative contribution of sex is 43.7 percent. So, as in Nonelectrical Machinery, aggregating IWS occupations into Census occupations in Banking does have an effect on the estimated contribution of an individual's sex to the wage gap, but the effect is small and is nowhere near large enough to explain the discrepancies between the results for the IWS and NWECD.

To summarize, in each of the three industries, aggregating up from detailed IWS occupations to Census occupations does increase the relative contribution of the female dummy variable to the overall sex wage gap.[19] But the qualitative conclusions one can draw from the analysis of the IWS are not affected by the aggregation of occupations. In the IWS, an individual's sex accounts for a relatively small portion of the overall wage gap, even when occupations are aggregated up to Census occupation codes. Moreover, in two of the three industries studied (Nonelectrical Machinery and Banking), the IWS results are markedly different from the NWECD results, even when the level of occupational classification used is identical. Thus, these results for the IWS show that differing levels of detail in occupational classifications cannot explain the discrepancies between results from the sample of NWECD workers in the three IWS industries, and results using the IWS data.

Additional exploration of differences between these two quite different data sources raised some caution flags regarding the IWS. Because the IWS for Banking was conducted in 1980, it can be compared with data from the 1980 Decennial Census. We extracted data from the 5 percent Public Use Microsample (PUMS), for all workers reporting that they worked in the Banking industry in 1979 in occupations represented in the IWS. Using similar individual-level sample restrictions to those in the NWECD, we obtained a sample of 37,710 workers in Banking in 1980. The mean wage of banking workers in the PUMS is $5.47 per hour, similar to the estimate of $5.60 per hour that we obtained in our IWS sample, while the percent female in banking is 79.9 percent in the PUMS, again very similar to the 82.8 percent we obtained in the IWS sample. In contrast, the unadjusted sex wage differences in the PUMS and IWS are vastly different. In the IWS, the sex wage difference is -0.372, while in the PUMS the sex wage difference is -0.614, almost double that in the IWS. In contrast, the PUMS estimate is very similar to the -0.689 sex wage difference in the NWECD. Of course, such a large discrepancy in unadjusted sex wage differences could lead to vastly different conclusions from a wage decomposition using the two data sets.

We can only speculate on why it is that the sex wage gap in Banking in 1980 is so much smaller in the IWS than in the 1980 PUMS. The IWS in Banking is likely to contain a nonrepresentative sample of banks, given that it was only conducted in twenty-nine large metropolitan areas, although it does not appear that these banks were nonrepresentative in terms of the average wages they paid or in terms of the sex mix of their workers. Another possibility is that at least some banks were hesitant to provide data suggesting that within narrowly defined occupations there was a pay gap between men and women,[20] and therefore both the overall sex wage gaps and the within job-cell sex wage gaps calculated in the IWS are artificially low. Regardless, given that the data for 1 of the 3 IWS industries for which we have data from another source seem not to be comparable to a nationally representative sample of workers in that same year, we think one should be very cautious in drawing conclusions about the importance of segregation in determining sex wage differences using the IWS. In contrast, as we discussed earlier, the NWECD, while not entirely representative, comes much closer to matching the critical moments from the distributions of wages and worker characteristics in the US population, and of course provides broad industry coverage.[21]

Table 12.7 Effects of aggregation in IWS on IWS vs. NWECD comparison[a]

	IWS data, IWS occupations		IWS data, Census occupations		NWECD	
	Coefficient estimate (1)	Relative contribution to wage gap (2)	Coefficient estimate (3)	Relative contribution to wage gap (4)	Coefficient estimate (5)	Relative contribution to wage gap (6)
A. Miscellaneous Plastics Products						
Female	−0.011 (0.003)	0.047	−0.033 (0.003)	0.138	−0.026 (0.053)	0.135
Proportion female in occupation	−0.245 (0.004)	0.497	−0.172 (0.004)	0.265	−0.186 (0.114)	0.172
Proportion female in establishment	−0.117 (0.004)	0.156	−0.122 (0.004)	0.162	−0.015 (0.113)	0.018
Proportion female in job cell	−0.093 (0.005)	0.300	−0.141 (0.005)	0.435	−0.159 (0.070)	0.675
R^2	0.332		0.308		0.079	
N	70,355		70,355		582	
B. Nonelectrical Machinery						
Female	0.003 (0.004)	−0.010	−0.022 (0.004)	0.073	−0.123 (0.033)	0.414
Proportion female in occupation	−0.452 (0.006)	0.406	−0.150 (0.007)	0.090	−0.104 (0.075)	0.063
Proportion female in establishment	−0.331 (0.007)	0.479	−0.318 (0.008)	0.460	−0.291 (0.133)	0.265
Proportion female in job cell	−0.057 (0.007)	0.124	−0.191 (0.008)	0.377	−0.147 (0.045)	0.259
R^2	0.358		0.299		0.098	
N	54,873		54,873		3,220	

C. Banking

Female	−0.009	0.024	−0.026	0.070	−0.301	0.437
	(0.004)		(0.003)		(0.053)	
Proportion female in occupation	−0.685	0.711	−0.603	0.608	−1.01	0.363
	(0.008)		(0.009)		(0.077)	
Proportion female in establishment	−0.385	0.048	−0.376	0.047	−0.072	0.019
	(0.012)		(0.013)		(0.084)	
Proportion female in job cell	−0.160	0.217	−0.216	0.274	−0.184	0.182
	(0.008)		(0.009)		(0.071)	
R^2	0.401		0.387		0.404	
N	74,501		74,501		1,830	

Note

a Standard errors of estimates are reported in parentheses. Following Groshen, in the estimates in this table we do not correct standard errors for correlation across individuals in an establishment. However, the corrected standard errors on the female dummy variable are virtually identical to the uncorrected standard errors.

Conclusions

We assembled a large matched employer–employee data set covering essentially all industries and occupations across all regions of the United States. We use this data set to re-examine the question of the relative contributions to the overall sex gap in wages of sex segregation vs. wage differences by sex within occupation, industry, establishment, and occupation-establishment cells. This is especially important given that earlier research on this topic relied on data sets that covered only a narrow range of industries, occupations, or regions.

Our results indicate that although a sizable fraction of the sex gap in wages is accounted for by the segregation of women into lower-paying occupations, industries, establishments, and occupations within establishments, a substantial part of this gap remains attributable to the individual's sex. Overall, our estimates indicate that approximately one-half of the sex wage gap takes the form of wage differences between men and women within narrowly defined occupations within establishments. These findings contrast sharply with the conclusions of previous research (especially Groshen, 1991) using more limited data, which indicated that sex segregation accounted for essentially all of the sex wage gap. While we do not attempt in this chapter to determine the underlying forces that cause men and women to have different wages within narrowly defined occupations in the same establishments, further research into the sources of within-establishment, within-occupation sex wage differences is apparently much more important than previously thought.

The policy implications of our findings are very different from those drawn from the earlier research. Our results suggest that identifying and eliminating the sources of within-occupation, within-establishment wage differences between men and women can play a large role in reducing wage differences between men and women. In particular, if within the narrowly defined occupations that we study the jobs performed by men and women require substantially equal skill, effort, responsibility, and working conditions, yet wages differ by sex, then enforcement of the Equal Pay Act can play a fundamental role in closing the wage gap between men and women. In contrast, if segregation along various dimensions accounts for most of the sex wage gap, then policies along the lines of comparable worth, equal opportunities in employment and promotion, and Affirmative Action would be central to any further closing of this gap, and stronger equal pay provisions would not be effective. Our findings suggest that stronger enforcement of equal pay legislation could further reduce the wage gap between men and women, perhaps substantially.

Appendix: matching employees to employers using location and industry information

The Census Bureau organizes the United States into different geographic areas, assigning codes to each. For the NWECD, there are five areas of interest: state, county, place, tract, and block.[22] The geographic coding process works primarily as a hierarchy. The Census Bureau assigns unique codes to every state in the country. Within states, each county is also assigned a unique code. In addition, in areas or townships with a population of 2,500 or more, the Census Bureau assigns a place code. Because an area or town can cross county boundaries, we can distinguish between areas in the same place but different counties. Tract codes are unique within counties and block codes are unique within tracts. The Census Bureau uses the same geographic codes in both the SSEL and the Decennial Census.[23]

In addition to geographic codes, the Census Bureau assigns industry codes to the SEDF and the SSEL. The Census Bureau asks long-form respondents to identify their employer's industry, which the Census Bureau codes into one of 236 Census Industry Classification (CIC) codes. Each CIC code corresponds roughly to a three-digit Standard Industrial Classification (SIC) code.[24] In the SSEL, the Census Bureau assigns each establishment a six-digit SIC code based on the plant's primary economic activity.[25] Since the CIC codes are more aggregated than SIC codes, we use a concordance table to assign a CIC to each SIC in the SSEL.[26]

The first step in the matching process is to assign all plants in the SSEL to industry-location cells. We divide the SSEL into plants that are unique in a state-county-place-industry (SCPI) cell, and those that are not, and retain all unique SCPI plants. In cases where there are multiple plants in an SCPI cell, we first retain the cell only if all plants in the cell have tract and block codes. We then keep only those plants that are unique within a state-county-place-tract-block-industry cell. Next, we assign workers in the SEDF to industry-location cells based on information provided in the SEDF. Unlike the SSEL, the Census Bureau assigns detailed geographic codes to all observations in the SEDF.[27] Once we have workers assigned to industry-location cells and have establishments that are unique within a cell, we can match the workers to the particular establishments where they work.

We take a number of additional steps to improve the quality of the match. First, to ensure that workers are matched properly to employers in the NWECD, we discard all workers and establishments from the matched sample where Census imputed either the worker's or the establishment's industry.[28] We also discard all workers from the matched sample if the worker's place-of-work code is imputed and if this imputed code is the source of the match.[29] Second, some matches lead to apparent inconsistencies, prompting us to discard matches when the number of workers matched to an establishment exceeds the number of employed workers as reported by the establishment in the SSEL. Although there may be legitimate reasons for the number of matched workers to exceed reported establishment employment, to avoid potentially incorrect matches we discard cases where this occurs.[30]

Acknowledgments

We thank Fran Blau, Bill Evans, Claudia Goldin, Erica Groshen, Larry Katz, Robert Lalonde, Jonathan Leonard, Brooks Pierce, Peter Schmidt, and seminar/conference participants at Princeton University, the University of Kentucky, the University of Maryland, UCLA, the NBER, the Center for Economic Studies at the US Census Bureau, the American Economics Association and Southern Economics Association meetings, the BLS, and the International Symposium on Matched Employer–Employee Data for helpful comments. We also thank Jennifer Foster, Nicole Nestoriak, and Scott Adams for outstanding research assistance.

This research was supported by NSF grant SBR95–10876 through the NBER. The research in this chapter was conducted while the last three authors were research associates with the Center for Economic Studies, US Bureau of the Census. Part of this research was conducted with restricted access to Bureau of Labor Statistics (BLS) data on-site at the BLS. Research results and conclusions expressed are those of the authors and do not indicate concurrence by the US Bureau of the Census, the Center for Economic Studies, or the Bureau of Labor Statistics. The main data used in this chapter were collected under the provisions of Title 13 US Code and are only available at the Center for Economic Studies, US Census Bureau. To obtain access to these data, contact the Center for Economic Studies, US Census Bureau, Rm. 211/WPII, Washington, DC, 20233.

Notes

1 See Troske (1998) and Bayard *et al.* (1999) for descriptions of these data sets.
2 Multiple job-holding rates are virtually identical among men and women. 1996 Current Population Survey (CPS) data indicate rates of 6.2 percent for men and 6.1 percent for women (Stinson, 1997). Thus, although multiple job-holding could affect our data, it is unlikely to influence the sex differences we estimate.
3 We used the March 1990 Basic CPS file and Income Supplement to attempt to gauge the extent to which these restrictions accomplish this. We first extracted a sample that corresponds to our SEDF sample along other dimensions. For this sample, we estimated the proportion that had not "changed jobs" over the period from the beginning of the previous calendar year to the March interview. We identified such individuals as those who held only one job over the course of the previous calendar year (the survey instructs respondents to ignore multiple jobs held at the same time), and who are working in the same three-digit industry at the March interview as in the last job held in the previous calendar year (the only available information on job change for this interval (Stewart, 1998)). Overall, 76.52 percent of the sample satisfies these criteria. When we impose the weeks and hours restrictions for the previous calendar year, this percentage rises to 78.62, indicating that the weeks and hours restrictions tend to screen job changers, but not in a very disproportionate fashion. Thus, measurement error in the wage because of job changing remains a problem. We do note, however, that this phenomenon is very similar for men and women, as the percentages that had not changed jobs (with or without the restrictions) differ by no more than 0.5 percentage point. Thus, it seems that any measurement error is not systematically related to sex.
4 It would be ideal to use actual hourly wages whenever possible, but these are not available in the SEDF. We therefore examined data from the March 1990 Basic CPS file and Income Supplement to gauge the possible sensitivity of the results to using a constructed wage. In particular, we extracted the outgoing rotation group with similar restrictions to those imposed on the SEDF sample we use. We restricted attention to hourly workers for whom the reported March hourly wage is an actual hourly rate, not constructed. For this same sample, we also constructed an hourly wage based on earned income in 1989 divided by an estimate of total hours worked, paralleling the SEDF measure. We then estimated standard wage regressions with similar controls to those used in the SEDF (except for the percent-female variables). The estimated wage

regressions—and in particular the coefficients of the sex dummy variable—were very similar using these two wage measures, indicating that use of this constructed wage in the SEDF is unlikely to be problematic.

5 For an example of what this occupational disaggregation entails, consider one of our 13 Census occupation codes, Technicians and Related Support Occupations. At the level of 72 total occupations, this category constitutes 3 separate occupations: (1) Health Technologists and Technicians; (2) Technologists and Technicians, Except Health Engineering and Related Technologists and Technicians; Science Technicians; and (3) Technicians, Except Health, Engineering, and Science. At the level of 491 total occupations, these three categories are further disaggregated into 22 distinct occupations, including such occupations as dental hygienists, survey and mapping technicians, and legal assistants. Because we do not look at establishment-industry cells (since all workers in an establishment are presumably in the same industry, and are so by construction in our data set), we face no constraint in disaggregating industries finely, and hence we always use the detailed Census industry codes.

6 We could, in principle, implement a formal correction for the measurement error bias that results from the sampling error in this case, as explained in Cockburn and Griliches (1987) and Mairesse and Greenan (1999). Cockburn and Griliches find that when they construct a consistent estimate of the measurement error covariance matrix, allowing the error variances to differ across observations (as is necessary in this case, because the cell sizes differ), the resulting error-corrected covariance matrix is near-singular. Mairesse and Greenan are able to successfully invert their error-corrected covariance matrix, but their model contains many fewer covariates that are measured with error.

7 All of our coefficient estimates are highly significant, so while standard errors are reported, we do not continually discuss their statistical significance.

8 Macpherson and Hirsch (1995) caution that the percent female in the worker's occupation may be a proxy for other job-related characteristics, so that the estimated negative effect on wages may partially reflect compensating differentials based on workers' preferences, and perhaps also different skill requirements. Their evidence is consistent with this, as the longitudinal estimate of the effect of percent female in the occupation is much smaller than the cross-sectional estimate. Sorensen (1989) presents similar evidence for women only, based on a comparison of OLS estimates with estimates that account for selectivity into employment and into female-dominated occupations (although one can raise questions regarding identification of this model). In both papers, despite the evidence of bias, occupational segregation continues to lower wages.

9 Examples of n.e.c. occupations include: engineers, n.e.c. (within the occupational category of engineers, which includes aerospace, chemical, nuclear, etc.); social science teachers, n.e.c. (within the occupational category of postsecondary teachers, which includes psychology, economics, history, political science, and sociology teachers); and office machine operators, n.e.c. (within the occupational category of duplication, mail and other office machine operators, which includes duplicating machine operators and mail preparing and paper handling machine operators).

10 To assess the robustness of our basic results and those using different levels of occupational disaggregation, we also estimated these same specifications including controls for establishment size and whether the establishment belongs to a multi-unit firm. To the extent that these reflect establishment-level characteristics, they may "over-control" for establishment-level differences, because they may capture dimensions of sex segregation. On the other hand, these variables may be related to unobserved human capital, calling for their inclusion along with the other human capital controls. The estimates scarcely changed upon including these additional control variables.

11 The results were similar excluding the n.e.c. occupations.

12 When job-cell dummy variables are included in the regression specifications, the estimated effects of the individual's sex in these specifications are, literally, within-job-cell

sex differences in wages. Up to this point, we have not used this label in describing the effect of an individual's sex; however, because the results from this specification are quite similar to those using the proportion-female variables, from this point on we use the more transparent "within-job-cell" expression.

13 We also used this specification to verify that the relationship we estimate between wages and sex is driven by the rate of pay. Because our wage variable is a constructed wage, it is possible that it is not rates of pay that differ by sex within job cells, but rather weeks or hours. For women to have lower constructed wages within job cells, however, it would have to be the case that their weeks or hours were higher within job cells, which seems unlikely (although our "stylized facts" do not refer to within-job-cell differences). To check this, we estimated specifications for log weeks and for log hours, including a dummy variable for females and job-cell fixed effects. For the different levels of occupational disaggregation, the estimated coefficient on the female dummy variable in the weeks regression ranged from -0.005 to -0.007, while in the hours regression it ranged from -0.030 to -0.044. These negative coefficients imply that dividing through by weeks and hours tends to make constructed wages look, if anything, more equal by sex within job cell.

14 Note that we have substituted age dummy variables for the linear and quadratic terms.

15 This variable is available in the SEDF only for women. One can of course measure whether there are currently children in the household for men and women, but this variable does not capture the effects of past childbearing and child rearing. Using the variable only available for women implies that we simply restrict the effect on men's wages of children to be zero.

16 Since the IWS data do not contain the basic control variables we used, comparisons with the NWECD estimates should be based on the estimates without these controls (in Panel A of Table 12.4); these controls are also excluded in the NWECD estimations presented in this section.

17 There is of course no way to do the reverse exercise, disaggregating the NWECD occupations to correspond to those in the IWS.

18 There are 582 workers working in 105 establishments in Plastics, 3,220 workers in 191 establishments in Nonelectrical Machinery, and 1,830 workers in 390 establishments in Banking. NWECD samples sizes in Computer and Data Processing and Life Insurance are much smaller.

19 As expected, this aggregation reduces the estimated contribution of occupational segregation to the wage gap, and increases the estimated contribution of job-cell segregation.

20 The Equal Pay Act places the burden of proof on the employer to show that unequal pay for equal work is based on a factor other than sex, such as seniority.

21 This is true not only for the NWECD in general, but also specifically for Banking. For example, the sex wage difference for NWECD workers in Banking is -0.689, whereas for all workers in Banking in the SEDF it is -0.617. This is a very small discrepancy relative to the difference between the unadjusted wage gap in the IWS in 1980 relative to that in the PUMS in 1980.

22 In some geographic areas, the Census Bureau uses Block Numbering Areas (BNAs) instead of tracts. For our purposes, a BNA is equivalent to a tract. The Census Bureau assigns tracts and blocks in tandem, so whenever an establishment is assigned a tract code, it is also always assigned a block code.

23 Two shortcomings of the geographic codes in the SSEL are (1) the absence of tract and block codes before 1992, and (2) the incomplete assignment of these codes to all establishments. To assign tract and block codes to the 1990 SSEL, we extracted each establishment's block and tract code (when available) from the 1992 SSEL, and then matched these codes back to the 1990 SSEL. Some establishments that ceased operation

between 1990 and 1992 do not appear in the 1992 SSEL, making it impossible to identify block and tract codes for these establishments. Due to address problems, not all establishments had tract and block codes assigned as of 1992. In the 1992 SSEL, Census had assigned tract and block codes to 45 percent of all establishments.

24 An exception is Construction. There is one CIC for Construction and this corresponds to the equivalent of three two-digit SIC codes.

25 The last two digits of the SIC code are product codes for goods-producing industries, or type of business codes for service establishments.

26 A few SIC's correspond to more than one CIC. We omitted establishments in these industries.

27 When long-form respondents omit geographic information, the Census Bureau imputes missing values.

28 This imputation occurs for plants when an incomplete SIC code (only the first two or three digits) is provided. For such cases, the Census Bureau randomly assigns the remaining digits.

29 To understand the exclusion based on imputed geographic data, consider the following example. When a worker is matched to an establishment unique in an SCPI cell, the match is based on the state, county, place, and industry of the worker and the establishment. If the worker's block code is imputed, then this imputed code has no bearing on the match, and we retain the match in the data. However, if the match relies on tract- and block-level information, and the worker's place-of-work block code is imputed, then we discard the worker from the matched data set.

30 There are several reasons why the number of matched workers might exceed total employment. First, there may be errors in the industry or geographic codes for some workers or establishments in the SEDF or SSEL. Second, there is a time difference built into the Census Bureau surveys of workers and employers. The Census asks workers where they worked on April 1 and employers how many workers they employed as of March 12; total employment may differ on the two dates. A third problem is that workers may be incorrectly assigned to locations because of imprecise SEDF questions. Because the SEDF asks workers only where they worked in the past week, workers who were working at a site other than their employer's primary location may be improperly assigned to an establishment. Fourth, in the SSEL total employment includes only a plant's employees, not its owners. In the SEDF, however, both owners and employees are assigned to a particular establishment.

References

Bayard, Kimberly, Judith Hellerstein, David Neumark, and Kenneth Troske. 1999. "Why Are Racial and Ethnic Wage Gaps Larger for Men than for Women? Exploring the Role of Segregation Using the New Worker-Establishment Characteristics Database." In *The Creation and Analysis of Employer–Employee Matched Data*, eds John Haltiwanger, Julia Lane, James Spletzer, Jules Theeuwes, and Kenneth Troske, pp. 175–203. Amsterdam: Elsevier Science B.V.

Bielby, William, and James Baron. 1984. "A Woman's Place is with Other Women: Sex Segregation Within Organizations." In *Sex Segregation in the Workplace: Trends, Explanations, Remedies*, ed. Barbara Reskin, pp. 27–55. Washington, DC: National Academy Press.

Blau, Francine D. 1977. *Equal Pay in the Office*. Lexington, MA: D.C. Heath.

——. 1998. "Trends in the Well-Being of American Women, 1970–1995." *Journal of Economic Literature* 36: 112–65.

Brown, Charles and James L. Medoff. 1989. "The Employer Size Wage Effect." *Journal of Political Economy* 97: 1027–59.

Carrington, William J. and Kenneth R. Troske. 1998. "Sex Segregation in U.S. Manufacturing." *Industrial and Labor Relations Review* 51: 445–64.

Cockburn, Ian and Zvi Griliches. 1987. "Industry Effects and Appropriability Measures in the Stock Market's Valuation of R&D and Patents." Working Paper No. 2465. Cambridge, MA: National Bureau of Economic Research.

Fields, Judith and Edward N. Wolff. 1995. "Interindustry Wage Differentials and the Gender Wage Gap." *Industrial and Labor Relations Review* 49: 105–20.

Groshen, Erica L. 1991. "The Structure of the Female/Male Wage Differential: Is it Who You Are, What You Do, or Where You Work?" *Journal of Human Resources* 26: 457–72.

Johnson, George and Gary Solon. 1986. "Estimates of the Direct Effects of Comparable Worth Policy." *American Economic Review* 76: 1117–25.

Korenman, Sanders and David Neumark. 1992. "Marriage, Motherhood, and Wages." *Journal of Human Resources* 27: 233–55.

Macpherson, David A. and Barry T. Hirsch. 1995. "Wages and Gender Composition: Why Do Women's Jobs Pay Less?" *Journal of Labor Economics* 13: 426–71.

Mairesse, Jacques and Nathalie Greenan. 1999. "Using Employee Level Data in a Firm Level Econometric Study." In *The Creation and Analysis of Employer–Employee Matched Data*, eds John Haltiwanger, Julia Lane, James Spletzer, Jules Theeuwes, and Kenneth Troske, pp. 489–512. Amsterdam: Elsevier Science B.V.

Neumark, David. 1988. "Employers' Discriminatory Behavior and the Estimation of Wage Discrimination." *Journal of Human Resources* 23: 279–95.

Oaxaca, Ronald. 1973. "Male–Female Wage Differentials in Urban Labor Markets." *International Economic Review* 14: 693–709.

Polachek, Solomon. 1975. "Differences in Post-School Investment as a Determinant of Market Wage Differentials." *International Economic Review* 16: 451–70.

Sorensen, Elaine. 1989. "Measuring the Pay Disparity Between Typically Female Occupations and Other Jobs: A Bivariate Selectivity Approach." *Industrial and Labor Relations Review* 42: 624–39.

Stewart, Jay. 1998. "Has Job Mobility Increased? Evidence from the Current Population Survey: 1975–1995." Working Paper No. 308. Washington, DC: US Bureau of Labor Statistics.

Stinson, John F. Jr. 1997. "New Data on Multiple Jobholding Available from the CPS." *Monthly Labor Review* March: 3–8.

Troske, Kenneth R. 1998. "The Worker-Establishment Characteristics Database." In *Labor Statistics Measurement Issues*, eds John Haltiwanger, Marilyn Manser, and Robert Topel, pp. 371–404. Chicago: University of Chicago Press, 1998.

13 Are Affirmative Action hires less qualified?

Evidence from employer–employee data on new hires

(with Harry J. Holzer)

Introduction

Affirmative Action policies have always been controversial, largely because of the allegation that they cause employers to give preference in hiring to less-qualified minorities or females over more-qualified white males. Survey evidence suggests that, even among whites, there is widespread public support for outlawing employment discrimination and also for policies that compensate the past victims of discrimination through targeted education, job training, and recruitment efforts. At the same time, policies that give "preference" in employment (or university admissions) to less-qualified members of these groups are strongly opposed (e.g. Lipset and Schneider, 1978; Bobo and Smith, 1994).[1]

Similarly, many critics of Affirmative Action policies support strong enforcement of EEO laws and even compensatory recruitment and training, but argue that the alleged preferences for less-qualified minorities and females in most current Affirmative Action practices create labor market inefficiencies and/or inequities.[2] In contrast, proponents of Affirmative Action policies frequently argue that labor market discrimination continues to be prevalent, despite EEO laws.[3] They also argue that gaps between different groups in relative qualifications measured by educational attainment, experience, etc., likely reflect past or current discrimination (Bergmann, 1989), and that such qualifications are weak predictors of actual performance on the job, which itself may be difficult to measure, especially in the short term.[4] In this view, the efficiency costs of preferential policies are considered very small or even negative.

To a large extent the debate over Affirmative Action hinges on whether labor markets in the absence of Affirmative Action are better characterized by competition or by discrimination. If Affirmative Action is used in establishments that otherwise would discriminate in hiring, there would not necessarily be any shortfall in the qualifications of minorities or females hired there relative to white males. In fact, if more qualified minorities and women were being passed up because of discrimination, Affirmative Action could lead to the hiring of *more productive* minorities and females. On the other hand, if Affirmative Action is imposed on (or chosen by) firms with no such discriminatory practices, it could lead to the hiring of employees with weaker qualifications or performance, since such firms were presumably already hiring the best-qualified individuals regardless of race or sex.

The likelihood that Affirmative Action leads to the hiring of less-qualified minorities and women may be reinforced because the educational attainment of minorities (especially among Hispanics) continues to lag behind that of whites, as do their average test scores (Mare, 1995; Neal and Johnson, 1996). These shortfalls in average qualifications might reflect past discrimination in the labor market or current discrimination in the housing market, either of which could lead to lower schooling attainment of young people through their effects on family incomes or neighborhood quality (Yinger, 1995; Cutler and Glaeser, 1997). Of course, as we emphasize later, education (and test scores) may represent only a narrow set of relevant job qualifications. Regardless, lower distributions of qualifications among some groups of minorities or women would make it more likely that Affirmative Action would lead to less-qualified minority or female hires in both discriminating and nondiscriminating companies. Thus, evidence on the presence or absence of discrimination in labor markets is an important component of the Affirmative Action debate, but is not sufficient to fully evaluate the policy.

Given these considerations, the current debate on Affirmative Action turns heavily on the existence and empirical magnitudes of shortfalls in qualifications and job performance of women and minorities hired under Affirmative Action. Yet despite the intensity of the viewpoints held, the evidence to date on this issue remains quite thin. To the best of our knowledge, the only systematic empirical study of the effects of Affirmative Action on productivity is that of Jonathan Leonard (1984). He estimates production functions using state-by-two-digit industry data in manufacturing, in which the fractions of employment accounted for by minorities/females and by federal contractors (who are typically required to have Affirmative Action plans) appear as independent variables. But the usefulness of this approach is limited by the highly aggregated nature of the data and its focus only on manufacturing.[5] Also, Badgett (1995) provides more qualitative evidence on the effects of Affirmative Action on the qualifications of minority hires from a case study of a large manufacturing firm, and concludes that—at this company—Affirmative Action did not result in lower-quality hires, based in part on evidence that upper-level management promoted Affirmative Action as a means of finding the best employees.

In this chapter, we provide what we believe to be the first survey-based micro-level empirical evidence on the relative qualifications of workers hired under Affirmative Action. Using data on new hires collected from establishments, we are able to compare the qualifications of women or minorities hired under Affirmative Action to those of white men in comparable jobs, and to those of women or minorities or white men hired in establishments that do not use Affirmative Action. Because workers' qualifications and performance are multifaceted and difficult to measure, we take a broad-ranging approach, focusing on a variety of variables related to both qualifications and job performance.

The data

The sample

The data we use are from a survey that was administered to about 800 establishments in each of four metropolitan areas: Atlanta, Boston, Detroit, and Los Angeles (see Holzer, 1995, 1996, and 1998).[6] The survey was administered between June of 1992 and May of 1994, as the national economy was recovering from the recession of the early 1990s.[7]

The survey was administered over the phone, and averaged roughly 35 minutes in length. The sample of establishments was drawn from two sources: (1) a listing of establishments and their phone numbers provided by Survey Sampling, Inc. (SSI), which is drawn primarily from local phone directories and supplemented by other sources; and (2) the establishments of employment of respondents in the household surveys that were administered in each of these four metropolitan areas. The latter were drawn in order to generate a sample of "matched pairs" of individuals and establishments. For the establishments in the SSI part of the sample, the main respondent to the survey is the person who is responsible for hiring noncollege workers. For the sample drawn from the household survey, the respondent is the person responsible for hiring into the occupation of the household respondent.[8]

A number of steps were taken to ensure that the data could be used to draw inferences regarding the underlying population. Sample weights were generated to account for any differences in establishment characteristics that might be attributable to these different sampling strategies, so that we can pool data from these two sources. Despite the differences between these two sources, both were designed to generate employee-weighted samples of establishments. For the SSI sample, this was accomplished by *ex ante* stratification of the sample based on establishment size, with the distribution of establishments chosen to approximate the distribution of employees across size categories in the workforce.[9] For the household-generated sample, the distribution of establishments should approximate the distribution of employment in the population by construction, at least when household respondents are sample-weighted.[10] Thus, no additional size-weighting of establishments is necessary with this sample. When focusing on the characteristics of each establishment's most recently filled job, the sample will provide extra weight to establishments that do a lot of hiring because of their size (but not because of high turnover).[11] The sample of new jobs should thus approximate the stock of available jobs.

The overall response rate for the survey was 67 percent for establishments that were successfully screened.[12] This response rate compares favorably with other phone surveys of employers (e.g. US Department of Labor, 1993). In addition, because we have some measured characteristics of establishments in the SSI sample that did not respond to the survey (i.e. establishment size, industry, and location), we could check for differences in response rates across these observable categories that might generate sample selection bias. Few significant differences were found in response rates across the categories measured by these variables, and response rates for all categories were within 0.10 of the mean.

Comparisons of the industries and sizes of establishments in our sample were also made with the most recently available published data from *County Business Patterns* for these metropolitan areas, and the two samples appeared to be quite comparable. Finally, we compared the distributions of occupations among our most recently filled jobs with those in the 1990 Census of Population for these areas, and with the distributions of occupations and worker characteristics among all employees in our establishments, to see whether or not the sample of "marginal" employees (i.e. new hires) differs greatly from the "average." While we found only minor evidence of such differences, our results speak more directly to qualifications of new hires.

The Affirmative Action variable

The variables used in this study are primarily drawn from survey questions on the last job filled and the worker hired into that job. In particular, respondents were asked whether or not "Affirmative Action or Equal Employment Opportunity Law play any role in your recruiting activities for this position," and also whether or not these factors "play any role in whom you actually hire."[13] The measure we use for Affirmative Action in this chapter is the latter, because lower qualifications or performance are more likely when Affirmative Action is used in hiring rather than in recruiting. In addition, data on Affirmative Action in hiring are obviously more pertinent to who actually gets hired, which is the focus of the debate.

Given the wording of the question, there is some ambiguity over whether we are picking up the effects of Affirmative Action or EEO law more generally. In addition, the variety of reasons a respondent might indicate use of Affirmative Action raises questions about the exogeneity of the variation in Affirmative Action across establishments. All firms with fifteen or more employees are bound by Title VII of the Civil Rights Act, which covers just over 80 percent of the private sector workforce (Bloch, 1994). On the other hand, explicit Affirmative Action plans are mandatory only for employers with federal contracts and fifty or more employees, or a contract worth $50,000 or more. In our sample, 60 percent of establishments report the use of some kind of Affirmative Action in recruiting, and 45 percent in hiring. Although our self-reported measure is not explicitly based on actual contractor status, the fraction of units reporting Affirmative Action and some of their characteristics are similar to what Leonard (1989) found regarding federal contractor status among firms required to file EEO-1 reports. Specifically, 60 percent of his sample were contractors who were therefore bound by Executive Orders mandating the use of Affirmative Action; and the use of Affirmative Action in Leonard's data was highly correlated with employer size (at the firm level, in his case), as it is in our data. On balance, then, we believe that our measure of Affirmative Action is likely to be related to contractor status—which is to some extent exogenous—and is therefore much more likely to be capturing explicit Affirmative Action in hiring, rather than mere compliance with EEO law.[14]

In addition to the role of contractor status, establishments or firms may behave *as if* they have an explicit Affirmative Action plan, even when they do not.[15] This might arise if management feels some pressure to improve the hiring and promotion of protected groups. We presume this is especially likely for establishments belonging to firms with 100 or more employees, which are required to file EEO-1 forms with the government. Although only compliance with EEO laws is required of firms without federal contracts, those who file EEO-1 reports may engage in Affirmative Action hiring to avoid litigation or other problems that could be triggered by these reports; as noted by Bloch (1994), employment discrimination suits can stem from charges brought by the EEOC based on review of EEO-1 reports, even without a single complainant. In this case, establishments belonging to such firms would likely report the use of Affirmative Action in hiring, and their use of Affirmative Action would be exogenously determined by their size and the practice of federal monitoring.

Of course, there may be other reasons why employers might report that they are using Affirmative Action besides their status as federal contractors or their size. In addition to requirements for contractors, explicit plans may be implemented by the courts as a remedy for a finding of past discrimination (see the discussion in Epstein, 1992, ch. 19), or implemented by companies as a deterrent to claims of discrimination under Title VII (see Badgett, 1995) or to increase workplace diversity for other reasons. These latter plans are voluntarily chosen, and have been permitted by the courts if they are based on a specific plan, correct a previous imbalance, protect the interests of non-Affirmative Action candidates, and will end when specific goals are met (Gold, 1993). We know of no actual count of the number of such plans that actually exist, and suspect that the number may be fairly small; but their existence at least raises the possibility that an employer's decision to use Affirmative Action may be endogenous with respect to other outcomes that we are measuring, an issue we explore further in the section "Descriptive statistics on differences in establishment, job, and employee characteristics by use of Affirmative Action."

Other variables used in the study

The other job-specific questions include whether or not a college degree is required for the job; whether or not high school, specific previous experience, vocational training, or references are each required;[16] whether each of a set of tasks (dealing with customers directly, reading or writing paragraphs, arithmetic, or computer use) is performed daily on the job; and a set of one-digit occupational dummies. The characteristics of the last worker hired include race/ethnicity, sex, age, and educational attainment, as well as information on wages, promotions, and a supervisor's performance rating. Establishment-specific characteristics include establishment size, percent of workforce covered by collective bargaining, one-digit industry dummy variables, and dummy variables for location within the central city of the MSA. We also use variables for the race and sex of the main respondent to the survey and the worker's supervisor, and the racial composition of the establishment's customer pool, to control as much as possible for determinants of racial or gender preferences among survey respondents or other agents.

Descriptive statistics on differences in establishment, job, and employee characteristics by use of Affirmative Action

Descriptive statistics

We begin in Table 13.1 by providing simple descriptive information on differences between worker-establishment matches in which Affirmative Action is used in hiring and those in which it is not. Looking first at demographic characteristics

Table 13.1 Descriptive statistics[a]

	Affirmative Action used in hiring		Affirmative Action not used in hiring	
	Mean (1)	Std. error (2)	Mean (3)	Std. error (4)
Worker demographic characteristics				
White male	0.24	0.01	0.30	0.01
White female	0.40	0.02	0.33	0.01
Black male	0.09	0.01	0.08	0.01
Black female	0.08	0.01	0.09	0.01
Hispanic male	0.07	0.01	0.10	0.01
Hispanic female	0.06	0.01	0.06	0.01
Asian	0.06	0.01	0.03	0.005
Worker education				
Dropout	0.03	0.01	0.06	0.01
GED	0.002	0.001	0.003	0.001
High school graduate	0.31	0.01	0.40	0.01
Trade school or some college	0.23	0.01	0.24	0.01
AA degree	0.04	0.01	0.04	0.01
Bachelor's degree	0.27	0.01	0.18	0.01
Some graduate school	0.01	0.003	0.03	0.004
Graduate degree	0.10	0.01	0.06	0.01
Job requirements				
High school degree	0.85	0.01	0.74	0.01
College degree	0.33	0.01	0.18	0.01
References	0.81	0.01	0.73	0.01
Vocational training	0.46	0.02	0.41	0.01
Specific experience	0.72	0.01	0.62	0.01
Customer contact	0.73	0.01	0.72	0.01
Reading/writing	0.75	0.01	0.65	0.01
Math	0.68	0.02	0.66	0.01
Computer	0.63	0.02	0.52	0.01

Table 13.1 Continued

	Affirmative Action used in hiring		Affirmative Action not used in hiring	
	Mean (1)	Std. error (2)	Mean (3)	Std. error (4)
Occupation				
Management/professional	0.30	0.01	0.25	0.01
Sales	0.13	0.01	0.14	0.01
Clerical	0.32	0.01	0.25	0.01
Agricultural	0.01	0.002	0.01	0.002
Crafts	0.04	0.01	0.09	0.01
Operative	0.08	0.01	0.11	0.01
Labor	0.03	0.005	0.04	0.01
Service	0.09	0.01	0.12	0.01
Establishment characteristics				
Employer size	572.5	47.8	177.0	17.3
Median	100.0	—	30.0	—
Central city	0.26	0.01	0.27	0.01
Noncentral city MSA	0.16	0.01	0.15	0.01
Percentage of workforce covered by collective bargaining	19.5	1.11	13.7	0.84
Percentage of customers black	19.0	0.73	16.8	0.60
Percentage of customers Hispanic	13.9	0.76	13.2	0.62
Construction	0.01	0.003	0.02	0.004
TCPU	0.07	0.01	0.05	0.01
Wholesale trade	0.06	0.01	0.08	0.01
Retail trade	0.11	0.01	0.18	0.01
FIRE	0.08	0.01	0.07	0.01
Services	0.46	0.02	0.37	0.01
Public	0.02	0.004	0.01	0.003
Nondurables manufacturing	0.10	0.01	0.09	0.01
Durables manufacturing	0.10	0.01	0.12	0.01
Respondent and supervisor characteristics				
Respondent's sex different from worker's sex	0.50	0.02	0.39	0.01
Respondent's race different from worker's race	0.37	0.02	0.36	0.01
Supervisor's sex different from worker's sex	0.62	0.02	0.68	0.01
Supervisor's race different from worker's race	0.30	0.01	0.28	0.01

Note

a There are 1,033 observations in columns (1) and (2), and 1,480 observations in columns (3) and (4). There are fewer observations for age, education, percentage of customers in each race group, and the demographic characteristics of the supervisor and respondent, because of missing data. In the following tables, a dummy variable for missing data on these variables is included, and the variables are set to zero.

of recent hires, we see that the largest absolute difference between hires in which Affirmative Action plays a role and those in which it does not is between white males and females, where the proportion of recent hires accounted for by these groups is 0.06 lower and 0.07 higher, respectively, when Affirmative Action is used in hiring. The proportions of recent hires among the other demographic groups are not very different between Affirmative Action and non-Affirmative Action hiring; the proportions of black females and Hispanic males are actually slightly lower. Of course, these are univariate comparisons, and the influence of Affirmative Action on hiring by demographic group may change once account is taken of establishment, job, and other individual characteristics.[17]

The second panel of Table 13.1 provides information on worker education, while the third panel provides descriptive information on job requirements for the jobs into which the recent hiring occurred. We see that workers hired under Affirmative Action tend to be more educated, and that skill requirements are higher for these jobs for each of the requirements included in the survey. These results suggest that we may have to compare qualifications of women and minorities relative to white males *within* the subset of establishments using Affirmative Action; otherwise, we might incorrectly conclude that Affirmative Action hires are more qualified.

Consistent with the above results, the fourth panel in Table 13.1 reveals that a greater proportion of hiring in establishments using Affirmative Action is into management/professional and clerical jobs than into blue-collar or service jobs.[18] Of course, these results do not indicate whether Affirmative Action hiring is used more for such occupations, or whether Affirmative Action leads to more hiring into such occupations. Given these questions, it is unclear whether it is always appropriate to control for occupation (or required skills), which generates only within-job estimates of Affirmative Action effects.

The fifth panel of Table 13.1 provides descriptive information on establishment characteristics, broken down by whether or not Affirmative Action was used in recent hiring. Establishments using Affirmative Action are much larger, have a significantly higher proportion of the workforce covered by collective bargaining, and are significantly more likely to be in the services industry. These establishments also have higher percentages of black and Hispanic customers.

Finally, the sixth panel of Table 13.1 reports on the demographic characteristics of supervisors and respondents to the survey. We see that respondents—who are responsible for hiring—are more likely to be the opposite sex from the new hire in establishments that report using Affirmative Action in hiring, although this is not true of supervisors. In the analyses that follow, we control for the possibility that these characteristics of respondents or supervisors affect the outcomes over which respondents or supervisors exert some control—such as promotions and performance ratings.

The effects of Affirmative Action on hiring of women and minorities

Table 13.2 presents a multivariate descriptive analysis of the relationship between Affirmative Action hiring and the demographic group of the recent hire, based on logit or multinomial logit estimates accounting—in different specifications— for differences in establishment characteristics, in the occupational distribution of hires, and in job requirements.[19] In columns (1) and (1′) the dependent variable is

Table 13.2 Logit and multinomial logit estimates of effects of Affirmative Action on demographic group of hire[a]

	(1)	(1')	(2)	(2')
Minority or white female	0.027	0.036	—	—
	(0.019)	(0.019)		
White female	—	—	0.077	0.051
			(0.023)	(0.025)
Black male	—	—	0.002	0.015
			(0.011)	(0.011)
Black female	—	—	−0.014	−0.010
			(0.009)	(0.009)
Hispanic male	—	—	−0.016	−0.003
			(0.007)	(0.006)
Hispanic female	—	—	−0.006	−0.003
			(0.008)	(0.007)
White male	−0.042	−0.051	−0.060	−0.071
	(0.019)	(0.019)	(0.022)	(0.025)
Occupation and job requirement controls	No	Yes	No	Yes

Note

a The table reports partial derivatives of the probability of each outcome with respect to the Affirmative Action dummy variable, evaluated at the weighted means. Standard errors calculated from a linear approximation to these derivatives treating the means as fixed are reported in parentheses. Columns (1) and (1') are based on a logit model, and columns (2) and (2') on a multinomial logit model. There are 2,513 observations. All specifications include dummy variables for city and year and establishment controls. Asian hires are also included as an outcome, but results are not reported. In columns (1) and (1'), "minority" refers to blacks and Hispanics. Estimates are weighted.

a dummy variable for whether the hire was a woman or minority, and in columns (2) and (2') the dependent variable is a categorical indicator for the more-detailed demographic group of the hire. In columns (1) and (2) controls for city and year of hire, as well as establishment characteristics (listed in Table 13.1), are included. The probability that a minority or female was hired is estimated to be significantly higher, by 0.03, when Affirmative Action is used in hiring.[20] Columns (1') and (2') add controls for the occupations and job requirements listed in Table 13.1. The association between Affirmative Action and hiring of minorities or females strengthens slightly when we include these controls. The estimates in column (2') indicate that the probabilities that white females and black males are hired, relative to the probability that a white male is hired, are higher when Affirmative Action is used in hiring (significantly so only for white females); the hiring of black females and Hispanic males and females appears to be unaffected.[21] Comparing effects on probabilities to the means in Table 13.1 for each group, we see that Affirmative Action is associated with increases of about 15 percent in the probabilities of hiring white women and black men. On the other hand, the last row indicates that the probability that a white male is hired is lower by about 20 percent under

Affirmative Action.[22] Presumably, most of these white males are then hired in establishments not using Affirmative Action; these establishments likely pay less, among other reasons because they are smaller.[23]

These results, coupled with evidence of strengthened enforcement activity in 1989 and especially in 1993 (Anderson, 1996), suggest that Affirmative Action has real consequences for hiring behavior. We next turn to the more contentious issue of the relative qualifications and performance of women and minorities hired under Affirmative Action.

Relative qualifications and performance of Affirmative Action hires

The empirical approach

Having documented the associations between Affirmative Action and hiring of minorities and women, we now turn to the question of whether Affirmative Action leads to the hiring of less-qualified women or minorities. Our approach is to estimate equations for Q, a measure of the qualifications or performance of the last worker hired, of the form:

$$
\begin{aligned}
Q_{ijk} = {} & \alpha W M_{ijk} \cdot (1 - AA_{jk}) + \beta D_{ijk} \cdot AA_{jk} + \gamma W M_{ijk} \cdot AA_{jk} \\
& + \delta D_{ijk} \cdot (1 - AA_{jk}) + \theta X_j + \lambda Z_k + \varepsilon_{ijk},
\end{aligned} \tag{1}
$$

where AA is a dummy variable indicating that Affirmative Action was used in hiring, WM is a dummy variable for white males, D is a set of dummy variables for each other demographic group considered, X is a set of job characteristics, and Z a set of establishment characteristics; i, j, and k denote the last worker hired, the most recent job filled, and the establishment. Note that we include separate intercepts for each demographic group distinguished by the Affirmative Action status of the establishment, and no common intercept.

This specification provides us with a number of potential comparisons for estimating the effects of Affirmative Action in hiring. One interesting comparison is between women or minority hires and white male hires in establishments using Affirmative Action. The difference in Q for this comparison, which is given by $(\beta - \gamma)$, addresses the question of whether Affirmative Action leads to hiring of women or minorities who are less qualified than the white male workers hired in similar establishments. A second interesting comparison is between women or minority hires in establishments using Affirmative Action and women or minority hires in establishments not using Affirmative Action, which is captured by the difference $(\beta - \delta)$. A third comparison is between women or minority hires in establishments using Affirmative Action and white male hires in establishments not using Affirmative Action, which is measured by $(\beta - \alpha)$. This comparison might pertain to white male workers who would otherwise have been hired in establishments using Affirmative Action had the policy not been in place.

We suspect that the first difference, $(\beta - \gamma)$, may be most relevant to the policy debate. However, there is the potential for misleading inferences to be drawn because of differences in skills or qualifications between women or minorities and white males that exist independently of Affirmative Action. For example, suppose that the estimate of $(\beta - \gamma)$ is a large negative number, indicating that women or minorities hired into establishments using Affirmative Action are less qualified than white males hired into similar establishments. However, there may be an economy-wide shortfall in qualifications of women or minorities relative to white males, in which case workers in non-Affirmative Action establishments should serve as a control group for overall differences between minorities or women and white men. For example, Hispanics may be perceived as less qualified or perform less well because of language barriers, regardless of whether the establishments into which they are hired use Affirmative Action. Then to estimate the independent effects of Affirmative Action on differences between white male and Hispanic workers, we subtract off any shortfall in qualifications attributable to language in establishments not using Affirmative Action, and ask instead whether the shortfall is *relatively larger* in establishments using Affirmative Action. In general, the shortfall in qualifications (or performance) in establishments not using Affirmative Action is measured by $(\delta - \alpha)$, leading to the difference-in-differences estimate of $(\beta - \gamma) - (\delta - \alpha)$.[24] Thus, critics of Affirmative Action may make a potential error if they base their criticisms only on observed shortfalls in qualifications at establishments using Affirmative Action, rather than the net difference in these shortfalls between the two sectors.

On the other hand, the assumption underlying the difference-in-differences estimation is that the policy does not affect the control group—in this case, establishments not using Affirmative Action. Under this assumption, $(\delta - \alpha)$ measures the difference between women or minorities and white males in the absence of Affirmative Action. However, this assumption would be invalid if Affirmative Action affects who is hired at all types of establishments, whether or not they use Affirmative Action. In particular, Affirmative Action could create or enlarge a shortfall in qualifications among women and minorities at both types of establishments—by drawing the most-qualified women and minorities into establishments using Affirmative Action, and pushing the least-qualified white males out of these establishments—in which case the difference-in-differences estimate could understate or obscure the effect of Affirmative Action. As a simple example, suppose that initially establishment A employs some men with productivity (per unit of time) equal to 4 and other men with productivity of 3, while establishment B employs some women with productivity of 2, and other women with productivity of 1. After implementing Affirmative Action, establishment A hires the more productive women, and fires the less productive men, who are hired by establishment B. Thus, establishment A employs men with productivity of 4, and women with productivity of 2, while establishment B employs men with productivity of 3, and women with productivity of 1. In this case, Affirmative Action has led to the hiring of less-productive women, and $(\beta - \gamma)$, which equals -2, reflects this. But because $(\delta - \alpha)$ also equals -2, the difference-in-differences estimator gives

Table 13.3 Alternative estimators of differentials in qualifications or performance associated with Affirmative Action

---

Equation
$$Q_{ijk} = \alpha WM_{ijk} \cdot (1 - AA_{jk}) + \beta D_{ijk} \cdot AA_{jk} + \gamma WM_{ijk} \cdot AA_{jk}$$
$$+ \delta D_{ijk} \cdot (1 - AA_{jk}) + \theta X_j + \lambda Z_k + \varepsilon_{ijk}$$

Simple differences
$\beta - \gamma$ = woman/minority AA hire vs. white male AA hire
$\beta - \delta$ = woman/minority AA hire vs. woman/minority non-AA hire
$\beta - \alpha$ = woman/minority AA hire vs. white male non-AA hire

Difference-in-differences
$(\beta - \gamma) - (\delta - \alpha) = (\beta - \delta) - (\gamma - \alpha)$
= (woman/minority AA hire vs. white male AA hire)
  −(woman/minority non-AA hire vs. white male non-AA hire)
= (woman/minority AA hire vs. woman/minority non-AA hire)
  −(white male AA hire vs. white male non-AA hire)

---

no indication that Affirmative Action led establishment A to hire less-productive women over more-productive men.[25] Although this is a contrived example, it illustrates why the simple difference may be preferable to the difference-in-differences estimator. Throughout, we report both. Table 13.3 summarizes the alternative estimates we present.

Table 13.4 presents simple means for the dependent variables we analyze, by demographic group and whether the firm reports using Affirmative Action. This table is useful when examining the estimates of equation (1) in the tables that follow, since it provides information on the levels of the dependent variables for each of these groups. In addition, the table is useful in providing an illustration of our empirical approach. Consider, for example, educational levels of black men vs. white men. If we simply look at firms reporting using Affirmative Action, the educational difference is -1.39 years ($13.22 - 14.60$). This corresponds to $(\beta - \gamma)$ in equation (1). Note, though, that the educational attainment of black men also falls short in the non-Affirmative Action sector, by 0.89 years, which corresponds to $(\delta - \alpha)$ in equation (1). Thus, the difference-in-differences estimate, which measures how much *greater* the shortfall is among firms using Affirmative Action, is -0.5 ($-1.39 - (-0.89)$). Of course, in the estimations that follow, control variables are introduced to remove the influence of confounding factors; consequently, here we do not go through the whole set of estimated differences.

There are three potential econometric problems in estimating equation (1). First, the differentials associated with Affirmative Action may reflect unmeasured job or establishment characteristics that differ across establishments that use Affirmative Action in hiring and hire minorities or women, and establishments that use Affirmative Action but do not hire minorities or women—that is, unobserved characteristics that vary within the subset of establishments using Affirmative Action in such a way as to be correlated with minority or female hiring. Without data on multiple hires from different demographic groups for the same job in the same establishment, we must simply make the assumption that unobserved job

Table 13.4 Means for dependent variables by demographic characteristics and use of Affirmative Action[a]

	Jobs filled using Affirmative Action (1)	Jobs filled not using Affirmative Action (2)
Educational level		
White male	14.60	13.66
White female	14.29	13.63
Black male	13.21	12.77
Black female	13.22	12.70
Hispanic male	12.03	13.31
Hispanic female	12.81	12.50
Less than reported education requirement		
White male	0.048	0.033
White female	0.056	0.055
Black male	0.089	0.023
Black female	0.128	0.024
Hispanic male	0.065	0.042
Hispanic female	0.106	0.034
Log starting wage		
White male	2.38	2.36
White female	2.28	2.20
Black male	2.20	1.98
Black female	2.10	1.92
Hispanic male	2.05	2.10
Hispanic female	2.12	2.00
Log current wage		
White male	2.43	2.42
White female	2.33	2.25
Black male	2.26	2.04
Black female	2.11	1.97
Hispanic male	2.12	2.15
Hispanic female	2.18	2.10
Promoted		
White male	0.060	0.101
White female	0.033	0.086
Black male	0.098	0.080
Black female	0.058	0.050
Hispanic male	0.094	0.048
Hispanic female	0.195	0.029
Performance rating — typical rating for job		
White male	3.05	3.50
White female	2.43	2.15
Black male	2.07	−0.06
Black female	5.33	−0.44
Hispanic male	−2.95	4.55
Hispanic female	1.86	0.83

Note

a Sample sizes are given in following tables with regression/logit analyses of dependent variables.

or establishment characteristics are not correlated with the Affirmative Action–demographic group interactions (e.g. $D{\cdot}AA$) as well as with qualifications or performance, in order to identify relative differentials in qualifications or performance among minorities or women hired under Affirmative Action.

Second, if the decision to use Affirmative Action is partly endogenous—as discussed earlier—then $D{\cdot}AA$ may be correlated with the error term. For example, if establishments facing smaller skill differentials between minorities and females, on the one hand, and white males, on the other, are most likely to embrace such hiring (since they may face lower costs from using Affirmative Action), our estimates may be biased in the direction of finding no shortfall in qualifications among women or minorities hired under Affirmative Action, relative to the estimates we would obtain from an exogenously imposed policy. Alternatively, if establishments that voluntarily adopt Affirmative Action tend to be those whose owners or managers are favorably disposed toward women or minorities, we might expect higher ratings of women or minorities in such establishments, leading to a positive correlation between the error term and the $D{\cdot}AA$ interactions, and hence bias against finding that women or minorities hired under Affirmative Action perform worse on the job. However, we argued earlier that it appears that much of the variation in reported use of Affirmative Action in our data is induced by policy and therefore likely to be largely exogenous. Nonetheless, toward the end of the chapter we present some separate estimates for firms with less than 50 or less than 100 employees. As discussed earlier, federal regulations make both of these employment levels points at which the actual use of Affirmative Action is likely to increase, so the use of Affirmative Action is more likely to be exogenous above these cutoffs than below. Comparisons of estimates between samples of smaller and larger establishments should thus indicate the relative importance of any such endogeneity.

Finally, the estimates we obtain are informative even if one views our estimates as reflecting in part endogenous variation in Affirmative Action. In particular, we can still draw inferences regarding Affirmative Action as it is used in practice, which is an important input into the policy debate, because we know little about differences in hiring under Affirmative Action. However, drawing conclusions regarding changes in Affirmative Action from our evidence requires that one interpret the variation in reported use of Affirmative Action as exogenous.

Third, as discussed earlier, there is some ambiguity in the classification of establishments using Affirmative Action. Though we believe it is small, measurement error from misclassification is likely to bias the results toward finding no effect of Affirmative Action. Since some of our results point to no effect, the results must be interpreted cautiously, pending development of superior data sources to re-examine some of the questions we consider in this chapter.

Educational qualifications

The qualification we can most easily identify with workers is their education. Table 13.5 reports alternative simple differences and difference-in-differences estimates for years of education of the last worker hired. The estimates in Panel A

Table 13.5 OLS estimates for educational level of last hire[a]

AA hire	Difference relative to			Difference-in-differences
	White male, AA hire (1)	Same demographic group, non-AA hire (2)	White male, non-AA hire (3)	(4)
A. Establishment controls only				
White female	−0.48	0.45	0.19	−0.23
	(0.16)	(0.13)	(0.14)	(0.20)
Black male	−1.47	0.30	−0.80	−0.38
	(0.23)	(0.27)	(0.22)	(0.31)
Black female	−1.72	0.26	−1.05	−0.42
	(0.24)	(0.27)	(0.23)	(0.31)
Hispanic male	−2.48	−0.96	−1.81	−1.63
	(0.26)	(0.28)	(0.25)	(0.32)
Hispanic female	−2.49	−0.20	−1.81	−0.87
	(0.28)	(0.32)	(0.27)	(0.35)
B. Occupation and job requirement controls added				
White female	−0.65	0.22	−0.28	−0.15
	(0.14)	(0.11)	(0.12)	(0.17)
Black male	−0.77	0.24	−0.40	−0.13
	(0.20)	(0.23)	(0.19)	(0.27)
Black female	−1.32	0.18	−0.95	−0.19
	(0.21)	(0.23)	(0.20)	(0.27)
Hispanic male	−1.51	−0.55	−1.14	−0.92
	(0.23)	(0.24)	(0.22)	(0.28)
Hispanic female	−2.00	−0.46	−1.63	−0.83
	(0.24)	(0.27)	(0.23)	(0.30)

Note

a There are 2,381 observations. Standard errors are reported in parentheses. All specifications include dummy variables for city and year and establishment controls, as well as dummy variables and interactions for Asian males and females. In Panel B educational requirements are not included. There are fewer observations than in the previous tables because of missing data on the recent hire's actual schooling. The educational variable is coded as follows: drop out (10 years); GED (11 years); high school graduate (12 years); trade school or some college (13 years); Associate's degree (14 years); Bachelor's degree (16 years); some graduate school (17 years); and graduate degree (18 years). Estimates are weighted. The difference-in-differences estimates in column (4) correspond to either of the following two equivalent relative comparisons: (woman/minority AA hire vs. white male AA hire) − (woman/minority non-AA hire vs. white male non-AA hire); or (woman/minority AA hire vs. woman/minority non-AA hire) − (white male AA hire vs. white male non-AA hire). A relevant difference-in-differences estimate with respect to the estimates in column (3) is (woman/minority AA hire vs. white male non-AA hire) − (woman/minority non-AA hire vs. white male non-AA hire). This estimate corresponds to those in column (2).

are based on specifications that include only city and year dummy variables and establishment characteristics as control variables. The estimates in column (1) measure $(\beta - \gamma)$, the differences between women or minorities and white males hired at establishments using Affirmative Action. For all five groups, the educational level of women or minority Affirmative Action hires is significantly lower than that of white males hired into similar establishments; the differential is less than one-half year for white females, but about one and one-half years for blacks, and two and one-half years for Hispanics. However, the estimates of $(\beta - \alpha)$ in column (3) indicate that these educational shortfalls also appear—although to a lesser extent—between women and minorities hired in establishments using Affirmative Action, and white males hired in establishments not using Affirmative Action. At the same time, the estimates in column (2) indicate that, with the exception of Hispanic males, there are negligible differences between women and minorities in establishments using Affirmative Action and in establishments not using Affirmative Action. The combined evidence implies that the educational shortfalls in column (1) may overstate the shortfalls that can be attributed to Affirmative Action hiring, if the differences in the establishments not using Affirmative Action reflect overall differences that would occur in the absence of Affirmative Action hiring at any establishment. This is reflected in the difference-in-differences estimates in column (4), which indicate considerably smaller educational shortfalls of women and minorities attributable to Affirmative Action hiring. The differentials for white females and blacks are small and relatively insignificant, while only those for Hispanics (especially men) remain large and significant.

In Panel B we present similar estimates adding controls for occupation and job requirements, looking at differences in qualifications within more narrowly defined jobs. The most relevant policy question probably concerns the relative skills of individuals hired to do the same job. If the educational shortfalls of some groups of minorities or women are much smaller with the occupation and job controls than they are in Panel A, this would suggest that minorities or women hired under Affirmative Action are matched to less-demanding jobs that are appropriate for their lower skill levels. On the other hand, occupation and job requirements likely reflect the characteristics of the worker hired as well as the job, in which case we may be over-controlling by including them as independent variables; that is, Affirmative Action may lead to the hiring of less-skilled women or minorities who are then allocated to less-demanding jobs. Given these ambiguities regarding the choice of specification, we think it best to present both types of evidence.

In Panel B the estimated education differentials between women or minority workers hired by establishments using Affirmative Action and other workers are a bit smaller for most groups, while for Hispanic males they are substantially smaller. This implies that only Hispanic males are allocated to significantly less demanding jobs when hired under Affirmative Action. However, the overall conclusion is the same; the simple difference estimates of $(\beta - \gamma)$ indicate educational shortfalls among women and minorities hired under Affirmative Action, while the difference-in-differences estimates of $(\beta - \gamma) - (\delta - \alpha)$ reflect a shortfall only for Hispanics.

The evidence from the difference-in-differences estimation of lower qualifications of Hispanics hired under Affirmative Action may appear inconsistent with the results in Table 13.2 suggesting that the hiring of Hispanics is not boosted by Affirmative Action. However, we examined data on the percentage of applicants at the establishment accounted for by each demographic group, as reported by the respondent. These data reveal that, in establishments using Affirmative Action, the percentage of applications from blacks is higher (by roughly 2 percentage points) than in establishments not using Affirmative Action, while this percentage is lower for Hispanics (by 0.8 percentage point). Given their higher overall skill needs and lower application rates from this group, establishments that use Affirmative Action may have to be less selective in hiring Hispanic applicants to hire the same proportion of Hispanics as establishments not using Affirmative Action. One reason for the lower application rate of Hispanics at establishments using Affirmative Action might be that Hispanic immigrants are more likely to work in smaller establishments that are owned or operated by co-ethnics, especially in Los Angeles. On the other hand, Table 13.2 suggested that hiring of white women and of black men is boosted by Affirmative Action, so the results in column (1) of Table 13.5 indicating lower qualifications of these groups are more easily reconciled.

An alternative approach to the issue of educational qualifications is to ask whether minorities or women hired under Affirmative Action are less qualified relative to the educational requirements of the job, rather than simply relative to white males. We refer to this outcome as indicating that the employee is "underqualified," rather than "less qualified." For example, if black men are sufficiently qualified for the jobs they hold, while white males are either overqualified or allocated to more demanding jobs, then the criticism of Affirmative Action on the grounds of lower educational levels of black men would be blunted. Conversely, it is possible that women or minorities hired under Affirmative Action are more underqualified relative to the jobs that they hold.[26]

To examine this question, we use information on the educational requirement for the job reported by the employer, and estimate logit models for whether the individual hired had less than the reported required amount of education. There is some ambiguity in the coding of this dependent variable, since employers were asked whether a college degree was required, without specifying whether this was an Associate's or Bachelor's degree. We assume that they were referring to the latter.[27]

The results are reported in Table 13.6; the control variables are the same as in Table 13.5. In column (1) in Panel A, the positive signs of the estimates indicate that for all groups, women or minorities hired under Affirmative Action are relatively more likely to be underqualified than white males hired into establishments using Affirmative Action. The difference-in-differences estimates are quite similar, although because of increased standard errors the only significant evidence of underqualification of women or minorities hired under Affirmative Action is for black females. In Panel B, where we add the occupation and job controls, the evidence is similar (although slightly weaker); because this specification looks at education relative to educational requirements, it is not surprising that controlling for other job characteristics has relatively little influence on the estimates.[28] The fact that we find no evidence of higher probabilities that Hispanics hired under Affirmative Action are more likely to be underqualified is consistent with the conclusion we drew from Table 13.5 that such Hispanic hires are allocated to less-demanding jobs. Conversely, the evidence for black females in Tables 13.5 and 13.6 suggests that this allocation does not occur for them.

Table 13.6 Logit estimates for probability that last hire had less than reported education requirement[a]

AA hire	Difference relative to			Difference-in-differences
	White male, AA hire (1)	Same demographic group, non-AA hire (2)	White male, non-AA hire (3)	(4)
A. Establishment controls only				
White female	0.011	−0.0002	0.023	−0.011
	(0.014)	(0.012)	(0.014)	(0.020)
Black male	0.029	0.045	0.040	0.034
	(0.019)	(0.028)	(0.018)	(0.032)
Black female	0.051	0.069	0.062	0.057
	(0.018)	(0.026)	(0.018)	(0.031)
Hispanic male	0.009	0.009	0.020	−0.002
	(0.023)	(0.025)	(0.022)	(0.030)
Hispanic female	0.031	0.045	0.042	0.034
	(0.021)	(0.029)	(0.021)	(0.033)
B. Occupation and job requirement controls added				
White female	0.005	−0.001	0.018	−0.014
	(0.014)	(0.011)	(0.013)	(0.018)
Black male	0.029	0.036	0.042	0.023
	(0.018)	(0.026)	(0.017)	(0.030)
Black female	0.045	0.058	0.058	0.045
	(0.017)	(0.024)	(0.017)	(0.028)
Hispanic male	0.018	0.011	0.031	−0.002
	(0.021)	(0.023)	(0.021)	(0.027)
Hispanic female	0.027	0.035	0.040	0.022
	(0.020)	(0.026)	(0.019)	(0.030)

Note

a There are 2,027 observations in both panels. The table reports partial derivatives of the probability of being underqualified, evaluated at the weighted means. Standard errors calculated from a linear approximation to these derivatives treating the means as fixed are reported in parentheses. All specifications include dummy variables for city and year and establishment controls, as well as dummy variables and interactions for Asians. The dependent variable is coded as 1 if the job requires a college degree and the hire has less than a college degree, or the job requires a high school degree and the hire has less than a high school degree (including a GED). We assume that a required college degree refers to a Bachelor's degree. In Panel B the educational requirements are not included. The sample is smaller than in the previous table because data on the education requirement for the job is needed. Estimates are weighted.

Job-related outcomes

The results in the preceding sections provide some evidence of relatively lower educational or skill qualifications of women or minorities hired under Affirmative Action. But there remains the question of whether the shortfalls in these two observable measures of qualifications imply inferior performance on the job. If they do not, then there is perhaps no reason to be concerned with the apparent lower qualifications of women or minorities hired under Affirmative Action.[29]

Consequently, in this subsection we look at three employment outcomes that should be related to actual job performance: starting wages, current wages, and promotions. Looking at this broader set of job-related outcomes is useful for another important reason—namely, educational levels and job requirements are only a subset of the many dimensions along which a worker's qualifications can be measured. Measures such as wages and promotions should, if they are related to productivity, provide more of a summary or "sufficient" statistic for a worker's qualifications. A potential objection, however, is that the same pressures that may lead to the hiring of less-qualified workers under Affirmative Action may also lead employers to pay and promote women and minorities at a rate that is more than commensurate with their productivity, in which case wages and promotions would not be useful as measures of relative qualifications or job performance.[30]

To obtain a more independent measure of worker performance in these jobs, we use a rating of the worker's job performance (measured on a scale of 1–100) elicited from the person interviewed.[31] The survey also asked for the supervisor's rating of the typical new hire into the job, which lets us standardize across establishments and jobs by looking at the deviation of the new hire's performance rating from the usual or typical rating. If the performance ratings were the product of a formal evaluation procedure used to set wages and determine promotions, the ratings might be contaminated in the same way as data on wages and promotions (as employers might feel constrained to manipulate performance ratings to back up their wage and promotion decisions). However, these ratings are informal and not explicitly related to actual pay and promotion decisions, and survey respondents were promised full confidentiality. Therefore, the ratings seem likely to provide an unbiased measure of a worker's true job performance. Although even the standardized performance ratings are likely to be measured with error, if the measurement error is random with respect to true performance and the independent variables, it should lead to larger standard errors of the estimated coefficients, but not to bias in the estimated magnitudes or signs of these coefficients. Thus, if we find positive rather than negative effects of Affirmative Action on these ratings, it would be difficult to interpret such findings as stemming solely from measurement error.

Wages

Regressions for logs of starting and current wages are reported in Panels A and B of Table 13.7. In addition to the establishment, occupation, and job requirement controls, we also add standard human capital controls (education and age to both sets of equations, and tenure to the equations for current wages).[32] As a means of assessing the reliability of the data, it is worth noting that wage differentials between women or minorities and white males in establishments not using Affirmative Action, which can be calculated from the estimates in column (3) minus the estimates in column (2), indicate significantly lower wages paid to women and minorities. The estimated differentials are -0.15 for white women, -0.16 for black men, -0.25 for black women, and -0.29 for Hispanic men and women.

Table 13.7 OLS estimates of log wage regressions, and promotion logits[a]

AA hire	Difference relative to			Difference-in-differences
	White male, AA hire (1)	Same demographic group, non-AA hire (2)	White male, non-AA hire (3)	(4)
A. Log starting wage				
White female	−0.10 (0.03)	−0.05 (0.02)	−0.20 (0.03)	0.05 (0.04)
Black male	0.03 (0.04)	0.09 (0.05)	−0.07 (0.04)	0.19 (0.06)
Black female	−0.14 (0.04)	0.01 (0.05)	−0.24 (0.04)	0.10 (0.06)
Hispanic male	−0.09 (0.05)	0.10 (0.05)	−0.19 (0.04)	0.19 (0.06)
Hispanic female	−0.23 (0.05)	−0.04 (0.06)	−0.33 (0.05)	0.05 (0.06)
B. Log current wage				
White female	−0.10 (0.03)	−0.04 (0.03)	−0.20 (0.03)	0.06 (0.04)
Black male	0.04 (0.05)	0.08 (0.05)	−0.06 (0.05)	0.18 (0.06)
Black female	−0.15 (0.05)	−0.01 (0.05)	−0.25 (0.05)	0.09 (0.06)
Hispanic male	−0.07 (0.05)	0.13 (0.05)	−0.17 (0.05)	0.23 (0.06)
Hispanic female	−0.20 (0.06)	−0.05 (0.06)	−0.30 (0.05)	0.05 (0.07)
C. Promotions				
White female	−0.019 (0.017)	−0.029 (0.014)	−0.038 (0.015)	−0.011 (0.020)
Black male	0.029 (0.023)	−0.003 (0.022)	0.010 (0.021)	0.016 (0.026)
Black female	0.025 (0.025)	0.015 (0.026)	0.007 (0.024)	0.033 (0.029)
Hispanic male	0.027 (0.025)	0.025 (0.024)	0.009 (0.023)	0.044 (0.028)
Hispanic female	0.073 (0.023)	0.108 (0.031)	0.054 (0.021)	0.127 (0.034)

Note

a There are 2,135 observations in Panels A and B, and 2,438 in Panel C. In Panels A and B, regression coefficients and standard errors are reported. Panel C reports partial derivatives of the probability of each outcome, evaluated at the weighted means; standard errors calculated from a linear approximation to these derivatives treating the means as fixed are reported in parentheses. All specifications include dummy variables for city and year, establishment, occupation, and job requirement controls, and controls for age and years of education, as well as dummy variables and interactions for Asian males and females. In addition, controls for tenure are included in the current wage and promotion specifications, and dummy variables for different race or sex of respondent or supervisor are included in the promotion specification only. Estimates are weighted.

Turning to the three alternative comparisons for women or minority workers in establishments using Affirmative Action, column (1) indicates that the wage differentials between these workers and white males in similar establishments are considerably smaller than the wage differentials in establishments not using Affirmative Action, noted earlier.[33] In fact, for black men the wage differential is erased. Because the wage differentials compared with white males in establishments not using Affirmative Action are somewhat larger, as reported in column (3), and the differences between women and minorities in the two types of establishments are small, as reported in column (2), the difference-in-differences estimates in column (4) indicate that Affirmative Action raises the relative wages of women and minorities, although most groups still earn less than comparable white males in establishments using Affirmative Action; the increase is substantial for black and Hispanic men, on the order of 20 percent.[34] The results are quite similar for starting and current wages, indicating no differences in wage growth.

Promotions

Panel C of Table 13.7 reports logit estimates of equations for whether the newly hired worker was promoted.[35] The independent variables are the same as in the other panels, with the exception of the inclusion of controls for whether the race or sex of the supervisor differed from that of the worker. The results in column (1) suggest that the probability of promotion for blacks and Hispanics hired in establishments using Affirmative Action is higher than for white males in similar establishments, although the differential is statistically significant only for Hispanic females. The difference-in-differences estimates in column (4) convey the same result. Finally, again subtracting the estimates in column (2) from those in column (3), we see that in establishments not using Affirmative Action, promotion probabilities are lower for 4 of the 5 groups of minorities or women. However, in contrast to wages, the estimates suggest that the negative promotion differentials for Hispanics and blacks in these establishments is reversed in establishments using Affirmative Action. This is so despite the earlier evidence that blacks and Hispanics are relatively less qualified in terms of educational attainment. These higher promotion rates for women and minorities hired under Affirmative Action may reflect performance that at least compensates for lower educational qualifications, although they may also reflect Affirmative Action pressures themselves. As a consequence, we next turn to the performance ratings.

Performance ratings

Given our uncertainty over whether the wage and promotion results reflect better performance of blacks and Hispanics, or preferential treatment, we turn in Table 13.8 to the performance rating regressions, in which the dependent variable is the measured rating minus the typical rating. We report results including only the establishment (and city and year) controls in Panel A, and adding in the occupation, job requirement, and other controls in Panel B. The estimates in column (1) indicate that black females hired under Affirmative Action obtain higher performance

Table 13.8 OLS estimates of (performance rating − typical rating for job) regressions[a]

AA hire	Difference relative to			Difference-in-differences
	White male, AA hire (1)	Same demographic group, non-AA hire (2)	White male, non-AA hire (3)	(4)
A. Establishment controls only				
White female	−1.16	−0.16	0.74	−0.58
	(1.50)	(1.16)	(1.19)	(1.89)
Black male	0.49	2.32	0.91	1.90
	(2.24)	(2.40)	(2.07)	(2.82)
Black female	3.10	5.18	3.52	4.76
	(2.39)	(2.53)	(2.23)	(2.94)
Hispanic male	−6.31	−5.93	−5.89	−6.35
	(2.33)	(2.39)	(2.17)	(2.82)
Hispanic female	−3.49	0.39	−3.07	−0.03
	(2.56)	(2.88)	(2.42)	(3.24)
B. Occupation, job requirement, education, age, tenure, and different *race or sex of respondent or supervisor controls added*				
White female	−1.94	−0.59	−1.51	−1.01
	(1.55)	(1.18)	(1.28)	(1.91)
Black male	2.91	1.23	3.34	0.80
	(2.45)	(2.41)	(2.31)	(2.84)
Black female	5.06	4.48	5.49	4.05
	(2.62)	(2.53)	(2.49)	(2.94)
Hispanic male	−2.72	−6.08	−2.29	−6.51
	(2.66)	(2.41)	(2.53)	(2.84)
Hispanic female	−1.23	−0.97	−0.81	−1.40
	(2.86)	(2.89)	(2.75)	(3.24)

Note
a There are 2,130 observations. Standard errors are reported in parentheses. All specifications include dummy variables for city and year and establishment controls, as well as dummy variables and interactions for Asian males and females. Estimates are weighted.

ratings than white males hired in similar establishments, although the differential is not significant at the 10-percent level. The evidence for white females and black males also indicates that their performance is not lower than that of white males in similar establishments. On the other hand, the performance ratings of Hispanic males and females at these establishments are lower, although significantly so only for Hispanic males.

The estimates in column (3) suggest that the differentials between each group of women or minorities in establishments using Affirmative Action and white males in establishments that do not use Affirmative Action are similar to the corresponding differentials within establishments that use Affirmative Action. But the estimates in column (2) also indicate that similar differentials exist between women or minorities hired at the two types of establishments. As a result, the difference-in-differences estimates in column (4) are somewhat similar to those in column (1); the only changes are that the relative performance advantage of black women hired in establishments using Affirmative Action is now stronger, and the performance shortfall for Hispanic women is erased. The evidence is very similar in Panel B, when the more extensive set of controls is added.[36]

Thus, the evidence for Hispanics tells a relatively consistent story, especially for men. We generally find that Hispanic men and women hired under Affirmative Action are less qualified in terms of education, and at least the men are matched to less-demanding jobs and get worse performance ratings.[37] On the other hand, while we find some evidence that blacks are less qualified, we find no evidence that they receive lower performance ratings, which (like their wage and promotion rates) are relatively higher in these establishments than elsewhere. This is the case despite the fact that they are not allocated to less-demanding jobs, suggesting that employers using Affirmative Action find ways to hire blacks who are qualified on grounds other than education. For white females, who appear to be the primary beneficiaries of Affirmative Action (in terms of numbers of hires), we find relatively little evidence of weaker (or stronger) qualifications or performance.[38,39]

Sources of variation in the use of Affirmative Action in hiring

The results to this point describe average differences in qualifications or performance of women or minorities hired under Affirmative Action relative to other workers, based on self-reported use of Affirmative Action by the owners or managers who responded to the survey. Previously, we noted some of the similarities between our self-reported measure, and more exogenous measures based on EEO-1 reporting or regulations for federal contractors. However, we acknowledged that the potential endogeneity of self-reported use of Affirmative Action, and the biases this could generate, limit our ability to infer causal effects, and hence limit the ability of our evidence to answer questions regarding the likely effects of imposing, eliminating, or otherwise changing Affirmative Action policies.

In this section, we assess the sensitivity of our conclusions to this potential endogeneity problem by estimating the effects of Affirmative Action only for a sample of relatively small establishments, among which the use of Affirmative Action is more likely to be voluntarily chosen, and therefore *more endogenous*. We use cutoffs of 50 and 100 to delineate the relevant size categories; the former reflects the point at which federal contractors must have Affirmative Action plans, while the latter reflects the point at which firms must file EEO-1 forms (and thus be subject to monitoring that may induce hiring behavior comparable to that induced by explicit Affirmative Action plans). Since the cutoffs are based on employer rather than establishment size, we focus on the subset of establishments in our sample that constitute the entire firm (which we refer to as "single-unit firms").

Because the sample of single-unit firms includes a bit less than half of the establishments used so far, we adopt a more restrictive version of equation (1), in which D is a single dummy variable for being female or minority. Also, we adopt a linear probability model for the educational underqualification equation. To show that these changes are relatively inconsequential, in Table 13.9 we first

Table 13.9 Estimates of performance rating and educational qualification regressions, alternative sources of variation in use of Affirmative Action, single-unit firms[a]

Women/minority, AA hire	Difference relative to			Difference-in-differences	No. of observations
	White male, AA hire (1)	Women/minority, non-AA hire (2)	White male, non-AA hire (3)	(4)	(5)
A. OLS estimates of restricted model for full sample of single-unit firms					
Educational level	−0.85	−0.02	−0.49	−0.38	890
	(0.23)	(0.14)	(0.17)	(0.27)	
Less than required education	0.03	0.06	0.08	0.01	751
	(0.04)	(0.02)	(0.03)	(0.04)	
Performance rating–typical rating for job	2.87	0.82	2.07	1.61	796
	(2.65)	(1.56)	(1.98)	(2.96)	
B. OLS Estimates for single-unit firms with <50 employees					
Educational level	−0.82	−0.06	−0.57	−0.31	632
	(0.30)	(0.19)	(0.22)	(0.34)	
Less than required education	0.07	0.10	0.14	0.04	507
	(0.06)	(0.04)	(0.04)	(0.06)	
Performance rating–typical rating for job	3.55	−0.26	1.11	2.19	580
	(3.38)	(2.01)	(2.45)	(3.71)	
C. OLS estimates for single-unit firms with <100 employees					
Educational level	−0.91	−0.05	−0.52	−0.43	720
	(0.26)	(0.17)	(0.20)	(0.30)	
Less than required education	0.07	0.07	0.11	0.04	590
	(0.05)	(0.03)	(0.04)	(0.05)	
Performance rating–typical rating for job	3.44	0.19	1.37	2.27	662
	(3.04)	(1.84)	(2.25)	(3.36)	

Note

a Specifications are restricted to include a single dummy variable for white women or minorities. Asians are dropped from the sample. Finally, for the specification for underqualification in terms of education, linear probability estimates are reported. Standard errors are reported in parentheses. All specifications also include dummy variables for city and year. The control variables correspond to those in the corresponding specifications in Panel B of Tables 13.5, 13.6, and 13.8. Estimates are weighted.

report results for the full sample of single-establishment firms using this restricted specification, for the three dependent variables we consider most interesting: educational level, education less than required education, and standardized performance rating. These estimates are qualitatively similar to those for the full sample, with the less restricted specification, that were reported in the earlier tables (as were the results for this restricted specification when we did not restrict the sample to single-establishment firms). Looking at educational level, there is some evidence that women or minorities hired at firms using Affirmative Action are less qualified (but more so relative to white males hired at similar firms than in the difference-in-differences estimation). The probability that educational levels are less than required also seems somewhat higher for women or minorities hired under Affirmative Action, though the differences once again are not always significant. Finally, with respect to performance ratings, there is no evidence that women or minorities hired at firms using Affirmative Action perform any worse on the job; if anything, the point estimates for their ratings are higher.

These estimates are followed in Panels B and C by results for the sample of single-unit firms with less than 50 and then less than 100 employees. Because Affirmative Action is more likely to be voluntary in smaller firms, any potential endogeneity bias should be worse, and therefore we might expect any evidence of lower qualifications or performance of Affirmative Action hires to be weaker in these subsamples if endogeneity bias is important. However, the estimates in Panels B and C are qualitatively and quantitatively similar to those in Panel A, suggesting that there is little bias due to endogeneity (either because endogenous choices are not correlated with the outcomes we are studying, or because there are in fact few cases of voluntary adoption of Affirmative Action).[40]

To summarize, the results in size categories in which the use of Affirmative Action is more plausibly endogenous also indicate that women or minorities hired under Affirmative Action are somewhat less qualified in terms of education, but perform as well or better on the job. Because this evidence is very similar to that based on estimates for the full sample, we are more inclined to interpret our results as informative with regard to the causal effects of Affirmative Action.

Conclusions

We use micro-level data on employers and employees to investigate whether minority or female employees hired under Affirmative Action are less qualified, relative to other groups of workers. Our measures of qualifications include educational attainment of the workers hired (in absolute levels and relative to job requirements), skill requirements on the job, and a variety of outcome measures that presumably are linked to worker performance on the job. The analysis is based on data from a new survey of establishments in four major metropolitan areas in the United States.

On average, we find some evidence that minority employees hired under Affirmative Action have lower educational attainment, and are somewhat more likely to fall short of formal educational "requirements" on these jobs when they are hired,

although we find very little evidence of this for white females hired under Affirmative Action. However, when we consider measures of outcomes for workers
in these jobs, we find that minorities and females hired under Affirmative Action
do relatively well. On average, their wages are relatively higher, as are their
probabilities of promotion. But since these outcomes might themselves be driven
by Affirmative Action policies, and not just by the performance of the workers,
we also consider employers' ratings of employee performance. The results show
that ratings of white female or black employees in establishments using Affirmative Action are generally at least as high as those of other comparable workers.
These results are reversed only for Hispanic men, who receive significantly lower
performance ratings.

Taken together, the results of this chapter suggest that critics of Affirmative
Action may be right in pointing to *some* shortfalls in qualifications among women
or minorities hired under Affirmative Action. However, these critics may be focusing too narrowly on one or two easily-observable measures of qualifications that
are not the only predictors of what is ultimately the most important measure—job
performance. Our results suggest that most women or minorities hired under Affirmative Action make up in some way—presumably through qualifications or skills
other than those measures we observe, or perhaps through effort—for the educational and skill shortfalls that we find. Thus, there may be some redistribution of
employment away from white males toward minorities and females at establishments using Affirmative Action, but there does not appear to be substitution of
less-able women or minority workers for more-able white male workers.

This does not necessarily imply that there are no costs from using Affirmative
Action. One possibility is that these establishments hire relatively more less-skilled
workers than they would in the absence of Affirmative Action, which might entail
some cost in efficiency. Another is that the same number of less-skilled workers
are hired as before, but that there is relatively more redistribution of employment
away from less-skilled white males within these establishments. Without panel
data on establishments both before and after their use of Affirmative Action, it is
impossible to distinguish among these interpretations.

We should also note a number of further caveats with respect to these findings.
Given the data that we have, we are only able to estimate the effects of Affirmative
Action on the last worker hired in each establishment, which is not necessarily
a representative sample of all employees hired under these procedures. We are also
not able to compare different hires into comparable jobs within each establishment.
The focus on recent hires also forces us to consider only short-term outcomes
for a sample of employees with very low job tenure. Finally, our self-reported
measure of use of Affirmative Action may not allow us to define the relevant set
of establishments or activities as clearly as in those studies that use more objective
measures, such as federal contractor status or EEO-1 filing, although we have
argued that our measure appears to mimic more objective measures quite well,
and could conceivably be preferable.

Despite these caveats, we believe that our data provide useful information on the
effects of Affirmative Action, by providing the first micro-level evidence linking

Affirmative Action to worker qualifications and performance. We interpret the overall evidence as indicating that while Affirmative Action may lead to the hiring of women and minorities with shortfalls in terms of some observable qualifications, most groups of women and minorities hired under Affirmative Action perform their jobs as well as white males.

Acknowledgments

We are grateful to Jess Reaser for outstanding research assistance, to the Rockefeller Foundation for financial support, and to Jeff Biddle, Bill Evans, Robert Lalonde, Angelo Melino, Ed Montgomery, and seminar participants at Maryland, Michigan State, the NBER, Ohio State, Rochester, Toronto, and the Upjohn Institute for helpful comments.

Notes

1 In these data, much hinges on the wording of questions describing Affirmative Action; references to "quotas" or "reverse discrimination" generally elicit the most negative responses. There is also some evidence of more tolerance for compensatory policies in education than in employment, though quotas or other forms of preferences in university admissions are still widely opposed. For a view that distinguishes Affirmative Action in universities from that in employment see Carter (1991).

2 Critics of current Affirmative Action policies that stress both inefficiencies and inequities (from violating principles of rewards based on individual merit) include Glazer (1975), Epstein (1992) and Sowell (1990). Coate and Loury (1993) argue that Affirmative Action can reduce the incentives of "preferred" groups to invest in human capital formation, while Carter (1991) also emphasizes the stigma borne by qualified minorities because of these policies.

3 Evidence of discrimination against minorities or females, even when controlling for observable credentials, can be found in several recent "audit" studies of employers (e.g. Fix and Struyk, 1994; Neumark, 1996), in which matched pairs of applicants with comparable credentials but of different races or sexes are sent out to apply for identical jobs.

4 The difficulty of predicting or observing individual-level productivity has been stressed in the "statistical discrimination" literature (e.g. Cain, 1986), and more recently by Oettinger (1996) and Altonji and Pierret (1996). The question of whether required qualifications accurately predict job performance, and whether any resulting "disparate impacts" across demographic group can be considered discrimination, has been addressed in a variety of court cases (e.g. *Griggs* v. *Duke Power* in 1971 and *Ward Cove* v. *Atonio* in 1989) and in the Civil Rights Act of 1991. The debate over the latter, including the allegations of critics that such legislation constituted a "quota bill," indicates the difficulties of distinguishing strong EEO policies from Affirmative Action.

5 Most of Leonard's papers deal with the effects of Affirmative Action on relative employment, occupational status, and the like. These are reviewed in various survey papers (1989, 1990). See also Smith and Welch (1984). Given the small effects of Affirmative Action on the overall composition of employment that Leonard shows in his other work, it is very unlikely that he would find strong effects on productivity at the two-digit industry level.

6 The data are drawn from a broader project known as the Multi-City Study of Urban Inequality, which also consists of household surveys and an in-depth, qualitative study of a smaller sample of establishments.

7 The survey was administered to establishments in Detroit between June 1992 and February 1993, and the other areas between March 1993 and May 1994. The timing was deliberately chosen in order to coordinate with the surveying of households in each area, as part of the Multi-City Study. Monthly unemployment rates averaged under 6 percent in Atlanta and Boston during the survey period, and between 8 and 10 percent in Detroit and Los Angeles. Dummy variables for metropolitan area and year are included in the multivariate analyses that follow to control for these differences in local labor market conditions.

8 Most characteristics of workers and jobs do not differ significantly across the samples of establishments generated by the two data sources.

9 The stratification scheme was: 25 percent in establishments with fewer than 20 employees; 50 percent in establishments with 20–99 employees; and 25 percent in those with 100 or more employees. These distributions were drawn from a weighted sample of establishments in the Employment Opportunity Pilot Project (EOPP) of 1980 and 1982.

10 Sample weights are applied to the household-generated establishments that adjust for: (1) the underrepresentation of jobs requiring college, since the SSI sample focused on noncollege jobs; (2) the oversampling of low-income and minority residents in the household surveys; and (3) the incompleteness of the Boston and Los Angeles samples of households from which establishments were drawn. More information on the construction of these weights is available from the authors.

11 The lack of extra weighting for high-turnover establishments seems appropriate, since a single job that turns over frequently is only available to a single worker at any time. Unfortunately, there was no easy way to put extra weight on establishments whose rate of hiring is temporarily high due to their net employment growth.

12 Successfully screened establishments were those where the correct establishment and the person responsible for new hiring into the relevant types of positions were contacted.

13 Clearly a positive response to this latter question does not necessarily mean that the worker was an "Affirmative Action hire," but just that Affirmative Action played a role in the decision. This is reflected in the considerable number of observations in which employers provide a positive response to this question but hire a white male (see Table 13.1). An instructive example comes from academic hiring, where Affirmative Action nearly always plays a role in the hiring decision, but by no means precludes hiring white males.

14 Because the survey used in this chapter was not designed explicitly to study Affirmative Action, it did not elicit information that might further clarify the interpretation of the question, such as federal contractor status or the size of federal contracts.

15 Conversely, given that there is imperfect compliance with Affirmative Action guidelines for federal contractors (as emphasized, e.g. by Leonard, 1989), employers in principle bound by such guidelines may not in fact be adhering to them. Thus, a self-reported measure of Affirmative Action use may be preferable to a measure based on federal contractor status or explicit Affirmative Action plans.

16 We code most of these requirements as dummy variables which take on a value of 1 if the requirement is "absolutely necessary" or "strongly preferred" at the time of hiring and zero if it is "mildly preferred" or "doesn't matter." In contrast, the college requirement is based on an explicit "yes" or "no" question in the survey.

17 These results also differ somewhat from those of Leonard (1989) for the 1970s, who finds proportionately bigger effects on black males and females than on white females. But during the 1980s Leonard finds relative employment of black males and females *declining* at contractor establishments (relative to noncontractors).

18 This evidence is broadly consistent with Leonard's (1989) findings that Affirmative Action has created the most opportunities for white women in white-collar trainee positions, and for black females in managerial, sales, clerical, laborer, and white-collar trainee positions.

19 In this table and all that follow, estimates are sample-weighted (as they were in Table 13.1), to produce more accurate estimates of "average" effects. We recomputed the specifications unweighted, and most of the results were very similar. One exception is discussed later.

20 "Minority or female" refers to white women, blacks, and Hispanics. All of the models estimated in the chapter also included categories for Asian men and women. However, we do not focus on (or report) results for Asians, since most of the debate seems to be about the treatment of relatively disadvantaged subgroups of the population, a categorization which may not apply to Asians. Omitting the Asians had virtually no effect on the reported results.

21 The results are partly consistent with those reported by Rodgers and Spriggs (1996), who find that federal contractor status is associated with a higher percentage of black workers (by 12 percent) and a lower percentage of Hispanic workers (by 0.45 percent) in 1992.

22 Note that the combined marginal effects reported for minorities or white females are smaller in absolute value than those for white males. This is because Asians are also included in the estimation, and their hiring appears to be boosted by Affirmative Action.

23 Further, if there is some job segregation by demographic characteristics, or if overall hiring at establishments using Affirmative Action falls because of the policy, the wages of white males in non-Affirmative Action establishments will be lower because of an outward labor supply shift. However, Table 13.7 shows that these white males still earn higher wages on average than women or minorities hired at either type of establishment.

24 Note that the difference-in-differences estimator $(\beta - \gamma) - (\delta - \alpha)$ is equal to the difference between the first and third comparisons, $(\beta - \gamma) - (\beta - \alpha)$, plus the second comparison, $(\beta - \delta)$. Note also that this estimator does not distinguish between a larger difference in qualifications in establishments using Affirmative Action that arises from lower standards for women or minorities, or higher standards for white men, relative to establishments not using Affirmative Action.

25 One might argue that in this simple example, Affirmative Action is irrelevant because it simply results in a reshuffling of workers. But if wages are partly attached to jobs and do not just reflect productivity, perhaps because of restrictions on paying men and women different wages at the same establishment, then the men in this example are likely to suffer wage declines, and the women to gain wage increases.

26 Note that this still could be relevant in Panel B of Table 13.5, because educational requirements are excluded from the set of job requirements.

27 About 6 percent of the sample is underqualified using the data this way. If we instead assume that employers were referring to Associate's degrees, about 5 percent of the sample is underqualified. In either case, more than half of the underqualified workers were those without high school degrees in jobs reported to require high school degrees.

28 This is the one dependent variable for which the results differ for unweighted estimates. In particular, although the signs of the estimates are the same, the results are not statistically significant. This occurs because the shortfall in education relative to requirements among some minorities arises with respect to college degrees. Since, as noted earlier, the original sample strongly oversampled jobs requiring a high school degree (for other reasons related to the purposes of the survey), in the unweighted sample jobs requiring college degrees are underrepresented, and this shortfall is therefore harder to detect if we fail to account for the nonrepresentative sampling.

29 As an example, Bloch (1994) discusses *James* v. *Stockham Valves and Fittings Company*, in which an employer charged with discrimination claimed that formal education requirements for manual laborers led to hiring of more whites than blacks. But the court ruled that education was unrelated to job performance.

30 Nonetheless, the wage and promotion results are still of interest because there is virtually no empirical evidence to date on the relationship of Affirmative Action to these outcomes.

31 A similar variable is used in the EOPP Survey (e.g. Barron *et al.*, 1989) and a more recent, similar survey of members of the National Federation of Independent Businesses (Bishop, 1993). Since the main survey respondent was the person responsible for hiring, in small- and medium-sized companies the performance rating was typically elicited from this respondent, who was likely to be a manager or owner, and who should therefore be able to speak knowledgeably about a worker's job performance. In large companies, these functions are more likely to be separated. As a result, in these cases the interviewer generally elicited the performance rating from a supervisor.

32 One might object that by controlling for differences in qualifications (education), we bias the results against finding poorer performance, as measured by wages (or promotions). However, the results reported in Table 13.7 turned out to be insensitive to the inclusion of these variables.

33 Leonard (1990) reports similar evidence indicating that wages of minorities relative to white males are higher in cities and industries with high proportions of employment in establishments subject to Affirmative Action.

34 Table 13.1 indicates that the percentage of the workforce covered by collective bargaining is higher in establishments using Affirmative Action. However, the relatively higher wages paid to women and minorities in such establishments do not appear to be attributable to the well-documented tendency for race and sex differentials in wages to be lower among union workers. We re-estimated the models adding a set of interactions between the demographic dummy variables D and two alternative measures of unionization: the percentage covered by collective bargaining, and a dummy variable indicating whether this percentage was greater than zero. The relatively higher wages paid to women or minorities in establishments using Affirmative Action, based on the difference-in-differences estimates, did not diminish in this augmented specification.

35 A limitation of the promotions variable is that median tenure with the employer is roughly 2–3 months in our sample. The proportion of workers promoted is only 0.08.

36 Earlier we noted the possibility that stronger ratings given to women or minorities in establishments using Affirmative Action might reflect relatively favorable views of these workers at establishments that have voluntarily chosen to use Affirmative Action. But it is unclear why this would be true for blacks and not Hispanic males. Our controls for the racial composition of customers and for the race/sex of the respondent should also help to control for such factors. We also note that our job requirement controls include information on customer contact, where immigrant Hispanics might be at some disadvantage relative to native-born whites and blacks. Finally, we consider evidence on the sensitivity of the estimates to endogeneity. The estimated coefficients of the dummy variables for different race or sex of the respondent or supervisor indicated that supervisors or respondents of the opposite sex resulted in performance ratings that were significantly higher, by about 2 points, whereas supervisors or respondents of the opposite race resulted in ratings that were lower by about 1–2 points (significantly so for supervisors of the opposite race).

37 Although Hispanics in this sample are heavily concentrated in Los Angeles (with 70 percent of the newly hired Hispanics being located there), the finding of low performance ratings for Hispanic men is not unique to Los Angeles; if anything, the negative difference-in-differences estimates for Hispanic males in Los Angeles were somewhat smaller than those in other cities.

38 When we add these performance measures to the current wage equations in Table 13.7, we generally find that they generate positive and significant effects on wages. But the various race/sex differentials presented there are little changed by their inclusion. On one hand, this suggests that the relatively higher wages paid to women and minorities hired under Affirmative Action may reflect preferential treatment. On the other hand, these results are based on using the performance ratings as an independent variable; the presumed measurement error in these ratings inhibits our ability to ask whether performance ratings explain these higher wages.

39 One potential problem with the standardized performance ratings is that when we look at a worker hired by an establishment using Affirmative Action, the typical rating that is subtracted off may also apply to an Affirmative Action hire. In this case, the standardization may erase any relative differences in performance between Affirmative Action and non-Affirmative Action hires, leading the estimate of the effect of Affirmative Action on performance to be zero. To examine this possibility, we re-estimated the equations in Table 13.8 using the raw performance ratings. The column (4) estimates using the raw ratings were not generally further from zero than the corresponding estimates in Table 13.8, suggesting that standardization does not force the estimated effects of Affirmative Action toward zero.

40 We have also estimated some equations using dummy variables for establishment sizes of 50–99 and 100 or more employees as instruments for reported use of Affirmative Action. These results were qualitatively similar to those reported in the chapter, although the estimates were considerably less precise, and identification is tenuous because employer size may directly affect the outcomes we study.

References

Altonji, Joseph and Charles Pierret. 1996. "Employer Learning and the Signaling Value of Education." National Bureau of Economic Research Working Paper No. 5438.

Anderson, Bernard E. 1996. "The Ebb and Flow of Enforcing Executive Order 11246." *American Economic Review Papers and Proceedings* 86: 298–301.

Badgett, M. V. Lee. 1995. "Affirmative Action in a Changing Legal and Economic Environment." *Industrial Relations* 34: 489–506.

Barron, John, Mark Berger, and Dan Black. 1989. "Job Matching and On-the-Job Training." *Journal of Labor Economics* 7: 1–19.

Bergmann, Barbara R. 1989. "Does the Market for Women's Labor Need Fixing?" *Journal of Economic Perspectives* 3: 43–60.

Bishop, John. 1993. "Improving Job Matches in the U.S. Labor Market." *Brooking Papers on Economic Activity: Microeconomics* 1: 335–90.

Bloch, Ferrel. 1994. *Anti-Discrimination Law and Minority Employment*. Chicago: University of Chicago Press.

Bobo, Lawrence and Ryan Smith. 1994. "Antipoverty Policy, Affirmative Action, and Racial Attitudes." In *Confronting Poverty: Prescriptions for Change*, eds Sheldon Danziger, Gary Sandefur, and Daniel Weinberg, pp. 365–95. Cambridge MA: Harvard University Press.

Cain, Glen. 1986. "The Economic Analysis of Labor Market Discrimination: A Survey." In *The Handbook of Labor Economics*, Vol. 1, eds Orley C. Ashenfelter and Richard Layard, pp. 693–785. Amsterdam: North-Holland.

Carter, Stephen. 1991. *Reflections of an Affirmative-Action Baby*. New York: Basic Books.

Coate, Stephen and Glenn Loury. 1993. "Will Affirmative Action Policies Eliminate Negative Stereotypes?" *American Economic Review* 83: 1220–40.

Cutler, David and Edward Glaeser. 1997. "Are Ghettoes Good or Bad?" *Quarterly Journal of Economics* 112: 827–72.

Epstein, Richard A. 1992. *Forbidden Grounds: The Case Against Employment Discrimination Laws*. Cambridge, MA: Harvard University Press.

Fix, Michael and Raymond Struyk. 1994. *Clear and Convincing Evidence*. Washington DC: Urban Institute Press.

Glazer, Nathan. 1975. *Affirmative Discrimination: Ethnic Inequality and Public Policy*. New York: Basic Books.

Gold, Michael Evan. 1993. *An Introduction to the Law of Employment Discrimination.* ILR Bulletin 68. Ithaca, NY: ILR Press.

Holzer, Harry J. 1995. "Employer Skill Needs and Labor Market Outcomes Across Groups." Russell Sage Foundation Working Paper.

——. 1996. *What Employers Want: Job Prospects for Less-Educated Workers.* New York: Russell Sage Foundation.

——. 1998. "Employer Hiring Decisions and Antidiscrimination Policy." In *Generating Jobs: How To Increase Demand for Less-Skilled Workers*, eds Richard Freeman and Peter Gottschalk, pp. 223–57. New York: Russell Sage Foundation.

Leonard, Jonathan S. 1984. "Anti-Discrimination or Reverse Discrimination: The Impact of Changing Demographics, Title VII and Affirmative Action on Productivity."*Journal of Human Resources* 19: 145–74.

——. 1989. "Women and Affirmative Action." *Journal of Economic Perspectives* 3: 61–76.

——. 1990. "The Impact of Affirmative Action Regulation and Equal Opportunity Law on Black Employment." *Journal of Economic Perspectives* 4: 47–64.

Lipset, Seymour Martin and William Schneider. 1978. "The Bakke Case: How Would It Be Decided at the Bar of Public Opinion?" *Public Opinion* (March–April): 38–48.

Mare, Robert. 1995. "Changes in Educational Attainment and School Enrollment." In *State of the Union*, Vol. 1, ed. Reynolds Farley, pp. 155–214. New York: Russell Sage Foundation, 1995.

Neal, Derek and William Johnson. 1996. "The Role of Premarket Factors in Black–White Wage Differences." *Journal of Political Economy* 104: 869–95.

Neumark, David. 1996. "Sex Discrimination in Restaurant Hiring: An Audit Study." *Quarterly Journal of Economics* 111: 915–942.

Oettinger, Gerald. 1996. "Statistical Discrimination and the Early Career Evolution of the Black–White Wage Gap." *Journal of Labor Economics* 14: 52–78.

Rodgers, William M. and William E. Spriggs. 1996. "The Effect of Federal Contractor Status on Racial Differences in Establishment-Level Employment Shares: 1979–1992." *American Economic Review* 86: 290–3.

Smith, James and Finis Welch. 1984. "Affirmative Action and Labor Markets."*Journal of Labor Economics* 2: 269–301.

Sowell, Thomas. 1990. *Preferential Policies: An International Perspective.* New York: W. Morrow.

US Department of Labor. 1993. "High Performance Work Systems and Establishment Performance." Mimeograph.

Yinger, John. 1995. *Closed Doors, Opportunities Lost.* New York: Russell Sage Foundation.

14 What does Affirmative Action do?

(with Harry J. Holzer)

Introduction

Affirmative Action remains a highly controversial issue in the United States. Recent court decisions (such as *Adarand* v. *Pena*, US Supreme Court) or state-level referenda (such as Proposition 209 in California) are likely to influence the use of Affirmative Action in employment and/or education, and other actions by courts and legislatures are pending.[1] Yet the effects of Affirmative Action on employment outcomes are not particularly well understood to date. The seminal work by Jonathan Leonard (summarized in his paper in 1990) provides evidence that Affirmative Action affects the employment and occupational status of women and minorities, which has been confirmed elsewhere (e.g. Leonard, 1985a; Rodgers and Spriggs, 1996; Holzer and Neumark, 1999).[2] But the exact mechanisms by which these effects occur, and their consequences for a wide range of performance measures of firms or employees, have received little attention.

The reason for this is that much of the empirical analysis of Affirmative Action to date treats the program as a "black box," and generates only reduced-form estimates on employment (or occupational status) by race and gender. For instance, Leonard (as well as Rodgers and Spriggs) have analyzed the effects of being a Federal contractor on employment outcomes across establishments, while Holzer and Neumark analyze the relationship between self-reported use of Affirmative Action and employment outcomes in a cross-section of establishments.[3]

In reality, however, "Affirmative Action" can incorporate and influence a wide variety of activities by employers. These include: "outreach" or special recruitment efforts; changes in screening practices; changes in hiring, pay, or promotion standards; and/or special assistance programs to members of "protected groups" who are hired (Caplan, 1997). This chapter differs from previous work on Affirmative Action by attempting to go inside the black box, providing a fuller answer to the question "What does Affirmative Action do?" We use data from a survey of employers to attempt to understand how Affirmative Action influences a wide array of employer hiring practices, personnel policies, and ultimately employment outcomes. Among the policies and outcomes we study are: recruiting and screening practices; applicant flows; hiring criteria and standards; characteristics of employees hired; training and evaluation practices; and relative employee performance. In most of our analysis, we attempt to distinguish between the effects of Affirmative Action in recruitment and Affirmative Action in hiring.

The intense public scrutiny and debate over Affirmative Action makes it critical to understand how Affirmative Action actually affects employers' personnel and employment policies. In the court of public opinion, some types of Affirmative Action are much more unpopular than others. Specifically, survey data in the United States suggest that whites are much more sympathetic to special recruiting and training efforts targeted toward minorities and women than to "preferential treatment" in hiring and promotion (Lipset and Schneider, 1978; Kluegel and Smith, 1986; Kinder and Sanders, 1990). Appendix Table 14.A1 documents the results of public opinion polls reflecting differences in opinions regarding the two "types" of Affirmative Action.

These two ways of thinking about Affirmative Action correspond to alternative ways in which economists might interpret the policy, with one interpretation more benign than the other. First, Affirmative Action might create inducements for employers to use methods of search (i.e. recruitment and screening) that are nontraditional for them, but which enable them to find qualified women and minorities. This would be particularly true in the presence of imperfect information among employers or minority/female applicants, especially if the traditional methods lead to statistical discrimination against these groups. The methods of search used under Affirmative Action may be more expensive, but need not lead to hiring of less-qualified workers. In addition, Affirmative Action might lead employers to engage more intensively in activities such as training, to bring otherwise less-qualified women and minorities up to par. Alternatively, a more negative view is that Affirmative Action operates largely as a quota system. In the face of some skill shortfalls among minorities, and especially in the absence of imperfect information or discrimination, Affirmative Action would necessarily lead to the hiring and employment of less-qualified workers.[4,5]

We suspect that the debate over whether to eliminate or how to change Affirmative Action will ultimately hinge on which of these alternative interpretations comes to be accepted. Does Affirmative Action put in place a set of incentives that move us toward equally qualified men, women, and minorities in the workplace? Or does it instead force employers to hire less-productive female and minority workers, leading to inefficiencies in the workplace? In our view, we do not know enough about what Affirmative Action actually does to accurately characterize it one way or the other. Our goal in this chapter is to generate additional knowledge about precisely these issues.

Our results show that Affirmative Action increases the number of recruitment and screening practices used by employers, raises their willingness to hire stigmatized applicants (such as persons with criminal records or long unemployment durations), increases the number of minority or female applicants as well as employees, and increases employers' tendencies to provide training and to formally evaluate employee performance. When Affirmative Action is used in recruiting, it does not lower either the credentials or performance of women and minorities hired; if anything, it seems to draw in more-qualified women and minorities. These results suggest that the principal effect of Affirmative Action in recruiting is to lead employers to search more widely and gain more information about potential employees. When Affirmative Action is used in hiring, however, it yields female and minority employees whose credentials are somewhat weaker, but whose performance is not, perhaps because of additional training and evaluation. Overall, then, the more intensive search, evaluation, and training that accompany Affirmative Action appear to offset any tendency of the policy to lead to hiring of less-qualified or less-productive women and minorities.

Data, outcomes, and estimation strategies

The data set

The survey of employers that we use was administered between June 1992 and May 1994 to over 3,200 employers in four metropolitan areas: Atlanta, Boston, Detroit, and Los Angeles. The survey was administered over the phone to individuals responsible for hiring, and focused on the characteristics of employees, vacant jobs, and the most recently filled job and hired worker at each establishment. Other characteristics of the establishment, such as its size, presence of collective bargaining, and the demographic composition of its applicants and customers, were covered as well.

The sample of firms surveyed was drawn from two sources: roughly 30 percent were generated by employees who were respondents in a corresponding household survey in the same metropolitan areas, and the rest were generated by lists provided by Survey Sampling Inc. (SSI).[6] The latter sample was stratified *ex ante* to reflect the distribution of workers across establishment sizes in the labor force, while the former sample implicitly reflects this distribution. Both samples are therefore already weighted by employee size, permitting us to analyze either individual jobs (such as the one most recently filled) at these firms or overall employment.[7] Response rates to the survey among firms that passed the screening averaged 67 percent, and there is little evidence of selection bias induced by nonrandom response patterns in the data.[8]

Our data include two different variables regarding the role of Affirmative Action in hiring for the last position filled. Respondents to the survey were asked "whether or not Affirmative Action or Equal Opportunity Law plays any role in *recruiting* for this position," and also whether or not it plays any role in who is actually *hired*.[9] Though responses to these questions are highly correlated, there appears to be enough independent variation to distinguish between the differing effects of Affirmative Action in hiring and in recruiting on hiring practices, personnel policies, and employment outcomes.

Affirmative Action, EEO, and causality

One potential problem with the Affirmative Action questions is that responses to them could confound the effects of Equal Employment Opportunity (EEO) laws with the effects of Affirmative Action. All establishments with fifteen or more employees (over 80 percent of the workforce) are bound by Title VII of the Civil Rights Act, while explicit Affirmative Action plans are mandatory only for employers with federal contracts and fifty or more employees, or a contract worth $50,000 or more. In our sample, 56 percent of establishments report the use of some kind of Affirmative Action in recruiting, and 42 percent in hiring. Although our self-reported measure is not explicitly based on actual contractor status, the fraction of units reporting Affirmative Action and some of their characteristics are similar to what Leonard (1989) found regarding federal contractor status among firms required to file EEO-1 reports. In particular, in Leonard's data and in our data the use of Affirmative Action is highly correlated with employer size (at the firm level, in his case). In addition, around 60 percent of his sample were contractors who were bound by Executive Orders mandating the use of Affirmative Action; this number is a bit higher than ours, but his sample tends to exclude smaller firms that are less likely to use Affirmative Action. On balance, then, we believe that our measure of Affirmative Action is strongly related to contractor status, and is therefore likely often to be capturing use of Affirmative Action rather than mere compliance with EEO law.[10]

But establishments or firms may behave *as if* they are contractors, even when they are not, for other reasons. For example, this is especially likely to be true for establishments belonging to firms with 100 or more employees, which are required to file EEO-1 forms with the government. Although only compliance with EEO laws is required of firms without federal contracts, those who file EEO-1 reports may engage in Affirmative Action hiring to avoid litigation or other problems that could be triggered by these reports; as noted by Bloch (1994), employment discrimination suits can stem from charges brought by the EEOC based on review of EEO-1 reports, even without a single complainant. In this case, establishments belonging to such firms would likely report the use of Affirmative Action in hiring, and their use of Affirmative Action would be exogenously determined by their size and the practice of federal monitoring. We therefore explore differences in our results by establishment size below.

In addition to requirements for contractors or large firms, explicit Affirmative Action plans may be implemented by the courts as a remedy for a finding of past discrimination (Epstein, 1992), or by companies fearing potential lawsuits that could be caused by an underrepresentation of women or minorities in hiring or promotions.[11] In these cases, the distinction between compliance with EEO and the practice of Affirmative Action becomes blurred, both in name and in practice.[12] Some employers might choose to engage in Affirmative Action for other reasons as well, such as a perception that a diverse workforce is profitable for their company, or because they value it personally.[13]

Given that some employers voluntarily choose to engage in it, our measure of Affirmative Action use might potentially be spuriously correlated with (or endogenous with respect to) some of our outcome variables, such as performance ratings of individual minority employees. But it is hard to understand why this would be the case for the full range of dependent variables that we consider in the next section.[14]

We return to this issue later, when we consider evidence from more institutional research on firm behavior in response to government EEO laws and Affirmative Action rules. Also, because there are reasons why the use of Affirmative Action in larger firms is more likely to be exogenous, we consider evidence on the effects of Affirmative Action in different size firms to assess the likelihood of endogeneity bias. While we would not argue that we decisively uncover the causal effects of Affirmative Action, we do interpret the evidence as indicating that endogenous selection is relatively unimportant as an explanation of our results. Nonetheless, we think caution is in order in drawing conclusions from our evidence regarding exogenous variation in the use of Affirmative Action (such as would be generated by its elimination, for example). Rather, our evidence is probably most compelling as an empirical description of how behavior differs among employers using and not using Affirmative Action—an empirical description that is sorely lacking in the debate over Affirmative Action.

Dependent variables

As stated in the previous section, our goal is to understand how Affirmative Action affects a wide array of hiring practices, personnel policies, and employment outcomes. Consequently, in this chapter we examine the entire process of recruiting, hiring, and utilizing employees. Of course, we do not claim that the steps of this process that we study are the only ones that might be considered; but we believe they provide a relatively thorough picture of the recruitment, screening, hiring, and employment process. In the sections that follow, we describe in detail the types of data we have on each component of this process, and the specifications we estimate to study the effects of Affirmative Action on each of these.

Recruitment methods

We begin by examining the relationship between Affirmative Action in recruiting and the recruitment methods that employers use. We have data on six alternative recruitment methods: walk in/sign; referral from employees/others; state/community agency; private agency; newspaper; and referral from unions/schools.[15] The data on recruitment methods are reported two ways: one for whether each of a series of methods was used at all during the recruitment process for the position; and one for which of the methods actually generated the applicant who was ultimately hired. Thus, only one of the latter set of methods can be chosen, while any number of the former might be. To examine the effects of Affirmative Action on recruitment methods, we estimate equations of the form:

$$Z_{jk} = f(X_{jk}, X_k, AA_{jk}, v_{jk}). \tag{1}$$

In equation (1) Z denotes recruitment methods. The subscripts j and k denote the last job filled/most recent hire and the establishment respectively; the j subscript is needed because survey questions sometimes refer to the most recent hire. X_{jk} represents characteristics of the last job filled at the establishment, and X_k

instead represents general establishment characteristics; these control variables are described below. v_{jk} captures unobservables. Finally, AA reflects the use of Affirmative Action at the establishment (with reference to the most recent hire).

When we study recruitment methods, it is presumably Affirmative Action in recruiting rather than hiring that is relevant, so we restrict attention to the differences between establishments that do and do not use Affirmative Action in recruiting. When we use the data on all methods used, we estimate logit models for each method, whereas when we use the data on the method that generated the last hire, we estimate a multinomial logit model.

Demographic characteristics of applicants

The natural next step after estimating the effects of Affirmative Action (in recruiting) on recruitment methods used is to study its effects on the demographic characteristics of the applicant pool, since influencing these characteristics is presumably a major goal of Affirmative Action in recruiting. Our data here consist of the percentages of the applicants for the most recently filled job who were black males, black females, and Hispanics.[16] Because these percentages are bounded at 0 and 100, we estimate two-tailed Tobit models of the form:

$$PD_k = g(X_{jk}, X_k, AA_{jk}, v_{jk}; Z_{jk}). \tag{2}$$

PD_k refers to the percentage of the applicant pool in each demographic group covered. The recruitment methods Z_{jk} are sometimes included in these specifications, and sometimes excluded, to see the extent to which these methods can account for the effects of Affirmative Action on the applicant pool.[17] As for recruitment methods, in estimating equation (2) we focus on Affirmative Action in recruiting.

Screening methods and hiring criteria

We next turn from recruitment to hiring. We have data on what we regard as two conceptually distinct inputs into the hiring process: screening methods and hiring criteria. We have data on seven different screening methods used for the position of the most recent hire, including: whether a test/work sample is required; whether a drug test/physical is required; whether the employer checks references; whether the employer checks education; whether the employer checks criminal records; whether a written application is required; and whether an interview is required.[18] We have data on five different hiring criteria questions regarding whom the employer would hire, including: someone with a criminal record; a welfare recipient; a person with government training or a GED; a person with a short-term/part-time work history; and a person unemployed for one year or more.[19] For these screening methods and hiring criteria, we estimate models like equation (1), although in this case we always estimate separate logit models for each of the questions.

In looking at recruitment methods and applicants, we restricted attention to Affirmative Action in recruiting. From this point, though, because we begin to look at hiring policies, we estimate separate equations first looking at the effects of Affirmative Action in recruiting, and then at Affirmative Action in hiring. The two types of Affirmative Action may have different effects; for example, the former might be more likely to lead to recruitment methods that cast a wider net, while the latter may be more likely to lead to preferential hiring. Of course most employers who use Affirmative Action in hiring also use it in recruiting, although some do not, so our estimates of the effects of Affirmative Action in hiring should be interpreted as the effects of using Affirmative Action in recruiting and hiring. On the other hand, many establishments in our sample use Affirmative Action in recruiting but not hiring. Thus, we suspect the dichotomy between Affirmative Action in recruiting and Affirmative Action in hiring is not an either/or one, but rather one of degree, capturing the extent to which employers focus more on recruiting, or more on hiring. Nonetheless, the fact that different subsamples of establishments in our data set report using Affirmative Action in recruiting and in hiring allows us to use the data to characterize how these two types of Affirmative Action operate.[20]

Hires: demographic characteristics and qualifications

The product of recruitment, screening, and hiring criteria are new hires. We first report evidence on the effects of Affirmative Action in recruiting and hiring on the demographic characteristics of workers hired. This evidence, of course, most closely parallels the kinds of evidence reported in the literature on Affirmative Action, although from other sources. Next, we look at qualifications of workers hired, asking in particular whether female or minority Affirmative Action hires appear to be particularly less qualified.

Turning first to the effects of Affirmative Action on the demographic characteristics of the workers hired, since the Affirmative Action question in the survey refers to the most recently filled job, the most pertinent information is the demographic group of the person who filled that job. We therefore estimate multinomial logit models of the form:

$$D_{ijk} = g(X_{jk}, X_k, AA_{jk}, v_{ijk}; Z_{jk}, PD_k, S_{jk}).$$ (3)

D_{ijk} is a set of dummy variables for the demographic group of the last worker hired; it has an 'ijk' subscript to denote that it refers to a specific worker in the most recently filled job in the establishment. We also estimate these models focusing separately on the effects of Affirmative Action in recruiting and Affirmative Action in hiring. In addition, we explore the extent to which the differences in recruitment methods (Z_{jk}), applicant demographics (PD_k), and screening methods and hiring criteria (S_{jk}) that are attributable to Affirmative Action account for differences in hiring of minority or female workers depending upon whether establishments use Affirmative Action, to gauge the extent to which race/ethnicity or sex is being used as an explicit hiring criterion conditional on all of these other changes; we do this by alternately including these variables as controls. We also estimate models for the overall percentage of the workforce that is white male, white female, black male, black female, and Hispanic.[21]

We next ask whether Affirmative Action leads to hiring of less-qualified women or minorities. In terms of formal qualifications, one useful piece of information we have is whether the most recently hired worker falls short of the educational requirement for the job (whether that is a college or high school degree).[22] Here we are comparing the employee's actual educational attainment with the stated requirements by employers in a separate question.[23] For the analysis of this outcome, we estimate logit equations of the form:

$$U_{ijk} = g(X_{jk}, X_k, D'_{ijk}, AA_{jk}, v_{ijk}).$$ (4)

U_{ijk} is a dummy variable for whether the worker was underqualified for the job. The control variables here include all of the X_{jk} and X_k. D'_{ijk} is a vector of dummy variables for the demographic group of the worker actually hired, as explained below. Prior to looking at whether or not the worker is underqualified, we also look at qualifications in terms of educational levels, using a linear model. Again, we separately consider the effects of Affirmative Action in recruiting and hiring.

Once we start to compare qualifications (or, as below, performance) of workers in different demographic groups, we have to be careful to attempt to sort out effects of Affirmative Action from those differences that would exist even in its absence. To do this in equation (4), we interact the Affirmative Action dummy variables with a set of dummy variables capturing the race and sex of the last hired worker (D'). Then the estimated equation takes the form:

$$U_{ijk} = \alpha WM_{ijk} \cdot (1 - AA_{jk}) + \beta D_{ijk} \cdot AA_{jk} + \gamma WM_{ijk} \cdot AA_{jk}$$
$$+ \delta D_{ijk} \cdot (1 - AA_{jk}) + \theta(X_k, X_{jk}) + v_{ijk}.$$ (5)

WM_{ijk} is a dummy variable for white males and D_{ijk} is a set of dummy variables for each other demographic group considered.[24] One relevant comparison might be between women/minority hires and white male hires in establishments using Affirmative Action. The difference in U for this comparison, which is given by $(\beta - \gamma)$, addresses whether Affirmative Action leads to hiring of women or minorities who are less qualified than the white male workers hired in similar establishments.[25] However, this can lead to misleading inferences regarding the effects of Affirmative Action *per se*, because of differences in skills or qualifications between women/minorities and white males that exist independently of Affirmative Action.

For example, suppose that the estimate of $(\beta - \gamma)$ is a large negative number, indicating that women or minorities hired into establishments using Affirmative Action are less qualified than white males hired into similar establishments. There may, however, be an economy-wide shortfall in qualifications of women/minorities relative to white males, in which case workers in non-Affirmative Action establishments should serve as a control group for overall differences between these groups.

To estimate the independent effects of Affirmative Action on differences between white male and other workers, we then subtract off any shortfall in qualifications in establishments not using Affirmative Action, and ask instead whether the short-fall is *relatively larger* in establishments using Affirmative Action. In general, the shortfall in qualifications (or performance) in establishments not using Affir-mative Action is measured by $(\delta - \alpha)$, leading to the "difference-in-differences" estimate of $(\beta - \gamma) - (\delta - \alpha)$. We regard these difference-in-differences estimates as more meaningful indicators of whether Affirmative Action leads to the hiring of less-qualified women or minorities.[26]

Evaluation, reward, and training

The skills and qualifications possessed by new hires are not set in stone, but can be influenced by training. In addition, performance can be affected by both pay and evaluation systems, in the latter case resulting in both constructive feedback as well as weeding out of employees who turn out to be unsatisfactory. Affirmative Action may influence evaluation, reward, and training as employers attempt to upgrade the skills of workers hired under Affirmative Action, or use pay and evaluation mechanisms to ensure better performance. In terms of evaluation and pay "personnel" policies, we have data on: whether formal systems are in place for evaluating employee performance; whether performance-based pay policies are used; and whether there is a probationary period for the employee.

For each of these three variables, we estimate logit models of the same form as equation (1), estimating separate equations for Affirmative Action in recruiting and hiring. We also estimate models for hours of formal and informal training the new hire receives (where informal training reflects time spent with supervisors or coworkers). The training equations are estimated as Tobits.[27]

Current performance

Finally, the net result from all of the steps of the recruitment, screening, hiring, and employment process is the current performance of the employee. The performance measure we have is a supervisor's rating of the employee on a scale of 1–100. To scale this, the survey also asked the supervisor to rate the "typical" employee on this job, which we subtract off of the rating for the most recent hire.[28] As with educational underqualification, we report difference-in-difference estimates to isolate the effects of Affirmative Action *per se*; the specification is the same as equation (5).

Control variables

Most of the specifications we estimate include a full set of control variables for establishment and job characteristics. The establishment characteristics include industry, collective bargaining coverage, location (including dummy variables for each MSA and for areas within MSAs), racial composition of customers, and establishment size. We also control for whether or not the establishment has a personnel or human resources department, since those that do will no doubt use a different set of recruiting and hiring behaviors than those that do not.[29] The job characteristics for which we control include year of hire, occupation dummy variables, and dummy variables for the daily performance of a variety of tasks (e.g. reading/writing paragraphs, arithmetic, computer use, etc.) and for job requirements (e.g. college or high school degrees, specific experience, previous training, etc.).[30] The precise control variables included in each specification are detailed in the footnotes to the tables that follow.

Results

Summary statistics on establishments' use of Affirmative Action

In Table 14.1 we present summary data on establishments reporting the use of Affirmative Action in recruiting and hiring. Panel A simply tabulates the use of each type of Affirmative Action, indicating that 56 percent of establishments use Affirmative Action in recruiting, while 42 percent use it in hiring. In addition, the panel shows that of those establishments using Affirmative Action in recruiting, 70 percent also report using it in hiring, while of those using Affirmative Action in hiring, 93 percent also report using it in recruiting. Thus, almost all establishments that use Affirmative Action in hiring also do so in recruiting, so that we can think of Affirmative Action in hiring as essentially always accompanied by Affirmative Action in recruiting. However, the reverse is not as true, as there is a sizable fraction (0.30) of establishments that report using Affirmative Action in recruiting only. Thus, we can hope to identify differential effects of Affirmative Action in recruiting and Affirmative Action in hiring.

In Panel B we present means (and standard deviations, for nonbinary variables) of establishment characteristics for establishments using each type of Affirmative Action and those using no Affirmative Action. The results indicate that establishments using Affirmative Action tend to be significantly larger and more heavily unionized, and are much more likely to have personnel departments. By industry, establishments using Affirmative Action are more likely to be in the services sector, and less likely to be in wholesale or retail trade. Although not reported in this table, it is also the case that the jobs for which establishments report using Affirmative Action require relatively higher skills (Holzer and Neumark, 1999).

The positive association between Affirmative Action, establishment size, and the presence of a personnel department (which presumably implies more formal methods of recruitment and hiring) is noteworthy, since all are likely to affect the procedures by which establishments recruit or hire and all are likely to be positively correlated with the hiring of minorities (Holzer, 1987, 1998). On the other hand, the generally higher skill requirements at these establishments would, all else equal, result in fewer minority employees there. The importance of controlling for a wide range of observable establishment and job characteristics is thus underscored by these results.

Table 14.1 Descriptive statistics on use of Affirmative Action in recruiting and hiring[a]

	Total	Of those using Affirmative Action in	
		Recruiting	Hiring
A. Proportion using			
Affirmative Action—recruiting	0.55	—	0.93
Affirmative Action—hiring	0.42	0.70	—

	Affirmative Action— recruiting (1)	Affirmative Action— hiring (2)	No Affirmative Action (3)
B. Mean characteristics of establishments			
Central city	0.29	0.25	0.24
Non-central city MSA	0.16	0.16	0.16
Number of employees	504	560	116
	(1,407)	(1,493)	(444)
Percent unionized	18.48	19.31	11.46
	(35.45)	(35.71)	(29.96)
Employer has personnel dept.	0.42	0.43	0.17
Construction	0.02	0.01	0.02
Transportation, communications, and utilities	0.07	0.07	0.06
Manufacturing, durables	0.11	0.10	0.12
Manufacturing, nondurables	0.09	0.10	0.11
Wholesale trade	0.05	0.04	0.09
Retail trade	0.12	0.11	0.20
Finance, insurance, and real estate	0.08	0.08	0.07
Services	0.46	0.46	0.33
Public	0.02	0.01	0.003
N	1,172	865	928
Percentage of customers black	19.04	18.93	16.23
	(19.68)	(19.57)	(19.95)
N	815	599	703
Percentage of customers Hispanic	16.11	14.06	10.44
	(24.16)	(20.86)	(14.78)
N	809	591	692

Note

a Means are reported, with standard deviations in parentheses.

Summary statistics on outcome variables

Table 14.2 provides descriptive statistics, broken down by the use of Affirmative Action, on each of the outcome variables that we study in this chapter. In addition to foreshadowing some of the results, this table provides a "road map" for the empirical analyses we conduct in this chapter. For each set of outcomes, we provide descriptive statistics broken out by the types of Affirmative Action used in the multivariate analysis that follows (as explained in the previous section). Thus, for example, for recruitment methods we only look at whether establishments use

	Affirmative Action in		No Affirmative Action
	Recruiting (1)	Hiring (2)	(3)
Recruitment methods, all methods used			
Walk in/sign	0.77	—	0.66
Referral from current employees/others	0.91	—	0.87
State/community agency	0.50	—	0.31
Private agency	0.26	—	0.18
Newspaper	0.52	—	0.45
Referral from unions/schools	0.46	—	0.33
Recruitment methods, method that generated last hire			
Walk in/sign	0.15	—	0.16
Referral from current employees/others	0.37	—	0.46
State/community agency	0.04	—	0.04
Private agency	0.08	—	0.03
Newspaper	0.31	—	0.27
Referral from unions/schools	0.05	—	0.05
Applicant demographics			
Percentage black male	14.63	—	14.86
	(19.79)	—	(22.09)
Percentage black female	13.50	—	9.93
	(18.33)	—	(17.70)
Percentage Hispanic	17.38	—	12.54
	(27.07)	—	(23.83)
Screening methods			
Test/work sample (required)	0.42	0.40	0.41
Drug test/physical (required)	0.18	0.17	0.11
Check references (always)	0.81	0.82	0.67
Check education (always)	0.45	0.48	0.25
Check criminal record (always)	0.39	0.36	0.21
Require written application (always)	0.88	0.89	0.76
Require interview (always)	0.88	0.88	0.89
Hiring criteria—would definitely/probably hire			
Person with criminal record	0.40	0.40	0.35
Welfare recipient	0.92	0.93	0.90
Person with govt. training/GED	0.97	0.97	0.97
Person with short-term/part-time work history	0.60	0.60	0.55
Person unemployed more than 1 year	0.84	0.84	0.79
Last worker hired			
White male	0.25	0.24	0.33
White female	0.40	0.44	0.35
Black male	0.09	0.09	0.09
Black female	0.09	0.08	0.08
Hispanic	0.17	0.15	0.15
Percentage of workforce			
White male	29.89	30.84	36.54
	(25.05)	(24.85)	(30.63)
White female	35.82	35.48	35.22
	(27.40)	(27.46)	(30.47)

Table 14.2 Continued

	Affirmative Action in		No Affirmative Action
	Recruiting (1)	Hiring (2)	(3)
Black male	9.34	9.53	7.90
	(14.08)	(14.16)	(14.67)
Black female	10.24	9.90	7.96
	(16.75)	(16.55)	(16.50)
Hispanic	14.71	14.24	12.39
	(24.30)	(24.00)	(24.17)
Education			
Years of education	13.84	13.90	13.26
	(2.15)	(2.16)	(2.06)
White male	14.47	14.66	13.58
White female	14.10	14.29	13.62
Black male	13.25	13.32	12.75
Black female	12.87	12.95	12.63
Hispanic	13.13	12.33	12.27
Last worker hired underqualified			
Based on degree	0.05	0.06	0.04
White male	0.04	0.03	0.03
White female	0.05	0.06	0.06
Black male	0.03	0.03	0.02
Black female	0.11	0.15	0.03
Hispanic	0.06	0.09	0.02
Based on degree/GED	0.05	0.06	0.04
White male	0.04	0.03	0.03
White female	0.05	0.06	0.06
Black male	0.02	0.02	0.03
Black female	0.11	0.17	0.02
Hispanic	0.05	0.10	0.03
Evaluation/pay systems			
Formal performance evaluation system	0.85	0.84	0.60
Pay for performance	0.60	0.59	0.62
Probationary period	0.73	0.69	0.72
Training			
Hours of formal training	25.41	26.00	18.72
	(45.32)	(46.39)	(39.13)
Hours of informal training	61.33	61.90	55.38
	(52.21)	(53.40)	(52.94)
Performance rating			
Normalized rating	1.92	1.22	2.54
	(15.04)	(16.44)	(17.98)
White male	1.05	2.75	5.28
White female	1.74	0.41	2.29
Black male	1.57	1.44	−0.38
Black female	4.33	5.56	−1.23
Hispanic	2.46	−0.72	0.90

Note

a Means are reported, with standard deviations in parentheses. Sample sizes and other details regarding variables are provided in corresponding tables for the multivariate analyses that follow. Training hours are capped at 160.

Affirmative Action in recruiting, whereas for the demographic characteristics of hires, we look at Affirmative Action in both recruiting and hiring.[31]

We begin by looking at the relationship between Affirmative Action in recruiting and recruitment methods used. The figures for all methods used indicate that establishments using Affirmative Action in recruiting use a wider array of recruitment methods, as the proportion reporting use of each type of method is higher for the establishments using Affirmative Action in recruiting. The figures for the method reported to have generated the last hire are perhaps more revealing, then, since respondents can only select one of these. The means are consistent with Affirmative Action in recruiting encouraging use of methods more likely to cast a wide net and to reach all types of workers (like newspaper advertisements), and discouraging use of methods that are more likely to result in hiring a workforce demographically similar to the existing workforce or the local population (walk in/signs or referrals from current employees/others).

Recruitment methods are presumably linked to applicants, so the next set of descriptive statistics looks at applicant flows. These figures reveal a considerably higher proportion of black female and Hispanic (but not black male) applicants to establishments using Affirmative Action in recruiting (and apparently using more "open" recruitment methods). Among the questions we will address in the multivariate analysis is the extent to which the differences in recruitment methods account for the differences in applicant flows at establishments using Affirmative Action in recruiting.

The next stage in the process is screening and the application of hiring criteria. The descriptive statistics on screening methods used indicate that, with the exception of requiring an interview, establishments using Affirmative Action in either recruiting or hiring are more likely to make use of each type of screening method. This suggests that establishments using Affirmative Action not only cast a wider net in recruitment, but also invest more heavily in screening applicants to identify those with desirable characteristics.[32] The findings for hiring criteria are consistent with employers obtaining more information about applicants when they use Affirmative Action, enabling them to hire applicants with traditionally "stigmatizing" characteristics.[33] At establishments using Affirmative Action in recruiting or hiring, employers are more willing to hire workers with criminal records, workers who are welfare recipients, and workers with spottier employment histories.

Table 14.2 next turns to the demographic characteristics of workers hired, first looking at the last worker hired, and then at the overall composition of the workforce.[34] Looking at the last worker hired, establishments using Affirmative Action in recruiting or hiring are considerably less likely to hire a white male, and considerably more likely to hire a white female. The proportion hiring black females and Hispanics is slightly higher only for Affirmative Action in recruiting. Turning to the overall composition of the workforce, we again find the proportion white male lower at establishments using Affirmative Action in either recruiting or hiring, while for this variable Affirmative Action in recruiting or hiring is associated with more hiring of black males and females and of Hispanics.

The next panels of Table 14.2 refer to the qualifications of the workers hired under Affirmative Action, looking at their educational levels as well whether they are underqualified (relative to educational requirements). Education levels are higher in establishments using Affirmative Action in either recruiting or hiring. This is true for all demographic groups, although much less pronounced for Hispanics when Affirmative Action is used in hiring. In general, women and minorities hired in establishments using Affirmative Action in either recruiting or hiring are less highly educated than white males hired in those establishments. However, here the difference-in-difference estimator is appropriate, to obtain a comparison relative to the female/minority vs. white male difference in the non-Affirmative Action sector. For example, the educational shortfall among Hispanics in establishments using Affirmative Action in hiring is 2.33 (i.e. 14.66 − 12.33), while the difference between these groups in establishments not using Affirmative Action is 1.31 (13.58 − 12.27). Thus, the difference-in-difference estimator of the shortfall in education, which measures how much greater this shortfall of Hispanics is in the Affirmative Action sector, is 1.02 (2.33 − 1.31).

The proportion underqualified is higher at establishments using Affirmative Action in recruiting, and higher still at establishments using Affirmative Action in hiring. The descriptive statistics disaggregated by demographic group reveal that in establishments using Affirmative Action in recruiting or in hiring, black female and Hispanic hires are considerably more likely to be underqualified; for both groups the shortfall is greater when Affirmative Action is used in hiring. We can also use the disaggregated means to compute the difference-in-differences estimator. For example, using the means in the first panel, the difference in the proportion underqualified between black females and white males in establishments using Affirmative Action in hiring is 0.12 (0.15 − 0.03). Among establishments not using Affirmative Action, this proportion is equal for white males and black females, leading to a difference-in-difference estimate of 0.12. For Hispanic hires, as well, the difference-in-differences estimator indicates a higher probability of underqualification relative to white males.

Having examined who gets hired and their qualifications, Table 14.2 next turns to personnel policies used to evaluate, motivate, and train employees. Although there appear to be no notable differences across establishments in the use of pay for performance, establishments using Affirmative Action in recruiting or hiring are considerably more likely to use formal performance evaluation systems. However, whereas establishments using Affirmative Action in recruiting have a higher tendency to use probationary periods, those using Affirmative Action in hiring have a lower tendency to use them. Turning to training, we see that establishments using Affirmative Action in either recruiting or hiring report more hours of both formal and informal training.

Finally, the last panel reports normalized performance ratings, which we interpret as a summary measure of current performance. There appears to be no sizable performance shortfall among hires in establishments using Affirmative Action in recruiting or in hiring. In fact, among black male and black female hires performance appears to be higher; for example, the difference-in-differences estimate for black females relative to white males in establishments using Affirmative Action in hiring is 9.32 (i.e. $5.56 - 2.75 - \{-1.23 - 5.28\}$). Note that performance of these groups is at or above that of white males even in the simple difference.

As a provisional summary, the univariate comparisons in Table 14.2 suggest that Affirmative Action is associated with substantial shifts in hiring practices, personnel policies, and employment outcomes. These univariate comparisons suggest that Affirmative Action encourages employers to use recruitment methods more likely to result in demographically diverse applicant pools, and that this shift in applicants actually occurs. Affirmative Action is also associated with more intensive screening of applicants, and with more flexible hiring criteria. This suggests that casting a wider net will, on the one hand, bring in more women and minorities. On the other hand, it may also entail hiring more workers with some less-desirable characteristics (because of population-wide differences between race/ethnic groups, such as higher crime rates and lower education levels for minorities); employers may initially screen on these characteristics, but the more intensive screening associated with Affirmative Action may lead them to identify other characteristics that at least partially offset these factors. Affirmative Action appears to be successful in terms of boosting the hiring of women and minorities, although when used in hiring, in particular, results in a higher likelihood of less-qualified or underqualified hires. Employers using Affirmative Action do, however, appear to take some steps to help these workers, using formal evaluation systems and providing more training. Coupled with more intensive screening, the ultimate effect appears to be that current performance of women/minority employees at establishments using Affirmative Action is as high as that of otherwise comparable workers.

The following sections explore this evidence more fully in a multivariate setting that controls for other establishment characteristics, and considers some of the effects of Affirmative Action on applicant flows and hires taking account of differences in recruitment methods, screening methods, etc.

Recruitment methods and applicant flows

Table 14.3 presents estimates of logit and multinomial logit models for recruitment methods used for the most recently filled job. Both versions of recruitment methods are used here: one for whether each of a series of methods was used at all during the recruitment process for this position; and one for which method generated the applicant who was ultimately hired. Column (1) presents results from a series of independent logit equations for the former recruitment measure, and column (2) presents results from a multinomial logit equation for the latter measure. The table reports partial derivatives of the probability of each outcome with respect to the Affirmative Action variable, with standard errors of these partial derivatives in parentheses. In these estimations, we look only at the effects of Affirmative Action in recruiting. Control variables in each equation include the full set of establishment and job characteristics, as described in the footnote to the table.

The results in column (1) show that the use of Affirmative Action in recruiting tends to raise the use of virtually each recruitment method. The effect is

Table 14.3 Estimated effects of Affirmative Action in recruiting on method of recruitment[a]

	All methods used to fill position, logit estimates of effect of Affirmative Action in recruiting (1)	Method that generated last hire, multinomial logit estimates of effect of Affirmative Action in recruiting (2)
Walk in/sign	0.083**	0.007
	(0.021)	(0.017)
Referral from current employees/others	0.012	−0.082**
	(0.013)	(0.025)
State/community agency	0.128**	0.005
	(0.025)	(0.006)
Private agency	0.034	0.021**
	(0.019)	(0.008)
Newspaper	0.070**	0.055**
	(0.025)	(0.023)
Referral from unions/schools	0.079**	−0.007
	(0.025)	(0.008)
N	2,162	2,162

Notes

* statistically significant at the 10-percent level.
** statistically significant at the 5-percent level.
a Partial derivatives of probabilities of outcomes are reported (evaluated at sample means), with standard errors of these partial derivatives in parentheses. All specifications include the following controls: dummy variables for city, year of hire, central city and noncentral city SMSA, whether the employer has a personnel department, industry, occupation, job tasks and requirements, and the race or sex of the interview respondent; and controls for percent covered by collective bargaining, size, and percentage of black and Hispanic customers. Column (1) reports estimated coefficients of the Affirmative Action—recruiting variable from separate logit estimations; column (2) reports estimates of the coefficient of the Affirmative Action—recruiting variable from a single multinomial logit estimation. In each table all estimates are weighted.

smallest and least significant for the use of informal referrals from current and other employees. On the other hand, the probabilities of using walk ins/signs, state/community agencies, newspapers, and referrals from unions/schools—that is, methods likely to attract more diverse applicants—are significantly increased. Turning to the method reported to have generated the last hire, in column (2), the estimates indicate that Affirmative Action significantly boosts the use of private agencies and newspapers in generating new hires, and decreases the use of informal referrals from current employees/others. Thus, both the overall number of recruitment methods used (and therefore the overall intensity of recruitment activity) as well as their composition change under Affirmative Action. The composition shift is, to some extent, away from methods that are less likely to generate demographically diverse applicants (such as informal referrals from current employees/others) and toward the opposite types of methods (such as newspapers).

The evidence of changes in recruitment practices used under Affirmative Action suggests that Affirmative Action may increase the flow of minority and/or female applicants to establishments. In Table 14.4 we present Tobit estimates of the effects of Affirmative Action in recruiting on the percentages of applicants for these positions who were black males, black females, and Hispanics. For each equation, two specifications are presented: one with the same controls as in Table 14.3, and another in which we also control for the recruitment methods used in hiring for this position. By comparing the latter estimates to the former, we can infer the extent to which any observed effects of Affirmative Action operate indirectly through the effects of Affirmative Action in recruiting on the recruitment methods chosen.

The results in columns (1), (3), and (5), which exclude the recruitment methods, show that Affirmative Action in recruiting has positive and significant effects on the flows of black female applicants and Hispanic applicants. More specifically, Affirmative Action in recruiting raises the percentages of applicants who are black female or Hispanic by 3–4 percentage points each; these represent large percentage

Table 14.4 Estimated effects of Affirmative Action and recruiting methods on applicant demographics[a]

	Percent black male		Percent black female		Percent hispanic	
	(1)	*(2)*	*(3)*	*(4)*	*(5)*	*(6)*
Affirmative	0.010	0.0005	0.038**	0.028**	0.033**	0.030**
Action-recruiting	(0.012)	(0.012)	(0.011)	(0.011)	(0.012)	(0.012)
Recruiting methods, among all methods used to fill position						
Walk in/sign	—	−0.010	—	0.020	—	0.024*
		(0.013)		(0.013)		(0.014)
Referral from current employees/others	—	0.049**	—	0.010	—	0.047**
		(0.018)		(0.017)		(0.020)
State/community agency	—	0.075**	—	0.047**	—	0.013
		(0.013)		(0.012)		(0.013)
Private agency	—	0.028*	—	0.016	—	0.014
		(0.015)		(0.014)		(0.015)
Newspaper	—	0.038**	—	0.035**	—	−0.011
		(0.011)		(0.011)		(0.012)
Referral from unions/schools	—	0.008	—	0.010	—	0.018
		(0.012)		(0.011)		(0.013)
N	1,648	1,648	1,678	1,678	1,817	1,817

Note

a Estimates are from two-tailed Tobit models. All specifications include the following controls: dummy variables for city, year, central city and noncentral city SMSA, whether the employer has a personnel department, industry, occupation, job tasks and requirements, and the race or sex of the interview respondent; and controls for percent covered by collective bargaining, size, and percentage of black and Hispanic customers. See footnote to Table 14.3 for additional details.

changes, since (as Table 14.2 shows) the percentage of black female (Hispanic) applicants at establishments not using Affirmative Action in recruiting is 9.92 (13.28). The results in columns (2), (4), and (6), when the recruitment methods are included, indicate slightly smaller direct effects of Affirmative Action in recruiting, although the estimates do not appear to be significantly different from those in the odd-numbered columns. Thus, these results suggest that recruitment methods *per se* account for only a fraction of the shift in applicant demographics associated with the use of Affirmative Action in recruiting.[35,36]

Screening methods and hiring criteria

The evidence to this point indicates that Affirmative Action in recruiting generates more minority applicants, in part perhaps by changing the recruitment methods that employers use. We might expect employers facing larger pools of minority applicants because of Affirmative Action to use additional screening methods as well. In the absence of Affirmative Action employers may have been screening efficiently. For example, education and race may have been relatively cheap and efficient screens. Having recruited an applicant pool with more minorities, however, employers would have to use additional screening methods to look for characteristics for which they previously used race as a screen (such as lower educational quality, higher rates of participation in illegal activities, etc.).

Panel A of Table 14.5 reports logit estimates for each type of screening method, as a function of Affirmative Action in recruiting and the other control variables included previously. The estimates indicate that employers using Affirmative Action in recruiting make significantly higher use of most screening methods, including: drug test/physical; checking references, education, and criminal records; and requiring a written application. In Panel B, we instead use Affirmative Action in hiring as the independent variable of most interest, to see whether the results differ for the smaller set of establishments that report that Affirmative Action affects not only recruiting but also hiring. However, the results are generally quite similar, and (except for the use of drug tests/physicals), continue to indicate that employers using Affirmative Action appear to use considerably more screening methods.[37]

In Table 14.6, we look instead at hiring criteria. In particular, we ask whether the employer's willingness to hire a worker with less desirable characteristics is higher for employers using Affirmative Action, for the same reasons outlined above. The results in Panel A indicate that Affirmative Action in recruiting is associated with a significantly greater likelihood that an employer is willing to hire a worker with a criminal record or who has been unemployed for more than a year. The results in Panel B indicate that the signs are the same for Affirmative Action in hiring, although the evidence is weaker. This differential suggests that Affirmative Action in recruiting, in particular, may lead employers to gather more information about prospective employees so that they are willing to hire employees who have some negative characteristics, perhaps because their more intensive screening has identified other positive characteristics.

Table 14.5 Estimated effects of Affirmative Action in recruiting and hiring on screening mechanisms used by employers[a]

	Test/ work sample (1)	Drug test/ physical (2)	Check references (3)	Check education (4)	Check criminal record (5)	Require written application (6)	Require interview (7)
A. Effects of Affirmative Action in recruiting							
Affirmative Action—recruiting	−0.007 (0.024)	0.039** (0.013)	0.065** (0.019)	0.108** (0.024)	0.137** (0.022)	0.066** (0.015)	−0.025* (0.013)
B. Effects of Affirmative Action in hiring							
Affirmative Action—hiring	−0.033 (0.024)	0.002 (0.012)	0.046** (0.019)	0.114** (0.023)	0.054** (0.021)	0.075** (0.016)	−0.019* (0.012)
N	2,187	2,358	2,351	2,343	2,316	2,353	2,358

Note

a Partial derivatives of probabilities of outcomes are reported, with standard errors of these partial derivatives in parentheses. Each estimate is from a separate logit estimation. All specifications include the following controls: dummy variables for city, year, central city and noncentral city SMSA, whether the employer has a personnel department, industry, occupation, job tasks and requirements, and the race or sex of the interview respondent; and controls for percent covered by collective bargaining, size, and percentage of black and Hispanic customers. See footnote to Table 14.3 for additional details.

Table 14.6 Estimated effects of Affirmative Action in recruiting and hiring on hiring criteria of employers, for jobs not requiring college degree[a]

	Would definitely/probably hire				
	Person with criminal record (1)	Welfare recipient (2)	Person with govt. training/ GED (3)	Person with short-term/ part-time work history (4)	Person unemployed more than 1 year (5)
A. Effects of Affirmative Action in recruiting					
Affirmative Action—recruiting	0.065** (0.024)	−0.007 (0.010)	0.006 (0.005)	0.038 (0.025)	0.034** (0.017)
B. Effects of Affirmative Action in hiring					
Affirmative Action—hiring	0.042* (0.025)	0.004 (0.011)	−0.0002 (0.005)	0.024 (0.025)	0.027 (0.017)
N	1,974	2,004	1,954	1,957	1,936

Note

a Partial derivatives of probabilities of outcomes are reported, with standard errors of these partial derivatives in parentheses. Each estimate is from a separate logit estimation. All specifications include the following controls: dummy variables for city, year, central city and noncentral city SMSA, whether the employer has a personnel department, industry, occupation, job tasks and requirements, and the race or sex of the interview respondent; and controls for percent covered by collective bargaining, size, and percentage of black and Hispanic customers. See footnote to Table 14.3 for additional details. The data on hiring criteria are available only for jobs not requiring a college degree.

Demographic characteristics and qualifications of hires

The results thus far indicate that the processes of recruiting and screening job applicants is quite different between firms that do or do not use Affirmative Action.

Those who use it recruit more extensively and screen more intensively, generate more minority applicants, and appear more willing to consider hiring those with stigmatizing personal characteristics and histories. How do all of these factors affect the race/gender mix of those who are hired? And, if more women or minorities are hired under Affirmative Action, do they have weaker credentials than those of white males hired at similar establishments?

We begin to address these questions in Table 14.7, where we present estimates of multinomial logit models in which the dependent variable is the demographic group of the last worker hired. In Table 14.8, we instead report Tobit estimates for the percentages of the establishment's workforce that belong to a particular demographic group. In both tables, we look at Affirmative Action in recruiting as well as Affirmative Action in hiring. We also report estimates with and without controlling for recruitment methods, applicant demographics, screening methods, and hiring criteria, to gauge the extent to which the shifts in these variables associated with Affirmative Action explain hiring differences associated with Affirmative Action.

The estimates in Panel A of Table 14.7, which study the last worker hired, indicate that Affirmative Action in recruiting is weakly associated with increased hiring of white women, black men, and Hispanics, and with decreased hiring of white men. The only statistically significant shift (at the 10-percent level) associated with Affirmative Action in recruiting is in favor of Hispanic hires in jobs not requiring college degrees (columns (8) and (9)). Although many of these estimates are at best marginally significant, it is also the case that the estimated effects on hiring generally do not get much smaller when we control for the other shifts that Affirmative Action in recruiting induces.

Panel B turns to the narrower subset of employers using Affirmative Action in hiring. In this case, the effects on the demographic characteristics of the last worker hired are much more pronounced, with significant increases in the probability that white females (by as much as 0.08) or black males (by as much as 0.03) are hired, and significant decreases in the probability that white males are hired (by about $0.05 - 0.07$). Thus, in contrast to Affirmative Action in recruiting, Affirmative Action in hiring induces larger, more statistically significant shifts in hiring toward underrepresented groups. It is also the case that controlling for the other shifts that Affirmative Action induces does relatively little to explain the differences in the demographic characteristics of the last worker hired. In columns (6)–(7), in particular, which look at screening methods—the one type of policy for which we already documented apparent effects of Affirmative Action in hiring—the increase in the probability that a white female is hired and decrease in the probability that a white male is hired are both larger in absolute value once the controls for screening methods are added. Thus, it appears that Affirmative Action in hiring generates increased hiring of women and minorities that cannot be explained by changes in recruitment methods, screening methods, and hiring criteria that might be expected to widen the pool of minority and female applicants, which is perhaps more consistent with outright preferential treatment in hiring.

In Table 14.8 we turn to estimates of the effects of Affirmative Action in recruiting and hiring on the overall demographic composition of establishments'

Table 14.7 Estimates of effects of Affirmative Action in recruiting and hiring on demographic characteristics of last worker hired, with and without controls for recruitment methods, applicant demographics, screening methods, and hiring criteria[a]

	Recruitment methods			Applicant demographics		Screening methods		Jobs not requiring college degree	
	(1)	(2)	(3)	(4)	(5)	(6)	(7)	(8)	(9)
A. Affirmative Action used in recruiting									
White female	0.037 (0.028)	0.044 (0.029)	0.027 (0.029)	0.018 (0.033)	0.024 (0.034)	0.029 (0.028)	0.042 (0.029)	-0.013 (0.032)	-0.015 (0.032)
Black male	0.011 (0.010)	0.007 (0.010)	0.011 (0.010)	-0.002 (0.013)	0.002 (0.012)	0.003 (0.010)	0.004 (0.010)	0.015 (0.013)	0.012 (0.013)
Black female	-0.005 (0.010)	-0.008 (0.010)	-0.006 (0.010)	0.004 (0.013)	0.001 (0.011)	-0.007 (0.011)	-0.009 (0.011)	-0.0004 (0.014)	0.004 (0.014)
Hispanic	-0.005 (0.015)	-0.003 (0.015)	-0.007 (0.015)	-0.001 (0.018)	-0.006 (0.021)	-0.001 (0.015)	-0.002 (0.015)	0.031* (0.018)	0.034* (0.019)
White male	-0.037 (0.027)	-0.039 (0.027)	-0.024 (0.027)	-0.020 (0.033)	-0.020 (0.034)	-0.024 (0.027)	-0.034 (0.028)	-0.032 (0.031)	-0.035 (0.031)
B. Affirmative Action used in hiring									
White female	0.068** (0.028)	0.073** (0.029)	0.060** (0.029)	0.040 (0.034)	0.041 (0.035)	0.072** (0.028)	0.084** (0.029)	0.016 (0.032)	0.014 (0.033)
Black male	0.022** (0.010)	0.016 (0.010)	0.021** (0.010)	0.017 (0.013)	0.014 (0.012)	0.011 (0.010)	0.011 (0.010)	0.026** (0.013)	0.023* (0.013)
Black female	-0.016 (0.010)	-0.017* (0.010)	-0.018* (0.010)	-0.015 (0.012)	-0.013 (0.012)	-0.012 (0.010)	-0.015 (0.011)	-0.015 (0.014)	-0.012 (0.014)
Hispanic	-0.012 (0.014)	-0.010 (0.015)	-0.013 (0.014)	-0.0001 (0.018)	0.002 (0.020)	-0.007 (0.014)	-0.011 (0.014)	0.020 (0.018)	0.023 (0.018)
White male	-0.063** (0.027)	-0.063** (0.027)	-0.051* (0.027)	-0.041 (0.033)	-0.045 (0.034)	-0.063** (0.027)	-0.070** (0.028)	-0.047 (0.031)	-0.049 (0.032)
Other controls considered:									
	No	Yes, all methods	Yes, method generating hire	No	Yes	No	Yes	No	Yes
	Recruitment methods			Applicant demographics		Screening methods		Hiring criteria	
N	2,162	2,162	2,162	1,584	1,584	2,135	2,135	1,701	1,701

Note

a Partial derivatives of probabilities of outcomes (evaluated at sample means) are reported, with standard errors of these partial derivatives in parentheses. Each column in each panel reports results from a multinomial logit estimation. All specifications include the following controls: dummy variables for city, year, central city and noncentral city SMSA, whether the employer has a personnel department, industry, occupation, job tasks and requirements, and the race or sex of the interview respondent; and controls for percent covered by collective bargaining, size, and percentage of black and Hispanic customers. See footnote to Table 14.3 for additional details. The data on hiring criteria are available only for jobs not requiring a college degree.

Table 14.8 Estimates of effects of Affirmative Action in recruiting and hiring on demographic composition in noncollege jobs, with and without controls for recruitment methods, applicant demographics, screening methods, and hiring criteria[a]

	(1)	(2)	(3)	(4)	(5)	(6)	(7)	(8)
A. Affirmative Action used in recruiting								
White female	0.032**	0.034**	0.040**	0.033**	0.039**	0.042**	0.025*	0.026**
	(0.013)	(0.013)	(0.015)	(0.014)	(0.013)	(0.013)	(0.015)	(0.015)
Black male	0.020**	0.015	0.0004	0.012	0.014	0.006	0.018	0.017
	(0.009)	(0.009)	(0.012)	(0.010)	(0.010)	(0.010)	(0.011)	(0.011)
Black female	0.029**	0.024**	0.021	0.013	0.021*	0.012	0.006	0.008
	(0.011)	(0.011)	(0.013)	(0.011)	(0.011)	(0.011)	(0.012)	(0.012)
Hispanic	0.005	0.006	0.013	0.013	0.008	0.010	0.004	0.004
	(0.013)	(0.013)	(0.016)	(0.013)	(0.014)	(0.014)	(0.015)	(0.015)
White male	−0.023*	−0.024*	−0.027*	−0.022	−0.025*	−0.027*	−0.013	−0.014
	(0.013)	(0.013)	(0.016)	(0.015)	(0.014)	(0.014)	(0.015)	(0.015)
B. Affirmative Action used in hiring								
White female	0.013	0.015	0.021	0.015	0.016	0.017	0.047**	0.047**
	(0.013)	(0.013)	(0.015)	(0.014)	(0.013)	(0.013)	(0.015)	(0.015)
Black male	0.012	0.008	−0.006	−0.001	0.010	0.006	0.009	0.009
	(0.009)	(0.009)	(0.012)	(0.010)	(0.009)	(0.010)	(0.011)	(0.011)
Black female	0.012	0.007	−0.011	−0.010	−0.001	−0.010	−0.006	−0.005
	(0.010)	(0.011)	(0.013)	(0.011)	(0.011)	(0.011)	(0.013)	(0.012)
Hispanic	0.030**	0.030**	0.039**	0.047**	0.029**	0.030**	0.008	0.009
	(0.013)	(0.013)	(0.015)	(0.013)	(0.013)	(0.013)	(0.015)	(0.015)
White male	−0.012	−0.014	−0.017	−0.021	−0.009	−0.007	−0.025*	−0.024*
	(0.013)	(0.013)	(0.016)	(0.015)	(0.013)	(0.013)	(0.015)	(0.015)
Other controls considered:								
	Recruitment methods		Applicant demographics		Screening methods		Hiring criteria	
	No	Yes	No	Yes	No	Yes	No	Yes
N	2,304	2,304	1,625	1,625	2,125	2,125	1,720	1,720

Note

a Each column in each panel reports results from a two-tailed Tobit estimation. All specifications include the following controls: dummy variables for city, year, central city and noncentral city SMSA, whether the employer has a personnel department, industry; and controls for percent covered by collective bargaining, size, and percentage of black and Hispanic customers. (The controls for occupation and job tasks and requirements are dropped because the dependent variable in this table covers the entire workforce in noncollege jobs.) See footnote to Table 14.3 for additional details. The data on hiring criteria are available only for jobs not requiring a college degree. Recruitment methods in this table refer to all methods used.

workforces; recall that this variable is restricted to noncollege jobs. In this case, the effects of Affirmative Action in recruiting, reported in Panel A, are a lot stronger. We find at least some specifications indicating significant increases in the proportions of white females, black males (at the 10-percent level), and black females, and significant decreases in the proportion of white males. The stronger effects when we look at the entire workforce rather than the last worker hired are probably due to better measurement of workforce demographics—owing to less random variation—although they may also be attributable to weakened enforcement of Affirmative Action in recent years (Leonard, 1990; Rodgers and Spriggs, 1996). There is again little evidence that changes in recruitment methods, screening methods, etc. explain the shifts in hires. However, in this table there is some evidence that applicant demographics partly explain the hiring differences, as their inclusion in column (4) weakens the effects of Affirmative Action on the proportions white female, black female, and white male.[38] At least to some extent, then, the effects of Affirmative Action in recruiting in boosting minority and female hiring appear attributable to the role of Affirmative Action in widening the potential applicant pool to encompass more women and minorities.

Finally, Panel B looks at the effects of Affirmative Action in hiring on the demographic composition of the workforce. In this case, the significant effects appear for increased proportions of white females and Hispanics, and a decreased proportion of white males. In contrast to the effects of Affirmative Action in recruiting, these shifts associated with Affirmative Action in hiring do not appear to be attributable to induced changes in applicant demographics, as the addition of these controls does nothing to reduce the hiring shifts associated with Affirmative Action. Rather, Affirmative Action in hiring appears to generate direct increases in female and minority hiring, more consistent with preferential treatment.

Tables 14.9 and 14.10 take us from the effects of Affirmative Action on the demographic characteristics of workers hired to their educational qualifications, reporting regressions for educational levels in Table 14.9, and logit estimates for whether or not workers are underqualified in Table 14.10. Both tables report difference-in-differences estimates that measure the extent to which Affirmative Action leads to the hiring of females/minorities who are either relatively less educated or more likely to be underqualified than white males, by comparing differences in qualifications between these groups in establishments using Affirmative Action relative to the differences in establishments that do not.

The estimates in Table 14.9 indicate that Affirmative Action in recruiting leads to the hiring of white females with educational levels that are relatively lower by about one-quarter of a year, with the estimate significant at the 10-percent level; the estimate for Affirmative Action in hiring is a bit smaller and insignificant. Affirmative Action in hiring leads to the hiring of Hispanic workers whose relative education is significantly lower by more than one-half year. The estimates in Panel A of Table 14.10, for Affirmative Action in recruiting, indicate no significant differences in the probability that women or minorities hired by employers using Affirmative Action are underqualified. But the estimates in Panel B, for Affirmative Action in hiring, indicate that black females hired under Affirmative

Table 14.9 Estimated effects of Affirmative Action in recruiting and hiring on educational levels, difference-in-differences estimates, minority/female vs. white male in Affirmative Action establishments vs. non-Affirmative Action establishments[a]

A. Affirmative Action used in recruiting	
White female	−0.269*
	(0.155)
Black male	0.241
	(0.237)
Black female	−0.224
	(0.240)
Hispanic	0.065
	(0.194)
B. Affirmative Action used in hiring	
White female	−0.185
	(0.157)
Black male	0.244
	(0.242)
Black female	−0.246
	(0.242)
Hispanic	−0.507**
	(0.199)
N	2,058

Note
a The table reports OLS difference-in-difference estimates discussed in reference to equation (5) in the text. All specifications include the following controls: dummy variables for city, year, central city and noncentral city SMSA, whether the employer has a personnel department, industry, occupation, and job tasks and requirements; and controls for percent covered by collective bargaining, size, and percentage of black and Hispanic customers. See footnote to Table 14.3 for additional details.

Action are considerably more likely to be underqualified (by 0.07–0.09). Similar results, although smaller and less significant, can be found for Hispanics.

Thus, Affirmative Action in hiring appears more likely to lead to the hiring of less-qualified minority workers. The difference between the results for Affirmative Action in recruiting and hiring is consistent with Affirmative Action in recruiting widening the pool of potential applicants, without resulting in less-qualified hires, while Affirmative Action in hiring—either because of weaker recruitment efforts or weaker hiring standards—results in less-qualified hires for some minority groups.

Evaluation, reward, and training

The results to this point suggest two provisional conclusions. First, Affirmative Action in recruiting and in hiring boost the employment of some groups of women

Table 14.10 Estimated effects of Affirmative Action in recruiting and hiring on educational underqualification, difference-in-differences estimates, minority/female vs. white male in Affirmative Action establishments vs. non-Affirmative Action establishments[a]

	Degree (1)	Degree/GED (2)
A. Affirmative Action used in recruiting		
White female	−0.024	−0.018
	(0.019)	(0.019)
Black male	−0.001	−0.018
	(0.035)	(0.038)
Black female	0.026	0.047
	(0.030)	(0.035)
Hispanic	−0.017	−0.016
	(0.022)	(0.022)
B. Affirmative Action used in hiring		
White female	−0.003	0.006
	(0.019)	(0.019)
Black male	0.0005	0.003
	(0.033)	(0.037)
Black female	0.067**	0.086**
	(0.028)	(0.030)
Hispanic	0.023	0.031
	(0.022)	(0.022)
N	2,058	1,887

Note
a Partial derivatives of probabilities of outcomes (evaluated at sample means) are reported, with standard errors of these partial derivatives in parentheses. Estimates in each column and panel are from a single logit estimation. In column (2) if a high school degree is reported as required, but the employer indicates he would definitely or probably accept a GED and the worker has a GED, the worker is coded as qualified. All specifications include the following controls: dummy variables for city, year, central city and noncentral city SMSA, whether the employer has a personnel department, industry, occupation, and job tasks and requirements, except for educational requirements; and controls for percent covered by collective bargaining, size, and percentage of black and Hispanic customers. See footnote to Tables 14.3 and 14.9 for additional details.

and minorities in the relevant establishments. Second, there is some evidence that the effects of Affirmative Action in recruiting are at least in part attributable to employers widening the pool of minority applicants. More generally, employers using Affirmative Action appear to use different screening methods and hiring criteria that may enable them to identify qualified women and minority applicants. Apparently as a result, Affirmative Action in recruiting does not appear to result in less-qualified hires. In contrast, Affirmative Action in hiring seems to operate more as simple preferential treatment in hiring, and appears at least for some groups to result in less-qualified hires.

As a result, employers may take steps to elicit better performance from such workers, or to enhance their skills. The estimates in Tables 14.11 and 14.12 turn to evidence on these questions. Table 14.11 reports estimates of logits for employers' use of formal performance evaluation systems, pay for performance, and probationary periods. The evidence indicates that employers using Affirmative Action in either recruiting or hiring are more likely to use formal performance evaluation systems.

The evidence on training, in Table 14.12, reveals a couple of things. First, the levels estimates suggest that new employees in establishments using Affirmative Action receive more training. Perhaps more significantly, the difference-in-differences estimates indicate that when employers use Affirmative Action in hiring, most groups of women and minorities receive relatively more training (where the comparison is with female/minority vs. white differences in the non-Affirmative Action sector).

Interestingly, our previous results suggested that it was the use of Affirmative Action in hiring, more so than in recruitment, that led to the hiring of less-qualified workers and hence to the potential need for remedial training. Here we find positive and sometimes significant results for formal training for the three groups of workers for which we found some evidence that Affirmative Action in hiring led to less-qualified hires—white females, black females (although for them the estimates are not significant), and Hispanics. For informal training, the estimated differential for black males is also positive and significant (at the 10-percent level). In our view, the training results, in particular, suggest that employers use training to improve the quality of women and minorities brought in because of Affirmative Action in hiring, who might otherwise be less-productive workers.[39]

Table 14.11 Estimated effects of Affirmative Action in recruiting and hiring on performance evaluation and pay systems[a]

	Employer uses		
	Formal performance evaluation system (1)	*Pay for performance* (2)	*Probationary period* (3)
A. Affirmative Action used in recruiting			
Affirmative Action—recruiting	0.129**	−0.015	0.019
	(0.017)	(0.024)	(0.020)
B. Affirmative Action used in hiring			
Affirmative Action—hiring	0.090**	−0.018	−0.040**
	(0.018)	(0.024)	(0.020)
N	2,353	2,337	2,357

Note

a Partial derivatives of probabilities of outcomes (evaluated at sample means) are reported, with standard errors of these partial derivatives in parentheses. Estimates in each column and panel are from a single logit estimation. All specifications include the following controls: dummy variables for city, year, central city and noncentral city SMSA, whether the employer has a personnel department, industry, occupation, and job tasks and requirements; and controls for percent covered by collective bargaining, size, and percentage of black and Hispanic customers. See footnote to Table 14.3 for additional details.

Table 14.12 Estimated effects of Affirmative Action in recruiting and hiring on hours of formal and informal training of most recent hire[a]

	Formal training (1)	Informal training (2)
A. Affirmative Action used in recruiting		
Levels		
Affirmative Action—recruiting	11.60**	5.90*
	(4.95)	(3.23)
Difference-in-differences		
White female	−6.81	12.74*
	(11.72)	(7.47)
Black male	−32.64*	12.83
	(17.83)	(11.56)
Black female	8.64	12.30
	(17.72)	(11.11)
Hispanic	−17.18	22.83**
	(14.81)	(9.62)
B. Affirmative Action used in hiring		
Levels		
Affirmative Action—hiring	10.50**	4.90
	(4.82)	(3.13)
Difference-in-differences		
White female	20.14*	21.70**
	(11.70)	(7.52)
Black male	−9.81	21.86*
	(18.04)	(11.62)
Black female	24.57	16.72
	(17.16)	(11.11)
Hispanic	24.37*	10.32
	(14.91)	(9.66)
N	2,255	1,843

Note

a Estimates in each column of Panel A and B are from a Tobit estimation with an upper limit of 160 hours (above which there were a few outliers). Below the levels estimates, the table reports estimates corresponding to equation (5) in the text. Estimates of $[(\beta - \gamma) - (\delta - \alpha)]$ are reported. All specifications include the following controls: dummy variables for city, year, central city and noncentral city SMSA, whether the employer has a personnel department, industry, occupation, and job tasks and requirements; and controls for percent covered by collective bargaining, size, and percentage of black and Hispanic customers. See footnote to Table 14.3 for additional details.

Current performance

The final outcome we study is the relative performance of women and minorities hired under Affirmative Action. We have seen relatively little evidence that women and minorities hired by employers reporting Affirmative Action in recruiting are less qualified, although we clearly cannot measure all qualifications. We have seen somewhat more evidence that Affirmative Action in hiring leads to less-qualified hires, but that employers take steps (such as increased training) that may offset this. In addition, the more intensive recruiting and screening methods spurred by Affirmative Action may result in employers finding hires who are less qualified in terms of credentials such as education, but more qualified in terms of characteristics we cannot observe. Table 14.13 therefore reports difference-in-differences estimates for performance ratings assigned by supervisors, relative to the "typical" employee in the job.

The results indicate that minorities and women in establishments using Affirmative Action in recruiting perform, if anything, better than white males; the ratings differentials are positive for all groups, and significant for black males (at the 10-percent level) and black females. The results for Affirmative Action in hiring are somewhat different. First, there is no evidence of better performance of women and minorities. Second, although the evidence is not significant, the point estimates suggest that Hispanics, who were the least qualified in terms of

Table 14.13 Estimated effects of Affirmative Action in recruiting and hiring on normalized performance rating, difference-in-differences estimates, minority/female vs. white male in Affirmative Action establishments vs. non-Affirmative Action establishments[a]

A. Affirmative Action used in recruiting	
White female	3.11
	(1.92)
Black male	4.85*
	(2.90)
Black female	7.70**
	(3.00)
Hispanic	3.27
	(2.38)
B. Affirmative Action used in hiring	
White female	−2.94
	(1.99)
Black male	1.38
	(2.99)
Black female	4.84
	(3.09)
Hispanic	−3.53
	(2.46)
N	2,066

Note
a The table reports OLS difference-in-differences estimates discussed in reference to equation (5) in the text; estimates of $[(\beta-\gamma)-(\delta-\alpha)]$ are reported. All specifications include the following controls: dummy variables for city, year, central city and noncentral city SMSA, whether the employer has a personnel department, industry, occupation, and job tasks and requirements; and controls for percent covered by collective bargaining, size, and percentage of black and Hispanic customers. See footnote to Table 14.3 for additional details.

educational levels, exhibit worse performance.[40] Overall, it appears that perhaps because of employers' efforts when they use Affirmative Action in recruiting to widen the applicant pool and screen more carefully, and perhaps because of employers' remedial efforts to offset the relatively lower credentials among some women and minorities who are hired when Affirmative Action in hiring is used, Affirmative Action generally does not translate into weaker job performance of the women and minorities who are hired.

Are we identifying causal effects of Affirmative Action?

As we noted earlier, some important questions remain about the extent to which the estimates we have presented reflect causal effects for employers who engage in Affirmative Action, as opposed to unobserved characteristics of their establishments or firms that are associated with the use of Affirmative Action (perhaps because of self-selection). In this section we present some additional evidence on this issue, drawing on additional information in our data, as well as on studies that examine changes in firm policies over time to attempt to infer causality.

As we noted in the previous section, firms with 100 or more workers must file EEO-1 forms that report their hiring activity by race and gender, and firms with 50 or more employees must undertake Affirmative Action if they are federal contractors. Thus, the use of Affirmative Action in recruiting and hiring is more likely to be endogenous for firms with less than 50 or less than 100 employees. The strategy we follow to assess the role of endogeneity bias, therefore, is to compare estimates of the effects of Affirmative Action in the full sample with estimates in samples of firms with less than 50 or less than 100 employees. In the full sample, variation in the use of Affirmative Action may come from endogenous selection, but—in contrast to the sample of small firms—much of it is likely to come from differences between large and small firms and from variation among large firms, both of which may be driven by policy rules. Thus, if the estimates are similar in the full sample and the sample of smaller firms, and more specifically if the estimated differentials associated with Affirmative Action are no larger in the sample of small firms, this would indicate a minimal role for bias from endogenous selection in generating the apparent effects of Affirmative Action reported in the earlier tables.

Table 14.14 presents results of estimated equations for samples of firms disaggregated by firm size. Since the rules cited above apply to *firms* rather than establishments, we limit our samples of employers to those that are single-establishment firms. Also, because of the small sample sizes and cell sizes we encounter when disaggregating the data, for the difference-in-differences specifications we collapse the variables for each demographic group into a single "minority/female" variable. We therefore first report, in columns (1) and (2), estimates for the full sample using this more restricted specification; in the panels that are not difference-in-differences estimates, these simply replicate results from earlier tables. In columns (3) and (4) we report results for all single-site or single-establishment firms, to provide a baseline with which to compare the estimates for smaller establishments. Finally, columns (5)–(8) report results for the subset of firms with less than 100 employees, and then the subset of firms with less than 50 employees. Each panel of Table 14.14 reports results corresponding to each of the dependent variables explored in the earlier tables. In cases where there were multiple specifications reported in the earlier tables, we have chosen the most basic one, as indicated in the table.

First, note that in most cases the results for the single-site firms are similar to those for the full sample. The important exception is training; for the full sample minorities and women hired under Affirmative Action receive relatively more training, while in the single-site firms this result does not appear. This may be because the largest firms are multi-site firms, and training is much more likely to occur in large firms (Holzer and Reaser, 1999). But replicating the full-sample results, among single-site firms those that report using Affirmative Action in recruiting use more recruiting methods (especially those likely to cast a wide net), get more minority applicants, screen more intensively, are more willing to hire workers with a recent history of unemployment, and are more likely to use formal evaluation systems.

Turning to the estimates for the smaller firms, the results are remarkably similar to the full sample (single-site) results, whether we use the cutoff of 100 employees, or the more stringent cutoff of 50 employees—below which we might most expect the use of Affirmative Action to be endogenous. Some of the point estimates are larger for the smaller firms (such as using formal evaluation systems and checking references), while some are smaller (such as using newspaper ads and requiring a written application). Overall, though, most of the estimates are of very similar magnitudes across columns (3)–(8), and the pattern of statistically significant estimates is generally alike.

Since we do not generally find stronger associations between our measures of recruiting, screening, etc., and the use of Affirmative Action in firms where the use of Affirmative Action is more likely to be endogenous, we believe that our estimates in large part capture exogenous effects of Affirmative Action on employer recruiting and hiring behavior. This view receives additional support in earlier literature on firm behavioral responses to the passage of EEO laws and enforcement of Affirmative Action regulations by the federal government. Dobbin *et al.* (1993) and Edelman (1990) demonstrate that employment practices changed significantly during the late 1960s and even more so during the early 1970s, as employers became more likely to use formal job evaluations and job descriptions and to have formal personnel offices (among other changes). They also present evidence from the Personnel/Human Resources literature of that period tying these changes to growing company concerns over compliance with EEO law as well as Affirmative Action regulations.[41]

Stronger evidence comes from Freeman (1981), who reports that employer recruitment activity at historically black colleges rose substantially in the late 1960s, presumably in response to these developments. He also cites results from a Bureau of National Affairs report indicating that, during the late 1960s and early 1970s, most large companies incorporated special recruiting efforts for minority

Table 14.14 Summary of results for single-site firms, different size categories, estimated effects of Affirmative Action in specifications corresponding to Tables 14.3–14.13[a]

	All establishments		All single-site firms		<100 employees		<50 employees	
	Recruiting (1)	Hiring (2)	Recruiting (3)	Hiring (4)	Recruiting (5)	Hiring (6)	Recruiting (7)	Hiring (8)
Table 14.3—Recruitment methods, all methods used								
Walk in/sign	0.083**	—	0.069**	—	0.114**	—	0.119**	—
Referral from current employees/others	0.012	—	0.039**	—	0.057**	—	0.051*	—
State/community agency	0.128**	—	0.093**	—	0.073**	—	0.050	—
Private agency	0.034*	—	0.030	—	0.007	—	−0.004	—
Newspaper	0.070**	—	0.124**	—	0.078*	—	0.082	—
Referral from unions/schools	0.079**	—	0.034	—	0.048	—	0.042	—
Table 14.4, columns (1), (3), and (5)— Applicant demographics								
Percentage black male	0.010	—	0.002	—	−0.022	—	−0.024	—
Percentage black female	0.038**	—	0.064**	—	0.054**	—	0.057**	—
Percentage Hispanic	0.033**	—	0.035	—	0.007	—	0.014	—
Table 14.5—Screening methods								
Test/work sample (required)	−0.007	−0.033	0.007	−0.042	−0.007	−0.042	0.019	0.010
Drug test/physical (required)	0.039**	0.002	0.049**	0.028*	0.024**	0.019**	0.017**	0.010
Check references (always)	0.065**	0.046**	0.064**	0.050	0.080*	0.073	0.082*	0.076
Check education (always)	0.108**	0.114**	0.139**	0.107**	0.123**	0.103**	0.118**	0.088**
Check criminal record (always)	0.137**	0.054**	0.092**	0.017	0.083**	0.025	0.093**	0.021
Require written application (always)	0.066**	0.075**	0.102**	0.117**	0.091**	0.116**	0.079*	0.115**
Require interview (always)	−0.025*	−0.019*	−0.041**	−0.030	−0.068**	−0.058**	−0.059**	−0.062**
Table 14.6—Hiring criteria— Would definitely/probably hire								
Person with criminal record	0.065**	0.042*	0.023	0.035	0.060	0.042	0.031	0.048
Welfare recipient	−0.007	0.004	0.006	0.001	0.006	−0.008	−0.005	−0.027
Person with govt. training/GED	0.006	−0.0002	0.002	−0.002	0.002	−0.002	−0.003	−0.005
Person with short-term/ part-time work history	0.038	0.024	0.069	0.042	0.100**	0.070	0.073	0.067
Person unemployed more than 1 year	0.034**	0.027	0.069**	0.047*	0.068**	0.062*	0.056	0.071*

	(1)	(2)	(3)	(4)	(5)	(6)	(7)	(8)
Table 14.7, column (1)—Last worker hired								
Minority/female	0.030	0.048**	0.043	0.047	0.032	0.057	−0.0001	0.041
Table 14.8, column (1)—Percentage of workforce								
Minority/female	0.022*	0.013	0.052*	0.048*	0.055	0.065*	0.052	0.073*
Table 14.9—Education								
Minority/female	−0.116	−0.173	−0.324	−0.166	−0.302	−0.154	−0.353	−0.254
Table 14.10—Last worker hired underqualified								
Minority/female	−0.016	0.012	0.012	0.012	0.010	0.016	0.014	0.021
Table 14.11—Evaluation/pay systems								
Formal performance evaluation system	0.129**	0.090**	0.181**	0.159**	0.195**	0.188**	0.190**	0.196**
Pay for performance	−0.015	−0.018	−0.038	−0.007	−0.050	0.003	−0.070	−0.035
Probationary period	0.019	−0.040**	0.022	0.019	0.001	0.026	−0.019	−0.013
Table 14.12—Formal training								
Minority/female	−10.21	18.25*	12.70	−5.61	15.84	−16.27	16.11	−23.75
Table 14.12—Informal training								
Minority/female	14.62**	18.68**	10.85	−1.47	8.36	−6.67	0.47	−13.49
Table 14.13—Performance rating								
Minority/female	3.86**	−1.78	3.59	2.05	3.81	1.88	4.94	1.72

Notes

* statistically significant at the 10-percent level.
** statistically significant at the 5-percent level.
a Estimates corresponding to the indicated earlier tables are reported. For panels corresponding to Tables 14.9, 14.10, 14.12, and 14.13, difference-in-differences estimates are reported. For the other tables, the estimated coefficients of the Affirmative Action variables are reported. In the various samples used, approximately 40 percent are single-site firms, and of these 20 percent have more than 100 employees, 80 percent less than 100, and 70 percent less than 50. For some panels, the estimates in columns (1) and (2) repeat those from earlier tables. All estimates are weighted. Standard errors are not reported.

workers and changed their selection practices to ensure greater minority representation at their workplaces. As we noted earlier, the finding that recruitment practices were affected strengthens the case that firms are engaging in Affirmative Action rather than simple compliance with EEO, because extra recruiting activity reflects practices that go well beyond simple nondiscrimination in employment.

Thus, while some employers may voluntarily choose to engage in Affirmative Action for a variety of reasons, the evidence overall suggests that government enforcement of EEO laws and especially Affirmative Action rules have generated changes in employer recruiting and hiring behavior and employment outcomes.

Conclusions

We find that hiring practices, personnel policies, and employment outcomes differ between establishments that use Affirmative Action in recruiting, those that use Affirmative Action in hiring, and those that do not use Affirmative Action. When we look at establishments that use Affirmative Action in recruiting, we find that such establishments recruit applicants much more extensively and screen them more intensively; they rely more heavily on formal rather than informal means of evaluation (both before and after a worker is hired); they are more likely to ignore stigmatizing personal characteristics and histories when they hire; and they are more likely to provide training to candidates whom they do hire. Partly as a result of these differences, and partly as a direct result of Affirmative Action, establishments using Affirmative Action generate greater flows of minority applicants, and more recent hires (or employees) who are minority or female. For the most part, though, the minority and female hires at these establishment do not have lower qualifications or current performance (as measured by supervisor ratings).

The narrower set of establishments that use Affirmative Action in hiring use many of these same strategies, but some to a lesser extent than establishments that use Affirmative Action in recruiting. Presumably as a result, these establishments are more likely to hire women or minorities with lower qualifications. On the other hand, these same establishments also provide more training to these hires. For most groups of minorities and females, job performance is not relatively lower in these establishments than in establishments that do not use Affirmative Action.

Overall, the results suggest that employers who undertake Affirmative Action in recruiting—either voluntarily or because of the requirements imposed on federal contractors—cast a wider net than they otherwise would, thus generating more minority and female job candidates. By using more screening methods (particularly more formal ones), they obtain more information about each candidate and pay less attention to more obvious but potentially noisier signals of quality (such as education or previous employment and criminal histories).[42] As a result, these employers likely practice less *statistical discrimination* (and perhaps less pure discrimination as well). While there is no doubt some cost to employers from obtaining the extra information, it probably enables them to avoid hiring candidates whose productivity might otherwise be considerably weaker as a result of

Affirmative Action. The extra training that these establishments appear to provide their employees might also be a way to compensate for any initially weaker credentials and/or performance among their "protected group" hires and thus to offset potential productivity losses.

This interpretation is consistent with anecdotal evidence provided by Caplan (1997), who argues that Affirmative Action requirements are flexible enough that employers can adapt to them in ways that are not very costly (and are sometimes beneficial) over the longer term. It is also consistent with two studies of doctors in California (Penn *et al.*, 1986; Davidson and Lewis, 1997) that found weaker credentials on paper but little difference in observable performance between minorities/females admitted to medical school under Affirmative Action and their white male counterparts.[43]

There may still be other costs of Affirmative Action, especially for the white males who are hired less frequently into establishments using Affirmative Action. Furthermore, our results suggest that Affirmative Action that focuses more on hiring probably leads to higher costs, as less-qualified women and minorities, who probably require more remedial help, are hired.[44] But, as we argued in our earlier chapter, the redistribution of earnings from white males to minorities/females is not likely to be very large, and must be balanced against the gains experienced by minorities and females who enter the labor market with known disadvantages and who often face discrimination there in the absence of these forces. We think that the latter argument is particularly compelling in light of evidence that when less-qualified workers are hired, the differences in performance appear to be erased because of actions employers take. Thus, the costs that employers are bearing as a result of Affirmative Action in hiring are more likely to be one-time costs associated with bringing skills up to speed, rather than continuing efficiency costs from the employment of less-productive workers (possibly coupled with constraints on paying correspondingly lower wages).

Finally, it is instructive to interpret our findings in light of the public's attitudes toward Affirmative Action, indicating support for special training and other programs that help disadvantaged groups advance, but opposition toward preferential treatment. Our evidence on Affirmative Action in recruiting suggests that it is consistent with the policies that receive broad public support, since it encourages more extensive and intensive search for qualified minority (and female) candidates, but not "preferential treatment." In contrast, Affirmative Action in hiring seems more consistent with preferential treatment that the public opposes. But even here, the preferential hiring appears to be coupled with increased training of minority/female hires, consistent with the "special training" that receives more widespread public support. In addition, either this training or unobserved (to us) individual characteristics result in equal performance among most groups of women or minorities hired under Affirmative Action. Thus, even Affirmative Action in hiring, and the preferential treatment it may entail, does not appear to result in the employment of less-productive women and minorities in place of more-qualified white males.

Appendix

Table 14.A1 Public opinion polls on Affirmative Action

A. New York Times/CBS News, October 1977

First of all, would you approve or disapprove of requiring business to hire a certain number of minority workers?

	Whites	Blacks
Approve	35%	64%
Disapprove	60%	26%

How about requiring large companies to set up special training programs for members of minority groups?

	Whites	Blacks
Approve	63%	88%
Disapprove	32%	9%

B. Independent Survey, 1980

Affirmative Action programs that help blacks and other minorities to get ahead should be supported.

	Whites	Blacks
Strongly agree	6%	26%
Agree	70%	70%
Disagree	21%	4%
Strongly disagree	3%	0%
N	1,276	524

Employers should set aside a certain number of places to hire qualified blacks and other minorities.

	Whites	Blacks
Strongly agree	3%	16%
Agree	48%	57%
Disagree	40%	24%
Strongly disagree	9%	3%
N	727	283

Do you personally feel that such preferential treatment (for blacks) is/would be:

	Whites	Blacks
Fair	35%	42%
Unfair	65%	58%
N	1,223	486

C. National Election Pilot Study, 1985

Some people say that because of past discrimination against blacks, preference in hiring and promotion should be given to blacks. Others say preferential hiring and promotion of blacks is wrong because it discriminates against whites. What about your opinion—are you for or against preferential hiring and promotion of blacks?

Favor strongly	6%
Favor not strongly	7%
Oppose not strongly	20%
Oppose strongly	67%
N	380

Sources: Panel A, Lipset and Schneider (1978); Panel B, Kluegel and Smith (1986); Panel C, Kinder and Sanders (1990).

Acknowledgments

We thank Jess Reaser for excellent computational assistance, and Peter Cappelli, John Donohue, Larry Kahn, Larry Katz, Steffanie Wilk, and seminar participants at Michigan State and the NBER for helpful discussions.

Notes

1 *Adarand* v. *Pena* concerns minority set-asides, but these may have strong influences on minority employment (Bates, 1993). We expect future court decisions to address Affirmative Action in employment directly, as almost occurred in the recent case involving teachers in Piscataway, New Jersey.

2 Effects on educational as opposed to employment outcomes have been analyzed by Kane (1996), Attiyeh and Attiyeh (1997), and Bowen and Bok (1998).

3 An exception is a paper by Leonard (1985a), which analyzes the targeting of compliance reviews across companies by the Office of Federal Contract Compliance Programs (OFCCP).

4 If Affirmative Action is strictly used to counter "pure" (as opposed to statistical) discrimination in the labor market, it should not lead to the hiring of underqualified workers.

5 Eastland (1996) characterizes Affirmative Action that takes the form of more aggressive recruitment or special training as "good" Affirmative Action, and the use of race or sex preferences to determine who gets jobs as "bad" Affirmative Action. As Radford (1997) points out, however, the distinction is not hard and fast, since more investment in resources for recruiting and training women or minorities is likely to involve some denial of positions or resources to white males.

6 The household and employer surveys in the four metropolitan areas are part of the Multi-City Study of Urban Inequality (MCSUI) sponsored by the Russell Sage Foundation.

7 Sample weights are still necessary to adjust for an underrepresentation of jobs in the sample that require college degrees (since the SSI part of the sample only asked about jobs that do not require college degrees). Sample weights also adjust for the nonrandomness of the household samples that generated some of the firms. All estimation below is sample-weighted.

8 Since SSI provided data on industry, location, and establishment size for all establishments, we could test for differences in response rates across these observable dimensions. We found only small and/or insignificant differences in most cases. The distributions of our establishments across industry and size categories are quite comparable to those found in *County Business Patterns* data in the same areas, and occupational distributions are quite comparable to those found in the 1990 Census of Population. For more information see the appendix to chapter 1 of Holzer (1996).

9 They were also asked whether or not Affirmative Action affects their promotion decisions. However, we do not study this response since the question was asked only for the subset of jobs for which there were promotion possibilities.

10 It seems unlikely that firms interpreted this question as being mostly about compliance with EEO law, since this would imply that roughly half of the establishments in our survey report being out of compliance. Another possibility, consistent with this interpretation, is that most companies comply with EEO law but only some respond affirmatively to this question because of ambiguities in its wording. In this case we would expect to find few differences between employers that report using Affirmative Action and those that do not, in contrast to the actual results.

11 For instance, Epstein claims that published EEOC guidelines on what constitutes underrepresentation of minority hires relative to applicants in the 1970s (with regard to concerns over "disparate impact" of hiring rules) led many noncontractor companies to

engage in Affirmative Action. The claim by many Senators and the White House that the Civil Rights Act of 1991 was really a "quota bill" reflects this perception as well.

12　For instance, Freeman (1981) cites a Bureau of National Affairs report on "Equal Employment Opportunity Programs compete with Affirmative Action plans," indicating that the latter are often part of the former. But the evidence that these firms are really engaging in some type of Affirmative Action, and not just compliance with EEO, can be found in the fact that over 60 percent of those with an EEO program engage in special efforts to *recruit* minorities (in addition to efforts to ensure that minority applicants are screened fairly).

13　For instance, companies that want to expand their sales among minority customer groups might consider it profitable to have a more diverse workforce. Evidence that employers' perceptions of customer preferences can affect their employment decisions appears in Holzer and Ihlanfeldt (1998).

14　For example, if the owners or managers of a company have preferences for minority workers, they may choose to engage in Affirmative Action and give these employees relatively high performance ratings; but it is not clear why they would engage in the broad range of different recruiting and screening behaviors that we document below *independently* of their practice of Affirmative Action. On the other hand, companies who choose to engage in Affirmative Action because of its potential profitability might recruit and screen differently, but they have little reason to rate their minority employees more positively.

15　We have combined a few categories from the original survey.

16　No such questions were asked about white females or about Hispanics broken down by sex. Comparable questions were asked about Asian applicants, but we do not include this group in any of our analyses reported in this chapter.

17　We suspect that the method used to generate the hire might be more endogenous with respect to the race/gender of the worker chosen, and therefore might be less valid as a predictor of those outcomes.

18　The first two of these are coded as required or not required. The last five are coded as used if the respondent indicated that the information was always checked or the application/interview was always required, as opposed to sometimes or never.

19　These are coded as affirmative if the respondent indicated they would definitely or probably hire such a person.

20　In principle, we could estimate separate effects (in the same specification) for establishments that use Affirmative Action in recruiting and Affirmative Action in hiring, although we have some reservations about the reliability and interpretation of the data for establishments reporting Affirmative Action in hiring only. When we estimated the specifications reported in this chapter for the Affirmative Action variable broken down this way, we reached very similar conclusions regarding the different effects of Affirmative Action in recruiting and hiring that we report in the chapter. Specifically, the independent effects of Affirmative Action in hiring largely reflect the differences between Affirmative Action in recruiting and Affirmative Action in hiring that we report in this chapter, and the summed effects of Affirmative Action in recruiting and in hiring largely parallel the effects of Affirmative Action in hiring reported in this chapter.

21　Again, because these percentages are bounded at 0 and 100, we estimate two-tailed Tobit models. The data on last worker hired also break out Hispanic men and women, but the questions regarding the composition of the total workforce do not, so we use the consistent measures.

22　The survey asked whether or not a college degree was required for the job; we interpret this to mean a four-year bachelor's degree (rather than an associate's degree). The question about high school asks whether the degree is absolutely necessary, strongly preferred, etc; we interpret either of the first two categories as indicating a requirement.

In some runs, for employers who state that they require a high school degree but who separately indicate that they would accept a candidate with a GED, we count employees with GEDs as qualified.

23 Over 90 percent of the new hires met the stated requirement, and far more newly hired workers exceeded the requirement than fell short of it.

24 Note that we include separate intercepts for each group, and hence no constant. β and δ are row vectors of coefficients.

25 β is actually a vector of coefficients.

26 More complete results for qualifications and performance, including estimates of alternative "differences," are discussed in Holzer and Neumark (1999).

27 Given that a small number of cases have extremely high values of hours of training, we cap the number of hours at 160 (i.e. a month of full-time formal training) and estimate two-tailed Tobits, with zero being the other tail. Variation in the level at which we cap the training hours does not qualitatively affect the results.

28 The results turn out to be insensitive to whether the typical rating is subtracted. In Holzer and Neumark (1999) we also look at wages and promotions as indicators of qualifications or productivity, and find no evidence (if anything, the reverse) that women or minorities hired under Affirmative Action are less productive. However, the disadvantage of wage and promotion data, compared with confidential supervisors' ratings, is that they may be influenced by the same Affirmative Action pressures that influence hiring, rendering them uninformative as independent measures of performance.

29 We gauge this by whether or not the respondent to the survey reports that he/she is a personnel department official as opposed to the owner/manager of the establishment. Given that the respondent is always the person responsible for entry-level hiring, the presence of a personnel department at the establishment should be indicated by whether or not the respondent has such a position.

30 The educational requirements are omitted from the controls when the dependent variable is defined as whether or not the last hired worker has met formal educational requirements for the job.

31 In this discussion we do not report on the statistical significance of the differences; since the control variables are often quite important, we instead provide this discussion when we report the multivariate results later.

32 Barron *et al.* (1985) label "extensive" and "intensive" search for employees as approaches which generate more applicants and more information per applicant, respectively. Our evidence suggests that Affirmative Action increases both types of search.

33 Data on hiring criteria are available only for jobs not requiring a college degree.

34 The latter variable refers only to jobs not requiring a college degree.

35 We estimated similar specifications including dummy variables for the method used to generate the last hire. These estimates provided less evidence that recruitment methods *per se* account for the effect of Affirmative Action on flows of minority applicants.

36 The effects of recruitment methods on applicant flows are different for Hispanics, with positive estimated effects of using walk ins/signs and informal referrals from current employees or others, and no significant effects of newspaper ads or use of agencies. These differences are consistent with the notion of an "ethnic economy" in areas like Los Angeles where informal methods are relatively more important in generating applicants from the relevant ethnic community (Falcon and Melendez, 1997).

37 Although this may appear to contradict the failure of employers using Affirmative Action to require interviews more frequently, much research suggests that interviews—especially when unstructured—can be unreliable screening mechanisms (Karren, 1980; Harris, 1989; Huffcutt and Arthur, 1994). In contrast to unstructured interviews, structured interviews are "characterized by the use of the same questions across interviews,

detailed rating scales, multiple interviewers per candidate, extensive interviewer training, note taking, and consensus processes" (Pulakos *et al.*, 1996, p. 87). We suspect that the interviews to which our respondents refer are better characterized as unstructured and hence are likely to be perceived by employers as unreliable. Moss and Tilly (1995) discuss the potential for racial stereotypes to influence hiring decisions made on the basis of employer interviews, which may be another reason Affirmative Action is associated with less reliance on interviews.

38 Because we are looking at the entire workforce, we restrict attention to all recruitment methods used, and do not examine the recruitment method tied explicitly to the last hire.

39 In these data, training does increase wage growth and performance ratings of most newly hired workers (Holzer and Reaser, 1999).

40 In Holzer and Neumark (1999) we break out results for Hispanic men and women, and find significantly lower performance ratings for Hispanic men hired under Affirmative Action. In this chapter we aggregate these groups, because some of our other related variables (such as the percentage of Hispanic applicants to the establishment) are defined that way.

41 Variables indicating contractor status have significant effects on the presence of personnel offices in Edelman's study but not on the use of formal evaluations and job descriptions in the study by Dobbin *et al*. However, since the latter study controlled for the presence of personnel offices (which themselves have significant effects on the use of formal evaluations and descriptions), it is possible that contractor status worked indirectly through that variable. Since we control for the presence of personnel offices in all of our estimates above, it is also possible that we are presenting lower bounds for the true estimates of the effects of Affirmative Action on hiring procedures and outcomes.

42 While informal recruitment has often been seen as a mechanism for generating accurate information about potential employees (e.g. Rees, 1966), there has been some evidence that it leads to lower employment among blacks (Holzer, 1987).

43 For similar findings in the case of women police officers see Steel and Lovrich (1987).

44 For evidence on administrative and enforcement costs of EEO and Affirmative Action see Conrad (1995).

References

Attiyeh, Gregory and Richard Attiyeh. 1997. "Testing for Bias in Graduate School Admissions." *Journal of Human Resources* 32(3): 524–48.

Barron, John, John Bishop, and William Dunkelberg. 1985. "Employer Search: The Interviewing and Hiring of New Employees." *The Review of Economics and Statistics* 67(1): 43–52.

Bates, Timothy. 1993. *Banking on Black Enterprise*. Washington, DC: Joint Center for Political and Economic Studies.

Bloch, Ferrel. 1994. *Anti-Discrimination Law and Minority Employment*. Chicago: University of Chicago Press.

Bowen, William G. and Derek C. Bok. 1998. *The Shape of the River*. Princeton, NJ: Princeton University Press.

Caplan, Lincoln. 1997. *Up Against the Law: Affirmative Action and the Supreme Court*. Washington DC: Brookings Institution.

Conrad, Cecelia. 1995. "The Economic Cost of Affirmative Action." In *Economic Perspectives on Affirmative Action*, ed. M. Simms, pp. 31–54. Washington, DC: Joint Center for Political and Economic Studies.

Davidson, Robert and Ernest Lewis. 1997. "Affirmative Action and Other Special Consideration Admissions at the University of California, Davis, School of Medicine." *Journal of the American Medical Association* 278(14): 1153–8.

Dobbin, Frank, John Sutton, John Meyer, and Richard Scott. 1993. "Equal Opportunity Law and the Construction of Internal Labor Markets." *American Journal of Sociology* 99(2): 396–427.

Eastland, Terry. 1996. "Special to *Insight*: Should Washington Halt Race-based Policies for Hiring and Contracting? Yes: Restore the Standard of the Civil Rights Act of 1964." *Insight Magazine*, May 6.

Edelman, Lauren. 1990. "Legal Environments and Organizational Governance: The Expansion of Due Process in the American Workplace." *American Journal of Sociology*, 95(6): 1401–40.

Epstein, Richard. 1992. *Forbidden Grounds: The Case Against Employment Discrimination Laws*. Cambridge MA: Harvard University Press.

Falcon, Luis and Edwin Melendez. 1997. "The Social Context of Job Searching for Racial Groups in Urban Centers." Mimeograph, Northeastern University.

Freeman, Richard B. 1981. "Black Economic Progress After 1964: Who has Gained and Why." In *Studies in Labor Markets*, ed. S. Rosen, pp. 247–94. Chicago: University of Chicago Press

Harris, Michael M. 1989. "Reconsidering the Employment Interview: A Review of Recent Literature and Suggestions for Future Research." *Personnel Psychology* 42: 691–726.

Holzer, Harry. 1987. "Informal Job Search and Black Youth Unemployment." *American Economic Review* 77(3): 446–52.

——. 1996. *What Employers Want: Job Prospects for Less-Educated Workers*. New York: Russell Sage Foundation.

——. 1998. "Why Do Small Establishments Hire Fewer Blacks than Larger Ones?" *Journal of Human Resources* 33(4): 896–914.

Holzer, Harry and Keith Ihlanfeldt. 1998. "Customer Discrimination and Employment Outcomes for Minority Workers." *Quarterly Journal of Economics* 113(3): 835–67.

Holzer, Harry and David Neumark. 1999. "Are Affirmative Action Hires Less Qualified? Evidence from Employer–Employee Survey Data." *Journal of Labor Economics* 17(3): 534–69.

Holzer, Harry and Jess Reaser. 1999. "Firm-Level Training for Newly Hired Workers: Its Determinants and Effects." *Research in Labor Economics* 18: 377–402

Huffcutt, Allen I. and Winfred Arthur. 1994. "Hunter and Hunter (1984) Revisited: Interview Validity for Entry-Level Jobs." *Journal of Applied Psychology*, 79(2): 184–90.

Kane, Thomas. 1996. "Racial Preferences in College Admissions." Mimeograph, Harvard University.

Karren, Robert. 1980. "The Selection Interview: A Review of the Literature." US Office of Personnel Management.

Kinder, Donald R. and Lynn M. Sanders. 1990. "Mimicking Political Debate with Survey Questions: The Case of White Opinion on Affirmative Action for Blacks." *Social Cognition* 8(1): 73–103.

Kluegel, James R. and Eliot R. Smith. 1986. *Beliefs About Inequality: Americans' Views of What Is and What Ought to Be*. New York: Aldine De Gruyter.

Leonard, Jonathan. 1985a. "Affirmative Action as Earnings Redistribution: The Targeting of Compliance Reviews." *Journal of Labor Economics* 3(3): 363–84.

Leonard, Jonathan. 1985b. "What Promises are Worth: The Impact of Affirmative Action Goals." *Journal of Human Resources* 20(1): 3–20.

Leonard, Jonathan. 1989. "Women and Affirmative Action." *Journal of Economic Perspectives* 3(1): 61–76.

——. 1990. "The Impact of Affirmative Action Regulation and Equal Employment Opportunity Law on Black Employment." *Journal of Economic Perspectives* 4(4): 47–64.

Lipset, Seymour Martin and William Schneider. 1978. "The Bakke Case: How Would It Be Decided at the Bar of Public Opinion?" *Public Opinion* March–April: 38–48.

Moss, Philip and Chris Tilly. 1995. "Soft Skills and Race." Working Paper, Russell Sage Foundation.

Penn, Nolan, Percy Russell, and Harold Simon. 1986. "Affirmative Action at Work: A Survey of Graduates of the University of California, San Diego, Medical School." *American Journal of Public Health* 76(9): 1144–6.

Pulakos, Elaine D., Neal Schmitt, David Whitney, and Matthew Smith. 1996. "Individual Differences in Interviewer Ratings: The Impact of Standardization, Consensus Discussion, and Sampling Error on the Validity of a Structured Interview." *Personnel Psychology* 49: 85–102.

Radford, Mary F. 1997. "The Affirmative Action Debate." In *Government Regulation of the Employment Relationship* ed. B. Kaufman. Madison, WI: Industrial Relations Research Association.

Rees, Albert. 1966. "Information Networks in Job Markets." *American Economic Review* 56(2): 559–66.

Rodgers, William and William Spriggs. 1996. "The Effect of Federal Contractor Status on Racial Differences in Establishment-Level Employment Shares: 1979–1992." *American Economic Review* 86(2): 290–3.

Steel, Brent and Nicholas Lovrich. 1987. "Equality and Efficiency Tradeoffs in Affirmative Action—Real or Imagined? The Case of Women in Policing." *Social Science Journal* 24(1): 53–70.

Index

For Product Safety Concerns and Information please contact our EU representative GPSR@taylorandfrancis.com Taylor & Francis Verlag GmbH, Kaufingerstraße 24, 80331 München, Germany

Printed and bound by CPI Group (UK) Ltd, Croydon, CR0 4YY

08/05/2025

01864517-0001